THE GERMAN RIGHT, 1860–1920: POLITICAL LIMITS OF THE AUTHOR IMAGINATION

Before the rise of Hitler and the Nazis, Germany was undergoing convulsive socio-economic and political change. With unification as a nation-state under Bismarck in 1871, Germany experienced the advent of mass politics, based on the principle of one man, one vote. The dynamic, diverse political culture that emerged challenged the adaptability of the 'interlocking directorate of the Right.' To serve as a bulwark of the authoritarian state, the Right needed to exploit traditional sources of power while mobilizing new political recruits, but until Emperor Wilhelm II's abdication in 1918 these aims could not easily be reconciled.

In *The German Right, 1860–1920*, James Retallack examines how the authoritarian imagination inspired the Right and how political pragmatism constrained it. He explores the Right's regional and ideological diversity, and refuses to privilege the 1890s as the tipping point when the traditional politics of notables gave way to mass politics. Retallack also challenges the assumption that, if Imperial Germany was modern, it could not also have been authoritarian. Written with clear, persuasive prose, this wide-ranging analysis draws together threads of reasoning from German and Anglo-American scholars over the past thirty years and points the way for future research into unexplored areas.

(German and European Studies)

JAMES RETALLACK is a professor in the Department of History at the University of Toronto.

GERMAN AND EUROPEAN STUDIES

General Editor: James Retallack

THE GERMAN RIGHT, 1860–1920

Political Limits of the Authoritarian Imagination

James Retallack

UNIVERSITY OF TORONTO PRESS
Toronto Buffalo London

© University of Toronto Press Incorporated 2006
Toronto Buffalo London
Printed in Canada

ISBN-13 978-0-8020-9145-1 (cloth)
ISBN-10 0-8020-9145-8 (cloth)

ISBN-13 978-0-8020-9419-3 (paper)
ISBN-10 0-8020-9419-8 (paper)

Printed on acid-free paper

Library and Archives Canada Cataloguing in Publication

Retallack, James N.
  The German right, 1860–1920 : political limits of the authoritarian imagination / James Retallack.

  Includes index.
  ISBN-13: 978-0-8020-9145-1 (bound).
  ISBN-10: 0-8020-9145-8 (bound).
  ISBN-13: 978-0-8020-9419-3 (pbk).
  ISBN-10: 0-8020-9419-8 (pbk).

  1. Germany – Politics and government – 1871–1933. 2. Germany – Politics and government – 1848–1870. 3. Conservatism – Germany – History – 19th century. 4. Conservatism – Germany – History – 20th century. 5. Authoritarianism – Germany – History – 19th century. 6. Authoritarianism – Germany – History – 20th century. I. Title.

  DD221.R49 2006   320.943'09'034   C2006-900662-8

Cover illustrations: (front) *Suits of Armour Standing* (1866) by Adolph Menzel (1815–1905), gouache and pencil on light brown paper, 43.9 x 56.7 cm. This study (*Stehende Rüstungen*) was part of a collection of 20 drawings ('Fantasies from the Arms Room') sketched during the winter of 1865–6 in the Garde-du-Corps-Saal of the royal palace in Berlin. Image (Inv. 35.803) courtesy of the Albertina, Vienna; (back) *Peasants in Conversation* (1876–7) by Wilhelm Leibl (1844–1900), oil on canvas, 76 x 97 cm. Leibl titled his work *Bauern in Gespräch*, but it is best known under the designation given it by the contemporary art trade: 'The Village Politicians' (*Die Dorfpolitiker*). Image courtesy of the Art Renewal Center, www.artrenewal.org.

University of Toronto Press acknowledges the financial assistance to its publishing program of the Canada Council for the Arts and the Ontario Arts Council.

University of Toronto Press acknowledges the financial support for its publishing activities of the Government of Canada through the Book Publishing Industry Development Program (BPIDP).

For L.S.R. and N.F.R.

Contents

Illustrations   ix
Tables and Figures   xi
Abbreviations   xii

Introduction   3

PART ONE: 'TRADITION IS HOW WE CHANGE'

1 Habitus and Hubris   35

2 'Fishing for Popularity'   76

3 Meanings of Stasis   108

PART TWO: CULTURES OF CONSERVATISM

4 Culture/Power/Territoriality   137

5 Governmentality in Transition   168

6 Citadels against Democracy   192

PART THREE: TENSION AND DÉTENTE

7 Publicity and Partisanship   225

8 Building a People's Party   273

9 Conservatives *contra* Chancellor   325

10 The Road to Philippi   370

Acknowledgments   407

Index   413

Illustrations

I.1 The German Empire, 1871–1918   4–5
I.2 Berlin election rallies, 1890   21
1.1 First election news, 1881   53
1.2 *If I Were the Kaiser – Political Truths and Necessities*   64
2.1 Campaigning in Bavaria   86
2.2 The Reichstag in session, 1870s   93
2.3 A Berlin polling station, January 1912   98
3.1 'At the helm'   118
3.2 'The man at the helm'   119
3.3 'Unresolved questions'   125
4.1 Mediating power   155
4.2 Schloss Rötha   158
5.1 Baron Richard von Friesen   171
5.2 The Saxon *Landtag* am Schlossplatz, Dresden   182
6.1 The 'uplifting' of the middle classes   194
6.2 Election spending: a balance of voices?   195
7.1 News fanciers or connoisseurs?   232
7.2 Complacent or anxious?   246
7.3 A popular Berlin newspaper hits the streets   253
7.4 *The Newspaper Reader*   259
8.1 Baron Heinrich von Friesen-Rötha   288
8.2 Schloss Rötha, interior   289
8.3 Two antisemites: Heinrich von Friesen-Rötha and Hermann Ahlwardt   301
8.4 Capitalism in crisis!   305
9.1 Otto von Helldorff-Bedra and members of the Conservative Reichstag caucus, 1889   335

9.2 'A German seven who do not love the Jews' 338
9.3 Court Preacher Adolf Stöcker 343
9.4 *Deutschtum* endangered 350
10.1 'Chancellor's love,' 1882 373
10.2 'The feeling of dependency,' 1910 377
10.3 The 'uncrowned king of Prussia' 388

Tables and Figures

Tables

6.1 Leipzig municipal elections, 1889–93   199
6.2 Occupational profile of Chemnitz city councillors, 1905   210
7.1 Images of the journalist before 1900   241

Figures

8.1 Occupational profiles of Baden, Saxony, and the Reich, 1882   284
8.2 Religious profiles of Baden, Saxony, and the Reich, 1871   285
8.3 Reichstag elections in Baden, 1871–1912   286
8.4 Reichstag elections in Saxony, 1871–1912   287
8.5 Saxon Conservative State Association, social profile, c. 1877   292

Abbreviations

AGB	*Archiv für Geschichte des Buchwesens*
BA	Bundesarchiv (Federal Archive: formerly BA Koblenz, BA Abteilungen Potsdam, Zentrales Staatsarchiv I Potsdam; now Berlin-Lichterfelde and Koblenz)
BA-MA	Bundesarchiv-Militärarchiv (Federal Archive–Military Archive)
BdL	Bund der Landwirte (Agrarian League)
Bl.	Blatt / Blätter (folio/folios)
CSP	Christlichsoziale Partei (Christian Social Party)
DKP	Deutschkonservative Partei (German Conservative Party)
FO	(British) Foreign Office
GDR	Deutsche Demokratische Republik (German Democratic Republic, East Germany)
GLA	Generallandesarchiv (General State Archive)
GStAPK	Geheimes Staatsarchiv Preußischer Kulturbesitz (Prussian Privy State Archive; formerly Zentrales Staatsarchiv II Merseburg or GStA Berlin-Dahlem; now Berlin-Dahlem)
Kl. Erw.	Kleine Erwerbungen (minor collections)
LBI YB	*Leo Baeck Institute Yearbook*
LT	*Landtag* (state parliament)
NASG	*Neues Archiv für sächsische Geschichte*
NL	Nachlaß (unpublished private papers)
NLP	Nationalliberale Partei (National Liberal Party)
Nr., Nrn.	Nummer, Nummern (no./nos.)

PA AA	Politisches Archiv des Auswärtigen Amts (Political Archive of the Foreign Office; formerly Bonn, now Berlin)
PRO	Public Record Office, Kew, now the (British) National Archives
RG Rötha	Rittergut Rötha mit Trachenau (Knight's Estate Rötha and Trachenau)
Rkz.	Reichskanzlei-Akten (Reich chancellery files)
RT	Reichstag (imperial parliament)
RT Sten. Ber.	*Stenographische Berichte über die Verhandlungen des Deutschen Reichstages* (Stenographic Reports of German Reichstag Debates)
SächsHStA	Sächsisches Hauptstaatsarchiv (Saxon Central State Archive; Dresden)
SächsStA	Sächsisches Staatsarchiv (Saxon State Archive; Leipzig)
Sg F	Sammlung Karl von Fechenbach (Karl von Fechenbach Collection)
Staatsbibliothek Berlin I, II	Staatsbibliothek zu Berlin Preußischer Kulturbesitz, Haus I (Unter den Linden), Haus II (Potsdamer Straße) (Berlin State Library, House I and House II)
StadtA	Stadtarchiv (municipal archive)
SPD	Sozialdemokratische Partei Deutschlands (German Social Democratic Party)
Pr. St. Min.	Preußisches Staatsministerium (Prussian State Ministry)
ZGO	*Zeitschrift für die Geschichte des Oberrheins*
ZSg	Zeitgeschichtliche Sammlung (Contemporary Historical Collection)
ZStA I, II	Zentrales Staatsarchiv I (Potsdam) and Zentrales Staatsarchiv II (Merseburg) (former GDR Central State Archive I [Potsdam] and II [Merseburg]; now BA Berlin-Lichterfelde and GStAPK Berlin-Dahlem)

Other Titles by the Same Author

Wilhelminism and Its Legacies: German Modernities, Imperialism, and the Meanings of Reform, 1890–1930, ed. with Geoff Eley.

Zwischen Markt und Staat. Stifter und Stiftungen im transatlantischen Vergleich, ed. with Thomas Adam.

Saxony in German History: Culture, Society, and Politics, 1830–1933, ed.

Sachsen in Deutschland. Politik, Kultur und Gesellschaft 1830–1918, ed.

Saxon Signposts, ed.

Germany in the Age of Kaiser Wilhelm II.

Modernisierung und Region im wilhelminischen Deutschland. Wahlen, Wahlrecht und Politische Kultur, ed. with Simone Lässig and Karl Heinrich Pohl.

Between Reform, Reaction, and Resistance: Studies in the History of German Conservatism from 1789 to 1945, ed. with Larry Eugene Jones.

Elections, Mass Politics, and Social Change in Modern Germany: New Perspectives, ed. with Larry Eugene Jones.

Notables of the Right: The Conservative Party and Political Mobilization in Germany, 1876–1918.

THE GERMAN RIGHT, 1860–1920:
POLITICAL LIMITS OF THE AUTHORITARIAN
IMAGINATION

Introduction

In Heinrich Mann's 1918 novel *The Loyal Subject*,[1] the middle-class protagonist Diederich Heßling finds himself in a 'private and confidential conclave' with a 'real feudal aristocrat,' Herr von Barnim. Von Barnim's political ideal entails 'a permanent system of popular representation as in the happy Middle Ages: knights, clergy, craftsmen and artisans.' For such a system Diederich expresses warm approval: these ideas 'fully corresponded with his desire, as a member of a profession and a gentleman, to take his stand in life collectively rather than individually.' Diederich also agrees with Herr von Barnim that the Jews are 'the root of all disorder and revolution, of confusion and disrespect, the principle of evil itself.' As they reach consensus on this point, von Barnim's 'pious face' is 'convulsed with hatred' – and 'Diederich felt with him.'

But Heßling is forced to reconsider things when he reports this conversation to another friend, Herr Wiebel, who observes: 'That is all very well, and I have a particular regard for the idealistic viewpoint of my friend, von Barnim, but in the long run it will not get us anywhere.' Referring to recent tumults at antisemitic rallies in Berlin, Wiebel suggests that conservatives are courting danger with their 'damned experiments with democracy.' Whether it is a matter of 'Christian or un-Christian democracy, I don't know,' he declares. But he is sure of one thing: 'Things have got too far for that. Today only one course is still open: to hit out hard so long as we have the power.' This conclusion, too, leaves Heßling greatly relieved: 'To go round converting Christians had at once struck him as rather laborious.'

These two fictional conversations illustrate motifs also found in this book on the German Right: relations between bourgeois and aristocratic

I.1. The German Empire, 1871–1918

Introduction 5

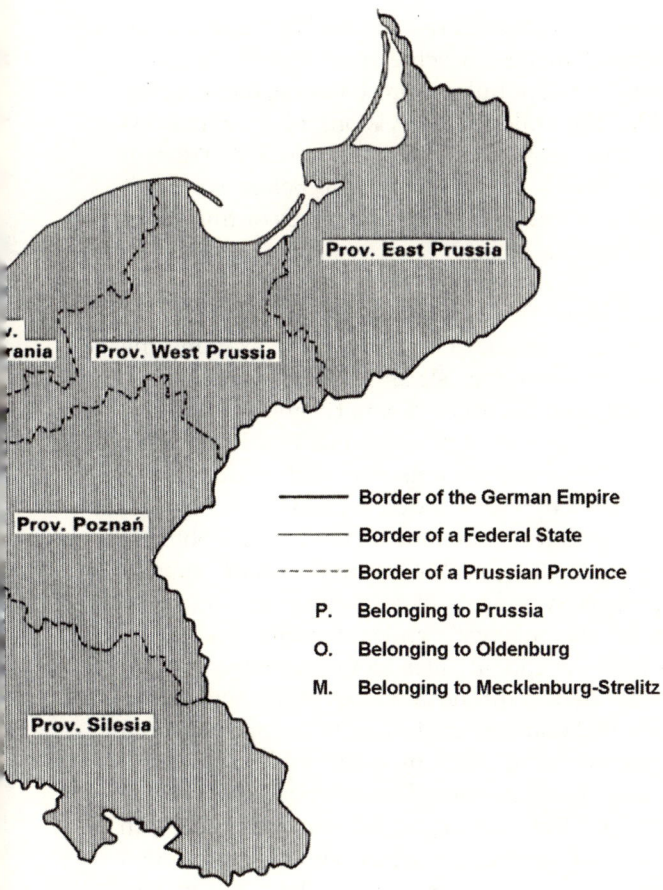

Germans, attempts to reinvigorate the 'Christian state' by targeting the Jews, the use of 'democratic' means to achieve undemocratic ends, efforts to institute an ideal form of popular representation, the determination to 'take a stand in life collectively,' visions of a calamitous political future, and the raw exercise of power to avoid it. We will return to *The Loyal Subject* later in this introduction. Before we do, it may be helpful to readers to identify the central themes of this study and their methodological ramifications.

These chapters collectively chart the dynamic political adaptation of right-wing political groups in Imperial Germany. They examine the German Right's position between the 'state' and the 'masses,' its accommodation of regional and doctrinal diversity, and its political strategies to retain traditional sources of power while mobilizing new political recruits. Each of these developments was part of Germany's political modernization in the sixty years under scrutiny.

The challenges and opportunities inherent in the Right's political orientation between the people (*Volk*) and the state (*Staat*) are considered from a number of perspectives. Particular attention falls on right-wing attempts to mobilize the 'masses' while retaining ties to the monarch, the state, and their functional elites (court, nobility, bureaucracy, army). As classic defenders of throne and altar, politically powerful members of the Right hoped that their ranks would be supplemented in number, but not supplanted in influence, by lower-middle-class and even working-class recruits. They attempted to reconcile mass inclusion and political exclusivity. But campaigns to gain influence with groups at one end of Imperial Germany's social hierarchy presented members of the Right with difficult choices, forcing them to consider the relative merits and liabilities of alienating groups at the other end. This book is about the political choices they made – and the decisions they skirted.

The significance of the German Right's regional and doctrinal heterogeneity requires somewhat fuller elaboration, not least because these two kinds of disunity were linked. Although a 'sense of place' informs every chapter of this book, geography alone cannot explain the range of opinion on the Right about how best to accommodate universal manhood suffrage and other new features of German political life after 1867.[2] Conversely, despite the range of ideological positions adopted by different factions on the Right, contemporaries were not blind to the fact that some adaptive strategies promised more success in one region of the empire than in another.

Historians of political movements, like party leaders, often equate unity with success and fragmentation with failure. In Imperial Germany, regional variations and internal rivalries certainly made it difficult for leaders of right-wing parties to demand obedience from their own followers as consistently as they would have liked. Centralized party structures emerged relatively late in the imperial era, particularly on the Right.[3] But historians should not forget that contemporary Germans often invoked a familiar dictum for success: 'March separately, strike together.' For this reason we must not overlook elements of a right-wing consensus that helped to secure different factions within what George L. Mosse once called the 'interlocking directorate of the Right.' Such groups included 'moderate' conservatives, 'radical' nationalists, 'extreme' agrarians, advocates of the lower middle classes (*Mittelständler*), antisemites, and other elements of the *völkisch* movement.[4] That 'interlocking directorate' was national in one sense, but it was very local in structure and orientation as well. Heinrich Mann's *Loyal Subject* illustrates how and why these interlocking dimensions of local politics were so important. Diederich Heßling's personal journey to financial independence, high social status, and political power is predicated on his penetration of every sphere of real or potential influence in the fictional town of Netzig. Thus the plot of the novel and Heßling's triumphal rise both make sense only because they unfold in Netzig's largest factory, its veterans association, its municipal council, its courthouse, its theatre, its public square, and its tavern.

Competing factions on the German Right also operated simultaneously in more than one sphere and on more than one plane of politics. What merits emphasis here is that members of the Right who were not included in national party councils often took the lead in articulating the challenges of political adaptation. This group included editors of newspapers, pamphleteers, rank-and-file functionaries, and regional chairmen. As a group, they could hardly be more heterogeneous socially. But by studying them outside conservatism's traditional power bases in rural Prussia, we can utilize a kind of spatial and ideological triangulation to overcome the constraints of a top-down, Prusso-centric perspective. This approach in turn enriches our understanding of how members of the German Right believed authority and nationality were related. As historians, we may choose to travel analytically from smaller to larger spaces, as do some chapters of this book – from local manifestations of burgher pride through state-level patriotism to the emergence of mentalities and identities that fed into a nationalist consensus about what it meant to be German. But it is not necessary to structure the analysis this way. Uncharted journeys into unfamiliar territory are welcome: they remind us that contemporary conceptions of *Deutschtum* were never uniform, static, or uncontested.

The challenge of mobilizing previously unenfranchised or politically passive social groups was *the* central dilemma facing all parties that were trying to adapt to a new political age from the 1860s onwards. This book examines the erosion of the older 'politics of notables' (*Honoratiorenpolitik*) as a consequence of many factors: rapid economic change, social dislocation, and the long-term impact of the constitutional structures put in place in the years 1867–71. This challenge was met with more success by those parties that were able to mobilize relatively homogeneous social milieux based on class or confession. The Social Democratic and the Catholic Centre parties were the first 'mass' parties (some historians would say the only ones) in pre-1918 Germany. By contrast, the challenge to adapt was especially convulsive for the right-wing parties, whose strategies for popular mobilization had to be squared with respect for the authority of the state. As a result, the politics of notables persisted longer on the Right.

Some historians claim to have discovered how 'notable politics' was superseded by 'mass politics' and when the tipping point was reached (almost invariably they choose the decade of the 1890s). These chapters argue for a different approach, one that considers the *longue durée* and refuses to single out one decade as 'a moment of fission' in modern Germany's political history. With this approach these chapters also seek to integrate new archival findings[5] into analytical concepts that consider political modernization in broader terms and over longer time spans – for example, the 'fundamental democratization of society' (Karl Mannheim), the advent of a 'political mass market' (Hans Rosenberg), and the rise of 'politics in a new key' (Carl Schorske).[6]

Even though these framing devices have stood the test of time, they can be given still sharper contours. In a previous study of the German Conservative Party,[7] two contemporary observations were cited to identify Conservatism's central dilemma, and they remain relevant to this book's broader consideration of the German Right. Bismarck remarked after his dismissal from office in March 1890 that Conservatives regarded politics and parliamentary life as 'mere sport.' 'One enjoys living a few months in Berlin,' Bismarck observed, 'going to breakfast in the House, and, when the bell for a plenary vote rings, quickly wiping one's mouth, rushing into the chamber, and asking, "How do we vote?"'[8] This was wishful thinking. A more candid appraisal was provided a few years later by Baron Julius von Mirbach-Sorquitten. 'Eminent statesmen,' declared Mirbach, 'have often expressed to me the wish to resurrect a Conservative Party as it once existed. Indeed, Gentlemen, we would be exceedingly happy to allow ourselves this retired life, if this universal, equal, and secret suffrage had not grown so hot under our feet. Now every party is more or less dependent on the large masses and must reckon with them, whether or not it wants to, whether or not it finds it comfortable to do so.'[9] The practice of politics on the Right was anything but mere sport. It was a hard-headed enterprise designed to preserve cherished ideals, privileges, and interests. It was debilitated by ambivalence towards the means for generating popular support. But it was deadly serious business, and as such, it deserves our attention.

Among the methodological ramifications mentioned earlier, which are paramount? First is the need to provide a working definition of 'authoritarian,' 'authoritarianism,' and the 'authoritarian imagination' – in each case, within the specific historical context of the German Empire's political system. We will do so in a moment. But any definition of German authoritarianism must stress its ambiguities, breadth, and fluidity. Authoritarianism is a relational category – like gender and region, for example – and it must be analysed by locating it securely in overlapping systems of political practice and intellectual thought.

Another methodological issue concerns the differences of opinion and competing research priorities that have come to the fore in German and Anglo-American scholarship on pre-1918 Germany. These differences have not, on balance, undermined the rich international collaboration that has marked the study of Imperial Germany's political history for decades. More than once, however, scholars on both sides of the Atlantic have ended up talking past each other when debating the overall contours of Imperial Germany, its developmental tendencies, and the best theories with which to analyse it.[10] Some of these scholarly wrangles reached a low point in the mid-1990s, in both tone and substance. Others should now be allowed to expire of their own lethargy.[11] By contrast, a discussion of Imperial Germany's authoritarian features can open up new questions for debate and advance scholarly research on a broad front.

This proposition is itself contentious. Two distinguished émigré historians recently claimed that to speak of the 'authoritarian' German Empire is to invoke an empty cliché.[12] Others insist on debating Germany's 'special path' (*Sonderweg*) to modernity. Still others believe that studying the multivalency of Imperial Germany's 'modernity' should be historians' highest priority.[13] Each of these arguments tends to present a caricature of authoritarian Germany as sclerotic, backward-looking, and ruled by pre-modern elites. This caricature is then used to support three further claims (each of which is challenged in this book): that if Imperial Germany was 'modern,' it cannot also have been authoritarian;[14] that a sharp chronological caesura (1890) divides Bismarckian and Wilhelmine styles of politics;[15] and that an 'old' Right comprised mainly of traditional elites was superseded not long after 1890 by a 'new' Right that drew its strength and élan from the masses.

To help redress such one-sided or polarized views of Imperial Germany, this book adopts methods derived from the 'social history of politics' and a 'cultural history of politics.'[16] It does so without pursuing theories that spiral inward on themselves and without following research agendas that have become narrow and self-referential. Instead it proposes two working hypotheses. It suggests, first, that the German Empire *was* marked by authoritarian structures, practices, and habits of mind in all areas of politics. And it suggests, second, that historians' recent efforts to document dynamism and restlessness in Imperial Germany do not refute the reality of constitutional stasis or the Right's central role in perpetuating blockages to political reform.

These chapters thus depict a flexible, dynamic German Right that was always dependent upon flexible, dynamic forms of German authoritarianism. Both the adaptation of the Right and the evolution of authoritarianism are considered as a part of broad-gauged political modernization, rather than as a narrow, static set of political institutions. These hypotheses are meant to pull together the scattered conversations that have been taking place among German and Anglo-American historians, to draw from them threads of reasoning that contribute to a cohesive assessment of Germany's political development, and to point the way for future research into unexplored areas. To put it differently, by taking up ambitious questions and providing modest, contingent answers, this book reviews the state of our scholarly *learning* about Imperial Germany while also stressing the limits of our *knowledge*.

This study tries to integrate concepts drawn from the field of political science into a fuller account of Imperial Germany's political contours and trajectories.[17] It discusses political modernization, democratization, and parliamentarization, asking whether these descriptors are compatible with shorthand accounts of an authoritarian system of rule. Here we consider analytical concepts currently attracting the attention of political scientists – for example, 'hybrid regimes,' 'semi-authoritarianism,' and 'elections without democracy.' Does the concept of hybrid regimes serve us well when we speak of 'democracy in the undemocratic state'? Were Germans 'practising democracy' *avant la lettre* by pushing turnout rates for Reichstag elections sky-high; or was Tom Stoppard on to something when he wrote: 'It's not the voting that's democracy, it's the counting.'[18] Germany after 1871 was a constitutional monarchy. But how did the German Right shape its political strategies to privilege one part of the equation and undermine the other? Although this social science literature is addressed more implicitly than explicitly in the chapters that follow, a political scientist suggested the subtitle of this book when he wrote that authoritarian rulers may break the links in 'the chain of democratic choice': 'the limits of the authoritarian imagination are not logical, but empirical.'[19] With the sociologist Max Weber as our guide, we will return to this proposition.

To reunite studies of political styles with studies of political mentalities is another aim of this book. Much work on the German Right[20] has focused on strategies for popular mobilization but neglected the larger mental frameworks within which those strategies – especially their anti-democratic, anti-liberal, antisemitic, anti-feminist, and anti-parliamentary aspects – were devised. Studying the medium without the message simply will not do. Consider, for example, the gulf that divided the political philosophy of Dubslav von Stechlin, the central figure in Theodor Fontane's last novel (1899),[21] from that of Heinrich Claß, the antisemitic leader of the Pan-German League, who fantasized publicly in 1912 about what the future would look like if he, not Wilhelm II, ruled Germany.[22] Both figures indulged in anti-establishment rhetoric, ranging from good-natured grumbling to outright treason. These two figures can be said to define the two ends of the spectrum, from tolerance to intolerance, on the German Right. Yet neither of them ever intended, should their imagined Germany become reality, that such a Germany would be politically more liberal, more democratic, or more pluralistic than the empire already was, as we see when we follow the leaders of the Right into and through the First World War.[23]

Once we establish that a pronounced anti-establishment effect cannot be equated with a disavowal of the principle of authority, it becomes more important to ask where the 'self-activation of subaltern groups' on the Right actually led. These groups were allegedly motivated by a 'soured emancipatory impulse.'[24] But what exactly did they want to liberate (besides others' wallets and their own frustrated career ambitions)? When one German chancellor dismissed the 'beer-bench politics' of the Pan-German League and another referred to leading conspirators in the German Conservative Party as the new 'pirates of public opinion,' they were criticizing the 'popular' means adopted by the Right but not its anti-democratic ends. Heinrich Claß's pseudonymous pamphlet of 1912, *If I Were the Kaiser*, was an invitation to Wilhelm II to walk the plank (Wilhelm refused the offer). But it was not an attempt to delegitimize the principle of authority or diminish its centrality in the governance of a future Germany.

Examining the political destinations to which right-wing imaginations pointed, we discover that different factions on the Right vied constantly with one another to explore the limits of political partisanship. However, we also discover that most of them practised very limited tolerance of heterodox political views; they adhered with much more determination to political ideals (monarchy, hierarchy, order) that bolstered the principle of authority in its most unvarnished form. Moreover, the Right devised new ways to rig the old rules of the game – not only in the realms of 'pure' politics but in many 'unpolitical' realms as well, including municipal administration, associational life, economic interest groups, nationalist lobby groups, the schools, the press, even in the streets. Though their goals were the same as Diederich Heßling's interlocutor Herr Wiebel, members of the German Right did not always have to 'hit out hard' to retain power. Jabbing strategically, back pedalling when necessary, even offering the feint of a roundhouse blow – a *coup d'état* against the Reichstag – they developed innovative, flexible means to achieve authoritarian ends.

This line of argument differs from that of historians who believe that by the dawn of the twentieth century, Germany was well embarked on a 'transition to democracy.' According to this latter view, pressed vigorously in recent studies by Margaret Lavinia Anderson and Brett Fairbairn, 'affirming' German voters regularly cast ballots in national elections untainted by administrative chicanery, state control, and Prussian traditionalism.[25] German scholars are more sceptical.[26] Similarly, this book does not support the argument that radical nationalist competitors on the Right undermined the politics of notables to the point that old-style conservatism was marginalized both on the Right and in national politics.[27] As chapter 2 explains, a more convincing scenario depicts the interpenetration of an 'old' and a 'new' Right and acknowledges the adaptation (not demise) of older practices in the face of new challenges.[28] Such interpenetration and adaptation occurred on constantly shifting political terrain, to be sure. But Adolf Hitler was correct in pointing out in the early 1920s that stuffy *Honoratiorenpolitik* was still very much in evidence, even on the radical nationalist Right.

Is it reasonable to ask whether the history of the German Right is a story of success or failure? At first glance this question appears wrongheaded. Yet upon reflection, we see that historians tend to elide two quite different historical narratives in attempting to answer it. One story depicts the failure of right-wing political parties to maintain their electoral strength into the late Wilhelmine era. Thus the 'red elections' of January 1912 demonstrate the Right's loss of legitimacy and popularity. The other story is predicated on the success of 'newer' and more 'radical' elements of the Right in mobilizing a popular constituency. In this account, these extremists succeed in putting radical nationalist goals on the political agenda, brutalizing the general level of civility in political discourse by giving priority to *völkisch* rhetoric.

As historians, we are inclined to think that right-wing diehards deserved the dismal fate that awaited them at the polls. We don't like their politics, and so we tend to see the tide of world history arrayed against them. But as German scholars have pointed out with increasing vehemence in the last half-decade, this emphasis on failure does not take full account of the persistent power of those institutions of authority in Imperial Germany on whose survival or demise the fortunes of the German Right hinged. Conversely, living in democratic and multicultural societies today, we find it easy to applaud the self-mobilization and self-emancipation of the masses. But telling this story with too much fervour skews our conclusions, to the point that any self-mobilized social group can be seen as contributing to the pluralization of political culture. To slip between the horns of this dilemma, historians need to take seriously the inner logic of the Right's authoritarian values *and* the range of historical contingencies that contributed to the triumph of Hitler and the Nazis.

'Authority,' *Obrigkeit* – what is it? Did it permeate Imperial Germany's political culture? This book tries to demonstrate that between 1860 and 1920 Germans rarely thought or spoke or wrote about liberty and democracy, about mass politics and the nation, about revolution and religion and race, without also thinking, speaking, and writing about the principle of authority itself. This finding requires the reader to draw together two scripts – one that was proclaimed and invoked publicly and one that was fashioned and articulated privately in the less-bounded realm of the imagination. To qualify for sustained historical analysis, the recorded sentiment and the exercise of power both have to be far enough away from the private opinion to communicate some other meaning, yet close enough that the historian can connect them to the unspoken thought.

In Imperial Germany the struggle to control the exercise of authority was a contest to sustain relationships of super- and subordination – to deploy power rather than to become the object of its deployment. One might argue that right-wing Germans could scarcely imagine their world any other way. Or one might claim that they could not foresee any outcome to political struggle that did not perpetuate established relations of authority. But both suppositions would be historically wrong and analytically limiting. A successful defence of the principle of authority required something more of right-wing Germans than blinkered, single-minded conviction. It required a larger and more dynamic mental image of how state and society could be linked in ways that reconciled tradition and change, stasis and adaptation. (As Thomas Mann put it once: 'And waiting means hurrying on ahead.')[29] In this imaginary world the principles of authority and order trumped political practicality. In today's vernacular, authoritarianism provided the 'vision thing' – something that mere ideologues could never understand.

Absolute authority can never be attained. Like pure liberty and full democracy, it is a chimera. The same is true of something for which Germans have one word, *Herrschaft*, and English speakers have many: rule, domination, mastery, governance, perhaps also hegemony.[30] Authority and *Herrschaft* may be perfect in theory, but they are always imperfect and always incomplete in practice. They can be striven for, rehearsed, practised, or defended, but the striving and defending never end. Moreover, before the quest to achieve or perpetuate authoritarian rule can even begin, it has to be conceived and endorsed. This is where the authoritarian imagination operates – in a number of registers but with a consistent core logic. No less an authority than Max Weber suggested as much in the spring of 1917, at a moment when the legitimacy of the authoritarian German state was dying in the slaughter of the Western Front and when he could no longer conceal his outrage over the bankruptcy of Germany's monarchy, its nobility, and its warmongering *littérateurs*. The logic of authoritarianism, Weber suggested, was unimpeachable: 'If there is anyone whose deepest conviction places *every* form of authoritarian rule exercised for its own sake above *all* the political interests of the nation,' he wrote, 'let him confess his beliefs openly. *He cannot be proved wrong.*'[31]

It is difficult to know precisely what kind of person Weber was writing about here. But if that person defended authoritarian rule in the way Weber described, he would fit comfortably among the thinkers and activists examined in this book. Heuristically, it may be acceptable to concede that conservatives and other 'moderates' of the 'old' Right were usually more interested than Weber in the *power of the state* as an end in itself (though they were clearly also interested in preserving their own power, privilege, and economic advantage). Conversely, one may argue that radical nationalists and other 'extremists' on the 'new' Right were usually more directly concerned with the *fate of the nation* (which likewise was invoked in the name of the people but often masked status anxiety and profit-seeking). Nevertheless, in 1917, just as in 1867, it is permissible to speak of a German Right in the singular. This Right endorsed the logic of authoritarianism for its own sake *and* sought to transform the principle of authority into political practice on its own terms, albeit in a contest whose rules were constantly evolving. This finding cannot easily be squared with past descriptions of the German Right as having been fundamentally reshaped by 'populists' who overcame the liabilities of traditional right-wing politics around 1900.

Members of the German Right were consistent in one thing: they sought to be responsive to the masses without ever wishing to be truly responsible to the people. They imagined and they practised authoritarianism in ways that premised the autonomy of established authority on the political subordination of the people's democratically expressed will. Some of them fostered new styles of politics that fished for popularity in uncharted waters and claimed to sound the direct voice of the people. Others continued to look to the monarchy, the bureaucracy, the army, and the uniqueness of Prussia to preserve the hard kernel of authoritarian order in the empire. But none of them sought salvation in the devolution of power to a *demos* worthy of the name. Instead, they bound the future of their movement to the survival of the nation, to the power of the state, and to the fateful unboundedness of authority itself.

Samuel Johnson was only half-right: 'Definitions are tricks for pedants.' Perhaps we can accept instead that 'the meaning of a proposition is the method of its verification.'[32] Many of the key terms used in this book are contingent on place and time. Nevertheless, these terms need to be clarified for readers through the provision of working definitions, however contentious and inadequate such definitions may be.

The adjective *authoritarian* and the noun *authoritarianism* are simple to define in a narrow sense and difficult in almost every other way.

Authoritarianism favours the principle of authority over that of individual liberty. Hence the *authoritarian imagination* is a mental map in which authority is found at the very centre and liberty is relegated to the margins (if not beyond). Before we elaborate on this concept, let us try to define and describe an authoritarian regime.

Such a regime is based on a type of rule that is dependent on centralized control and coercion.[33] That centralized authority may be a single ruler, but not a ruler who enjoys the autonomous power of the autocrat. It may constitute a larger ruling group, an executive; but if it is said to be an oligarchy, who belongs and who does not belong to such an oligarchy is difficult to specify. An authoritarian regime may grant wide powers of law enforcement and punishment to institutions of the state, but only in extreme cases does this way of exercising authority lead to a police state. If an authoritarian state is governed by the rule of law, legal and political corruption are generally contained. In a state like the imperial German *Rechtsstaat*, where the rule of law prevailed, existing laws and procedures are applied in ways that may seem intrusive, unjust, or excessive, but they are not arbitrary or routinely ignored. Nevertheless, it requires only a slight change of perspective to see that the rigour with which laws (including minor statutes and ordinances) are applied can make the rule of law oppressive and, in certain circumstances, authoritarian. An authoritarian regime also does its utmost to enforce public conformity and limit intellectual, artistic, and political freedom – if necessary, with force. It seeks to exert control over demands emanating from below, even when it cannot reject them outright and especially when it cannot gain the explicit consent of the majority of the population. Such a regime enjoys 'substantial leeway in the determination of the goals that the regime will pursue.' It is not responsible to the people.

In contradistinction to absolutism and totalitarianism, any definition of authoritarianism will stress the state's *limited* control and its *partial* toleration of pluralism, opposition, and freedom of ideas. The tendency of authoritarianism as a Weberian ideal type is always to attempt to subvert or destroy autonomous behaviour (individual, collective, or institutional). Legally and de facto, however, rulers and elites in authoritarian systems have to accept that change is unstoppable, that total autonomy of the state from society is unrealizable, and that groups and organizations independent of the regime will have some political influence. Authoritarian regimes therefore pay considerable attention to developing political structures and practices that deal with the problems of individual, social, and political mobilization as well as with other features of modernization.

Most attempts to define and analyse authoritarianism have considered regimes that came into existence after 1918, particularly military, bureaucratic, and/or one-party dictatorships (the classic example is Franco's Spain). Much of this literature follows the lead of Juan Linz, who was one of the first scholars to elaborate the problems inherent in a typology of authoritarian regimes. Linz also set a trend in dismissing nineteenth-century variants, including Imperial Germany, as far less interesting than more recent types and subtypes.[34] For him and others, 'semi-constitutional monarchies' such as the German Empire were 'halfway between traditional legitimate and authoritarian rule (with monarchical, estate, and even feudal elements mixed with emerging democratic institutions).' This dismissiveness is unfortunate. But the political hybridity that Linz identified here can focus our attention on what Marina Ottaway has termed the 'games semi-authoritarian regimes play.'[35] And those games, in turn, permit a fuller consideration of political mentalities, imaginations, and styles.[36] Thus the authoritarian imagination can be integrated into scholarly writing on political culture.

By speaking of *political culture*, we signal an interest in exploring the subjective dimension of politics: the social-psychological ambiance of a system of rule, the subjective relationship between the state and its citizens, and the system of norms, values, beliefs, attitudes, and sentiments that seem self-evident to groups and people involved in political activity. Those norms and values condition people's appraisals of what is and what is not possible in the political realm. Thus political culture research is concerned with the 'how' and 'why' of politics as much as with the 'what.' Moreover, such research posits no clear separation between the social and political dimensions of life; it is closely and logically associated with research on (political) social cultures, (political) mentalities, and (political) ways of life. As such, it focuses on the ensemble of codes and signs that condition the way citizens behave politically and how they interact with one another or with political institutions.

To return to Linz's analysis, it is possible to see how the authoritarian imagination fits into his typology of authoritarian regimes in two ways. First, authoritarianism, like political culture, can be conceived of as a kind of political medium through which interconnections among elections, party politics, and the state were experienced and reassessed over time. This medium ensured that shocks to the system generated in one battle zone would be felt in other battle zones as well. Second, by tilting the analysis in the direction of perception and experience, we are able to emphasize the range of hopes and fears found on the German Right as its members tried to make sense of political change and its uncertain trajectories. These Germans were linked less by a discrete, cohesive political ideology than by a multifarious, fractured authoritarian imagination that maps directly onto Linz's 'authoritarian mentality':

> Mentality is an intellectual attitude; ideology is intellectual content. Mentality is psychic predisposition, ideology is reflection, self-interpretation; mentality is previous, ideology later; mentality is formless, fluctuating – ideology, however, is firmly formed ... Ideologies have a strong utopian element, mentalities are closer to the present or the past ...
>
> Mentalities are ... more difficult to use as a test of loyalty. The range of issues for which an answer can be derived from them, the degree of precision of those answers, the logic of the process of derivation, and the visibility of the contradictions between them and policies are very different. Their constraining power to legitimate and delegitimate actions are very different.[37]

As this volume's subtitle suggests, the relationship between human imagination and the political constraints that determine how thought is transformed into action is an important one. The authoritarian imagination links successes and failures of the German Right to something broader than a party program and narrower than a *Weltanschauung*. As such, it has little to do with 'the mind of Germany,' 'theories of the elite,' or the 'Germanic ideology.'[38] But it has everything to do with Germany's turn away from liberalism and democracy and the steps in that direction that were taken during the imperial era. By examining the history of the Right and the authoritarian imagination together, this book explores the intermediate, shifting ground between historical 'facts' and imaginative 'truths.' And by stressing the role of individual thought and human emotions in larger narratives, it illustrates how history is made by the intersection of character and circumstance.

Other working definitions can be dispatched more quickly. Throughout this book, the *state* is deemed to include local, regional, and national governments, their bureaucracies, and other agents of governance, always in the context of the constitutions, laws, and administrative practices that gave it legitimacy (or not). In fact, to refer to 'the state' in the singular is to begin on the wrong foot; therefore the following chapters strive for precision when referring to imperial (*Reich*) authorities, to Prussian authorities, or to other embodiments of the German state at the federal, provincial, and local levels. It is also useful to remember that the state itself was 'neither unchanging nor an entity that stood outside society.'[39]

Use of an upper-case C is reserved for the *German Conservative Party* or its members. A lower-case *c* is used to refer to either of the two principal conservative parties (the second being the Imperial and Free Conservative Party)[40] and to those Germans who espoused conservative principles, policies, or habits of mind but affiliated themselves with no party. The first chapter of this book charts the genesis, evolution, and diversity of political *conservatism* in German history, and it reviews the contending interpretative positions taken by historians since the 1930s. Problems of definition have figured prominently in this literature, at least for historians not willing to follow John Stuart Mill's famous description of conservatives as 'the stupid party.'[41] As a starting point for the following analysis – but only a starting point – we can list the six canons of conservative thought identified by one intellectual historian: belief in a transcendent order that rules society as well as conscience; affection for the proliferating variety and mystery of human existence, as opposed to uniformity, egalitarianism, and pure logic; conviction that civilized society requires orders and classes; a belief that freedom and property are closely linked; distrust of sophistry and 'totalizing' constitutional systems, with a corresponding preference for custom, convention, and prescription; and recognition that change, and especially hasty innovation, may not be salutary reform. Thus, for conservatives, a statesman's chief virtue is prudence.[42]

As should be apparent already, conservatives made up only one part of the German *Right*. The term *radical nationalist* is reserved for those who gave priority to national goals and whose radicalism stood in at least latent conflict with conservatism. In large measure the radical nationalists overlapped with members of the *völkisch movement*, who likewise espoused strong nationalist views but whose thinking was also typically imbued with strongly racialist and reformist strains.[43] What may surprise readers is the degree to which the *radical Right* in Imperial Germany corresponds to a definition of the radical Right in twenty-first-century Germany: both comprised 'parties, organizations, and individuals whose self-knowledge and activities are formed by the majority, if not all, of the following characteristics: nationalism; ethnocentrism; xenophobia, particularly in the guise of anti-Semitism and racism; anti-pluralism; anti-communism [in Imperial Germany, anti-socialism]; anti-parliamentarism; militarism; a law and order mentality; the longing for an authoritarian state under one leader; often a sympathy for conspiracy theories; and the acceptance of violence as a suitable means of political discourse.'[44]

Most *Junkers*, members of the lower Prussian nobility, were *agrarians* in that they owned and managed relatively large grain-growing estates east of the Elbe River. There were of course many aristocratic Germans who farmed estates outside Prussia; but as one socialist in the Kingdom of Saxony remarked, it was inconceivable to call such landowners 'Junkers' because the term was so closely associated with Prussianism. Peasants and independent farmers of small-scale agricultural holdings, which predominated in southwestern Germany, were also agrarians. According to conventional usage in histories of Imperial Germany, not all agrarians actually tilled the soil: some served as editors of leading newspapers affiliated with Imperial Germany's broad and diverse agrarian movement; others were politically active as functionaries, travelling speakers, or clerks in one or more interest groups dedicated to the prosperity of German agriculture. Both types of 'agrarians' would rarely have left the cities or come into contact with the German soil about which they wrote.[45]

The opportunity to distinguish between *antisemites* and conservatives is taken up in chapter 8. As Richard S. Levy has recently written, historians often have to leave it to antisemites of the day to decide who should be included in this category. Popular usage was not fastidious or consistent: that much is clear. Yet after it was first coined in 1879 by Wilhelm Marr, the term *antisemitism* described 'thinking and behaviour intended to do harm to the reputation, rights, and/or physical well-being of Jews for a wide variety of motives.' Levy has also provided a compelling rationale for using both terms in their unhyphenated form.[46]

Political modernization and *popular mobilization* are not used interchangeably in this book, but they are closely linked.[47] Over the sixty years examined here, broad sections of the population came to play a dramatically new role in German politics: this was Mannheim's fundamental democratization of German society. As the 'masses' were organized, they did not take over the state in the sense of instituting a democratic form of government. But they ceased to be merely the masses; as Baron von Mirbach-Sorquitten noted (with regret), they became the enfranchised population. Soon new structures and practices

I.2. Berlin election rallies, 1890. The captions read (clockwise from top): speakers of various parties; unauthorized posting of placards; urban listeners; invoking house rules (to clear an assembly hall); rural meeting; maiden speech (in parliament). 'Aus Berliner Wahlversammlungen,' wood engraving after a sketch by Carl Koch, 1890, in the *Leipziger Illustrierte Zeitung*, no. 94, 178. Image courtesy of the Bildarchiv Preußischer Kulturbesitz, Berlin.

facilitated their permanent, institutionalized, and legally enforced involvement in voting. With increasing energy and commitment they supported the activities of political parties and interest groups, subscribed to the political press, and turned out for small discussion groups and mammoth political rallies.

The way we conceive such participation is contentious, falling somewhere on the spectrum between participation-as-emancipation and participation-as-regimentation. When does a street demonstration fall into one category or the other? When does securing a black-market ticket to the visitors' gallery of the Reichstag represent dissent, when conformity? Readers will choose how to answer such vexing questions, but they should be aware that imperial German politics was an almost exclusively male affair, at least as conceived in the relatively narrow sense relating to parties and elections. German women won the vote only after the revolution of November 1918; until 1908 they were not even allowed to join parties or attend meetings where politics was discussed. Since 1992, when Eve Rosenhaft called on scholars to devise research strategies that could account for women's silences in the historical record, historians have begun to integrate gender into the history of Germany's political modernization generally and histories of the Right specifically.[48] But such research will always be constrained by the fact that male participation in the public sphere was privileged in innumerable ways. In the meantime, concluded Rosenhaft, perhaps 'the best we can hope for is an account that regretfully and self-consciously excludes women.'[49]

Both popular mobilization and political modernization should be distinguished from older versions of modernization theory.[50] Few historians any longer deploy a concept of modernization that sees parochial remnants receding on all fronts in the face of modern industrial capitalism, democratization, and parliamentarization. On the contrary, most scholars would agree with the anthropologist Marshall Sahlins, who once wrote that cultural continuity, cultural authenticity, and tradition are all too important to be associated exclusively with backwardness, conservatism, or custom. They are too multivalent to be set in opposition to rationality, development, or modernity. Rather, tradition is how we change.[51] This insight allows us to explore Germany's political modernization with due attention to its diverse forms, its surface textures, its reversible patterns, its constituent dilemmas.

In what corner of Germany, finally, are we to look for the 'essential' empire? In the late 1990s, historians responded negatively to attempts to sum up Imperial Germany by painting it in shades of grey. Tempering bold programmatic statements with caveats and second thoughts, concluding that the German Empire faced forward and backward at the same time – these balanced approaches satisfied few scholars.[52]

Every epoch is a transitional one. Yet not every epoch finds its protagonists imbued with the feeling that their times are contradictory, filled with shrill dissonances, out of joint.[53] What, then, do we make of another dissonance, this one in the scholarly literature about Imperial Germany's apparent hybridity? This dissonance contrasts anti-democratic, anti-parliamentary, and anti-liberal encumbrances from the Bismarckian age with an image of Wilhelmine society and culture as extraordinarily pluralistic, reformist, and modern. As Dieter Langewiesche recently put it: 'What does this conjoining of political *unambiguousness* and social-cultural *pluralism* signify for the question of political styles and of the relationship between politics and the public sphere?'[54] We might surmise that when Germans in the imperial era were confronted with political clarity and socio-cultural confusion together, they would have endorsed a subdued 'yes, but ...' assessment of both the *Zeitgeist* and their own lived experiences. But surely this is a dissatisfying way to take stock of twenty-five years of historiography on the German Empire; it veils, rather than sharpens, Imperial Germany's distinctive historical contours.[55]

As this introduction has suggested, historians have made great strides in revising earlier depictions of Imperial Germany as drab, brutish, and unchanging.[56] But there is no reason to conclude that the history of Germany's political modernization is best told in the style of Thomas Mann's *Buddenbrooks* (1901) either. In that story, decline into irrationality is graceful. A bustling metropolis, Lübeck, provides the setting for patricians jostling politely for power. Is this what Imperial Germany *really* looked like? Not necessarily. Imperial Germany had plenty of Netzigs, too – the nasty little town in which Diederich Heßling first imagines and then finds himself. Heinrich Mann's Netzig is filled with little emperors, rabid antisemites, and parochial sycophants, each of whom reflects features of the authoritarian imagination. There is precious little room for tolerance or pluralism or positively inflected provincial modernity here: by the novel's end, Netzig's liberal tradition has been snuffed out. As the personification of bourgeois Germany's public soul, updated for a new age, Diederich Heßling has carried the day.

To point out these contrasting facets of Imperial Germany is *not* to suggest that Lübeck or Netzig represents the 'real' Germany. Nor should it imply that scholarly quarrels are unhealthy if they leave historians uncertain about the political limits of the authoritarian imagination. On the contrary: as Gordon Craig once wrote, Thomas and Heinrich Mann became aware of their own creative gifts by quarrelling with each other – over 'the nature of the creative task, the social responsibility of the intellectual, and their country's role in modern history.'[57] Yet Imperial Germany's dissonances led Friedrich Nietzsche and others to diagnose the sign of the times as 'brutality' combined with an 'indulgence of meaning,' a 'dependency of judgment,' and a 'pliability of conduct.'[58] Thus, when weighing the ironic mode of *Buddenbrooks* against the uncompromising starkness of *The Loyal Subject*, historians would do well to heed an observation Thomas Mann made after Germany's self-destruction in 1945. At that time Thomas wrote that it was the other Mann – his brother Heinrich – who 'knew the score earlier and suffered no disillusionment.'[59]

NOTES

1 Heinrich Mann, *Man of Straw* (London and New York, 1984), 39. This is the translated title of *Der Untertan*, which appeared in a first edition of 100,000 copies in November 1918. A recent Continuum edition provides an improved translation and restores previously omitted scenes: *The Loyal Subject*, ed. Helmut Peitsch, trans. Ernst Boyd and Daniel Theisen, The German Library, 64 (New York, 1998).
2 See David Blackbourn, *A Sense of Place: New Directions in German History*, 1998 Annual Lecture of the German Historical Institute, London (London, 1999); David Blackbourn and James Retallack, eds., *Localism, Landscape, and the Ambiguities of Place: Germany, 1871–1918* (forthcoming); and further reflections in chap. 4.
3 Thomas Nipperdey, *Die Organisation der deutschen Parteien vor 1918* (Düsseldorf, 1961), esp. 241–64; Maurice Duverger, *Political Parties: Their Organization and Activity in the Modern State*, trans. Barbara and Robert North, 3rd ed. (London, 1978); Gerhard A. Ritter, *Die deutschen Parteien 1830–1914* (Göttingen, 1985).
4 On the interpenetration of the antisemitic and *völksich* milieus, see Stefan Breuer, 'Gescheiterte Milieubildung. Die Völkischen im deutschen Kaiserreich,' *Zeitschrift für Geschichtswissenschaft* 52, no. 2 (2004): 995–1016; and Massimo Ferrari Zumbini, *Die Wurzeln des Bösen. Gründerjahre des Antisemitismus* (Frankfurt a.M., 2003). On militarism among veterans groups and others, see Benjamin Ziemann, 'Sozialmilitarismus und

militärische Sozialisation im deutschen Kaiserreich 1870–1914,' *Geschichte in Wissenschaft und Unterricht* 53, no. 2 (2002): 148–64; Bernd Ulrich, Jakob Vogel, and Benjamin Ziemann, eds., *Untertan in Uniform* (Frankfurt a.M., 2001), esp. 9–11; and Thomas Rohkrämer, *Der Militarismus der 'kleinen Leute'* (Munich, 1990).

5 All archival documents in the notes are cited according to the name, file number, and location in which they were originally used over the period 1980–2005. Specialists will be familiar with the many changes in Germany's archival landscape since 1990.

6 See Karl Mannheim, *Man and Society in an Age of Reconstruction* (orig. 1935), trans. Edward Shils (New York, 1967), 44; Hans Rosenberg, *Große Depression und Bismarckzeit* (Berlin, 1967), 123 and passim; Carl Schorske, 'Politics in a New Key: An Austrian Trio,' *Journal of Modern History* 39 (1967): 343–86.

7 James Retallack, *Notables of the Right: The German Conservative Party and Political Mobilization in Germany, 1876–1918* (London and Boston, 1988).

8 Bismarck's comments made in Friedrichsruh in 1891, cited in the *Frankfurter Zeitung*, 6 April 1895.

9 From Mirbach's speech in the Prussian House of Lords on 26 March 1896; *Stenographische Berichte über die Verhandlungen des Preußischen Herrenhauses* (Berlin, 1896), 1:132. See also Andreas Biefang, 'Modernität wider Willen. Bemerkungen zur Entstehung des demokratischen Wahlrechts des Kaiserreichs,' in *Gestaltungskraft des Politischen*, ed. Wolfram Pyta and Ludwig Richter (Berlin, 1998), 239–59.

10 Thirty years ago James J. Sheehan tried to set a fruitful pattern for transatlantic dialogue with his edited collection *Imperial Germany* (New York, London, 1976).

11 For one particularly acerbic exchange, see Geoff Eley, 'Introduction 1: Is There a History of the Kaiserreich?' and Eley, 'German History and the Contradictions of Modernity: The Bourgeoisie, the State, and the Mastery of Reform,' in *Society, Culture, and the State in Germany, 1870–1930*, ed. Eley (Ann Arbor, 1996), 1–42 and 67–104; Hans-Ulrich Wehler, 'A Guide to Future Research on the Kaiserreich?' *Central European History* 29, no. 4 (1996): 541–72; and Roger Chickering's review in the *American Historical Review* 103, no. 1 (1998): 213–14. Eley replied to Wehler in 'Theory and the Kaiserreich. Problems with Culture: German History after the Linguistic Turn,' *Central European History* 31, no. 3 (1998): 197–227. These polemics appeared shortly after I tried to take stock of the debate in James Retallack, *Germany in the Age of Kaiser Wilhelm II* (Basingstoke, London, New York, 1996).

12 Konrad H. Jarausch and Michael Geyer, *Shattered Past: Reconstructing German Histories* (Princeton and Oxford, 2003), 19.
13 For programmatic statements about the need to focus on German modernities, see Geoff Eley, 'Bismarckian Germany,' in *Modern Germany Reconsidered, 1870–1945*, ed. Gordon Martel (London and New York, 1992), 1–32, esp. 7 and 25–6; Eley, 'Modernity at the Limit: Rethinking German Exceptionalism Before 1914,' in a special issue ('Conservative Modernity') of *New Formations* 28 (1996): 21–45, esp. 26; Eley, 'Making a Place in the Nation: Meanings of "Citizenship" in Wilhelmine Germany,' in *Wilhelminism and Its Legacies: German Modernities, Imperialism, and the Meanings of Reform, 1890–1930*, ed. Eley and James Retallack (Oxford and New York, 2003), 16–33.
14 See, for example, David Blackbourn and Geoff Eley, *The Peculiarities of German History: Bourgeois Society and Politics in Nineteenth-Century Germany* (orig. German ed., 1980; Oxford and New York, 1984), 37–155, esp. 127, 132–2, and 141–2. See also Geoff Eley, *Reshaping the German Right: Radical Nationalism and Political Change after Bismarck* (New Haven, 1980), esp. 7, 198.
15 Anglo-American scholars' tendency to focus on the years after 1890 is reflected in their neglect of important German studies that address a longer time frame. See, for example, Lothar Gall, ed., *Regierung, Parlament und Öffentlichkeit im Zeitalter Bismarcks* (Paderborn, 2003); Gall, ed., *Otto von Bismarck und Wilhelm II.* (Paderborn, 2000); Gerhard A. Ritter, ed., *Wahlen und Wahlkämpfe in Deutschland* (Düsseldorf, 1997); and Lothar Gall and Dieter Langewiesche, eds., *Liberalismus und Region* (Munich, 1995).
16 See James J. Sheehan, 'Klasse und Partei im Kaiserreich: Einige Gedanken zur Sozialgeschichte der deutschen Politik,' in *Innenpolitische Probleme des Bismarck-Reiches*, ed. Otto Pflanze (Munich, 1983), 1–24; Georg Iggers, ed., *The Social History of Politics* (Leamington Spa, 1985); Thomas Mergel, 'Überlegungen zu einer Kulturgeschichte der Politik,' *Geschichte und Gesellschaft* 28, no. 4 (2002): 574–606, esp. 593–4.
17 See *inter alia* Peter Steinbach, 'Modernisierungstheorie und politische Beteiligung – Zur Analyse politischer Partizipation im langfristigen Wandel,' in *Arbeit, Mobilität, Partizipation, Protest*, ed. Jürgen Bergman et al. (Opladen, 1986), 36–65; Steinbach, ed., *Probleme politischer Partizipation im Modernisierungsprozeß* (Stuttgart, 1982); M. Rainer Lepsius, *Demokratie in Deutschland* (Göttingen, 1993); and Karl Rohe, *Wahlen und Wählertraditionen in Deutschland* (Frankfurt a.M., 1992).
18 Tom Stoppard, *Jumpers* (1972), act I, cited in *The Oxford Dictionary of Quotations*, ed. Elizabeth Knowles, 5th ed. (Oxford, 1999), 743. Turnout rates for Reichstag elections reached 77.5 per cent as early as 1887.

19 Andreas Schedler, 'The Menu of Manipulation,' *Journal of Democracy* 13, no. 2 (Apr. 2002), 36–50, here 41. This journal issue was devoted to 'Elections without Democracy'; the following articles from the same issue also inform the general argument of this book: Larry Diamond, 'Thinking about Hybrid Regimes,' 21–35; Steven Levitsky and Lucan A. Way, 'The Rise of Competitive Authoritarianism,' 51–65. See also Thomas Carothers, 'The End of the Transition Paradigm,' *Journal of Democracy* 13, no. 1 (Jan. 2002): 5–21.
20 Including Retallack, *Notables of the Right*.
21 Theodor Fontane, *The Stechlin*, trans. with intro. by William L. Zwiebel (Columbia, SC, 1995).
22 Daniel Frymann [pseud. for Heinrich Claß], *Wenn ich der Kaiser wär' – Politische Wahrheiten und Notwendigkeiten*, 3rd ed. (Leipzig, 1912), esp. 206–227 and 230–1, 'Herrscher und Volk.'
23 See Rainer Hering, *Konstruierte Nation. Der Alldeutsche Verband 1890–1939* (Hamburg, 2003); Roger Chickering, *We Men Who Feel Most German: A Cultural Study of the Pan-German League, 1886–1914* (London and Boston, 1984).
24 David Blackbourn, 'The Politics of Demagogy in Imperial Germany,' in Blackbourn, *Populists and Patricians: Essays in Modern German History* (London, 1987), 217–45, here 239; Eley, *Reshaping*, 218.
25 See Margaret Lavinia Anderson, *Practicing Democracy: Elections and Political Culture in Imperial Germany* (Princeton, 2000); Brett Fairbairn, *Democracy in the Undemocratic State: The German Reichstag Elections of 1898 and 1903* (Toronto, 1997); Stanley Suval, *Electoral Politics in Wilhelmine Germany* (Chapel Hill, 1985). More sceptical: Robert Arsenschek, *Der Kampf um die Wahlfreiheit im Kaiserreich* (Düsseldorf, 2003); Gerhard A. Ritter, 'Die Reichstagswahlen und die Wurzeln der deutschen Demokratie im Kaiserreich,' *Historische Zeitschrift* 275 (2002): 385–404.
26 On the importance of Prussian traditions, see Hartwin Spenkuch, 'Vergleichsweise besonders? Politisches System und Strukturen Preußens als Kern des "deutschen Sonderwegs,"' *Geschichte und Gesellschaft* 29, no. 3 (2003): 262–93; Spenkuch, *Das Preussische Herrenhaus. Adel und Bürgertum in der Ersten Kammer des Landtages 1854–1918* (Düsseldorf, 1998); Thomas Kühne, *Dreiklassenwahlrecht und Wahlkultur in Preussen 1867–1914* (Düsseldorf, 1994). On democratization and parliamentarization, see the résumés in Thomas Kühne, 'Das Deutsche Kaiserreich 1871–1918 und seine politische Kultur: Demokratisierung, Segmentierung, Militarisierung,' *Neue Politische Literatur* 43, no. 2 (1998): 206–63; Kühne, "Demokratisierung und Parlamentarisierung: Neue Forschungen zur politischen Entwick-

lungsfähigkeit Deutschlands vor dem Ersten Weltkrieg,' *Geschichte und Gesellschaft* 31, no. 2 (2005): 293–316; also Andreas Biefang, *'Der Reichsgründer'? Bismarck, die nationale Verfassungsbewegung und die Entstehung des Deutschen Kaiserreichs* (Friedrichsruh, 1999); Biefang, 'Der Reichstag als Symbol der politischen Nation. Parlament und Öffentlichkeit 1867–1890,' in *Regierung*, ed. Gall, 23–42; Winfried Becker, *Das Bismarck-Reich – ein Obrigkeitsstaat?* (Friedrichsruh, 2000).

27 This line of argument is found in Eley, *Reshaping*; and Eley, *From Unification to Nazism: Reinterpreting the German Past* (Boston, 1986).
28 See Chickering, *We Men*; Heinz Hagenlücke, *Deutsche Vaterlandspartei. Die nationale Rechte am Ende des Kaiserreiches* (Düsseldorf, 1997).
29 Thomas Mann, *The Magic Mountain* (1924), chap. 5, sec. 5, cited in *Oxford Dictionary of Quotations*, 494.
30 See the multiauthored article 'Herrschaft' in *Geschichtliche Grundbegriffe. Historisches Lexikon zur politisch-sozialen Sprache in Deutschland*, ed. Otto Brunner, Werner Conze, and Reinhart Koselleck, 9 vols. in 8 (Stuttgart, 1972–97), 3:1–102.
31 Max Weber, 'Parliament and Government in Germany under a New Political Order: Towards a Political Critique of Officialdom and the Party System' (orig. 1917), in Weber, *Political Writings*, ed. Peter Lassman and Ronald Speirs (Cambridge, 1994), 130–271, here 132 (emphasis added only to the last sentence). See also Weber, 'Suffrage and Democracy in Germany,' ibid., 80–129.
32 The German philosopher Moritz Schlick, cited in *Oxford Dictionary of Quotations*, 648.
33 This and the following paragraph derive in part from Amos Perlmutter, *Modern Authoritarianism* (New Haven and London, 1981), 24–5.
34 For the following, see Juan Linz, *Totalitarian and Authoritarian Regimes* (orig. 1975; Boulder and London, 2000), 54 and 160–5; Paul Brooker, *Non-Democratic Regimes: Theory, Government and Politics* (Basingstoke and London, 2000), 22–35.
35 Marina Ottaway, *Democracy Challenged: The Rise of Semi-Authoritarianism* (Washington, DC, 2003), 137–60, esp. 137–8: 'Game playing is an intrinsic part of democracy ... Simply put, semi-authoritarian regimes play rougher games because they can get away with it.'
36 See also Francisco Panizza, ed., *Populism and the Mirror of Democracy* (London and New York, 2005).
37 Linz, *Totalitarian and Authoritarian Regimes*, 162–3.
38 See Theodor W. Adorno et al., *The Authoritarian Personality* (New York,

1950); Richard Christie and Marie Jahoda, eds., *Studies in the Scope and Method of 'The Authoritarian Personality'* (Glencoe, Ill., 1954); Renato Cristi, *Carl Schmitt and Authoritarian Liberalism* (Cardiff, 1998); Walter Struve, *Elites against Democracy: Leadership Ideals in Bourgeois Political Thought in Germany, 1890–1933* (Princeton, 1973); Hans Kohn, *The Mind of Germany: The Education of a Nation* (New York, 1960); Fritz Stern, *The Politics of Cultural Despair: The Rise of the Germanic Ideology* (Berkeley, 1961).

39 Blackbourn, *Populists*, 18.

40 Volker Stalmann, *Die Partei Bismarcks. Die Deutsche Reichs- und Freikonservative Partei, 1866–1890* (Düsseldorf, 2000); Matthias Alexander, *Die Freikonservative Partei 1890–1918. Gemäßigter Konservatismus in der konstitutionellen Monarchie* (Düsseldorf, 2000).

41 See Axel Schildt, *Konservatismus in Deutschland. Von den Anfängen im 18. Jahrhundert bis zur Gegenwart* (Munich, 1998), and works cited in chap. 1; Rudolf Vierhaus, 'Konservativ, Konservatismus,' in *Geschichtliche Grundbegriffe*, ed. Brunner et al., 3:531–65; Karl Mannheim, *Conservatism: A Contribution to the Sociology of Knowledge*, ed. David Kettler, Volker Meja, and Nico Stehr (London and New York, 1986); Caspar von Schrenck-Notzing, *Lexikon des Konservatismus* (Graz, Stuttgart, 1996); Stefan Breuer, *Ordnungen der Ungleichheit – die deutsche Rechte im Widerstreit ihrer Ideen 1871–1945* (Darmstadt, 2001); and Larry Eugene Jones and James Retallack, eds., *Between Reform, Reaction, and Resistance: Studies in the History of German Conservatism from 1789 to 1945* (Providence, RI, and Oxford; 1993).

42 Russell Kirk, *The Conservative Mind: From Burke to Eliot*, 7th rev. ed. (Washington, DC, 2001), 8–9.

43 See Uwe Puschner, *Die völkische Bewegung im wilhelminischen Kaiserreich* (Darmstadt, 2001); Puschner, Walter Schmitz, and Justus H. Ulbricht, eds., *Handbuch zur 'Völkischen Bewegung' 1871–1918* (Munich, 1996); Diethart Kerbs and Jürgen Reulecke, eds., *Handbuch der deutschen Reformbewegungen 1880–1933* (Wuppertal, 1998).

44 Lee McGowan, *The Radical Right in Germany, 1870 to the Present* (London, New York, Toronto, 2002), 5–6.

45 The standard work is Hans-Jürgen Puhle, *Agrarische Interessenpolitik und preußischer Konservatismus im wilhelminischen Reich 1893–1914* (orig. 1966), 2nd ed. (Bonn–Bad Godesberg, 1975); on the nobility, besides works cited in chap. 1, see Eckart Conze, ed., *Kleines Lexikon des Adels. Titel, Throne, Traditionen* (Munich, 2005), including Heinz Reif, 'Junker,' 123–9.

46 Richard S. Levy, ed., *Antisemitism: A Historical Encyclopedia of Prejudice and Persecution*, 2 vols. (Santa Barbara, Denver, Oxford, 2005), 1:xxix–xxx; Levy,

30 The German Right, 1860–1920

> *Antisemitism in the Modern World: An Anthology of Texts* (Lexington, Mass., and Toronto, 1991), 2–11. 'Anti-Semitism is not only a misnomer – it does not apply to the majority of Semites, that is, the Arab peoples – but it also gives continued life to a pernicious myth. "Semitism," a collection of exclusively negative traits comprising a monolithic Jewish essence, existed only in the minds of the enemies of the Jews. Jews and their allies who opposed the antisemites were defending not this imaginary "Semitism" but their human rights' (from Levy's preface to Binjamin W. Segel, *A Lie and a Libel: The History of the 'Protocols of the Elders of Zion,'* ed. and trans. Richard S. Levy [Lincoln and London, 1996], x).

47 The following draws on Brett Fairbairn, 'Political Mobilization,' in *Imperial Germany: A Historiographical Companion*, ed. Roger Chickering (Westport, Conn., 1986), 303–42; see also Larry Eugene Jones and James Retallack, eds., *Elections, Mass Politics, and Social Change in Modern Germany: New Perspectives* (Cambridge and New York, 1992).

48 See *inter alia* Ute Planert, *Antifeminismus im Kaiserreich* (Göttingen, 1998); Andrea Süchting-Hänger, *Das 'Gewissen der Nation'* (Düsseldorf, 2002); Christiane Streubel, 'Frauen der politischen Rechten in Kaiserreich und Republik,' *Historische Literatur. Rezensionszeitschrift von H-Soz-u-Kult* 1, no. 2 (2003): 10–39; and other works cited in ch. 1.

49 Eve Rosenhaft, 'Women, Gender, and the Limits of Political History in the Age of "Mass" Politics,' in *Elections*, ed. Jones and Retallack, 149–73, here 150.

50 See Peter Steinbach, 'Deutungsmuster der historischen Modernisierungstheorie für die Analyse westeuropäischer Wahlen,' in *Vergleichende europäische Wahlgeschichte*, ed. Otto Büsch and Steinbach (Berlin, 1982), 158–246; Thomas Mergel, 'Geht es weiterhin voran? Die Modernisierungstheorie auf dem Weg zu einer Theorie der Moderne,' in *Geschichte zwischen Kultur und Gesellschaft*, ed. Mergel and Thomas Welskopp (Munich, 1997), 203–32.

51 Marshall Sahlins, *Culture in Practice: Selected Essays* (New York, 2000), esp. 419 and 514–15.

52 See, for example, Thomas Nipperdey, *Deutsche Geschichte 1866–1918*, 2 vols. (Munich, 1992), 2:905.

53 See the perceptive argument in Dieter Langewiesche, *Politikstile im Kaiserreich. Zum Wandel von Politik und Öffentlichkeit im Zeitalter des 'politischen Massenmarktes'* (Friedrichsruh, 2002), esp. 6–9.

54 Ibid., 9; emphasis added.

55 Ibid., 28.

56 See Ewald Frie, *Das Deutsche Kaiserreich* (Darmstadt, 2004), esp. 118–24.

57 Gordon A. Craig, 'The Other Mann,' *New York Review of Books* 45, no. 6 (9 April 1998): 21.
58 Nietzsche cited in Reinhard Alter, *Die bereinigte Moderne. Heinrich Manns 'Untertan'* (Tübingen, 1995), 29; Thomas Ziegler (1899) cited in Langewiesche, *Politikstile*, 9.
59 Craig, 'Other Mann,' 21. See also Alter, *Bereinigte Moderne*, 64.

PART ONE

'Tradition is how we change'

1 Habitus and Hubris

Questions about political fairness and personal honour have always intertwined in the German authoritarian imagination. To begin the discussion of how this intertwining shaped the political agendas of the German Right in the nineteenth century, we might consider 'the ancient opinions and rules of life,' whose imminent demise pained the English conservative Edmund Burke more than two hundred years ago. This discussion in turn argues for a narrowing of focus, to take in not the German Right as a whole but those social and political groups to which Burke principally directed his message: aristocrats and conservatives.

It has been said that European conservatism was born in 1789 because before that date there was nothing else. The fate of aristocrats in society and the fortunes of conservatives in politics, however, were linked long before the storming of the Bastille. Referring to a less faraway past, Karl Mannheim wrote that the typical conservative wants to preserve 'not only his interests, but also the world in which his interests are embedded.'[1] As later chapters of this book reveal in more detail, the struggle to reconcile ideals and interests raged within conservative ranks as much as it did between conservatives and their antagonists. It pitted conservatives who were said to lack principles against other conservatives who drew praise for their determined struggle to preserve aristocratic or other codes of honour. Legitimists, pragmatists, romantics, reformers, reactionaries, resisters – these conservatives all faced the challenge of adapting means to ends, tactics to strategy, survival to virtue, ideology to vision.

To assess the degree to which conservatives met the challenge of reconciling interests and ideals, we can examine them at those turning points in their history when they confronted revolutionary situations (real or imagined). If we take this path, our investigation is steered toward those historical intersections where we find conservatives – often dazed and uncomprehending, as after a traffic accident – at the moment when they recognize that their party has come to a fork in the road. Or we can try to get close to conservatives as they enjoy the everyday comforts and challenges of life, deporting themselves in ways that reflected hybrid identities (as conservative landowners, most conspicuously, but also as conservative journalists, conservative parliamentarians, conservative advisers to the king, and so on). As we seek out conservatives in their salons and clubs, we can try to listen carefully to their conversations, just as in other studies we parse the words they committed to the printed page. As we follow conservatives onto their landed estates in backwoods Prussia, we can explore their activities in smaller social networks, just as with other approaches we study how they performed on a national stage.

Three historians whose work is highlighted in this chapter have suggested innovative ways to relate the habitus of nineteenth-century conservatives to their political ideals.[2] Each author in his own way reminds us that that a conservative ideology took shape gradually, hesitantly, and in piecemeal fashion. Robert Berdahl has studied the emergence of a conservative ideology from the agrarian, patrimonial existence of Prussian nobles on their landed estates before 1848. Wolfgang Schwentker has considered the mobilization of new political resources and conservatives' learning processes in the revolutionary upheavals of 1848–9. Willi Füßl has explored conservatives' slow adaptation to new parliamentary regimes – regimes that were mainly unforeseen and unloved – through the eyes of the greatest conservative thinker at mid-century, Friedrich Julius Stahl. These studies, and others like them highlighted later in this chapter, remind us that both momentous events and everyday routines are part of the same story. Political fireworks and programmatic texts, career highlights and parliamentary rituals – these must be considered in the light of less-dramatic changes in the lifestyles, social bearing, and mental orientation of conservatives.

Conservatives have always been more insistent than forthright when they declare that they operate in history without theories or programs. A.J.P. Taylor knew as much, even though he once declared baldly that liberals put ideas into history and conservatives take them out. Such pronouncements remind us that conservatives' ability to accommodate historical change has always depended on more than intellectual thought or party doctrine. Following a lead provided by Panajotis Kondylis, this chapter argues that not only ideologies of power but the *interpretation* of power must be brought into closer proximity with the exercise of power. Like Kondylis, we need to ask: 'Who embodies *Ordnung*, who determines its rituals, who is its custodian?'[3]

But how exactly do we embed conservatives within their interlocking worlds of experience and domination (*Herrschaft*)? We must investigate how they embraced the principles of legitimacy, Christianity, hierarchy, political inequality, and the organic development of state and society; but we must also continually ask how they *felt* about the task of inventing an ideology and all the traditions that go with it. By differentiating between the veil and the mask, between intent and perceived intent, we can attend more carefully to unexpected consequences.

Such distinctions are apposite to a discussion that runs, like this one, on parallel tracks. One track charts conservatives as they attempted to defend their habitus by devising a new ideology. The second track leads to another, as yet unexplored, destination. This one carried conservatives on a historical journey that imbued *neither* their personal conduct nor their political ideology with a broader, positive vision.[4] These tracks, because they are parallel, cannot meet at any agreed point, let alone one called 'modernity.' This chapter does not explore German conservatism's dilemmas beyond 1920. Instead it seeks to illuminate how habitus and hubris each contributed to a story of great success and great failure – a story that may have begun its real denouement only after Imperial Germany collapsed.

Trajectories of Scholarship

In the 1960s and 1970s, conservatism was the stepchild of German historical scholarship. Socialism, liberalism, imperialism – these drew the most attention. In the mid-1980s Wolfgang Schwentker reported that things were finally beginning to happen in research on German conservatism.[5] Seven years later an anthology of essays on German conservatism provided more even coverage for the period 1789 to 1945.[6] Such research is still being outpaced by work on German socialism and liberalism. But the disparity is shrinking.

A comparative assessment of German conservatism recommended itself early on. When he wrote *The Role of Force in History*, Friedrich Engels asked why German Junkers were incapable of playing the historical role that British aristocrats seemed to accept with such good grace.[7] Others have since posed essentially the same question in different ways, seeking to explain why Germany's Junker class survived so long and with such unfortunate consequences. Survivors are rarely the most articulate of historical sources. Neither are conservatives. No matter whether conservatives are asked to choose between reform and reaction or between reaction and resistance: they are always caught in the paradox of defending a status quo whose legitimacy they questioned before it came into being. Hence one scholar's observation that 'the essence of conservatism is continual treason unto itself.'[8]

Perhaps for this reason, historians have found it difficult to understand the sense of fatalism that accompanied aristocratic conservatives' sometimes gracious, more often ungracious, decline.[9] However, an empathetic approach pays dividends, assuming that empathy does not become apology. It is not difficult to conjure up sympathy for a figure such as Dubslav von Stechlin, who remarks in the novel *The Stechlin* by Theodor Fontane that the Prussian nobility, since the time of Frederick the Great, had become a service elite and little more: 'We had the honour of being allowed to go hungry and thirsty and to die for king and fatherland, but we were never asked whether it suited us to do so. Yes, now and then we were told that we were "noblemen" and hence had more "honour." But that was it.'[10]

Recent accounts of society and politics in nineteenth-century Germany suggest that the time has come to take the burden of twentieth-century disasters off the backs of the Junkers. Whether or not they actually retreated into the 'inner fastnesses' of the royal court, foreign service, cavalry and guards regiments, and the local Prussian bureaucracy,[11] the Junkers saw the writing on the wall even before 1900. As today's electronic media would have it, they read their fate 'up close and personal.' There is much truth in this view. Historians today no longer portray German landowners as pre-industrial or feudal. Although its commitment to exploiting industrialization for profit was always ambiguous, the Junker class cannot be described as anything but capitalist from at least the 1820s and 1830s onward. (This characterization also gives the lie to descriptions of the German bourgeoisie as having been 'feudalized.')[12] Moreover, we no longer believe that Prussia's landowning elite had everything its own way. Even in the countryside, the tugging of forelocks and the politics of *Ja* and *Amen* passed into the history books before the nineteenth century itself did.

A central question remains unanswered, however. Were German (not just Prussian) conservatives perhaps already watching the curtain descend on the first act of their historical drama in the era of revolution and reaction from 1789 to 1848? Were conservative reactions to revolution already proving insufficient in the middle of the nineteenth century? The jury is still out, but recent reports of conservatism's *political* demise before 1848 are greatly exaggerated. Indeed, when we look more closely at the interwoven strands of political conservatism before mid-century, we find that strategies to cope with new challenges were high on the conservative agenda well before violence broke out.[13] Those strategies proved so effective in the crucible of revolution that even conservatives were astounded.

Conservative politics of both the defensive and the offensive type were rooted in the direct experience of lordly domination on landed estates and the gradual erosion of myths idealizing a system of paternalism. In practice, the appeal to broad segments of the populace was carefully calculated and refined during the mobilization of conservative voters in 1849. And the ministrations of compromise with which the conservative ideologue Friedrich Julius Stahl stifled his colleagues' allergic reactions to constitutional monarchy and parliamentarism were crucial in ensuring that conservatives would not be swept aside after 1848. Thus, although one may date the genesis of 'programmatic' conservatism to various moments in German history, conservatives' strategies to sidestep extinction had important implications, not only for the nobility but also for the long-term evolution of German political culture.

The study of German conservatism has also been frustrated by disagreements over what the term 'conservatism' actually means – a problem already noted in this volume's introduction. 'Conservatism,' wrote Clinton Rossiter in 1968, 'is a word whose usefulness is matched only by its capacity to confuse, distort, and irritate.'[14] Such problems arise in part because conservatism, unlike liberalism or socialism, did not originate as an ideology with a fully articulated concept of human nature, the state, and society, but rather as a reaction to the sudden and dramatic changes that began to transform the face of Europe in the second half of the eighteenth century. Insofar as it was identified with a defence of the status quo, conservatism clearly antedated the French and industrial revolutions. As a result, the term came to connote both a disposition frequently identified as 'traditionalist' and the specific ideology within which this disposition was articulated. Historians and social theorists have thus found it convenient to differentiate between traditionalism as a means of identifying the subjective, instinctive, and natural disposition to keep things the way they are and a formally articulated ideology of conservative principles, values, and ideas. This distinction, however, tends to be more artificial than real. It obscures the extent to which traditionalism and conservatism complement each other as the two poles of an analytical tension. That tension also defines the parameters of recent research on the subject.

The historiography of German conservatism since the 1920s has reflected changing emphases in the research and writing of German history. Initially, historians focused on the intellectual roots of German conservatism and its contribution to the German *Sonderweg*. Attempts were made to identify various strands of conservative ideology or stages in conservative development and then to link these with prominent individuals and their writings. Early and conceptually innovative forays into the field of social history were interrupted or ignored, only to be launched again at a later stage with new vigour and insight. Gradually, methodological tools adopted from the social sciences broadened the scope of the inquiry and introduced much-needed theoretical considerations, though generally 1933 continued to be taken as the terminal point of conservative development. In the most recent phase, a new pluralism of method in the historical guild has impelled research in promising new directions. Nevertheless, the separate strands of research on conservatism have all too often remained isolated from one another: theory and empiricism coexist unhappily, while studies of the nineteenth century often say nothing about the twentieth (or vice versa). Great works are studied without any attempt to identify their readership or political impact. And the tactics of parliamentary parties are divorced from the ideology that allegedly underpinned them. How have these deficiencies coloured past scholarship on German conservatism, and how might they be overcome?

The sociologist Karl Mannheim, writing in the 1920s, was one of the first to explore the intellectual roots of conservatism. To the concept of traditionalism, he opposed a type of conservatism 'oriented to meanings that contain different objective contents in different epochs.'[15] Mannheim's pioneering contribution remains undiminished, not least because his habilitation thesis was recently published in full in both German and English. Since Mannheim first raised the question of locating conservatism within its concrete historical context, historians have suggested many categories or 'ideal types' for the analysis of German conservatism. Usually these ideal types are presented in one of two ways: either as components of a comprehensive 'system' of conservative thought (less frequently a system of politics or a social order) or as chronological stages through which conservatism allegedly passed on the way to some more or less 'modern' form.

Sigmund Neumann's book on the 'stages' of Prussian conservatism (1930) set the pattern for these lines of analysis in three respects: Neumann combined the ideal-typical and the chronological models; he linked prominent individuals with each distinct brand of conservatism; and he identified two antithetical strands within nineteenth-century conservatism – Romantic conservatism and liberal conservatism – that combined to produce a synthesis, identified by Neumann as realistic conservatism, which purportedly dominated the period after 1848. As representative figures of these three stages, he selected the 'romantic' conservatives Justus Möser and Ludwig von der Marwitz,[16] the 'liberal' conservatives Joseph Maria von Radowitz and Moritz August von Bethmann Hollweg, and the 'realistic' conservative Otto von Bismarck.[17]

Mannheim's and Neumann's concentration on political thought rather than political action, their interest in ideal types, and their emphasis on the period from 1770 to 1848 influenced writing on the subject for many decades. In his study of German constitutional history since 1789, Ernst Huber identified four categories of conservatives: estate-bound (*ständisch*) conservatives, social conservatives, national conservatives, and state conservatives.[18] Fritz Valjavec was somewhat less categorical in his 1951 study of the emergence of political movements in Germany between 1770 and 1815. He pointed instead to the interplay between political forces of the late Enlightenment and early Romantic periods. Though his contribution was seldom acknowledged, he provided the first analysis of key conservative individuals and texts.[19]

The most important American contribution to this discussion was Klaus Epstein's seminal study of the genesis of German conservative thought from 1770 to 1806. Building on Valjavec's work, Epstein stressed the specificity of German conservatism as a defence of the *ancien régime* against the universalist principles of the Enlightenment and the French Revolution. But he also offered a comprehensive definition of conservatism that embraced three distinct ideal types: status quo conservatives, reform conservatives, and reactionaries.[20] Epstein's book, like Valjavec's, was theoretically less challenging than Mannheim's. Yet it surpassed any work of its era in the richness of its empirical detail.

By the time of Epstein's early death in 1967, students of conservative ideas had begun to turn their attention to the period after 1871. In this respect, the work of two émigré historians, Fritz Stern and George Mosse, merits special consideration. Stern was most interested in the emergence of a particular brand of conservatism known in the Weimar Republic as 'revolutionary conservatism.' By studying the writings of three self-styled 'conservative revolutionaries' – Paul de Lagarde, Julius Langbehn, and Arthur Moeller van den Bruck – Stern depicted the irrational, anti-modernist, and racialist currents that helped to create the cultural environment in which the Nazis could come to power.[21] Mosse directed his attention to the emergence, dissemination, and institutionalization of a *völkisch* ideology from the beginning of the nineteenth century through the Nazi seizure of power in 1933.[22]

By focusing on 'cultural despair' and 'liturgical impulses,' Stern and Mosse explored the more virulent forms of conservative ideology and charted later strains of antisemitism, anti-modernism, and nihilism back to their roots in the nineteenth century. Their work paralleled that of Peter Pulzer, an English scholar whose work on political antisemitism in Germany and Austria represented the beginnings of a socio-political analysis of what had certainly become one of the most vexing problems of modern German history.[23] The work of all three, but particularly that of Stern and Mosse, was predicated upon the assumption that a fundamental liberal deficit in Germany's political culture made the collapse of the Weimar Republic and the triumph of Nazism virtually inevitable.[24]

Neumann's argument that German conservatism developed in coherent stages also led historians to distinguish between two styles of conservative politics: one that derived from a comprehensive view of the world (*Weltanschauungspolitik*) and one geared towards the defence of conservative interests (*Interessenpolitik*). Those who made this distinction tended to argue that these styles were mutually exclusive and that they appeared sequentially. Thus they identified many variations and alleged turning points in conservative development – for instance, the 'Junker Parliament' of 1848, the Agrarian League, and the antidemocratic condominium of big business and agrarianism after 1930. These models included normative assumptions that were more often implied than explicitly argued. Ignoble, unreflective, and materialist motives were ascribed to German conservatives, while high-mindedness, insight, and a continuing attachment to idealism allegedly inspired conservatives in other countries, particularly in western Europe. In making such a distinction, however, historians were conflating social and political categories. By identifying conservatism exclusively with aristocrats, they failed to appreciate the extent to which conservatism penetrated the ranks of the middle and lower classes. Whereas this error of interpretation has been addressed recently by historians of liberalism, little attention has been devoted to the way in which such imprecision has skewed our understanding of conservatism.

Normative assumptions were found in even the most innovative studies of German conservatism by social historians such as Hans Rosenberg and Alexander Gerschenkron. Junkers and other German nobles were again condemned for not playing the historical role that British lords accepted after 1910. According to this line of analysis, the British aristocracy learned to preserve the semblance of status and power while waving the white flag of economic decline as a class. In effect, they voluntarily submitted and contributed to their own demise. But the Junkers were anomalous. Refusing to do the gentlemanly thing, they ignored the pronouncement of the elite theorist Vilfredo Pareto that history is the graveyard of aristocracies. Instead they fought ruthlessly to preserve their many privileges.

The political consequences of this rearguard action were enormous. As Gerschenkron expressed it in applying his model of 'backwardness' to Germany, the price of bread and the fate of democracy were not unconnected. Because the power of the Junkers on their landed estates was preserved through protective tariffs on grain, German history was encumbered with a fateful legacy.[25] As we will see in chapter 2, Hans Rosenberg believed that the Junkers' 'pseudo-democratization' involved the incorporation of populist techniques of mass mobilization that also contributed to their survival into the twentieth century.[26] In this way, too, the Junkers differed from elites anywhere else in the Western world.

By 1970 this view of German conservatism had become a crucial component of *Sonderweg* theory. Perhaps no book was more influential in defining the essential contours of this theory than Ralf Dahrendorf's *Society and Democracy in Germany*. Dahrendorf asked: 'Why is it that so few in Germany embraced the principle of liberal democracy?'[27] The rapid pace of German economic modernization after 1871, he answered, took place within a social and political system that was still essentially feudal. The net effect of this lack of 'synchronization' was to retard the social and political development of the German bourgeoisie. This line of analysis found immediate echoes in works written by Hans-Ulrich Wehler and others at the University of Bielefeld in the 1960s and 1970s. These confirmed the essential elements of Dahrendorf's thesis with a wide range of empirical and theoretical studies.

In 1966 one of Wehler's Bielefeld colleagues, Hans-Jürgen Puhle, published a densely empirical study of the Agrarian League. In this book Puhle argued that German conservatives abandoned their distaste for mass politics in the 1890s and learned better than their rivals how to mobilize a rural constituency for the defence of elite interests. Having adopted a political style that Puhle called 'pre-fascist,' German conservatism bequeathed a tragic inheritance to the Weimar Republic.[28] An equally critical view of German conservatism was found in Wehler's influential book *The German Empire* (1973).[29] Wehler painted a picture of conservatives working with tragic effectiveness to counter the threat of democracy by manipulating interest-group politics, religious and secular education, class justice, constitutionalism, imperialism, and alleged foreign threats. Mirroring A.J.P. Taylor's famous quip that 1848 was the turning point when German history failed to turn, Wehler's analysis seemed to suggest that German conservatives single-handedly brought history to a halt.

From the perspective of Puhle and Wehler, the political mobilization of the 'little man' in Wilhelmine society was nothing more than the penultimate act in a drama of political manipulation that stretched from the failed bourgeois revolution of the mid-nineteenth century to the failed conservative counter-revolution of January 1933. The same argument was espoused, though informed by different presuppositions, by Theodore S. Hamerow in the United States, Volker Berghahn in Britain, and Fritz Fischer and his circle of students from the University of Hamburg.[30] Meanwhile East German historians equated conservatism with fascism; they focused unremittingly on the united opposition of the Junkers and the bourgeoisie to Germany's working classes.[31]

By the end of the 1970s a reaction against this particular reading of German history had begun to materialize. The next decade witnessed a continuation and intensification of the assault on the Bielefeld paradigm. This, in turn, has led to a fundamental reassessment of the Right and its place in modern German history. One of the major weaknesses of the Bielefeld model was its tendency to refer to right-wing elites without regard to their actual positions in the hierarchies of wealth, prestige, and power. Depending on the requirements of the argument, these elites included not only Junkers but also members of the Prussian army, court, and bureaucracy, heavy industrialists, imperialists, Protestant clergy, educators, and – in the broadest view – all those who opposed the advance of Social Democracy and the threat of revolution. As historians began to appreciate the great diversity of social and ideological interests espoused by members of the Right, they grew increasingly sceptical of the argument that the German Right could have devised, much less implemented, a grand strategy to deflect the threat of modernization. Far from taking the initiative to steer economic, social, and political modernization into paths that did not threaten their material interests, members of the Right were forced to respond to these challenges as best they could – inadequately in some ways, more than adequately in others.

Some of the most exciting new work also took a fresh look at social and political relationships in the German countryside. An American observer wrote from Berlin in 1833 that this world was populated by only two classes: 'the von's and the not von's.'[32] But a richer and more complicated picture emerged in which patterns of authority and subordination between Junkers and peasants were more differentiated than previously believed. This has been illustrated by William W. Hagen's recent book (previewed in a battery of seminal essays) on the 'Junkers' faithless servants' in rural Brandenburg;[33] by two volumes of essays on the German peasantry in the nineteenth and twentieth centuries;[34] by Francis Carsten's survey history of the Junkers;[35] by René Schiller's and Ulrike Hindersmann's studies of noble landowners in Brandenburg and Hanover;[36] and by Robert Berdahl's exploration of conservative ideology, discussed in the next section. The newer studies among this group draw on sources that provide a much more intimate picture of landed estate life than was possible just twenty years ago. Such sources include tax tables, mortgage, debt, and servants' records, the minutes of agricultural credit associations, court proceedings, instructional primers written for landlords, and much more. Just as recent studies of the German bourgeoisie have put to rest the notion that the middle classes were 'feudalized' by a pre-industrial Junker elite, studies of peasants and lords have undermined the notion of a single cohesive conservative constituency in the countryside.

Ideology and Land

Robert Berdahl's book on *The Politics of the Prussian Nobility* broke new conceptual ground when it appeared in 1988. Berdahl's study was concerned with the genesis of a conservative ideology and a distinctly conservative style of politics.[37] Much more than earlier scholars, Berdahl saw both the theory and the practice of Prussian conservatism as emanating from the nobility's experience on the land. Prussian noblemen's perceptions of state and society, he argued, were immediate and direct. They were formulated – at least initially and for the majority – not at court, not in war, not in literary salons. Rather, class consciousness, economic self-interest, and political opinion all developed out of the everyday experiences of Prussian nobles on their estates in the rural east and their practice of *Herrschaft*. A seventeenth-century writer quoted by Berdahl expressed this idea didactically but with insight: 'A *Hausvater* should fear God, work with his wife, educate his children, rule his servants and subjects, and manage his estates from month to month.'[38] Only when his daily chores were done did the Prussian Junker have time to contemplate the larger world of politics and government.

At the time of writing, Berdahl had only a relatively small body of literature on estate life on which to draw. Appropriately, he mined the work of such historians as Otto Brunner, Hanna Schissler, and Hans Rosenberg, and he took note of comparative and theoretical insights offered first by E.P. Thompson, Pierre Bourdieu, and others.[39] Still, Berdahl's achievement was remarkable. He compelled us finally to dispense with the idea of German conservatism as emanating from the literary and philosophical musings of non-rural, non-farming, non-'lording' Prussians – of Romantics, in short, who had not yet seen the light of *Realpolitik*. Berdahl believed that *Weltanschauung* politics and interest politics were intertwined and complementary from the outset: 'Because the experience of domination was personal and immediate, it had to be justified in terms that were personal and private, in this case through an ideology that can best be described as paternalistic.'[40] To the perceived ignorance and immorality of the peasantry, the landowning nobility offered guidance and control; both duties were believed to belong to the intertwined 'offices' of which Ludwig von der Marwitz and others spoke. Thus 'the eternal conflict between honour and profit' conditioned Junker 'interests' as a way of life, a view of the world, a system of relationships, and a complex interplay of tradition and innovation. While interest politics on the Right may have had its genesis in the Junker Parliament of 1848, interests and their problematic relationship with ideologies had already been central to German conservatism for decades.

The nobility's practice of patrimonial rule rested in part on important distinctions between categories of peasants. As a result of the cruel treatment suffered by peasants, their increasing service obligations, and the effective confiscation of their lands, social unrest mounted in the 1840s. Yet large-scale rebellions did not occur before 1848. Social control combined with the uneven emergence of class consciousness among the lower orders to keep rural society both unfair and in flux. Thus the social differentiation of the peasantry 'functioned to enhance the lord's means of social control over the peasants at the same time that it offered opportunity for upward mobility for peasants locked within the framework of servile bondage.'[41]

The patrimonial *Hausvater* literature of the day transmitted and tried to instrumentalize images of the lowly peasant. Those images revealed the numbing effect of work processes and social underprivilege. But they gave a hint of later rebelliousness – the 'hidden conflict at the core of rural society.' Thus peasant youths presented a challenge to their masters in faces 'whose one eye, or perhaps both, squint furtively beneath half-closed eyelids, whose mouth is twisted open in a scornful, somewhat dumb smile, whose head hangs on his chest or even sinks toward the ground as if trying to conceal itself: in a word, faces in which fear, stupidity, and simplicity are mixed with ridicule and antipathy.'[42]

What instruments of social coercion preserved class domination in the countryside? And how were these integrated with instruments of cultural hegemony? Berdahl addressed these questions by examining patrimonial justice, the exercise of police powers, and the Junkers' influence on schooling and the appointment of local pastors. In each instance, the system of symbolic *Herrschaft* complicated the concept of paternalism. Whereas paternalism stressed the mutuality of rights and obligations within the peasant-lord relationship, often based on the model of the family, symbolic *Herrschaft* worked to legitimize the structures of subordination and superordination. These did not necessarily contradict paternalism; instead the 'structures of symbolic domination worked to show that those who governed were a different order of persons altogether from those whom they governed.' In other words, the Prussian nobility needed symbols to emphasize both its 'intimacy' with and its 'distance' from the peasants. There were instances where these symbols and strategies obviously failed, where the dominant class was unmasked and shown to be exercising 'arbitrary, raw privilege.'[43] The issue of noble hunting rights underlines this point well. On the whole, however, estate-bound (*ständisch*) distinctions persisted in the system of patrimonial justice, in codes of honour, and – as illustrated by the vacant chair left between nobles and commoners at dinner – in the rites and ceremonies of village life. The General Civil Code of 1794 systematized such relationships: it was a conserving document.

Berdahl also addressed a question to which recent historians of nineteenth-century conservatism have provided a half-dozen different answers: Who drew up Prussian conservatism's first coherent program?

Berdahl's first candidate was Ludwig von der Marwitz. In his polemics against the Prussian reforms of Baron Karl vom und zum Stein, the 'destroyer' of the Prussian nobility, Marwitz helped to establish the main motifs of conservative discourse for the rest of the century. He wrote that Stein had 'initiated the revolutionizing of the fatherland, the war of the propertyless against property, industry against agriculture, the mobile against the stabile, crass materialism against the God-given order.' Because he formulated the essential anti-capitalist, anti-liberal, and anti-revolutionary components of conservative ideology, Marwitz may indeed have provided 'the first fairly systematic expression of political conservatism.'[44]

After discussing the place of intellectuals and political theorists in political society, Berdahl next identified Adam Müller as 'beyond doubt, [the] author of the first conservative political ideology that defended the interests of the nobility.' This claim corrected early views of Müller as a representative of German Romanticism and little more. Müller's world view was concrete enough to be understood and appreciated by estate owners. It provided the Prussian landowning elite with 'an ideological framework that justified – one is tempted to say, sanctified – its traditional role.'[45] Nonetheless, Berdahl's conclusion ran contrary to the work of Klaus Epstein, Fritz Valjavec, and Jörn Garber, all of whom identified other possible authors of conservative ideology, including men who wrote before the French Revolution.[46] Indeed, to what extent can any one person be the 'author' of a political ideology? While his lectures on Frederick the Great 'provided the Prussian nobility with a clear-cut ideology,' Müller hardly seems a likely candidate for the role of father to conservatism.[47]

Why not? Given that most conservatives at this time stood in opposition to the government, Müller's paternity is called into doubt on four counts. First, Müller applied to the Prussian ministry to publish two newspapers, one supporting Stein's reforms and one anonymously in opposition. Second, he was viewed by many contemporary conservatives as a poseur, a pedant, and a fraud; as a student in Göttingen, he closed his shutters on bright days and lit candles, simply to be poetic and genteel. Third, his writings were received even by leading conservatives as 'falsehoods' and 'a remarkable jumble of ideas.' Lastly, Friedrich von Gentz suggested to Müller early in his career that he write something – anything? we wonder – that would win him 'a colossal reputation' and 'a highly comfortable existence.' These are not the normal motives for someone about to draw up a coherent, principled, or viable 'ideology' of any sort. Still less are they the hallmarks of a visionary.

In the end, Berdahl conceded that Müller failed to provide an effective guide to future conservative statesmen. The same is true of the next candidate for the job, Karl Ludwig von Haller, who 'provided conservatives with a formal ideology that could be used against both absolutism and revolution.'[48] Here, too, Epstein and Valjavec had previously demonstrated the force of anti-absolutist and anti-revolutionary strains in pre-1789 conservatism. No matter: by book's end it was clear that Berdahl's final choice as the father of a conservative ideology was Friedrich Julius Stahl, a prominent constitutional theorist, a professor, and a Jew. Stahl 'offered a conservative theory of a modern state that could accommodate change and give a place for the new social forces, while it retained the personal element in authority embodied in monarchy and nobility.' Berdahl may have erred when he claimed that Stahl's pre-eminence rested on his role as 'the first conservative thinker to give weight to public opinion.' As chapter 7 of this volume suggests, many other right-wing publicists from the 1770s to the 1840s were aware of the need to engage liberals in the expanding public sphere (*Öffentlichkeit*). But Stahl was able to formulate a world view for conservatives that was comprehensive and flexible. The message he had presented in *The Monarchical Principle* (1845) proved to be correct: 'It was possible to construct a constitutional monarchy that would not inevitably evolve into a parliamentary democracy.' This deceptively simple contribution was enough for Berdahl to give Stahl the nod over all other contenders: it was Stahl who forged the weapons Prussian aristocrats needed to recoup their power and recover their nerve after the shock of March 1848.

Lords and Peasants

Robert Berdahl was not alone in suggesting that the 'faithlessness' of villagers was inherent in the structures of rural societies. In his prize-winning book *Ordinary Prussians*, William W. Hagen chronicled the litigiousness of rural society that belied its reputation for dormancy. His conclusions about the Junker-villager relationship sounded uncannily like Berdahl's: 'The noble landlords wielded government-backed disciplinary and police powers, but whether these could be effectively and profitably applied depended on a constantly tested and renegotiated manor-village power balance.'[49] In his introduction, Hagen wrote that historians had been too 'Junker-obsessed' to take note of the village and its networks. However, this assertion overlooked two edited collections, both published in 1986, that addressed this lacuna and provided a quantum leap in our knowledge about German lords and peasants.[50]

Robert Moeller introduced his collection of essays by illustrating the insufficiency of a view of rural society that draws sharp divisions between exploitative employers and exploited workers.[51] Two early essays, by Hanna Schissler and Hans-Jürgen Puhle, made a hesitant start in this direction.[52] But in concentrating on the history of an entire class and restricting their analyses to the national sphere, they offered something close to an orthodox account of Germany's agrarian sector – one that subsequent authors attacked with success.

In an essay on property and wood theft in Westphalia, Josef Mooser discussed the alleged class nature of social conflict in the early nineteenth century. For a later period, Ian Farr analysed peasant protest through the example of the Bavarian Peasants League. Asking why deferential politics no longer operated in Germany after the 1890s, Farr emphasized the volatility, not the 'idiocy,' of rural life. He demonstrated that traditional parties responded to challenges from below, rather than working out manipulatory schemes on their own terms. And he showed that the peasants were less backward than previously imagined in determining where their real economic interests lay.

The contributors to the collection edited by Richard J. Evans and W.R. Lee took a different approach. First, they covered a longer time frame. Hartmut Harnisch and William Hagen concentrated on the latter half of the eighteenth century, examining the interplay between the rationalization of agricultural production and the development of social antagonisms in the countryside. Wolfgang Kaschuba explored the historical contours of village class society before and after the Nazi period, while Utz Jeggle – like Kaschuba, an anthropologist – claimed to be interested 'only in the present.' Second, this volume was distinguished by the inclusion of historians from the German Democratic Republic, where a major school of agrarian history flourished before 1990. Hainer Plaul, Gisela Griepentrog, and Christel Heinrich focused on the black-earth region (*Börde*) around the city of Magdeburg. Without even a tip of the hat to vulgar Marxist interpretations, their chapters analysed the everyday life of rural labourers before 1880, the interplay of demographic, economic, and political factors in peasant and working-class families before the Second World War, and peasant customs in the 1920s as revealed through local marriage festivals.

Third – and here the two volumes were most alike – the contributing authors portrayed Germany's rural worlds not as traditional, passive, and undifferentiated but as seething with inner conflicts, inner contradictions – indeed, with inner demons. The range of issues and personalities they examined extended from the sabotage practised on the Stavenow estate in Prussia to the 'rules of the village' laid down by the elders of Kiebingen in Swabia (who, as Jeggle ruefully admitted, almost frustrated efforts to penetrate their inner world).[53] This approach introduced the reader to the social hierarchy differentiating horse, cow, and goat farmers in the Weimar Republic; the female farm servants in Bavaria who carried with them more than one kind of reputation; even the German wedding gifts in the 1920s that were appraised with as keen an eye for their snob value as they are today. Thus an important feature of *The German Peasantry* was its interdisciplinary approach. Oral history, ethnography, folklore studies, social anthropology, and the history of *mentalités* combined to provide a broader analysis of German rural society than was possible before the 1980s. These two volumes did not offer the last word on relations between peasants and masters. But they did yeoman service, preparing the way for monographic studies such as those authored by Berdahl and Hagen.

Ideology and the State

Thomas Nipperdey built his analysis of German history after 1866 on two pillars: the world of burghers and the 'strong state.' These pillars also supported Lothar Dittmer's study of conservatives in the Prussian bureaucracy in the first half of the nineteenth century. For Dittmer, conservative responses to the challenges of Restoration Europe constituted the prehistory of the Conservative Party in Prussia.[54]

Like the other key authors discussed in this chapter, Dittmer was aware that the development of conservative ideology, propaganda, and associational life were strongly influenced by those close to the throne. But he pushed early conservative journalism into the limelight. He argued that in the 1830s the editorial staffs of conservative newspapers and journals provided the only adequate vehicle for developing a conservative 'program' qua ideology. Before the appearance of political parties, these editors offered the most effective means to disseminate conservative ideology to the functionaries and opinion-makers whom conservative bureaucrats in Prussia imagined to be bulwarks against liberal, democratic, and rationalist doctrines. Through them, Prussian ministers came to believe that the conservative and semi-official press could be used to communicate the government's views to 'the people.' Unfortunately, Dittmer presented only one side of the equation, leaving readers in the dark as to the administration's view of the liberal press. For all the evidence he provided about the circulation of conservative journals and the subsidies granted to them by officials, he never considered the strength of the conservative press relative to the liberal press. This omission led to a conclusion that, while not wrong, was contradictory.

On the one hand, Dittmer claimed that the public relations policy (*Öffentlichkeitspolitik*) of Prussian officials was a 'sensibly constructed and effective whole.'[55] The publicity that was supported and steered by the Prussian ministry of culture 'reached its intended audience and was read by the members of newspapers' editorial staffs and by important makers of public opinion.'[56] Because the government-subsidized press 'conducted an on-the-whole successful campaign with liberal and democratic forces,' it allegedly reached a 'wide range of social strata.'[57] On the other hand, Dittmer showed that conservative propaganda was most popular where its ideological content was least obvious; that is, in the rare cases where Prussian bureaucrats allowed conservative editors sufficient freedom to satisfy their readers' thirst for up-to-the-minute news and entertainment. According to this reading – the more correct reading, as chapter 7 of this volume argues – the administration's public relations policy was debilitated by 'dilemmas,' 'contradictions,' 'dead ends,' and unresolved paradoxes. Indeed, it was *so* conflicted in these ways that, if it achieved success at all, it did so according only to its own criteria.

Those criteria reflected the administration's wish to provide the public with both 'polemics' and 'non-partisanship.' Polemics sold copies and attacked the liberals head-on. But non-partisanship accorded with the pre-constitutional ethos of the bureaucracy itself. Thus post-1848 publicity was undermined by the same liabilities as in the pre-March era, 'as though the revolution had left not a trace on governmental publicity ... Frequent changes of editors, abrupt changes of direction in planning, mismanagement, lack of attractiveness, business failures, meddling from government offices, and not least the need to tow the official line' – these were the hallmarks of official journalism in this era.[58] This, surely, is the more realistic portrait of conservative journalism at mid-century: not effectively challenging the liberals for hegemony in the public sphere, not reaching the desired audience, and not

Habitus and Hubris 53

1.1. First election news, 1881. Scene outside a Berlin newspaper printing-shop. *Reichstagswahl am 27. Oktober 1881. Vor einer Berliner Zeitungsdruckerei*, wood engraving after a sketch by Carl Koch, n.d. Image courtesy of the Bildarchiv Preußischer Kulturbesitz Berlin.

reconciling the demands of elite and popular politics, but merely tempering liberal ascendancy in the press.

Dittmer's analysis also bundled together the threads that in 1848 led to the founding of the first conservative party in German history. Over time, conservatives in the Prussian administration were forced to supplement a negative, censorial stance toward the challenge of liberal publicity with a more proactive response. In this sense, Dittmer anticipated the direction of newer work on the 1850s and early 1860s, which has also demonstrated the positive contributions of 'reactionary' statesmen in these decades.[59] After mid-century, official public relations policy demanded substantial sums of money and support from the king. Both were granted only grudgingly. Yet with Metternich's repressive Carlsbad decrees long forgotten, neither Prussian officials nor conservative publicists could rest on complacent assumptions about the inherent plausibility, let alone the popular appeal, of the conservative message. As they agonized over ways to communicate their political ideology to the reading public, they also took hesitant steps into a new public sphere. In this task they were helped most conspicuously not by aristocratic landowners or court *frondeurs* but by a Jewish intellectual who provided the right-wing cause with both an overarching ideology and tactical savvy.

Ideology as Program

The strength of Wilhelm Füßl's political biography of Friedrich Julius Stahl lay in its ability to juxtapose theory and practice in Stahl's career.[60] Stressing the continuities rather than the caesuras in his political life, Füßl showed that Stahl sympathized with left-wing positions before 1848. In his journalistic pursuits and in the Bavarian *Landtag* in the 1830s, Stahl was already aware of the need for greater personal freedoms for individual citizens. He also knew Germany's progress towards an industrial capitalist economy was unstoppable. He shed few tears for the demise of a patrimonial and patriarchal society as enshrined in the political philosophy of Karl Ludwig von Haller. These enlightened aspects of Stahl's thought, to be sure, were tempered by more recognizable features of the conservative *Weltanschauung*: firm opposition to absolutism, to the French Revolution, to the idea of natural law, and to rationalism. Stahl also refused to recognize Jews as politically responsible actors in the public realm.[61] Nonetheless, it was the *combination* of liberalism and conservatism in his thought that gave him a pivotal role in 1848 and after.

Not all Stahl's talents were apparent early on. When he was called to a professorial chair in Berlin in 1840, his reputation as a 'pietist,' 'reactionary,' and 'absolutist' was already firmly in place. In his inaugural lecture, Stahl's remarks equating natural law and revolution so provoked his students that the podium was buffeted by notes, books, and umbrellas. One story has it that shouts and foot-stamping finally drove him from the lecture hall. But another account is more believable, wherein Stahl prevailed over his hecklers with the words: 'Gentlemen, I am here *to teach; you* are here *to listen.*'[62] This pronouncement presaged Stahl's most famous dictum, 'Authority, not majority.'

In the early 1840s many conservatives were suspicious of Stahl's political philosophy, including the social activist Victor Aimé Huber and the historian Heinrich Leo.[63] For Huber, Stahl was 'too constitutional.' For Leo, Stahl's Jewishness provoked a 'general antipathy' to his teachings. (Even liberal satirical journals such as *Kladderadatsch* regularly caricatured Stahl's Jewish features.) Twenty-one years of educating Berlin students, however, together with Stahl's practice of placing like-minded colleagues in professorial chairs elsewhere, were not without their effect on German political thought. Thus Füßl's short title, *Professor in Politics*, is appropriate: Stahl's role in the formation of political ideology rested on teaching, indoctrination, and communication.

Whereas 1848 was a watershed for conservatives, it was not a caesura for Stahl himself. Consider his article in the pages of the staunchly conservative newspaper, the *Neue Preußische Zeitung*, known as the *Kreuzzeitung* because of the prominent Iron Cross on its masthead. Stahl's article appeared on 20 July 1848 and was entitled 'The Conservatives' Banner.' Although the establishment of the *Kreuzzeitung* a few weeks earlier had broken no new ground programmatically, suddenly Prussian conservatives realized that they had no option but to turn to Stahl for leadership.[64] In this article he in effect established the 'program' (*Programmatik*) for Prussian conservatism after 1848 by declaring the royal accommodation of March and April to be evolutionary – as he wrote, it was an 'actual and legally based revision of the constitution of the land.' In this way Stahl prevented conservatism from stewing in the remnants of a system of social estates (*Stände*) or trying to resurrect relations of authority that pre-dated 1848.[65]

Two important points emerged from Füßl's analysis of these events, and both of them are controversial. First, Stahl was uniquely successful in helping conservatives to learn to defend institutions or circumstances that they had previously declared unacceptable. By the end of 1848 he was both 'anti-revolutionary' and in favour of the constitution imposed on 5 December. That constitution included many of the goals for which revolutionaries had fought and died the previous March. But it also offered Prussia's King Friedrich Wilhelm IV an opportunity to end what he called the 'constitutional comedy with no constitution.'

Stahl's 'reinterpretation' hinged on the question of what *sort* of revolution had occurred. But he was hardly the first to consider this issue. Nor was he quite so original as Füßl argued in the way he theorized about the meaning of revolution itself.[66] Just as the Left was disunited in 1848 about what kind of revolution should be supported or opposed, conservatives faced a similarly disquieting range of alternatives. Their reaction confirmed the observation of Clinton Rossiter: 'If ... the pace of history gets out of control, the conservative can no longer fall back on the simple, instinctive acts of conservation. He, like the liberal, must reason and discriminate; he, like the radical, may have to plan and gamble.'[67] Whereas one historian might see nothing problematic in this conservative response, others might see conservatism's essential dilemma.

The second point concerns Stahl's effort to bring the power of the church to bear against *both* the revolution and the conservative reaction to it. Stahl saw Protestantism as a 'political principle' in a way that differed from the views of both Ernst Wilhelm Hengstenberg, editor of the high-church *Evangelische Kirchenzeitung*,[68] and Ludwig von Gerlach, a member of Friedrich Wilhelm IV's camarilla. Gerlach allegedly jolted conservatives out of their lethargy in the summer of 1848 with the declaration: 'We must give our consciousness of God a political form.' Hengstenberg's *Evangelische Kirchenzeitung* sought to 'establish the biblical justification for the conservative concept of political authority.'[69] Before we can assess the novelty of Stahl's assertions – that the Christian church had a duty to defend the Christian state and that Protestantism itself is a political principle – we need to be able to place them more firmly in their contemporary context. We should also recall that Stahl was not alone in criticizing Ernst von Bülow-Cummerow and other members of the so-called Junker Parliament, an ad hoc body that met in the summer of 1848 to defend the economic interests of Prussian landowners. Stahl wrote in 1863 that 'not aristocracy, but only Junkerdom, is an evil.'[70] Exactly the same point, however, was made during the Junker Parliament itself by Ludwig von Gerlach.

This issue of timing raises more general questions. If Stahl may be said to have educated German conservatives to the realities of political life, how much of this schooling really stuck?[71] If *Realpolitik* and the spirit of compromise blew conservatives back into the political mainstream in late 1848 and early 1849, it did not keep them on the same course for long. As part three of the present volume suggests, conservatives either drifted or fished in opposition waters under every chancellor from Otto von Bismarck to Theobald von Bethmann Hollweg. How many times did conservatives surrender to the same apocalyptic forecasts that marked their initial reactions to revolution? In 1848–9 Stahl is alleged to have infused the conservative creed with confidence and breadth of perspective. But how do we reconcile this claim with the statements of men such as Moritz von Blanckenburg, Bismarck's political intimate, who complained in the late 1860s that conservatives were being 'forced to drink the liberal cup to the dregs'?[72] The London *Economist* once wrote that 'one of the disadvantages of disillusion is that politicians are never likely to be lucid in expressing it.' Seen in this context, Stahl's contribution to German conservatism was less to dispel disillusion itself than to provide the tools that made its political expression more articulate.

At a number of points, Füßl made a plea for exactly the book Wolfgang Schwentker published in the same year. For instance, he cited Heinrich Leo's observation in July 1848 that a newspaper and a voluntary association (*Verein*) constituted everything necessary for a political party. He uncovered a document from Hermann Wagener's private papers that stressed the need for the 'appearance' of democracy from below within the nascent conservative party. And he chronicled the sudden proliferation of conservative propaganda in January and February 1849. But Füßl also set the stage for the base-level research needed to address these issues in that he left open some tantalizing questions. If conservatives recognized the need for mass influence in 1848, how did their efforts in this direction compare with those undertaken on the Left? It may be true that newspapers and other forms of partisan publicity were conservatism's 'most effective instruments' in the 1849 Prussian *Landtag* election campaign.[73] But a question that is also taken up in chapter 7 cannot be avoided: how did conservative publicity compare with the propaganda campaign mounted by liberals? And why did conservatives' enthusiasm for mass politics wane so quickly after the crisis was passed? These questions run through other chapters in the present volume; they also provided a leitmotif for Wolfgang Schwentker's monumental study of local conservative clubs in the revolution of 1848–9.

Ideology as Mobilization

Ludwig von Gerlach wrote in his memoirs that before the revolutionary outburst of 1848, 'no one was inclined to establish a [political] party – a laborious, delicate, lofty enterprise! Only in 1848, when necessity drove us to it, did we come upon the idea, twenty years too late.' Wolfgang Schwentker's study, like its subject, sprang to life somewhat overdue but as a labour of love. Still, did it recast our understanding of political mobilization in mid-nineteenth-century Germany? Yes, it did – in three ways.

Schwentker demonstrated, first, that the evolution of conservative ideology and the establishment of formal party structures were intimately bound up with the ad hoc appearance of conservative associations in Prussian localities after June 1848 and with conservative attempts to define 'party' itself. The role of associations in the birth of a German party system has already been explored from other standpoints. Liberals, we know, had ambivalent feelings about the interrelationships among *Volk, Staat, Partei,* and *Verein.* Nor have historians of the German Right been unaware that conservatives made only the most reluctant and ambiguous accommodation with mass politics. But in recent years it has become more difficult to say when conservatives actually entered the age of 'mass' politics. Similarly, if antisemitism, *völkisch* nationalism, and other components of the German Right are said to have achieved their decisive 'breakthrough' to popularity on a number of occasions, how many breakthroughs can we legitimately identify?

Schwentker did not claim to sort out this confusion. No single historian could. But his decision to take the summer of 1849 as the terminal date of his study was appropriate. Between December 1848 and the spring of 1849, the number of conservative associations in Prussia grew from about 105 to over 300, with a total membership that rose from about 20,000 to about 60,000.[74] These numbers permit comparison with the level of activity inaugurated by the Prussian People's Association[75] in the 1860s and the Agrarian League after 1893. However, after the summer of 1849, the conservatives' counter-revolutionary activity disappeared almost overnight. It was replaced by the indolence and apathy that had previously characterized right-wing politics and constituted the kernel of what persisted as the politics of notables.

Second, Schwentker echoed Füßl and Dittmer in emphasizing the role of conservative publicity in the revolutionary era, including petitions, addresses to the king, pamphlets, placards, broadsheets, newspapers, and journals. These diverse materials helped to shape the self-image of conservatives, much as the 'illuminations' – the lighting of windows by homeowners loyal to the king – and the parades celebrating the return of the Prussian prince from exile helped to overcome conservatives' initial defeatism and sense of isolation. When the curtain rose on a new era of political mobilization in March 1848, initial stage fright cost the conservatives dearly. But the founding of the *Kreuzzeitung* in June 1848 and these other means of propaganda allowed them to make a dramatic entrance onto the public stage. Schwentker noted that 'for those who take part directly in revolutions, there is no time for leisure.' Conservatives had no time for caricature, satire, or other forms of humour either. But did this deficit make their propaganda less subtle than the Left's? In many instances, conservative propaganda caused a sensation in the ranks of liberals and democrats precisely because the advertisement of political ideology did not stand in the foreground.[76]

Third, Schwentker addressed a question that runs through the present volume too: did the impetus for the political mobilization of the Right come from above (the 'manipulation' thesis) or from below (the 'self-mobilization' thesis)? Other studies of conservative associations in 1848 sided strongly with the self-mobilization thesis; they downplayed the role of conservative 'ultras' associated with the *Kreuzzeitung* or the court camarilla.[77] Schwentker avoided this one-sided approach by casting his analytical light both from above and from below. He argued that the spontaneous founding of electoral committees in the countryside helped to offset conservative weakness in the Frankfurt and Berlin parliaments. These local organizations developed their own momentum and a political independence that confounded the efforts of distant party leaders to control their activities from afar.[78] Furthermore, in contrast to the early phase of the revolution, by December 1848 conservatives actually wanted to *preserve* civil liberties in the face of reactionaries seeking to abolish the right of free association and freedom of expression. Thus the statutes of conservative associations founded during the winter of 1848–9 signalled 'a completely new understanding of politics,' one that brought into closer proximity the individual burgher and the state. 'No longer were demands raised for political quiescence and trust in the authoritative power of the royal government.'[79] Once the crisis had passed in mid-1849, conservatives were free to fall back into political slumber – as free as they had previously been to choose the style of politics most suited to their own tastes. But this conclusion does not lead us back to any received wisdom about conservative indolence.

It pulls us forward instead, compelling us to consider anew the variety and importance of local politics in the evolution of the Right.[80]

Ideology as Political Economy

In 1931 Kurt Tucholsky wrote that although German agriculture had been living on the edge of extinction for the past quarter-century, it now seemed to be doing 'quite well.' With irony in the fire, Tucholsky voiced what others had been saying about the Junkers for decades: they had mastered the art of 'complaining without suffering.' With his 1990 study of Prussian estate owners, Klaus Heß suggested that Tucholsky came closer to the mark than he knew.[81]

In Heß's view, much of the previous scholarship on the Prussian Junkers hinged on two questions: whether a 'permanent crisis' confronted German agriculture after the early 1870s and whether that crisis was responsible for the preservation of a social class that was no longer economically viable but helped to pave the way for National Socialism. One of the most pointed statements of this thesis was Hans-Jürgen Puhle's slim volume of 1972, claiming a direct line 'from the agrarian crisis to pre-fascism.'[82] Unfortunately, Heß missed an opportunity to address broader questions about property, class, and ideology that Puhle and others had raised before him. Thus Heß was unfair when he stated that previous work on German agriculture had tended to offer 'handbook' accounts and narrow monographic studies.[83] His own book provided just as little context about the Junkers' survival skills.

What Heß did, he did well. He examined the legal status of knightly or entailed estates (*Rittergüter* and *Fideikommisse*) together with their debt structures, tax exposures, profit margins, marketability, and geographical distribution (mainly in the six eastern provinces of Prussia). Having bolstered his text with 114 tables and charts, Heß concluded that the Junkers conjured up the notion of an agrarian crisis where none existed. German agriculture was not doing so badly that large landowners in either the western or the eastern provinces of Prussia were forced to sell their estates en masse. Nor were agricultural prices so low or debts so high as to substantiate the politically opportune myth of an agrarian crisis. This scenario held true even in the 1890s, when the Junkers first mobilized the rural sector for their own political defence: 'to put it simply, agriculture in Imperial Germany experienced an efflorescence that may have undergone market fluctuations but was in no way interrupted by a serious crisis.'[84] This conclusion substantiated the view that the 'Great Depression' of 1873–96 was largely mythical, and it highlighted important regional disparities in German agriculture's development. However, Heß's study was not unlike other handbooks whose main argument need not be properly digested to be cited. By advertising the summaries that concluded each chapter (designed to help the 'reader in a hurry'), the author implicitly sanctioned such use of his book. Perhaps he knew best.

A riskier but ultimately more satisfying study also sought to reconsider the political economies of Junker landed estates. The intellectual journey that took Shearer Davis Bowman from his roots in the American South to the Berkeley seminars of Reinhard Bendix and Gerald Feldman informed the argument of *Masters and Lords*, a study comparing mid-nineteenth-century US planters with Prussian Junkers.[85] Bowman attempted to head off criticism of his comparative premise by conceding that he was far more familiar with the history of the Old South than of east-Elbian Prussia, that his German sources were limited to published material, and that his analysis concentrated on the middle decades of the nineteenth century alone. These limitations might have yielded a mechanical juxtaposition of two very different histories: the Prussians did this, while the southern planters did that – or didn't. But these fears prove unfounded. Bowman successfully wove two histories together by focusing on contentious terms with which historians, political scientists, and sociologists have grappled for years.

Happily, Bowman distributed this theoretical analysis throughout the book, rather than front-loading it in the German manner. Despite the author's hope that his 'freewheeling' approach would enhance the reputation of 'universal history,'[86] his analysis sometimes hit a dead end. Instead of taking stock of the histories of these two landed elites over the long term, the epilogue included repeated references to their 'political clout,' their 'electoral and ecclesiastical clout,' and even their 'regional clout.' By repeating this infelicitous term, Bowman showed that he had too quickly abandoned his exploration of local politics. And although the 'crucial difference' between southern planters and Junkers was identified as 'the former's libertarian but racist republicanism versus the latter's militarist and corporatist monarchism,'[87] the author was more successful in discussing the two nouns (republicanism, monarchism) than the four qualifying adjectives.

More convincing were Bowman's conclusions about how both elites became 'the font of an authentic and powerful conservatism.' Like Berdahl, Bowman identified an 'ambiguous and problematic' relationship between intellectual and pragmatic conservatives before 1848. Noting that even intellectuals vacillated between 'transcendence and partisanship,'[88] he argued that conservatism cannot be properly understood in either the United States or Prussia 'apart from a fluctuating, often muted tension between what can be termed doctrinaire (romantic and idealistic) and pragmatic (realistic and interest-oriented) defences of the status quo.' Thus the author insisted that although these elites were pre-modern, they were certainly not pre-capitalist. He also underscored the regional power base of both groups.

Was this comparative history at its best?[89] Perhaps not. Bowman's book did not substantively change the way historians think about either the American South or nineteenth-century Prussia. But by combining analytical verve and good sense, his approach was more refreshing and sophisticated than the tired old 'compare and contrast' trope.

Ideology and Proto-fascism

To leap from German conservatism in the first two-thirds of the nineteenth century to fascism's emerging potential in the third decade of the twentieth century is to step across a historical threshold that divides the politics of notables from 'politics in a new key.' Other chapters of this book examine these years (1867–1914) to suggest why that threshold continues to be rethought by historians of the German Right and why the interpenetration of notable politics and mass politics is the most interesting feature of this transformation. Here it remains only to sketch the analytical terrain on which historians land when they jump from 1848 to the German Time of Troubles between 1917 and 1923. One way to attempt this feat is to consider Heinz Hagenlücke's study of the German Fatherland Party, published in 1997.

At the time, everyone thought that this was the book the Lüneburg historian Dirk Stegmann was going to write.[90] But Hagenlücke was not alone in the 1990s when he raised new questions about the transformation of the German Right during and immediately after the First World War. Other studies, many with a strong biographical impulse, provided a sense of the direction this newer work was taking. One was Norbert Friedrich's biography of the antisemitic leader Reinhard Mumm, who drew to his camp a significant portion of the *völkisch* Right during the war years.[91] Two other books of note were by Raffael Scheck. Scheck's study of Alfred von Tirpitz[92] was the natural complement of Hagenlücke's, not because of Tirpitz's role in building the German battle fleet, but because Tirpitz was the figurehead of the Fatherland Party in 1917–18. Scheck's study of the mobilization of right-wing women in the Weimar Republic also addressed the question of how opposing groups within the right-wing camp sought to contain, or even to reverse, the fragmentation that ultimately rendered their parties defenceless against the Nazis.[93] Just as Hagenlücke's study focused on the Fatherland Party's founder, Wolfgang Kapp, without allowing 'the man' to overwhelm 'his times,' Friedrich's study and Scheck's first book tied the failure of right-wing reform attempts to long-neglected figures of major historical significance. The same was true of Stephan Malinowski's monumental study of social decline and political radicalization among German aristocrats.[94] Examining the difficult transference of aristocratic allegiances 'from king to Führer,' Malinowski's book is only one of a growing number that considers modern nobilities in their German and European contexts.[95]

Hagenlücke argued that Stegmann's earlier characterization of the Fatherland Party as 'pre-' or 'proto-fascist' could not withstand critical scrutiny. In Hagenlücke's opinion, only the smaller and more radical parties led after 1918 by Anton Drexler and, later, Adolf Hitler deserve to be considered proto-fascist. In suggesting that the Fatherland Party's leaders were unable to overcome the constraints of the politics of notables, Hagenlücke developed an argument to which we return in chapter 2. He showed that even leaders of the new Right were prone to give speeches every bit as pretentious, boring, and irrelevant as those delivered decades earlier by members of the old Right. Only the Pan-German Heinrich Claß emerged as a figure ruthless enough to merit comparison with Hitler. Yet Claß was completely unable to speak in front of an audience. As Hagenlücke reminded us, another thing distinguished pretenders from real fascists: the latter's willingness to resort to physical violence to achieve their aims.[96]

A critical appreciation of Hagenlücke's path-breaking study is in order, for his book raised more questions than it answered.[97] First, Wolfgang Kapp's private papers in Berlin suggest that the disaffection of non-Prussian chapters of the Fatherland Party in the summer of 1918 was foreshortened in Hagenlücke's account. How did the party's federal structure constrain its core group of Prussian activists? Second, the author identified the Fatherland Party as a 'populist-nationalist movement dominated by a few activists.'[98] But just how few activists – or

Daniel Frymann: Wenn ich der Kaiser wär' – politische Wahrheiten und Notwendigkeiten

Dritte Auflage
11. bis 15. Tausend

Viel Feind' — viel Ehr'

Erschienen in Leipzig 1912 in der Dieterich'schen Verlagsbuchhandlung, Theodor Weicher, Inselstraße 10

1.2. *If I Were the Kaiser – Political Truths and Necessities*, title page. Because of its radical anti-establishment tenor, the chairman of the Pan-German League, Heinrich Claß, published this work (1912) under the pseudonym 'Daniel Frymann.' The epigraph reads: 'Many enemies, much honour.' From the author's collection.

how many – can a 'movement' (*Bewegung*) actually have and still deserve the label Hitler preferred for his own party? Third, Hagenlücke never explained systematically why the party failed to expand beyond the 'nationalist camp.' The concept of camps (*Lager*) provides part of the answer, but its relevance remained veiled in Hagenlücke's account. Lastly, the author pulled up short in suggesting, but then not elaborating, how the Fatherland Party attempted a 'one-sided, emotional appropriation of the concept of Fatherland.'[99] Arguably, it is the *emotional* power of nationalism that most needs attention in future research on the German Right. Except for a brief treatment of the 'spirit of 1914,' Hagenlücke did not grapple with right-wing strategies calculated to draw emotional strength from the reservoir of national sentiment, national spirit, and national 'will.' If he had gone farther down this road, he could have hammered home a point to which we also return in the next chapter, namely, that although Hitler successfully used demagogic means to instrumentalize radical nationalism in the 1930s, similar efforts fell surprisingly flat in previous epochs – including the years 1909 to 1920, when the new Right is thought to have eclipsed the old.

Hagenlücke was more successful in demonstrating that the self-aggrandizement practised by the Fatherland Party's leaders duped Stegmann and other historians into believing that the party was a success. Wolfgang Kapp and other party leaders conceded privately that the first year of activity had brought mainly disappointment and failure: 'The party did not succeed in realizing a single one of its high-sounding program points.'[100] The failure of the party was apparent to most insiders even in the spring of 1918, when the German offensive in the west ground to a halt; that is, *not* only in the early autumn of 1918, when the other pillars of German authoritarianism began to crumble. After May 1918 the Fatherland Party's propaganda slowed to a trickle. Its financial situation became desperate (about half of all members were in arrears on their membership dues at this time). And its local and regional chapters baulked at the haughty pronouncements issued from the party's headquarters in Berlin.

By mid-1918 others were already engaged in fashioning a new popular basis for the German Right. Heinrich Claß's critical (though not entirely hostile) appraisals of the party's activities demonstrate that the Fatherland Party failed to exploit its many initial advantages: its connections to power brokers, its impressive membership figures, and its sophisticated propaganda distribution network. Almost at the outset of the party's activities, Claß identified three obstacles that the Fatherland Party never overcame.[101] The first was the governmental timidity of its leaders and patrons, particularly Alfred von Tirpitz, which prevented them from working openly against the government and its war aims. The second obstacle was Kapp's headstrong insistence on naming the new organization a 'party,' when it neither acted like a party nor really wanted to be one. The third was the contradiction between the Fatherland Party's declared aim of supporting a strong government and its leaders' actual goal of *creating* a strong government where (they claimed) none existed.

In light of this assessment, one conclusion seems incontrovertible: the revolutionary impulse that culminated in the Kapp Putsch of 1920 was latent in the Fatherland Party all along. This revolutionary potential was never forthrightly acknowledged by sycophants like Tirpitz. Nor was it resolved in the public's muddled understanding of what the party actually stood for. But in contrast to January 1933, the attempted juxtaposition of traditional parliamentarism and revolutionary putschism in 1917–18 constituted a weakness, not a strength.

These findings suggest that the Fatherland Party's history should not be cited as evidence of the power of a new Right, at least not in the Wilhelmine era. Hagenlücke demolished the notion – favoured by Stegmann, Geoff Eley, and others – that the so-called Cartel of Productive Estates (1913) had a tangible impact on German politics or represented a theoretical new departure. Eley was also the victim of Hagenlücke's conclusion that 'one cannot justifiably speak of any "self-mobilization of the grass roots" or of the lower middle classes.'[102] Between the opposing views of Eley and Roger Chickering on this point, Hagenlücke decisively opted for the latter. His book showed that the Fatherland Party never solved 'the central problem of the Right in Germany' – how to find a popular call to arms with which to mobilize the masses.

All in all, no existing study has come closer than Hagenlücke's to explaining why even a reshaped Right failed to supplant the politics of notables during the German Empire's dying years. Hagenlücke charted the interweaving of conflict and consensus that we find on the Right even before the founding of the Fatherland Party, and he carried the story beyond the revolution of November 1918. Although he was not alone in seeking to span the caesura of 1918, Hagenlücke illuminated trajectories that achieved major historical significance in the Weimar Republic, but also those that did not.

Conclusions

In retrospect, the study of German conservatism has demonstrated remarkable vitality since the 1920s, and never more than in the last two decades. It remains to be seen how far the scholarly trajectories charted in this chapter will transform the interpretative landscape in the future. Major areas of investigation still require attention. Historians are waiting for the kind of comprehensive social history of the Junkers that Hans Rosenberg promised but never wrote. Recent studies of estate life before 1848 have shown just how much remains to be learned for the later periods as well: historians know very little about the rhythms and rituals of aristocratic culture and everyday life on rural estates.[103] At the very least, it is safe to say that the agenda for future research on the history of German conservatism is far from exhausted. Perhaps greater accessibility to archives in the former German Democratic Republic and Poland will spur historians to this task. In a more traditional vein, accessibility to these resources might also encourage historians to undertake full-scale studies of the National Liberal and Christian Social parties at both the regional and national levels. Another promising sign is that gendered histories of conservatism have come to the fore in the last five years.[104]

All of this suggests that it would be premature to relegate even overtly 'political' histories of German conservatism to Karl Marx's infamous dustheap of history. Like Tucholsky writing in the 1930s, the liberal nationalist Friedrich Naumann thought he knew exactly what the conservatives were up to in history. He argued that 'pseudo-democratic' strategies first employed in 1848–9 were still effective fifty years later. 'Today's conservative,' wrote Naumann in 1900, 'is of a compromising nature – an authoritarian type [*Herrenmensch*] with democratic gloves.'[105] But a rather different take on the same problem had been offered by Ludwig von Gerlach in his monthly review of politics for the *Kreuzzeitung* in March 1849. In this review Gerlach attempted to draw up a balance sheet of conservative successes and failures over the previous twelve months. Conservatism, he admitted, remained an 'ideology without vision.' Having failed to find high-minded leaders to sustain it as a political movement, it had become the party 'of those who want to lose as slowly as possible what they possess.'[106] In other words, by the middle of the nineteenth century, not just at its end, German conservatives seemed to have no regard for the great goals of conservatism that Edmund Burke had outlined in his *Thoughts on the*

68 'Tradition is how we change'

Cause of the Present Discontents (1770). 'It is ... our business,' Burke had written, 'carefully to cultivate in our minds, to rear to the most perfect vigour and maturity, every sort of generous and honest feeling that belongs to our nature. To bring the dispositions that are lovely in private life into the service and conduct of the commonwealth.'[107] Although they differed in every other way, Burke's and Gerlach's definitions of conservatism both posited the theoretical convergence of habitus and ideology.

In the study of German conservative practice, not theory, the greater convergence is where habitus meets hubris. The work of Robert Berdahl, Wilhelm Füßl, Wolfgang Schwentker, and other historians of the German Right demonstrates that the aims of conservatism were never as simple as Naumann or Gerlach or Burke believed. The strategies conservatives devised to accommodate the nineteenth century's 'participation revolution' forced them time and again to forge new political weapons – weapons with which they still had not become comfortable six decades after the advent of universal male suffrage. That those political weapons were always two-edged is now clear. But it has taken a great deal of study to illustrate this ambiguity. One can only hope that the scholarly works surveyed in this chapter will inspire more research of the same high calibre.

NOTES

1 Karl Mannheim, *Konservatismus*, 71, cited in Axel Schildt, *Konservatismus in Deutschland* (Munich, 1998), 17. Mannheim's study has been translated as *Conservatism: A Contribution to the Sociology of Knowledge*, ed. David Kettler, Volker Meja, and Nico Stehr (London and New York, 1986).
2 Robert M. Berdahl, *The Politics of the Prussian Nobility: The Development of a Conservative Ideology, 1770–1848* (Princeton, 1988); Wolfgang Schwentker, *Konservative Vereine und Revolution in Preussen 1848/49. Die Konstituierung des Konservativismus als Partei* (Düsseldorf, 1988); and Wilhelm Füßl, *Professor in der Politik. Friedrich Julius Stahl (1802–1861)* (Göttingen, 1988).
3 Panajotis Kondylis, *Konservatismus. Geschichtlicher Gehalt und Untergang* (Stuttgart, 1986), 22.
4 See Ludwig von Gerlach's 1849 commentary, cited in this chapter's conclusion.
5 Wolfgang Schwentker, 'Conservatism in Nineteenth and Twentieth Century German History,' *Bulletin of the German Historical Institute, London*,

no. 23 (Autumn 1986): 3. See also Ludwig Elm, ed., *Falsche Propheten* (Berlin [GDR], 1984); Kurt Lenk, *Deutscher Konservatismus* (Frankfurt and New York, 1989); Wilhelm Ribhegge, *Konservative Politik in Deutschland* (Darmstadt, 1989); Stefan Breuer, *Grundpositionen der deutschen Rechten, 1871–1945* (Tübingen, 1999); Breuer, *Ordnungen der Ungleichheit. Die deutsche Rechte im Widerstreit ihrer Ideen 1871–1945* (Darmstadt, 2001); Hans-Christof Kraus, ed., *Konservative Politiker in Deutschland* (Berlin, 1995). The bibliography in Schildt, *Konservatismus*, is indispensable; English readers can consult the bibliography (503–23) in the anthology listed in the next note.

6 Larry Eugene Jones and James Retallack, eds., *Between Reform, Reaction, and Resistance: Studies in the History of German Conservatism from 1789 to 1945* (Providence, RI, and Oxford, 1993).

7 Friedrich Engels, *The Role of Force in History*, ed. Ernst Wangermann, trans. Jack Cohen (London, 1968), 106.

8 Leo Kofler, *Der Konservatismus. Zwischen Dekadenz und Reaktion* (Hamburg, 1984), 74, cited in Schildt, *Konservatismus*, 16.

9 A notable exception is Francis L. Carsten, *A History of the Prussian Junkers* (Aldershot, 1989). See also Heinz Reif, *Adel im 19. und 20. Jahrhundert* (Munich, 1999); Hans-Ulrich Wehler, ed., *Europäischer Adel 1750–1950* (Göttingen, 1990).

10 Theodor Fontane, *The Stechlin*, trans. with intro. by William L. Zwiebel (Columbia, SC, 1995); this citation from Joachim Remak, *The Gentle Critic: Theodor Fontane and German Politics, 1848–1898* (Syracuse, 1984), 20–1.

11 David Blackbourn and Geoff Eley, *The Peculiarities of German History* (Oxford, 1984), 246.

12 See Heinz Reif, ed., *Adel und Bürgertum in Deutschland*, vol. 1, *Entwicklungslinien und Wendepunkte im 19. Jahrhundert* (Berlin, 2000).

13 Hans Rosenberg, 'The Pseudo-Democratisation of the Junker Class' (orig. 1958), in *The Social History of Politics*, ed. Georg Iggers (Leamington Spa, 1985), 81–112; Alexander Gerschenkron, *Bread and Democracy in Germany* (New York, 1946).

14 Clinton Rossiter, 'Conservatism,' in *International Encyclopedia of the Social Sciences*, ed. David L. Sills, 19 vols. (New York, 1968–91), 3:290. See also Rudolf Vierhaus, 'Konservativ, Konservatismus,' in *Geschichtliche Grundbegriffe*, ed. Otto Brunner et al., 9 vols. in 8 (Stuttgart, 1972–97), 3:531–65, and other works cited in this book's introduction.

15 See the editors' 'Introduction' in Mannheim, *Conservatism*, 1–26, also 72–7.

16 See also Ewald Frie, *Friedrich August Ludwig von der Marwitz 1777–1837* (Paderborn, 2001).

70 'Tradition is how we change'

17 Sigmund Neumann, *Die Stufen des preußischen Konservatismus* (Berlin, 1930).
18 Ernst R. Huber, *Deutsche Verfassungsgeschichte seit 1789*, 4 vols. (Stuttgart, 1957–69), 2:331ff.
19 Fritz Valjavec, *Die Entstehung der politischen Strömungen in Deutschland 1770–1815*, 2nd ed. (Kronberg/Ts. and Düsseldorf, 1978).
20 Klaus Epstein, *The Genesis of German Conservatism* (Princeton, 1966), esp. 7–11.
21 Fritz Stern, *The Politics of Cultural Despair* (Berkeley, 1961).
22 George Mosse, *The Crisis of German Ideology* (New York, 1964); and Mosse, *The Nationalization of the Masses* (New York, 1975).
23 Peter G.J. Pulzer, *The Rise of Political Anti-Semitism in Germany and Austria* (orig. 1964; rev. ed., Cambridge, Mass., 1988).
24 See Fritz Stern, *The Failure of Illiberalism* (New York, 1972), xi–xliv.
25 Gerschenkron, *Bread and Democracy*.
26 Rosenberg, 'Pseudo-Democratisation'; Rosenberg, *Bureaucracy, Aristocracy and Autocracy: The Prussian Experience, 1660–1815* (Boston, 1958).
27 Ralf Dahrendorf, *Society and Democracy in Germany* (New York, 1967), 14.
28 Hans-Jürgen Puhle, *Agrarische Interessenpolitik und preußischer Konservatismus im wilhelminischen Reich 1893–1914* (orig. 1966), 2nd ed. (Bonn–Bad Godesberg, 1975). See also Puhle, *Von der Agrarkrise zum Präfaschismus* (Wiesbaden, 1972).
29 Hans-Ulrich Wehler, *The German Empire, 1871–1918*, trans. Kim Traynor (Leamington Spa, 1985, rpt. 1997).
30 Theodore S. Hamerow, *The Social Foundations of German Unification, 1858–1871: Ideas and Institutions* (Princeton, 1969), 181–221; Volker R. Berghahn, *Der Tirpitz-Plan* (Düsseldorf, 1971); Dirk Stegmann, Bernd-Jürgen Wendt, and Peter-Christian Witt, eds., *Deutscher Konservatismus im 19. und 20. Jahrhundert* (Bonn, 1983).
31 See the special issue on 'Konservative Politik und Ideologie,' edited by Herbert Gottwald, in the *Jenaer Beiträge zur Parteiengeschichte* 44 (July 1980); Kurt Gossweiler, 'Junkertum und Faschismus,' in *Preußen in der deutschen Geschichte nach 1789*, ed. Gustav Seeber and K.-H. Noack (Berlin [GDR], 1983), 290–302; and Elm, *Falsche Propheten*.
32 John Lothrop Motley, 4 Nov. 1833, cited in Ernst Engelberg, *Bismarck*, 2 vols. (Berlin, 1985–90), 1:126.
33 William W. Hagen, 'The Junkers' Faithless Servants: Peasant Insubordination and the Breakdown of Serfdom in Brandenburg-Prussia, 1763–1811,' in *The German Peasantry: Conflict and Community in Rural Society*, ed. Richard J. Evans and W.R. Lee (New York, 1986), 71–101; see now Hagen,

Ordinary Prussians: Brandenburg Junkers and Villagers, 1500–1840 (Cambridge, 2002).
34 See Ian Farr, '"Tradition" and the Peasantry: On the Modern Historiography of Rural Germany,' in *German Peasantry*, ed. Evans and Lee, 1–36; Robert G. Moeller's introduction in *Peasants and Lords in Modern Germany*, ed. Moeller (Boston, 1986), 1–23.
35 Carsten, *History*.
36 René Schiller, *Vom Rittergut zum Großgrundbesitz* (Berlin, 2003); Ulrike Hindersmann, *Der ritterschaftliche Adel im Königreich Hannover 1814–1866* (Hanover, 2001).
37 See also Berdahl's unpublished study 'The Transformation of the Prussian Conservative Party, 1866–1876' (PhD diss., University of Minnesota, 1965).
38 Berdahl, *Politics*, 46–7.
39 See Otto Brunner, *Land und Herrschaft*, 5th ed. (Vienna, 1965); Hanna Schissler, *Preußische Agrargesellschaft im Wandel* (Gottingen, 1978).
40 Berdahl, *Politics*, 5; for the following, 333.
41 Ibid., 41.
42 Ibid., 49–50.
43 For the preceding, ibid., 66, 72.
44 Ibid., 139, 140.
45 Ibid., 164, 179.
46 See Epstein, *Genesis*, chaps. 9–11; Valjavec, *Entstehung*, 255ff.; Jörn Garber, 'Politische Spätaufklärung und vorromantischer Frühkonservatismus. Aspekte der Forschung,' in Valjavec, *Entstehung*, 543–92; Ursula Vogel, *Konservative Kritik an der bürgerlichen Revolution. August Wilhelm Rehberg* (Darmstadt, 1972).
47 Berdahl, *Politics*, 167.
48 Ibid., 245; for subsequent citations in this paragraph, 349, 370, 373.
49 Hagen, *Ordinary Prussians*, 122.
50 Moeller, ed., *Peasants*; Evans and Lee, eds., *German Peasantry*. The latest contribution is Patrick Wagner, *Bauern, Junker und Beamte. Der Wandel lokaler Herrschaft und Partizipation im Ostelbien des 19. Jahrhunderts* (Göttingen, 2005).
51 Moeller, ed., *Peasants*, 8; for the following, 17.
52 Hans-Jürgen Puhle, 'Lords and Peasants in the Kaiserreich,' in *Peasants*, ed. Moeller, 82.
53 In *German Peasants*, ed. Evans and Lee, 238.
54 Lothar Dittmer, *Beamtenkonservatismus und Modernisierung. Untersuchungen zur Vorgeschichte der Konservativen Partei in Preußen 1810–1848/49* (Stuttgart, 1992).

72 'Tradition is how we change'

55 Ibid., 320.
56 Ibid., 319.
57 Ibid., 408.
58 Ibid., 414.
59 Andreas Neemann, *Landtag und Politik in der Reaktionszeit. Sachsen 1849/50–1866* (Düsseldorf, 2000); Abigail Green, 'Intervening in the Public Sphere: German Governments and the Press, 1815–1870,' *Historical Journal* 44, no. 1 (2001): 155–75.
60 See note 2. See also Hanns-Jürgen Wiegand, *Das Vermächtnis Friedrich Julius Stahls* (Königstein/Ts., 1980); Arie Nabrings, *Friedrich Julius Stahl* (Bielefeld, 1983).
61 Friedrich Julius Stahl, *Der christliche Staat und sein Verhältnis zu Deismus und Judenthum* (1847).
62 Füßl, *Professor*, 111.
63 See Wolfgang Schwentker, 'Victor Aimé Huber and the Emergence of Social Conservatism,' in *Between Reform*, ed. Jones and Retallack, 95–121; Heinrich Leo, *Was ist konservativ?* (Berlin, 1864); Carolyn Rebecca Henderson, 'Heinrich Leo: A Study in German Conservatism' (PhD diss., University of Wisconsin, 1977).
64 William J. Orr Jr, 'The Foundation of the Kreuzzeitung Party in Prussia, 1848–1850' (PhD diss., University of Wisconsin, 1971); Marjorie Lamberti, 'The Rise of the Prussian Conservative Party, 1840–1858' (PhD diss., Yale University, 1966).
65 Füßl, *Professor*, 134.
66 See esp. Jörn Garber, *Kritik der Revolution. Theorien des deutschen Frühkonservatismus 1790–1810*, vol. 1, *Dokumentation* (Kronberg/Ts., 1976).
67 Rossiter, 'Conservatism,' 3:292.
68 Marshall K. Christensen, 'Ernst Wilhelm Hengstenberg and the Kirchenzeitung Faction: Throne and Altar in Nineteenth Century Prussia' (PhD diss., University of Oregon, 1972), chaps. 5–7; William O. Shanahan, *German Protestants Face the Social Question*, vol. 1, *The Conservative Phase, 1815–1871* (Notre Dame, 1954).
69 Füßl, *Professor*, 140.
70 In *Die gegenwärtigen Parteien in Staat und Kirche* (1863).
71 Stahl is labelled the 'classicist of conservatism' in 'Konservatismus und Junkertum,' *Konservative Monatsschrift* 67, no. 2 (Nov. 1909): 200–4.
72 This and the quotation from the *Economist* are cited in Frederick Aandahl, 'The Rise of German Free Conservatism' (PhD diss., Princeton University,

1955), 78 and 264. See also Heinz Reif, 'Bismarck und die Konservativen,' in *Otto von Bismarck und die Parteien*, ed. Lothar Gall (Paderborn, 2001); less illuminating is Bernhard Ruetz, *Der preussische Konservatismus im Kampf gegen Einheit und Freiheit* (Berlin, 2001).

73 Füßl, *Professor*, 171.
74 See Schwentker, *Konservative Vereine*, table 4, 168.
75 Hugo Müller, 'Der Preußische Volks-Verein' (PhD diss., University of Berlin, 1914).
76 Ibid., 178.
77 Most notably, Richard Schult, 'Partei wider Willen. Kalküle und Potentiale konservativer Parteigründer in Preußen zwischen Erstem Vereinigten Landtag und Nationalversammlung (1847/48),' and Hubertus Fischer, 'Konservatismus von unten. Wahlen im ländlichen Preußen 1849/52 – Organisation, Agitation, Manipulation,' in *Deutscher Konservatismus*, ed. Stegmann et al., 33–68 and 69–128 respectively.
78 Schwentker, *Konservative Vereine*, 145.
79 Ibid., 256.
80 Local party affairs are highlighted in Thomas Nipperdey's classic study *Die Organisation der deutschen Parteien vor 1918* (Düsseldorf, 1961).
81 Klaus Heß, *Junker und bürgerliche Großgrundbesitzer im Kaiserreich. Landwirtschaftlicher Großbetrieb, Großgrundbesitz und Familienfideikommiß in Preußen (1867–71–1914)* (Stuttgart, 1990). For Tucholsky's remark about *'klagen ohne zu leiden,'* 316.
82 Puhle, *Von der Agrarkrise*.
83 Heß, *Junker*, 17.
84 Ibid., 315. The following are analytically thin: Stefan Biland, *Die Deutsch-Konservative Partei und der Bunde der Landwirte im Württemberg vor 1914* (Stuttgart, 2002); Elke Kimmel, *Methoden antisemitischer Propaganda im Ersten Weltkrieg* (Berlin, 2001); Volker Stalmann, *Die Deutschkonservative Partei und die Deutsche Reichspartei in Bayern 1890–1914* (Frankfurt a.M. etc., 2002); Stefan Ph. Wolf, *Konservativismus im liberalen Baden* (Karlruhe, 1990).
85 Shearer Davis Bowman, *Masters and Lords: Mid-19th-Century U.S. Planters and Prussian Junkers* (New York and Oxford, 1993).
86 Ibid., 81.
87 Ibid., 112.
88 Ibid., 208. For the following, 206.
89 Theda Skocpol and Margaret Somers, 'The Uses of Comparative History in Macrosocial Inquiry,' *Comparative Studies in Society and History* 22 (1980): 174–97.

74 'Tradition is how we change'

90 Heinz Hagenlücke, *Deutsche Vaterlandspartei. Die nationale Rechte am Ende des Kaiserreiches* (Düsseldorf, 1997). An important recent addition is Rainer Hering, *Konstruierte Nation. Der Alldeutsche Verband 1890 bis 1939* (Hamburg, 2003).
91 Norbert Friedrich, *'Die christlich-soziale Fahne empor!' Reinhard Mumm und die christlich-soziale Bewegung* (Stuttgart, 1997).
92 Raffael Scheck, *Alfred von Tirpitz and German Right-Wing Politics, 1914–1930* (Atlantic Highlands, 1998).
93 Raffael Scheck, *Mothers of the Nation: Right-Wing Women in Weimar Germany* (Oxford and New York, 2004); see also note 104 below.
94 Stephan Malinowski, *Vom König zum Führer. Sozialer Niedergang und politische Radikalisierung im deutschen Adel zwischen Kaiserreich und NS-Staat* (Berlin, 2003).
95 Eckart Conze and Monika Wienfort, eds., *Adel und Moderne. Deutschland im europäischen Vergleich im 19. und 20. Jahrhundert* (Cologne, 2004); Günther Schulz and Markus A. Denzel, eds., *Deutscher Adel im 19. und 20. Jahrhundert* (St Katharinen, 2004); see also Eckart Conze, *Von deutschem Adel. Die Grafen von Bernstorff im zwanzigsten Jahrhundert* (Stuttgart, 2000).
96 Hagenlücke, *Deutsche Vaterlandspartei*, 410–11.
97 For example, Hagenlücke insists (291) that the German Fatherland Party was an 'almost purely Prussian party.' Then he notes (300) that the Saxon Landesverband, the strongest of any regional group, had over 80,000 members.
98 Hagenlücke, *Deutsche Vaterlandspartei*, 408.
99 Ibid., 405.
100 Ibid.
101 Ibid., 353–4.
102 Ibid., 187.
103 See Heinz Reif, ed., *Ostelbische Agrargesellschaft im Kaiserreich und in der Weimarer Republik* (Berlin, 1994).
104 See Andrea Süchting-Hänger, *Das 'Gewissen der Nation.' Nationales Engagement und politisches Handeln konservativer Frauenorganisationen 1900 bis 1937* (Düsseldorf, 2002); Eva Schoeck-Quinteros and Christiane Streubel, eds., *Frauen der politischen Rechten (1890–1933). Aktionen – Organisationen – Ideologien* (Berlin, 2003); Ute Planert, *Antifeminismus im Kaiserreich* (Göttingen, 1998); Planert, ed., *Nation, Politik und Geschlecht* (Frankfurt, New York, 2000), including Kirsten Heinsohn, 'Im Dienste der deutschen Volksgemeinschaft: Die "Frauenfrage" und conservative Parteien vor und nach dem Ersten Weltkrieg.' For other references, see Scheck, *Mothers*.
105 Friedrich Naumann, *Demokratie und Kaisertum* (Berlin, 1900), 92–3.

106 Ernst Ludwig von Gerlach, cited in Schwentker, *Konservative Vereine*, 277. The definitive study is Hans-Christof Kraus, *Ernst Ludwig von Gerlach*, 2 vols. (Göttingen, 1994). A.J.P. Taylor was more dismissive: 'just as Bismarck gave national Germany the unity which it lacked the confidence to achieve for itself, so he tried to give the Junkers the vision and commonsense which they could not find in their own brains' (*The Course of German History* [orig. 1945; London, 1976], 134).

107 Edmund Burke, cited in *The Oxford Dictionary of Quotations*, 5th ed., ed. Elizabeth Knowles (Oxford, 2001), 164.

2 'Fishing for Popularity'

'To demagogue.' (*v.*) This awkward verb came suddenly into fashion during the U.S. presidential campaign of 1992. In that campaign the Democratic 'outsider,' Bill Clinton, defeated the wealthy Republican incumbent, George H.W. Bush. Significantly, this verb 'to demagogue' was used only occasionally – and then mainly by the electronic media – to describe the political tactics of the 'populist billionaire' from Texas, Ross Perot. Perot was unpretentious and had the 'common touch.' No one cared whether he belonged to the Left or the Right. Even though (or because) he said next to nothing about his policies, Perot was seen as someone who would simply 'get things done' in Washington. Untainted by professional politics, he spoke for the people, pure and simple.

By contrast, when President George Bush and Bill Clinton 'demagogued' the American electorate, they were roundly condemned. Because these men were the official ('partisan') candidates of the two established parties, political observers judged their campaign tactics by a different moral standard from the one they applied to the independent Perot. Bush was allegedly forced to demagogue the issue of riots in Los Angeles because he needed to put a favourable spin on the crisis and undercut its propaganda value to his challengers on the Right. Clinton demagogued the larger questions of urban crime and mass poverty in order to retain, or recapture, his standing as the quintessential Washington outsider. Both official candidates, as it happened, had good reason to attack Perot's temperamental character and authoritarian inclinations. They were also correct that his preference for conspiracy theories had a flip side: his refusal to play by the rules. Nevertheless, at the height of the campaign, Clinton's and Bush's staffers dared only whisper the 'P' word, standing not for 'partisan' or 'populist' but for Perot.

Remarkably, American broadcasters assumed that their listeners would understand this verb 'to demagogue' in an unproblematic way. One reason may lie in the two meanings commonly associated with the noun 'demagogue.' In the first – good – sense, a demagogue is virtually indistinguishable from a populist. He is a leader who, as in ancient times, champions the cause of the people against other factions in the state. In the second – bad – sense, a demagogue is an unprincipled agitator or orator, one who seeks to gain personal or partisan advantage by arousing mass prejudices and popular passions through specious, extravagant, or impossible demands.[1] During the 1992 campaign, no one lost sleep over the fact that demagoguery in *either* sense might undermine traditional political institutions. But demagoguery is a two-edged sword, by definition and in fact. One edge is sharp. It glimmers with the righteousness that for centuries has inspired outsiders to storm the fortresses of political orthodoxy in the name of 'the people.' The other edge is dull and self-destructive. It is indiscriminate in its blood-letting, and it betrays a popular trust. It wounds friend and foe alike.

If Americans have not always been sensitive to this dualism, neither have historians. One aim of this chapter is to discuss the usefulness of the term 'demagoguery' in tandem with two others that are equally slippery in definition: 'populism' and the more quixotic German word *Volkstümlichkeit*.[2] The latter term is important because it also had two connotations in contemporary usage. The first, negative, connotation implied 'fishing for popularity' among the people, a practice that was conjured up by the more literal but less benign term *Popularitätshascherei*. The second, more positive connotation of *Volkstümlichkeit* subsumed a variety of meanings that included popularity, closeness to the people, or 'possessing the popular touch.'

Each of these terms informs current historical writing about new political styles in Germany after 1871.[3] This chapter considers how 'licit' and 'illicit' forms of mass mobilization became increasingly indistinct after 1871. But like other chapters in this volume, this one has a historical and a historiographical component. On the one hand, it explores contemporary notions of 'dirty politics' as a means to explain how 'politics in a new key' intersected with politics in an *off* key.[4] This intersection, or intertwining, was an important factor determining the outcome of struggles for, first, legitimacy and then hegemony on the German Right. On the other hand, this chapter also interrogates today's leading historians of the Wilhelmine Right. It asks how *they* have deployed the concepts of demagoguery and populism to explain the dynamics of Imperial Germany's political modernization and its long-term significance up to 1933. Here a mixed assessment is in order. David Blackbourn's thesis of an escalating spiral of demagoguery – between rabble-rousing 'free-booters' on the Right and more traditional notables – provided an original interpretative key to understanding political change after 1890. But this chapter argues that the 'self-mobilization from below' thesis, advocated by Geoff Eley, downplays the political battles that were won by notables on the Right up to 1918 and beyond.

As a critical appreciation of Blackbourn's and Eley's work, this reassessment has three components. It argues that the concepts of demagoguery and populism have been used inconsistently and have now outlived their usefulness. Second, historians continue to neglect the 1870s and 1880s as decades when new political strategies to win popularity were also being worked out on the Right. Third, the idea of a demagogic spiral of 'challenge and response' tends to neglect the wide political terrain on which the 'old Right' and the 'new Right' found consensus. As an alternative, this chapter suggests that there are richer ways to see the dynamics of political change than through a winner-take-all interpretation, especially one that focuses narrowly on the years 1890 to 1909. By demonstrating that politics already looked frighteningly modern to many Germans in 1867 and that Hitler was not incorrect in the 1920s to disdain the ability of even the new Right to mobilize the masses, this chapter casts light on the changing discourses of politics over more than half a century. Like the next chapter, it contributes to a re-evaluation of what changed, and what remained the same, in German political culture from the time of Bismarck to the rise of Nazism.

Defining Styles

Long before the terms 'populism' and 'demagoguery' gained cachet among historians of the Right, another paradigmatic superweapon, the concept of 'illiberalism,' had been used to explain continuities that linked radical nationalism in the German Empire to the rise of Nazism.[5] The concept of illiberalism fell out of favour in the 1980s – so much so that by the 1990s many historians were stressing everything that was modern and dynamic about German society and culture before 1914.

The concepts of demagoguery and populism underpinned an impressive number of studies of the German Right in the 1980s; but as they became encumbered with more and more explanatory weight, they began to lose their usefulness as heuristic devices. In 2006, advocates of these concepts are suffering the same fate that befell their antagonists in the 'Bielefeld school' during the 1970s and 1980s, when a liberating interpretative model became a constraining one. Anglo-American historians who continue to deploy demagoguery and populism as explanatory concepts are now beginning to assume answers to questions about continuity in Germany history that these concepts were originally designed to raise.

One difficulty has been historians' tendency to see populism and demagoguery as two sides of the same coin, but with the moral and political signs reversed. In this usage neither concept is two-edged. Rather: *My* politics are enlightened and serve the people's interest; that is, they are populist. *Your* politics are dishonest and mislead the people; they are demagogic. Such polarized views arise as easily in scholarly analysis as they do in everyday life. If someone declares, 'You are a nationalist, but I am a patriot,' it is difficult for historians to sort out the complexities that actually define or distinguish nationalists and patriots, even though the *intended* effect of this rhetoric is transparent.

To be sure, historians no longer focus exclusively on the bad demagoguery of 'fearful' and 'defensive' elites or the illiberal structures that once were seen to have 'deformed' and 'deflected' German history. But along the way attention has shifted towards a good (or at least morally neutral) brand of populism that, in contrast to demagoguery, stands in a more benign relationship to democracy. That relationship is benign and especially close when democracy is unqualified – preceded by no qualifiers. But when historians claim that contemporary politicians endorsed 'mass democracy' or that 'pseudo-democratic' elites manipulated the methods of 'direct democracy,' those contemporaries are deemed to have flirted with a style of politics that had detached itself from the tether of democratic intentions and latched onto a new, more modern kind of demagoguery that instigated a twentieth-century 'revolt of the masses.'

A second difficulty arises in that populism confounds attempts to reduce it to a habit of mind or an ideology. Because it is a political style, or idiom, it is not just another 'ism' like liberalism, conservatism, or socialism. Rendering populism as a political idiom increases its attractiveness to historians who have abandoned structural history but who still hope to integrate political, cultural, and intellectual history. At the same time it is easier to apply to individuals and groups in history who wanted to 'shake things up.' Many historians of Germany use the term 'populism' to connote the mode of political activism embraced by those who were confident about the future. That confidence took many forms. Thus German populists were allegedly confident that change was on their side, that the destruction of exclusivity and privilege would usher in a new age, and that the realm of political decision-making in the state would expand with new forms of mass communication, the rise of the popular press, and the penetration of national issues into local affairs. Above all, populists were confident that they alone spoke for 'the people.'

Whom do these confident types bring to mind? Don't they look remarkably like liberals? These populists are said to have displayed the civic virtues that in Wilhelmine Germany allowed them to break the mould of the 'politics of notables' and in the Weimar Republic might even have allowed them to resist the appeals of the Nazis. Some historians even see such populism as a dominant paradigm over the long term. According to this viewpoint, expressed most forcefully by Geoff Eley, populists included the radical nationalists in the 1890s, who were the 'confident beneficiaries of Germany's capitalist transformation,' who portrayed themselves as 'free independent men,' and who often had emerged from the liberal milieu.[6] But they also included members of the German bourgeoisie in the mid-1920s who, as Peter Fritzsche has argued, were empowered by the 'Jacobin spirit of an independent citizenry,' who were struggling for 'genuine enfranchisement,' who 'now stepped into the public arena with greater and greater confidence,' and who embraced a 'robust' and 'reformist' politics with 'self-reliance,' 'vigor,' and 'poise.'[7] Self-reliant, vigorous, poised – again, these types sound very much like classic liberals.

This interpretative trajectory leads to conclusions that are counterintuitive: Populism in the good sense is ascribed to liberals whom we thought were always suspicious of the uneducated, unpropertied rabble. And demagoguery in the bad sense is ascribed to conservatives whom we thought were always in favour of authority and *Ordnung*. How did it come to this?

'A Handful of Junkers'

Even before the collapse of the Third Reich, Hitler was described as the quintessential demagogue: the *terrible simplificateur* who preferred the Big Lie and brutally unsophisticated propaganda. Some historians, indeed, contended that German political culture had been healthy and vibrant until defeat and revolution in 1918/19 opened the door to demagogues of both the Left and the Right. Gerhard Ritter argued in the 1950s that Germans turned to National Socialism not because liberal democracy failed but because German politics had become democratic and demagogic at the same time.[8] 'The parties were no longer composed of groups of notables, of clubs whose members were men who were socially and financially independent, who knew something about politics and were interested in them. They became mass organizations ... Political education, real discussion, individual thought ceased to be important; instead, what was required was mass appeal. In order to interest the masses, they must be attracted by sensationalism. He who is best at sensationalism is also the most popular ... Thus did it become possible to make a reality of the theory of the sovereignty of the people, in a radical manner that was completely new.'

In the 1960s most German historians discarded this interpretation. Scholars such as Hans Rosenberg, Fritz Stern, and George Mosse charted the roots of the Nazi triumph back to the nineteenth century. In this competing interpretation, the poles of Ritter's argument were reversed: Imperial Germany's ruling elites were *not* bulwarks against demagoguery; they were its patrons and perpetrators. As we saw in chapter 1, Alexander Gerschenkron in the 1940s had already argued that the 'machinery' of Junker protectionism, coupled with the Junker 'philosophy,' delayed the development of democratic institutions in Germany. According to Gerschenkron, the 'egocentric' German Junkers duped the peasantry into supporting policies contrary to their own economic interests through the vocal and unscrupulous propaganda of the Agrarian League (founded in 1893). He was able to cite Heinrich Heine's observation from the middle of the nineteenth century condemning the Junkers for the same crime. 'A handful of Junkers,' wrote Heine, 'who have learned nothing but a bit of horse-trading, card-sharping, dice-throwing or other stupid rascally tricks with which at best peasants at fairs can be duped, think that they can befool an entire people.'[9] The Junkers were demagogic in another way: they failed to serve their king. As Gerschenkron noted, the agrarians threatened to resort to the methods of Social Democrats unless their demands were satisfied: they spoke of refusing to pay taxes or give military recruits to the state, and they menaced the government's legislative program.[10]

In an essay first published in 1958, the German émigré historian Hans Rosenberg coined the term 'pseudo-democratization'[11] to describe the political strategy of these same Junkers. Rosenberg was not much impressed with Gerschenkron's work: he criticized Gerschenkron's 'alarming use of the word democracy and of undefined clichés such as "immature democracies," "semicoma [sic] democracies," "complete democracy," "democracy without democrats," "democratic strategy," etc.'[12] Rosenberg nonetheless came to many of the same conclusions as had Gerschenkron. The Agrarian League, in Rosenberg's view, was organized in a more 'modern' way than any previous political movement; its tactics were more ruthless and its ideology was more militant. The league had the character of 'a bureaucratized, undemocratic, and illiberally oriented plebicitary agrarian mass movement under the leadership of rural Junker demagogues and professional functionaries.'[13]

Like Gerschenkron, Rosenberg cited an influential nineteenth-century critic of the Junkers to reinforce his point. His choice was the liberal nationalist Friedrich Naumann. In his popular book *Democracy and Kaiserdom* (1900), Naumann had written about the Junkers with such passion that his words, often cited in short excerpts, deserve fuller attention: 'The old master caste [*Herrenschicht*] of about 24,000 individuals has fallen into a defensive position and now uses all possible means in order to maintain itself above water in a democratizing age. In the effort to attract new followers, it has become friendly to farmers, friendly to artisans, indeed sometimes even friendly to workers. For the same reason it makes alliances with industrial capitalism and with the Centre Party. It understands better than any other political group the art of accommodating fellow travellers ... From a purely aesthetic standpoint, it could be termed tragic that modern times demand such a thing from the old exclusive ruling aristocracy! We understand why conservatives cannot deal well with the universal suffrage. It ruins their character, for it is not possible to stand before an election meeting and defend the principle: Authority, not majority! ... Therefore the conservative today is of a compromising nature, an authoritarian type [*Herrenmensch*] with democratic gloves. He wanders through the age of freedom of movement, of the [universal] suffrage, and of a global grain trade, with the bearing of a head of a great old establishment who through circumstances is forced to humour even smaller clients. An agitating aristocracy! Even this is a consequence of the democratic tendency of the age.'[14]

Soon other scholars followed the same interpretative line.[15] Pauline Anderson's study of agrarian interest politics, for example, identified the Junkers' modern demagogic tactics as keys to their success. Ralf Dahrendorf's *Society and Democracy in Germany* highlighted the way

Imperial Germany's leading elites – the 'cartel of anxiety' – displayed a 'remarkable inventiveness' to deflect the onslaught of modernity.[16] George Mosse agreed, observing that 'what we call the fascist style was in reality the climax of a "new politics" based upon the emerging eighteenth-century idea of popular sovereignty.'[17]

Fritz Stern added his own indictment when he defined the Germanic 'ideology of resentment' as having affinities to American Populism. For Stern, German illiberalism became politically virulent when it was organized by agitators and writers who 'denounced,' 'attacked,' and 'maligned' modern civilization. 'The absence of a true conservative party,' he added, 'was a great loss to the political education of Germans. The power of delusion was great.'[18] For contemporary confirmation of this linkage, Stern cited Thomas Mann: 'Obscurantism – in politics we call it reaction – is brutality; it is sentimental brutality insofar as it tries to hide its brutal and irrational character "under the impressive mask" of Germanic temperament and loyalty.' On another occasion Stern advanced the same line: '[The Junkers in the 1890s] reached out to demagogic politics,' he wrote. 'The Conservative party bolstered its nationalistic rhetoric with an undertone of anti-Semitism and appealed to large segments of the non-proletarian world with an ideology of strident illiberalism.' Stern also cited Theodor Fontane's observation of 1896 that his 'unhappy love affair' with the Prussian nobility was over. Junker demagoguery was again to blame. 'The stance of the nobility,' wrote Fontane, 'almost going beyond the purely political, has taken on a shameless character, not externally, but internally ... a horrible mixture of narrowness, arrogance, and selfishness fills the whole brood.'

Hans-Jürgen Puhle's study of the Agrarian League, published in 1966, drew together these elements of the argument. Redirecting attention back to the German *Sonderweg*, Puhle presented the 'Junkers-as-demagogues' argument in its most rigorous form, thereby ensuring its survival into the 1980s.[19] According to him, the Agrarian League 'deformed' the Conservative Party structurally and ideologically. But along with new ideological strains on the Right – which, according to Puhle, became the 'exclusive ideology of the propertied classes' during the Wilhelmine era – went a new political *style*. The terms he used to describe the proponents of this demagogic style are revealing.[20] Whereas the old Conservatives were 'weak,' 'hopelessly outdated,' and 'moribund' by 1890, the new Right was dominated by 'desperados' and 'outcasts,' by 'professional politicians, managers, and publicists.' These men preferred 'rhetoric' and 'dogma' over rational political discourse:

theirs was a 'corporatist vocabulary' and a 'motley ideology.' Nonetheless, they proved willing to serve the rigidly centralized Agrarian League, which provided them the opportunity to move the people in new ways. Thus demagogues used the 'instruments of modern direct democracy' and 'manipulative popular ideological methods' to contribute to 'the extreme radicalization of political debate' and the 'rule by public acclaim [that] later became so politically effective.' In this way, democratic (qua demagogic) means served reactionary ends. This new relationship between ends and means, concluded Puhle, fundamentally transformed the German Right – well before 1918 – into something he labelled 'pre-fascism.' 'The new element in the era after Bismarck is not the fact of "interest politics" ... but rather ... the conscious practice of demagoguery [*Demagogisierung*], [which] became a correlate of democratization.'[21] 'It was this dual potential, the fusion of reactionary aims and modern, seemingly "progressive," and often revolutionary methods and ideologies, which actually makes the new Right pre-fascist and establishes a clear line of descent from it to the National Socialist takeover and Nazi rule.'[22]

Writing almost thirty years after Puhle, Dieter Langewiesche in 1994 endorsed essentially the same position. 'In so far as conservatism became nationalist, it could renew itself in a populist manner and find resonance among the masses,' Langewiesche wrote. 'The usurping of nationalism by conservatism and its nationalist modernization towards populism – this reciprocal process fuelled what was probably the most fundamental transformation of politics that Europe experienced after the revolutions of the eighteenth century. The older conservatism belonged among the losers as much as did liberalism. New, more nimble forces exploited the social energies that this dynamic mixture of nationalism and populism released. These were, after the First World War, above all the fascist movements.'[23]

The Spiral of Demagoguery

By the late 1970s this general interpretation of the dynamics of political modernization from Imperial Germany to the Third Reich was eliciting a sprinkling of dissent, mainly from Anglo-American scholars. Soon the sprinkle turned into a torrent. It did so in large measure because the twin concepts of demagoguery and populism were taken up by Geoff Eley and David Blackbourn in their co-authored book *The Peculiarities of German History*, which was published in Germany in 1980 and in a revised English edition in 1984. In the English version, Blackbourn's attempt to grapple with these concepts was programmatic:

> I have also questioned the idea of 'manipulation' ... This, once again, does not entail denying the elements of political dishonesty which characterized Imperial Germany; but it is easy to misidentify the range of would-be manipulators, and to approach the question of political manipulation itself one-sidedly. I am sceptical of accounts that depict the political process, in [Antonio] Gramsci's words, as 'a continuous *marche de dupes*, a competition in conjuring and sleight of hand.' It does greater justice to a complex historical process to recognize that if we are to talk of manipulation at all – and I prefer the term demagogy – we should at least recognize that it was a two-way process which was politically unpredictable and potentially dangerous. This approach need be neither ingenuous nor 'populist.' The purpose of questioning the idea of manipulation by a particular élite is not to substitute a view that everything happened 'from below' (which might be called the populist heresy), or that it happened because of the entry of 'the masses' into politics (the older conservative orthodoxy).'[24]

Blackbourn's reconsideration of changing political styles in Imperial Germany was elaborated not only in *Peculiarities* but in his own first monograph and a battery of related essays. Each work introduced innovative ways of thinking about populism and demagoguery. In Blackbourn's view, although the politics of notables and its alleged consensual style still prevailed in the 1870s and 1880s, more radical and 'chauvinistic' brands of nationalism came to the fore after 1890. These developments dovetailed with rapid increases in turnout at the polls, improved communication and transportation opportunities for the common man, and the expansion of the Social Democratic movement. Radical nationalists organized in the Pan-German League and the Navy League, in particular, challenged the 'élitist *insouciance*' of the old establishment, Blackbourn argued. Although these radical nationalists, like more traditional conservatives, claimed that the national ideal stood above political horse-trading, their challenge was marked by an 'energy' and a 'cutting contempt' that was directed against the complacency of *Honoratiorenpolitik*.[25] According to Blackbourn, politics in a new key was itself only a 'transitional mode of politics,' one that was 'contradictory and unstable, less self-assured and more febrile than what had preceded it.'[26] An important element of this new mode of

2.1. Campaigning in Bavaria. A Catholic priest solicits support from rural voters in southern Germany. *Wahltag im Bayerischen Gebirge*, wood engraving, ca. 1870, after a sketch by Julius Noerr. Image courtesy of the Bildarchiv Preußischer Kulturbesitz, Berlin.

politics was *Mittelstandspolitik* – advocacy of lower-middle-class interests – which was characterized by 'rhetorical excess and dishonesty.' But far from being the exclusive preserve of Conservatives and agrarians, *Mittelstandspolitik* was embraced by National Liberal and Centre Party leaders, even by left liberals, all of whom, Blackbourn wrote, could be 'startlingly demagogic.' This development allegedly 'injected a new measure of mendacity into political debate' because such demagogues 'offered panaceas which they often knew to be bogus.'[27]

The precise form in which such panaceas were articulated depended on class and sectional interests, and also on 'local identity, local grievances and local aspirations.'[28] But outsiders everywhere conceived of 'a direct form of popular, even populist politics which would, so they hoped, make parliaments irrelevant.' In this way, Blackbourn claimed, the congenial 'drama' of politics by and for notables was 'rudely interrupted from offstage as new voices demanded to be heard.'[29] The new leaders who emerged in the 1890s to lead the Centre Party in Württemberg – the subject of Blackbourn's monograph – proved at least as 'opportunistic' as the Conservatives: by wrapping anti-liberal, anti-capitalist, and anti-urban elements into an all-embracing ideological package, Blackbourn concluded, the Centre 'sustained its political position by means of a demagogic popular appeal.'[30]

Self-Mobilization from Below?

In his own monograph of 1980, *Reshaping the German Right*, Geoff Eley argued that the challenge from below 'registered a profound seismic shift at the base of German society.' That shift, he continued, 'sent heavy tremors of social aspiration upwards to the political surface of the new German nation-state.'[31] The different strategies adopted by right-wing mobilizers in order to win 'mass popular support' engaged Eley's attention directly. Like Blackbourn, he agreed with one of Puhle's premises: that the Agrarian League overran the Conservative Party, making its popular base broader and its political style demagogic.[32] In the main, however, Eley's demagogues and populists were not 'manipulators' in any sense of the word. Because he disagreed with Puhle's model of a 'manipulative self-modernization of the existing [Conservative] leadership,' he quickly left behind Diederich Hahn and other Agrarian League functionaries. Instead he looked for 'outsiders' among the radical nationalist associations. These outsiders constituted for Eley the 'self-activated' 'subaltern' groups in society who resisted manipulation from above. Rather, they waged 'unprecedented demagogic campaigns' against the authorities.[33] 'Denied political access by the ingrained etiquette of *Honoratiorenpolitik*,'[34] these people tended to invoke 'the higher legitimacy of the people's purpose.' This, wrote Eley, was 'something quite new' on the Right.[35]

A central chapter in *Reshaping the German Right* was entitled 'The New Terrain of Popular Politics.' This chapter was immediately preceded by a long section in which Eley addressed the conceptual problem of populism head-on.[36] Populism in its radical nationalist form was closely related to a 'generational anomie,' he argued. But he added that it would be a mistake to identify the inclination to invoke 'the people' exclusively with an 'anti-modern' or 'backward-looking' ideology. Less fearful than aggressive, Eley's protagonists – for example, the Navy League's Hermann Rassow and August Keim – were willing 'to fish on the edges of the opposition.' They were *not* 'shrinking violets.'

Gradually, these radicals developed 'a general philosophy of confrontation' and an 'angry critique' of established politicians, 'whom they accused of debilitating caution, social élitism, blindness to Germany's national needs, and a refusal to obey the dictates of the new mass politics.' For their pains, these populists were greeted with charges from 'on high' that they were demagogues. Why? Because 'they overrode opposition with extravagant appeals to imponderable popular sentiments.' And that is exactly what they did, argued Eley – consciously and with intent.[37]

In the course of the 1980s, Eley's thoughts about the long-term development of the German Right began more and more to stress populism as a binding link between the old Right and later German fascists. For example, he wrote that 'the possibility of a German fascism became inscribed in the political and ideological structures of the [Wilhelmine] power bloc at that moment when the struggle to recompose its unity became displaced on to populist terrain.'[38] Yet essays Eley published in 1983 and 1990 had very different emphases.[39] In 1983 Eley argued that 'dissenting radical-nationalist politics' was 'a new kind of right-wing populism' in the imperial era. In the context of the late Weimar years too, he implied, it was motivated 'by a growing anger at the alleged faint-heartedness of the constitutional government, the old-style conservatives, and above all the liberal parties.'[40] Populism thus was principally the demand 'for a radical propagandist effort to win the right to speak for the "people in general,"' a kind of 'right-wing Jacobinism.' This effort, Eley continued, had by the end of the Weimar Republic become critical for the German Left as well as for the Right: the Left's 'classic dilemma' was 'how to win popular support for socialism by electoral means.' Like the conservatives, the Socialists and Communists recognized that 'it was vital to conceive of other than class collectivities' by rallying the people according to new categories and interests, though not in the manner of 'some opportunist and eclectic pluralism of discrete campaigns, but as the coherent basis for the broadest possible democratic unity.' In this endeavour, ideology might have served the Left as well as Puhle claimed it served the Right, Eley wrote, but only if we adopt 'an expanded definition' in which ideology becomes 'not only the fascist movement's formal aims, but its style of activism, modes of organization and forms of public display.' However, for Left *and* Right, failure to achieve 'this wider popular democratic mobilization' was fatal, for 'it was precisely here that fascism showed its superiority.'[41]

In 1990 Eley went over the same conceptual ground again. But now he emphasized everything that *distinguished* fascists from conservatives. His list of distinctions is illuminating: 'The recourse to political violence – to repressive and coercive forms of rule, to guns rather than words, to beating up one's opponents rather than denouncing them from the speaker's platform – was ultimately what distinguished fascism, in Germany and elsewhere, from existing forms of right-wing politics.'[42] 'Hitler's parliamentary and "legal" strategy [after 1923] was very far from the practical parliamentarism of the Conservative parties before 1914. Whereas the Wilhelmine Right observed the rules of liberal political discourse until shortly before 1914, the Nazis treated them with complete and bare-faced cynicism ... The repudiation of the parliamentary legitimacy that had previously constrained the Right from this kind of extremism is the essence of the transition described here.'[43]

Conservatives in Imperial Germany, Eley noted, had neither terrorized nor killed socialists. Even the 'pluralistic logic' of the Weimar Republic's constitution imposed 'a practical scenario of compromise and negotiation.' Both Imperial and republican Germany, in other words, represented political systems that supported such traditional conservative leaders as Count Kuno von Westarp, who 'remained hostile to the populist and demagogic posture of "nationalist opposition."' What then, in Eley's view, consigned politicians like Westarp to the margins after 1928? 'An appeal to the "will of the people,"' he concluded, 'was something quite *new* for the Right.'[44] Thus German fascism was 'self-consciously and blusteringly plebeian.' Its vocabulary was 'crude and violent.' And it embraced an 'egalitarianism appropriate to its broadly based popular appeal.' In short, fascism embodied the twin ideas of 'activism and popular mobilization.' This dualism, argued Eley, lent it a 'distinctive political style.'[45]

'Letting the Dogs Bark'

That the concepts of demagoguery and populism remained central to Blackbourn's own interpretative paradigm was demonstrated in 1987 when he gave a collection of his essays the short title *Populists and Patricians*. No fewer than four of these essays were seminal: they dealt with peasant politics, antisemitism, metaphors of the stage, and the 'politics of demagoguery.'[46] But how did Blackbourn elaborate demagogic and populist practices now? Had his conclusions shifted since 1980 to the same degree that Eley's had?

Blackbourn noted, first, that manipulative models of politics in Imperial Germany used terms such as 'national demagoguery' to refer to such allegedly instrumentalist policies as social imperialism and *Weltpolitik*. Next, he reminded us that the charge of demagoguery was hurled frequently and more than a little arbitrarily during the Imperial period – at Bismarck by many liberals and at almost everyone by Max Weber.[47] The charge of right-wing demagoguery, noted Blackbourn, came in 'a smaller and larger version,' corresponding to the arguments Puhle and others had used to describe the Agrarian League specifically and illiberal elites broadly. The peasantry and the lower middle classes figured prominently in the protest movements that exhibited demagogic tendencies. But Blackbourn expanded the analysis. Now he included not only the antisemites, radical nationalists, and right-wing publicists who challenged the status quo but also the moderate conservatives and government ministers who attempted to manipulate and co-opt these forces to their own ends. However, 'letting the dogs bark,' as Foreign Secretary Alfred von Kiderlen-Wächter once put it, did not domesticate the wolf at the door. Quite the contrary. This strategy unleashed 'a politics of disrespect' that rebounded on conservatives. According to Blackbourn, the whole political system was destabilized because the demagogic 'idiom' compelled political outsiders *and* established government leaders to 'promise anything' to the people. Moreover, the continuing necessity of parliamentary horse-trading and compromise effectively reduced the chances that those promises would be redeemed.

One of Blackbourn's greatest contributions to the debate lay in his discussion of demagogic practices at the level of everyday politics. He noted, for example, that typewriters and slide shows provided some of the modern hardware that facilitated new forms of demagoguery after 1890. He also discussed the 'verbal shot-gun scatter of resentment' that characterized the public speeches of parish-pump activists. As well, Blackbourn addressed the dominant motifs of demagogic agitation and the social background that was typical of the Imperial era's most famous demagogues. It was not coincidental, he noted, that these men were labelled 'political speculators' and 'adventurers,' though Blackbourn preferred the terms 'maverick' and 'political free-booters.' Such mavericks gambled recklessly with the truth in order to win popularity. They gambled so recklessly, in fact, that they could end up as easily at the bottom of the heap as at the top: either in prison on charges of libel, embezzlement, and blackmail or else in the Reichstag as an esteemed member of parliament (*'hochverehrter MdR'*).

These mavericks and free-booters nonetheless encountered many of the same obstacles faced by Eley's populists, regardless of whether they considered themselves citizens, patriots, or tribunes of the people. According to Blackbourn, by confusing the distinction between private 'affairs' and public 'duties,' they lent a 'new public legitimacy to sentiments which, even two decades earlier, would have remained the stuff of private grumbles.' Moreover, disclosures, unveilings, and hints of 'betrayal in high places' did not remain – *could* not remain – trivial or benign. Instead such disclosures 'brought the prejudices of the *Stammtisch* into the public meeting and parliamentary debate.' In this sense, the old Conservative Party chairman Otto von Helldorff (profiled in chapter 9) hit the mark in 1892 when he complained that demagogues were contributing to 'a frightful brutalization of public opinion.' Demagoguery brutalized public life at all levels and in all camps. The 'new political formations' that emerged from this process represented 'an unstable amalgam of soured emancipatory impulse and illiberalism.'

Thus Blackbourn concluded that previous historians, including Puhle, were correct in charging that Junkers, imperialists, members of the other leading elites, and even government ministers were 'undeniably demagogic.' The deeper irony for Blackbourn, though, was that previous interpretations actually *underestimated* the long-term impact of this demagoguery and its 'potential explosiveness.' 'For elite efforts did more to make populist and chauvinist demagoguery respectable than to defuse them. The attempts to meet one form of demagoguery with another ("demagoguery in the good sense") established ... one dangerous element of continuity between Wilhelmine and Weimar Germany ... Far from being an accident, Hitler was the final revenge of those demagogues "in the bad sense" whose appetites had grown rather than diminished through the years of attempted co-optation.'[48]

The 'Cinderella Complex'

The concept of populism is still plagued by a disorder that Isaiah Berlin once labelled the 'Cinderella complex.'[49] Berlin put it this way: 'there exists a shoe – the word "populism" – for which somewhere there exists a foot. There are all kinds of feet which it *nearly* fits, but we must not be trapped by these nearly fitting feet. The prince is always wandering about with the shoe; and somewhere, we feel sure, there awaits a limb called pure populism.' Other critics have been more dismissive. To talk of populism in certain political contexts, Kenneth Minogue once observed, 'looks at first like talking of Spanish champagne; it's plausible, but there ought to be a law against it.'[50] So why attempt any longer to define populism at all? Why seek another charmed solution to a heavily burdened tale? As historians, should we not stop snapping at this stale bait?[51]

To ask this question is *not* to propose that we abandon our study of the relationship between politics and 'the people.' Quite the contrary. Historians of Imperial Germany have nonetheless used the twin concepts of populism and demagoguery in inconsistent, unsystematic, even contradictory ways. One symptom of this *Teufelskreis* is that historians continue to try to identify a particular decade in which the relationship between political leaders and 'the people' was allegedly transformed – transformed, that is, in such a decisive way that a new, 'modern,' 'popular' form of politics was suddenly born. The difficulty here, of course, is that historians disagree fundamentally about which decade to choose.

Some have identified the emergence of voluntary associations in the early nineteenth century as a 'key' development in the problematic encounter between liberalism and the *Volk*.[52] According to this argument, German liberals in the nineteenth century, like later leaders, wanted to get 'close' to the people – but not too close. Other historians look to the revolution of 1848 or the period after 1873 as decisive. Though Hans Rosenberg's notion of an emerging 'political mass market' in the 1870s and 1880s has not won universal acceptance, others identify the founding of the empire in 1871, the onset of the *Kulturkampf*

2.2. The Reichstag in session, 1870s. This scene depicts the left-liberal deputy Hermann Schulze-Delitzsch at the speaker's podium; Bismarck can be seen at left. Wood engraving, 1874, after a drawing by H. Luders. Image courtesy of the Bildarchiv Preußischer Kulturbesitz, Berlin.

against the Catholic Church, the rise of antisemitism, the appearance of powerful economic pressure groups, or Bismarck's 'charismatic dictatorship' as having produced a decisive shift in the relationship between leaders and led – in each case well before 1890.

Geoff Eley sees the 1890s as a 'moment of fission' in German politics, and David Blackbourn's examples of demagoguery have been drawn mainly from the same decade. Indeed, the 1890s are so often identified as the decade in which 'popular' politics was born that graduate students can be forgiven if they do not dare to tackle research on the 1870s and 1880s. The nationalist opposition to Chancellor Theobald von Bethmann Hollweg between 1909 and 1917 is also considered by some to have been decisive in bringing the German Right into greater proximity to 'the people'[53] (even though a recent study of the Army League speaks of the period after 1914 as the 'twilight of the demagogues').[54] And historians who focus on bourgeois organizational life believe that the period 1917–23 was a watershed. In those years, the argument goes, 'the notion of an all-embracing national community' and 'demands for inclusion in the political order' first resonated in bourgeois political discourse.[55] The paramilitary Steel Helmets (Stahlhelm) in the 1920s, for example, is taken as 'one of the first organizations to successfully cast nationalism in a popular mould, to encourage widespread public participation, and to embrace the bourgeois community in its entirety.'[56] Nevertheless, most historians agree that there was something qualitatively and quantitatively unprecedented about the Nazis' ability to mobilize popular forces. This distinction has now become one of the most durable orthodoxies of modern German history.[57] What, in the end, are we do make of all those other allegedly 'key' developments in previous decades?

One way to address the issue of continuity is to pay special attention to the evolving discourses that linked questions of 'popular' politics to the notion of political 'honour.' Honour as a concept was just as protean and elusive as 'genuine' popularity itself. In an essay on duelling, Ute Frevert wrote: 'Honour was a quality, the contents of which eluded positive definition: it was discernible solely through the perceptions of others, and materialized itself through continuing processes of social communication.'[58] Exactly the same can be said of attempts to use concepts of honour and morality to define 'dirty politics' in both the nineteenth and twentieth centuries. Here, too, theory and practice diverged. Max Weber expressed this syndrome succinctly: 'Certainly, politics is not an ethical business. But there does nevertheless exist a certain minimum of shame and obligation to behave decently which cannot be violated with impunity, even in politics.'[59] In the Weimar Republic, Robert Hopwood once observed, German burghers expected that a leader would provide 'moral as well as political guidance.' Nevertheless, what Hopwood identified as a development peculiar to the 1920s – the 'introspective frenzy' of middle-class Germans as they 'clawed at their cultural heritage to find guidelines or models for daily behaviour and for the means of regaining power' – was arguably just as pronounced in previous epochs. Hopwood himself provided a verse from 1912 that caught the desperation of these middle-class Germans:

> We want men, not weathervanes,
> Who at the first sight of a storm,
> Shrug and spin like a plane.
> We want men, who in order to win,
> Will go through hell and risk their skin.'[60]

Members of the German Right were neither uniformly mendacious nor uniformly high-minded, but they were not political weathervanes either. As the sociologist José G. Merquior once suggested with his metaphor of 'the veil and the mask,'[61] whereas an elite's conscious attempts to deceive and manipulate others may mask base intentions, the elite itself may see the world only through veils of misperception that are less odious.[62] This distinction should not be overdrawn: human motivations are usually mixed. Yet the concept of honour attunes us to the complex, intertwining motives that conditioned the relationship between Germans' personal value orientations and more programmatic statements that guided their social and political action.[63] It can do so even when we ask whether contemporary Germans felt they were 'honour-bound' to serve the *Volk* above all else.

Historians still disagree about whether invoking 'the people' as the highest authority was undertaken with 'sincere' motives. Indeed, this distinction lies close to the heart of the populism/demagoguery dualism. The logic of authoritarianism argued strongly in another direction, refusing to place the authority of 'the people' higher than the legitimacy of the Kaiser, the state, or the nation.[64] Our judgment as to whether members of the Right were acting honourably or not falls differently as we chart the evolution of German politics from the 1860s to the First World War and beyond – that is, to the moment when a young Adolf Hitler makes his appearance and we consider the Right's complicity in undermining the Weimar Republic. But this chapter and this book are premised on the belief that larger questions about what went so terribly wrong after 1920 necessarily draw us back to debates that troubled Germans during the nineteenth century. Identifying the question of honour helps to explain why those debates touched a raw nerve on the German Right well before the *terrible simplificateur* made his sudden entrance on the political stage.[65]

Old Right, New Right

In what waters, then, should *we* fish for clues to contemporary definitions of personal honour and political fairness? The history of associational life offers good prospects, though only if we range across the notional historical divide of 1918. 'Terrible, terrible,' was how Hitler described the first meetings of the German Workers Party he attended: 'This was club life [*Vereinsmeierei*] of the worst manner and sort.'[66] In a memorandum of January 1922, Hitler identified bourgeois party life as 'the mixture of goodwill, harmless naïveté, theoretical knowledge, and utter lack of instinct.'[67] With their obsessive adherence to statutes, rules of debate, and voting rites, these organizations subscribed to the same parliamentary 'lunacy' Hitler was driven to destroy.[68] But besides ridiculing the 'gossip societies,' 'literary tea clubs,' and '*spießbürgerlich* bowling societies' of pre-war days,[69] Hitler also ridiculed those *völkisch* nationalist groups that had allegedly provided Wilhelmine politics with its populist and demagogic character. He recalled a patriotic meeting he attended in Munich: 'On the platform sat the committee. To the left a monocle, to the right a monocle, and in between one without a monocle.'[70] Soon the audience, listening to a 'dignified old gentleman,' was 'dozing along in a state of trance,' from which only yawns, beer, or an early exit promised relief.

This is an important point missed by Blackbourn and Eley. The political free-booters that figure so prominently in their analyses had largely relinquished formal leadership of their voluntary associations – had they ever won it? – to right-wing notables. Those notables were described by Hitler himself as 'highly honourable but fantastically naïve men of learning, professors, district councillors, schoolmasters and barristers – in short a bourgeois, idealistic, and refined class. It lacked the warm breath of the nation's youthful vigour. The impetuous force of headstrong fire-eaters was rejected as demagoguery.'[71] Lacking 'discipline or form,' Hitler believed, the pre-war *völkisch* movement had 'utterly failed in its main task of winning the broad masses for the national cause.'[72] Who, then, would achieve this task? Hitler had the answer, as he always did: *he* would lead it – at the head of 'a racialist movement with a firm social base, a hold over the broad masses, welded together in an iron-hard organisation, instilled with blind obedience and inspired by a brutal will, a party of struggle and action.'[73]

Naturally, we cannot take Hitler's judgment at face value. But his consistency on this point prompts reflection: how far had 'politics in a new key' actually penetrated to the level of individual clubs before the mid-1920s? If the 'new key' is the idea of mass participation, one must immediately ask: 'mass' by what standard, and 'participation' on whose terms? About the actual course of the typical association evening meeting we remain remarkably ignorant, despite the flowering of local and regional studies in the past ten years. In these studies the demagogues of Imperial Germany are conspicuous mainly by their absence. For the period before 1900, it is true, a few declamatory speeches and malicious pamphlets are well known: one thinks of Adolf Stöcker's famous 'appeal' to the Jews (1879) or Hermann Ahlwardt's libellous *Jewish Rifles* pamphlet (1892). But next to nothing has been written about how 'rabble-rousers' conducted their meetings and structured their organizations – two features of modern politics to which Hitler gave considerable thought and attention.

Even the processes whereby the 'beer-bench politics' of the Pan-German League was upgraded into a 'nationalist opposition' remain obscure in crucial details. Far from putting into practice the populist ideals of community and participation, and far from opening the field to all the 'little people' who had grievances to express in public, groups such as the Navy League and Pan-German League recreated the formalized, highly articulated, and generally elitist structures for which their more vocal members condemned the established parties. As Roger Chickering once noted in a critical review of *Reshaping the German Right*, there is a certain irony that Eley chose the Navy League as indicative of the populist moment within radical nationalism,[74] because the Navy League proved more susceptible to manipulation from the government than most other nationalist associations. Members of the Pan-German League and the Agrarian League were better able to resist outside pressure from the government. But manipulation from above was found in these organizations too. Hence one should speak of a complex interplay among manipulation from above, self-mobilization from below, *and* a fragile but genuine consensus among radical nationalist associa-

98   'Tradition is how we change'

2.3. A Berlin polling station, January 1912. The ballot box is marked 'Wahlurne.' Image courtesy of the Bildarchiv Preußischer Kulturbesitz, Berlin.

tions and more conservative factions on the Right. If there always existed a latent tension between populist and elitist styles of politics, its effect remained just that: more latent than real. The practical effect of German populism was generally to endorse, not dismantle, bourgeois traditions.

Rather than giving in to the temptation to cite Hitler again, we can more profitably draw from the musings of a radical nationalist whose career spanned the Wilhelmine and Weimar eras: Franz Sontag, a Pan-German publicist who also wrote for mainstream conservative newspapers.[75] Like Hitler, Sontag was utterly dismissive of failed right-wing attempts to mobilize the masses both before and after November 1918. Sontag was so wedded to the Wilhelmine style of associational life, however, that by 1930 he could barely comprehend the 'strange forms' the nationalist movement had assumed: 'Gone are the days in which one passed resolutions in meetings of the membership or in similar fashion unleashed a little storm in a water glass. What does a resolution, a petition, or even a national congress mean any more ...? Mass has become trump; in these circumstances the power of arms and fists counts for more as a means of political expression and persuasion than the most pithy lecture ... All the old voluntary associations ... have become practically meaningless ... [Under] the symbols of the Steel Helmets or the swastika of the National Socialists ... the spirit of a new, younger generation takes flight towards goals that are at present still distant and hazy.'[76]

One can only applaud historians who are trying to apply lessons learned from the early 1930s to the period before 1918. Two such historians are Thomas Childers and Roger Chickering. With close attention to the language and imagery used in Nazi propaganda, on the one hand, and to the structure and style of local Nazi clubs, on the other, Childers and Chickering have suggested that the Nazis did not invade, penetrate, or take over the German public realm in the 1920s at all.[77] Instead the Nazi Party in its early days actually recreated the dominant organizational features and political vocabularies from an earlier era. 'The rituals of club life,' Chickering has written, could not simply be dismissed by Hitler; instead he familiarized himself with them and 'became their virtuoso.' At the local level especially, 'the *similarities* between the Nazi clubs and other local *Vereine* [associations] represented the party's most enduring success.'[78] Childers came to much the same conclusion. The Nazis were uniquely successful in persuading middle-class Germans to define themselves in the corporatist vocabulary that placed the Nazis on fertile political terrain; but that language itself was 'reinforced by social convention, economic organization, and official government usage, ... whether or not its users fully appreciated its historical origins or ideological implications.'[79]

'Respectability and Familiarity'

To take stock, this chapter has tried to narrow, not widen, the distance between the politics of notables and the politics of demagogues. It has argued against making strict social and ideological distinctions between 'populists' who tried to invoke the legitimacy of the people and 'notables' – who attempted the same trick. And rather than stressing the 1890s as a turning point in the birth of a political mass market, this chapter has opted to highlight long-term continuities, ambiguities, and complexities in the processes of political modernization. For reasons that will become clear in a moment, the 1860s and 1870s were at least as important as the 1890s in fostering fundamental political change in Germany. That said, both Sontag and Hitler were correct in dismissing the idea that the old Right had successfully transformed itself into something new, or that a new Right had supplanted it, before 1918.

This chapter can be concluded by establishing one final link between political modernization and the practice of 'fishing for popularity' among the people. Most readers will be able to discern the author of the following passage from internal references. But those who are not able to catch these hints may wonder about the stage of political development this particular author believed Germany had reached when he wrote these lines. This stage of political development would surely have been a very advanced one, we might suppose from the account itself – when the brutalization of public opinion was far advanced, when the politics of notables was a thing of the past, when populist and demagogic appeals to baser human emotions was widespread, when anti-Marxist rhetoric was already paying dividends, and when Germans appeared ready to throw off the fetters of democracy.

> A general election fever has broken out ... Let me relate the story of a comical trip [to Erfurt] ... March to a large, desolate meeting room, in which the voters were dutifully sitting smoking and drinking beer. ... Then a thundering, angry knock was heard at a small door ... When it was opened, a throng of contrary-minded voters pushed through into the hallowed spaces of the [nominating] committee and threateningly arrayed themselves behind us in a semicircle ...; these were unkempt journeymen and red-bearded, insolent Lassalleans ...
>
> In the knowledge that I had on a black dress coat and gray trousers – that is, the right mix of respectability and familiarity [*Hochachtung und Vertraulichkeit*] – I began to stir my punch, with feeling, drawing from the well-proven lines of the *Grenzboten* [a liberal middle-class journal] with profound observations about fate and the human condition. This pleased the lads ... Coarseness carried the day: ... with a loud cry and shaking of hands all around, I was proclaimed the chosen one. A sculptor requested that I model for him; a court photographer asked for sittings too; the publisher of the *Thüringische Zeitung* declared that his wife had just given birth and that I should serve as the child's godfather; a peasant regaled me with a short speech and expressed the wish that he might own a copy of *Debit and Credit* [*Soll und Haben*] – he could buy one, of course, but he would prefer that I present him with it as a gift. On the next day I obliged the sculptor, sat for the photographer, attended a baptismal breakfast with the new father, and sent the book to the peasant ...
>
> From all sides come demands from my voters that I visit them and

provide them with an evening's entertainment, and the correspondence with influential lawyers and innkeepers is becoming enormous. Oh, this universal suffrage ruins a man's character: for fifty years I didn't give popularity a second thought, and now I send a bouquet of flowers to a woman in childbed without knowing whether she had a boy or a girl, and I shake the hands of a hundred dear friends whose names I don't know and never will know. Fie, Bismarck, that was no master stroke! Worst of all, no one knows whether he'll be elected or not.[80]

This account of 'modern,' 'mass' politics was written *not* by one of Germany's most determined antidemocrats but by the liberal publicist Gustav Freytag. And it was written not when German democracy was on the ropes in the early 1930s but in January 1867, at the height of Germany's first national election campaign conducted under universal manhood suffrage. And so, when Freytag succumbed to these allegedly irresistible pressures to fish for popularity among the masses, was he witnessing the demise of the politics of notables? Was he contributing to the rise of modern demagoguery? Or had he simply discovered, like Bill Clinton in 1992 (and then again in 1996), that one could be popular, populist, and eminently electable all at the same time?

Had Freytag learned 'to demagogue'?

NOTES

1 *The Shorter Oxford English Dictionary*, 2 vols. (Oxford, 1973), 1:514, offers this definition of 'demagogue': '1. In ancient times, a leader of the people as against other parties in the state ... 2. In bad sense: A leader of a popular faction, or of the mob; an unprincipled or factious mob orator or political agitator.' The *Shorter Oxford* does not include 'demagogue' as a verb, whereas *Webster's Third New International Dictionary of the English Language, Unabridged* (Springfield, 1981), 598, does. The latter defines demagogue (*n.*) as: '1: a leader or orator in ancient times who championed the cause of the common people: a leader of the popular or plebeian party or faction in the state 2: one who employs demagogic methods; *esp*: a political leader who seeks to gain personal or partisan advantage by specious or extravagant claims, promises, or charges : rabble-rouser.' It also defines 'demagogue' (*v.*): 'to act the part of a demagogue : behave like a demagogue.'

2 These terms resurfaced in analyses of the September 2005 general elections

in Germany and the 'upstart' Leftist Party. See, for example, Ulrich Reitz, 'Old-New Left Alternative,' *Atlantic Times: A Monthly Newspaper from Germany* 2, no. 8 (Aug. 2005): A3, referring to Oskar Lafontaine and Gregor Gysi: 'both are lone wolves and not team players; both have an extraordinary talent for rhetoric and don't shrink from populism and even demagoguery.'

3 See Carl Schorske, 'Politics in a New Key: An Austria Trio,' *Journal of Modern History* 39 (1967): 343–86.

4 The latter term was first used by Peter Hayes in a critical review of David Abraham's book *The Collapse of the Weimar Republic* (Princeton, 1981).

5 Konrad H. Jarausch, 'Illiberalism and Beyond: German History in Search of a Paradigm,' *Journal of Modern History* 55 (1983): 268–84, here 281.

6 Geoff Eley, *Reshaping the German Right: Radical Nationalism and Political Change after Bismarck* (New Haven and London, 1980), 199–200; compare Roger Chickering, *We Men Who Feel Most German: A Cultural Study of the Pan-German League, 1886–1914* (Boston, 1984), 303: 'as a description of a historical phenomenon in Germany the term [illiberal] is misleading at best. The Pan-German League was a child of German liberalism. It retained the pretension of the *Bildungsbürgertum* [educated bourgeoisie] to speak in the name of the German nation, which it defined as the *Volk* [the people].'

7 Peter Fritzsche, 'Between Fragmentation and Fraternity: Civic Patriotism and the Stahlhelm in Bourgeois Neighborhoods during the Weimar Republic,' *Tel Aviver Jahrbuch für deutsche Geschichte* 17 (1988): 123–44, here 141, 144; Fritzsche, 'Presidential Victory and Popular Festivity in Weimar Germany: Hindenburg's 1925 Election,' *Central European History* 23, nos. 2/3 (1990): 205–24, here 221, 224; Fritzsche, 'Weimar Populism and National Socialism in Local Perspective,' in *Elections, Mass Politics, and Social Change in Modern Germany: New Perspectives*, ed. Larry Eugene Jones and James Retallack (New York and Cambridge, 1992), 287–306, here 288, 299–305; Fritzsche, 'Breakdown or Breakthrough? Conservatives and the November Revolution,' in *Between Reform, Reaction, and Resistance: Studies in the History of German Conservatism from 1789 to 1945*, ed. Larry Eugene Jones and James Retallack (Providence, RI, and Oxford, 1993), 299–328; and Fritzsche, *Rehearsals for Fascism* (New York and Oxford, 1990), 6–15.

8 For an English statement of this influential interpretation, see Gerhard Ritter, 'The Historical Foundations of the Rise of National-Socialism,' in International Council for Philosophy and Humanistic Studies and UNESCO, eds., *The Third Reich* (London, 1955), 381–416, esp. 390–7, with citations from 391, 394. See also Georg Iggers, 'Introduction,' to *The Social*

History of Politics, ed. Iggers (Leamington Spa, 1985), 20; Richard J. Evans, 'Wilhelm II's Germany and the Historians,' in Evans, *Rethinking German History* (London, 1987), 25–54, here 25–31.
9 Heinrich Heine, *Französische Zustände*, cited in Alexander Gerschenkron, *Bread and Democracy in Germany* (Ithaca and London, 1989), 26.
10 Gerschenkron, *Bread and Democracy*, 55.
11 Hans Rosenberg, 'Die Pseudodemokratiserung der Rittergutsbesitzerklasse' (orig. 1958), in Hans-Ulrich Wehler, ed., *Moderne deutsche Sozialgeschichte* (Cologne and Berlin, 1973), 287–308. This essay is reprinted in English in *Social History*, ed. Iggers.
12 Hans Rosenberg, 'Aristokratischer Agrarismus in Österreich und Preußen,' in Rosenberg, *Machteliten und Wirtschaftskonjunkuren* (Göttingen, 1978), 279–80.
13 Rosenberg, 'Zur sozialen Funktion der Agrarpolitik im Zweiten Reich,' in ibid., 102–17, here 110.
14 Friedrich Naumann, *Demokratie und Kaisertum* (Berlin, 1900), 92–3.
15 Heinz Haushofer, *Die deutsche Landwirtschaft im technischen Zeitalter* (Stuttgart, 1963), 213, still claimed that leaders of the Agrarian League were 'in no way demagogues.' Cited by David Blackbourn in 'Peasants and Politics in Germany, 1871–1914,' in Blackbourn, *Populists and Patricians* (London, 1987), 116.
16 Ralf Dahrendorf, *Society and Democracy in Germany* (New York, 1967), 207–8, 195, 108–9, 368, 327. Two other influential works with related theses were William Kornhauser, *The Politics of Mass Society* (Glencoe, Ill., 1959), and Barrington Moore Jr, *Social Origins of Dictatorship and Democracy* (Boston, 1966), esp. 448–50.
17 George L. Mosse, *The Nationalization of the Masses* (New York, 1975).
18 For this and the following, see Fritz Stern, *The Politics of Cultural Despair* (orig. 1961; Berkeley, 1974), xxii–xxx; Stern, 'Prussia,' in *European Landed Elites in the Nineteenth Century*, ed. David Spring (Baltimore, 1977), 59–63. See also Hans-Jürgen Perrey, *'Nirgends ist ihm ganz zu trauen.' Bismarck im Urteil Theodor Fontanes* (Friedrichsruh, 2002).
19 It is not my intention to detract from Puhle's path-breaking research.
20 The following account is a composite drawn from Hans-Jürgen Puhle, 'Conservatism in Modern German History,' *Journal of Contemporary History* 13, no. 4 (1978): 689–720, esp. 703–6; Puhle, 'Lords and Peasants in the Kaiserreich,' in *Peasants and Lords in Modern Germany*, ed. Robert G. Moeller (Boston, 1986), 81–109; and Puhle, *Agrarische Interessenpolitik und preußischer Konservatismus im wilhelminischen Reich (1893–1914)*, 2nd ed. (orig. 1966; Bonn-Bad Godesberg, 1975), esp. 274–89.

21 Puhle, *Agrarische Interessenpolitik*, 286.
22 Puhle, 'Conservatism,' 706; also Puhle, 'Lords,' 93: 'A mix between a political party and a pressure group, [the Agrarian League] pursued reactionary goals with direct democratic techniques and a proto-fascist ideology.'
23 Dieter Langewiesche, *Nationalismus im 19. und 20. Jahrhundert. Zwischen Partizipation und Aggression* (Bonn, 1994), 14–15.
24 David Blackbourn and Geoff Eley, *The Peculiarities of German History* (New York and Oxford, 1984), 290.
25 Ibid., 264.
26 Ibid., 266.
27 Ibid., 271, 272.
28 David Blackbourn, *Class, Religion and Local Politics in Wilhelmine Germany* (New Haven, 1980), 18.
29 Blackbourn and Eley, *Peculiarities*, 280, 285.
30 Blackbourn, *Class*, chap. 7, esp. 230.
31 Geoff Eley, 'The Wilhelmine Right: How it Changed,' in *Society and Politics in Wilhelmine Germany*, ed. Richard J. Evans (London, 1978), 112–35, here 124.
32 See ibid., 129; Eley, *Reshaping*, 9–11, 188, 218; Blackbourn, *Class*, 12, 226; and Blackbourn, 'Peasants and Politics,' 130; see also Chickering, *We Men*, 203.
33 See esp. Eley, *Reshaping*, 218.
34 Ibid., 184.
35 Ibid., 188.
36 For the following, see ibid., 184–205, passim.
37 See ibid., 193–5.
38 Ibid., 205.
39 Eley, 'What Produces Fascism: Pre-Industrial Traditions or a Crisis of the Capitalist State?' (orig. 1983) in Eley, *From Unification to Nazism* (Boston, 1986), 254–82; Eley, 'Conservatives and Radical Nationalists in Germany: The Production of Fascist Potentials, 1912–28,' in *Fascists and Conservatives*, ed. Martin Blinkhorn (London, 1990), 50–70, here 50, 69. See also Jeremy Noakes, 'German Conservatives and the Third Reich: An Ambiguous Relationship,' in ibid., 71–97.
40 Eley, 'What Produces Fascism,' 265–6.
41 Ibid., 269–70.
42 Eley, 'Conservatives,' 50.
43 Ibid., 69n8.
44 Ibid., 64; original emphasis.

45 Ibid., 52.
46 See 'Peasants and Politics in Germany, 1871–1914'; 'Catholics, the Centre Party and Anti-Semitism'; 'The Politics of Demagogy in Imperial Germany' (from which most citations below are taken); and 'Politics as Theatre: Metaphors of the Stage in German History, 1848–1933,' in Blackbourn, *Populists*, 114–39, 168–87, 217–45, and 246–64 respectively. Also Blackbourn's 'Introduction,' ibid., esp. 19–24.
47 For example: 'As is generally known, the present franchise for elections to the Reichstag was introduced by Bismarck for purely demagogic reasons' (Max Weber, *Political Writings*, ed. Peter Lassman and Ronald Speirs [Cambridge, 1994], 80).
48 Blackbourn, 'Politics of Demagogy,' 240.
49 Cited in J.B. Allcock, '"Populism": A Brief Biography,' *Sociology* 5 (1971): 385.
50 Kenneth Minogue, 'Populism as a Political Movement,' in *Populism*, ed. Ernest Gellner and Ghita Ionescu (London, 1969), 197–211, here 197, 200.
51 See Helmut Dubiel, ed., *Populismus und Aufklärung* (Frankfurt a.M., 1986); Ernesto Laclau, 'Towards a Theory of Populism,' in Laclau, *Politics and Ideology in Marxist Theory* (London, 1977), 143–98; Gino Germani, *Authoritarianism, Fascism, and National Populism* (New Brunswick, NJ, 1978); *Populism*, ed. Gellner and Ionescu; Margaret Canovan, *Populism* (New York and London, 1981); and Kenneth Barkin, 'A Case Study in Comparative History: Populism in Germany and America,' in *The State of American History*, ed. Herbert J. Bass (Chicago, 1970), 373–404. The concept has experienced a revival lately: see John Lukacs, *Democracy and Populism: Fear and Hatred* (New Haven and London, 2005); Francisco Panizza, ed., *Populism and the Mirror of Democracy* (London and New York, 2005).
52 James J. Sheehan, 'Partei, *Volk*, and Staat. Some Reflections on the Relationship between Liberal Thought and Action in Vormärz,' in *Sozialgeschichte Heute*, ed. Hans-Ulrich Wehler (Göttingen, 1974), 162–74; Sheehan, *German Liberalism in the Nineteenth Century* (Chicago and London, 1978), esp. secs. 1 and 3; Sheehan, reviewing Eley's *Reshaping the German Right*, in *Social History* 7, no. 2 (1982): 235–8; Thomas Nipperdey, 'Verein als soziale Struktur in Deutschland im späten 18. und frühen 19. Jahrhundert,' in Nipperdey, *Gesellschaft, Kultur, Theorie* (Göttingen, 1976), 174–205.
53 See Dirk Stegmann, 'Zwischen Repression und Manipulation: Konservative Machteliten und Arbeiter- und Angestelltenbewegung 1910–1918. Ein Beitrag zur Vorgeschichte der DAP/NSDAP,' *Archiv für Sozialgeschichte* 12 (1972): 351–432; Stegmann, 'Konservativismus und nationale Verbände

im Kaiserreich. Bemerkungen zu einigen neueren Veröffentlichungen,' *Geschichte und Gesellschaft* 10 (1984): 409–20; Stegmann, 'Vom Neokonservatismus zum Proto-Faschismus: Konservative Partei, Vereine und Verbände 1893–1920,' in *Deutscher Konservatismus im 19. und 20. Jahrhundert*, ed. Stegmann, Bernd-Jürgen Wendt, and Peter-Christian Witt (Bonn, 1983), 199–230; Stegmann, 'Between Economic Interests and Radical Nationalism: Attempts to Found a New Right-Wing Party in Imperial Germany, 1887–94,' in *Between Reform*, ed. Jones and Retallack, 157–86. Chickering, *We Men*, is seminal.

54 Marilyn Shevin Coetzee, *The German Army League* (New York, 1990), chap. 6.
55 Rudy Koshar, *Social Life, Local Politics, and Nazism: Marburg, 1880–1935* (Chapel Hill and London, 1986), 146; Fritzsche, 'Weimar Populism,' 301.
56 Fritzsche, 'Between Fragmentation,' 143.
57 Compare *inter alia* Leon Poliakov, 'The Weapon of Anti-Semitism,' in *Third Reich*, ed. International Council for Philosophy and Humanistic Studies and UNESCO, 832; Eley, 'Conservatives,' 65–6; Chickering, *We Men*, 300; and Moshe Zimmermann's insightful essay, 'Two Generations in the History of German Antisemitism: The Letters of Theodor Fritsch to Wilhelm Marr,' *LBI YB* 23 (1978): 89–99, esp. 94.
58 Ute Frevert, 'Bourgeois Honour: Middle-Class Duellists in Germany from the Late Eighteenth to the Early Twentieth Century,' in *The German Bourgeoisie*, ed. David Blackbourn and Richard J. Evans (London, 1991), 255–92, here 269.
59 See Max Weber, 'Suffrage and Democracy in Germany' (orig. 1917), in Weber, *Political Writings*, 80–129, here 83.
60 Cited in Robert Hopwood, 'Paladins of the Bürgertum: Cultural Clubs and Politics in Small German Towns, 1918–1925,' *Historical Papers* (1974): 213–35, here 216.
61 José G. Merquior, *The Veil and the Mask: Essays on Culture and Ideology* (London and Boston, 1979), esp. 20–1 and 27.
62 See Blackbourn, *Populists*, 23.
63 See Merquior, *Veil*, 38.
64 For a sharply divergent view, see Eley, *Reshaping*.
65 Søren Kierkegaard's common-sense truth seems relevant to this long-term development: 'it is possible to be *both* good and bad, but it is impossible *at one and the same time* to become both good and bad' (cited in Lukacs, *Democracy*, 242). Less insightful: Chris Lorenz, 'Beyond Good and Evil? The German Empire of 1871 and Modern German Historiography,' *Journal of Contemporary History* 30, no. 4 (1995): 729–65.

66 Adolf Hitler, *Mein Kampf*, 400–404th ed. (Munich, 1939), 241; see also Roger Chickering, 'Political Mobilization and Associational Life: Some Thoughts on the National Socialist German Workers' Club (e.V.),' in *Elections*, ed. Jones and Retallack, 307–30, citing Hitler on 309. Hitler's reflections from 1929 in *Nazism, 1919–1945*, ed. Jeremy Noakes and Geoffrey Pridham, 4 vols. (Exeter, 1983–97), 1:16.
67 Adolf Hitler, memorandum of 7 Jan. 1922, in Noakes and Pridham, eds., *Nazism*, 1:23.
68 Hitler, *Mein Kampf*, 660.
69 Ibid., 392, 378.
70 Ibid., 539.
71 Hitler, memorandum of 7 Jan. 1922, in Noakes and Pridham, eds., *Nazism*, 1:23.
72 Ibid.
73 Ibid.
74 *American Historical Review* 86, no. 1 (Feb. 1981): 159–60.
75 Sontag's unpublished papers are found under his pseudonym, Junius Alter, in BA Koblenz; see esp. Nr. 6, 'Kampfjahre der Vorkriegszeit' (MS.).
76 Junius Alter [Franz Sontag], *Nationalisten. Deutschlands nationales Führertum der Nachkriegszeit* (Leipzig, 1930), 24, cited in Chickering, *We Men*, 301.
77 For a critique of Childers's and Eley's linguistic analyses, see Roger Chickering, 'Language and the Social Foundations of Radical Nationalism in the Wilhelmine Era,' in *1870/71–1989/90: German Unifications and the Change of Literary Discourse*, ed. Walter Pape (Berlin and New York, 1993), 61–78, esp. 72.
78 Chickering, 'Political Mobilization,' 319; emphasis added.
79 Thomas Childers, 'The Social Language of Politics in Germany: The Sociology of Political Discourse in the Weimar Republic,' *American Historical Review* 95 (1990): 331–58, here 357; Childers, 'Languages of Liberalism: Liberal Political Discourse in the Weimar Republic,' in *In Search of a Liberal Germany*, ed. Konrad H. Jarausch and Larry Eugene Jones (New York, 1990), 324.
80 Gustav Freytag to Duke Ernst of Coburg, 21/30 Jan. 1867, in *Gustav Freytag und Herzog Ernst von Coburg im Briefwechsel 1853 bis 1893*, ed. Eduard Tempeltey (Leipzig, 1904), 212–17.

3 Meanings of Stasis

Of all civilized peoples, the German submits most readily and permanently to the regime under which he lives and is, for the most part, not at all fond of innovations ... His character combines understanding with phlegma: he neither indulges in subtilizations about the established order nor devises one himself ... In keeping with their penchant for order and rule, [Germans] will rather submit to despotism than venture on innovations (especially unauthorized reforms in government). – That is their good side.
          Immanuel Kant, *Anthropology from a Pragmatic Point of View* (1797)[1]

Whole books could be filled citing Germans who felt that every dimension of their personal, communal, and political existence was in flux between 1890 and 1914. With the possible exceptions of the Nazi era or the 1990s, there is hardly another period in which German society, culture, and politics were allegedly more 'turbulent,' 'tumultuous,' or 'disorienting.' Thus many historians argue that Germany in these years was undergoing its transition to 'modernity.' Nevertheless, debates about the nature of these changes continue to exercise scholars, as do disagreements about their magnitude and trajectory.[2] Hence there exists an opportunity to take stock of competing viewpoints and to consider whether Imperial Germany was fundamentally transformed between 1871 and 1918.

Commonly, this problem has been approached as one of political continuity: what lines of development extend across the divides of 1866–71, 1888–90, and 1917–23? This chapter offers a shift of focus – away from the search for epochal thresholds, watersheds, and turning points,[3] away from analyses of the rise or decline of Germany's 'great power' status,[4] away from personalistic appraisals of distinctions between the Bismarckian and Wilhelmine eras,[5] away from questions about the regional diversity of the empire (not because such questions are uninteresting but because they have attracted growing attention elsewhere), and *towards* the question of why Germany's basic political institutions remained consonant with so many of its citizens' desires and expectations until the autumn of 1918. Thus this chapter explores aspects of political life in the empire that were deemed by contemporaries to be closely aligned to their own interests and ideals – closely enough, that is, that they deserved to be defended or not challenged openly. Our aim is to rethink the multiple meanings and varied consequences of both liberal reform and conservative stasis in Imperial Germany.

How should we set about appraising contemporaries' preference for reform or stasis? Recent studies that examine centennial or millennial turning points as representative of a distinctive *Zeitgeist* illustrate the benefits of an interdisciplinary approach.[6] Hence we might consider the contours of the 'second' industrial revolution after 1890 and ask what aspects of industrial production or management underwent changes as fundamental as those occurring in the years 1830–70. We might consider the emergence of an increasingly differentiated class society and ask whether the social fabric was torn at all and, if it was, whether it was rent more conspicuously in this period than in those preceding and following it. We might consider the breakthroughs associated with Expressionism and other avant-garde movements and ask whether most Germans on the eve of the First World War perceived, let alone condoned, a shift in cultural sensibilities. And we might consider turn-of-the-century advances in medicine, anthropology, physics, quantum mechanics, and the social sciences, asking whether they underscored a distinctively Wilhelminian outlook on the future. Only by taking stock of economic, social, and cultural developments in these years can we say whether Wilhelmine Germany is best described in terms of its edginess or its immobility.

It is in the political sphere that historians of the German Empire can profit most directly from a new appraisal of the blockages to reform that remained in place up to 1918. In asking why so many aspects of Germany's political institutions and processes did *not* fundamentally change during the Wilhelmine age – this is the thesis presented in the first two-thirds of this chapter – it is patently unwise to cut selected examples of political change from their historical context and fix them to the static conceptual backdrop encapsulated in the phrase 'life goes on.' To address crises and continuities together, we must concern ourselves not only with aims and ambitions but also with underlying values; not only with strivings and successes but also with lingering regrets. This approach is appropriate when dealing with an age in which new motifs of liberation became tied to actual embodiments of vitality. Hence the following analysis is built upon the twin observations that the quest for emancipation often falls short of the act of rebellion and that bodies gradually become less vital with the passage of time. Taking the pulse of the German body politic in subjective as well as objective ways helps to explain why Wilhelminians did not *want* to rebel against their government before 1918.

On the other hand, this chapter's penultimate section, 'Nemesis,' suggests that exploring elements of stasis and reform together in the post-1900 period does in fact reveal compelling political transitions. Precisely because preceding acts of restraint were so successful, precisely because persistent political blockages had created a backlog of reforms too massive – too *embarrassing* – for twentieth-century Germans to ignore, conservative stasis itself facilitated new ways of bringing ideas into politics. It nevertheless bears emphasizing that in this argument the idea of nemesis does not make sense without its antecedent. Only once the dynamic, dialectical relationship between stasis and reform is established can we understand why contemporaries after 1900 came to accept certain means of crisis management (qua system stabilization) that they had previously considered unthinkable or unacceptable. Only then can we begin to determine why the solutions proposed to problems of political deadlock after 1909 were so radical. And only then can we discover a new meaning of reform in Wilhelmine Germany, namely, reform as a reluctant response to stasis, rather than a ringing endorsement of change.

Economy, Society, Culture

We are often told that the accelerating pace of economic change in the Wilhelmine era was palpable at every level of German society and in every corner of the land. But if we consider the disruptive and disquieting transformations Germans had experienced during the so-called Great Depression of 1873–96, might Germans not have seen the subsequent years as an era of consolidation or even, after such periodic downturns as 1900–2, of retrenchment? Here we should remember that the anti-cyclical economic and political measures deployed during the 1870s and 1880s continued, albeit with refinements, in the following decades. For example: The growth of giant cartels in German big business is generally taken as one feature of the 'full-throttle capitalist transformation between the 1890s and 1914.'[7] But cartels are meant to stabilize things, not encourage change willy-nilly. They make forward planning easier, simplify industrial relations, and insulate both individual enterprises and larger economic sectors from shocks to the economic system.[8] Cartels, in other words, freeze economic advantages that are already in place.

Much the same could be said of other 'corporatist' features of the economy and society. Klaus Tenfelde has argued that these social aspects did not differ as much as we suppose from those of an earlier age. 'The concept of "social estate" [*das Ständische*] continued to have a virulent but real effect – even an increased one, possibly, but at the very least one that decisively conditioned perceptions well beyond its time ... It may be too much to claim that milieux can be conceived as surrogates for [social] estates, but arguably there was a certain functional equivalency nonetheless.'[9] Thomas Kühne and Gerhard A. Ritter have demonstrated that corporatism also infused German political thought, and Prussian political practice, much longer than we have believed.[10] The Nazis were not the first to recognize the political dividends to be reaped from freezing labour relations and the organization of key industries in corporatist modes or extolling the virtues of a stable *Mittelstand* of peasants, artisans, and small shopkeepers. Even the role of banks in the Wilhelmine era tended in the same direction. Long-term financing gave bankers a tangible motive to favour stability and security over upheaval and risk. The investment of huge amounts of capital inclined them to opt instinctively for steady growth and continuity: 'By tying up their capital, they tied their own hands.'[11]

In many other economic sectors, too, continuity and gradual change were as easily discernable as upheaval and breakthrough. Despite the much-talked-about transition of the German economy from a mainly agrarian to a mainly industrial one around 1900, 35 per cent of the economically active population in 1907 was still working in agriculture, forestry, or fishing: that is, almost four times the level in Britain. This rural population, not the Junker class alone, was supported throughout the Bismarckian and Wilhelmine periods by high agricultural tariffs.

Those tariffs were legitimized by the argument that Germany needed to be as close to self-sufficient in foodstuffs as possible in order to feed its population if war should come. In manufacturing and mining, the subsectors that had provided the bedrock of industrial success at mid-century – coal, iron, steel, engineering, machine-building, construction – retained their leading roles after 1890. Although newer and more dynamic branches such as petrochemicals, electrical engineering, and precision instruments emerged after 1890, the drive towards concentration lent continuing political influence to older industrial sectors. After 1905 the Hansa League, representing mainly newer and secondary industries, attempted to challenge the older and better-established organizations of heavy industry. But its campaign yielded meagre political results.

In short, although the Wilhelmine era can rightly be seen as an age in which the distance between economic interests and politics diminished, we should not identify the modern aspects of this relationship unequivocally with a tendency towards economic experimentation or accelerating change. It may be true that government ministers and party leaders asked themselves every day whether stability was 'best served by traditional, paternalist nostrums, or by more modern policies geared to the new kind of society that had emerged.'[12] Yet even contemporaries who opted for 'modern policies' were seeking to ensure steady economic growth, social harmony, and political stability.

In turn-of-the-century Germany, time was controlled in many ways – had been controlled since the advent of the first industrial revolution. But that did not change the rhythm of the seasons one whit. The kinetic energy of German society was increasing. But psychosomatic suffering hobbled more and more Germans. Joachim Radkau has explained that his grandfather could date precisely the arrival of his own personal pathology of nervousness: it occurred on the morning of 28 January 1901, after which he acquired – nerves.[13] But like the knotted *Zeitgeist* itself, personal 'nervousness' was not necessarily channelled into excitable aggressiveness. It might foster a reaction akin to that of the proverbial deer caught in the headlights. Or it might foster new faith in an old adage: 'The good things in life come to those who wait.'

University education took longer than ever before in German history. So did the making of a career, the decision to marry, the planning of children, the path to death. More time than ever was needed to wring decisions from an expanding bureaucracy and increasingly complex industrial management. Even the new kinds of fast food and refreshments available on Wilhelmine street corners required greater time (and effort) to digest. So did the task of recuperating from things unwisely ingested, for instance, by bringing the daily alcohol-coffee drinking cycle into balance. The German lifestyle reform movement focused on exactly these kinds of novelties and targeted them for criticism and study. However, that very criticism fuelled a new dialectic between the changing pace of life and the confused, pragmatic, stubborn efforts of contemporaries to understand and deal with it. Often, lifestyle reformers' lobbying efforts merely fed a bad conscience or led to closer self-inspection. As reported in the records of a rehabilitative centre in Ahrweiler, a corpulent pastor once spent half a day reclining on a sofa, thinking of nothing but passing his next stool.[14]

Cramping and constipation: are these the proper subjects of political history? Could reduced motility of the intestines – stasis – possibly be relevant to the fate of political reform in Wilhelmine Germany, even metaphorically? Does stasiphobia, the fear of standing upright, bear any relation to the tugging of German forelocks, identified by Immanuel Kant in this chapter's epigraph, or to German democracy's alleged self-abasement long before the Nazis or the East German secret police appeared on the scene? Could bacteriostasis describe Germans' desire to inhibit the growth of foreign elements in their body politic? Were Wilhelminians more anal-retentive than their Victorian counterparts?

Such quixotic leaps between personal and political pathologies do not require as much analytical athleticism as one might suppose. After all, Wilhelmine reformers regularly drew linkages among the modern problems of unhealthy lifestyles, dysfunctions of class society, and bottlenecks in governmentality. They moved away from the 'sterile equilibrium' or the 'static balance among opposing tendencies' that are also listed among definitions of the word 'stasis.' Doing so, they moved towards a new condition, in which conservative equipoise and other impediments to 'the normal flow of fluids in an organ' could be progressively removed. As this process unfolded in late Wilhelmine Germany, previously unimagined strategies to overcome political immobility were considered plausible for the first time. Quiescence and stagnation gave way to new (or renewed) creative activity. However, anxiety and self-reflection were not removed from the equation. Radkau has written illuminatingly about this phenomenon: 'Social counter-reactions and stress effects of the modernization process do not as a rule follow promptly but rather are delayed ... It is precisely the hindrances that contribute to the fact that particular features of modernization, as soon as the hindrance is removed, proceed in reverse and give rise to severe upheavals. That was apparently the case in the "age of nervousness." And more: between the process and the reaction it elicits, there frequently occurs not a calm equilibrium but a knotting-up, which itself produces new tensions.'[15]

What, next, of culture? The best discussions of both high- and lowbrow culture in the Wilhelmine era stress its 'extraordinary richness,' creative energy, and diversity. Nor do the fluidity and indeterminacy of Wilhelmine high culture often go unmentioned. One recent account, for example, posits a 'general identification by most Germans with the ideas of newness, regeneration, and change.'[16] But only at their peril do historians forget that most of Kaiser Wilhelm II's subjects retained their conservative artistic tastes. Pre-war Germany's avant-garde actually generated only a tiny following before the war. Thus Peter Jelavich has reminded us that 'movements' within Wilhelmine Germany's modern artistic scene developed 'against the backdrop of, and often in direct hostility to, a persistent tradition of idealized realism in literature and academic painting.'[17]

Against this backdrop we can test reactions to the attack on German *Kultur* allegedly unleashed by the Allies in August 1914. Was German vitriol generated because Germans wanted to defend change? Or did most of them believe instead that German *Kultur* was threatened by the same 'superficiality, caprice, and ephemera' that they had ascribed to the works of their own avant-garde before 1914? Friedrich Nietzsche had predicted many years earlier that the European response to German 'effervescence' would be to pronounce it 'invariably *evil*, wanting as it does to break through the old limits and subvert the old pieties.' But Germans themselves, whom Nietzsche also labelled 'procrastinators *par excellence*,'[18] were at least as bloody-minded as their enemies: they declared that the Germany of Goethe and Schiller (not Nolde or Wedekind) had to be preserved and enshrined for the sake of 'honesty and sincerity.'[19] In any case, the victories that Expressionists won in the half-decade before 1914 or that German academics won (so rhetorically) in the first months of the war did not contribute to overcoming political stasis.

They did the exact opposite. Wolfgang J. Mommsen has written that German artists and writers may have tried to resist the instrumentalizing intentions of Germany's rulers and political parties; nevertheless, he adds, the tendency towards 'purely theoretical negation' of the existing order – for example, *against* large cities and other aspects of modernity – 'accelerated the emergence of largely non-political subsystems within Wilhelmine society and thereby contributed indirectly to the weakening of reformist forces' in the empire.[20] In making much the same point, Modris Eksteins has stressed the darker irony in this process: 'The modern temper had been forged; the avant-garde had won. It tried to fight new battles, but these turned out to be the same old battles, or in fact no battles at all because the infamous bourgeoisie now often bowed with polite, if silent, respect. The "adversary culture" had become the dominant culture, irony and anxiety the mode and the mood, hallucination and neurosis the state of mind.'[21]

Plus ça change ...

The list of political institutions that retained their contours between 1871 and 1918 is familiar to most scholars. First to be mentioned is the federal structure of the German Empire. The constitutional arrangement devised by Bismarck left to the individual federal states considerable autonomy in the realms of culture, education, policing, religion, and health. While a centralizing Reich government made inroads in some of these areas, federalism itself blocked many political initiatives that might otherwise have contributed to significant constitutional reform.

Related to this point is the overwhelming dominance of Prussia within the empire. Quite apart from the unchanging demographic and geographical preponderance of Prussia – constituting roughly two-thirds of the empire – the Prusso-German dualism that was readily apparent to constitutional experts and politicians alike in 1871 had diminished hardly at all by 1918. For that reason, reformist efforts to devise a new order (*neue Ordnung*) during the last years of the war were directed against this particular anomaly of German national life. The Prussian *Landtag* (state parliament) and the Prussian bureaucracy remained such bastions of conservative interests that the wheels of state in the empire seemed to turn, or more often stop, at the command of Prussian civil servants and conservative *Landtag* deputies. The constitutional dualism between the Federal Council (*Bundesrat*) and the Reichstag also acted as a brake on many legislative initiatives. The influence of the Federal Council diminished over time, as the popular imagination listened more closely and intently to the voices of those in the Reichstag. Nevertheless, Manfred Rauh's thesis that these developments constituted a de facto or 'silent' parliamentarization of Imperial Germany has been rightly discarded.[22] Much the same conclusion arises from recent work on the Kaiser's role as supreme warlord, on the survival of the Prussian aristocracy, and on other aspects of the constitutional order.

Whereas recent studies of Wilhelmine elections acknowledge that ministerial responsibility and the formation of national governments on the basis of parliamentary majorities were never within the realm of practical possibility in Imperial Germany, they point to the increasing importance of national elections based on the principle of 'one man, one vote.'[23] However, historians still direct their gaze too infrequently towards elements of political stasis in the empire. As just one among many possible examples, constituency boundaries for Reichstag elections were never redrawn between 1871 and 1918. Not only the government but the majority parties themselves refused to endorse legislation that would have made reapportionment a reality, even after population shifts made a mockery of the original principle behind such geometry. Over time, the relatively underpopulated constituencies of rural Prussia continued to send conservative landowners into parliament, whereas the refusal to consider reapportionment effectively devalued the votes of Socialist supporters in the huge urban constituencies. This apparently mundane aspect of constitutional stasis set parameters of far-reaching importance for larger political contests.

It is helpful to differentiate between two kinds of continuity discernible within Wilhelmine politics: continuity of political alignments and continuity of political styles. Recent studies of political activity at the sub-national level have shown that liberals as well as conservatives changed their voting habits, party alignments, and styles of campaigning much more slowly in local and regional political environments than in national politics. The ingrained rituals of Prussian *Landtag* voting, for example, persisted until the end of the empire. Up to a week might be required to complete the complicated two-stage voting procedure in Prussian elections: this practice found its analogy in the parties' unwillingness to break with the face-to-face style of campaigning characteristic of the 'politics of notables,' in voters' clear preference for home-grown candidates, and in the survival of relatively fixed party coalitions at the local and regional levels.[24]

Nor have studies of Wilhelmine political culture undermined an interlocking group of three hypotheses, each of which points not to dramatic changes in the political culture of Wilhelmine Germany but to the resiliency and longevity of political alignments that arose during the empire's first decade. The first of these theses, though not unchallenged, suggests the continuity of German social-moral milieux from the dawn of the Imperial era to the Nazis' breakthrough after 1928. Second, historians and political scientists continue to work through the significance of four persistent cleavages within Wilhelmine political society: between the centre and the periphery, between state and church, between the agrarian and industrial sectors, and between employers and employees. Third, the concept of political 'camps' focuses on sets of political allegiances that were at least as resilient as milieux and cleavages. For example, the gulf between the working classes and bourgeois society, which itself was both constitutive and a mirror of German authoritarianism, found its parallel in the enduring political division between the socialist and nationalist camps. Two points are worth emphasizing here. On the one hand, although historians continue to disagree about the function of these camps and the degree of flux within them, they recognize that changes in Wilhelmine political culture confirmed divisions between these camps. On the other hand, a camp is defined as something more than a convenient or momentary coalition: it is built on powerful historical, cultural, and emotional foundations. By definition, only political continuity lends it historical significance. It is predicated, in a word, on stasis.

Real Men, Skirted Decisions

On Thursday, 25 July 1912, the man who has been called Wilhelmine Germany's 'grand master of capitalism' dined with Chancellor Theobald von Bethmann Hollweg at his country estate. Later, in his diary, Walther Rathenau described the course of the evening's discussion. He did so in a way that speaks volumes about how the most far-reaching reformist ideas concerning Germany's future were – and were not – translated into practice by those who had the power to do so.

> Dined at Hohen-Finow ... Chancellor [Bethmann Hollweg] ... asked what I meant by what I had called political goals. He saw no such goals for Germany. Long discussion on this after dinner. I put forward: (1) Economy ... (2) Foreign Policy ... (3) Domestic. Reform of parliament. Prussian fran-

118 'Tradition is how we change'

Am Steuer.

Die liberale Speiche zu den anderen Beiden:
Ueberhebt euch nur nicht! Sobald der Wind sich dreht, bin ich wieder oben.

3.1. 'At the helm.' In this 1879 cartoon from the satirical journal *Kladderadatsch*, the liberal reminds the conservative and the (Catholic) ultramontane that with Otto von Bismarck steering the ship of state, they should not become haughty: 'As soon as the wind shifts I'll be on top again.' 'Am Steuer,' from Wilhelm Scholz et al., *Bismarck-Album des Kladderadatsch 1848–1989*, 31st ed. (Berlin: A. Hofmann & Comp., 1915), 117. From the author's collection.

3.2. 'The man at the helm.' Chancellor Theobald von Bethmann Hollweg declares: 'So finally we are to steer a *Bismarckian course*! Now we'll have to see what can be made of it.' 'Der Mann am Steuer,' *Kladderadatsch* 67, no. 28, 1. Beiblatt (12 July 1914): 461. Image courtesy of the Universitätsbibliothek, Universität Heidelberg.

chise. Reich [Reichstag] constituencies. Proportion [proportional representation]. These are all ways to a full parliamentary system.

Bethmann in overall agreement; arguing against 3 (*a*) inferiority of the Reichstag, lack of political personalities. Reply: No one wants to enter a mere debating machine. (*b*) [He]: we have the most perfect self-government (municipal, country, provincial). Reply: Only as far as the kitchen, not as far as the drawing-room.

I went on to explain. He could not very well dispute that change would come. Answer: No (!). Hence: either it would come as a result of unfortunate circumstances, or 'heroically' amid sunshine, through a new Hardenberg ...

Bethmann urged me three times, the last time as he accompanied me to the car, to elaborate my ideas regarding electoral reform for him. *Each time I declined: he has better people for that among his staff.*[25]

This diary entry illuminates how Rathenau and many other Germans felt about the limits of reform, enthusiasm for reform, fear of reform, love of reform, and – not least – satisfaction with particular but not inconsequential aspects of the political status quo. Rathenau's words substantiate Mark Hewitson's observation that although the relationship between the nation and politics in Imperial Germany was invariably close, it was also 'brittle, opaque, and frequently taboo.'[26] When Rathenau remarked that Bethmann Hollweg had 'better people ... among his staff' to undertake the drafting of reforms – reforms for which he had just spent a full evening serving as impassioned advocate – both the brittleness and the taboo-like qualities of reform come into focus. For Rathenau, it was one thing to counsel 'a full parliamentary system' or other equally far-reaching departures from the political status quo. It was quite another thing to carry those proposals to fruition.

At this point we should also pause and consider how our perspective shifts when we convert the unexciting passive voice used so often in analyses of Imperial Germany to the more affirmative active voice. Thus, rather than claiming that 'skirted decisions' and 'delaying compromises'[27] persisted from the beginning to the end of the empire – as resilient regional identities, as lingering fears about national solidarity and racial homogeneity, as a pervasive respect for authority – it is more helpful and more accurate to say that specific individuals actually wanted such things 'to persist.' Why? Because they believed that conservative stasis accrued to their own and to Germany's material, cultural, and spiritual benefit.

In practice, although real men might make political decisions to realize (or avoid) thoroughgoing reform or complete stasis, more often they sought to mediate between change and no change. Any future, no matter how boldly or timidly envisioned, could not be reconciled with the present except via compromise or gradualism. Seen in this light, Rathenau displayed the same mixture of conflicted feelings, ranging from self-righteousness to self-contempt and everything in between, that was typical of other Wilhelmine figures unwilling to leap into an unknown future. These conflicted responses to change caution against accepting at face value the argument that the German Empire's founding constitutional structure had fallen into disrepute by 1914 as a result of social and political fragmentation, the pillarization of its party system, or the overwhelming dominance of Prussia. Most Germans probably felt that the skirted decisions of 1871 were best left undone after all.

On a different plane, we might also consider whether Rathenau was very different from the constitutional theorists about whom Mark Hewitson has written or the left-liberal politicians Alastair Thompson has studied. Hewitson has argued that support for the existing idea of German constitutionalism in Wilhelmine Germany 'prevented the practice of parliamentarization from extending beyond certain critical thresholds.' This debate suggested that 'the meaning of "parliamentarism" and "constitutionalism" remained in flux and thus contributed for a time to a feeling of crisis.' Yet – and this is the more important point – it 'eventually led to a *stabilization* of the German regime' by 'serving to reinforce contemporary support for the *Kaiserreich*.'[28] Even the liberal Friedrich Naumann acknowledged in 1908 that 'the constitution, as it was fashioned by Bismarck's hand, was to be accepted as the fixed property of the German people.'[29] Like many of his liberal contemporaries, Naumann 'had accepted the institutional structure of the *Kaiserreich* as the invisible framework of his political thought.'[30] That 'invisible framework,' too, both constituted and reflected the nature of German authoritarianism. Thus when the Conservative Party leader Ernst von Heydebrand und der Lase asked fellow members of the Reichstag whether they wanted a republic – his question was posed in 1908 during debate on the Kaiser's notorious *Daily Telegraph* interview – his colleagues did not rise from their seats in outrage or take up his question in earnest; they responded exactly as Heydebrand knew they would: with laughter. That laughter, most Germans would have agreed, was the only appropriate response to such an absurd, impossible proposal.

In his study of left liberals such as Theodor Barth, Conrad Haußmann, and Friedrich von Payer, Alastair Thompson sidestepped the unpersuasive version of history that depicts liberalism's failure. Indeed, wrote Thompson, on this point 'there is even some danger of historians exaggerating those aspects of Imperial Germany which were successful and "modern."'[31] Nevertheless, he acknowledged that the pressure on liberal politicians to be pragmatic increased in the final pre-war years; left liberals 'increasingly identified with the Wilhelmine state and yearned for practical results after over two decades in opposition.'[32] Although most left liberals in Prussia shared Rathenau's support for electoral reform, responsible government, and the rule of law, they were also, like him, 'visibly patriotic and not *insistent* on full parliamentary rule.'[33] When these men added up the numbers, they saw no need 'to trouble their heads' about the imminent introduction of a system whereby shifting parliamentary majorities could force a change of government. As Friedrich von Payer declared in December 1908: 'We can leave this question to future generations; for we lack the unavoidable prerequisite for it, namely a closed, capable, enduring majority, as in England.'[34]

If we follow the liberals' preference for stability and pragmatism into the years 1914–18, do we find 'defeat in victory' and 'victory in defeat,' as Thompson suggested? Do we discover that bourgeois liberals 'came to appreciate the power of the state because of their inability to reconcile their own desire for social, cultural and political unity with the reality of ever-increasing social and confessional division'?[35] This conclusion was suggested by Jan Palmowski when he asked '*how* liberals combined opposition to state authoritarianism with trust in state reform.' One way to answer these questions is to look again to illustrative examples drawn from the sub-national level. Doing so, we might consider what the National Liberal government that came to power in Saxony in October 1918 actually attempted in terms of overturning the political status quo. We discover that liberals were not as fixated on change as many historians believe.

Well into 1918 the National Liberals, left liberals, and Social Democrats in the Saxon *Landtag* had agreed to bury their domestic quarrels for the sake of the common war effort. Although these parties from time to time 'asked for the rudder to Saxony's ship of state,' until the final weeks of the war 'they did not rock the boat when their request was denied.'[36] Then on 26 October 1918 Saxony's king appointed the National Liberal leader in Saxony, Rudolf Heinze, government leader.

For over a fortnight Saxony was ruled according to the principles of parliamentary government. Because this experiment was effectively freed from the death throes of the Hohenzollern dynasty, it provides a hint of how Germany's political system might have evolved if liberals elsewhere had found themselves at the helm before revolution broke out on 9 November. What did Saxony's National Liberals do with this opportunity?

Not very much. They proclaimed on 5 November that they would 'keep the wheels of the state bureaucracy well oiled.' Otherwise they proposed a hybrid system of governance that was 'neither democratic nor authoritarian, but a delicate mixture of both, with a corporatist flavour.' The liberals would enjoy a free rein in the fields of industry and commerce. The Social Democrats would preside over a ministry of labour, while Saxon Conservatives would be allowed to dominate the ministries of finance, justice, and culture. A state of parliamentary equipoise appears also to have been the liberals' goal. They proposed introducing proportional representation, without, however, abolishing the upper house of the Saxon *Landtag*, the very institution against which they had lobbied for more than two decades. For these reasons, inverted commas are appropriate when referring to the 'modern' political system that the National Liberals in Saxony intended to inaugurate with their 'new course' in early November 1918. In fact the slipperiness of the term 'modern' should make us doubly cautious – cautious about seeing parliamentary democracy as the desired end point of an evolving imperial political culture, and cautious about imagining that all reformers were in a hurry to embrace change. When given the opportunity, National Liberals in Saxony introduced a political system that was more corporatist than democratic. And to implement it, they favoured a political process designed to slow down, not speed up, the pace of future developments.

The aim of this section has *not* been to suggest that contemporaries, when they opted for stasis over reform, were somehow dilatory, or insufficiently 'modern,' or in favour of the unalloyed hegemony of established elites in the economic, social, and cultural spheres. To argue that many defining features of the empire's political system remained in place between January 1871 and November 1918 is not to resurrect an outdated view of Imperial Germany as rigid and unchanging.[37] It suggests, rather, that more Germans avoided firm decisions in favour of political reform, and did so at more important turning points in their history, than scholars have generally thought. If Germans did not necessarily get the system of governance they envisioned or deserved before 1918, they seem to have gotten what they actually wanted.[38]

Nemesis

It is ironic that historians who consistently stress the 'modern,' dynamic nature of German politics after 1890 have themselves provided arguments that highlight conservative stasis after 1871.[39] For example, David Blackbourn convincingly demonstrated the newness of political institutions set in place by Bismarck at the founding of the empire, including the constitutional, administrative, parliamentary, and electoral institutions that remained largely unchanged over the next half-century. Geoff Eley has drawn attention to the relatively early date – not later than the mid-1870s – by which time both bourgeois and (national) liberal Germans can be said to have exerted not only economic, social, and cultural dominance but something approaching political dominance as well. Margaret Lavinia Anderson and Helmut Walser Smith, among others, have illustrated that although openness and dynamism characterized the 1870s as a result of conflicts pitting the authoritarian state against the Catholic Church and Social Democracy, those battle lines had already hardened by the early 1880s into political polarities that remained largely static until the end of the empire. All new? New and improved? Surely these labels apply to Germany in 1871 and 1919, not in 1900 or 1913.

Much of the revisionist scholarship of the 1980s and 1990s argued that the decade of the 1890s witnessed the 'reconstitution of the political nation.' In that literature any number of recurring phrases were used to give analytical priority to change over stasis. Thus we read that the 1890s constituted 'a major moment of flux,' a 'vital moment of transition,' a time of political 'fission,' a 'populist moment,' a 'major enlargement of the public sphere,' a 'reordering of the public domain,' and 'a fundamental change in the scale and intensity of public life.'[40] As other chapters of this volume argue, though, and as a growing number of historians agree, it is wrong to single out the 1890s so categorically.[41] When we consider the decades in which genuinely innovative strategies were not just formulated but actually implemented by the political parties and leading interest groups, the 1890s recede as a time when the fundamental politicization and democratization of Imperial Germany occurred.[42] And when we consider larger changes in political ideologies, styles, discourses,

3.3. 'Unresolved questions.' The central figure of this painting is likely a liberal journalist or lawyer, perhaps Jewish. He appears to take issue with the arrogant views and dismissive postures of his two interlocutors: on the left, a figure who might be a National Liberal or Conservative landowner; on the right, a priest or a professor. Bismarck looms over all three figures. *Ungelöste Fragen*, by Emil Schwabe, 1887. Image courtesy of the Bildarchiv Preußischer Kulturbesitz, Berlin.

and means of mobilization, the discontinuities of 1871 and 1918 seem far more compelling than the alleged watershed of 1890.

Nevertheless – and here we come to the hinge of this chapter's argument – after 1900 Wilhelminians began to feel that conservative stasis was itself a destabilizing factor in politics. Stasis began to generate its antithesis. It was *this* dialectic, at least as much as the activities and arguments of flesh-and-blood advocates of political reform, that now necessitated the accommodation of social, economic, and cultural changes from which politics had been largely insulated up to that point. And it was this dialectic that eventually dissipated a confidence shared by many Wilhelminians that they could continue to build on the achievements of the past. In the final years before the war, Wilhelmine Germans began to recognize that they had no choice – no skirts to hide behind – in confronting challenges that were distinctively twentieth-century in nature.

By and large, such recognition brought with it a clearer, more hard-nosed vision of the future. Thus, for example, Wilhelm's personal rule, precisely because it rested on traditional pillars of Prussian strength, eventually generated its own devastating critiques.[43] The Prussian three-class suffrage, precisely because it remained unreformed up to 1910 and beyond, fuelled suffrage debates in both the Reich and the individual federal states – debates that questioned the political status quo more fundamentally than was possible even in the 1890s.[44] The Bülow Bloc (1907–9), which seemed to epitomize the balancing of Right and Left, blew apart because of, not despite, the flaw in its founding logic. Subsequent political detonations released more heat than light, but their frequency and resonance increased over time. The Black-Blue Bloc (1909–14) satisfied no one, whereupon a continuing left-liberal renaissance in the final pre-war years soon brought alternative alignments into focus. In the years 1914–18, Social Democracy's integration into the political system, which had been underway long before 1914 but which became apparent to all in the early war years, generated its own internal challenge from an alienated, pacifist rank and file. And Conservative hotheads opted increasingly for *va banque* solutions to their own marginalization.

What evidence points to a new political dialectic between stasis and reform after 1900?[45] First, the older Bismarckian dichotomy between 'friends' and 'enemies' of the empire became increasingly irrelevant as another division arose: that between producers and consumers.[46]

Founded upon a commodification of politics that was perceived clearly by contemporaries, this conflict shifted the initiative towards reformers. After the turn of the century, those reformers began to wrest from the state the power to determine which political discourses resonated most loudly in the public sphere. Second, it was only after 1899 that Wilhelmine debates about civil liberties moved from the realm of discourse (challenges and threats) to one of practical action. When we consider the efforts of Bismarck and his ministers in the 1870s and 1880s to curtail such rights as freedom of association, freedom of the press, parliamentary immunity, and universal manhood suffrage, we see that in the 1890s there was nothing new under the sun. At the end of this long period of constitutional incubation and especially during the Reichstag election campaign of 1898, the Catholic Centre and left-liberal parties successfully called attention to the government's and the right-wing parties' plans to amend the Reichstag suffrage.

In quick order, other new ideas were subsequently floated about the possibility of plural voting, proportional representation, the abolishment of upper houses of parliament, and the female vote. To be sure, the pillarization of political parties conspired against the realization of many of these ideas before 1918. Nonetheless, the broad front on which suffrage reform and other fairness issues were pushed after 1900 suggests that the former Bismarckian consensus began to unravel not with the Iron Chancellor's dismissal from office in March 1890 but only upon his death in July 1898.[47]

Third and lastly, the pluralization of social and regional allegiances after the turn of the century changed the largely static party alignments of the previous three decades. Whereas electoral coalitions had previously formed around constitutional questions of a demonstratively national type (*Kulturkampf*, military budget, anti-socialist laws), whereby enemies of the empire could be targeted with relative ease, conflicts that fell along the urban/rural and consumer/producer axes sundered the old Bismarckian *Kartell* of 'state-supporting' parties. The most conspicuous aspect of this sundering was to free the National Liberals and a new generation of liberal politicians from their client relationship with the two conservative parties. After 1900 both the German Conservative and the Free Conservative parties began to follow the lead of the *völkisch* movement,[48] most of whose members offered some combination of *mittelständisch*, hyper-nationalist, reform-oriented promises to overcome stasis on the Right. By contrast, the National Liberal and the left-liberal parties produced a new generation of spokesmen who were willing to undertake what has been called both a programmatic and a mental reorientation.

The early career of Gustav Stresemann, foreign minister in the Weimar Republic, epitomizes three aspects of this new political orientation: its endorsement of imperialist *Weltpolitik* (world policy), its advocacy of urban and industrial interests, and its fixation on suffrage reform in Germany's federal states. In each respect, the National Liberals' redefinition of their core political goals tended to increase their distance from the conservative parties and lessen the distance to the left liberals and Social Democrats. These shifts are easily recognizable at the regional and local levels; changes at the base of left-wing constituencies forced party leaders to move in the same direction. Thus the learning processes we commonly regard as characteristic of the late Wilhelmine years began to overshadow and displace the conservative stasis inherited from the Bismarckian era. Granted, those learning processes were slow, uneven, and incomplete. However, they would contribute by 1914 to the relative isolation of Wilhelminians who continued to insist that the status quo was the only option. As Thomas Kühne has written: 'The processes of democratization did not overcome the authoritarian essence[49] of Imperial Germany; nor did the beginnings of pluralization and integration neutralize the socio-cultural fragmentation of the party system. But in the half-decade around 1900, these processes developed a momentum they did not exhibit either before or after in the German Empire.'[50]

Conclusions

The puzzles, paradoxes, and ironies of Wilhelmine Germany cannot be contained within the framework of 'either/or' questions. The incongruent dualisms taken up as topics of debate in recent historical overviews are dissatisfying to many readers, yet they contribute to larger reinterpretations in a positive way. In the case of Wilhelmine Germany, they demonstrate that the growing complexity of the political system (and its individual parts) was balanced by more persistent features already present at the birth of the empire. These features included the institutionalization of diversity through federalism, the fracturing of political consensus, the persistence of antagonistic political camps, and the accumulation of skirted decisions.

As we cast our gaze back over the imperial era as a whole, we tend to highlight the dynamic aspect of Wilhelminism because it is the nearer, sharper end of the historical stick we pick up. That dynamism seems all the more compelling when it is associated with a man who was disparaged even in his own time as His Impulsive Majesty and Wilhelm the Sudden. However, Kaiser Wilhelm II has also been described in a different way: as a monarch who fulfilled a commitment to an anachronistic Bismarckian legacy but *not* one who inaugurated or personified a new age.[51] Count Harry Kessler recalled: 'As life's purpose, he [Wilhelm II] offered us youthful Germans a political retirement, the defence and the enjoyment of what had already been attained ... As was painfully evident to the eye, he represented no beginning but rather an end, a grandiose final chord – a fulfiller, not a herald [*ein Erfüller, kein Verkünder*]!'

A careful attempt to balance elements of reform and stasis, of progressivism and traditionalism, can recover important aspects of Imperial Germany's historiography that may have had their heyday in the 1970s but do not deserve to be disregarded today. Reassessing the degree to which traditionalism continued to influence German life reminds us that many contemporaries foresaw the possibility that the German Empire would not only continue to exist but actually thrive in the third decade of the twentieth century. To try to monitor, manage, and control change, rather than embrace it across the board or reject it out of hand – these are aspects of state governance and bourgeois taste that are certainly characteristic of the Wilhelmine era, but they can be discerned in German history between 1860 and 1900 too. Therefore we must take account of the many compromises struck between Germans who sought emancipation of one sort or another and those who defended authoritarianism over a span of many decades. To neglect such compromises skews our understanding of Imperial Germany by deflecting attention away from those moments when Germans such as Rathenau consciously sidestepped meaningful political reform of the empire's central institutions. It is one thing to emphasize how 'modern,' pluralistic, and dynamic life in the empire was after 1900 and to document the important growth of the Wilhelmine Left. It is quite another thing to suggest that the 'remarkable success'[52] of the opposition parties did not also entail disappointments and outright failures – not ephemeral failures but, arguably, ones that reached from the margins of the respective ideologies to their very core.

Are historians guilty of boosterism if they study the meanings of reform in the German Empire without also studying the meanings of stasis?[53] Not at all. Yet to do one without the other presents the sound of only one hand clapping – a non-event that provides neither confirmation of what came before nor transition to something new. It makes more sense to recover elements of political stasis, cast them in the light of transformations in the social, economic, and cultural spheres, and then try to explain why they remained so important until November 1918. Doing so juxtaposes the more resounding measures of Wilhelmine history with the political silences that also deserve our attention. By listening carefully for both, we may discover some new harmonics – muted and not always benign – lying in between.

NOTES

1 Immanuel Kant, *Anthropology from a Pragmatic Point of View*, trans. Mary J. Gregor (The Hague, 1974), 179–80.
2 See *inter alia* Volker R. Berghahn, 'The German Empire, 1871–1914: Reflections on the Direction of Recent Research,' and Margaret Lavinia Anderson, 'Reply to Volker Berghahn,' *Central European History* 35, no. 1 (2002): 75–82, 83–90.
3 For example, Dietrich Papenfuß and Wolfgang Schieder, eds., *Deutsche Umbrüche im 20. Jahrhundert* (Cologne etc., 2000); Eberhard Kolb, *Umbrüche deutscher Geschichte 1866/71, 1918/19, 1929/33*, ed. Dieter Langewiesche and Klaus Schönhoven (Munich, 1993).
4 For example, Volker Ullrich, *Die nervöse Großmacht 1871–1918* (Frankfurt a.M., 1999).
5 For example, Lothar Gall, ed., *Otto von Bismarck und Wilhelm II. Repräsentanten eines Epochenwechsels?* (Paderborn, 2000).
6 See Martin Doerry, *Übergangsmenschen* (Weinheim, 1986); Ute Frevert, ed., *Das Neue Jahrhundert* (Göttingen, 2000); August Nitschke et al., eds., *Jahrhundertwende*, 2 vols. (Reinbek, 1990); Barbara Beßlich, *Wege in den 'Kulturkrieg'* (Darmstadt, 2000); Thomas Rohkrämer, *Eine andere Moderne?* (Paderborn, 1999).
7 See Geoff Eley, 'Making a Place in the Nation: Meanings of "Citizenship" in Wilhelmine Germany,' in *Wilhelminism and Its Legacies: German Modernities, Imperialism, and the Meanings of Reform, 1890–1930*, ed. Geoff Eley and James Retallack (New York and Oxford, 2003), 31.
8 The following draws on David Blackbourn, *The Fontana History of Germany, 1780–1918: The Long Nineteenth Century* (London, 1997), esp. chaps. 7–8.
9 Klaus Tenfelde, '1890–1914: Durchbruch der Moderne? Über Gesellschaft im späten Kaiserreich,' in *Otto von Bismarck und Wilhelm II.*, ed. Gall, 119–41, here 136.

10 Gerhard A. Ritter, 'Politische Repräsentation durch Berufsstände. Konzepte und Realität in Deutschland 1871–1933,' in *Gestaltungskraft des Politischen*, ed. Wolfram Pyta and Ludwig Richter (Berlin, 1998), 261–80, esp. 269–74. See also Thomas Kühne, *Dreiklassenwahlrecht und Wahlkultur in Preussen 1867–1914. Landtagswahlen zwischen korporativer Tradition und politischem Massenmarkt* (Düsseldorf, 1994). The 'between' in Kühne's subtitle, as in many others, appropriately suggests that traditional and modern political styles persisted in uneasy tension throughout the Imperial period.
11 Blackbourn, *Fontana History*, 313, 323, and subsequent pages for much of the following.
12 Ibid., 347–8.
13 See Joachim Radkau, *Das Zeitalter der Nervosität* (Darmstadt, 1998).
14 Cited ibid., 26.
15 Ibid., 25.
16 Modris Eksteins, 'When Death Was Young ... : Germany, Modernism, and the Great War,' in *Ideas into Politics*, ed. R.J. Bullen, H. Pogge von Strandmann, and A.B. Polonsky (London, 1984), 25–35, here 29; see also Wolfgang J. Mommsen, *Bürgerliche Kultur und Künstlerische Avantgarde 1870–1918* (Frankfurt a.M. and Berlin, 1994), 98.
17 Peter Jelavich, 'Literature and the Arts,' in *Imperial Germany: A Historiographical Companion*, ed. Roger Chickering (Westport, Conn., 1996), 377.
18 Nietzsche, *Der Fall Wagner*, cited in Mommsen, *Bürgerliche Kultur*, 104.
19 Eksteins, 'When Death,' 31, citing the German sexual reformer Magnus Hirschfeld.
20 Mommsen, *Bürgerliche Kultur*, 107; Mommsen, ed., *Kultur und Krieg* (Munich, 1996), esp. 13–14.
21 Eksteins, 'When Death,' 33.
22 See Dieter Langewiesche, 'Das Deutsche Kaiserreich: Bemerkungen zur Diskussion über Parlamentarisierung und Demokratisierung Deutschlands,' *Archiv für Sozialgeschichte* 19 (1979): 628–42. More recently, see Marcus Kreuzer, 'Parliamentarization and the Question of German Exceptionalism, 1867–1918,' *Central European History* 36, no. 3 (2003): 327–57, and the gentle rebukes by Jonathan Sperber and Kenneth Ledford in the same issue of *Central European History*; and Thomas Kühne, "Demokratisierung und Parlamentarisierung: Neue Forschungen zur politischen Entwicklungsfähigkeit Deutschlands vor dem Ersten Weltkrieg,' *Geschichte und Gesellschaft* 31, no. 2 (2005): 293–316.
23 See Brett Fairbairn, *Democracy in the Undemocratic State* (Toronto, 1997); Margaret Lavinia Anderson, *Practicing Democracy: Elections and Political Culture in Imperial Germany* (Princeton, 2000).

24 Thomas Kühne, 'Die Liberalen bei den preußischen Landtagswahlen im Kaiserreich. Wahlmanipulation, Lokalismus und Wahlkompromisse,' in *Liberalismus und Region*, ed. Lothar Gall and Dieter Langewiesche (Munich, 1995), 277–305; Kühne, 'From Electoral Campaigning to the Politics of Togetherness: Localism and Democracy,' in *Localism, Landscape, and the Ambiguities of Place: Germany, 1871–1918*, ed. David Blackbourn and James Retallack (forthcoming). See also Andreas Gawatz, *Wahl-kämpfe in Württemberg* (Düsseldorf, 2001); Elvira Döscher and Wolfgang Schröder, *Sächsische Parlamentarier 1869–1918* (Droste, 2001); Detlef Lehnert, *Kommunale Institutionen zwischen Honoratiorenverwaltung und Massendemokratie* (Baden-Baden, 1994); and Thomas Mergel, 'Gegenbild, Vorbild und Schreckbild. Die amerikanischen Parteien in der Wahrnehmung der deutschen politischen Öffentlichkeit 1890–1920,' in *Parteien im Wandel*, ed. Dieter Dowe, Jürgen Kocka, and Heinrich August Winkler (Munich, 1999), 363–95.

25 Hartmut Pogge von Strandmann, ed., *Walther Rathenau. Industrialist, Banker, Intellectual, and Politician* (Oxford, 1985), 163–4; emphasis added.

26 Mark Hewitson, *National Identity and Political Thought in Germany* (Oxford, 2000), 253.

27 See Wolfgang J. Mommsen, 'The German Empire as a System of Skirted Decisions,' and 'A Delaying Compromise: The Division of Authority in the German Imperial Constitution of 1871,' in Mommsen, *Imperial Germany, 1867–1918* (London, 1994), 1–19 and 20–40 respectively.

28 Mark Hewitson, 'The *Kaiserreich* in Question: Constitutional Crisis in Germany before the First World War,' *Journal of Modern History* 73 (2001): 725–80, here 725–30; emphasis added. See also Hewitson, *National Identity*, 253.

29 Friedrich Naumann, 'Die Umwandlung der deutschen Verfassung,' *Patria*, 1908, 84, cited in Hewitson, '*Kaiserreich*,' 733–4.

30 Hewitson, '*Kaiserreich*,' 734, and 734–5 for the following.

31 Alastair P. Thompson, *Left Liberals, the State, and Popular Politics in Wilhelmine Germany* (Oxford, 2000), 7.

32 Ibid., 23.

33 Ibid., 24; emphasis added.

34 Payer speech to the Reichstag, 2 Dec. 1908, cited in Hewitson, '*Kaiserreich*,' 770.

35 Jan Palmowski, 'Mediating the Nation: Liberalism and the Polity in Nineteenth-Century Germany,' *German History* 18, no. 4 (2001): 573–98, here 584 and 597–8.

36 Christoph Nonn, 'Saxon Politics during the First World War: Moderniza-

tion, National Liberal Style,' in *Saxony in German History: Culture, Society, and Politics, 1830–1933*, ed. James Retallack (Ann Arbor, 2000), 309–21, esp. 315–21; see also Ralph Czychun, 'Political Modernisation, Democratisation and Reform during the First World War: The Case of Saxony' (MA diss., University of Toronto, 1998).

37 See David Blackbourn's review of Thomas Nipperdey in the *English Historical Review* 109, no. 432 (June 1994): 667.

38 As Jan Palmowski commented on reading an earlier version of this chapter, a more cautious assertion would be that *Protestant, bourgeois* Germans got what they wanted.

39 For the following, see David Blackbourn, 'New Legislatures: Germany, 1871–1914,' *Historical Research* 65 (1992): 201–14; Geoff Eley, 'Society and Politics in Bismarckian Germany,' *German History* 15 (1997): 101–32, esp. 111, 121, 128; Margaret Lavinia Anderson, 'Voter, Junker, *Landrat*, Priest: The Old Authorities and the New Franchise in Imperial Germany,' *American Historical Review* 98 (1993): 1448–74; and Helmut Walser Smith, *German Nationalism and Religious Conflict* (Princeton, 1995). Smith emphasized the 'persistence' and 'hardening' of tensions that were already fully apparent in the 1870s: 'The two religious groups thus *stood opposed*, though the geography of their opposition was quite complex: in some areas conflict was *strung taut* by the pressures of integration, in others *reinforced* by social division and confessional organization' (113, emphasis added).

40 These terms are found in Geoff Eley, 'Anti-Semitism, Agrarian Mobilization, and the Conservative Party: Radicalism and Containment in the Founding of the Agrarian League, 1890–93,' in *Between Reform, Reaction, and Resistance: Studies in the History of German Conservatism from 1789 to 1945*, ed. Larry Eugene Jones and James Retallack (Providence, RI, and Oxford, 1993), 187–227, here 194; and Eley, 'Notable Politics, the Crisis of German Liberalism, and the Electoral Transition of the 1890s,' in *In Search of a Liberal Germany*, ed. Konrad H. Jarausch and Larry Eugene Jones (New York, Oxford, and Munich, 1990), 187–216, here 192, 210–11.

41 'The intensification of popular politics took place at different times and to differing degrees. Singling out the 1890s as the crucial decade of popular mobilization, as Geoff Eley and others have done, tends to understate what had already taken place ... Nor was the pre-war decade just a continuation of the "new politics" of the 1890s ...; the pre-war years also saw substantial changes in political fashion, issues, and allegiances ... Mobilization is best seen as a process stretching across the whole of the [imperial] period, with many of the political, economic, and social seeds sown at the outset' (Thompson, *Left Liberals*, 21).

134 'Tradition is how we change'

42 See Axel Grießmer, *Massenverbände und Massenparteien im wilhelminischen Reich* (Düsseldorf, 2000), esp. 49–50. Here I can only sketch in the arguments behind this interpretation: Reichstag turnout rates rose until 1887 and then levelled off, before rising again after 1898; the Catholic and Social Democratic milieux were mobilized in the 1870s and 1880s respectively; SPD membership took off after 1903; and the nationalist 'camp' – if it actually existed at all – was consolidated only once the agrarian movement, mass imperialist agitation, and popular anti-socialism were fully functional, that is, after the turn of the century.
43 See, e.g., Ludwig Quidde, *Caligula*, ed. Hans-Ulrich Wehler (Frankfurt a.M., 1977).
44 See also Thomas Kühne, 'Wahlrecht – Wahlverhalten – Wahlkultur. Tradition und Innovation in der historischen Wahlforschung,' *Archiv für Sozialgeschichte* 33 (1993): 481–547; Kühne, 'Entwicklungstendenzen der preußischen Wahlkultur im Kaiserreich,' in *Wahlen und Wahlkämpfe in Deutschland*, ed. Gerhard A. Ritter (Düsseldorf, 1997), 131–67; and Kühne, 'Das Deutsche Kaiserreich 1871–1918 und seine politische Kultur: Demokratisierung, Segmentierung, Militarisierung,' *Neue Politische Literatur* 43 (1998): 206–63.
45 This analysis is indebted to Thomas Kühne, 'Die Jahrhundertwende, die "lange" Bismarckzeit und die Demokratisierung der politischen Kultur,' in *Otto von Bismarck und Wilhelm II.*, ed. Gall, 85–118.
46 See Christoph Nonn, *Verbraucherprotest und Parteiensystem im wilhelminischen Deutschland* (Düsseldorf, 1996).
47 See Kühne, 'Jahrhundertwende,' 118.
48 See Uwe Puschner, *Die völkische Bewegung im wilhelminischen Kaiserreich* (Darmstadt, 2001); also Uwe Puschner et al., eds, *Handbuch zur 'Völkischen Bewegung' 1871–1918* (Munich, 1996); Diethart Kerbs and Jürgen Reulecke, eds., *Handbuch der deutschen Reformbewegungen 1880–1933* (Wuppertal, 1998).
49 Kühne's German term is '*obrigkeitsstaatliche Verfaßtheit*.'
50 Kühne, 'Jahrhundertwende,' 117.
51 Lothar Gall, 'Otto von Bismarck und Wilhelm II.: Repräsentanten eines Epochenwechsels?' in *Otto von Bismarck und Wilhelm II.*, ed. Gall, 1–12, including (8) the following passage from Kessler's memoirs.
52 Anderson, 'Reply,' 88.
53 The implicit reference here is to the 'meanings of reform' taken up by Geoff Eley and other contributors to *Wilhelminism and Its Legacies*, ed. Eley and Retallack.

PART TWO

Cultures of Conservatism

4 Culture/Power/Territoriality

Geography without *History* hath life and motion, but very unstable and at random; but *History* without *Geography*, like a dead carkasse, hath neither life nor motion at all.

Peter Heylyn (1600–62)[1]

This chapter explores sites – conceptual and actual sites – where culture and power intersect in Germany history. It does so by examining a collection of political visions drawn from the experience of conservatives and liberals in the nineteenth century. Although the focus of this chapter is not on party politics, it addresses issues that conditioned the possibilities for political renewal on the Right. Such issues included attempts by bourgeois Germans to carve out political space between working-class and aristocratic competitors, efforts to revitalize the authoritarian state, middle-class fears of revolution, ambivalence towards democracy, and the collision of individual rights and group solidarities in sub-national territorial units.

This argument proposes that the study of political history is enriched in often unanticipated ways by examining the intersection of culture and power locally – *vor Ort*. To give specificity to the argument, the focus sometimes falls on the history and historiography of the Kingdom of Saxony. But we could as easily have chosen another region. Indeed, rather than giving priority to any point of reference close to the 'heart' of national politics, this chapter examines the exercise of power, as Michel Foucault once put it, at 'those points where it becomes capillary, that is, in its more regional and local forms and institutions.'[2] These are the points where the 'ambiguities of place' were most palpable in German history – no matter whether their effects were enervating or neuralgic.

The culture/power/history nexus has been explored elsewhere and needs little elaboration here.[3] But what does the politics of place add to the equation? Has the linguistic turn been followed by a spatial turn, as some recent observers have suggested, or perhaps even by a topographical turn?[4] Can the concept of symbolic territoriality (*symbolische Ortsbezogenheit*) augment the practice of local and regional history?[5] And what, if anything, does local history have to do with national aggregates, long trends, and international contexts?[6]

In one sense, the spatial turn signals historians' increasing awareness since the 1970s that regions – like nations, classes, and communities – are discovered, constructed, forgotten, and remade in history. Reminding ourselves as historians about the 'constructedness' of regions has allowed us to go beyond a metaphoric use of culture, so common these days in professional and public discourse, to speak of culture in the sense of symbolic representations that shaped and were shaped by social and political conditions. Discussing culture in a regional setting provides a means to gather together ideas about identities, mentalities, and loyalties without implying that there is something parochial about this exercise. Doing so also allows historians to explore how regional and national cultures commingle, diverge, and influence each other.

A region's history is rooted in a matrix of direct spatial relationships that change over time. E.P. Thompson reminded us that 'class' does not simply exist: class *happens*. But regions also happen, though not always in a manner of their inhabitants' own choosing. Historians now take the geography in historical geography much more seriously than they did twenty years ago. They pay closer attention to the physical boundaries – rivers, coastlines, valleys, mountain ranges, concentrations of natural resources – that define regions. But they also link physical boundaries to historical maps and the maps that reside in people's minds. Physical boundaries and mental maps are most significant when they come together, when they delimit particular horizons of understanding. With this in mind, Celia Applegate has written that historians need to consider 'why people loved and hated the regional places in which they found themselves, why they worked to strengthen them, hastened to escape them, praised them, poured invective upon them, thought about them all the time, ignored them completely, and yet for all that dwelt many days of their lives within the "networks of experience" that these regions sustained.'[7]

Historians are immeasurably better attuned to the comparability of regions than they were a quarter-century ago. To some scholars, the history of a region is of special interest because it undermines the uniformity of German history. It disproves previous assumptions about what was going on at the 'centre,' and yet it illuminates dimensions of German history that no other region can. Thus a region may be particularly revealing because it has represented, at various points in its history, a worst-case scenario or the best of all possible worlds. Other historians ask whether a regional case study can ever be broadly representative, or even typical, of developments everywhere in Germany. Still others try to add a human dimension to these questions by exploring identities, mentalities, and perceptions. Did Berliners have a different outlook on the world than Rhinelanders did, even though both groups resided in the state of Prussia and paid allegiance – some with more conviction, some with less – to the German nation? What analyses can be built on the tension between the diversity of Prussia (or any state) and whatever ideas of Prussianness (etc.) may have united its people?

Federalism has always been a contentious issue in German history. But it has too rarely been explored in cultural terms. Therefore this chapter asks how Germans appraised the legacies and prospects of federalism at various times in their history. For citizens of any given federal state, to what extent was their social, economic, and political integration into a national community congruent with their sense that they belonged together culturally? Here it is possible to take the linguistic and spatial turns together, for example, by interrogating 'that awful German language' (Mark Twain) to ask how Germans reflected critically on their *landsmannschaftliches Zusammengehörigkeitsgefühl* – their own sense of rootedness in a territorial community. When Germans perceived that their villages and towns were becoming more like villages and towns elsewhere in the empire, did they fear that industrialization, urbanization, and democratization on a national scale were eroding everything that was distinctive about local life? Or could larger modernizing processes actually have perpetuated local particularities, reinforced them, and enhanced their positive valence?

Innovative thinking about a sense of place has helped historians overcome a Prusso-centric bias in German historical writing. Taken as a whole, local and regional studies have contributed to a picture of nineteenth-century Germany that deviates substantially from a view of Bismarck's national state as the inevitable outcome of German unification. The latter view has been under attack for at least twenty-five years. Yet it has not disappeared from standard textbook accounts.

Indeed, if it is important to see that a Prussianized Germany emerging from 1870/71 wasn't necessarily the way things had to turn out, it is more important still to recognize that a Prussianized Germany wasn't *in fact* the way things turned out either. In this sense, historians' concern to write German histories, in the plural, has provided a salutary reminder that pride in German unification after 1871 looked very different depending where you were in the empire – and how you got there.

How, then, does this chapter bring the politics of place into closer proximity with themes more familiar to mainstream German historians? This proximity is explored on more than one front. These fronts run obliquely to a history of the Right narrowly defined, but they squarely address the political limits of the authoritarian imagination. The following argument examines the attempts of liberal reformers, burgher activists, and other culture-builders to challenge the authoritarian state and to modernize the exercise of power in Imperial Germany. It analyses the diffusion and circulation of power in modern societies, not only between the centre and the periphery but also around and through these spaces. And it considers how frontiers and other symbolic representations of territoriality facilitated local efforts at identity-building. This analysis makes no attempt to take stock of a vast body of literature on these subjects; instead it aims to draw new linkages among the three concepts identified in this chapter's title.

The argument unfolds in three sections. The first of these examines the tension between territorial history (*Landesgeschichte*) and regional history (*Regionalgeschichte*). A brief discussion of how this tension has conditioned historical writing on Saxony introduces more general reflections on how historians are 'doing' regional history today. The second section examines politics and culture together. Again, the conceptual tension between these terms is highlighted. That tension is partially resolved in political culture research; but it is still complicated by choices historians make about how to chart change over time and how they answer the question of what really constitutes a region. The third and last section considers how German identities were constructed in smaller settings by culture-builders, nation-builders, and identity-builders. This section examines liberals and conservatives in 'their' spaces.[8] But it considers them on the move, too, as they tried to reconcile traditional sources of local power with new identities created by Germany's growth as a national and international power. How has research on civil society, the public sphere, and citizenship rights illuminated the challenges and opportunities faced by Germans journeying across boundaries of political or imaginative space? Why did cosmopolitan or transnational tropes come to play such a role in political 'conversations' that began at the local *Stammtisch*? And how, the conclusion asks, can the politics of place help to integrate 'provincial' research into 'total' history?

Territorial History and Regional History

In choosing to study local, regional, and national political cultures together, the historian faces many potential pitfalls. On the one hand, it is easy to become too focused on the particular and the unique. As the comparative framework is sacrificed, however reluctantly, to the need for a deeper understanding of local peculiarities, the links between different tiers of political activity become tenuous. In the end they are often ignored altogether. On the other hand, studies that give precedence to national developments are rarely able to demonstrate how national politics are conditioned by different political cultures in one or more regions. Too often, building a composite picture of Germany's political culture becomes a mechanical, cumulative exercise: Wait long enough, and one day sufficient work will have been done on each locality to bring the national picture magically into focus. But of course historical scholarship (at its best) does not work this way. Analysis a mile wide and an inch deep is generally of little interest to local specialists, whose archival knowledge and detailed studies are indispensable. Scholars who are determined to produce a synthesis can rarely acquire the precise knowledge of local conditions necessary to shed genuinely new light on the national picture. And so, like partners in a bad marriage, these two approaches – local history and national history – coexist unhappily; with a bare minimum of contact, they each struggle to realize their incompatible goals in separate spheres.

Although it is frequently regarded as an unwelcome interloper, regional history can offer useful counsel to those wishing to escape this predicament.[9] Here it is helpful to distinguish between territorial history and regional history, because the dialogue between these two subfields of history has not always been congenial.

Already by the 1970s, territorial history had lost much of its resonance among students and the lay public, who tended to regard it as traditional and stuffy. But as regional studies multiplied in the 1980s, the term *Regionalgeschichte* came into vogue, though it was more a symptom than a cause of deepening interest. Around 1985 the debate about regional history in Germany reached a high-water mark. Considering the much more acrimonious controversy over the history of everyday life (*Alltagsgeschichte*) and the so-called war of the German historians (*Historikerstreit*), that debate remained relatively muted. Scholars willingly climbed on board for a trip across fresh historical landscapes, regions, territories, provinces, and localities. Interdisciplinary and comparative approaches began to make progress too – in practice, not just in theory. For example, the lines soon blurred between local history (*Lokalgeschichte*), urban history (*Stadtgeschichte*), the history of urbanization (*Urbanisierungsgeschichte*), and the history of municipal administration.[10]

The regional history train, in other words, had clearly left the station by the middle of the 1980s. Yet still historians wanted to get off at different stops. Some were willing to travel to the end of the line, while others wished to remain close enough to reach for the brake. As early as 1981, Peter Steinbach suggested why regional history should be practised with critical, reflective distance. He warned that those who brought a regional perspective to either economic history or the history of everyday life needed to avoid identifying too closely with their subject; in particular, they should not treat the 'region' as though it were reality itself.[11] (This warning was formulated in almost identical terms as recently as 2000.)[12] Instead, Steinbach wrote, regional history at its best functions as a corrective science: it can 'examine claims about general historical developments and about universality' and yet also 'explore their penetration down to the lower levels of human collectivity.'[13]

Steinbach was not alone in suggesting that the goal of regional history should be something less than a *histoire totale* and something more than 'merely' a methodology. As Ernst Hinrichs noted in 1985, the gradual and incomplete detachment of regional history from territorial history had brought with it progressively less interest in studying a 'political' space and more interest in studying a 'socio-anthropological' one. The development of closer links between regional history and the history of everyday life in these same years verified this observation. But still many practitioners of territorial history could not make this leap. As Hinrichs wrote: 'With the ideas of social history, regional history, the history of mentalities, historical anthropology, [and] the history of everyday life, we find fields of research that the territorial historian of the traditional stamp can understand as a constitutive element of territorial research only reluctantly or not at all.'[14] However, he continued, this need not remain the case: a more open brand of territorial history could carry forward valuable traditions and yet also 'conquer new terrain.' To argue about 'whether it should be called regional history or should retain the old name,' added Hinrichs, was fruitless.[15]

There is no longer any need to retain the designation 'territorial history' to describe what regional historians do. Nonetheless, the baby of traditional political history is in danger of being thrown out with the bathwater of a methodology condemned as passé. If the child is to be saved, regional history must take on board whatever insights are thrown up by cognate disciplines but not allow the history of society to become disengaged from the history of the state. By focusing on a specific geographical space (*Raum*), regional history, like territorial history before it, can use the constraints imposed by actual political and administrative borders in a positive way.

One example may suffice to illustrate this point concretely. In the modern era, Germany has been Europe's chameleon. But the same is not true of all its federal states. Although the Kingdom of Saxony suffered repeated defeats and partial dismemberment at the hands of Prussia between 1756 and 1815, it retained the same size and shape on the map of Germany for the next 137 years. After 1815 the territoriality of the Saxon state was a 'given.' Does this circumstance shape or constrict analyses of Saxon history in the nineteenth century? One answer begins with the term *Land*, a word that is notoriously difficult to translate precisely. *Land* has had different political and cultural connotations in different historical periods. Moreover, the term can be considered functionally equivalent to a single state within a federation; but it can also be used to designate a 'homeland,' which is patently less easy to demarcate on a map or describe as a discrete political unit.

Nevertheless, the indeterminacy of *Land* has limits. Sometimes historians become interested in political institutions for which the word *Land* is linguistically constitutive: state parliaments (*Landtage*), for example, or state suffrages (*Landtagswahlrechte*), state constitutions (*Landesverfassungen*), even local county councillors (*Landräte*). These terms suggest that scholars interested in the history of Germany's federal states are not concerned only with imagined communities. Indeed, the way we study Germans who were striving for political emancipation, protesting injustice, or otherwise seeking a better future is linked closely with both physical and administrative borders. All too often, contemporaries were frustrated when they rubbed up against such boundaries and found that they constrained their everyday lives materially, politically, and in myriad other ways. But the real point is that the conceptual limits we impose upon ourselves when we 'do' regional history can be used positively in not one but two ways: they help us understand how relatively impermeable political borders defined certain types of political activity, and they illuminate linkages between different *kinds* of borders (permeable or not).

For the study of political parties and elections in Imperial Germany, a regional perspective that takes territoriality seriously can meet a number of challenges. These include, first, the challenge issued over forty years ago by Thomas Nipperdey when he set the highest possible standard for the study of party organizations in their regional diversity.[16] Regional history, second, can rise to the challenge issued thirty years ago by Gerhard A. Ritter when he identified the need for more regional studies in his introduction to a volume of essays on German parties.[17] Third, it can offer a means for political historians to update their craft by integrating insights drawn from social history, cultural history, and *Alltagsgeschichte*. Peter Steinbach addressed this issue twenty-five years ago, but he could as easily have been writing today: 'Whereas previously, histories of parties, associations, and elections would jump all too quickly from the social structure of a district to the articulation of politics, research on the history of everyday life offers the opportunity to draw connections between the social and political dimensions of human behaviour and to describe more precisely the social structures that are considered primarily as statistical categories: status, life expectancy, perception, neighbourhood communication – these should all at least be recognized as problems of historical research on a regional basis. Even though the much cited "linkage problem" between social structure and political articulation can be resolved at the empirical level only in the rarest cases, this does not eliminate the historian's duty to recognize that it is a new task of historical-sociological regional history to find a solution.'[18] How far can regional history take us in directions signposted by these historians? It may not take us to the end of the line. But we need not be left standing at the station either.

If the typical regional historian pursues his or her craft with a sense of obligation to those who have gone before, this is markedly so for the historian of Saxony. A great debt is owed to scholars who before, during, and after the 'historical epoch' of the German Democratic Republic made a unique contribution to Saxon regional history. One need only mention the names of Karl Lamprecht, Rudolf Kötzschke, Hellmut Kretzschmar, and Walter Schlesinger, among an older group, or Karlheinz Blaschke, Karl Czok, and Hartmut Zwahr, among more recent scholars, to hint at the importance of Saxony as a centre of pioneering work. Yet retrospective surveys of East German historiography have shown that regional history hung by a thread through the 1960s and 1970s. The effects of this precarious status are being felt still.

In the early 1960s, regional history was clearly articulated in East Germany for the first time. It was recognized as problematic even by those Saxon historians who were willing to tolerate the intrusion of the state into historical scholarship. Nonetheless, such historians were in little doubt as to why territorial history should be abandoned. Karlheinz Blaschke, a strong advocate of territorial history who resisted the trend toward regional historiography under the East German dictatorship, once explained the antipathy felt by GDR regional historians. In their view, 'territorial history was associated exclusively with the individual German states, with their dynasties, with monarchical court histories, and with German particularism.'[19] By contrast, continued Blaschke, 'the German labour movement, whose leaders now possessed political power, had always been oriented against particularism and had been centrally organized; its field [of action] was the whole German nation, not the single state.'[20] Territorial history in East Germany was thus considered 'reactionary' – triply so. It was *emancipatory* in that it suggested 'sympathy for the independence, or even the striving for self-determination, of particular geographical areas within the national and political unit.' It was *anomalous* because it did not correspond to internal East German administrative boundaries, which had eliminated the individual states (*Länder*) in 1952 and replaced them with fourteen districts (*Bezirke*). And it was *nonconformist* in providing a banner to critics of the regime and impeding the elevation of regional history into a canon of communist scholarship.

Historians can be thankful that local and regional archivists, church archivists, and a small community of nonconformist historians like Blaschke continued to resist the historiographical orthodoxy imposed by a dictatorial regime. Work done in those archives and the preservation of materials that can now be studied without ideological restrictions must not be forgotten. Nor can we disregard the many studies of individual industrial concerns, localities, and institutions of higher learning that flourished in these years. Even the East German *Jahrbuch für Regionalgeschichte*, first published in Leipzig in 1965 under Karl Czok's editorship, provided an opportunity for Saxon historians to publish their findings, though only as long as they did not challenge ideological orthodoxy.[21]

Regional history, as developed by Czok and others, brought with it emphases that deflected East German historiography in problematic ways.[22] In fact, the history of Social Democracy was *the* starting point for research on Saxony for so long that this tendency persisted into the 1990s. And the ill will generated by thirty years of struggle over competing conceptions of regional history has not entirely dissipated. Nevertheless, the signals now point toward a bright future. The re-establishment of Saxony as a Free State, increased accessibility to document collections there, the eagerness of Saxon scholars to establish new ties with western colleagues, the revival of the flagship journal *Neues Archiv für sächsische Geschichte*, the establishment or reconstitution of such organizations as the Institute for Saxon History, the Dresden Historical Association, the Hannah Arendt Institute for the Study of Totalitarianism, and the Simon Dubnow Institute for Jewish History and Culture – all these developments suggest that an optimistic prognosis is in order. The study of Saxon history is more exciting now than seemed imaginable only fifteen years ago.

'Doing' Regional History Today

Isaiah Berlin once warned against a 'naïve craving for unity and symmetry at the expense of experience.' He made this observation in the context of the Germans' national hangover after revolution and unification in 1989–90, but elsewhere he advocated 'allowing curiosity into the airless chamber of fixed certainty.'[23] When we consider the practice of regional history today, such curiosity underpins a healthy resistance to any 'craving for symmetry.' Nevertheless, resistance has its positive and negative aspects.

On the positive side, scholars sustain this resistance by using a wide range of analytical tools in their regional histories. Only rarely do they still fall into the trap of identifying too closely with their favourite *Ländl* or of believing that the region they study constitutes historical 'reality' itself. Nevertheless, Celia Applegate has noted that there is 'something both liberating *and* demoralizing about our current suspicion of allegedly overdeterministic explanations of change and its organizing categories.' The anti-explanatory mode demands critical distancing from our method of historical investigation (regional history) and from the object of study itself (the region). But this pose of ironic detachment can be overdone, in the manner of an awkward personal encounter: 'Let me introduce you to my spouse, but I'm not really committed to this relationship and it could well turn out to be something entirely different from a marriage and it's certainly in flux and under negotiation and filled with other possibilities and contingently related to all the other things going on in my life, and I wouldn't wish to suggest that there is some normative value adhering to this particular relationship.'[24] What might take the place of these normative values? Let us consider three possible answers in turn.

First, regional historians have begun to devote more attention to change over time. They look at people on the move, for instance, to consider migration as a factor reflecting the connections between identity and geography.[25] They also consider how the 'nuts and bolts' of regional consciousness – church or military institutions, dialects, networks of family connections, and myriad other cultural practices – are set in motion by challenges to the status quo. When did contemporaries reflect on their particular era as perpetuating or overcoming something special in their lives, and when did they focus on the arrival of something better in the future? Do historians accurately capture this sense of change over time when they write, for example, about a 'post-revolutionary' epoch or a 'pre-emancipatory' stage of development? Does it make sense to denote certain political movements as 'rising,' to say that others are in danger of 'disappearing' from history, or to search for liberals seizing a 'second chance' to change the course of history?

Such considerations can be couched in less-abstract terms. Suffrage laws and railway maps, drawn and redrawn over the years, illustrate the way things have already evolved in the past; but they also capture potential sources of legitimacy or profit in the future. A sense of place usually evolves in tandem with a sense of time. However, a sense of time is still too rarely included among the 'modern' ways of seeing that regional historians consider. When do identities remain rooted, and when do they change at a recognizably accelerating pace? At what rate do spatial memories fade away? What is their relationship to the perceived 'newness' of places and groups in which displaced persons find themselves? Ironically, such questions about change over time actually de-emphasize the priority historians have placed on the region-nation nexus as a process; they tend to reconceptualize it as a tension – a tension with many layers and facets.

Second, historians may be well advised to ask, not 'What is a region?' but rather, What set of practices define a sense of place? What identities adhere to 'region,' and what experiences constitute it? In considering shifting practices, identities, and experiences, historians still risk losing track of the specificities of place. Yet by discussing the importance of neighbourhood boundaries, of states' territorial sovereignty, or of networks of transportation and communication, scholars are moving towards the better integration of mental and physical topography, that is, towards a better understanding of the symbolic *and* the geographic 'placeness' of place. That understanding will in turn help them rethink the 'discernible patterns, identifiable limits, commonalities of experience – mental, physical, social, political – and even trends that at least felt inexorable at the time, even if they may not have been so.'[26]

Lastly, 'doing' regional history today continues to raise questions about modernization as a concept. The liabilities of modernization theory in its extreme form have always been clear to local and regional historians – no less clear, in fact, than to practitioners of microhistory and the history of everyday life. For too long, the local and the regional were studied exclusively as the sites of resistance to modernity and nationalism, as the bastions of parochial outlooks and particularist navel-gazing – the narcissism of small differences. On the other hand, moving beyond the 'generalizing social-science approach to the past' allows us to sidestep the teleologies that tend to wipe out 'the cultural distance between the past and the present, losing the strangeness and individuality of the past in the process.'[27] Bringing a sense of place back in restores one small part of that fascinating, frustrating strangeness of far-off historical epochs.

Geoff Eley has criticized the 'connotative continuum of "bourgeoisie = liberalism = democracy."'[28] This is the continuum of classic modernization theory. Yet at the regional level this 'implied causal chain' remains just that: implied, not proven. Mere interdependence among the social and cultural components of political modernization should not be taken as tending inevitably towards a good fit. Thus, to choose to explore these issues is not to lock oneself into the iron cage of modernization theory or to accept rigid patterns of development from which no person or region or collectivity can possibly deviate. Rather, it is to suggest that questions of power and domination, patterns of social upheaval and economic development, and problems of social inequality are still important in German history. Concepts of structured change – like the concepts of political mobilization, participation, activization, pillarization, polarization, integration, and nationalization – these concepts must be used flexibly; they must be used contingently; but they can be used nevertheless. Similarly, constructs of identity may be more or less useful when they are used as heuristic tools, but the extent of their usefulness has to be proven.

Sceptics will argue that more than a mere vestige of such polarities (modern, not-modern) and other trail-markers laid down long ago by the advocates of modernization theory are still pushing regional historians of Germany towards depicting a surprisingly familiar, well-trodden path. Yet regional historians are answering the call to put the telos of modernization at arm's length by explaining both the erosion and the persistence of traditional ways of seeing. National patterns thus yield pride of place to local and regional particularities, to sudden turning points, to individuals whose role on the national stage was unexceptional.[29]

In the process of such investigations, we find that contemporaries' attempts to hasten the arrival of 'the modern' cannot neatly be placed in opposition to attempts to preserve tradition. The two projects jumble and jostle together. This jostling makes it more difficult for historians to dress 'national' modernizers alone as the protagonists of German history.[30] And it helps us avoid the trap of dichotomous thinking. By discarding the notion of a German *Sonderweg* in the singular, we can more easily avoid both sentimentality and censure.

One can only hope that scholars will continue to work hard at writing regional histories that are methodologically self-conscious, inventive, and demanding, but also respectful of the historical record. In bridging the unfruitful divides between empiricism and theory, between solid, careful history and the search for nuance and insight, regional studies can reorient Germany's multiple histories, as though one were observing them through telephoto and wide-angle lenses at the same time.

Politics / Culture / Political Culture

By joining the two words 'politics' and 'culture,' one can begin to link two very different, perhaps opposite, worlds of human endeavour.[31] As Eva Kolinsky and John Gaffney once observed: '[Do not] politics concern themselves with the issues of the day [and] adopt a pragmatic, even opportunistic, approach ...? [Does] not culture, by contrast, rise above the fray, articulate lasting values and reveal beauty and ideals behind everyday mediocrity and confusion?'[32] Other dualisms have been suggested to reveal both the strengths and weaknesses of political culture research. In Max Kaase's famous quip, trying to define political culture is like trying 'to nail a pudding against the wall.' Dirk Berg-Schlosser, another political scientist, elaborated on the metaphor and cast it in a more positive light: he compared political culture to a

150 Cultures of Conservatism

'multilayered cake with numerous tasty ingredients, a variety of lighter and darker sections.'

The concept of political culture has enjoyed star quality for many years now. Yet the practice of regional history still has much to gain from a more intimate relationship with political science. Clarity of purpose is important here, because students of political culture are sometimes presumed to want to move political history (back) closer to centre stage: uncomfortable and disillusioned in the postmodern arena and determined to win back their 'rightful' share of the spotlight, such scholars are accused of wanting to upstage their colleagues in related sub-fields of history and shuffle their competitors off to the wings. Such small-mindedness is unnecessary. Regional historians are committed to exploring broader relationships between politics and society, politics and culture, politics and modernization, politics and everyday life. After all, students of political culture (not merely *Staatskultur*) who study one federal state or region are usually also interested in the stability of political systems, crises of legitimacy, processes of political polarization, bureaucratization, confessionalization, and the 're-regionalization' or 'de-regionalization' of politics.[33]

Again Saxon historiography is illustrative. The contours of bourgeois politics in Saxony are beginning to come into focus in ways that heed Geoff Eley's warnings about equating the bourgeoisie exclusively with liberalism. Thus historians of Saxon political culture are aware of the danger of conceptual slippage when they study, say, local chapters of the Pan-German League in Dresden and Leipzig in relation to their national organizations. Some historians might argue that members of these local chapters saw themselves as 'little people' battling against the elitist politics of notables. In reality they belonged to social groups that already dominated the local hierarchies of income, privilege, and power. It is true, moreover, that some members saw their activity within these organizations as exclusively local: providing an evening's entertainment, offering escape from a tiresome spouse (not necessarily the wife), or serving to launch a campaign for municipal office. Even in this sense, everyday life and local politics were intertwined. But other members were surely drawn principally by the 'other-sidedness' of Pan-German ideology itself. Just as the historian Heinrich von Treitschke did everything possible to disavow and disparage his Saxon roots in writing his history of nineteenth-century Germany, these nationalists tried to transcend local allegiances that constrained their enthusiasm for Germany's national mission. For better or worse, they were not always up to the task. But why this was so can be best explored through further research at the levels of local and regional political cultures.

Culture-Builders

The explosion of scholarship on German liberals and on the German bourgeoisie has intersected at many places with efforts to revisit Jürgen Habermas's theories of the public sphere. Today, far more than even a decade ago, scholars are focusing their attention on German liberals in both public and private spaces, charting the micropractices of power against liberals' larger visions.[34] On the one hand, this trend has produced a rich array of studies in which prominent liberals (and their family histories) have been situated within the overlapping local, regional, and national spheres of bourgeois activity that lent them influence.[35] On the other hand, German liberals' sense of space and time is also is being considered in ways that necessarily enrich our understanding of the German Right and relations of authority on many tiers of political activity.

Most liberals identified closely with the accelerating pace of life in the nineteenth century. They defined themselves in ways that fitted comfortably with unprecedented opportunities to communicate across continents and to change the natural rhythms of life. Hence many liberals are depicted on the move – emphatically so – seizing unprecedented and often unanticipated opportunities as wealth was redistributed, social status renegotiated, distant authorities challenged. But liberals were not always in the driver's seat. Many shared the fears of conservatives that the tempo of modern life was contributing to social atomization and their own isolation. These liberals suspected (even if they did not often concede the point publicly) that they no longer exerted cultural or political hegemony in 'their' urban spaces. Nor did their claim to be seeking social cohesion and class harmony convince conservatives, socialists, and Catholics that their definition of the natural political order was the only one available.

Often liberals did not know where to turn when their prescriptions for social cohesion were resisted by authorities who themselves responded inadequately or inflexibly to change. In such cases, liberals sometimes advocated a political or aesthetic release from the bonds of authority that in more normal circumstances they might have supported. For example, liberals staging ethnographic displays of people and artefacts from far-flung cultures claimed to be searching for world peace and authenticity; but they resorted to constructed authenticity by masking, rather than uncovering, the distinctiveness of particular classes and people. Museum directors, too, appeared to be searching for alternative means to promote tolerance and respect. But by working to redefine the power that previously lay 'elsewhere' (at the 'centre'), German liberals became too certain that the logic of their own solution to Germany's ills was watertight.

Liberals disappointed even themselves when they proved vulnerable to the physicality of local protests that they had initiated. In Leipzig in 1830, for example, the same protesters who burned a corrupt city official's residence during a night-time riot might be found the next morning among members of the civil guard charged with restoring public peace. The public and private contexts in which liberals operated conditioned their targeted outbursts against authority. Yet at the same time they favoured the liberals' own encroachments on the autonomy of the individual. Liberal concepts of professionalism, the common good, the classless society, tolerance for difference, respect for foreign cultures, appreciation for the varieties of human endeavour – these concepts proved to be remarkably protean, depending on the manner in which liberal culture was fashioned and controlled locally. Liberals believed that authority, to be legitimate, had to be enlightened and tempered. Yet their own enlightenment was frequently insufficient to steer them away from a preference for uniformity over diversity.

While facing a challenge from one quarter, liberals were likely to undertake reform in another. Effective local governance was seen to be essential to the general welfare. As the Saxon constitutional theorist Wilhelm Traugott Krug wrote in 1831: 'A good local government law is as necessary for a well-organized state as a good constitution. Indeed, one is the indispensable complement of the other, since the cities themselves are nothing other than small states within larger ones.'[36] Liberals nevertheless knew that good government was also conducive to the exercise of authority. Recent studies of German liberalism have therefore explored the interdependence of state and civil society. They have shown that liberal influence was generally reinforced by the decisions of local parliaments, by bureaucratic regulators, and even by political opponents who disagreed with liberals about what sorts of political rights inhere in the possession of private property (a topic taken up in the next two chapters).

Many histories of German liberalism in urban settings hinge on economic issues. These range from personal thrift to national economic policy, from the solvency of individual entrepreneurs to the fiscal propriety of communal administrators, from the privileges of home ownership to the international networks of acquisition and exchange.[37] Fund-raising and prestige-building often went hand in hand, as when liberals raised funds for cultural institutions or lobbied for tax concessions. This attention to the material aspects of culture-building is a significant departure from historians' earlier preoccupation with liberal failure. It reinforces our sense that cultural emulation, business competition, and feelings of superiority fitted together naturally for self-made Germans.

Along these lines, Robert Beachy has demonstrated the significance of public debt and taxation in conditioning the rise of a modern civil society that rested squarely on the principle of private property. Leipzig's reputation as a university and trading centre of major importance, the locus of *Geist und Geld*, emerged intact from the Napoleonic Wars. By contrast, the settlement of 1815 tarnished Dresden's own reputation for power and display – *Macht und Pracht*. For a time, the rigid conservatism of the Saxon state and of Leipzig's city council appeared resilient enough to resist competing claims on the public purse. But the old order could not deflect demands for more equitable taxation and participation rights without calling into question its own legitimacy. Leipzig's civic elites proved themselves willing and able to challenge royal authority emanating from Dresden. Such battles for fiscal autonomy flowed directly into the reconstituting of Saxon state power in the 1830s.

Later in the century, too, battles raged between groups trying to establish local control over the symbols of German national culture. Such battles have previously received scrutiny mainly in their national contexts. But regional historians are more often taking the lead here, as in two recent essays by Glenn Penny and Marline Otte. Otte has explored the world of popular culture through her study of the Sarrasani circus in Dresden. Penny has juxtaposed the local and cosmopolitan outlooks of museum-builders in Leipzig to illustrate how local identities evolved amidst national and international competitions for superiority. In each study one discovers that cultural battles were fought on local terrain at least as often and at least as intensely as they were fought nationally or internationally.

Such local studies underline the insufficiency of any historical approach that is not to some degree interdisciplinary. They examine spaces where commerce and culture came together, where business and beautification were advanced in tandem, and where civic pride and worldly competition were not seen as incompatible. How, after all, except with an interdisciplinary approach, can we study the political economy of municipal tax reform in the context of local debates about street violence and political grandstanding? How, except by considering commercial success, public acclaim, and political influence-peddling, can we deduce the calculations of circus directors trying to find the perfect mix of entertainment genres for their target audience? And how can we understand the determination of museum boosters to trumpet German science and the superiority of German *Bildung* without gauging the resonance of their arguments against yardsticks calibrated to both local and cosmopolitan standards? Such questions compel us to integrate economic, social, political, intellectual, and cultural perspectives to a degree that is still too rarely found in sub-national histories.

Nation-Builders

Few historians view local or regional politics exclusively as the target of domination by the centralizing state. Nevertheless, the move away from the study of high politics towards a focus on everyday experience has sometimes gone too far in allowing the state and its agendas to recede into the background.

Michel Foucault has provided guidance on this question. On the one hand, in *Power/Knowledge* he wrote that 'the important thing is not to attempt some kind of deduction of power starting from its centre and aimed at the discovery of the extent to which it permeates into the base ... One must rather conduct an *ascending* analysis of power, starting, that is, from its infinitesimal mechanisms, which each have their own history, their own trajectory, their own techniques and tactics.'[38] On the other hand, Foucault also argued that power should be seen as something that circulates in and through social spaces. From this vantage point, power is constituted not only (or even mainly) by the official agents of social control and cultural production but by their unofficial agents as well.

These observations apply to histories of the German authoritarian state and its agents at every level of politics. In grappling with this state and its activities, historians still commonly buy into polarized thinking that contrasts despotism with legitimation, repression with rights. But German authorities exercising power locally and regionally were usually operating on both sides of the line. Contemporaries understood this when they used labels such as 'petty tyrant' or the 'uncrowned king

4.1. Mediating power. This scene depicts Dresden's lord mayor, Friedrich Wilhelm Pfotenhauer (hand outstretched), and the Conservative Party's leading *Mittelstand* advocate, Karl Ackermann (standing to his right), greeting Saxon Crown Prince Albert on 11 July 1871, after the Franco-German War. *Die feierliche Begrüßung Sr. Königlichen Hoheit des Kronprinzen Albert von Sachsen als Feldmarschall und Obercommandeur der Maasarmee an der Spitze der Sächsischen Truppen durch den Rath der Stadt Dresden am 11. Juli 1871*, by Friedrich Wilhelm Heine (detail), 1879. Image courtesy of the Stadtmuseum Dresden.

of X' to suggest that local and provincial power brokers did not always call the shots.[39] Put another way, this nomenclature reflected contemporary Germans' awareness that smaller, local practices of authoritarian rule were inseparable from larger means to deploy power. Hence the idea of abandoning an ascending analysis of power makes good sense. 'Power is employed and exercised through a net-like organization,' Foucault has written. 'And not only do individuals circulate between its threads; they are always in the position of simultaneously undergoing and exercising this power. They are not only its inert or consenting target; they are always also the elements of its articulation.'

Against this backdrop we might consider how nineteenth-century Saxons and other Germans planted signposts pointing toward a culture of rights.[40] If we accept that the dispersal of power outward from the state toward a variety of agents (each with more or less legitimate claims to autonomy) is characteristic of a modern form of rule, then local and regional perspectives can illuminate at least three important aspects of attempts to establish a culture of rights. First, many liberals hoped that their aspirations in the local, regional, and national spheres could be brought into harmony. As the bonds constraining behaviour in family, neighbourhood, and village settings were loosened during transitions to the modern era; as state governments developed the institutions of governance (constitutions, state parliaments, taxation, etc.) that set new limits on the autonomy of individuals and communities; as the nation began to exert symbolic power over the allegiances of the common man – as all three processes unfolded simultaneously, the task of reconciling individual rights and the welfare of the larger community at every tier of politics became more complex and impermanent. Such complexity and impermanence were characteristic of political transitions besides those that narrowly concern the expansion of individual rights; but rights were nonetheless central to a host of cultural and political activities we commonly associate with modernization.

Second, most liberals hoped that a culture of rights would provide an opportunity for members of religious and ethnic minorities, underprivileged classes, and, indeed, all citizens to join together in communities characterized by a high degree of solidarity and consensus. Others hoped that by negotiating such a culture of rights, they would bring Germany incrementally closer to what we today call a multicultural society. Liberals and conservatives each set limits to such diversity – limits beyond which their ideal society could no longer be brought into focus. Thus they defended their political ideals up to certain boundaries (for example, defining the limits of Jewish emancipation), beyond which they would not go. Exactly where those boundaries lay needs further investigation and analysis, but local historical research provides a start in this direction.

Third, the establishment of a culture of rights was conceived by many Germans as a means to achieve their personal goals as members of a civil society simultaneously in the realms of culture, education, and self-fulfilment. Most conspicuous in this quest for *Bildung*, but in fact infusing all three aspects, was the feeling that a culture of rights would have to be attained in the cultural and political realms together. Thus liberals sought to become free and responsible citizens, members of stable, prosperous communities, and Germans whose level of *Bildung* set them apart from their neighbours.

At the national level we know a great deal about why these aspirations ended in the disaster of Nazism. We know much less about how struggles to attain a culture of rights unfolded in Germany's federal states, in its cities, and in the villages and rural districts that also made up the whole. Although it is here that historians have experienced particular difficulty in bringing culture and politics together, promising efforts are underway to correct this deficiency.[41] For example, the trope of 'emancipation' illuminates how a culture of rights engaged the attention of Germany's middle classes in many ways, from liberal parliamentarians' formal efforts to enhance the power of parliaments to a variety of public campaigns rooted in the idea of self-help. In this vein Simone Lässig has considered the regional guise of Jewish emancipation, emphasizing the connections between the processes of Jewish emancipation and cultural embourgeoisement on a sub-national scale. The German model of conditional emancipation from above was successful in the small state of Anhalt-Dessau, but it proved problematic in other German lands, including Saxony, where state policies of conditional emancipation perpetuated the notion that Jews were persons of 'lesser rights' (and hence of 'lesser worth'). Whatever rights Jews received in Saxony were up to the discretion of the state, and even those rights were subject to being revoked.[42]

Does this discussion lead us to conclude that national history is passé? No. Few regional historians today would wish to deny the gradual emergence of national consciousness in nineteenth- and early twentieth-century Germany. Nor would they deny that industrializa-

4.2. Schloss Rötha. Baron Heinrich von Friesen-Rötha's estate, located about fifteen kilometres south of Leipzig. From *Der Leipziger. Illustrierte Wochenschrift*, no. 12 (8 Dec. 1906): 10–12, in SächsStA Leipzig, RG Rötha, Nr. 1579. Image courtesy of the Sächsisches Staatsarchiv Leipzig.

tion, urbanization, the rise of mass politics, and the transformation of popular culture left few corners of everyday life untouched – untouched, that is, by trends and patterns whose larger contours are most recognizable at the national level. Nevertheless, the actual relationship between these transitions and the exercise of power 'where it becomes capillary' has been explored so seldom that modern German authoritarianism is still seen principally as a national phenomenon. This is the implication behind Hans-Ulrich Wehler's term 'imperial nationalism' (*Reichsnationalismus*), with its strongly negative connotations. But national feelings did not have to displace traditional attachments to *Heimat*. They actually emerged and drew strength from them. In this sense, recent scholarship postulates no direct opposition between the local and the national.[43] Even in the imperial(ist) era, the political topography of nationalism did not lead ordinary Germans far from home.

Identity-Builders

This discussion brings us back to the terrain on which issues of power and identity intersect with ideas of place. Here we discover that liberals and other identity-builders regularly questioned their subordination to the centre and found ways to outflank it. Thus rather than concentrating on victims, local historical research increasingly depicts enterprising citizens, shapers of public opinion, acclaimed scientific leaders, self-confident entrepreneurs. Historians are also exploring power and its diffusion in society by looking for sites of resistance outside the realms of conventional power and 'between its threads.' As Foucault has written, there is 'no single locus of great Refusal, no soul of revolt, source of all rebellions, or pure law of the revolutionary.'[44] Recent work confirms this view. By carrying the analysis away from central institutions, it suggests that power *and* resistance existed in the strategies of individuals and groups seeking to fashion new identities for themselves. Leipzig's museum-builders and the ethnologists who helped them muster collections of artefacts from around the world after 1880 were bent, in Glenn Penny's telling phrase, on 'doing' or 'being' something remarkable. Circus director Hans Stosch-Sarrasani was determined to take the stage as an 'oriental' emperor, and he pulled it off (more or less). Throughout the nineteenth century, the civic pride of Leipzig's and other municipalities' city fathers was empowering in other ways: it helped to keep at bay residual fears of provincialism and generated support for new financial institutions and cultural displays.

Nevertheless, the opponents of these self-willed individuals must not be allowed to disappear from view. Municipal parliamentarians and state ministers had to react to the insubordination of subaltern groups. City fathers and museum directors were forced to reconfigure multicultural visions under the impact of globalization. And regulators of the entertainment industry were compelled to adapt to changing political moods and aesthetic conventions. Ultimately, of course, the real sparks began to fly when these contending groups rubbed together – when active, enthusiastic, innovative Germans met obsessed, blinkered, clamorous Germans. Both groups were self-aware and self-confident, despite inverted political polarities. One group is not historically more significant than the other. But their mutual attempts to fashion new identities within shared communities cannot be understood unless both groups are examined together.

Whether challengers or defenders of the old order, whether of high moral character or prone to personal calamity, such individuals belong to the historical record because they served as guides to discourses that animated millions of Germans and underpinned authoritarian practices. In surveys of those discourses that have lately captured the imagination of local historians, conflict seems to outweigh consensus, exclusion triumphs over inclusion, and boundaries figure more prominently than bridges in the processes of identity formation. The black and white contrasts found in lowbrow adventure stories do not seem entirely out of place when we read about Germans who wished to escape from bourgeois codes of conduct, who levelled their sights on social groups ready for exploitation, and who sought to tame contrasting cultural and political visions. To be sure, one also discovers in these accounts Germans who tried to 'connect' in more benign ways with the greater world beyond their borders. But more commonly, such Germans were constrained by cultural idioms that flowed with the grain of imperialism, not international brotherhood.

Property owners and museum directors in Leipzig, antisemites and circus directors in Dresden – each of these groups developed an 'us-against-the-world' mentality that *tended* to offer binary choices about where they fitted into Saxon and German society. There was plenty of combativeness to go around. Leipzig's municipal parliamentarians fought among themselves, but they also struggled to liberate themselves from the king's ministers in Dresden. German adventurers competed with the British in Africa and with each other at home. Circus directors entered into cut-throat competition to mount the most impressive exhibitions of foreign exotica and German derring-do, only to discover after 1914 that the supply of talented German performers could not keep pace with the public's demand for ever more violent displays.

This combativeness was reflected in a new coarseness of language – not unlike the coarseness we will encounter in the last three chapters of this book, where one side was likely to label the views of the other side 'pernicious,' 'poisonous,' 'ruinous,' 'demagogic,' or simply 'artificial.' Aggression and blame, negotiation and exoneration: these tropes appear again and again, in smaller cultural worlds as often as in national politics. In local contexts, the lines dividing camps and genres frequently became blurred. It may be true, as Marline Otte has suggested, that circus directors and performers attempted to construct new 'zones without boundaries,' where a democratization of the senses and the levelling of social distinctions could proceed hand in hand. More often than not, however – as when the Saxon king (almost) came into contact with his subjects while attending a Dresden circus performance – our attention is drawn to 'highly charged social spaces' where one side tried to invade the territory of the other.

The long-term repercussions of such negative identity politics should not be overdrawn. There is no reason to see a descent into violence as symptomatic of imperial German political culture. There were other, less-violent dialogues going on at the same time. In fact, these were not really dialogues at all. Nor were they mere rants. Rather, they were conversations – about man, nature, and what it meant to be German. These conversations constituted the look and feel of local protest just as much as did adversarial confrontations. Often they were polite enough to reveal the underlying economic dimensions of local protest that typically remain unheard in political battles. The commercial city of Leipzig had to define its place in the world benignly just to survive; no one could coerce traders, tourists, and students to come to Leipzig against their will. Hence backwardness, insolvency, and unworldliness were simply not options for the city's leading citizens. Similarly, transformations in the production values of local theatre performance were seen as 'monumental'; and indeed they were, driven by new economic realities transcending Saxony's borders. The larger point is that even as Germans fashioned their identities in opposition to a definable 'other,' they did so in ways that cut across and undermined polarized views of the world (and their place in it).

Drawing attention to these cross-cutting themes and practices provides an appropriate end point to this section. Recent findings drawn from the smaller corners of nineteenth-century Germany are unlikely to elicit consensus for long; so rapid is the expansion of new knowledge about power and culture that arguments about their interrelationship can never be timeless, even given the limited geographic scale of illustrative examples cited in this chapter. A more rigorous comparative framework would further illuminate the mental maps of Germans who were trying simultaneously to pursue strategies of self-affirmation and to transcend frontiers of geography, class, and power. Nevertheless, current writing on local and regional history has already mapped a multiplicity of paths, charting historical developments that do not converge at a familiar time *or* space. Given that so much work remains to be done on relatively under-researched regions of Germany and for other periods of history, one can only hope that scholars will continue to search for other signposts: those that pointed contemporary Germans on their way and those that still illustrate the difficulty of moving from the conceptually familiar towards the unknown.

Conclusions

A quarter-century ago James J. Sheehan considered a question that had exercised the Leipzig cultural historian Karl Lamprecht a hundred years earlier: How do we 'bring general and provincial research into contact and reconcile them'? Sheehan substituted the terms 'national' for 'general' and 'local' for 'provincial' in posing the question 'What is German history?' And his tone was more cautious than Lamprecht's. But their conclusions did not diverge as much as the span of years might suggest. After warning against the tendency to read the shape of the future Germany from fragmentary evidence of economic or cultural unity in central Europe before 1866, Sheehan turned to politics specifically.[45] 'Even in the political realm,' he wrote, 'we should be wary of false assumptions about institutional symmetry and cohesion ... After all, a great deal of the political activity that goes on at the national level is designed to simplify issues, to clarify alignments, to reduce politics to a set of binary choices ... But this activity at the center obscures as much as it reflects the political life of the nation, as we all know from our everyday experience. In the worlds of local politics, choices are frequently more fluid, alliances more uncertain, combinations more complex ... It is not that local affairs are somehow more real or basic than national ones, but rather that they are often different.'

This 'differentness' suggests why it remains difficult to conceive of local history as 'total history.'[46] As Lamprecht understood, it is incorrect to eliminate the transition from the particular to the general by positing the identity of the two. Local diversity is not irrelevant or incidental; historians are agreed on that point. But a more interesting point of convergence leads us back to the culture/power/territoriality nexus. This point was raised by a contemporary admirer of Lamprecht who understood that the boldness of Lamprecht's argument surpassed its conclusiveness. Perhaps, in the end, the greatest asset that local and regional historians bring to their craft is the interpretative boldness of their approach, rather than the conclusiveness of their findings. Such boldness functions as a corrective science: it confounds historians who are determined to retain their national, transnational, or global generalizations, particularly if they insist on doing so in the face of details that threaten to invalidate them. Thus local history and regional history convey a sense of the openness and ambiguity of all history. In doing so, each of them provides not the premise of total history but rather its perfect complement.

NOTES

1 As cited in publicity materials for Robert Mayhew, ed., *Historical Cultures and Geography, 1600–1750*, 8 vols. (Bristol, 2003), and, slightly differently, in David Blackbourn, *A Sense of Place: New Directions in German History*, The 1998 Annual Lecture, German Historical Institute, London (London, 1999), 8.
2 Michel Foucault, *Power/Knowledge: Selected Interviews and Other Writings, 1972–1977*, ed. Colin Gordon (New York, 1980), 96.
3 See Nicholas B. Dirks, Geoff Eley, and Sherry B. Ortner, eds., *Culture/Power/History* (Princeton, 1994).
4 See *inter alia* Sigrid Weigel, 'Zum "topographical turn." Kartographie, Topographie und Raumkonzepte in der Kulturwissenschaften,' *Kultur-Poetik* 2, no. 2 (2002): 151–65; Wolfgang Hardtwig, 'Politische Topographie und Nationalismus. Städtegeist, Landespatriotismus und Reichsbewußtsein in München 1871–1914', in Hardtwig, *Nationalismus und Bürgerkultur in Deutschland 1500–1914* (Göttingen, 1994), 219–45; and Thomas Mergel, 'Mapping Milieus Regionally: On the Spatial Rootedness of Collective Identities in the Nineteenth Century,' in *Saxony in German History: Culture, Society, and Politics, 1830–1933*, ed. James Retallack (Ann Arbor, 2000), 77–95.
5 Heiner Treinen, 'Symbolische Ortsbezogenheit. Eine Soziologische Untersuchung zum Heimatproblem,' *Kölner Zeitschrift für Soziologie und Sozialpsychologie* 17 (1965): 73–97, 254–97.
6 Charles Tilly, *Big Structures, Large Processes, Huge Comparisons* (New York, 1984).
7 From Applegate's commentary at the conference 'Memory, Democracy, and the Mediated Nation: Political Cultures and Regional Identities in Germany, 1848–1998,' held at the University of Toronto, 18–20 Sept. 1998. Other points raised in this chapter also derive from Applegate's commentary.
8 On this plurality, see David Blackbourn and James Retallack, eds., *Localism, Landscape, and the Ambiguities of Place: Germany, 1871–1918* (forthcoming).
9 The literature is vast. Among those works I found most useful in writing

this section were Otto Dann, 'Die Region als Gegenstand der Geschichtswissenschaft,' *Archiv für Sozialgeschichte* 23 (1983): 652–61; Carl-Hans Hauptmeyer, ed., *Landesgeschichte heute* (Göttingen, 1987); Friedrich Lenger, 'Urbanisierungs- und Stadtgeschichte – Geschichte der Stadt, Verstädterungsgeschichte oder Geschichte in der Stadt?' *Archiv für Sozialgeschichte* 26 (1986): 429–79; Ernst Hinrichs and Wilhelm Norden, eds., *Regionalgeschichte. Probleme und Beispiele* (Hildesheim, 1980); Gert Zang, *Die unaufhaltsame Annäherung an das Einzelne* (Konstanz, 1985); and Ernst Hinrichs, ed., *Regionalität* (Frankfurt a.M., 1990).

10 The journal *Informationen zur modernen Stadtgeschichte* documents these developments.
11 See, for example, Gert Zang, ed., *Provinzialisierung einer Region* (Frankfurt a.M., 1978).
12 Thomas Kühne, 'Imagined Regions: The Construction of Traditional, Democratic, and Other Identities,' in *Saxony*, ed. Retallack, 51–62, esp. 52.
13 Peter Steinbach, 'Zur Diskussion über den Begriff "Region" – eine Grundsatzfrage der modernen Landesgeschichte,' *Hessisches Jahrbuch für Landesgeschichte* 31 (1981): 185–210, here 208.
14 Ernst Hinrichs, 'Zum gegenwärtigen Standort der Landesgeschichte,' *Niedersächsisches Jahrbuch für Landesgeschichte* 57 (1985): 1–18, here 9.
15 Ibid., 18. See also Hinrichs, 'Regionale Sozialgeschichte als Methode der modernen Geschichtswissenschaft,' in *Regionalgeschichte*, ed. Hinrichs and Norden, 16.
16 Thomas Nipperdey, *Die Organisation der deutschen Parteien vor 1918* (Düsseldorf, 1961).
17 Gerhard A. Ritter, ed., *Die deutschen Parteien vor 1918* (Cologne, 1973), 13, 20.
18 Peter Steinbach, 'Alltagsleben und Landesgeschichte. Zur Kritik an einem neuen Forschungsinteresse,' *Hessisches Jahrbuch für Landesgeschichte* 29 (1979): 304.
19 For the following, see Karlheinz Blaschke, 'Die Landesgeschichte und ihre Probleme in Sachsen,' *Blätter für deutsche Landesgeschichte* 94 (1958): 120–45; Blaschke, 'Die Landesgeschichte in der DDR – ein Rückblick,' *Blätter für deutsche Landesgeschichte* 126 (1990): 243–61; Blaschke, 'Die sächsische Landesgeschichte zwischen Tradition und neuem Anfang,' *Neues Archiv für sächsische Geschichte* 64 (1993): 7–28; Karl Czok, 'DDR-Regionalgeschichte im Zwiespalt zwischen Wissenschaft und Politik,' in ibid., 185–99.
20 Blaschke, 'Landesgeschichte in der DDR,' 250.
21 See Peter Steinbach, 'Territorial- oder Regionalgeschichte: Wege der modernen Landesgeschichte. Ein Vergleich der "Blätter für deutsche

Landesgeschichte" und des "Jahrbuchs für Regionalgeschichte,"' *Geschichte und Gesellschaft* 11 (1985): 528–40.

22 Detailed references in James Retallack, 'Society and Politics in Saxony in the Nineteenth and Twentieth Centuries: Reflections on Recent Research,' *Archiv für Sozialgeschichte* 38 (1998): 396–457.

23 Cited in a retrospective on Berlin's life by William Thorsell, *The Globe and Mail* (Toronto), 15 Nov. 1997; see also Michael Ignatieff, *Isaiah Berlin* (Toronto, 1998).

24 Celia Applegate; see note 7.

25 See Helmut Walser Smith, 'The Boundaries of the Local in Modern German History,' in *Saxony*, ed. Retallack, 63–76.

26 Celia Applegate; see note 7.

27 See Richard J. Evans, *Rituals of Retribution: Capital Punishment in Germany, 1600–1987* (Oxford, 1996), ix.

28 Geoff Eley, 'German History and the Contradictions of Modernity: The Bourgeoisie, the State, and the Mastery of Reform,' in *Society, Culture, and the State in Germany, 1870–1933*, ed. Eley (Ann Arbor, 1996), 67–103, here 87.

29 Peter Steinbach, 'Deutungsmuster der historischen Modernisierungstheorie für die Analyse westeuropäischer Wahlen,' in *Vergleichende europäische Wahlgeschichte*, ed. Otto Büsch and Steinbach (Berlin, 1982), 158–246; Thomas Mergel, 'Geht es weiterhin voran? Die Modernisierungstheorie auf dem Weg zu einer Theorie der Moderne,' in *Geschichte zwischen Kultur und Gesellschaft*, ed. Mergel and Thomas Welskopp (Munich, 1997), 203–32.

30 David Blackbourn refers to the 'martinets of modernity' in *Marpingen: Apparitions of the Virgin Mary in Bismarckian Germany* (Oxford, 1993), 14.

31 Peter Reichel, ed., *Politische Kultur in Westeuropa* (Frankfurt a.M., 1984), 9.

32 Eva Kolinsky and John Gaffney, eds., *Political Culture in France and Germany* (London, 1991), 1–12, here 5–8. See also Hans-Georg Wehling, ed., *Regionale politische Kultur* (Stuttgart, 1985); Siegfried Quandt and Jörg Calließ, eds., *Die Regionalisierung der historisch-politischen Kultur* (Gießen, 1984); Dirk Berg-Schlosser and Jakob Schissler, eds., *Politische Kultur in Deutschland* (Opladen, 1987).

33 See Karl Rohe, 'Regionale (politische) Kultur: Ein sinnvolles Konzept für die Wahl- und Parteienforschung?' in *Parteien und regionale politische Traditionen in der Bundesrepublik Deutschland*, ed. Dieter Oberndörfer and Karl Schmitt (Berlin, 1991), 17–37.

34 See *inter alia* Páll Björnsson, 'Making the New Man: Liberal Politics and Associational Life in Leipzig, 1845–1871' (PhD diss., University of Roches-

ter, 1999), or, for Sweden, Jonas Frykman and Orvar Löfgren, *Culture Builders: A Historical Anthropology of Middle-Class Life*, trans. Alan Crozier (New Brunswick, NJ, 1987).

35 See Karl Heinrich Pohl, 'Liberalismus und Bürgertum 1880–1918,' in *Bürgertum und bürgerlich-liberale Bewegung in Mitteleuropa seit dem 18. Jahrhundert*, ed. Lothar Gall, Historische Zeitschrift, Sonderheft 17 (Munich, 1997), 231–91, esp. 244–51; also Lothar Gall and Dieter Langewiesche, eds., *Liberalismus und Region*, Historische Zeitschrift, Beiheft 19 (Munich, 1995).

36 Cited in Robert Beachy, 'Local Protest and Territorial Reform: Public Debt and Constitutionalism in Early-Nineteenth-Century Saxony,' in *Saxon Signposts*, ed. James Retallack (special issue, *German History* 17, no. 4 [1999]), 471–88, here 471. For the following, see also Glenn Penny, 'Fashioning Local Identities in an Age of Nation-Building: Museums, Cosmopolitan Visions, and Intra-German Competition,' and Marline Otte, 'Sarrasani's Theatre of the World: Monumental Circus Entertainment in Dresden, from Kaiserreich to Third Reich,' ibid., 489–506 and 527–42 respectively.

37 See also chap. 6.

38 For this and following passages, see Foucault, *Power/Knowledge*, 98–9.

39 Ernst von Heydebrand und der Lase was the 'uncrowned king of Prussia.' Paul Mehnert Jr was the 'uncrowned king of Saxony.' This list could be extended to a half-dozen other individuals in Imperial Germany, not all of them on the Right.

40 Manfred Berg and Martin Geyer, eds., *Two Cultures of Rights* (Cambridge, 2002).

41 See Celia Applegate, 'The Mediated Nation: Regions, Readers, and the German Past,' in *Saxony*, ed. Retallack, 33–50.

42 Simone Lässig, 'Emancipation and Embourgeoisement: The Jews, the State, and the Middle Classes in Saxony and Anhalt-Dessau,' in *Saxony*, ed. Retallack, 99–118; see also Lässig's recent prize-winning study, *Jüdische Wege ins Bürgertum. Kulturelles Kapital und sozialer Aufstieg* (Göttingen, 2004); and Till van Rahden, 'Jews and the Ambivalences of Civil Society in Germany, 1800–1933: Assessment and Reassessment,' *Journal of Modern History* 77, no. 4 (Dec. 2005): 1024–47.

43 See three important works that take culture seriously: Celia Applegate, *A Nation of Provincials: The German Idea of Heimat* (Berkeley, 1990); Pieter M. Judson, *Exclusive Revolutionaries: Liberal Politics, Social Experience, and National Identity in the Austrian Empire, 1848–1914* (Ann Arbor, 1996); and

Alon Confino, *The Nation as a Local Metaphor: Württemberg, Imperial Germany, and National Memory, 1871–1918* (Chapel Hill, 1997).
44 Michel Foucault, *History of Sexuality*, vol. 1 (New York, 1978), cited in *Culture*, ed. Dirks et al., 8.
45 James J. Sheehan, 'What Is German History? Reflections on the Role of the *Nation* in German History and Historiography,' *Journal of Modern History* 53 (1981): 1–23, here 21–2.
46 See Roger Chickering, 'Local History as *histoire totale*? Locating Freiburg in Breisgau in the Age of Total War' (unpublished position paper delivered at the conference 'Memory, Democracy, and the Mediated Nation: Political Cultures and Regional Identities in Germany, 1848–1998,' University of Toronto, 18–20 Sept. 1998): 'Far from marginalizing local and regional history, total war demands closer attention to it ... As it has been traditionally, so too in total war, local history is the natural ally of total history' (2). See also Deborah Neill and Lisa M. Todd, 'Local History as Total History: A Symposium Held at the Munk Centre for International Studies, University of Toronto, 25 February 2002,' in *German History* 20, no. 3 (2002): 373–8; and Blackbourn and Retallack, eds., *Localism*.

5 Governmentality in Transition

In world history the 1860s was a decade of political renewal. It was dominated by reformist conservatives who sought to sidestep the revolutionary aspects of political modernization.[1] If we think initially of Bismarck in Prussia and Cavour in Italy, we are soon prompted to consider Napoleon III in France, Disraeli in England, Lincoln in America, John A. Macdonald in Canada, and the oligarchs behind the Meiji Restoration in Japan. Even in the calmer corners of central Europe – in the cantons of Switzerland,[2] in Vienna,[3] in Württemberg[4] – we find transitions to more democratic forms that involved the fundamental realignment of parliamentary suffrages.[5]

In this era, reformist conservatives were remarkably successful in drawing (or redrawing) the boundaries of new nation-states. They revitalized the sources of state legitimation. And they redefined national electorates. Some of them did all three things at the same time, laying the basis of the modern state. As David Blackbourn has pointed out, most of these developments unfolded against a common background of 'growing national sentiment, argument over sovereignty, and civil war.'[6] Yet when we consider how arguments over sovereignty actually unfolded, we discover a striking incongruity. Many reformist conservatives did not stake their new claim to legitimacy on the kinds of polarizing discourses that are typically fuelled by national disputes, wars, and the battle of public interests. Instead they proclaimed the existence of a broad, popular consensus that made political reform irresistible.[7] Often referring to 'the new requirements of the age' or 'the sign of the times,' such arguments stressed reform over any instinct to conserve. This, at least, was the dominant motif in parliamentary debates that preceded suffrage reform in Saxony's *Landtag* (state parliament) in 1868.[8]

This chapter considers how suffrage reform debates illuminate broader cultural responses on the part of states to the challenges of social, economic, and political change. It suggests that suffrage reform in Saxony was not untypical in revealing both positive and negative reactions to such change. Such reactions were conditioned by two interconnected historical developments: the transition from a corporatist society of occupational estates (*Stände*) to one of interests and classes, and the transition of German political culture from one that identified and balanced group rights to one where the rights of individuals, although far from paramount, were given a more positive weight. As we will see, like reformist conservatives elsewhere in the world, Saxon statesmen appreciated the opportunity – not just the threat – inherent in the need to align Saxon political culture with new realities. The final section of the chapter suggests that only comparative and long-term analyses can reveal whether we should evaluate this response in terms of continuity or of discontinuity.[9]

Rationales for Reform

In nineteenth-century Germany, state legitimation on the basis of rights was problematic. German liberals frequently cited individual rights as sacrosanct or transcendent in the construction of a modern civil society. But the liberals' universalizing vision had no place for rights they designated particularist or parochial. On no issue were liberals more vulnerable than on the extension of the suffrage to the common man (let alone woman).[10] Conversely, conservatives opposed individual rights because they undermined the notion of a hierarchical, organic society. When it came to incorporating the concept of individual rights into suffrage legislation, Saxons on both the Left and the Right expressed fears that granting the vote to individuals (as under the Reichstag suffrage) would undermine social peace, group cohesion, and Saxon identity itself.

But if only social groups were to have rights, what made a particular group legitimate in the eyes of the state? Social pre-eminence, education, or property ownership? Annual tax payment? Other service to the state? These questions became acute when legislators and state ministers tried to peg suffrage thresholds at levels that rewarded 'state-supporting' citizens and excluded the 'dangerous classes.' Yet far from dipping their toe into unfamiliar democratic waters with fear and loathing, as historians have generally argued, Saxon state ministers understood that moderate, limited reform offered the best prospects for state legitimation if it was not forced upon them but was freely given.

Only a few lines are required to set up the historical context of Saxony's suffrage reform and to outline the principal revisions implemented in the legislation of 1868. After Saxony was defeated at Austria's side in the German civil war of 1866, it was forced to enter the Prussian-dominated North German Confederation. At that point a new set of government ministers inaugurated what has been called Saxony's only liberal era, which lasted until the mid-1870s.[11] The government leader was Baron Richard von Friesen, who replaced the much-hated Count Friedrich Ferdinand von Beust. With his rather pedantic emphasis on fiscal discipline and administrative propriety, Friesen lacked the flair of his hot-headed predecessor. But he shared the liberals' familiarity with Saxony's dynamic industrial economy. He also sympathized with their preference for undertaking (and thus controlling) constitutional experiments legally and rationally.

The most conspicuous change actually enacted in the Saxon suffrage reform of 1868 was abandonment of representation according to occupational estates (*ständische Vertretung*).[12] Under the old *Landtag* suffrage, the eighty-member lower house was composed of twenty deputies representing large estate owners, twenty-five representing farmers, twenty-five representing town dwellers, and ten representing commercial and industrial circles. The 1868 reform substituted a system whereby forty-five deputies were elected from rural constituencies and thirty-five from urban ones. Saxony's suffrage also became direct, secret, and nearly universal. Apart from relatively minor exclusions, all male citizens over the age of twenty-five who paid at least 1 thaler (3 marks) in state taxes annually were allowed to vote.[13] This threshold corresponded to an annual taxable income of about 600 marks. Whereas it is difficult to gauge the size of the Saxon electorate before 1868, about 245,000 Saxon males (or about 10 per cent of the population) were entitled to vote after the suffrage reform.[14] Yet one in two Reichstag voters in Saxony was still disqualified from *Landtag* voting even after the reform of 1868.[15]

Baron von Friesen's *Landtag* suffrage reform provided the cornerstone for major administrative, judicial, press, and educational reforms in the early 1870s.[16] If we swallowed liberal pronouncements, we might believe that the force of public opinion alone had compelled Friesen to accept these changes. As a liberal member of Saxony's lower house put it: 'The call for reform of our constitution and of our suffrage is no

5.1. Baron Richard von Friesen (1808–84), Saxon government leader after 1866. From Richard Freiherr von Friesen, *Erinnerungen aus meinem Leben*, 3 vols. (Dresden: Wilhelm Baensch, 1880–1910), 3: frontispiece. From the author's collection.

longer a demand voiced merely by one political party in the land. It is voiced by all classes and strata of the people without distinction according to party line. It is rooted in the requirements of the age [*Bedürfnissen der Zeit*], and it has received nourishment and legitimation through the mighty transformation ... of 1866.'[17] Yet Friesen, recognizing that Saxon political culture was still in its formative stage, saw a more vigorous state parliament as an inherent good, as a means to co-opt potential enemies of the state. Such sharing of power was considered acceptable only if state ministers did not become formally responsible to parliament. This point was never in doubt. Nevertheless, in 1870, as the first session elected under the new suffrage neared its close, Friesen acknowledged that a positive new spirit had invigorated the *Landtag*. 'We have drawn nearer to each other,' he told the liberals, 'and a great deal of mistrust has been removed.'[18]

How do we explain Friesen's willingness not only to accommodate but actually to embrace suffrage reform? Guidance is provided by the political scientist Larry Diamond, who has written that 'we observe during democratic consolidation the emergence of an elite political culture featuring moderation, accommodation, restrained partisanship, system loyalty, and trust. These norms enhance the predictability and mitigate the intensity of political conflict.'[19] Friesen had come to ministerial office just in time to assist in the suppression of the Dresden Uprising in May 1849. He had left Beust's cabinet in the 1850s in protest over his more repressive measures. And in September 1866 he witnessed first-hand in Berlin how Bismarck overcame the determined opposition of liberals in Prussia's House of Deputies. Hence Friesen was well aware of the dividends to be reaped by mitigating the intensity of political conflict.

To what extent was suffrage reform premised on new ideas about the relationship between the authoritarian state and civil society? The strategies deployed by Friesen and other reformist conservatives suggest that state and society were no longer seen only as rivals. Rather, social groups and the parties that soon came to represent their interests were considered legitimate participants in modern political life – not in the sense of overseeing or controlling the state, but in cooperating with it and helping to set its agenda. Conversely, suffrage reforms allowed states more explicitly to draw legitimacy and security from such participation. Voting rights were often appraised as a kind of reward for service (*Gegenleistung*) to society or the state, a point elaborated in the next chapter. Eventually, service to the state came to include a new and more abstract sense of national loyalty. But long before ideas of national citizenship became ingrained, the undertaking of novel social and economic tasks by the state was seen to constitute an opportunity for the state to extend its hegemony in untraditional and far-reaching ways.

Antonio Gramsci's distinction between hegemonic and coercive forms of rule helps to explain the willingness of reformist conservatives to eat away at local autonomies and traditional privileges while favouring 'a politically more modern but still hegemonic form of political control.' Gramsci might almost have been describing the Saxon suffrage reform of 1868 when he wrote that 'in the ancient and medieval state alike, centralization, whether political-territorial or social ..., was minimal. The state was, in a certain sense, a mechanical bloc of social groups ... The modern state substitutes for the mechanical bloc of social groups their subordination to the active hegemony of the directive and dominant group, hence abolishes certain autonomies, which nevertheless are reborn in other forms, as parties, trade unions, cultural associations.'[20] New public figures in the age of 'mass' politics appealed to universal interests rather than particular estates, classes, or other sets of persons; in such an age, 'what you say will carry force not because of who you are but despite who you are.'[21]

And yet suffrage reform in Saxony *was* contentious. On the one hand, a remarkable array of suffrage schemes was proposed by democrats, liberals, conservatives, and government bureaucrats before a final compromise was hammered out.[22] These proposals ranged from the prescient to the hare-brained. On the other hand, it is no accident that Baron von Friesen first acknowledged the desirability of suffrage reform at the moment when Saxony's sovereignty was most threatened, in mid-September 1866. Writing from Berlin while awaiting the Prussians' peace proposals, he observed that 'next to a federal parliament elected under universal suffrage, a *Landtag* based on the principle of occupational estates cannot exist.'[23]

Friesen was hardly thinking of dismantling the Saxon *Landtag*. Quite the contrary: he did everything in his power to ensure that Saxony's parliament *not* become redundant. Thus he made sure that the *Landtag* voting scheduled for the autumn of 1866 proceeded according to plan. Why? By demonstrating the continued independence of Saxony's own state parliament, Friesen believed that the Saxon people would see him as the determined defender of Saxon interests just when the Prussian occupation was most onerous and when rumours were flying that Saxony would be annexed outright.[24] However, these elections convinced no one that Saxony's sovereignty remained fully intact. The public registered very little interest in the *Landtag* campaign.

During 1867 Saxon liberals relentlessly drew the contrast between the Reichstag's universal male suffrage and the *Landtag*'s restricted suffrage. This disparity made Saxony's own parliament seem more anachronistic than ever. Karl Biedermann, a former 1848er and leader of the Saxon National Liberals, asked: 'Is not the common weal of the individual state inextricably linked to that of the Confederation? ... Can this larger body tolerate a diseased limb?'[25] For sixteen years since the government's *coup d'état* of 1850, wrote Biedermann, the reactionary *Landtag* in Dresden had condemned Saxon political life to 'deathly silence' (as Beust himself had famously boasted). This silence had not retarded economic modernization, Biedermann conceded; but it had prevented the attainment of civil liberties and religious tolerance: 'When have these reactivated estates[26] ever demonstrated any understanding for timely reform? Where can one find a single law passed [by parliament] that corresponds to the people's legitimate claim for the protection of those rights without which a true and genuine political life is unthinkable? ... Have the old reactivated [assembly of] estates protected freedom of religion? The law of July 1852, which restricted the Jews to Leipzig and Dresden and resurrected the medieval law of 1838, says enough about that. Have the estates protected the rights of the press or recognized the freedoms of expression and assembly? Not in the least!'

In the *Landtag* session of 1866–7, another liberal complained that the 'glaring' discrepancy between the *Landtag* and Reichstag suffrages 'screamed' for immediate redress. One of his colleagues proposed a motion designed to address 'the legitimate wishes of the people for a progressive widening of the threshold for the active and passive suffrage and for a more up-to-date [*zeitgemäßer*] composition of parliament.' And a university professor representing Leipzig declared in the upper house: 'Political wisdom dictates that one not only have a hand on the pulse of the times but also take into account the healthy, moral spirit of the people and seize the initiative accordingly in a timely, honourable fashion.'[27]

Saxon liberals offered innumerable variations on this theme. Writers in the *Constitutionelle Zeitung* and the *Grenzboten* argued that dismantling the upper house of the Saxon *Landtag* would streamline legislation and eliminate 'the bastion of particularism, governmental complacency, and agrarian interests.' The prominent Progressive deputy Hermann Schreck declared in the lower house that the estate-bound suffrage was 'unfit for the requirements of the day.' He therefore called on the government to dissolve the *Landtag*, submit a new suffrage reform package, and seek a bill of indemnity. Such a bill would exactly parallel Bismarck's indemnity bill, which was passed by the Prussian *Landtag* in September 1866. The National Liberal Moritz Heinrich Lorenz ostentatiously resigned his Saxon *Landtag* seat, declaring that he did not recognize the legality of *Landtag* proceedings since 1850. Leipzig's liberal mayor told the upper house that the *Landtag* should confine itself to the passing of the two-year budget and a new suffrage bill. After a dissolution, he added, Saxony 'should be governed *ad interim* according to the constitution of the North German Confederation.' In contrast to National Liberal agitation, petitions sent to the *Landtag* by left liberals and Social Democrats stressed the minimum level of voting rights necessary to transform the *Landtag* into a 'true people's parliament.'[28]

Members of the Saxon Right of course disagreed with both positions. One of them argued that even the most moderate among the liberals' motions for reform was 'not as harmless as it appears.' What exactly is 'up-to-date'? asked this speaker, and what are the 'legitimate wishes' of the Saxon people? Another right-wing parliamentarian opposed plans to 'adapt' Saxony's suffrage to the North German Confederation, predicting that individual *Landtage* would soon be reduced to 'mere provincial parliaments.' These provincial parliaments, rather than concerning themselves with great national issues, should focus their attention on 'questions of practical importance.' Because 'practical businessmen' were best suited to such debates, this speaker added, universal suffrage was wholly unsuitable for Saxony.[29]

In the course of 1867, Saxon liberals became even further convinced that *Landtag* suffrage reform was the *sine qua non* for further reforms in state and society. An article published in the *Preußische Jahrbücher* in mid-1867, which may well have been written by Heinrich von Treitschke, hammered home the point: 'Freely elected representatives of the people will prevail not only over the sort of cranky particularism that so contemptuously abuses the name of patriotism, but also over the spirit of serfdom and servility that suffuses almost the entire civil service in Saxony and has even found its way into the circle of burghers who appear outwardly independent.' Indulging in the rhetorical excess that was so characteristic of Treitschke, this writer continued: 'Individuals and parties must ... demonstrate manly courage and resolution, they must unlearn the vacillation and seesawing, the glances to left and right, the fear of unfriendly looks from above and of unpopularity from below.' Increasing the register of his complaint, this writer doubted whether Saxons possessed either the national conviction or the manly courage to understand the mood of the times: 'Into their soft, pliant, submissive Saxon natures they must bring some steel ... If this regenerative process is completed, then Saxony will be one of the brightest pearls in the crown of our great German Fatherland. May God grant it!'[30]

Did these debates influence Friesen and his ministerial colleagues when they met in the autumn of 1867 to draw up the reform bill? Without doubt. At this time a pro-reform petition campaign was set in motion by groups stretching from Social Democrats on the extreme Left to National Liberals in the middle.[31] We must not overestimate the cohesion of this campaign or its immediate impact.[32] Yet Joseph Crowe, the British consul in Leipzig, was impressed enough to predict that 'this Saxon agitation is the prelude to change throughout the whole of Germany.' In following up this observation, Crowe noted that the National Liberals had already convinced many Germans about the compelling need for a more thoroughly integrated system of political representation in the new Germany. 'Nothing can be more clear,' he wrote, 'than that the tendency of German thought at this time is to admit the superiority of the one-chamber over the two-chamber system.' (By a two-chamber system, he meant a national Reichstag and independent *Landtage*, not upper and lower chambers.) 'A powerful party in Germany,' Crowe continued, 'favours the absorption of all legislative power into this body [the Reichstag] by gradually degrading the old chambers to the rank of provincial assemblies. The first step in this direction would be the assimilation of the electoral laws in Kingdoms and principalities to that of the federation; and the German press sounds the key note of agitation when it points out the anomaly of universal suffrage and a single parliament being enforced for the whole whilst restricted franchise and dual chambers govern the parts.'[33]

Saxony's interior minister, Hermann von Nostitz-Wallwitz, also felt it was important to see Saxony's reform in a federal context.[34] Nostitz-Wallwitz insisted that the North German Confederation's new constitution had no *direct* implications for the individual states. He also refuted the charge that the Saxon *Landtag* represented only privileged estates. The current *Landtag*, he declared, was already more representative than the English House of Commons and much more so than the Belgian parliament, with its tax threshold of approximately 11 thaler (33 marks).[35] Nostitz-Wallwitz also observed that most other German electoral laws included tax thresholds, residency requirements, or three-class voting, as in Prussia. Yet he conceded the confederation's *indirect* impact. Here he used an analogy that was common currency in German political debate at this time. 'When a number of people live together in a large house,' Nostitz-Wallwitz told the *Landtag*, 'certainly each one has the right to furnish his own room according to his tastes. But in doing so he will have to take into account certain structural features of the building, and if he is to live in peace with his fellow lodgers, he cannot prevent their customs and habits from influencing his own. I believe that in many respects we find ourselves in a similar relationship to the federal constitution.'

The preamble (*Motive*) to the government's suffrage bill rehearsed Nostitz-Wallwitz's remarks. The Reichstag and individual *Landtage*, it stated, necessarily 'influenced and complemented' each other. Therefore it was advisable that the two parliaments not differ greatly in their composition.[36] However – and this was the government's more important point – each tier of government required its own suffrage. The distance between national and local affairs was so great, the preamble argued, that the universal suffrage could not be extended either to *Landtag* or to local elections: 'The more universal in nature interests represented in the Reichstag have become, ... the wider it has been possible to set the limits of voting rights for Reichstag elections. By contrast, the main tasks of the *Landtag*e in individual federal states will continue to lie in the conscientious overseeing of the state budget and the prudent improvement of existing society and its institutions. Therefore the prerequisites for attaining the right to vote will be different ... Although no classes of the population are to be excluded from voting, only those persons can be included whose status as burghers [*bürgerliche Verhältnisse*] allows one to assume that they demonstrate the necessary concern for the tasks at hand.'

From Nostitz-Wallwitz's remarks in parliament and from this preamble, it is not difficult to discern the Saxon government's reasoning: Although social and economic modernization called for new tasks at each level of government, the 'new requirements of the age' could be given a positive spin to favour a particular set of reforms. Those reforms might modernize German legislatures at all three tiers of government, but they could not be allowed to subordinate state legislatures or sovereign territorial units to a single vision of democracy – least of all one based on natural rights.

A Balance Sheet

How do we draw up a balance sheet of the ways in which the 1868 suffrage bill reflected traditional and newer conceptions of civil society? We might begin with the Saxon government's most conspicuous break with the past: its endorsement of direct, rather than indirect, voting. There was 'no doubt,' the government's preamble stated, that direct voting 'expresses the will of the voters more completely and with less falsification' than indirect voting. Here the Saxon government shared Bismarck's conviction that liberals profited more than conservatives from indirect voting under the Prussian three-class system. Thus Baron von Friesen and his cabinet colleagues may have hoped to eliminate the liberals' successful mobilization ('falsification') of public opinion through their emerging network of constituency-level associations. Nevertheless, on balance the Saxon government appears to have been more confident than Bismarck that conservatives would profit from the deployment of local influence at election time. Second, the proposed bill broke with the traditional requirement that candidates must run in their home constituency – long a target of liberal attacks.[37] Third, each chamber of the *Landtag* was now empowered to examine the propriety of its own members' election; each could respond as it saw fit to charges of electoral chicanery. Fourth, the grounds on which voters or candidates could be excluded from participating in elections were narrowed. Taken together, these provisions represented a real break with the past.

When we consider the less-progressive features of the government's bill, we need to distinguish between obvious efforts to hold back the tide of democracy and other, more ambiguous measures that cannot be so neatly categorized. Prominent among the former would be provisions for grouping together urban constituencies that were not contiguous. If one looks at a contemporary map of Saxon *Landtag* constituencies, one sees immediately that as many as fifteen towns were deemed to constitute a single urban riding. Floating like islands in the larger sea of rural constituencies, these towns proved to be especially susceptible to conservative influence – precisely as the bill's drafters intended. The relatively underdeveloped network of local liberal associations was inadequate to organize a coherent campaign involving communication and travel across vast distances. The Saxon administration, by contrast, relying on police, local councils, pastors, foresters, and railway officials, could distribute propaganda and ballots in these far-flung locales.[38] Such materials were unlikely to advocate the election of liberal deputies.

The same conserving tendency is evident in the bill's preservation of the so-called rolling renewal of the *Landtag*. Under this system, one-third of *Landtag* seats were contested every two years (formerly three). The lack of general elections, plus the fact that the constituencies contested in any given year were scattered throughout the land, was designed to dampen the enthusiasm of both voters and their elected representatives. And it did just that. In any given year, no political issue, however contentious, could produce a landslide or change the whole complexion of the house. Moreover, the Saxon government foresaw that at least two-thirds of every *Landtag* would be composed of incumbents. This continuity would smooth the business of legislation and ensure the 'cautious consideration' of new bills. Why would any government *not* wish to preserve this congenial situation?

Among the more ambiguous features of the government's bill was the elimination of formal representation according to occupational estates. Even Friesen's conservative colleagues in the Saxon state ministry recognized the fruitlessness of holding to the outworn idea of an estate-bound (*ständisch*) suffrage.[39] Yet one historian has suggested that the goal of preserving a society of estates was abandoned not in 1868 but much earlier, in the Saxon suffrage law of 1831. That earlier reform, together with other far-reaching policy changes implemented in the 1830s, had recognized (and accelerated) the disintegration of estate-bound society.[40] This interpretation is correct. Even the government's preamble had conceded that a minor suffrage reform in 1861, which increased the number of industrial and commercial representatives from five to ten, demonstrated that the lower house already represented *interests*, not social estates. Tellingly, Prussian bureaucrats had discovered, while drafting their own suffrage reform in 1849, that it was impossible to 'draw up appropriate categories to designate corporative or occupational groups as the basis for elections according to occupational or corporative "interests."' As one constitutional expert wrote, 'the distinction between urban and rural constituencies was no longer conceived as representation according to estates or interests, but rather as a practical stipulation corresponding to the actual proclivities of the people.'[41]

Even the British chargé d'affaires in Dresden saw things in a similar light. One might argue that this diplomat was not attuned to the fine distinctions German constitutional theorists drew among 'estates,' 'interests,' and 'classes.' Hence he may not fully have understood what the Saxons were up to. Nonetheless, the British chargé felt strongly that 'the fundamental principle that every class interest shall be represented has in all material points been adhered to.' Thus he reported to the Foreign Office in London that the changes inaugurated by Saxony's suffrage reform were 'not numerous.'[42]

Democratization and System Stabilization

The most intriguing aspect of Saxony's suffrage debate in the 1860s hinged on the question of a tax threshold. At what level did contemporary Germans believe such a threshold should be pegged to ensure that the 'dangerous classes' would not be enfranchised? This and similar questions can be addressed comparatively.

One way to do so is to study the *process* whereby bureaucrats and legislators amended initial proposals and came up with often quite different interpretations of 'safe' thresholds. We know that the Saxon government's proposal in 1867 envisaged a tax threshold of 2 thaler. This was reduced to 1 thaler by the Conservatives, who feared that artisans and small farmers paying between 1 and 2 thaler would vote for the liberals. The parallel thinking undertaken by Bismarck, Disraeli, and other conservatives cries out for detailed analysis. So do the political calculations made by middle-level bureaucrats who actually drafted their reform bills. More than one member of Disraeli's cabinet spent 'a miserable arithmetical Sunday,' as Asa Briggs once put it, 'making precise calculations of what the government's proposals implied.'[43] But we should not forget that the best-laid plans of legislators elsewhere in the world have been confounded by faulty statistical forecasts provided by their advisers.

We should also consider the *context* of other suffrage stipulations that allowed tax thresholds to be pegged very low. Many of these stipulations offset the universal or near-universal nature of new suffrages. They did so by ensuring that certain social groups would enjoy privileges through extra votes, parallel chambers, nomination rights, and other entitlements. The redrawing of electoral boundaries, the publication of parliamentary debates, per diem allowances for deputies, the length of parliamentary periods, plans for future tax reform – these were practical issues that reformers invariably considered in conjunction with tax thresholds. One can argue, for example, that Disraeli in Britain and Friesen in Germany abandoned urban constituencies to the liberals in 1867 only because other features of their reforms tightened the conservatives' hold on rural seats.

Lastly, the *cultural* significance of tax thresholds can be gauged by considering the determination of reformist conservatives to 'measure up' as modern statesmen in the constitutional era. In 1867 Friesen shared with Saxon liberals a determination to devise a suffrage law that would stand up to international yardsticks of fairness and at the same time erase the lingering embarrassment of backwardness and pliability from the Beust era. Those yardsticks were always calibrated according to particular traditions. As we have seen, the issue of states' rights within a federal system was a pressing one for German reformers in 1867 – far more pressing than in Britain or Japan. Nevertheless, Germans grew more practised at drawing national and international comparisons as time went by. After 1900 Saxon ministers commissioned dozens of studies of suffrage reforms passed in neighbouring lands. Far from remaining behind closed doors, these comparisons invigorated public debate about electoral fairness. In late 1905, not long after the tsar handed down his October Manifesto in Russia, Saxon Social Democrats demonstrating in favour of suffrage reform at home declared ominously that they had learned to 'speak Russian.' Everyone knew exactly what they meant.

To turn the coin over, how did foreign observers report back to their superiors on reforms undertaken in German lands? Here it is surely important to know that Disraeli's Second Reform Act of 1867 had already passed the House of Commons when the British chargé d'affaires in Dresden reported to London that 'the qualifications of a vote [in Saxony] are made it appears to me as low as are consistent with safety, the line of one Thaler or 3 Shillings of taxation bringing it down almost to the Proletariat class.'[44] In October 1869 the chargé held much the same opinion: 'the Suffrage qualification has been put as low as it possibly can be without calling in the actual proletariat class.' This assessment was about right. Although Conservative diehards complained that the 1-thaler threshold would throw parliament into the arms of the 'communists,' Nostitz-Wallwitz claimed on behalf of the government that this threshold would give 'any worker who distinguishes himself through talent, intelligence, and hard work the opportunity to attain the vote.' Such a prospect, he added, would 'also enliven the interest of the well-off classes of the population in the elections.'[45]

One last example may suggest why far-flung comparisons need not be far-fetched. It is unlikely that Berlin was the only European capital visited – or Rudolf von Gneist, Hermann Roesler, and Lorenz von Stein the only constitutional experts consulted – when the Meiji reformers

5.2. The Saxon *Landtag* am Schlossplatz, Dresden. From *Dresdens Entwicklung in den Jahren 1903 bis 1909* (Dresden: Dr. Güntzsche Stiftung, 1910), facing 22.

sent a fact-finding mission abroad preparatory to drafting Japan's constitution of 1889. If members of that mission had learned to 'speak Saxon' before returning to Tokyo, would they still have set the tax threshold for Japan's legislature at 15 yen?[46] We cannot know. Saxon legislators who passed the watershed suffrage reform of 1868 emphasized practicality over theory at every turn. They seldom referred to Stein or any other expert. However, as Colin Gordon has written, elements of Stein's teachings have a relevance that extends beyond the German context. Stein was impatient for German administrators to move away from the 'archaic' and 'fragmented' polity of corporatist society towards what he called a 'social state' (but what in essence was a society of classes). We should not locate his class society unequivocally at the end point of the telos of modernization. Just as the taming of accidents of birth by formal democratization does not introduce 'modern' ideas of fairness, so the taming of regional particularities by a national parliament does not introduce 'modern' ideas of loyalty to a larger, more powerful ideal.

Nevertheless, as Ian Hacking has suggested, there is a connection between the 'taming of chance by statistics' and the introduction of 'a new liberty' in the life of a nation. Although the cause-and-effect relationship is not direct, discussions about where suffrage thresholds should be placed to ensure the continuity and safety of the modern state have a direct impact on the way citizens conceive of a given polity and act within the constraints it imposes upon their political behaviour. Hacking put it this way: 'The bureaucracy of statistics imposes not just by creating administrative rulings but by determining classifications within which people must think of themselves and of the actions that are open to them.'[47] The vision that German reformers took from Stein was a powerful one: as Colin Gordon has noted, it was 'the vision of a liberal state as active historic partner in the making of civil society; an exacting appraisal of the inner consistency of the social fabric; and, perhaps most strikingly, a tabling of the question of class formation as part of the state's agenda – a condition, one might add, of the state's security.'[48]

Conclusions

Saxony's suffrage debate in the late 1860s alerts us to the danger of accepting at face value either unsubstantiated historical claims about the force of public opinion upon lawmakers or undifferentiated contemporary arguments about an irresistible *Zeitgeist* in favour of democracy. It is less important to paint the Saxon suffrage reform of 1868 as either modern or unmodern than to consider in specific ways how it contributed to the transformation of electoral and political cultures and, in the context of this book, how those changing cultures induced Germans to rethink the goals of authoritarian governance.

In the 1860s, hierarchical society based on occupational estates was not only disintegrating in Germany; it was *seen* to be disintegrating. But socio-moral milieux based on solid class allegiances or confessional conflicts had not yet come into focus. The extraordinary degree of flux in the German party system generally, and its electoral culture specifically, determined the nature of suffrage reforms – those only contemplated and those actually implemented. Whereas the inadequacy of traditional or 'natural' arguments in favour of estate-bound suffrages was evident to contemporaries, compelling alternatives were elusive. Hence a simpler electoral law was conceived on the basis of 'rewarding' those who provided wealth or service to the state.

Even this partial solution was only one step on Saxony's odyssey towards democracy. The term 'odyssey' connotes a grand and epoch-making journey into uncharted territory. Yet as Friesen, Bismarck, and other reformist conservatives stated explicitly, it is better to make revolutions than to suffer them. For modernizing states in the 1860s, statistics and other electoral calculations provided illumination when constitutional leaps in the dark were unavoidable.

This chapter has also tried to demonstrate the value of making explicit comparisons among states whose leaders were rethinking durable assumptions about the bases of state legitimacy. Suffrage reform in the Kingdom of Württemberg was enacted at exactly the same time and broadly with the same result as Saxony's reform. Württemberg's reform provides a final example of how German statesmen in this era sought to accommodate political change in the interest of system stabilization. Its interior minister, Ernst von Geßler, recognized that a modern state could no longer be based on the support of traditional (agrarian) elites alone. Like Baron von Friesen in Saxony, this conservative reformer was not going to sacrifice Württemberg's vital interests on the altar of nationalism or liberalism. Yet Geßler was convinced that any struggle against the forces of change could never repeat the victory of 1848/9; therefore the modern state should never attempt one. Instead, timely suffrage reform should be conceived as the means to sidestep such a crisis.

Geßler elaborated his strategy to reach this goal in a memorandum that had previously made reference to universal suffrage at Frankfurt in 1849, in the Reichstag after 1867, and in the Second French Empire. He wrote: 'In consideration of these factors, I believe it is more prudent to initiate the step required by the logic of circumstances quickly and comprehensively at the outset, rather than to let it be wrung from us by stages in a struggle that the government will have to undertake not on its own behalf but for particular classes of citizens who have long enjoyed special privileges – a struggle, moreover, in which the government might well be abandoned by these classes at the decisive moment and would therefore have to take the entire weight of battle upon its own shoulders.' In a strikingly similar argument and at virtually the same time, Friesen observed that Saxon Conservatives lacked both the energy and the necessary organization to provide the government with the support it required. Hence he was prepared, with liberal support, to embark on a course of prudent reform as long as it promised broader and more durable support for the authoritarian state.[49]

Lastly, the preceding argument has suggested that when we peel back the rhetoric of class harmony, constitutional propriety, and administrative non-partisanship, we often find disturbing evidence of pedantry, prejudice, and the abuse of power. Such abuse is rarely mentioned in historical accounts of how states modernized by accepting the progressive expansion of voting rights. One of the foremost authorities on the subject, Karlheinz Blaschke, has suggested that of Saxony's three major suffrage reforms, enacted in 1868, 1896, and 1909, it was unequivocally the first that pulled the Saxon *Landtag* into the modern era. According to Blaschke, after 1868 Saxony's lower house became the 'locus of real political opinion-formation and political decision-making by a plurality of groups in constant touch with public opinion.'[50]

This rosy appraisal is difficult to accept. The Social Democratic leader August Bebel came closer to the truth when he described the Saxon *Landtag* during the 1880s very differently. For Bebel, Saxony's parliamentary culture twenty years after the suffrage reform of 1868 was no more modern, no more representative, no more tolerant of public opinion. Quite the contrary: 'A very considerable proportion of the [Saxon] chamber,' he wrote, 'was made up of rural deputies whose political horizons were as narrow as the boundaries of their own constituency. [These were] people who had only the most laughable conceptions of what we Social Democrats actually wanted. Along with them went a number of small-town mayors who lived in a parochial middle-class [*spießbürgerlich*] milieu and thought the same way. The remaining deputies were made up of some government officials, a few industrialists, and a large contingent of lawyers. With only a few exceptions, the deputies were Saxon particularists of the narrowest sort, whereby the so-called Progressives could hardly be distinguished from the Conservatives. There wasn't a single day when it was a pleasure to sit in such a chamber.'[51]

It is not necessary to choose categorically between the positive and negative appraisals offered here by Blaschke and Bebel. More important is that we develop a nuanced, contingent understanding of what reformist conservatives were actually trying to achieve when they sought to enhance the governmentality of their societies. In exploring the contentious nature of electoral rights, this chapter has attempted to recapture the ambivalence, but also the variety and boldness, of their reform proposals. Liberals and reformist conservatives each developed compelling strategies for political renewal. In the process they also found a common purpose: to accommodate the rapid emergence of a modern capitalist economy and to mitigate the social upheaval that it engendered, always in the interest of system stabilization. The middle ground upon which liberals and reformist conservatives met was often narrow and shifting. But it should not be ignored or folded into a story that portrays political modernization as a uniform, unstoppable juggernaut that destroys all sub-national allegiances in its path. Both groups of reformers developed original ideas that were diverse and complex. And both groups may have been more in tune with the spirit of the times than scholars admit. If this is so, then Germany's regional political cultures in this watershed era surely remain a worthy focus for comparative research in the future.

NOTES

1 Works pointing to this historical moment include David Blackbourn, *The Fontana History of Germany, 1780–1918: The Long Nineteenth Century* (London, 1997), 244; Theodore S. Hamerow, 'The Origins of Mass Politics in Germany 1866–1867,' in *Deutschland in der Weltpolitik des 19. und 20. Jahrhunderts*, ed. Imanuel Geiss et al. (Düsseldorf, 1973), 105–20, esp. 105; and Geoff Eley, 'Liberalismus 1860–1914. Deutschland und Großbritannien im Vergleich,' in *Liberalismus im 19. Jahrhundert*, ed. Dieter Langewiesche (Göttingen, 1988), 260–76. One of the most insightful recent contributions

is Andreas Biefang, 'Modernität wider Willen. Bemerkungen zur Entstehung des demokratischen Wahlrechts des Kaiserreichs,' in *Gestaltungskraft des Politischen. Festschrift für Eberhard Kolb*, ed. Wolfram Pyta and Ludwig Richter (Berlin, 1998), 239–59; see also Biefang, *'Der Reichsgründer'? Bismarck, die Nationale Verfassungsbewegung und die Entstehung des Deutschen Kaiserreichs*, Friedrichsrüher Beiträge, 7 (Friedrichsruh, 1999).

2 See the definitive study by Erich Gruner, *Die Wahlen in den schweizerischen Nationalrat 1849–1919*, 3 vols. in 4 (Bern, 1968).

3 See Pieter M. Judson, *Exclusive Revolutionaries: Liberal Politics, Social Experience, and National Identity in the Austrian Empire, 1848–1914* (Ann Arbor, 1997), 81–3; Maren Seliger and Karl Ucakar, *Wahlrecht und Wählerverhalten in Wien 1848–1932* (Vienna and Munich, 1984); John Boyer, *Political Radicalism in Late Imperial Vienna* (Chicago, 1981), esp. 273ff.

4 See Rosemarie Menzinger, *Verfassungsrevision und Demokratisierungsprozeß im Königreich Württemberg* (Stuttgart, 1969); Hartwig Brandt, *Parlamentarismus in Württemberg 1819–1870* (Düsseldorf, 1987), 162ff., on the 1868 suffrage reform.

5 Besides Biefang, 'Modernität,' see Markus Mattmüller, 'Die Durchsetzung des allgemeinen Wahlrechts als gesamteuropäischer Vorgang,' in *Geschichte und politische Wissenschaft*, ed. Beate Junker, Peter Gilg, and Richard Reich (Bern, 1975), 213–36; and Jürgen Kohl, 'Zur langfristigen Entwicklung der politischen Partizipation in Westeuropa,' in *Vergleichende europäische Wahlgeschichte*, ed. Otto Büsch and Peter Steinbach (Berlin, 1983), 377–411. On the extreme flux in the German party system following 1866, see Klaus-Erich Pollmann, 'Parlamentseinfluß während der Nationalstaatsbildung 1867–1871,' in *Regierung, Bürokratie und Parlament in Preußen und Deutschland von 1848 bis zur Gegenwart*, ed. Gerhard A. Ritter (Düsseldorf, 1983), 56–75; and Margaret Lavinia Anderson, 'Voter, Junker, *Landrat*, Priest: The Old Authorities and the New Franchise in Imperial Germany,' *American Historical Review* 98 (1993): 1448–74.

6 Blackbourn, *Fontana History of Germany*, 244.

7 Cf. Niels-Uwe Tödter, 'Die deutschen parlamentarischen Klassenwahlrechte im 19. und 20. Jahrhundert' (Jur. Diss., University of Hamburg, 1967), esp. 67–86 and 94–119.

8 See Simone Lässig, 'Wahlrechtsreformen in den deutschen Einzelstaaten. Indikatoren für Modernisierungstendenzen und Reformfähigkeit im Kaiserreich?' in *Modernisierung und Region im wilhelminischen Deutschland. Wahlen, Wahlrecht und Politische Kultur*, ed. Lässig, Karl Heinrich Pohl, and

James Retallack, 2nd rev. ed. (Bielefeld, 1998), 127–69; Gerhard Schmidt, 'Der sächsische Landtag 1833–1918. Sein Wahlrecht und seine soziale Zusammensetzung,' in *Beiträge zur Archivwissenschaft und Geschichtsforschung*, ed. Reiner Groß and Manfred Kobuch (Weimar, 1977), 445–65; Wolfgang Schröder, 'Wahlrecht und Wahlen im Königreich Sachsen 1866–1896,' in *Wahlen und Wahlkämpfe in Deutschland*, ed. Gerhard A. Ritter (Düsseldorf, 1997), 79–130; and Schröder, 'Sozialdemokratie und Wahlen im Königreich Sachsen 1867–1877,' *Beiträge zur Geschichte der Arbeiterbewegung* 36, no. 4 (1994): 3–18; James Retallack, '"Why Can't a Saxon Be More Like a Prussian?" Regional Identities and the Birth of Modern Political Culture in Germany, 1866–67,' *Canadian Journal of History* 32 (1997): 26–55.

9 See Elfi Bendikat, *Wahlkämpfe in Europa 1884 bis 1889* (Wiesbaden, 1988); Brett Fairbairn, *Democracy in the Undemocratic State* (Toronto, 1997); Stanley Suval, *Electoral Politics in Wilhelmine Germany* (Chapel Hill, NC, 1985); Thomas Kühne, 'Wahlrecht – Wahlverhalten – Wahlkultur. Tradition und Innovation in der historischen Wahlforschung,' *Archiv für Sozialgeschichte* 33 (1993): 481–547; Karl Rohe, *Wahlen und Wählertraditionen in Deutschland* (Frankfurt a.M., 1992); and Peter Steinbach, *Die Zähmung des politischen Massenmarktes*, 3 vols. (Passau, 1990).

10 For a contemporary view, see Friedrich von Raumer, *Über die geschichtliche Entwicklung der Begriffe von Recht, Staat und Politik*, 3rd ed. (Leipzig, 1861; rpt. Aalen, 1971), 306–7. See also Thomas Bridges, *The Culture of Citizenship: Inventing Postmodern Civic Culture* (Albany, 1994), esp. 5–15; and Caroline Daley and Melanie Nolan, eds., *Suffrage and Beyond: International Feminist Perspectives* (New York, 1994). Still useful is Jacques Droz, 'Liberale Anschauungen zur Wahlrechtsfrage und das preußische Dreiklassenwahlrecht,' in *Moderne deutsche Verfassungsgeschichte (1815–1918)*, ed. Ernst-Wolfgang Böckenförde (Cologne, 1972), 195–214.

11 For background, see Retallack, '"Why Can't a Saxon"'; Retallack, '"Something Magical in the Name of Prussia ..." British Perceptions of German Nation Building in the 1860s,' in *Germany's Two Unifications: Anticipations, Experiences, Responses*, ed. Ronald Speirs and John Breuilly (Basingstoke, 2005), 139–54; and chapters by Andreas Neemann, Siegfried Weichlein, and Wolfgang Schröder in *Saxony in German History: Culture, Society, and Politics, 1830–1930*, ed. James Retallack (Ann Arbor, 2000).

12 E. Otto Schimmel, *Die Entwicklung des Wahlrechts zur sächsischen Zweiten Kammer* (Nossen, 1912), 79–87.

13 That is, unless they were disqualified by active military service, withdrawal of citizen rights through a court sentence, residency of less than three years (a major exclusion), indebtedness, bankruptcy, or receipt of poor relief.

14 This figure of 10 per cent corresponds almost exactly to the proportion of Saxons entitled to vote for the Frankfurt parliament in 1848.
15 In 1871 about 18.5 percent of Saxony's total population was enfranchised for Reichstag elections. The *Landtag* electorate, as a result of rising wages, tax reform, and inflation, roughly doubled between 1869 and the mid-1890s, when it stood at about 500,000. The increase in the size of the Reichstag electorate was more modest: roughly 744,000 Saxons were enfranchised in 1893.
16 Richard Dietrich, 'Die Verwaltungsreform in Sachsen 1869–1873,' *Neues Archiv für sächsische Geschichte* 61 (1940): 49–85.
17 *Landtags-Mitteilungen* (hereafter cited as *LT-Mitt.*), 1866–8, II. Kammer, Bd. 3: 2636, Heinrich Theodor Koch, 23 Mar. 1868.
18 *Constitutionalle Zeitung*, 3 Mar. 1870; *Leipziger Zeitung*, 25 Feb. 1870; *Deutsche Allgemeine Zeitung*, 24 Feb. 1870; all cited in Albert Richter, 'Die öffentliche Meinung in Sachsen vom Friedensschlüsse 1866 bis zur Reichsgründung' (PhD diss., University of Leipzig, n.d. [1922]), 137.
19 Cited in Fairbairn, *Democracy*, 28.
20 Cited in Geoff Eley, 'Nations, Publics, and Political Cultures: Placing Habermas in the Nineteenth Century,' in *Habermas and the Public Sphere*, ed. Craig Calhoun (Cambridge, Mass., 1992), 289–339, here 324.
21 Michael Warner, 'The Mass Public and the Mass Subject,' ibid., 377–401.
22 See *inter alia* Wilhelm August Gersdorf, *Einige Sätze in Betreff eines neuen Wahlgesetzes für das Königreich Sachsen* (Crimmitschau, 1867).
23 Letter of 15 Sept. 1866, in Richard von Friesen, *Erinnerungen aus meinem Leben*, 3 vols. (Dresden, 1880–1910), 2:288.
24 See Richard Dietrich, 'Preußen als Besatzungsmacht im Königreich Sachsen 1866–1868,' *Jahrbuch für die Geschichte Mittel- und Ostdeutschlands* 5 (1956): 273–93; also Retallack, '"Why Can't a Saxon?"'
25 [Karl Biedermann], *Die reactivirten Stände und das verfassungsmäßige Wahlgesetz in Sachsen* (Leipzig, 1866), 12; see also Karl Biedermann, *Die Wiedereinberufung der alten Stände in Sachsen* (Leipzig, 1850).
26 By which Biedermann meant Saxony's state parliament, elected according to social estates (*Stände*).
27 *LT-Mitt.*, 1866–8, I. Kammer, Bd. 1: 96–8, debates of 6 Dec. 1866.
28 SächsHStA Dresden, Gesammt-Ministerium, Loc. 63, Nr. 4, Bl. 266, Resolution of 1 Nov. 1867.
29 *LT-Mitt.*, 1866–8, I. Kammer, Bd. 1: 27–35 and 81–101 (esp. 81–8), 4 and 20 Dec. 1866.
30 Anon., 'Zur Charakteristik des öffentlichen Geistes in Sachsen,' *Preußische Jahrbücher* 20, no. 2 (1867): 195–215.
31 SächsHStA Dresden, Gesammt-Ministerium, Loc. 63, Nr. 4, Bl. 269

(*Landtags-Akten*, 1866–8, Abt. 1, Bd. 3: 155ff., No. 77, Decret an die Stände ... 19 Nov. 1867, esp. 'Motive,' 170–82); SächsHStA Dresden, Ständeversammlung, Nr. 5948, Bl. 22–40v.
32 See the police report in SächsHStA Dresden, Ministerium des Innern (hereafter cited as MdI), Nr. 11039, Bl. 169.
33 PRO Kew, FO 68, Nr. 147, General no. 10, Joseph Crowe, Leipzig, to FO, 2 Dec. 1867. At this time Crowe enjoyed close relations with Leipzig's most prominent National Liberals. See also Bayrisches Hauptstaatsarchiv (hereafter cited as BayrHStA) Munich, Abt. II, MA III, Nr. 2841, reports no. 101 and 105, 3 and 8 Nov. 1867.
34 Here I draw on Nostitz-Wallwitz's arguments during debates a year earlier – before Disraeli's Second Reform Act had passed: *LT-Mitt.*, 1866–67, II. Kammer, 110–11, 6 Dec. 1866.
35 The Belgian constitution of 1831 was regularly cited as exemplary by nineteenth-century German liberals.
36 To those liberals who advocated abolishing Saxony's upper house, the government responded that a two-chamber system gave Saxony's 'national [*vaterländischen*] institutions the character of an independent state organism' ('Motive,' 172–5).
37 This was the so-called *Bezirkszwang*.
38 Schröder, 'Wahlrecht,' 94–102; compare Judson, *Exclusive Revolutionaries*, 88.
39 See the minutes of the Saxon cabinet meetings of 27 Sept. and 5 Nov. 1867 and 23 Feb. and 26 Mar. 1868, in SächsHStA Dresden, MdI Nr. 5372, Bl. 6–11, 17–21, 118d-e, 119b-c.
40 See Axel Flügel, 'Sozialer Wandel und politische Reform in Sachsen. Rittergüter und Gutsbesitzer im Übergang von der Landeshoheit zum Konstitutionalismus 1763–1843,' in *Wege zur Geschichte des Bürgertums*, ed. Klaus Tenfelde and Hans-Ulrich Wehler (Göttingen, 1994), 36–56, esp. 40–2; Günter Grünthal, *Parlamentarismus in Preußen 1848/49-1857/58* (Düsseldorf, 1982), 68, 72–7; and Klaus-Erich Pollmann, *Parlamentarismus im Norddeutschen Bund 1867–1870* (Düsseldorf, 1985).
41 C[arl] V. Fricker, ed., *Die Verfassungsgesetze des Königreichs Sachsen* (Leipzig, 1895), 65n2.
42 PRO Kew, FO 68, Nr. 149, J. Hume Burnley, Dresden, to FO, no. 3, 26 Feb. 1868, addendum.
43 Asa Briggs, in *Victorian People*; cited in Margaret Lavinia Anderson, *Practicing Democracy: Elections and Political Culture in Imperial Germany* (Princeton, 2000), 4.
44 Burnley continued: 'It is not safe to say what the aspect of the Chamber

will be at present, one thing however seems very certain that it will be decidedly more democratic than its predecessor' (PRO Kew, FO 68, Nr. 149, Burnley, Dresden, to FO, no. 34, 5 Oct. 1869.
45 Nostitz-Wallwitz, speaking in the lower house on 23 March 1868, cited in Schröder, 'Wahlrecht,' 99n54). See also report no. 101, 3 Nov. 1867, in BayrHStA Munich, Abt. II, MA III, Nr. 2841.
46 My preliminary understanding of the Meiji Restoration is based on the following: Nobutaka Ike, *The Beginnings of Political Democracy in Japan* (Baltimore, 1950); George M. Beckmann, *The Making of the Meiji Constitution* (Lawrence, Kans., 1957); Joseph Pittau, 'Ideology of a New Nation: Authoritarianism and Constitutionism, Japan: 1868–1890 (PhD diss., Harvard University, 1962), esp. chap. 7; George Akita, *Foundations of Constitutional Government in Modern Japan, 1868–1900* (Cambridge, Mass., 1967); and Robert A. Scalapino, *Democracy and the Party Movement in Prewar Japan* (Berkeley, 1967). The Japanese election law of 11 Feb. 1889 was consulted in *The Meiji Japan through Contemporary Sources*, ed. Centre for East Asian Cultural Studies, Tokyo, vol. 1, *Basic Documents, 1854–1989* (Tokyo, 1969), 131–52.
47 Ian Hacking, 'How Should We Do the History of Statistics?' in *The Foucault Effect: Studies in Governmentality*, ed. Graham Burchell, Colin Gordon, and Peter Miller (Chicago, 1991), 181–95, here 194.
48 See Colin Gordon, 'Governmental Rationality: An Introduction,' ibid., 1–51, here 30–1.
49 See Menzinger, *Verfassungsrevision*, 56–68, esp. 60; Friedrich von Eichmann, Dresden, to Prussian Foreign Minister Otto von Bismarck, no. 95 (confidential), 18 Dec. 1867, in PA AA Bonn, I.A.A.m. Sachsen (Königreich), Nr. 39, unfoliated.
50 Karlheinz Blaschke, 'Die Verwaltung in Sachsen und Thüringen,' in *Deutsche Verwaltungsgeschichte*, vol. 3, *Das deutsche Reich bis zum Ende der Monarchie*, ed. Kurt G.A. Jeserich et al. (Stuttgart, 1984), 778–97, here 781.
51 August Bebel, *Aus meinem Leben* (Berlin, 1961), 784.

6 Citadels against Democracy

This chapter examines municipal politics, philanthropy, and local efforts to recast the electoral rules of the game.[1] The Germans who appear to be in the driver's seat in this chapter cannot easily be fixed on the German Right; most of them would probably have described themselves as liberals. Few of them, however, would willingly have accepted the label 'democrat.' Indeed, not unlike Herr von Barnim, who was cited in this volume's introduction, the struggle against Social Democracy was often at the forefront of their thinking.

This discussion of power and privilege focuses on efforts to reform municipal voting rights in ways that rewarded the achievements of German burghers. Thus it provides another opportunity to explore the fine grain of politics in the German Empire. Again the analysis centres on tax thresholds and their significance: as the fruit of legislative infighting, as evidence of bourgeois fears about the stability of their local worlds, and as a means to incorporate particular social strata into the polity while excluding others. This analysis also permits reconsideration of one of the great lies of modern bureaucracies: the myth of nonpartisanship. The contention that cities in Imperial Germany were 'administered' in a neutral manner rather than 'governed' politically was sustained by an outlook that some historians have called 'apolitical.' By the late 1890s, though, this contention was being exposed for what it was: a myth.

This chapter also suggests that new meanings can be teased from the language used in turn-of-the-century Germany to describe how and why the 'dangerous classes' should be excluded from power locally. It does so by examining the vocabulary of political rights in the context of campaigns to enact specific pieces of legislation – in this case, voting laws in three Saxon cities – that excluded a certain proportion of Social Democratic supporters from influencing the outcome of elections.

These thresholds, vocabularies, and laws can only be understood in their local historical contexts. However, better-known struggles to hold back the tide of revolution on a national scale are not irrelevant to the story told here. Kaiser Wilhelm II's ill-fated campaign for 'Religion, Morality, and Order' in 1894–5 provides the framework within which anti-socialist groups at both the state level in Saxony and the municipal level in Leipzig devised plans to deal with socialist advances at the polls. The Kaiser's campaign at first glance appears more significant because it mobilized political parties throughout the empire. Those parties attracted national attention when their campaigns for or against repressive legislation occupied weeks of debate in the Reichstag and the Prussian House of Deputies. But the struggles to enact the more modest and less overtly authoritarian laws examined in this chapter raised important, abstract issues concerning the rights and duties of all citizens. They also moved beyond the party-political realm. The contending camps worked hard to avoid the language of partisan politics. They preferred instead to speak of individual achievement (*Leistung*). This achievement had been fought for and won in the realms of entrepreneurship, education, public works, and philanthropy. But it was to be acknowledged and rewarded, albeit secondarily, in the worlds of politics. *How* 'secondarily' remains to be shown.

Money, Politics, Achievement

Echoing across two centuries, complaints that politics is tainted by money have a familiar ring. Campaign finance reform – we need it today! Gerrymandering is an abomination. Statesmanship has disappeared. The electoral game is played with loaded dice. Party machines and special interests call the shots. Demagoguery is trump!

Frequently, such complaints are followed by larger, more vexing questions about citizenship roles, equality of opportunity, the fair distribution of tax burdens, constitutional symmetry, and access to power. Are elections nothing more than contrived ventriloquism? Did the U.S. Electoral College cheat Al Gore of the presidency in 2000? Should the little man bother to vote? What sane person enters public service willingly? Will democracy survive?

Even editorial cartoons depicting the contest between plutocracy and democracy are distinctly unoriginal. Illustrations 6.1 and 6.2 suggest

194   Cultures of Conservatism

6.1. The 'uplifting' of the middle classes. The caption reads: 'Why does a wealthy man count for more than a hundred less-affluent ones in the Prussian [*Landtag*] elections? For *weighty* reasons.' 'Die "Hebung" des Mittelstandes (Zur Dreiklassenwahl),' by F. Jüttner in *Lüstige Blätter. Humoristische Wochenschrift* 8, no. 45 (1893). Image courtesy of the Bildarchiv Preußischer Kulturbesitz, Berlin.

Citadels against Democracy 195

6.2. Election spending: a balance of voices? Editorial cartoon by Matt Wuerker, 2000. Image courtesy of Matt Wuerker.

that the public welfare in the twenty-first century, as in the nineteenth, is suspended between the unhealthy influence of moneyed interests and the virtues of the common people – or rather, the *multiplicity* of class identities that are taken to constitute 'the people.' The fulcrum of power lies just beyond the reach of the middle classes, who are perched precariously on the ballot box or who hang in exposed fashion from the half-hidden scales of justice. Most conspicuously of all, wealth, especially excessive wealth, throws everything out of kilter. The spectre conjured up by Albert Camus, depicting a world where 'tyrants indulge in monologues over millions of solitudes,' lies close at hand.[2] Money has triumphed over intellect – and everything else besides.

Historians have long known that most nineteenth-century liberals in Germany did not support the principle of 'one man, one vote.' Yet liberal conceptions of liberty and democracy were bound up with ideas about the role that education, independence, and achievement should play in the 'fair' allocation of political privilege. Because those ideas were part of an evolving discourse among many groups contending for power, we cannot speak, like Camus, of tyrants, monologues, or solitudes. Yet what *can* we say about the relationship between money and politics? To address this question we turn to two issues that are rarely brought into proximity: suffrage laws and philanthropy.

The concept of 'achievement' (an approximation of an untranslatable German word, *Leistung*) is important here. The idea of *Leistung* played a significant role in framing contemporary debates about how philanthropy, patronage, and politics were related. This chapter proposes the hypothesis that the German reformers who revised the municipal suffrage laws in Dresden, Leipzig, and Chemnitz staked their claim to civic leadership on such cultural practices as philanthropy.

Philanthropy was not the only kind of *Leistung* upon which wealthy German burghers based their arguments for unequal political privilege. Public and private discussions preceding suffrage reforms in each of these Saxon cities focused on two other factors: the *Leistung* of individuals, as defined and measured by either their income or their payment of taxes to the state, and the *Leistung* of particular social groups as bulwarks against the challenge of Social Democracy. Nevertheless, whether conceived in terms of an individual's level of tax exposure or his capacity to defend the existing social order against the threat of revolution, the belief that certain groups contributed more than others to the public good supported philanthropists' claim that what they did, too, deserved special rewards, including privileged access to power.

It follows, then, that a study of Leipzig's bourgeoisie and its pioneering role in implementing anti-democratic suffrage reforms should also be examined along parallel tracks: as a result of Leipzig burghers' willingness to stake their claim for social, cultural, and political leadership on the basis of their financial contributions to public works, and in terms of their determination to overturn a relatively equitable suffrage and replace it with a conspicuously plutocratic one. The suffrage reform inaugurated in Leipzig did not have its intended effect of quelling debate on the issue; strident proposals for reform resurfaced in later years. Yet the Leipzig reform served as a model for later suffrage reforms in Dresden and Chemnitz. Space does not permit a full-scale study of these reforms; they are simply too complex and diverse. But neither their complexity nor their diversity prevents us from emphasizing two related points that inform the central argument of this chapter. The first is that the institutions and practices of power in Imperial Germany were susceptible to both manipulation from above and scrutiny from below. The second point is that the contests between those advocating plutocratic and democratic electoral systems in pre-1914 Germany unfolded in ways that will be remarkably familiar to readers in the twenty-first century.

The Undemocratic State

Social Democratic contemporaries and historians alike have described the Kingdom of Saxony as one of the most undemocratic polities in the German Empire. In many respects it deserved its reputation as the playground of authoritarianism. Although recent scholarship has looked on Saxon authoritarianism from new angles and noted its ambiguity, such accounts suggest that the kingdom's highly urbanized society and industrial economy not only did not preclude, but actually *favoured*, anti-democratic habits of mind that we wrongly associate only with Prussian Junkers.

Such anti-democratic attitudes were the direct result of the early and rapid rise of Social Democracy in Saxony, which scored many of its successes in the 1860s and 1870s. With the fall of Bismarck in 1890 and the decision not to renew the anti-socialist laws he had inaugurated, Social Democrats registered some of their most important breakthroughs in the Reichstag elections of 1890 and 1893. But nowhere was their rise monitored and their strength feared more than in the Kingdom of Saxony. In the wake of failed attempts to combat the spectre of revolution with a national campaign in 1894–5, the leaders of all non-socialist parties in the Saxon *Landtag* collaborated in 1896 to introduce a three-tiered voting system, which approximated the three-class electoral system that had been in place in Prussia since 1850.[3]

The fact that political leaders in a highly modern state should move contrary to the general democratizing trends of the age further reinforced Saxony's reputation as a bastion of anti-democratic elites. Theirs was a pyrrhic victory, however, as the attempt to 'dish the Reds' produced its own backlash. In the Reichstag elections of 1903, the Saxon Socialists scored a huge victory. 'Red Saxony' was born overnight. But the story did not end there. In response, the Saxon government and the more insightful party leaders slowly came to the conclusion that the three-class system could not be sustained for state-level elections. As one government declaration put it, the 1896 reform had 'not had the intended effect,' in part because the electoral influence of the third class of voters, the least affluent, had sunk to a level that did not correspond with 'the principles of fairness.' The disparity between the Socialists' share of the popular vote and the number of seats they won in the national Reichstag and the Saxon *Landtag* was too obvious, and too galling, for the political system to bear.[4] And so finally, in 1909, Saxony's version of the three-class *Landtag* suffrage was replaced by a system of plural voting. In this system, extra ballots were awarded to individual voters according to criteria based on age, military service, tax payment, and land ownership.

Recent research has begun to bring this interplay between national and state-level electoral systems into focus.[5] By contrast, the evolution of suffrage laws at the third tier of government in Saxony, the municipal level, has received virtually no scholarly attention at all. There is no modern study of the comparatively liberal municipal suffrage laws inaugurated in Saxony in 1873. Nor can one find an adequate account of how Saxons actually reformed their municipal suffrages after 1890. While the present chapter cannot fill these lacunae, it can suggest which aspects of this story might contribute to a historical reconsideration of the cross-cutting motives for reform and retrenchment that animated members of other polities in this era.[6]

The revised municipal ordinance of 1873 divided the population of each Saxon city into so-called inhabitants (*Gemeindemitglieder*) and citizens (*Bürger*).[7] Everyone who did not depend on the state or charity for financial aid, who paid at least 3 marks annually in direct state taxes, and who possessed property or a trade was considered to be an inhabitant of the city. Inhabitants had the right to apply for municipal citizenship and to become eligible to vote in municipal elections. Voters elected members of the municipal parliament (*Stadtverordnetenkollegium*), who together with the municipal council (*Stadtrat*) administered the city. Fifty per cent of these municipal parliamentarians had to possess property within the city. The voters did not vote for individual candidates but for different lists, which eventually took on the character of what we now call party slates. The party, group, or coalition that received the most votes received all seats in the municipal parliament.[8]

Given Saxony's industrial character and its workers' relatively high wages, this municipal suffrage enfranchised most adult male inhabitants of Saxon cities. As 3 marks in annual state taxes would have been paid by people who earned 600 marks a year, most skilled workers in Dresden, Leipzig, and Chemnitz could meet this threshold easily. In Leipzig in 1889, for example, more than 70 per cent (totalling 43,298) of workers affiliated with the local health insurance plan (*Leipziger Ortskrankenkasse*) had an income of more than 600 marks.[9]

After the incorporation of many working-class suburbs into Leipzig city proper in 1889, and after the fall of Bismarck's anti-socialist laws in 1890, the Social Democratic Party decided to take up the political op-

Table 6.1. Leipzig municipal elections, 1889–93

Year	Number of enfranchised voters	Number of votes cast	Votes cast for non-socialist parties	Votes cast for Social Democracy
1889	13,061	6,809	6,795	–
1890	17,697	11,520	9,191	2,329
1891	21,706	14,674	10,361	4,313
1892	22,245	15,245	10,341	4,904
1893	24,308	15,770	9,835	5,935

Source: Leo Ludwig-Wolf, 'Leipzig,' in *Verfassungs- und Verwaltungsorganisation der Städte*, vol. 4, no. 1, *Königreich Sachsen*, ed. Verein für Socialpolitik, Schriften des Vereins für Socialpolitik, 120/I (Leipzig, 1905, rpt. Vaduz 1990), 123–61.

portunity offered by Saxony's municipal suffrage law.[10] In 1890 the Leipzig branch of the SPD participated in municipal elections for the first time. In the autumn of that year – the municipal elections were almost always held in the last two months of the year – they received about 20 per cent of the vote. The next four years were characterized by an unprecedented campaign to convince workers to apply for citizenship (the *Bürgerrecht*) in Leipzig and to turn out at the polls on election day. The success of Social Democrats in Leipzig's municipal elections rose correspondingly (see table 6.1). In the elections of 1893 the Social Democrats fell only a few thousand votes short of a majority. If these trends continued, it seemed certain that Socialists would dominate Leipzig's parliament after the next elections.[11]

Whereas most studies of municipal suffrage laws simply pass over Saxon cities,[12] those that focus on state-level suffrage laws typically describe Saxony as occupying a middle position between undemocratic Prussia and the 'more democratic' southern German states. In the 1990s Helga Grebing and Hans Mommsen developed their concept of the 'third Germany' (which included Saxony and Thuringia). They argued that this third Germany took a different path from the authoritarian Prussian path and the more liberal southern German path. It required something of a stretch to locate Saxony geographically between the northeastern and southwestern German territories in question. But historically it seemed plausible to describe Saxony's political culture as integrating aspects common to both its northern and its southern 'neighbours.'[13] This alleged constellation may be true – and even then only with significant caveats – if we concentrate on the state level. However, the analysis of municipal suffrages between 1873 and the late

1890s suggests that Saxony was in some respects more receptive to liberal reforms than even such 'democratic' states as Bavaria and Baden.

In southern German cities the right to vote was limited by a citizenship fee and other restrictions.[14] Merith Niehuss has argued that this fee was very high in order to exclude the lower classes from participation in political decisions.[15] To ensure that well-paid workers could not find their way into the privileged group of voters, secondary regulations accompanied the high citizenship fee. 'Apart from proof of property ownership ranging between 1,000 and 3,000 marks, and assets worth 300 marks if he was married, an aspirant for the *Bürgerrecht* in Baden, for example, also had to prove that he was neither a poor householder nor a drunkard, and that he did not lead a dissolute or disorderly life.'[16] In the end, the high citizenship fee and the secondary regulations ensured that only a relatively small proportion of a city's inhabitants were entitled to vote and that the lower classes would be under-represented.[17] In the case of Munich, fewer than 20 per cent of those entitled to vote in national elections were enfranchised for municipal elections. The class-based suffrage in Baden placed three-quarters of all those who were entitled to vote in the third class, which in turn elected only one-third of municipal parliamentarians.[18] These restrictions contributed to what has been called the 'liberal power monopoly' in German cities.[19]

Saxony's municipal suffrage laws differed significantly from these southern German examples. The Saxon law did not contain any secondary regulations as the law for Baden did. The character and the behaviour of the prospective candidate for citizenship was of no consequence to the local authorities. Only financial requirements were deemed important, and as has already been noted, the 3-mark threshold could be met easily by the majority of potential voters from the lower classes. Also in contrast to southern Germany, Saxony did not demand any citizenship fee. The only common denominator between the Saxon and the southern German laws was the age at which people could apply for citizenship: in both cases it was set at twenty-five years. Otherwise, Saxon municipal suffrage laws closely approximated the Reichstag's universal, direct, equal, and secret suffrage. But this picture changed dramatically after 1893.

No Representation without Taxation

In late 1893 Leipzig's burghers were horrified by the outcome of the municipal elections: they had dodged a bullet, and they knew it. A

Social Democratic municipal parliament seemed the inevitable consequence if the suffrage system were not changed. Within weeks, members of Leipzig's municipal parliament decided to reform the municipal suffrage. Interestingly, their first tactic was blocked by central Saxon authorities. Those authorities refused to allow the Leipzig parliament to use new but more vague criteria to determine whether a Leipzig citizen possessed enough 'intellectual or economic independence' to merit enfranchisement. In their opinion, anyone who paid income tax to the city was independent per se. Blocked on one front, the Leipzig parliamentarians tacked quickly and decided to copy parts – most parts – of the Prussian three-class system. In October 1894 the municipal parliament passed a new suffrage law that fundamentally changed political representation in the city.

Leipzigers copied the Prussian law in more ways than one. As their Prussian counterparts had decades earlier, they abandoned the chimera of dividing voters according to their *qualitative* differences (that is, according to social estates, as the Prussians had hoped to do, or by reference to an abstract notion of 'independence'). Instead both the Prussians in 1850 and the Leizpigers in 1894 opted for a scheme according to which voters' *quantitative* contribution to the state, their *Leistung*, could be assessed and rewarded. Thus the three-class suffrage was universal but unequal – unequal because all voters did not have equal weight in choosing their parliamentary representatives.

Voters were divided into classes by ranking each male taxpayer hierarchically according to the taxes he paid. At the top was the taxpayer who paid the highest state taxes annually. The lowest-paying taxpayer was at the bottom of the list. The taxes that were taken into account in this procedure included personal taxes (class and income taxes) and so-called real taxes (business and property taxes). A civil servant would go down the list, compiling a running total of the taxes paid until he reached a sum equivalent to five-twelfths of the total tax roll (for Prussian *Landtag* elections it was one-third). These taxpayers would constitute the first class of voters. The process was then continued, with the second class of voters being demarcated once the next 15 per cent of most highly taxed voters were included. Those remaining on the list, plus all eligible non-taxpayers, constituted the third voting class.

In 1902 a voter with an annual income of 15,000 marks or more (corresponding to annual taxes of about 780 marks or more) would be included in the first voting class; a voter with an annual income of about 4,000 marks (corresponding to annual taxes of about 155 marks) would vote in class II. All others would be included in class III.[20] Class I had very few voters in it because a relatively small proportion (typically about 5 per cent) of taxpayers accounted for five-twelfths of the total taxes paid. In 1902, 1,507 voters were included in this class. The second class had rather more voters, usually about 15 per cent (in 1902, 4,470 voters). Class III had the vast majority of voters, roughly 80 per cent, who paid little or no tax.[21] In 1902, 23,818 Leipzigers were enfranchised in class III.

In practice, the relatively well-off voters in classes I and II outvoted the poorer voters in class III. Initially they elected well-established men of property or higher education who represented their own class interests. This outcome was perfectly in tune with liberal conceptions of elite representation, including those advocated by John Stuart Mill, whereby the 'best and the brightest' were ascribed the right, and the duty, to legislate on behalf of the majority.[22] And it corresponded to popular conceptions of the state as a kind of joint-stock company, whereby votes were allocated to citizen 'shareholders' on the basis of each one's 'investment' (in the form of taxes) in the larger 'enterprise' of the state. Most notably of all, the emphasis on independence, refinement, *Intelligenz*, and concern for the public good corresponded to contemporary understandings of philanthropy itself. In any case, this model was not seen to be antagonistic to local social, economic, and cultural ties that bound voters together in groups arranged hierarchically.

The defenders of the new Leipzig municipal suffrage claimed that all three classes of voters at least had equal weight in choosing the seventy-two municipal parliamentarians. Such arguments, however, were a sham. Every vote cast in the first class carried far more weight – roughly sixteen times more weight – than every vote cast in the third class. This arrangement so disadvantaged voters in the third class that abstention was far higher there than in the first two classes. Apathy among the third class of voters grew significantly, no matter which three-class system was implemented. This was true after 1850 in Prussia, after 1894 in Leipzig municipal elections, and after 1896 in Saxon *Landtag* elections.[23]

Following Leipzig's Lead?

With the change in the municipal suffrage law, Leipzig became a testing ground for other Saxon communities and the state legislature. If such restrictive suffrage laws achieved their intended result in Leipzig, they might work elsewhere. Thus the plutocratic reform of the Leipzig municipal suffrage set the stage for the *Landtag* suffrage reform of 1896 and the suffrage reforms enacted in other Saxon cities over the next few years. However, Dresden and Chemnitz did not slavishly follow the path taken by Leipzig. To be sure, both cities introduced new municipal suffrage laws with the goal of disenfranchising, or at least disadvantaging, the lower classes. But these 'latecomer' reforms were not based only on the principle of tax exposure; they also considered the electoral weight given to voters according to their occupation and level of education.[24] Even more significant were the different motives, and different outcomes, that accompanied the revision of the state *Landtag* suffrage in 1896. That suffrage differed from Leipzig's municipal voting system in two important ways.[25]

First, whereas antisemites and members of the old *Mittelstand* in Saxony's largest cities generally favoured the move to more restrictive, class-based suffrages after 1894, these groups opposed the reform of the Saxon *Landtag* suffrage in 1896. They feared that the latter reform would diminish their influence in the state parliament (which it did). Second, Leipzig's voting system was far more direct than the Saxon system inaugurated in 1896. In Leipzig, members of the municipal parliament were elected directly from each of the three classes. The third class, for instance, would vote directly for candidates who would then represent them in the municipal parliament. After 1896, on the other hand, the Saxon *Landtag* suffrage featured indirect voting, whereby each *constituency* was divided into three classes. The voters of these three classes elected delegates who in turn elected a member of the legislature.

This difference between the systems might seem trivial, but it reflected quite different political strategies by members of both legislatures. Whereas the indirect three-class suffrage virtually excluded the possibility that Social Democrats would be elected to the Saxon *Landtag*, the direct three-class suffrage that prevailed for Leipzig's municipal parliament almost ensured this outcome. As a result, in Leipzig, even though the suffrage reform was undertaken in order to prevent Social Democrats from winning *all* seats in the municipal parliament, the reform actually permitted them to win some seats for the first time (recall the previous 'winner-take-all' arrangement). As such, this suffrage reform represented a strategy of limited inclusion, permitting those who had previously not participated in parliamentary affairs to do so.

In light of this evidence, it is difficult to sustain the argument that the authors of Leipzig's plutocratic suffrage of 1894 were attempting to destroy the Social Democratic movement in their city.[26] There can be no doubt that Leipzig burghers condemned the goals of the SPD and sought to limit the influence of its voters and parliamentary representatives. But because the three-class system virtually guaranteed the party one-third of the seats in the municipal parliament, we must conclude that members of Leipzig's bourgeoisie accepted the existence of a Social Democratic party on principle and made their peace with the idea that its representatives should be allowed to participate, to a limited extent, in the city's political affairs. The indirect three-class suffrage inaugurated for the Saxon *Landtag*, by contrast, represented a strategy of exclusion and confrontation. It succeeded admirably on both counts.

The motives for enacting new suffrage laws in Chemnitz and Dresden corresponded more closely to the (relatively) inclusive Leipzig strategy than to the confrontational path chosen by *Landtag* parliamentarians. In both cities, reformers eschewed the strategy of exclusion and sought possibilities of limited inclusion according to the existing Leipzig blueprint. However, they chose quite different paths in other respects. They did so, for example, by considering not only the income and tax exposure of the prospective voter but also his profession and level of education. In this respect, these reformers resurrected options that the Leipzigers had rejected as being too conducive to Social Democratic gains at the municipal level.

Parenthetically, the Leipzig reformers had considered proposals that foresaw the division of voting classes according to occupational estates, but they concluded that such divisions were difficult to make and would be in constant flux. They considered a system of plural voting, with extra ballots awarded for age, family status, ownership of property, and military service, but some parliamentarians believed these criteria would favour the SPD. They considered a system of proportional representation, but they worried that SPD influence in working-class neighbourhoods would have a 'paralysing' effect on the process. Advocates of a division of the electorate into four voting classes were defeated by those who argued that the possible emergence of two equally strong blocs might paralyse each other. These fears of electoral 'paralysis' capture the mindset of Leipzigers who felt that admitting the SPD to the political fold would result in the hegemony of a *single* party.[27]

Reformers in the industrial city of Chemnitz were the first to move in the direction of suffrage reform.[28] In 1898 the municipal parliament passed a new suffrage law based on the occupational status of its citizens. Chemnitz voters were divided into six classes, which elected fifty-seven members of the municipal parliament. All citizens who earned less than 2,500 marks belonged to class A (with a further division, A1 and A2, according to whether they earned more or less than 1,900 marks). All citizens who were required to pay fees for the old-age and invalid insurance schemes belonged to class B. Civil servants, teachers, physicians, and clergy were gathered in class C. Class D consisted of people who engaged in trade and manufacturing and who earned more than 2,500 marks annually. Class E included all owners and shareholders of manufacturing and joint-stock enterprises who had an annual income of more than 2,500 marks.[29]

In 1905 it was time for Dresden's municipal parliamentarians to follow suit. These legislators, too, preferred a voting scheme based on occupation. Voters were divided into five classes, who elected a total of eighty-four representatives. Class A consisted of people without any profession; class B included those who paid fees to the old-age and pension schemes; class C comprised civil servants, clergy, lawyers, physicians, and intellectuals; class D included those who were engaged in trade and industry but were not members of the Chamber of Commerce, while those who did belong to the latter were included in class E. The Dresdeners, too, added some new wrinkles. Their new suffrage law privileged those who had held local citizenship for more than ten years. Thus every class contained two groups of voters: those who had been citizens of Dresden for more than ten years and those who had not.[30]

Philanthropy and Political Representation

To dwell any longer on the details of these suffrage reforms would perpetuate a rather narrow perspective. The more interesting and important story concerns the specifically bourgeois character of these reforms and the mental orientation of the burghers who advocated them. Saxon burghers genuinely feared the spectre of the SPD. In the 1890s the majority of them likely believed that the Socialists were going to infiltrate, dominate, and then 'tyrannize' municipal parliaments in Saxony. This is the standard argument that historians offer to explain these suffrage reforms. But this explanation, focusing on the antagonism between political parties, raises more questions than it answers.[31] What was the mentality of those who claimed for themselves positions of leadership in local society? Did they conceive of themselves as playing different roles when they staked their claim to special privileges and disproportionate influence in local, regional, and national electoral cultures? Why did bourgeois Saxons accept a very liberal municipal suffrage law until the end of the nineteenth century but not after the turn of the century? Why was it possible to reform the three-class suffrage for the Saxon *Landtag* in 1909 but not the laws governing elections to municipal parliaments? Did the experience of living with the Leipzig reform of 1894 make *Landtag* legislators in 1909 confident that a partial opening to the Socialists would not have cataclysmic consequences?[32]

An investigation of Saxony's bourgeois culture and of its wealthiest citizens' philanthropic activities provides one means to situate this discussion of municipal suffrage reform in a broader social and cultural context – a context that in turn enables us better to discuss the interplay of authoritarian and liberal attitudes in dynamic urban settings. For to examine the philanthropic culture of Saxon cities is to engage with individuals whose interests spanned the philanthropic and political spheres. Such wealthy Dresdeners and Leipzigers as Herrmann Julius Meyer (Leipzig), Gustav Schwabe (Leipzig) and Johann Meyer (Dresden) represented an urban bourgeoisie that considered it a natural duty of well-placed citizens to organize, finance, and represent their community both inwardly and outwardly. Such wealthy citizens created countless civic organizations for the support of museums and art galleries. They provided social housing for working-class families. And they financed social security schemes, hospitals, and other 'good works.'[33] Religious beliefs are often cited as the reason for such philanthropic activity. However, the industrialist Gustav Schwabe believed that he owed part of his fortune and success to the community. He once observed that he felt obliged to contribute a portion of his wealth to improving the lot of working-class families because, as he put it, only their work had enabled him to amass such a fortune.[34]

While we should not dismiss such high-minded motives out of hand, giving money for social and cultural institutions is always tied up with the attempt to claim a position of leadership in society. Philanthropy is an instrument for defining the upper class. For this reason, the practice of philanthropy has historically stood in close relationship to other attempts to define who should exercise power and influence in political society. Such attempts include the reform of suffrage laws. From the mid-1870s to the mid-1890s, wealthy burghers in Leipzig, Dresden, and Chemnitz accepted liberal suffrage laws that granted the right to vote to nearly every male citizen, because those laws did not endanger the traditional order. The same bourgeois citizens, however, suddenly demanded a reform of the suffrage laws when the lower classes – the proper *target* of philanthropy – seemed on the verge of gaining decisive political influence in city parliaments.

Philanthropy in Saxony, in Germany, and elsewhere had always had a transparently paternalistic character. In part, this was unavoidable. Philanthropists preferred to support public institutions directly because indirect financing schemes at this point had not been invented. But they also did so because the lower classes were perceived to be unable to share the responsibility for these institutions. Philanthropists envisioned themselves as the only ones having the means and the will to support social and cultural enterprises. Therefore it was easy for them to articulate demands for political privilege based on the good of the community. Put another way: in advocating suffrage reforms that inaugurated systems of three-class voting or representation according to occupational status, these wealthy citizens granted themselves privileges because they believed that they contributed the most to the well-being of the community and best understood how to ensure that it would flourish. Conversely, it was natural for them to claim that the lower classes who deferred to their initiative and leadership in the philanthropic sphere should also do so in the parliamentary sphere.

The entire system of support for public works in Saxony underpinned such arguments. Saxony was the first German state to introduce personal income taxes, in 1887–8; it was followed by Prussia in 1892 and Bavaria in 1912.[35] Nevertheless, even in the 1880s, most of Saxony's social, cultural, and educational institutions were still financed directly by upper-class citizens. Moreover, we should keep in mind that philanthropy was not an extraordinary act of generosity made occasionally by a rich gentleman; it was an everyday habit practised in one form or another by the majority of bourgeois Germans. Museums, art galleries, hospitals, universities, and social housing – all these enterprises relied on direct donations. In the mind of bourgeois citizens, the city simply could not exist without a core group of generous, resourceful, dependable financial backers. From their vantage point, a city – *their* city – was less a thing of stone and iron than a 'human network,' a network of wealthy bourgeois citizens who organized, financed, and represented their community. By logical extension, then, anyone who lived in this community but did not contribute to its maintenance and expansion was not to be considered a citizen. This view was so firmly entrenched that neither the introduction of the income tax nor the suffrage reforms described above sufficed to undermine it. That change came with the dawn of the new century. It was only after 1904 that Leipzig's city government used tax revenues to support and assume financial responsibility for such important institutions as the Grassi Museum, the Art Museum (*Kunstmuseum*), and the symphony hall (*Gewandhaus*).[36]

The Leipzig bourgeoisie's notion that the city was, quite literally, its 'property,' also had deep roots.[37] The city had always constituted something that had to be nurtured and protected. But now, in the modern era, it could also be conceived as a commercial enterprise or a piece of private property. That property had to be defended against communists, levellers, or anyone else seeking to 'expropriate' something that was not legitimately theirs. The possible exclusion of the bourgeoisie from power – a distinct possibility within the context of the old suffrage laws – must have provoked real fear within Leipzig's bourgeoisie on exactly these grounds. Who could predict what levels of taxation might be imposed on the wealthy classes once Social Democrats stood at the helm? To what extent would socialist doctrine be implemented? Where would it lead? Would only the economy and social relations be affected, or might the very existence of the state be endangered? The suffrage reforms in 1894 in Leipzig, in 1898 in Chemnitz, and in 1905 in Dresden must be seen in the context of these contemporary anxieties. If the old suffrage laws had not been abolished in Leipzig in 1894, a Social Democratic majority the next year seemed a certainty. But what would follow was anyone's guess.

It is hardly surprising that Gustav Schwabe, one of Leipzig's leading philanthropists, was also an influential member of the parliamentary commission that proposed the three-class suffrage for the city in 1894.[38] Schwabe would have been blind not to see his own, and his class's, direct material interest in the outcome of the suffrage deliberations, just as he considered himself particularly well placed to judge his city's best interests. But we do not have to rely on Schwabe's testimony itself or even the deliberations of the parliamentary committee on which he sat to see how Saxony's urban elites viewed issues of philanthropy and political representation in such close proximity.

For the case of Chemnitz, consider the arguments in favour of reform that preceded the inauguration of an occupation-based suffrage in 1898. Those arguments are necessarily filtered through the eyes of Dr Johannes Hübschmann, a city councillor (*Stadtrat*) whose reportage formed the basis for the study commissioned by the Association for Social Policy (Verein für Sozialpolitik). In Hübschmann's account, the interweaving of philanthropic and political motives is unmistakable. 'Already in the wake of the municipal election of 1897,' wrote Hübschmann, 'the question was raised vehemently in various circles of the citizenry whether the existing electoral system could in the long run ensure the continued development of the common weal along its present path and also in accord with national principles; or whether it would not, or rather must not, lead to a situation where property – already heavily burdened – and intellect would be sacrificed to headcounts and where a single party would achieve domination [Herrschaft] in the municipal parliament. It was also emphasized that the equal suffrage for the municipal parliament had revealed itself as inopportune, because it did not allow those elements of society who were most important and beneficial for the flourishing and expansion of the city to come to the fore, and as illegitimate, because it virtually took away the rights of the burghers who, on the basis of their level of taxation, had to bear the largest portion of the city's financial burdens. For example, in recent times the election of a large industrialist had almost become an impossibility. These opinions found an echo in the halls of the municipal parliament itself.'[39]

In equally faithful fashion, the association's analyst summed up the opinion of Chemnitz burghers who, after 1898, had found the newly restrictive suffrage very much to their taste and even hailed their own role as pioneers. Hübschmann wrote: 'The new electoral system according to occupational estates, which Chemnitz was the first among large German cities to introduce (the electoral law in Bremen arose from different circumstances), enfranchises the most diverse strata of the population according to the measure of their interest in the common good and of their importance to it; it also opens to the most insightful and talented men the prospect of being elected. Far from being plutocratic, it accommodates the desire of the working classes to participate in the administration of the city according to their level of contribution to the community, and it ensures that under any circumstances burghers who belong to the working classes will have an appropriate representation in the municipal parliament in that they are in a position to fill the positions in class B with representatives drawn from their own level of income.' Writing in 1905, seven years after the reform, Hübschmann reported that Chemnitz burghers' experience with the new suffrage had been 'completely satisfactory.' He emphasized that the reform had increased the social diversity of Chemnitz's municipal parliament, a change documented in table 6.2.

Table 6.2. Occupational profile of Chemnitz city councillors, 1905

Occupation (German)	Occupation (English)	Number of city councillors
Großindustrielle	large industrialists	6
Angehörige des Kaufmannstandes	merchants, shopkeepers, businessmen	17
Handwerker, Gewerbetreibende	artisans, owners/operators of small enterprises	11
Architekten und Ingenieure	architects and engineers	4
Gast- und Schankwirte	hoteliers, publicans	3
Juristen	lawyers (3) and judges (1)	4
Ärtzte	doctors	2
Angehörige des Lehrerstandes	teachers	3
Privatbeamte (Krankenkassenvorstand, Expedient, Lagerhalter beim Konsumverein u.s.w.)	white-collar workers, service industry personnel	5
Rentner	retired persons	2

Source: Johannes Hübschmann, 'Chemnitz,' in *Verfassungs- und Verwaltungsorganisation der Städte*, vol. 4, no. 1, *Königreich Sachsen*, ed. Verein für Socialpolitik, Schriften des Vereins für Socialpolitik, 120/I (Leipzig, 1905, rpt. Vaduz, 1990), 170.

An analysis of the sociological make-up of Leipzig's three voting classes after 1894 suggests why Leipzig burghers, too, could be pleased with the political consequences of their reform. The restriction of the first voting class to 1,500–2,000 of Leipzig's most exclusive citizens helped to preserve the traditional politics of notables. A special committee of the most exclusive club in the city, the Harmony Society, virtually orchestrated elections to the first class in a way that few philanthropists could find offensive. As Michael Schäfer has written: 'The three-class suffrage only drew more sharply the contours of an upper-bourgeois leadership elite that was active in municipal affairs, socially exclusive, and bound by networks of intermarriage and common social circles.'[40]

The arguments Leipzig burghers used to base this exclusivity on entrepreneurial or philanthropic *Leistung* were diverse. They nevertheless reflected the same intermixing of philanthropic and political motifs. The Harmony Society's election committee praised its candidates for their independence, specialized knowledge, professional experience, and social status. Looking back from the perspective of 1912, a lawyer sitting in Leipzig's municipal parliament expressed the same satisfaction that Hübschmann had voiced with respect to Chemnitz: 'If, on the one hand, one proclaims as just the principle that all citizens of the state and the city should bear the state's and the city's burdens according to their achievement potential [*Leistungsfähigkeit*], then on the other hand, one must accept the implication that political rights should also be distributed according to one's share of the public burden.'

Once the logic of this relationship between *Leistung* and political rights had been firmly established, members of the Leipzig parliament elected by the first two voting classes were able to continue the philanthropic activities – now more often in the name of the state – that had allegedly made them the natural representatives of 'the people' in the first place. Still embodying the principle of independence and yet now dispensing the massive sums of money needed to run a modern city, these men saw no reason to differentiate between their political and their philanthropic engagement on behalf of those less fortunate than themselves. The associations that played a large role in promoting their candidacy for public office also straddled the line between politics and philanthropy. 'Financed through the contributions of association members or through the donations or foundations of wealthy burghers, these associations and institutions were part of a sphere of direct municipal self-administration, the dispensing of influence, and the exercise of power, all of which was more effectively insulated from the democratizing pressure of the lower social strata than were the municipal parliaments themselves.'[41]

As the interests of the first two classes of voters in Leipzig diverged more and more from those of the third class, this 'insulating' effect increased in political significance (or 'value'), principally because it continued to keep the Social Democratic movement in check. Over time, however, not even the rhetoric of philanthropists and the prognoses of social scientific observers could hide the fact that a gulf of sympathy separated the bourgeoisie from the working classes. Leipzigers in the first two voting classes escalated their attempt to mobilize all the sources of social and economic influence that lay at their disposal. But the Socialists attempted to counter these efforts through a highly organized party structure and the claim that justice lay with their cause. Thus the spiraling dynamic of competition among social groups that is so characteristic of the late Wilhelmine era in general also came to characterize Leipzig's political culture. Once that occurred, there was little chance that another, more 'generous' interpretation of the bourgeoisie's best interests would support a movement for a democratic suffrage at the local level.

This dynamic in Saxony precluded the divergence of liberal and conservative forces that occurred elsewhere in the Reich. Frequent skirmishes erupted between Leipzig's grand bourgeoisie (*Großbürgertum*), whose interests in commerce, industry, and the upper reaches of the bureaucracy dominated the first voting class, and the lower middle classes, whose influence was wielded in the second voting class through their *Mittelstand* and homeowners associations and whose political sympathies generally ran toward antisemitic, Conservative, or right-wing National Liberal positions. Yet these groups found enough common ground – with each other and with the Saxon government in Dresden – that neither was required to compromise its essential anti-socialist world view.[42] Paul Brandmann has identified the historical significance of this stasis in Leipzig's electoral system after 1894: 'In Leipzig the National Liberals and "their" municipal administration had seized the initiative, whereby they could be assured of the support of the Saxon ministry of the interior. The interests of the authoritarian, aristocratic state leaders and those of the liberal city burghers were thus reconciled in this central political question. At least when we speak of municipal politics in Leipzig, the binary distinction [that historians often draw] between a modern *Bürgertum*, liberalism, and democracy, on the one side, and older anti-democratic elites, on the other side, must give way to a more differentiated judgment.'[43]

Reform on Hold?

The issue of suffrage reform did not disappear. Even after the introduction of plural voting for *Landtag* elections in 1909, discussions about the further reform of municipal suffrage laws in Saxon cities continued. But the opportunity for fundamental change had passed.[44] Even when the future orientation of the *Landtag* suffrage was still in doubt in 1906, Leipzig's municipal parliamentarians discussed a possible second reform of their suffrage law. Many now favoured a model similar to Chemnitz's law based on occupational estates. The discussions ended with no tangible outcome, and the municipal suffrage was not changed before November 1918. Nevertheless, one reform proposal by a city councillor, Leo Ludwig-Wolf, is illuminating.

Like his counterpart in Chemnitz, Ludwig-Wolf was both an active participant in the debate and a scholarly observer eager to present his version of events to a broader public.[45] His proposal for a new suffrage in Leipzig foresaw six voting classes, organized according to occupation. In simple terms, it would have resulted in the replacement of the city's three-class system with Chemnitz's more complicated model. Revealingly, Ludwig-Wolf started from the bottom of the social ladder, not the top. In his scheme, class A would have included the bulk of Leipzig workers. Class B would have comprised civil servants with an income of more than 3,000 marks, and class C, merchants with an income of more than 3,000 marks. Class D would have included industrialists with an income of more than 10,000 marks. Classes E and F would have been so-called mixed classes, comprising citizens with an income of up to 3,000 marks in class E and with an income above 3,000 marks in class F.

This proposal would have sustained the principle embedded in the 1894 reform, whereby the limited participation of the Social Democrats was guaranteed even though the bourgeoisie would continue to dominate. Indeed, Leipzig's Social Democrats would have benefited greatly from this proposed reform, because it can be assumed – it *was* assumed at the time – that they would win all the seats in classes A and E. These victories alone would not have enabled the Socialists to achieve significantly more influence over the policies of the municipal government. But they would have nearly doubled the number of Social Democratic members sitting in the city's parliamentary body. Ironically, it was the more conservative city council that appeared prepared to approve Ludwig-Wolf's proposal. The bourgeois parties in the lower house, however, were not prepared to test such dangerous waters. They voted the law down decisively.[46]

This debate about reforming the municipal suffrage law in Leipzig pre-dated the reform of the Saxon *Landtag* suffrage by three years. But the two debates were not unconnected. As in the mid-1890s, discussions about possible changes in a municipal setting conditioned the tone and substance of changes contemplated at the state level, and in both cases the debates received a strong impulse from the public discourse that unfolded in Leipzig. The introduction of the three-class suffrage for Leipzig elections in 1894 represented an opportunity to test the outcome of reform, and at this time it contributed to a decision to introduce a quite different three-class system at the state level. The intention of Conservative Party leaders, who were much more firmly in the driver's seat in the Saxon *Landtag* than in Leipzig's municipal parliament, was obviously to expel Social Democrats from the state legislature entirely. In Leipzig, on the other hand, where Conservatives and National Liberals had to share power more even-handedly, a coalition endorsed a solution that guaranteed the limited participation of Social Democrats in municipal affairs. After reform of municipal suffrage laws in Chemnitz and Dresden, Leipzig's municipal parliament again launched a suffrage reform debate. This time it failed at the local level but fed into a wider debate that unfolded at the state level.

While it would be mistaken to overstate the significance of these sequential reforms, it appears that members of Saxony's bourgeois parties, once they were sure that the concept of limited Social Democratic participation functioned well at the municipal level, dared to assume that it would function at the state level too. This hypothesis is given further support in that the plural voting scheme finally introduced for Saxon *Landtag* elections in 1909 combined two essential elements of the preceding reforms at the municipal level: the concept of limited Social Democratic participation, as in Leipzig, and the (albeit modified) concept of suffrage laws based on occupational status, as inaugurated in Chemnitz and Dresden. The *Landtag* suffrage law did not copy any one model fully. And the Saxon suffrage law of 1909 was not taken as a blueprint for suffrage reform in either Prussia or the Reich before the November Revolution of 1918. Nevertheless, the complex interplay of local and regional factors in Saxony before 1909 and the way the Saxon case animated public discourse about suffrage reform elsewhere in Germany during these years confirms Saxony's reputation as a laboratory for political experiments of national import.

Looking Forward

Chemnitz, Dresden, and Leipzig retained their occupational and three-class suffrage laws, respectively, until the collapse of the German Empire. Only the events of October–November 1918 paved the way for a full democratization of municipal suffrage laws. After the revolution, one's wealth, tax exposure, and gender no longer determined whether one enjoyed the right to vote. In January 1919 Leipzig, Dresden, and Chemnitz electors chose their municipal parliamentarians for the first time under the new system. Proportional representation enabled Saxon Social Democrats to conquer city hall in all three cities and participate meaningfully in municipal government for the first time. The middle parties that had inherited their political mantle from the pre-war Conservatives and National Liberals were paralysed and unable to resist these developments. However, even the Social Democrats in Leipzig could not win a clear majority in the municipal parliament. Furthermore, the position of mayor remained in the hands of its wartime incumbent, Karl Rothe, who retained office from 1917 to 1929. The composition of the municipal council also remained largely unchanged.[47]

Despite these continuities in personnel, the organization and structure of municipal affairs changed tremendously. Developments leading towards municipal control over such cultural institutions as museums and art galleries were already underway. Under pressure from the Social Democrats, the provision of social housing for working-class families was now defined as a task for city government. Leipzig and Chemnitz organized housing enterprises run by municipal administrations.[48]

These changes slowly transformed communities of wealthy citizens who felt responsible for the common good into ones that resembled anonymous, bureaucratic, administrative units. As philanthropists no longer financed cultural and social institutions to the degree they once had, city and state governments assumed financial responsibility for these institutions. After the First World War the direct financing of public institutions was replaced by indirect financing, using tax money collected by the state. Philanthropy lost its importance as a central factor ensuring the smooth functioning of the community, and it slowly declined into insignificance. This change in turn had important implications for the way citizens identified with their cities and how they staked their own claim for leadership in society.

Leipzig in the 1920s had little in common with the city of the 1890s. For example, it had first supported an art museum in 1886, giving the museum board approval to spend 10,000 marks annually for the expansion of the art collection and providing about 40 per cent of the museum's annual costs. In 1909 the city finally assumed complete control over the museum. Soon thereafter, through a highly symbolic act, it excluded the possibility of any further philanthropic support. In 1912 Julius Vogel, the director of the museum, took the plaster-cast collection and presented it to Leipzig's schools. The original museum donors protested vehemently – to no avail. Vogel then proceeded to discard the pictures and busts of the very philanthropists who had donated so much money and *objets d'art* to the museum. Understandably, these actions had immediate consequences. The willingness of Leipzig's wealthy citizens to support the museum declined precipitously. The time of the philanthropists was over – not because of the actions of philanthropists themselves, but because of a city government that had chosen to exclude them from influence and prestige.[49]

On one hand, this 'mistreatment' caused cultural philanthropists to withdraw in alienation and frustration, relinquishing leadership in the community they had once believed to be 'theirs.' On the other hand, when the city assumed absolute control over Leipzig's public institutions of culture, it opened the doors of such institutions to the lower classes. Admission to the Art Museum and the *Gewandhaus* had been beyond the financial reach of the working classes until the First World War. Such exclusion had contributed to the success of the Social Democratic movement in establishing its own cultural world. Only in the crisis of war and revolution did these symbols of bourgeois culture lose their exclusive character, thus mitigating at least the cultural division within the city.[50] In this sense we can speak of a historic step having been taken towards the democratization of culture and the integration of the working classes into German society. However, these same years of crisis also changed the relationship between the wealthy citizens who financed these institutions and the city administration, as reflected in the trauma suffered by the philanthropists who saw their own images abused and neglected. They became less inclined to engage in other attempts to support culture and the arts. Philanthropy did not die overnight. But over the next three decades, it continued to decline, until it seemed hardly to play a role at all in the affairs of the city. One of the few exceptions remaining today is the Meyersche Foundation in Leipzig, which, despite forty years of communist rule, still fulfils the original intentions of its founder.

Although we must not read history backward, this epilogue throws light on the way philanthropic networks and habits of mind operated in Germany around the time of revolution in 1918–19. Because Leipzig's burghers believed that their role in support of cultural institutions was no longer valued, they did not offer much resistance to the democratization of the suffrage laws. The city was no longer the property of wealthy citizens, no longer a tightly knit community whose members knew one another well and shared common values. It had become a more autonomous social unit that now included – indeed, actively embraced – all strata of society. Virtually all social and cultural institutions were financed by public money. Those for which private money remained critical sources of support (including the *Gewandhaus* and the Meyersche Foundation) continued to be the exceptions that proved the rule. In this new environment, the universal suffrage was not anomalous at all.[51]

Conclusions

If money allegedly taints politics across the ages, we should not infer that the converse is always true. There is little to be gained in suggesting – and it has not been the intention of this chapter to argue – that philanthropists in Saxon cities invariably operated with ulterior motives. Some were undoubtedly self-interested and cynical in pursuing the political goals identified here. But the majority of them seem to have regarded it as self-evident and wholly natural to pursue their claim to leadership in the social, economic, cultural, and political spheres simultaneously. Space has not permitted a full discussion of how this frame of mind can be mapped onto familiar distinctions of Left and Right in turn-of-the-century Saxon cities. Still, what have we learned about the political boundaries that constrained authoritarian imaginations in this corner of Germany?

On the one hand, we have become less quick to identify wealthy philanthropists as the target of our historical condescension or contempt (the double irony here is intended). On the other hand, we still face the challenge of dissecting motives for retrenchment or reform in terms of personal dispositions and dilemmas. Recently, a student of left liberalism in Wilhelmine Germany put it this way in trying to strike the proper balance: 'Nowhere is the tendency to analyze politics according to what we want it to be, rather than what it was, more evident than in the area of economics and material self-interest. Too often accounts echo contemporary (mainly Liberal) complaints that politics are being overtaken and debased by competing material interests. But "pocket book" issues were an inevitable and important part of politics and need to be taken seriously. Indeed, ... left liberal rhetoric condemning the rise of interest politics was disingenuous. It was advanced to claim a moral superiority over opponents ... To understand Wilhelmine politics, a wide agenda of political causes and antagonisms must be examined, not just the great issues of "national" questions, constitutional reform, and class-conflict.'[52] In seconding this conclusion, one can only add that although class conflict, constitutional propriety, and political antagonisms are indeed the stuff of national histories, they are no less significant when, as in these three Saxon cities, they are writ small.

218 Cultures of Conservatism

NOTES

1 The original version of this chapter was co-authored with Thomas Adam.
2 Albert Camus, *Resistance, Rebellion, and Death*, cited in Allan Hutchinson, 'Election Spending: We Need a Balance of Voices,' *Globe and Mail* (Toronto), 25 Oct. 2000, A19.
3 See Thomas Kühne, *Dreiklassenwahlrecht und Wahlkultur in Preussen 1867– 1914* (Düsseldorf, 1994). For a contemporary account, see Victor Böhmert, *Der sächsische Wahlgesetzentwurf und seine Gefahren* (Dresden, 1896). Böhmert notes (2) that while most National Liberals in Leipzig were in favour of the government's proposed *Landtag* suffrage reform, many elsewhere in Saxony opposed it, in part because they feared it would disrupt employer-employee relations in the workplace (8–9).
4 In the Reichstag elections of 1903, the SPD won 58.8 per cent of the popular vote and twenty-two of twenty-three Saxon seats. In the last three *Landtag* elections fought under the three-class suffrage (1903, 1905, 1907), the SPD won 45.4 per cent of the vote but only one seat. The SPD's share of the vote in Dresden, Leipzig, and Chemnitz was 48.3, 51.1, and 59.0 per cent respectively. See Gerhard A. Ritter with Merith Niehuss, *Wahlgeschichtliches Arbeitsbuch* (Munich, 1980), 89, 176; Simone Lässig, *Reichstagswahlen im Königreich Sachsen 1871–1912, Beiheft zur Karte D IV 2. Atlas zur Geschichte und Landeskunde von Sachsen*, ed. Sächsische Akademie der Wissenschaften zu Leipzig (Leipzig and Dresden, 1998). On the rise of Social Democracy, see Mike Schmeitzner and Michael Rudloff, *Geschichte der Sozialdemokratie im Sächsischen Landtag. Darstellung und Dokumentation 1877–1997* (Dresden, 1997); Michael Rudloff, Thomas Adam, and Jürgen Schlimper, *Leipzig – Wiege der deutschen Sozialdemokratie* (Berlin, 1996); and Gerhard A. Ritter, 'Das Wahlrecht und die Wählerschaft der Sozialdemokratie im Königreich Sachsen 1867–1914,' in *Der Aufstieg der deutschen Arbeiterbewegung*, ed. Ritter with Elisabeth Müller-Luckner (Munich, 1990), 49–101.
5 On regional approaches see Gerhard A. Ritter, ed., *Wahlen und Wahlkämpfe in Deutschland* (Düsseldorf, 1997). The plutocratic features of the 1909 *Landtag* suffrage and their significance for the public discourse about suffrage reform remain only partially explored. See Ritter, 'Wahlrecht'; Ritter, 'Wahlen und Wahlpolitik im Königreich Sachsen 1867–1914,' in *Sachsen im Kaiserreich*, ed. Simone Lässig and Karl Heinrich Pohl (Dresden, 1997), 29–86; Simone Lässig, *Wahlrechtskampf und Wahlreform in Sachsen (1895–1909)* (Cologne, etc., 1996); and James Retallack, '"What Is to Be

Done?" The Red Specter, Franchise Questions, and the Crisis of Conservative Hegemony in Saxony, 1896–1909,' *Central European History* 23 (1990): 271–312.
6 Limits of space preclude a consideration of smaller Saxon cities.
7 'Revidierte Städteordnung vom 24. April 1873,' *Die Gesetzgebung des Königreichs Sachsen* (Leipzig, 1896), 3:178–92; see also Richard Dietrich, 'Die Verwaltungsreform in Sachsen 1869–1873,' *Neues Archiv für sächsische Geschichte* 61 (1940): 49–85.
8 The best single source, on which most later accounts rely, is Leo Ludwig-Wolf, 'Leipzig,' in *Verfassungs- und Verwaltungsorganisation der Städte*, vol. 4, no. 1, *Königreich Sachsen*, ed. Verein für Socialpolitik, Schriften des Vereins für Socialpolitik, 120/I (hereafter cited as VfS, *Sachsen*) (Leipzig, 1905; rpt. Vaduz, 1990), 123–61; the following analysis is also indebted to Michael Schäfer, 'Die Burg und die Bürger. Stadtbürgerliche Herrschaft und kommunale Selbstverwaltung in Leipzig im frühen 20. Jahrhundert,' in *Wirtschaft und Gesellschaft in Sachsen im 20. Jahrhundert*, ed. Werner Bramke and Ulrich Heß (Leipzig, 1998), 270–93, and Schäfer, 'Bürgertum, Arbeiterschaft und städtische Selbstverwaltung zwischen Jahrhundertwende und 1920er Jahren im deutsch-britischen Vergleich. Befunde einer vergleichenden Lokalstudie,' in *Mitteilungsblatt des Instituts zur Erforschung der europäischen Arbeiterbewegung (IGA)*, no. 20 (1998): 178–232. See also Schäfer, *Bürgertum in der Krise. Städtische Mittelklassen in Edinburgh und Leipzig 1890 bis 1930* (Göttingen, 2003), esp. pt. 2: 38–166; and Paul Brandmann, *Leipzig zwischen Klassenkampf und Sozialreform* (Cologne etc., 1998), esp. 45–56.
9 On the incomes of Saxon workers, see Thomas Adam, 'How Proletarian Was Leipzig's Social Democratic Milieu?' in *Saxony in German History: Culture, Society, and Politics, 1830–1933*, ed. James Retallack (Ann Arbor, 2000), 259–62; and Adam, *Arbeitermilieu und Arbeiterbewegung in Leipzig 1871–1933* (Cologne etc., 1999), 70–1.
10 See Karin Pontow, 'Bourgeoise Kommunalpolitik und Eingemeindungsfrage in Leipzig im letzten Viertel des 19. Jahrhunderts,' *Jahrbuch für Regionalgeschichte* 8 (1981): 84–106; Karl Czok, 'Die Stellung der Leipziger Sozialdemokratie zur Kommunalpolitik in der ersten Hälfte der neunziger Jahre des 19. Jahrhunderts,' *Arbeitsberichte zur Geschichte der Stadt Leipzig* 11, Heft 1 (Nr. 24) (1973): 5–54.
11 Adam, 'How Proletarian?' 293–5.
12 Exceptions include Helmuth Croon, 'Das Vordringen der politischen Parteien im Bereich der kommunalen Selbstverwaltung,' in *Kommunale*

Selbstverwaltung im Zeitalter der Industrialisierung, ed. Croon et al. (Stuttgart, 1971), 15–54; Karl Heinrich Pohl, 'Power in the City: Liberalism and Local Politics in Dresden and Munich,' in *Saxony*, ed. Retallack, 289–308.

13 Helga Grebing, Hans Mommsen, and Karsten Rudolph, eds., *Demokratie und Emanzipation zwischen Saale und Elbe* (Essen, 1993).
14 Merith Niehuss, 'Party Configurations in State and Municipal Elections in Southern Germany, 1871–1914,' in *Elections, Parties and Political Traditions*, ed. Karl Rohe (New York, Oxford, Munich, 1990), 101. See also Niehuss, 'Strategieen zur Machterhaltung bürgerlicher Éliten am Beispiel kommunaler Wahlrechtsänderungen im ausgehenden Kaiserreich,' in *Politik und Milieu*, ed. Heinrich Best (St Katharinen, 1989), 60–91.
15 Niehuss, 'Party Configurations,' 101–2.
16 Ibid., 102.
17 Ibid.
18 Ibid.
19 Hartmut Pogge von Strandmann, 'The Liberal Power Monopoly in the Cities of Imperial Germany,' in *Elections, Mass Politics, and Social Change in Modern Germany: New Perspectives*, ed. Larry Eugene Jones and James Retallack (New York and Cambridge, 1992), 93–118; see also the seminal essay by James J. Sheehan, 'Liberalism and the City in Nineteenth-Century Germany,' *Past and Present*, no. 51 (1971): 116–37.
20 Ludwig-Wolf, 'Leipzig,' 137–8; see also Schäfer, 'Burg,' 274.
21 Ritter, *Wahlgeschichtliches Arbeitsbuch*, 142, table 2.
22 See esp. Walter Gagel, *Die Wahlrechtsfrage in der Geschichte der deutschen liberalen Parteien 1848–1918* (Düsseldorf, 1958); James J. Sheehan, *German Liberalism in the Nineteenth Century* (Chicago, 1978), 105–7.
23 See StadtA Leipzig, Kap. 7, Nr. 36, Bd. 1, Bl. 147–9; Ludwig-Wolf, 'Leipzig,' 137–40; Schäfer, 'Burg,' 273–5; Adam, *Arbeitermilieu*, 293–7.
24 StadtA Leipzig, Kap. 7, Nr. 36, Bd. 1, Bl. 160.
25 Lässig, *Wahlrechtskampf*, 67–80; Schmeitzner and Rudloff, *Geschichte*, 25–36.
26 See F. Seger, *Dringliche Reformen. Einige Kapitel Leipziger Kommunalpolitik* (Leipzig, 1912), 29; Adam, *Arbeitermilieu*, 297–8.
27 See Ludwig-Wolf, 'Leipzig,' 137–8.
28 Chemnitz's population in 1905 stood at 243,476 persons, of whom about 16,500 held the right of citizenship (*Bürgerrecht*); see Johannes Hübschmann, 'Chemnitz,' in VfS, *Sachsen*, 163–79, here 165.
29 StadtA Leipzig, Kap. 7, Nr. 36, Bd. 1, Bl. 160; Johannes Hübschmann, 'Chemnitz,' in VfS, *Sachsen*, 165–9.
30 StadtA Leipzig, Kap. 7, Nr. 36, Bd. 1, Bl. 160; Rudolf Heinze, 'Dresden,' in VfS, *Sachsen*, 115–21.

Citadels against Democracy   221

31 Lässig, *Wahlrechtskampf*; Schäfer, 'Burg.'
32 The introduction of a plural voting system enabled Social Democrats to occupy twenty-five seats (nearly one-third of total) in the post-1909 *Landtag*. See Lässig, *Wahlrechtskampf*, 214–47.
33 Thomas Adam, 'Die Kommunalisierung von Kunst und Kultur als Grundkonsens der deutschen Gesellschaft ab dem ausgehenden 19. Jahrhundert,' *Die Alte Stadt* 2 (1999): 79– 99; Adam, *Allgemeine Ortskrankenkasse Leipzig 1887 bis 1997* (Leipzig, 1999); Adam, *Die Anfänge industriellen Bauens in Sachsen* (Leipzig, 1998); Adam, 'Das soziale Engagement Leipziger Unternehmer – die Tradition der Wohnstiftungen,' in *Unternehmer in Sachsen*, ed. Ulrich Heß and Michael Schäfer (Leipzig, 1998), 107–18; Margaret Menninger, 'Art and Civic Patronage in Leipzig, 1848–1914' (PhD diss., Harvard University, 1998).
34 Adam, *Allgemeine Ortskrankenkasse*, 32.
35 M.J. Daunton, 'Payment and Participation: Welfare and State Formation in Britain 1900–1951,' *Past and Present*, no. 150 (1996): 177.
36 Menninger, 'Art'; Adam, 'Kommunalisierung.'
37 See Robert Beachy, *The Soul of Commerce: Credit, Property, and Politics in Leipzig, 1750–1840* (Leiden and Boston, 2005).
38 Adam, *Allgemeine Ortskrankenkasse*, 30.
39 Hübschmann, 'Chemnitz,' 168–70, and for the following.
40 Schäfer, 'Burg,' 274; the following obervation from 1912 is cited ibid., 275–6, based on Ludwig-Wolf, 'Leipzig,' 141.
41 Schäfer, 'Burg,' 285.
42 Socialists in Leipzig, too, offered no hope of compromise: their position hardened in favour of nothing less than the universal, equal, and secret suffrage for municipal elections. However, they were not mistaken in seeing in later liberal reform proposals nothing more than an attempt to win members of the new *Mittelstand* to their own camp. See Brandmann, *Leipzig*, 54n109.
43 Ibid., 51–2.
44 Lässig, *Wahlrechtskampf*, 181–247; Schmeitzner and Rudloff, *Geschichte*, 30–41.
45 StadtA Leipzig, Kap. 7, Nr. 36, Bd. 1.
46 Ibid., Bl. 160.
47 For Leipzig, see Rudloff, Adam, and Schlimper, *Leipzig*, 111–34; Sebastian Thiem, '"... der Oberbürgermeister blieb aber weiter auf seinem Posten." Das Leipziger Oberbürgermeisteramt vom Vorabend des ersten Weltkrieges bis zum Ende der zwanziger Jahre,' in *Wirtschaft*, ed. Bramke and Heß, 293–325; for Dresden we have no comparable study; for Chemnitz

we must rely on the insubstantial study entitled *Die SPD im Chemnitzer Rathaus 1897–1997* (Hanover, 1997).
48 Within eight years, the city of Leipzig owned and operated not only the largest number of houses in Leipzig but also the largest number of communal houses among the German cities. See Thomas Adam, *125 Jahre Wohnreform in Sachsen. Zur Geschichte der Sächsischen Baugenossenschaften (1873–1998)* (Leipzig, 1999), 34–6.
49 Adam, 'Kommunalisierung,' 90–2; Menninger, 'Art,' 101–5; B. Rothbauer, 'Vom Stiftermuseum zur modernen Kunstsammlung. Bausteine zur Sozialgeschichte der Kunststiftungen in Leipzig,' in *150 Jahre Museum der bildenden Künste 1837–1987* (Leipzig, 1987), 30.
50 Adam, *Arbeitermilieu*, 145.
51 Adam, *125 Jahre*, 32–6; Rudloff, Adam, and Schlimper, *Leipzig*, 130–4; Urich Krüger, 'Leipzigs Stadtwirtschaft. Eine Skizze ihrer Entwicklung,' in *Sachsen und Mitteldeutschland*, ed. Werner Bramke and Ulrich Heß (Cologne etc., 1995), 215–40.
52 Alastair P. Thompson, *Left Liberals, the State, and Popular Politics in Wilhelmine Germany* (Oxford, 2000), 11.

PART THREE

Tension and Détente

7 Publicity and Partisanship

Worthless fellows, these gentlemen of the quill! Cowardly, malicious, deceitful in their irresponsibility.
Gustav Freytag, *Die Journalisten. Lustspiel in vier Akten* (1854), act 3, scene 1[1]

In 1980 a historian of the German Right noted that scholars faced a 'massive problem' in integrating analyses of the imperial German state and its political culture with 'the history of mass communications ... and the relation of propaganda to ideology.'[2] Other historians have since called for 'a social history of reading, writing, and publishing' in nineteenth-century Germany[3] and for a social history of professionalism (*Beruf*).[4] The challenge of integrating the histories of mass communication and right-wing politics still confronts historians of Germany, regardless whether they focus on the late Enlightenment or the early twentieth century. This chapter begins by returning to an age when journalists, as members of the learned estate in Germany, discovered that their quest for professional status compelled them to carve out their own political space – sometimes in direct opposition to the state, more often in an ambiguous relationship with it. That political space was a vital component of what scholars call the public sphere (*Öffentlichkeit*).[5]

Why has the history of German journalism been so often bypassed by scholars? Instead of linking histories of the German state with the social history of politics, most contributions to the field have studied individual journalists or publishing houses, on the one hand, or the repressive institutions of authority, on the other. With one notable exception,[6] these studies have rarely enlightened us about how journalists actually functioned in society and politics. Scholars who focus on the educated middle classes and the learned professions in Germany also tend to look right through journalists. They refuse to welcome journalists on the journey because they did not adhere to accepted models of professional behaviour.[7] Journalists' notoriously low socio-economic status, their inability to restrict entry to their field, their lack of specialized training, and their dependence on patrons and clients[8] – these factors seem to confirm Otto von Bismarck's verdict of 1862 that journalism was a dumping ground for those who had failed to find their calling in life.

This chapter addresses these lacunae by asking whether journalists in general and right-wing journalists in particular should be included among those members of the educated middle classes who 'saw professionalism as an attractive alternative to fuzzy intellectual idealism, the tainted profit motive, or the anonymous government bureaucracy.'[9] Was political journalism one of the first bourgeois pursuits in Germany to generate professional *Angst* in the nineteenth century? Any answer must consider the journalist in society and the self-definition of the profession as two sides of a single coin. How did journalists police themselves, and to what extent did they believe that the state should do the job for them? How were journalists' social status and political function related? And did right-wing attempts to limit political discourse in nineteenth-century Germany influence journalists' willingness to censure those 'unprofessional' colleagues who in other fields were labelled quacks, charlatans, and ambulance-chasers?

A social history of journalism demonstrates that German journalists' definition of their own social status and function did indeed depend on whether they belonged to the political Left or Right. Liberals favoured the abandonment of what they saw as socio-economic, cultural, and political 'residues' from the pre-modern era; hence they tended to accord relatively high status to journalism, whether or not it was overtly political. Conservatives, on the other hand, could not embrace change with the same enthusiasm. As a growing number of journalists became wealthy, respected, and powerful in their own right during the course of the nineteenth century, liberals applauded the structural changes in society and politics that allowed these men to exert unprecedented influence. Conservatives, in the main, condemned these changes, and often their displeasure with modernity fell on the shoulders of journalists (even right-wing journalists) who seemed to hasten its arrival.

The section following this introduction launches the discussion by describing the reading revolution in Germany after 1770, by differentiating between journalists and other writers, and by exploring the self-image of journalists before 1830. The next section provides an overview of how the everyday aspects of journalism – writing, publishing, gathering news, getting paid – changed between the Enlightenment and the foundation of the German Empire, while the subsequent section considers the role of journalists in efforts to modernize the political Right. The focus then returns to the 'professionalization project'[10] of German journalists between 1871 and 1920. Efforts to enhance the standing of the profession are examined through a discussion of the mass-based, advertisement-driven *Generalanzeiger* press, of new 'professional' organizations, and of the role of women in the field. Some concluding remarks suggest possible avenues for future research.

A Revolution in Print

Adelaide. Journalists are, as I notice, dangerous people, and it is well to have their goodwill, although I, an insignificant person, will take pains never to furnish material for a newspaper article.

Gustav Freytag, *Die Journalisten*, act 3, scene 1

The professionalization project of German journalists must be understood within the context of the transformation of the public sphere beginning in the late Enlightenment. Of the many events that transformed Europe between 1770 and 1815, cultural life in Germany was arguably most affected by a revolution in print. The number of German-language periodicals more than doubled during the last three decades of the eighteenth century. In the same period the number of reading circles and societies – leaving aside lending libraries – increased from a mere dozen to some two hundred.[11] Whereas only about 15 per cent of the inhabitants of German-speaking territories could read in 1764, this figure had reached about 33 per cent by 1800 and 40 per cent by 1830.[12] Each copy of a newspaper (*Zeitung*) was seen by an estimated average of ten readers and was read aloud to many more. Hence Germany's total production of about 300,000 newspapers in 1800 would have reached well over 3 million readers and listeners. To this picture can be added a 'few hundred' journals (*Zeitschriften*) appearing at any one time in the late eighteenth century. These reached an audience of perhaps 300,000 to 400,000.[13]

In this period Germans nonetheless witnessed only the first of several reading revolutions.[14] Periodical publishing took its largest leap forward between the 1770s and what the Austrian foreign minister Klemens von Metternich in 1808 labelled the 'century of words.'[15] But one could also point to the impact of revolutionary events in 1830 and (more obviously) 1848 as decisive. One estimate puts at 1,000 the number of newspapers appearing in the German Confederation before the revolution of 1848; of these, perhaps 100 could be considered political.[16] An estimate for 1850 already puts the total figure at 1,500.[17] Still another revolution occurred after unification in 1871, when literacy rates topped 70 per cent and kept climbing. Within the borders of the German Empire, the number of newspapers rose from about 2,400 in the 1870s to over 4,200 in 1914. The number of journals rose from about 3,300 in 1890 to 6,500 in 1914.

The total circulation of German newspapers and journals is notoriously difficult to estimate. Publishers' circulation statistics were inevitably inflated. But one estimate suggests that between 1885 and 1914 the average newspaper edition rose from 2,600 copies to 8,600 copies.[18] During the First World War and the period immediately after, Germany experienced two more reading revolutions of comparable magnitude, as the volume of available reading matter first plummeted and then rose to new heights.[19] In short, the scale as well as the character of German periodical publishing changed enormously from the late eighteenth century to the early twentieth, whether one speaks of one reading revolution or many. It is only natural that the working conditions, the social image, and the political function of the journalist were transformed just as fundamentally in the process.

That a new role for journals and newspapers facilitated the emergence of both organized 'public opinion' and the public sphere in Germany is well known.[20] Bounded on the one side by the private sphere and on the other side by the state, the public sphere also includes the network of voluntary associations, political parties, civil liberties, and public customs that foster the formulation and communication of public opinion.[21] As the German press evolved from 'the journalism of private men of letters to the public consumer services of the mass media,'[22] it helped to define the contours of the public sphere as a cultural phenomenon and as a class-bound product of social experience. Historians continue to debate the role of 'ideological' versus 'commercial' publishing in this era.

What distinguished literary from political journalism, and how were journalists' experiences distinct from those of poets, dramatists, novelists, pamphleteers, and other writers? In many respects, journalists can be included among those to whom the young poet Hermann Conradi addressed his call in 1884 for all German artists to become 'protectors and guardians, leaders and comforters, pathfinders and guides, physicians and priests of humanity.'[23] The terms Conradi used remind us that journalists – like doctors, clerics, lawyers, and others imbued with a professional ideology – saw themselves contributing to the good of society by both enlightening and leading the people. To describe this rhetoric as ideology is to note that it was self-serving, but this characterization should not imply that journalists sought to hoodwink the public. Like other professionals, they generally concluded that true talent, to be legitimate, was premised on virtue.[24]

At the dawn of the nineteenth century, most Germans would have agreed that journals and newspapers ought to have different functions: 'newspapers report, journals reflect.'[25] But newspapers were intended for an audience that already had sufficient cultivation and political understanding to make sense of a bare reporting of facts. By 1800 such newspapers were allegedly coming into the wrong hands. These of course were the hands of the lower classes, who were thought to lack the mature judgment for private political reflection and who (contemporary critics were equally certain) were unlikely to acquire it through reading the daily press. Such fears arose even before the French Revolution, and they haunted Germans throughout the nineteenth century. The 'dreadful' and 'vacuous' books that Jacob Grimm found in Hessian lending libraries in the 1830s and 1840s were dangerous because they appealed to popular tastes and modest budgets.[26] King Friedrich Wilhelm IV of Prussia agreed. In a cabinet order of February 1843 he wrote: 'What I do not wish is the degradation of science and literature into journalism or that the latter should be placed in a position of equal dignity with the former.'[27]

Public opinion and 'published opinion' were both theoretically concerned with providing universal truths to the reader. But liberals always believed more fervently than conservatives that demagoguery and lies would vanish as more 'general' information became 'generally available' – hence Johann Cotta's *Allgemeine Zeitung* and Karl Biedermann's *Deutsche Allgemeine Zeitung*.[28] Yet as Rudolf Vierhaus has observed, political journalism of all sorts involved a 'complicated process of working over experiences, assimilating and passing on knowledge, becoming sensitized to what had hitherto either been taken for granted or gone unnoticed, recognizing contradictions, and becoming and making others receptive to opinion and the formulation of aims. It took place within the context of general intellectual shifts and changes in *mentalité*, which in turn were inseparable from concrete socio-cultural and socio-economic change.'[29] The politicization of the public sphere, in other words, was not a social situation but a social activity. As such, it was always influenced by the process (not institution) of self-cultivation (*Bildung*).[30]

According to the editor of the *Vossische Zeitung*, Karl Philipp Moritz, the ideal newspaper of the 1780s was no longer a vehicle for the reporting of novelties and curiosities. Rather, it was a 'mouthpiece through which one can preach to the people and force the voice of truth into both the palaces of the mighty and the hovels of the lowly.'[31] In this enterprise, knowledge could not be merely communicated to the lower orders in neutral terms. It had to be general knowledge, but useful, comprehensible, served in manageable portions. And so the journalist took on the guise of other 'professionals' in the public sphere – as 'teacher, translator, distributor, and popularizer'; as adviser, neighbour, friend to humanity, reformer, and patron of the general welfare; and as discussant, evaluator, critic, litigator (*Räsonneur*), and judge (*Richter*).[32]

The Enlightenment passion for statistics was symptomatic here. It implied a 'professional' approach in the form of specialized knowledge combined with social altruism. Statistics provided the opportunity for drawing up a balance sheet of society's virtues and ills. With them one could draft a better order for the world. Statistics, Hans Erich Bödeker has written, 'became the method and raw material of political reasoning, and hunger for statistics the tool with which to engineer social and political emancipation.'[33] Thus August Ludwig Schlözer, editor of the *StatsAnzeigen* and probably the most influential German journalist of the late 1700s, sought to bring the veiled workings of the state into the light of day: 'Statistics and despotism are incompatible.'[34]

As we will discover, even in the 1770s right-wing journalists opposed such presumption with a vehemence that approached fanaticism. But the goal of making the press a 'fearsome tribunal' inspired only a small minority of journalists. Most agreed that it was not necessary to seek formal limits to the political power of the state or guarantees of popular participation in politics. Again, quite the contrary was true. Notions of a bourgeois public and advocacy of bourgeois reform were perfectly compatible with the holding of professional positions as servants of the state. The aim of the liberal publisher Johann Cotta was 'to define, and institutionalize, a realm of action beyond the control of the state, but short of opposition to it – a "public" realm in which intellectual independence and political loyalty would equally well be served.'[35] This aim inspired many journalists (and other writers) well into the middle of the nineteenth century. Thus a character in one of Karl Gutzkow's novels claimed that 'the basic rights of the people are basic duties of the knights of the spirit.'[36] Yet in the later era Gutzkow suffered state repression as a member of the Young Germany movement, whereas Cotta's announced goals did not keep him from making his peace with Metternich and his conservative ally Friedrich von Gentz.

Conservatives in the Napoleonic era did not need to challenge every conclusion reached by liberals who sought to expand the power of the press. What they more often criticized was the logic that led to those conclusions. They worried, for example, that not reading but 'excessive' reading (*Zuviel-Lesen, Zeitungsleserei, Lesesucht*) was to blame for social and political unrest. By catering to a half-educated public, newspapers allegedly foisted prefabricated opinion on readers too ignorant to distinguish between objectivity and partisanship or between substance and superficiality. And by supplying the masses with compelling accounts of the world, newspapers fuelled the 'pretentious' and mistaken belief of the common people that they were well informed about the world and hence should be allowed to participate in changing it. As James J. Sheehan has written, in the wake of the French Revolution many intellectuals began to see 'excessive' reading as a symptom of social upheaval and moral decline. An 'epidemic of compulsive reading,' such intellectuals believed, was 'leading to physiological, psychological, and social disabilities' – disabilities, moreover, to which 'disrespectful servants, overtrained teachers, nervous youths, and loose women were especially susceptible.'[37]

Journalists' assessments of their own role in society became more problematic as they were forced to show their political colours after 1789. Unlike other elites of service and culture, journalists gained little material compensation from the expansion of the public sphere; they did not fit into the 'comprehensive social theory' glorifying the educated bourgeoisie before 1848.[38] As successive waves of change swept across Germany in the form of invasion, occupation, and liberation, their forced entry into the world of politics brought journalists' nascent feelings of self-confidence and social importance into conflict with their equally strong feelings of 'astonishment, disaffection, anxiety, and even

7.1. News fanciers or connoisseurs? This caricature shows newspaper readers in a typical coffee house. *Die Zeitungsliebhaberey*, coloured etching by Andreas Geiger after a sketch by Johann Christian Schoeller, 1837. Image courtesy of the Deutsches Zeitungsmuseum, Wadgassen.

fear.'[39] 'It was truly a poetic epoch,' wrote Ernst Moritz Arndt in his memoirs, 'when, after long, dull dreams, our dear Germany awoke to a new literary and political existence.'[40] Johann Cotta's biographer has also noted the centrality of politics in the transformation of German journalism in these years: 'the newspapers Cotta read as a young man were remotely and inconsequentially *about* politics; those he published in his maturity would be most decidedly *in* politics – a development whose consequences, even for him, were difficult to judge.'[41] Moreover, the particular *mix* of self-confidence and anxiety registered by Cotta was itself conditioned by politics. After all, a predisposition towards change, positive or negative, is what helps to distinguish liberals from conservatives. If these two forces opposed each other in the sphere of public opinion, it was natural that liberals and conservatives should look on the enlargement of the public realm in different ways as well. If publicity was consensual in theory, it was also partisan in practice.

A Ruinous Career

Enemies? Who does not have them! But journalists have nerves like women. Everything stirs you up, every word that is said against you agitates you! I know you, you are sensitive people.

Gustav Freytag, *Die Journalisten*, act 1, scene 1

German journalists developed an early corporate ethos, but it remained more fragile than those adopted by other members of the educated middle classes. Factors that prevented the emergence of journalism as an acknowledged profession included the impossibility of limiting the number of recruits entering the field, the failure to develop a standard pattern of career advancement (the so-called career ladder), and the slow emergence of journalism as a full-time or lifetime pursuit. In examining these impediments to professionalization, we must not lose sight of differences between actual career patterns and *perceptions* about why individuals sought 'refuge' in the field of journalism.

How many journalists lived in Germany at the beginning and the end of the nineteenth century? Only the roughest guess can be attempted for the late Enlightenment, when perhaps a few thousand writers (*Schriftsteller*) had one foot planted firmly enough in the world of politics to allow them to call themselves 'publicists' (*Publizisten*).[42] Yet writing of any sort was still most commonly a secondary occupation that did not yield sufficient income on its own. Of these publicists, only a small proportion worked regularly for the periodical press and thus can be considered journalists in the narrow sense. A journalist's time, moreover, was typically divided between writing fiction and book reviews, contributing articles for encyclopedias, translating foreign texts, perhaps even checking page proofs or setting print. It is hardly surprising, therefore, that for most of the nineteenth century no reliable figures exist about the number of journalists in Germany. One historian has estimated that about 4,600 were active in Germany in 1904.[43]

Before 1848 the educational background of those journalists who became editors (always a minority) actually differed relatively little from that of other professionals. One study of ninety editors indicates that almost all of them had attended an institution of higher education, and a large proportion held a doctorate.[44] On the other hand, through much of the nineteenth century it was said that every journalist in Leipzig used the title of *Doktor* whether he held a PhD or not. Gradually, higher education became less, not more, important as an entrée to the field, increasing the social distance between journalists and doctors, lawyers, engineers, and other professionals.[45] This trend accelerated with the sudden emergence after the 1880s of the *Generalanzeiger* press, which was based on (relatively) non-partisan reporting, extensive advertisements, and mass circulations. Thus by 1923 another survey of editors revealed that 61 per cent classified themselves as 'academics' but only about 30 per cent had actually completed their studies.[46] Nonetheless, through much of the previous century most journalists were active either as 'educators' in the broad sense or in an occupation where they might handle printed matter as part of their daily routine: as librarians, officials, lawyers, book printers, or postmasters, for example.[47]

In the late eighteenth century many publishers composed, edited, and even printed their own material. But from about 1800 onward, publishers began increasingly to conceive of their function in managerial and commercial terms. In 1825, long before writers of any sort (let alone journalists) had their own professional association, German publishers formed the Association of German Book Dealers to represent their interests; by 1845 it included half of all publishers. In cities where the political press was expanding rapidly, the organization of publishers was sometimes followed more quickly by the organization of writers. Leipzig, for instance, was the centre of Germany's publishing industry and allegedly a 'mother lode' of opportunities for writers and publishers in the 1830s and 1840s. There the founding of a Book Dealers Association in 1833 preceded the founding of a Literary Association by only nine years.[48] But did the expansion of the German press augment the status or rewards of journalism? In many cases it did the exact opposite.

Publikum, Presse, Politikum

Because journalists were so sensitive to the charge of partisanship, they tried whenever possible to fudge the issue of where reportage ended and politics began. Local political circumstances often determined whether they were successful in this fudge. Again the case of Leipzig is illuminating. The founders of the Leipzig Literary Association were fully aware of Saxony's repressive press policies. Hence their statutes claimed (section 1) that the purpose of their organization was moral – not 'aesthetic,' still less 'political,' and certainly not designed to provide a 'comprehensive opinion' (*Gesammtmeinung*) about 'general matters of state.'[49] However, when the first German Assembly of Writers was held in Leipzig in 1845, many of the 110 writers in attendance would have agreed with a contributor to the liberal journal *Die Grenzboten* that this tactic had not been successful. This contributor wrote disapprovingly that 'political' and 'material' tendencies were more strongly represented at the Leipzig gathering than 'artistic' or 'idealistic' ones.[50]

The social status of German writers in general had improved slowly since the mid-eighteenth century, when to be labelled a 'novelist' was still an insult.[51] Journalists benefited from this trend, but only marginally. From the 1790s onward, journalism began to demand more work and to offer fewer rewards. It was not uncommon to hear references to the Roman slave trade when working conditions for ordinary newspaper writers were discussed. Parallels were also drawn between journalists and conscripted soldiers or forced labourers.[52] Friedrich Schiller, after working briefly (and obviously under duress) for the periodical press, wrote to a friend in 1788: 'May heaven protect you from the desperate thought of putting yourself in chains in the writer's galley [*Schriftstellergaleere*]. That I can warn my friend is the only real profit I derived from this experience.'[53] Many other famous writers tested the waters of journalism: Georg Wilhelm Friedrich Hegel, Karl Gutzkow, Ferdinand Freiligrath, Theodor Mommsen, Heinrich von Treitschke, and Karl Marx. It seems that most of them came to the same conclusion as Schiller. As editor of the *Schleswig-Holsteinische Zeitung* in 1848, Theodor Mommsen was typical in the bitterness of his reflections. After writing some sixty newspaper articles in the space of a few weeks during the revolution, he described journalism as so 'disreputable' and 'spiritually dissipating' that he would have come to ruin if he had been forced to endure it any longer.[54] Mommsen's fellow historian Heinrich von Treitschke agreed. In the 1870s, just one year before being called to the University of Berlin, he turned down a financially lucrative offer to edit the renowned *Spenersche Zeitung*. Treitschke reflected afterward: 'To write a lead editorial immediately upon receiving the latest telegram, and then to have to write the exact opposite eight days later – that is a business for other people.'[55]

As publishers and editors began to reassess the relationship between profitability, political independence, and literary excellence, it was more often the rank-and-file journalist who experienced the downside of an undersupply of conviction and an oversupply of manpower. By the 1850s Gustav Freytag's readers would have been familiar enough with this dilemma to appreciate the tragicomic quality of Schmock's famous lament in Freytag's drama *Die Journalisten*: 'My editor is a dishonest man. He cuts too much and pays too little ... How can I write pure brilliance for him at five *Pfennige* per line?'[56]

Nevertheless, as Lenore O'Boyle has written, in the 1830s and 1840s journalists and other writers were not poor because it was difficult to get into print; it was too easy. The small journals that proliferated in these years were willing to accept almost anything as long as they did not have to pay for it. And whereas the potential readership of political journals rose swiftly after 1840, production costs soared. The risk of offending Metternich's stable of censors also discouraged investment. As a result, holding the line on honoraria proved an effective way to reduce costs. This consideration continued to limit the number of salaried writers on the staffs of newspapers and journals well into the twentieth century: Hans Delbrück worried continually about the level of honoraria paid to writers who contributed to his *Preußische Jahrbücher*.[57] Hence, although there may have been what Heinrich Laube referred to as 'universal literary conscription'[58] in the nineteenth century, there also arose fine and increasingly oppressive distinctions of rank within the journalistic vocation. Theodor Fontane, who marshalled a national reputation as a writer of great fiction but also served as a literary foot soldier for the leading conservative newspaper, the *Kreuzzeitung*, understood how social antagonism and different roles in the creative process prevented the emergence of a corporate ethos among journalists. 'Only he who serves as his own editor,' Fontane observed once, 'can live from what he writes.'[59]

Although the relationship between editors and unsalaried journalists was not simply exploitative in the nineteenth century, editors were generally far better rewarded for their labours.[60] Yet only a tiny elite of editors received high remuneration. Around 1900 an editor of a small or medium-sized newspaper in a provincial capital might have earned somewhere between 3,000 and 10,000 marks annually. This salary would almost surely have placed such an editor among a small town's circle of notables. One thinks of the editor Nothgroschen in Heinrich Mann's novel *The Loyal Subject*, whom the protagonist described disparagingly – but inaccurately – as a 'broken-down scholar' and 'a starving penny-a-liner.'[61] Correspondents and editors with many years' experience might have earned between 10,000 and 20,000 marks, while a chief editor on the staff of a large national daily might have earned 40,000 to 50,000 marks annually.

The Image of the Journalist

To what extent does our knowledge about the working conditions and socio-economic status of journalists correspond to contemporaries' *perception* of the journalistic vocation? With what criteria did Germans appraise a journalist's 'product' – according to its literary merit, political influence, or market value? And why did they equate journalism with such a wide range of occupations, many of which were exceedingly low in status but some of which commanded as much respect as any learned profession?

One handbook for journalists (1901) observed that most Germans liked to complain about the government, the police, and the weather, but *everyone* complained about the newspapers of the day.[62] The number of critics who concentrated their attacks on the 'untrained' language and faulty grammar of journalists is legion. Well before 1848 and well after 1900, German journalists were being chided for their *Zeitungsdeutsch*, *Journalistendeutsch*, and *Kellerdeutsch*.[63] Nor was Gustav Freytag in the 1850s the first to recognize the dramatic potential of journalism. Other German playwrights had been levelling criticism against journalists for at least a century. The titles of their dramas make it abundantly clear that they associated newspaper work with hypocrisy, cant, parochialism, and the basest of personal motives.[64] Many of these observations sprang from an age when princely patronage was still indispensable to those who sought literary fame, when Germany lacked a national capital or intellectual centre equivalent to London and Paris, and when the low life of literature was colliding with the High Enlightenment.[65] Is it any wonder that early images of journalists' literary shortcomings, political naïveté, and crass self-interest persisted so long? 'Exaggeration of every sort,' wrote the philosopher Arthur Schopenhauer in 1851, 'is as inherent in journalism [*Zeitungsschreiberei*] as in the dramatic arts; for it is a matter of making as much as possible out of every action. That is why all newspaper writers, because of their craft, are alarmists. This is their way of making themselves interesting.'[66]

It was also said that journalism was a fine career – as long as you got out of it. But Germans always harboured grave suspicions about why certain types got into it. Bismarck's remark about journalism being a refuge for those who could not succeed in any other walk of life was only one among many such bons mots.[67] There has been an open season on German journalists for so long now that two scholars recently collected these potshots and filled a book.[68] Were all these snipers off the mark? It hardly seems possible. Gotthold Lessing, one of the most prominent writers and editors in Germany after 1750, wrote that 'today, every young man who is only passably competent in the German language and who has read the odd thing here and there, is editing a weekly journal.'[69] A long line of other critics emphasized the same connection between social and professional misdevelopment. Adolph von Knigge complained in 1785 that 'the fools are everywhere; whoever cannot do anything else writes [for] a journal,'[70] while the conservative social observer (and journalist) Wilhelm Heinrich Riehl noted in the mid-nineteenth century that 'whoever wants to reap without having first sown becomes a *Literat*.'[71]

Riehl believed that German journalism had been born 'socially premature.' But he was not the last to label journalists members of an 'intellectual proletariat' or to compare them to such other frustrated careerists as unsalaried lecturers, virtuosos, and comic actors.[72] Some contemporaries claimed that journalists functioned entirely outside the social organism. Parallels were drawn between journalists and gypsies, tinkers, actors, shepherds, ballad-mongers, and barrel organists. Other critics conceded that the press played a decisive role in modern society but noted that journalists were impossible to locate precisely on the social scale. More often the two viewpoints were mixed. The sociologist Max Weber, in his famous 1919 lecture 'Politics as a Vocation,' tried to defend the honour of journalists and their sense of responsibility as professionals. But he conveyed more strongly his notion of journalists as 'demagogues' and as a 'pariah caste' in society.[73] A last group of naysayers can be identified: those who postulated the indispensability of journalism but at the same time equated it with occupations that may be functionally necessary for society but whose practitioners often bring 'bad news': postal clerks, schoolmasters, lower officials, and – most revealingly of all – dentists.[74]

The simple ascription of negative status to journalists does not resolve the question of how and why they were so often judged according to standards established by other professional groups. Indeed, historians who cite these well-known observations often miss the political subtext that underlay them.[75] The frequency with which journalism was identified as the chosen profession of young, rootless, and poorly trained (or overtrained) school leavers 'on the make' reveals another important dimension of this problem. But it is not always possible to distinguish between liberal and conservative perceptions here. The liberal writers Karl Gutzkow and Heinrich Laube were among those who claimed that 'independence' ascribed 'outsider roles' to both journalism and liberalism. Whereas most of the ambitious and strong-willed students these men knew in their student days (the late 1820s and 1830s) desired a position connected with the state, 'every free activity that depended only on one's own independent strength was considered adventurous, even suspect.'[76] From a perspective even further left, Ferdinand Lassalle wrote that newspaper writers were 'a band of men who are unqualified to be elementary schoolteachers and too lazy to be postal clerks.'[77] Decades later Kaiser Wilhelm II was even more blunt. He described German journalists in 1890 as degenerate types destined to starve before they found gainful employment. In Wilhelm's view, German society was burdened by an 'overproduction of educated persons,' and journalists formed part of a new 'proletariat of school leavers.'[78] Max Weber's analysis in 1919 was more sophisticated and less negative than the Kaiser's. But Weber's conclusion also pointed to journalists' desperate need to earn a living and the lack of alternatives open to them. Thus he noted that journalists were among those professionals who now pursued politics as a vocation, not as a kind of voluntary service to society, as notables had (allegedly) pursued it in the nineteenth century. Journalists and other 'professionals' lived 'from' politics, Weber wrote, not 'for' politics.

Almost twenty-five years ago Cecelia von Studnitz attempted to draw up a balance sheet between journalists' social standing 'in reality' and the way they were portrayed in works of fiction (not quite all works in her sample were German).[79] Studnitz's principal conclusions can be summarized under five points.

First, in 62 per cent of her 183 cases where a journalist appeared as a fictional protagonist, Studnitz found that the journalist was presented in a generally positive light. In a limited sense, this may reflect the *self-image* of German journalists as well, because in over half these cases the author of the work had been active as a journalist. (Freytag is one of her examples.)

Second, Studnitz's study confirmed that journalists in fiction generally held liberal views and belonged to the middle classes. More than half the fictional journalists had middle-class origins, whereas only 6 per cent came from the upper classes. On the other hand, Studnitz noted that almost 30 per cent of fictional journalists came from the lower classes; in reality, she notes, this proportion was far lower.

Third, the relative socio-economic position of fictional journalists appears to have declined during the German Empire over what it had been in the period 1789–1870 and was again to be during the Weimar Republic. In the earlier and later eras, 43 per cent and 50 per cent of journalists were portrayed as 'comfortably situated.' In Imperial Germany only 32 per cent fell into this category.

Fourth, Studnitz also concluded that 'whereas one finds in works of fiction dependent, mercenary, starving journalistic protagonists who are striving for success,' in reality these types corresponded principally to those journalists who, as 'status changers' (*Statuswechsler*), pursued other occupations, including the more general designation *Schriftsteller-Publizist*. After 1870 the 'self-made journalist' appeared more frequently in reality, claimed Studnitz, though in works of fiction this figure was often portrayed as a parvenu or arriviste.

Lastly, Studnitz suggested that journalists in fictional works spanned the full range of positive and negative figures that we find personified by Bolz and Schmock in Freytag's *Die Journalisten*. On balance, however, these journalists' ethics and their motives for entering the field were neither as high-minded as one would expect (in theory) of modern professionals nor as suspect as many nineteenth-century observers charged.

Two sets of tentative conclusions can be drawn from Studnitz's study and the preceding argument. First, one must frequently rely on what journalists said about themselves – always a risky enterprise – as much as what others said about them. Just how much of the rhetoric about journalists' place in society can be taken at face value? In the end, it is impossible to distinguish categorically between the journalist's actual status in society, descriptions of the status that journalists would have *liked* to enjoy, and ascriptions of status based on comparisons with other groups against which Germans also ritually inveighed (the schoolteacher, the Catholic priest, the *Spießbürger*).

Second, the sharp polemical tone of political journalism in Germany clearly contributed to public distaste for the journalist as an individual. But what relative value was put on information, opinion, and style? Some readers voted with their feet when they selected a 'cheese and sausage rag' over a party organ because it offered more up-to-date stock prices. Others registered the opposite preference when they looked for a lead editorial spiced with a 'salty style.' But did readers consider journalists in their multiple identities – as public advocates, as employees in a commercial undertaking, as simple reporters of everyday events, and as professional politicians?[80]

Table 7.1. Images of the journalist before 1900

Characteristics	Positive protagonist	Negative protagonist
Label	• 'independent'	• 'dependent'
Social origins	• upper- or middle-class	• middle- or lower-class
Social mobility	• none	• declining, seldom ascending
Actual preparatory training	• 'academic journalist'	• '*Statuswechsler*' ('status-switcher')
Fictional preparatory training	• academic – higher education completed	• academic – higher education usually interrupted; seldom non-academic
Financial circumstances	• independent	• dependent
Principal activity	• writing	• editing
Field of activity	• *Gesinnungspresse* (political press)	• mainly *Gesinnungspresse*; seldom *Generalanzeigerpresse* (mass-based, advertisement-driven press)
Political engagement	• yes	• no
Preferred target group	• the people	• lobby groups
Imagined characteristics of readership	• positive: elite	• negative: elite
Perceived professional abilities	• talented	• untalented
Professional motives	• idealistic, political; to implement progressive ideas	• materialistic; to secure one's own material existence
Professional ethics	• yes	• no
Professional motivation		
(a) '*material*'		
• to earn money		27%
(b) '*egoistic*'		
• self-advancement		21%
• to exert power		12%
• to 'shock or destroy'		5%
(c) '*idealistic*'		
• to change things	21%	
• to enlighten	5%	
• to educate	4%	
• to control	3%	
• to help	1%	

Source: Based on Cecilia von Studnitz, *Kritik des Journalisten. Ein Berufsbild in Fiktion und Realität* (Munich, 1983), 71, 129–33; percentage figures for 'Professional motivation' refer to period 1789–1980s (N = 170 cases).

As noted previously, many liberals saw a 'modern' brand of journalism as a good thing. They tended to argue, for example, that political differences were anything but a handicap to the development of journalism. Could this attitude explain the willingness of liberal writers to satirize themselves, not only because it seemed both laudable and inevitable that they should do so but also because it reflected their opinions about talent, commitment, and professionalism? Conservatives, on the other hand, found far less comfort in the fact that a lively, up-to-date brand of journalism accurately reflected an anxiety-ridden age. Polemical journalism, by magnifying differences and divisions, could never appeal to those who prized social harmony and political stasis above all else. In their eyes, polemics could never be part of 'professional' journalism.

Maximilian Harden acknowledged the power of this conservative outlook in 1902. In an open letter to a New York journalist, he bitterly attacked the German establishment for its attitude towards journalists. 'Every year the Berlin Press Association holds a public ball,' wrote Harden; 'in attendance are dignitaries who perceive their own weakness and who hope for assistance from the great Babylonia in discreet matters; but as with visits to houses of ill-repute, they don't bring their wives with them ... This is the position of the press in the land of poets and philosophers ... Not only is the true journalist looked down upon – he who nimbly hauls in reports and toils away at them in editorial offices with pen, scissors, and pencil; no, [the same is true for] everyone who is associated with the press. It has come to the point that the disreputable social designation [of journalist] is avoided whenever possible: people who have no idea about law or political economy call themselves – both shamelessly and proudly – publicists.'[81]

Left and Right

Bolz. What do you desire from us, Roman slave? ... You want us to outrage your political convictions? To make you an apostate? ...
Schmock. Why do you bother yourself about that? I have learned ... to write in all directions. I have written Left and again Right. I can write in all directions.
Bolz. I see you have character. You cannot help but succeed on our newspaper.
Gustav Freytag, *Die Journalisten*, act 2, scene 2

When Gustav Freytag published *Die Journalisten* in 1854, he already had hands-on experience as editor of the influential Leipzig journal *Die*

Grenzboten. Yet he chose to explore journalism's dramatic potential by portraying German society as confronting the dual threats of political activism and journalistic irresponsibility. Early in his drama Freytag established the link between the 'maddening potion' of politics and the 'wicked spirit' of journalism. The noble heroine Adelaide at one point expresses the preference for security and tradition that so frequently coloured conservative criticisms of the press: 'These politics!' she exclaims. 'If I ever happen to take any man into my heart, I would place on him only one condition ...: Smoke tobacco, my husband, perhaps it does destroy the carpet; but don't ever dare to read a newspaper, that will ruin your character.'[82] Yet at the end of the story, Adelaide clandestinely purchases a liberal newspaper and sets herself up as publisher. Left standing in the wings are her hapless rivals: Schmock and his conspiratorial coterie of reactionary editors. Like so many others, they have proved unable to balance the conflicting demands of political conservatism and popular journalism.

Conservative journalists were always more ambivalent than their liberal colleagues about their perceived tasks in the public sphere. They had particular difficulty reconciling the need to write 'for the moment' with their faith in organic development and tradition. Though they sought to defend existing institutions, they were attacked for hastening change. Though empowered to cry out and tell all, they were expected to write cautiously and reveal nothing. When they composed polemical tracts for royal patrons or signed their name to an occasional journal article, they won personal recognition from those who were reluctant to arouse expectations about the future of public communication. But when they contributed anonymous articles to daily newspapers that promised more revelations on a continuing basis, they were damned. Conservative journalists were seen everywhere and welcomed nowhere.

Against this portrait of disappointed hopes and frustrated ambitions, one can also find in the historical record a compelling counter-image that stressed the tangible and (more often) the intangible rewards of journalism. But that counter-image was primarily a liberal one. Attempting to convince others that their calling deserved respect and preferment, liberals more often than conservatives blurred distinctions between their role in the literary and political spheres; indeed, they often claimed that their contribution was decisive in both.[83] Liberals tended to claim that they shouldered lightly the burden of their rootless existence, because such isolation was a necessary (if hardly welcome) guarantor of cultural creativity and political independence. From this perspective, liberal journalists wrote on their feet because they could never rest. They travelled without refuge because their home was the world. They accepted humble compensation for their labours because they did not pander to authority. And they belonged to no estate – much less a class – because they spoke for 'the people.'[84]

The great figures of the nineteenth-century press were liberals. The Wielands, the Cottas, the Sonnemanns, the Mosses – these men were no pariahs. Neither were Karl and Julius Bachem, Maximilian Harden, or Hans Delbrück, whose politics cannot easily be labelled but who might be described as moderate conservatives. By contrast, one is hard-pressed to think of a giant of conservative journalism at all, let alone one who was not tainted by scandal. Leopold Alois Hoffmann in the 1790s, Ernst Wilhelm Hengstenberg in the 1830s and 1840s, Hermann Wagener after 1848, and Wilhelm von Hammerstein-Schwartow in the 1880s and 1890s are only the most prominent among many examples.

A representative figure among this group was a hack writer who became editor of the first explicitly conservative journal in German lands, the *Wiener Zeitschrift* (1792–4). Leopold Alois Hoffmann has attracted more than his share of attention by virtue of the diatribes he unleashed against rationalism and the French Revolution.[85] Rather more interesting are his reflections on the function of political journalism itself. Those reflections help us avoid the mistake of reading back into the eighteenth century circumstances and attitudes that prevailed in the period 1819–48. One historian has argued that in pre-1848 Germany, periodicals had not progressed very far down the road from 'reflection' to 'criticism'; still only barely 'political,' they were not yet either fully 'politicized' or overtly 'politicizing.'[86] This characterization is misleading. The anti-revolutionary press was not a flower that could be nurtured carefully in the 1790s, but instead was brought to full bloom in the hothouse of revolutionary excitement. Hence there developed strains of German journalism that were politically (and aesthetically) less pleasing than some historians have acknowledged. For this reason a brief account of Hoffmann's contribution to the genre can illuminate the triangular relationship among the combating of a 'dangerous' press, the early growth of negative images of German journalism, and the genesis of political conservatism.

The style of the *Wiener Zeitschrift* in both tone and substance was set by Hoffmann in the first issue.[87] That issue covered almost every article of faith espoused by conservative journalists for decades to come. It attacked the 'intoxication with liberty' and 'the general atmosphere of political fermentation' in the wake of the French Revolution. It also attacked the practitioners of 'unbridled enlightenment': the 'horde of cosmopolitan and "philanthropic" authors' and 'subversive political assassins' who allegedly took Comte de Mirabeau as their model. Public opinion was 'completely in their hands,' Hoffmann argued, because their 'brazen loquaciousness [and] their flair for intrigue and manipulation,' when combined with the 'terrifying omnipotence' of secret societies, lent prestige to their 'disastrous principles.'

The quantity as well as the quality of reading material available to the German public concerned Hoffmann deeply. He believed that the basic truths of religion, philosophy, and ethics had been discovered long ago and found sufficient expression in existing books. Hence they did not need to be repeated, revised, or reflected upon. Condemning both the vulgar reading habits of the masses and the profit motive among publishers that forced authors to prostitute themselves in order to survive, Hoffmann believed that 'the good cause' would be served if books were once again published only in Latin, as in the Middle Ages. Public education was antithetical to true understanding, he wrote; it promoted only 'freshness, obtrusiveness, wild manners, [and] insolence.'[88]

Hoffmann was also in favour of strict censorship of the press. He once wrote that Germany need never fear 'intellectual despotism.'[89] On the other hand, he advocated the subsidization of conservative publicists, proposing that the state appoint a tribunal to review the credentials of every person who sought to enter the guild of writers. Here, too, he anticipated later conservative views of 'legitimate' journalistic qualifications when he declared that such a body must be composed only of men 'of known integrity, religious convictions, and solid learning.' Hoffmann could never have appreciated how decisively his own writing had called into question the integrity of political journalism itself.

After Hoffmann's journal collapsed, Robespierre, Napoleon, and the Prussian reformers provided conservative journalists with more vivid images to mobilize their readers. Always attacking the 'excesses' of rationalist and egalitarian thought, these writers set about the business of conservative journalism. They still earned meagre honoraria, but they honed their craft and gave the conservative ideology a recognizable profile.

To be sure, after 1815 conservative publishing became both more auspicious and more precarious. When the state officially endorsed conservative principles and then backed them up with the repressive

7.2. Complacent or anxious? A German newspaper editor is humbled by the statue of the state censor, who complains about the articles selected for publication. Yet the editor has merely cobbled together news items that have already been printed (and censored) in other periodicals. *Der bequeme und ängstliche Redakteur*, coloured lithograph, ca. 1835. Image courtesy of the Deutsches Zeitungsmuseum, Wadgassen.

Carlsbad Decrees of 1819, the conservative journalist's claim to independence was less willingly accepted by the reading public. With good reason: pro-establishment journalists between 1819 and 1848 tended to write official notices and translations rather than report events in the modern sense. Most of them offered citations instead of opinion – novelties taken from the press of foreign lands rather than analyses of events in Germany. In 1825, for example, it was said that the two important newspapers in Berlin, the *Vossische Zeitung* and the *Spenersche Zeitung*, could be relied on only to report on foreigners who lived beyond their hundredth birthday and on women who gave birth to triplets.[90] An English observer wrote in 1844 that Germany's political press was 'without interest – without influence – without character – without sympathy.'[91]

Yet Germany's political press was more piquant on the eve of the 1848 revolution than this English writer believed. As we saw in chapter 1, some conservatives were aware before 1848 that their newspapers needed a sharper political profile to be effective. In 1842 Leopold von Gerlach, who like his brother Ludwig was an influential conservative adviser of Friedrich Wilhelm IV, wrote to Ernst Hengstenberg, editor of the *Evangelische Kirchenzeitung*. Gerlach argued in this letter that it was mistaken to remain silent about political affairs that were uncomfortable to discuss or that could not be refuted: 'If an anti-revolutionary newspaper is to be successfully established,' he observed, 'no report can be passed on in a neutral manner, but rather must always be cast in the correct political light. This accomplishes more than treatises do: it awakens faith in the truth of our politics and allows one to preach positive Christianity in a practical way.' Nonetheless, Gerlach conceded that the conservative press suffered from the same stigma that afflicted the conservative journalist in society. 'The difficulty is to find co-workers,' he wrote, 'because many will not devote themselves to the maligned press, many believe it to be incompatible with their office and estate, [and] many shrink from the defamation, the insults, a[nd] the scorn. It is always more difficult to find co-workers than money.'[92]

As well as taking a stand on the increasingly dramatic political issues in this era, conservative journalists continued to identify and attack the abuses of the German press. Two examples suffice to suggest that the political press, well before 1848, had recaptured the partisan spirit of Leopold Hoffmann's day. The first example is an essay entitled 'The Good and the Bad Press,' published in 1840.[93] In this piece the anonymous essayist identified the press as a 'power' – albeit an 'often demonic' power – even in his (or her) day. The press, properly understood, was not an organ of public opinion, this writer argued, but rather 'a very significant means for the fabrication, seduction, and demagogic abuse' of public opinion. The reasons for the success of the 'bad press' were not difficult to identify. The 'unreflective reading appetite' of the lower classes demanded exciting reading materials: the most popular newspapers were those that 'best indulge the lusts of the masses, their wild ideas, and their *Schadenfreude,* that ... spread slander and rummage for scandal, [and] that dish up gossip of all sorts.' To their greater discredit, the German masses ignored the 'good' press – those newspapers 'that combat lies with calm, that convincingly point up the contradictions of the spokesmen of the day, and that make it their business to rectify [!] public opinion with intellect and, no less, with an appealing style.' More restraint, this essayist concluded, was what separated the 'good' press from 'the spiritual plague' of *Schnappsliteratur.*

The second example is from the 'New Year's Testament' of 1847, published by Karl Peter Berly, editor of Frankfurt's conservative *Oberpostamts-Zeitung*. Berly sought to distinguish between what he called the 'organic' and the 'chaotic' press in Germany.[94] Journalists contributing to the organic press, he suggested, worked from historical principles and investigated their stories with objectivity and insight. Their work was thoroughly imbued with the spirit of the times. Those who wrote for the 'chaotic' press, on the other hand, 'scraped together' the events they encountered. They inquired only about consequences and ignored causes. And they were satisfied with the temporary effect. Focusing on the failings of society, they also espoused the passions of the political parties – a double indictment. Berly recognized that 'the ideal of the organic press' could never be attained, but only because the chaotic press 'wins the applause of the masses.'

Berly's political testament accurately reflected how most conservative journalists saw their world. Conceived in dichotomous terms, their sort of journalism demanded a statement of principle for or against the masses, for or against contemporary public opinion, for or against the careful exercise of the journalistic vocation. Yet it remained impossible to separate – to 'quarantine' – the worlds of publicity and partisanship. As Berly stated later in his testament, the 'weapon of the word' had to be used carefully; 'speaking to the public daily,' he noted, 'is a rash, perhaps a presumptuous, beginning.' Newspapers should not 'anticipate' the thoughts of their readers. Nor should they presume to advise statesmen, because unsolicited advice 'is of no use and is usually rejected.' (One supposes that Berly was given the title *Hofrat*, court counsellor, because he never sought to give the court his counsel.) Berly hated the term 'leading article' because he believed newspapers should never lead; instead he boasted that over his career he had written some 4,000 'introductory articles.' Similarly, under the rubric 'Current Issues,' Berly liked to write essays with question marks at both the outset and the conclusion. In short, he never answered the stirring questions of the day; nor did he seek to. As Wilhelm Heinrich Riehl remarked some years later, this conservative journalist would likely have preferred the Sphinx to the trumpeting courier on the masthead of the *Oberpostamts-Zeitung*.

'Good' and 'Bad' Journalism

Bismarck's manipulation of the press from 1862 onward gave tangible advantages to conservative publicists while reinforcing images of the journalist as a Byzantine sycophant.[95] In subsequent decades conservative journalists continued to analyse the shortcomings of their press in terms of what it offered, or failed to offer, to the reading public. A few of them noted that their colleagues were too quick to disparage sensationalism and *Klatsch* in the liberal press. Such criticism, they charged, disregarded the fact that liberal newspapers provided their readers with well-written material of daily interest, while conservative organs put their readers to sleep. This point was only part of what eventually became a long litany of complaints about the right-wing press:[96] that it was too highbrow in language and expensive for the common man; that it neglected domestic politics; that it had no literary (*Feuilleton*) writers of any merit; that it offered few affordable newspapers in non-Prussian territories and none in the countryside; that its efforts to establish new organs were usually ill-prepared and ill-funded; that its leading editors displayed no sense of collegiality; that its publishers lacked business sense; and that it offered younger journalists neither 'schooling' or 'placement.'

Condescension mixed with suspicion undermined all efforts to reform the conservative press. Nothing less than a gulf of sympathy and understanding divided the first and fifth estates. Theodor Fontane observed this chasm first-hand when he was invited as a novice reporter to an aristocratic wedding celebration in 1847: 'So there you stand in your white tie, which, if ill luck has it, will be on a bit crooked, too, and what you read on most faces is: "Well, I suppose he'll want to write about it," something which everyone will at one and the same time very much like to see and consider rather low and almost common.'[97] There existed a gulf of both sympathy *and* understanding as a result of the ignorance displayed by members of the upper classes, who only occasionally came into contact with the world of journalism. Rudolf Stratz, theatre critic for the conservative *Kreuzzeitung* in the early 1890s, seemed to imply that much more than just class prejudice was involved when, in his memoirs, he recalled an encounter with an aristocratic lady on the streets of Berlin:

> A woman said to me: 'Who were the gentlemen with whom you were walking yesterday in the Tiergarten?'
> I: 'The chief editor of the "Kreuz-Zeitung," for which I am theatre critic, Baron [Wilhelm von] Hammerstein; the writer of the lead editorials, Baron [Eduard von] Ungern-Sternberg; Court Preacher [Adolf] Stöcker; plus a few other Reichstag deputies – all co-workers with the "Kreuz-Zeitung."'
> The woman, knowingly: 'Oh, I see! And thus you go through the streets, to see what has happened in the way of news, and write it up for the newspaper?'[98]

Social haughtiness, proximity to political power, and narrow intellectual horizons all contributed to conservatives' neglect and ignorance of their own press. Their anti-democratic and elitist prejudices inclined them to agree with the negative picture of journalists drawn by other critics. Conservative journalists deliberately undercut the importance of their own calling. Adam Röder, former editor of the conservative *Badische Post* and in 1914 editor of the *Süddeutsche Conservative Correspondenz*, once observed that it was misguided to believe that 'the people could be politically influenced in a decisive way by mass newspapers.' Röder reflected even deeper conservative prejudices when he added that the German farmer abandons newspaper reading altogether for a good third of the year, 'for he has *important* things to do.'[99]

If we consider the role of the press as a critic of contemporary society – as a conveyor of novelties in the present that conservatives have denied as possibilities in the past – it is understandable that conservatives greeted with suspicion any attempt on the part of their own journalists to achieve mass appeal. Paradoxically, they were relatively uninterested in attempts to raise the intellectual content of their press either. They never recognized the potential value of injecting humour into their publications or embracing the powerful literary device of satire. In 1848 conservatives had seen how decisively the liberal press benefited from satirical propaganda, but the lesson never stuck.[100] Instead their disinclination to 'pander' to the rabble, already evident in 1792 and 1850, remained as pronounced as ever.

In a typical (but anonymous) broadside against all those who wished to appear 'popular' before the masses, one conservative critic observed: 'Most writers who want to be popular are true beggars and toadies before the people: they stoop and submit, they try their best to affect the people's language and flatter the people, [and] in particular they have to adorn their title and contents with plenty of the word "*Volk*." Where there is real talent, the popular writer confronts the people as lecturer [*Lehrer*] and lord [*Herr*]!'[101] It is difficult to see how conservative journalists could have expected success in their attempt to win the masses by speaking to them as 'lecturer and lord.' It is even more remarkable that so few of them were conscious of this dilemma.

German journalists sought to steer between what the liberal journalist Theodor Barth identified in 1888 as the 'Scylla of boredom' and the 'Charybdis of sensationalism.'[102] But for right-wing journalists, doing so required navigating a much narrower course than for others. It revealed their most basic problem: how to defend authority, morality, and honest judgment, but at the same time capture the interest of the masses. Some conservative critics merely attacked such popular features of the modern press as the reporting of crime in local newspapers. Such reports, they claimed, inevitably led to sensationalism and public hysteria. Others feared that Germany was threatened by what they described as the 'revolver press,' which forced its victims to choose between losing their money or their honour.[103] Thus some conservatives advocated the abolition of anonymous authorship of newspaper articles. This proposal provoked a bitter debate among journalists, often with ideological and class overtones.[104] Richard Nordhausen wrote in 1908 that if political journalists allowed themselves to be denigrated as 'coolies' and 'writing-slaves,' 'then anonymity is to blame.'[105]

The 1890s also witnessed mounting attacks from the Right against the *Generalanzeiger* press.[106] A number of conservative writers suggested that paid advertisements should be banned from the political press altogether. Others argued for the taxation or state control of advertising. These were obvious ploys to compensate for the Right's poor record in attracting advertisers and making their publishing houses efficient. They nevertheless revealed an underlying moral imperative. Advertisements were believed to contribute to the reading of newspapers for all the wrong reasons. One reviewer agreed with a leading member of the Protestant Press Association who had attacked such advertisements for their 'filth' ('rubber products,' 'masseuses,' and 'discreet affairs') and 'swindle' ('moonlighting, loans, advantageous marriage, Galician butter, etc., quackery, [and] secret sciences'). By the end of the nineteenth century these reasons to avoid the 'bad press' no longer needed to be spelled out explicitly; readers would have understood another writer's cryptic attack on newspapers that accepted advertisements for 'secret sciences,' 'rubber products,' and apartments with separate entrances.[107]

The campaign against advertisements also condemned the intermixing of business and principle in the newspaper industry, which it labelled an American import.[108] But such attacks on the *Generalanzeiger* press were doomed to fail. Although the Association of German Newspaper Publishers was founded in 1894 partly to unite those who feared the challenge of the non-partisan publishers, it was a sign of the times that by 1901 this organization had had to open its ranks to *Generalanzeiger* publishers as well.

In the age of organization, individual virtue and prohibitive legislation could be supplemented with other sorts of collective action in defence of the 'good' press. As well as supporting a variety of activities to suppress the socialist press both before and after 1890, the Right undertook organizational initiatives to strengthen its own press.[109] The results varied greatly, however, and most practical initiatives occurred rather belatedly in the final years before the First World War. Catholics, for instance, founded a Central Information Bureau for the Catholic Press in 1900. This bureau annually investigated some 900–1,000 cases of false reports in the non-Catholic press, publishing rebuttals whenever possible.[110] In the 1880s and 1890s a number of auxiliary organizations also appeared with the aim of increasing the readership of Christian newspapers and journals.[111] These included the Association for the Distribution of Conservative Journals, founded in 1883; the Association for the People's Welfare, founded in 1884; the Association for the Distribution of Good, Popular Literature, founded in 1892 and numbering about 1,200 members in 1911; and the People's League to Combat Filth in Word and Image, with about 1,600 members in 1910. Outstripping all others in scale and influence was the Christian Journal Association.[112] These organizations supplemented the patriotic efforts of the more overtly political groups such as the Pan-German League and, later, the Imperial League against Social Democracy. They also provided a model for countless smaller initiatives to combat the 'subversive' press in all its forms.[113] Some of these groups understood how right-wing journal-

7.3. A popular Berlin newspaper hits the streets. *Die Ausgabe des Intelligenz-Blattes in Berlin*, wood engraving after a drawing by Th. Presuhn, 1878. Image courtesy of the Bildarchiv Preußischer Kulturbesitz, Berlin.

ism could be mobilized for nationalist causes. Others, however, dissipated enormous amounts of capital – financial and political capital – by continuing to address the masses as 'lecturer and lord.'

Right-wing journalists, in sum, were hamstrung in their efforts to expand their own press by two sorts of neglect, both of which inhered in the evolution of political journalism itself: the obvious and galling neglect accorded their efforts by readers, party leaders, and statesmen; and their own failure to confront the implications of pursuing antidemocratic strategies in political and cultural environments that heralded the coming of age of the masses. On each count, one can only guess the psychological costs to right-wing journalists, their career frustrations, and the temptations they faced to embrace radical political ideologies. When such journalists attacked the legitimacy of a critical reporting of events, they found themselves in the paradoxical situation of questioning their own status and function. Consequently they remained deeply ambivalent about the legitimate bounds of political discourse.

To this uncertainty was added a second paradox when members of the Right attacked liberal journalists who were, by turns, portrayed as dangerous revolutionaries who threatened the very existence of the state or as hack writers who represented no one. It was difficult for right-wing journalists to concede that their many opponents included talented writers and publishers. But it was equally difficult for them to determine when one of their own publishing ventures might be considered a success. The winning of a mass readership was often considered less essential than selfless service to a higher ideal (as when one conservative writer compared his martyrdom to that of Christians in Rome). As a result of these ambivalent attitudes, right-wing journalists never provided their parties with a propaganda apparatus that approached that of liberal and socialist opponents in scope, sophistication, or influence.

The Professionalization Project Unrealized

It is possible that sometime in the future I, too, ... will put a low value on our political rags, our party broils, and all that goes along with them ... Yes, it is highly possible that my own share in the fight will often be painful, wearying, and not at all what one would call a rewarding occupation; but all that does not restrain me from dedicating my life to the struggle of the age to which I belong; for in spite of everything, this fight is the highest and noblest that one finds today; ... not every century is fitted to make the men who live in it distinguished and happy.

Gustav Freytag, *Die Journalisten*, act 3, scene 1

Did a partial consummation of journalists' professionalization project occur after 1900? What reforms were initiated, what organizations were founded, and what mentalities were changed? Did efforts to improve the ethical standards of journalism pay off by measurably improving journalists' social prestige, salaries, or job security?

On one level, appeals for a more 'truthful,' 'patient,' and 'principled' approach to journalism persisted from an earlier era, with only the occasional new wrinkle.[114] One section of an 1883 handbook, for instance, was devoted to 'the honour of the journalistic estate.'[115] It stated that many modern newspapermen regarded principles and convictions as uncomfortable ballast to be thrown overboard before a successful career could be launched. The honour of the estate, however, demanded that individual journalists resist the temptations of indiscretion, scandal-seeking, *Klatsch*, and dogmatism. To help steady the will of those who might be so tempted, the author of this handbook felt the tone of Polonius was appropriate: 'Be truthful, be fair, be tolerant of the convictions of others and hold your own high; respect the law and what is right. Yours is indeed an estate of honour that stands second to none. You alone will illustrate that in the present organization of society, journalism is a moral factor of the highest power.'

On another level, however, the sheer number of handbooks promising 'practical tips' and 'professional advice' to journalists after the 1880s – as well as their growing size, their frequent reprintings, and their authors' effort to engage one another in debate – suggests that a new level of 'professional' consciousness had indeed been achieved, even if professional status still lay just beyond journalists' reach. The same conclusion arises from a survey of the many contemporary organs that addressed the material, intellectual, and ethical concerns of journalists.[116] Collective action by journalists on their own behalf was only partially successful. As one observer wrote in 1902, the number and diversity of organizations representing the interests of journalists reflected the field's weakness, not its strength.[117] In 1902 the splintering of the 'profession' had barely begun. Yet important strides had been taken during the previous century, strides that are unfairly and inaccurately measured by yardsticks calibrated exclusively to the experience of other professional groups.[118]

In the 1860s and 1870s the Saxon 1848er Karl Biedermann helped to organize German Journalists Congresses. At these gatherings, journalists formally represented their individual newspapers, not themselves or their peers.[119] Nonetheless, the lobbying effort undertaken at these congresses had an impact on the liberalization of Germany's press laws in 1874.[120] Local initiatives were even more successful: Viennese journalists founded their association Concordia in 1859. The Berlin Press Association, representing mainly liberal journalists and publishers, was founded in 1864.[121] Efforts to establish pension funds and other material benefits for journalists, on the other hand, often failed, especially when politics intruded. The Augustinus Association for the Cultivation of the Catholic Press was founded in 1878. It allegedly numbered over 1,000 members by 1911.[122] The socialist Berlin Workers Press was founded in April 1900. It too allegedly included about 1,000 members in 1911. Meanwhile, a General German Writers Club was established in 1878 and a rival German Writers Association in 1885. The latter more explicitly sought to represent journalists: it amalgamated with the former in

1887 to form the German Writers Club. Criticism arose immediately, however, that liberals dominated this new association. By 1902 it had only about 400 members, of whom a minority were journalists. A similar organization, the General Writers Association, founded in October 1900, numbered about 2,300 members in 1911. Playwrights had two or three separate organizations of their own.[123]

The most important developments in the organization of the 'profession' occurred in the mid-1890s. The Association of German Newspaper Publishers increasingly represented the interests of employers, though it claimed to support all journalists.[124] A Union of German Journalists and Writers Associations was established in Heidelberg in 1895. Led by Friedrich Spielhagen and Hans Delbrück, this umbrella organization in 1902 comprised twenty-six corporate associations with about 2,000 members. It reached its high point in 1909, when it included thirty-two corporate associations and more than 3,000 members. Although only perhaps 500 of these were active in the press, the founding of a separate organization for journalists in 1910 reduced the numerical strength and influence of this association substantially; its reorganization as the Cartel of German Writers Associations in 1911 was not a success.[125]

The notion that the social standing of journalism could be raised through agreement on professional credentials and standards became a mania at the turn of the century. Journalism courses, programs, and schools of vastly differing scholarly rigour were established at the universities of Heidelberg, Vienna, and Zurich, at the Technical University in Darmstadt, at the Trade Academy in Cologne, and at Richard Wrede's private institute in Berlin, all between the years 1895 and 1902.[126] Beginning in 1896/7, Professor Adolf Koch offered unpaid lectures and seminars on journalism at the University of Heidelberg each semester. His lectures regularly attracted two hundred listeners, his seminars sixty to seventy participants; of these, many followed their instructor on field trips to the editorial offices of local newspapers. Koch's efforts elicited a positive echo in academic journals. By 1909, efforts had begun to integrate journalism studies into an interdisciplinary program in Heidelberg and elsewhere.

Around the same time, historians, political economists, and members of the emerging field of sociology also began to emphasize the importance of the press in German culture and politics. For example, they championed a return to the statistical analysis of social issues through newspaper research. Characteristically, the scholars most interested in these developments were themselves outsiders: Hans Delbrück, Hermann Oncken, Adolf Grabowsky, Otto Hoetzsch, Martin Spahn, Karl Lamprecht, and Alfred Weber. That the notion of a 'newspaper science' remained contested through the First World War was demonstrated by Karl Bücher's avoidance of the term when he established his Institute for the Study of Newspapers[127] at the University of Leipzig in November 1916. The aim of this institute was not only to reform the German press and to educate journalists in practical matters but also to emphasize the role of the German (and international) press as a 'bearer of culture' (*Kulturträger*).

Meanwhile, by 1910 the splintering of interest groups representing journalists had accelerated. This occurred in part along party-political lines and in part hierarchically. An Association of German Editors was founded in February 1902. Initially numbering just 100 members, it rose to over 500 members in 1906–7 and then declined again to half that number by mid-1908.[128] Early the following year conservative editors, led by Justus Hermes of the *Kreuzzeitung*, founded a rival organization, the League of German Editors,[129] which promised to lobby on behalf of editors, not 'merely' journalists. Membership in this group appears to have numbered somewhere between 250 and 500. As political animosity between conservatives and liberals rose to new heights after 1909, the League of German Editors fused in November 1910 with those members of the Union of German Journalists and Writers Associations who held permanent positions in the field. Together they formed the Imperial German Press Club,[130] in which conservative editors appear to have found a congenial home. Although it is difficult to gauge how many journalists joined this organization before the war, by 1929 – after it had revised its statutes in 1918 to lobby more effectively against publishers – it numbered about 3,700 members.

Women in Journalism

It has been observed that the German professions emerged as overwhelmingly male preserves.[131] That this should also be true of journalism is revealing but ironic, for two reasons. Women played such an important role in literary movements of the nineteenth century that one would expect their interests and talents to have inclined them towards a field where distinctions between 'writer' and 'publicist' remained obscure and where anonymity was easily preserved. Moreover, the non-institutionalized character of journalism and the trend towards less-formal academic training might have provided an opportunity for women, who were barred from other pursuits by association laws and restricted access to higher education.

The role of women in political journalism remained very circumscribed until at least the First World War, and many believe it still is today.[132] In the census of 1895, only 410 women were listed as 'journalists, writers, and private scholars.' Of all Germans employed in this category, only 7 per cent were women. Ten years later, according to one study, the number of women journalists had grown in both absolute and relative terms.[133] Nonetheless, as for much of the previous century, only a tiny fraction of women writers were actually journalists, and of these, extremely few were associated with the 'political' aspects of journalism – according to one undefined sample published in 1905, only 3.5 per cent. Instead women journalists tended to contribute to, work in, or occasionally even oversee newspaper departments dealing with non-political affairs, such as art criticism or pedagogy. Of the newspaper publishers surveyed in 1905, 60 per cent claimed to have women as co-workers; but of these, only 43 per cent employed women in permanent positions. And of all the women journalists surveyed, only 18 per cent held editorial posts with daily newspapers. Most of these women complained that they received the same meagre honoraria (*Schundhonorare*) as their male colleagues, although the sources do not reveal whether they were markedly worse paid because of their gender.

Other impediments to the advancement of women journalists were more significant. In the first five years of Adolf Koch's lectures in Heidelberg, allegedly only four women attended; exactly why, we cannot know, as Koch's undertaking was inaugurated just when women were first permitted to attend lectures in German universities. Whereas women joined some journalists' organizations, they were barred from membership in the Berlin Press Association and other elitist clubs. One woman writer was outraged by this male 'clubbishness.' But professionalism was on her agenda too. As she wrote, it was 'extraordinarily important' for women journalists to be able to find 'a quiet place in the middle of the city where, after tours, interviews, lectures, concerts, and the theatre, they can write up their impressions and reports as quickly as possible, where they can read newspapers in peace, have a small meal, and solicit advice from male and female colleagues.'[134]

To most members of the Right, women journalists seemed just as threatening as women doctors and women lawyers. In a pamphlet entitled *The Female Danger in the Literary Field*, one right-wing editor

7.4. *The Newspaper Reader*. This painting by Wilhelm Leibl typifies the artist's realistic but sensitive portrayal of everyday life in rural Germany. The newspaper being read by the older peasant is the *Münchner Neueste Nachrichten*. Leibl's implied comment on the ceremonial, gendered nature of newspaper reading is amplified by the two motionless women, who gaze at each other but do not engage in conversation. *Der Zeitungsleser*, 1891. Image courtesy of The Yorck Project.

noted that women historically had contributed to 'flagellistic, masochistic, sadistic, and other perverse literature' in Germany. In the same breath this editor then labelled women as 'competitors' in the 'overproduction' of scholars. 'Floods,' he noted, 'are always caused by water, never by fine wine.'[135]

Unrealized Hopes

When the Imperial German Press Club revised its statutes in the summer of 1913, it stated categorically that journalism was now 'a free profession and presupposes its own professional abilities.'[136] Even at that point, however, the issue remained contentious. Debates persisted about whether the ideal journalist was 'born' or 'made' and whether a general humanistic education was preferable to specialized training in the field. Rebutting calls at the Press Club's 1913 meeting for the establishment of theoretical training requirements for journalists, a writer from the *Berliner Tageblatt* declared: 'Give up the idea of laying down any compulsion in any direction for the only free profession ... Give up the attempt to advance the training of journalists through institutes and seminar-like establishments ... Leave buried once and for all the question of preparatory training. Take my well-meant advice: let this wild, unregulated situation remain as it is.'[137]

The issue was not clarified when the Heidelberg program self-destructed in the wake of Koch's bitter personal quarrel with Max Weber, when Richard Wrede's Journalism Academy began to draw more scorn than admiration, and when Karl Bücher drew scathing criticism from patriotic writers during the First World War because he included German newspapers in his attacks on the modern press. The German *Kulturpresse*, Bücher believed, had fallen prey to commercialism.[138]

And so, as the Weimar Republic dawned, political, social, and cultural cleavages within the 'profession' rendered journalists free to serve no master unequivocally: neither the masses nor the good cause. Freedom meant the liberty to quarrel with one's own colleagues, to suffer neglect from one's own patrons, to see one's political idealism evaporate – and perhaps still to starve. Journalists now normally required some level of higher education to succeed, though far less than in the early nineteenth century. Yet the image (and self-image) of journalists had never been consolidated by a successful campaign to convince others (or themselves) that entry into the field was a commitment freely made: not as a last resort for those who were socially adrift and without alternatives, but as a first choice for those who recognized a higher calling.

In contrast to members of other professions, moreover, journalists still had little influence over their own fate. What publisher would permit employees to set their own standards, review and censure their own colleagues, establish uniform pay scales, or restrict the available pool of labour? Usually serving a single employer and contending with an authoritarian state that sought to mediate the flow of information, journalists employed a rhetoric that was still based on the assumption that these roles were compatible with their duties as the moral conscience of the people and the guardians of culture. But this divided allegiance made only more bitter their treatment as a mere 'commodity' – a commodity, as one of them put it, like 'herring and cheese.'[139] Nor could journalists any longer share the status of the literary artist. Whereas the public continued to value writers who revealed their soul and perhaps even revelled in their own *Weltschmerz*, the journalist was thought to hide behind a cloak of anonymity that masked sloth and ignorance. To be sure, few Germans in the twentieth century regarded journalists as politically impotent. Like other éminences grises, journalists had influence and power. But they left no shadow. Therefore they were both feared and abused; claiming to improve the world, they allegedly made it worse. Hence, on the threshold of Germany's great democratic experiment of the 1920s, journalists believed that professionalization had brought them few tangible rewards. They were free to act as advocates for all groups and interests in society – except their own.[140]

Conclusions

Bolz. We will fight our way together through the world. What do you say to a barrel organ, Bellmaus? We will go around to the fairs and sing your songs, I'll grind, and you will sing.

Gustav Freytag, *Die Journalisten*, act 4, scene 2

The findings of this chapter require little further elaboration. The social status of the German journalist from the late Enlightenment onward was closely bound up with contemporary understandings of intellectual talent, political engagement, professionalism, and the transformation of the public sphere. No consensus about the limits of public discourse ever welded together journalists of different ranks, styles, and political affiliations (though it is wrong to expect such a consensus to emerge as a logical or necessary consequence of modernization). By 1920 journalism was a vocation that had some of but not all the hallmarks of a free profession. Just as in the age of the French Revolution, journalists' efforts to develop a corporate ethos were undermined by a profound ambivalence about their own calling – no matter, it seemed, whether newspapers were 'about' or 'in' politics and whether journalists lived 'for' or 'from' politics. Thus Max Weber in 1919 correctly noted the irony that German journalism, despite its technical sophistication and its influence, continued to be judged by the standard of its *least* ethical representatives.

If politics played a central role in all this, that role can be properly understood only if we enlarge our conception of how political history should be written. Eve Rosenhaft has suggested how this might be done by arguing for a broader cultural analysis of mass politics. Drawing attention to fears about 'excessive' movie-going (*Kinosucht*) in the Germany of the 1920s, she has observed that the lower classes, youth, and women were believed to be particularly susceptible to forms of mass communication that embraced the genres of sensationalism and melodrama; by promising revelations every night of the week, movies seemed to be both theatrical and demagogic.[141] In an analogous way we can embed journalists and their alleged preference for exaggeration and grumbling (*Nörgelsucht*) in a wider set of contemporary fears. Certainly, those fears were similar to eighteenth-century concerns about 'excessive' reading – *Lesesucht* – but they were also fears about industrial capitalism, national identity, gender conflict, cultural decline, social dislocation, and political change.

This chapter has suggested that political partisanship played a large and hitherto unacknowledged role in shaping the image and self-image of the journalist in German society and politics. But more work is needed on this question, on a variety of fronts. In future it may prove helpful to retain the long chronological perspective provided here. It will be just as necessary to supplement this approach with a comparative one.[142] The dilemmas that confronted German journalists also vexed their colleagues in other nations, and not only in the nineteenth century.

NOTES

1 All citations from this drama are from the German edition (New York, 1889), translated by the author with reference to the English edition, *The Journalists* (Cambridge, Mass., 1888).
2 Geoff Eley, *Reshaping the German Right* (New Haven and London, 1980), 212.

3 Gary D. Stark, 'Vom Nutzen und Nachteil der Literatur für die Geschichtswissenschaft: A Historian's View,' *German Quarterly* 63, no. 1 (1990): 26.
4 See Anthony J. La Vopa, *Grace, Talent, and Merit* (Cambridge, 1988), 15.
5 Jürgen Habermas, *The Structural Transformation of the Public Sphere*, trans. Thomas Burger (Cambridge, Mass., 1989); Lucian Hölscher, 'Öffentlichkeit,' in *Geschichtliche Grundbegriffe*, ed. Otto Brunner et al., 9 vols. in 8 (Stuttgart, 1972–97), 4:413–67.
6 Jörg Requate, *Journalismus als Beruf. Entstehung und Entwicklung des Journalistenberufs im 19. Jahrhundert* (Göttingen, 1995). See esp. 16–18 for Requate's engagement with an earlier version of this chapter and his mild rebuke that nineteenth-century journalists were not undergoing professionalization. In fact, our conclusions merge or complement each other at more points than Requate's gentle critique suggested. Shortly before the First World War, Germans may still have been reluctant to consider German journalists as 'professionals,' but they seemed receptive to the idea that journalism had evolved into something very much like a profession. Moreover, drawing attention to the political aspect of the journalist's role does not fly in the face of the interesting contrast Requate drew between 'hegemonic' knowledge and the idea of a 'radical free field' – that is, a field of endeavour that in theory allowed journalists to resist the efforts of experts and governments to exert authoritarian rule. Journalists' social and political 'superiors' tried to control their writing, their activities, and their public appeal, but of course they did not always succeed. Thus this chapter considers the self-image and long-term political impact of rightwing journalists, not just their objective 'standing' in society.
7 See Konrad H. Jarausch, 'Die Not der geistigen Arbeiter: Akademiker in der Berufskrise, 1918–1933,' in *Die Weimarer Republik als Wohlfahrtsstaat*, ed. Werner Abelshauser (Stuttgart, 1987), 280–99. See also Werner Conze, 'Beruf,' in *Geschichtliche Grundbegriffe*, ed. Brunner et al., 1:490–507; Dietrich Rüschemeyer, 'Professionalisierung. Theoretische Probleme für die vergleichende Geschichtsforschung,' *Geschichte und Gesellschaft* 6 (1980): 311–25; Robert Dingwall and Philip Lewis, eds., *The Sociology of the Professions* (London, 1983); Hannes Siegrist, ed., *Bürgerliche Berufe* (Göttingen, 1988); Charles McClelland, *The German Experience of Professionalization* (Cambridge, 1991).
8 See Otto Groth, *Die unerkannte Kulturmacht. Grundlegung der Zeitungswissenschaft*, 7 vols. (Berlin, 1960–72); Rolf Engelsing, *Massenpublikum und Journalistentum im 19. Jahrhundert in Nordwestdeutschland* (Berlin, 1966); Kurt Koszyk, *Presse im 19. Jahrhundert* (Berlin, 1966); Elger Blühm and Rolf

Engelsing, eds., *Die Zeitung* (Bremen, 1967); Frederik Ohles, *Germany's Rude Awakening* (Kent, Ohio, 1992); and Daniel Moran, *Toward the Century of Words* (Berkeley, 1990).

9 Konrad H. Jarausch, 'The German Professions in History and Theory,' in *German Professions, 1800–1950*, ed. Geoffrey Cocks and Jarausch (New York and Oxford, 1990), 17.

10 Magali Sarfatti Larson, *The Rise of Professionalism* (Berkeley, 1977).

11 Hans-Ulrich Wehler, *Deutsche Gesellschaftsgeschichte*, 4 vols. to date (Munich, 1987–2003), 1:320. See also Kurt Koszyk, *Vorläufer der Massenpresse* (Munich, 1972); Margot Lindemann, *Deutsche Presse bis 1815* (Berlin, 1969); Georg Jäger and Jörg Schönert, eds., *Die Leihbibliothek als Institution des literarischen Lebens im 18. und 19. Jahrhundert* (Hamburg, 1980); Irene Jentsch, 'Zur Geschichte des Zeitungslesens in Deutschland am Ende des 18. Jahrhunderts' (PhD diss., University of Leipzig, 1937).

12 Moran, *Toward the Century*, 4; Thomas Nipperdey, *Deutsche Geschichte 1800–1866*, 2nd ed. (Munich, 1984), 587.

13 Wehler, *Deutsche Gesellschaftsgeschichte*, 1:306–10 and 2:529; also Hans Erich Bödeker, 'Journals and Public Opinion: The Politicization of the German Enlightenment in the Second Half of the Eighteenth Century,' in *The Transformation of Political Culture*, ed. Eckhart Hellmuth (Oxford, 1990), 423–45, esp. 428–35.

14 Rudolf Schenda, *Volk ohne Buch* (Frankfurt a.M., 1970); Schenda, *Die Lesestoffe der kleinen Leute* (Munich, 1976); Rolf Engelsing, *Analphabetentum und Lektüre* (Stuttgart, 1973); Engelsing, *Der Bürger als Leser* (Stuttgart, 1974); Engelsing, *Massenpublikum*.

15 Metternich to Philipp Stadion, 23 June 1808, cited in Moran, *Toward the Century*, 1.

16 Add to this figure perhaps 688 journals; Wehler, *Deutsche Gesellschaftsgeschichte*, 2:528–9.

17 See Thomas Nipperdey, *Deutsche Geschichte 1866–1918*, 2 vols. (Munich, 1991), 1:798–811, for selected statistics; Robert Goldstein, *Political Censorship of the Arts and the Press in Nineteenth-Century Europe* (Basingstoke, 1989), 56.

18 Gerhard Muser, *Statistische Untersuchung über die Zeitungen Deutschlands 1815–1914* (Leipzig, 1918), 58–63 and passim.

19 See *inter alia* ibid., 165; Kurt Koszyk, *Deutsche Pressepolitik im Ersten Weltkrieg* (Düsseldorf, 1968).

20 For the following and for further references, see Habermas, *Structural Transformation*; Bödeker, 'Journals'; Hans Jürgen Haferkorn, 'Der freie

Schriftsteller. Eine literatur-soziologische Studie über seine Entstehung und Lage in Deutschland zwischen 1750 und 1800,' *AGB* 5 (1962–4): 523– 711; Jeremy Popkin, 'Buchhandel und Presse im napoleonischen Deutschland,' *AGB* 26 (1986), 285–96; Rolf Engelsing, 'Zeitung und Zeitschrift in Nordwestdeutschland 1800–1850: Leser und Journalisten,' *AGB* 5 (1962–4): 850–955; Fritz Hodeige, 'Die Stellung von Dichter und Buch in der Gesellschaft: eine literar-soziologische Untersuchung,' *AGB* 1 (1956–8): 141–70; Hans Erich Bödeker and Ulrich Herrmann, eds., *Aufklärung als Politisierung – Politisierung der Aufklärung* (Hamburg, 1987). Still useful are Heinrich Wuttke, *Die deutschen Zeitschriften und die Entstehung der öffentlichen Meinung*, 3rd ed. (Leipzig, 1875); Joachim Kirchner, *Das deutsche Zeitschriftenwesen*, 2 pts. (Wiesbaden, 1958–62); and Wilmont Haacke, 'Geistesgeschichte der politischen Zeitschrift,' *Zeitschrift für Religions- und Geistesgeschichte* 21 (1969): 115–51.

21 Lenore O'Boyle, 'The Image of the Journalist in France, Germany, and England, 1815–1848,' *Comparative Studies in Society and History* 10 (1967–8): 290–317; A. Aspinall, 'The Social Status of Journalists at the Beginning of the Nineteenth Century,' *Review of English Studies* 21 (1945): 216–32.
22 Habermas, *Structural Transformation*, 181.
23 Cited in Katherine Roper, *German Encounters with Modernity* (Atlantic Highlands, 1991), 91.
24 See La Vopa, *Grace*, 12, 288.
25 Cited in Moran, *Toward the Century*, 33.
26 See Ohles, *Germany's Rude Awakening*, 72.
27 Cited in Carolyn R. Henderson, 'Heinrich Leo: A Study in German Conservatism' (PhD diss., University of Wisconsin, Madison, 1977), 111; Goldstein, *Political Censorship*, 43.
28 Moran, *Toward the Century*; Karl Biedermann, *Mein Leben und ein Stück Zeitgeschichte*, 2 vols. (Breslau, 1886), 2:192–243.
29 Cited in Bödeker, 'Journals,' 426.
30 See R. Steven Turner, 'The *Bildungsbürgertum* and the Learned Professions in Prussia, 1770–1830: The Origins of a Class,' *Social History* 13, no. 25 (1980): 105–35; Wolfgang Martens, 'Die Geburt des Journalisten in der Aufklärung,' *Wolfenbütteler Studien zur Aufklärung* 1 (1974): 84–98; Lenore O'Boyle, 'Klassische Bildung und soziale Struktur in Deutschland zwischen 1800 und 1848,' *Historische Zeitschrift* 207 (1968): 584–608.
31 Cited in Blühm and Engelsing, *Zeitung*, 124–31; see also Martens, 'Geburt,' 88 and passim.
32 Martens, 'Geburt,' 90–2.

33 Bödeker, 'Journals,' 437.
34 A.L. Schlözer, *Theorie der Statistik* (Göttingen, 1804), 54, cited ibid.
35 Moran, *Toward the Century*, 18.
36 *Die Ritter vom Geiste* (1850), cited in Roper, *German Encounters*, 74.
37 James J. Sheehan, *German History, 1770–1866* (Oxford, 1989), 215.
38 Turner, '*Bildungsbürgertum*,' 124–5.
39 Wolfgang von Ungern-Sternberg (1980), cited in Moran, *Toward the Century*, 6.
40 Cited in Sheehan, *German History*, 167.
41 Moran, *Toward the Century*, 11; emphasis added.
42 Koszyk, *Vorläufer*, esp. 83; Ludwig Sinzheimer, ed., *Die geistigen Arbeiter*, pt. 1, *Freies Schriftstellertum und Literaturverlag* (Munich and Leipzig, 1922), 9ff.
43 Nipperdey, *Deutsche Geschichte 1866–1918*, 1:805.
44 Kurt Brunöhler, 'Die Redakteure der mittleren und grösseren Zeitungen im heutigen Reichsgebiet von 1800 bis 1848' (PhD diss., University of Leipzig, 1933); also Engelsing, *Massenpublikum*, 160ff.; Koszyk, *Presse*, chap. 13; and Rudolf Oebsger-Röder, 'Untersuchungen über den Bildungsstand der deutschen Journalisten' (PhD diss., University of Leipzig, 1936), chs. 1–3.
45 W. Kahmann's study cited in Engelsing, *Massenpublikum*, 57; see also Paul Stoklossa, 'Der Arbeitsmarkt der Redakteure. Eine statistische Untersuchung,' *Schmollers Jahrbuch für Gesetzgebung* 35 (1911): 293–307; K. Thiess, 'Soziale Bestrebungen der deutschen Journalisten und Schriftsteller,' *Soziale Praxis* 14 (Nov. 1904): 188–91; Martin Wenck, 'Zur sozialen Lage der Redakteure und Journalisten,' *Patria!* 8 (1908): 139–44; Wilmont Haacke, *Publizistik und Gesellschaft* (Stuttgart, 1970), 438.
46 Cited in Cecilia von Studnitz, *Kritik des Journalisten* (Munich, 1983), 76.
47 See Koszyk, *Presse*, 220; Charles McClelland, 'Zur Professionalisierung der akademischen Berufe in Deutschland,' in *Bildungsbürgertum im 19. Jahrhundert*, pt. 1, ed. Werner Conze and Jürgen Kocka (Stuttgart, 1985), 233–47, here 237.
48 After 1846 renamed the Schriftstellerverein; see Bruno Rauecker, 'Die Fachvereine des freien deutschen Schriftstellertums,' 160, and H.H. Borcherdt, 'Das Schriftstellertum von der Mitte des 18. Jahrhunderts bis zur Gründung des Deutschen Reiches,' both in Sinzheimer, ed., *Die geistigen Arbeiter*; anon., *Die politische Tagespresse Sachsens* (Grimma, 1844).
49 Cited in Rauecker, 'Fachvereine,' 161.
50 *Die Grenzboten*, no. 2 (1845): 278ff., cited ibid., 163.
51 Albert Ward, *Book Production, Fiction and the German Reading Public*,

1740–1800 (Oxford, 1974), 25–8; Haferkorn, 'Freie Schriftsteller,' sec. 4; Koszyk, *Vorläufer*, 80–107.
52 See Rolf Engelsing, *Der literarische Arbeiter*, vol. 1, *Arbeit, Zeit und Werk im literarischen Beruf* (Göttingen, 1976), 403–9.
53 Schiller to Ferdinand Huber, 29 July 1788, cited ibid., 407.
54 Mommsen to Henzen, 5 April 1848, cited ibid., 408.
55 Cited ibid., 408.
56 Freytag, *Die Journalisten*, act 4, scene 1.
57 Staatsbibliothek Berlin I, NL Hans Delbrück, Abt. III, Fasz. 30, Nrn. 3–5, 'Honorar-Bestimmungen der "Preußischen Jahrbüchern."'
58 Cited in O'Boyle, 'Image,' 305.
59 Cited (n.d.) in Rauecker, 'Fachvereine,' 166.
60 For this and the following, see Engelsing, *Arbeit*, 404; Koszyk, *Presse*, 227–8.
61 Heinrich Mann, *Man of Straw* (Harmondsworth, 1984), 108–9.
62 Johannes Frizenschaf, *Die Praxis des Journalisten* (Leipzig, n.d. [1901]), 20.
63 E.g., Heinrich Keiter, *Praktische Winke für Schriftsteller, Journalisten und Zeitungs-Korrespondenten*, 8th ed. (Essen, 1911), 55.
64 See Willy Fentsch, 'Journalismus und Journalisten im Drama vor Gustav Freytag (1757–1848)' (PhD diss., University of Münster, 1922).
65 Robert Darnton, 'The High Enlightenment and the Low-Life of Literature,' in Darnton, *The Literary Underground of the Old Regime* (Cambridge, Mass., 1982), 17–20.
66 Cited in Blühm and Engelsing, *Zeitung*, 181.
67 Remark from 1862, cited in Richard Jacobi, *Der Journalist* (Hanover, 1902), 168.
68 Blühm and Engelsing, *Zeitung*.
69 Cited ibid., 168; cf. Koszyk, *Vorläufer*, 83.
70 Cited in Engelsing, *Massenpublikum*, 156.
71 Cited in Nipperdey, *Deutsche Geschichte 1800–1866*, 594.
72 Wilhelm Heinrich Riehl, *Die Naturgeschichte des Volkes*, cited in Engelsing, *Massenpublikum*, 52–3; for the following, see Blühm and Engelsing, *Zeitung*, passim.
73 Max Weber, 'Politik als Beruf' (October 1919), in Weber, *Gesammelte Politische Schriften*, ed. Johannes Winckelmann, 3rd rev. ed. (Tübingen, 1971), 505–60, esp. 525–8; Weber, 'Der Journalist,' *Deutsche Allgemeine Zeitung*, no. 610 (11 Dec. 1919): 2.
74 Leo Wörl (1881) and others, cited in Oebsger-Röder, 'Untersuchungen,' 33.
75 See also Heinz Schulze, *Die Presse im Urteil Bismarcks* (Leipzig, 1931).
76 Laube, cited in O'Boyle, 'Image,' 303.

77 Ferdinand Lassalle, *Die Feste, die Presse und der Frankfurter Abgeordnetentag*, 3rd ed. (Leipzig, 1871).
78 Cited in Frizenschaf, *Praxis*, 57.
79 Studnitz, *Kritik*.
80 See Weber, 'Politik als Beruf,' 519.
81 Maximilian Harden, 'Die Journalisten,' *Die Zukunft* 38 (March 1902): 382–5.
82 Freytag, *Die Journalisten*, act 2, scene 1.
83 Theodor Barth, 'Die Journalistik als Gewerbe und als Kunst,' *Die Nation* 5, no. 45 (Aug. 1888): 627–8.
84 See Haacke, *Publizistik*, 444–5.
85 The following account is drawn from Fritz Valjavec, 'Die Anfänge des österreichischen Konservativismus: L.A. Hoffmann,' in Valjavec, *Ausgewählte Aufsätze* (Munich, 1963), 331–42; Valjavec, *Die Entstehung der politischen Strömungen in Deutschland 1770–1815*, 2nd ed. (Düsseldorf, 1978), 312–27 (also the 'Nachwort' by Jörn Garber, 543–92); Friedrich Sommer, 'Die Wiener Zeitschrift (1792–93). Die Geschichte eines antirevolutionären Journals' (PhD diss., University of Bonn, 1932); Gerda Lettner, *Das Rückzugsgefecht der Aufklärung in Wien 1790–1792* (Frankfurt a.M., 1988); and Klaus Epstein, *The Genesis of German Conservatism* (Princeton, 1966), 485–594.
86 Haacke, 'Geistesgeschichte,' 131, 135.
87 *Wiener Zeitschrift* 1 (1792): 2–6; Sommer, 'Wiener Zeitschrift,' 16–90.
88 *Wiener Zeitschrift* 1 (1792): 73; Epstein, *Genesis*, 531.
89 See Sommer, 'Wiener Zeitschrift,' 91ff.; Epstein, *Genesis*, 529–31.
90 Cited in Johannes Bachmann, *Ernst Wilhelm Hengstenberg*, 3 vols. (Gütersloh, 1876–92), 1:175.
91 *Foreign Quarterly Review* (1844), cited in O'Boyle, 'Image,' 302.
92 Gerlach's descriptors were *Verleumdung, Schimpfe*, and *Spott*; see letter of 18 Nov. 1842, in Staatsbibliothek Berlin II, Handschriftenabteilung, NL Ernst Hengstenberg, Nr. 4 (Leopold von Gerlach), Bl. 3.
93 'Die gute und die schlechte Presse,' *Historisch-politische Blätter*, cited in Michael Schmolke, *Die schlechte Presse* (Münster, 1971), 57ff.
94 Wilhelm Heinrich Riehl, 'Ein vormärzlicher Redakteur,' excerpted in Blühm and Engelsing, *Zeitung*, 177–80.
95 Hans Herz, 'Zur Finanzierung konservativer Vereine durch die Bismarck-Regierung 1863,' *Zeitschrift für Geschichtswissenschaft* 33 (1985): 1097–110; Robert Keyserlingk, *Media Manipulation* (Montreal, 1977); Eberhard Naujoks, 'Bismarck und die Organisation der Regierungspresse,' *Historische Zeitschrift* 205 (1967): 46–80.

96 See *Die konservative Presse*, 'von einem konservativen Journalisten' (Berlin, 1885).
97 Theodor Fontane, *Von Zwanzig bis Dreißig. Autobiographisches*, 5th ed. (Berlin, 1910), 346–7, cited in Joachim Remak, *The Gentle Critic: Theodor Fontane and German Politics, 1848–1898* (Syracuse, 1964), 6, which also cites Fontane's unpublished essay 'Die gesellschaftliche Stellung des Schriftstellers in Deutschland,' in Fontane, 'Unveröffentlichte Aufzeichnungen und Briefe,' *Sinn und Form* 13, nos. 5–6 (1961): 704–49, here 721–3.
98 Rudolf Stratz, *Reisen und Reifen* (Berlin, 1926), 9.
99 *Süddeutsche Conservative Correspondenz*, 14 July 1914; original emphasis.
100 See Wolfgang Schwentker, *Konservative Vereine und Revolution in Preussen 1848/49* (Düsseldorf, 1988), 175–81; Christian Gehring, 'Die Entwicklung des politischen Witzblattes in Deutschland' (PhD diss., University of Leipzig, 1927).
101 Cited (n.d.) approvingly in Frizenschaf, *Praxis*, 64.
102 Barth, 'Journalistik,' 628.
103 See, e.g., 'Revolverjournalismus,' *Der Zeitungs-Verlag* 10, no. 41 (15 Oct. 1909): 771–2; 'Revolverpresse,' in Oskar Webel, ed., *Hand-Lexikon der deutschen Presse* (Leipzig, 1905), 749; Studnitz, *Kritik*, 49.
104 Frizenschaf, *Praxis*, 68–75; 'Über die Anonymität im modernen Zeitungswesen,' *Die Redaktion* 5, nos. 21–2 (1 Nov. 1906): 84–5.
105 *Der Tag* (1908), cited in Groth, *Unerkannte Kulturmacht*, 4:666; *Wie können die Schäden unserer periodischen Presse dauernd geheilt werden?* (Barmen, 1880), 14; Frizenschaf, *Praxis*, 69.
106 Hans-Wolfgang Wolter, *Generalanzeiger* (Bochum, 1981); Koszyk, *Presse*, chap. 16; Winfried Lerg and Michael Schmolke, *Massenpresse und Volkszeitung* (Assen, 1968).
107 *Der Zeitungs-Verlag* 8, no. 25 (20 June 1907), 749f., on Stanislaus Swierczewski, *Wider Schmutz und Schwindel im Inseratenwesen*, 3rd rev. ed. (Leipzig, 1907).
108 See *Die farblose Presse. Eine religiöse, politische u. soziale Pest* (Crefeld, n.d. [1894]); O. Arendt, 'Der Amerikanismus in der Fach- und Tagespresse,' *Die Redaktion* 3, nos. 38–9 (25 Sept. 1904): 298–9; Johannes Frizenschaf, *Die Wahrheit über die farblose Presse* (Bochum, n.d. [1912]); and W. Hammer, *Die Generalanzeigerpresse, ein Herd der Korruption* (Leipzig, 1911), reviewed in *Zeitungs-Verlag* 12, no. 39 (29 Sept. 1911): 851. See also Gangolf Hübinger, 'Politik mit Büchern und kulturelle Fragmentierung im Deutschen Kaiserreich,' in *Publishing Culture*, ed. Meike Werner (*Germanic Review* 76, no. 4) (Washington, DC, 2001), 290–307, esp. 302–3.

109 *Berliner Tageblatt*, 30 Sept. 1892; *Freisinnige Zeitung*, 18 June 1912; BA Potsdam, 61 Re 1 (Reichslandbund Pressearchiv), Nr. 2274, 'Konservative Presse.'
110 On the *Apologetische Mitteilungen*, see Schmolke, *Schlechte Presse*, 206–11.
111 See Karl Mühlhäußer, *Christentum und Presse* (Frankfurt a.M., 1876); *Neue Westfälische Volkszeitung*, 8 Sept. 1877, Beilage; *Deutsche Evangelische Kirchenzeitung* 5, no. 43 (24 Oct. 1891): 469.
112 See *Saat und Segen. Fünfzig Jahre Christlicher Zeitschriftenverein* (n.p., 1930); *Mitteilungen des Vereins zur Verbreitung Christlicher Zeitschriften*, nos. 5–75 (1881–93); *Mitteilungen des Christlichen Zeitschriftenvereins*, nos. 77–163 (1894–1914); *Bericht des Christlichen Zeitschriftenvereins* (1901–13); and *Mitteilungen des Vereins zur Verbreitung guter volkstümlicher Schriften*, 1–7 (1917–27) – all published in Berlin.
113 Vaterlands-Verein, *Die socialdemokratische Presse* (Berlin, 1896); Reichsverband gegen die Sozialdemokratie, *Handbuch für nichtsozialdemokratische Wähler*, 3rd ed. (Berlin, 1911), 582–90; Georg Jäger, 'Der Kampf gegen Schmutz und Schund. Die Reaktion der Gebildeten auf die Unterhaltungsindustrie,' *AGB* 31 (1988): 163–91.
114 Gustav Spiethoff, *Die Großmacht Presse und das deutsche Schriftsteller-Elend* (Düsseldorf, 1883); J. Publicus, *Die moderne Schandpresse*, 2nd ed. (Warnsdorf, n.d. [1899]); Eugen Buchholz, *Aus der Praxis eines Redakteurs und Schriftstellers* (Danzig, 1907); Werner Müller, *Das Elend unserer politischen Presse und seine Heilung* (Greiz, n.d. [1913]).
115 J.H. Wehle, *Die Zeitung*, 2nd ed. (Vienna, 1883), 146–9; see also Andreas Niedermeyer, *Die katholische Presse Deutschlands* (Freiburg i. Br., 1861); W. Drabitius, *Ueber den Klatsch und Quatsch in unseren Zeitungen* (Berlin, 1885).
116 This section draws on periodicals too numerous to list here.
117 Jacobi, *Journalist*, 178.
118 Compare Joseph Kürschner, ed., *Deutscher Litteratur-Kalender auf das Jahr 1885*, 7th ed. (Berlin and Stuttgart, 1885), and 22nd ed. (1900); Heinrich Klenz, ed., *Kürschners Deutscher Literatur-Kalender*, 36th ed. (Berlin and Leipzig, 1914).
119 Karl Biedermann, *Bericht über den ersten deutschen Journalistentag zu Eisenach am 22. Mai 1864* (Leipzig, 1864); Biedermann, *Mein Leben*, 2:214–16; Koszyk, *Presse*, 220–3.
120 Robert Keyserlingk, 'Bismarck and Freedom of the Press in Germany, 1866–1890,' *Canadian Journal of History* 11, no. 1 (1976): 31–3; Eberhard Naujoks, *Die parlamentarische Entstehung des Reichspressegesetzes in der*

Bismarckzeit (1848/74) (Düsseldorf, 1975); Hans-Wolfgang Wetzel, *Presseinnenpolitik im Bismarckreich (1874–1890)* (Frankfurt a.M., 1975).

121 Peter Eppel, *'Concordia soll ihr Name sein ...'* (Vienna, 1984); Gustav Dahms, ed., *Das Litterarische Berlin* (Berlin, n.d. [1895]); Paul Schlenther, *Der Verein Berliner Presse und seine Mitglieder 1862–1912* (Berlin, 1912).

122 This and following figures for 1911 are drawn from Kürschner, *Deutscher Literatur-Kalender* (Berlin, 1911). See also Klemens Löffler, *Geschichte der katholischen Presse Deutschlands* (Mönchen-Gladbach, 1924); Wilhelm Kisky, *Der Augustinus-Verein zur Pflege der katholischen Presse von 1878–1928* (Düsseldorf, 1928); and *Augustinus-Blatt* 1– (1897–).

123 Friedhelm Kron, *Schriftsteller und Schriftstellerverbände* (Stuttgart, 1976), 32–9.

124 *Zeitung als Aufgabe. 60 Jahre Verein Deutscher Zeitungsverleger, 1894–1954* (Wiesbaden, 1954).

125 Jacobi, *Journalist*, 178; Koszyk, *Presse*, 223; Kürschner, *Deutscher Literatur-Kalender* (1911); Kron, *Schriftsteller*, 38. On the professional undertakings of other German writers, see Eva Wolf, *Der Schriftsteller im Querschnitt* (Munich, 1978); Jere Hudson Link, 'Guardians of Culture: The Deutsche Schillerstiftung and German Writers, 1859–1917' (PhD diss., University of North Carolina, 1988), esp. 207ff.; and Kron, *Schriftsteller*. The German Writers Defence Association had been formed in 1909; two years later it had 250 members and its own organ, *Der Schriftsteller*.

126 Richard Wrede, *Was heißt und wie werde ich Journalist?* (Berlin, [1902]); and Wrede, *Handbuch der Journalistik*, 2nd rev. ed. (Berlin, 1906); discussed in Keiter, *Praktische Winke*, 55–8; and Frizenschaf, *Praxis*, 58, 64ff.; Ernst Posse, 'Journalistische Vorbildung und journalistische Fortbildung,' *Deutsche Presse* 1, no. 3 (18 Oct. 1913): 1–4; *Der Journalist und Redakteur*, 2nd ed. (Leipzig, [1902]); Friedrich Streißler, *Der Schriftsteller und Journalist* (Stuttgart, n.d. [1912]); *Deutsche Presse* 16, nos. 50–1 (24 Dec. 1926). See also Oebsger-Röder, 'Untersuchungen,' chap. 4; Rauecker, 'Fachvereine'; and for the following, Rüdiger vom Bruch, 'Zeitungswissenschaft zwischen Historie und Nationalökonomie. Ein Beitrag zur Vorgeschichte der Publizistik als Wissenschaft im späten deutschen Kaiserreich,' *Publizistik* 25 (1980): 579–607.

127 This institute was dedicated not to *Zeitungswissenschaft* but to *Zeitungskunde*.

128 *Die Redaktion* 5, nos. 17–18 (1 Sept. 1907): 65–6.

129 *Der Zeitungs-Verlag* 10, no. 3 (22 Jan. 1909): 40–1; Richard Wrede, 'Eine Faschingsgründung,' *Die Redaktion* 7, no. 2 (1 Feb. 1909): 9–10.

130 *Der Zeitungs-Verlag* 11, no. 49 (9 Dec. 1910): 958–60; Marie Matthies, *Journalisten in eigener Sache* (Berlin, 1969).
131 Jarausch, 'German Professions,' 17.
132 Studnitz, *Kritik*, 42. The first female protagonist Studnitz discovered in her sample appeared in a work published in 1901.
133 Eliza Ichenhäuser, *Die Journalistik als Frauenberuf* (Berlin and Leipzig, n.d. [1905]), 7ff. and passim.
134 Ibid., 37.
135 Theodor Wahl, *Die weibliche Gefahr auf literarischem Gebiete* (Stuttgart, 1906), 20–1; see also Philipp von Nathusius-Ludom, *Zur 'Frauenfrage'* (Halle, 1871); Josefine Trampler-Steiner, *Die Frau als Publizistin und Leserin* (Freiburg i. Br., 1938), 65ff.
136 Cited in Haacke, *Publizistik*, 437; see also Kron, *Schriftsteller*, 267.
137 Cited in vom Bruch, 'Zeitungswissenschaft,' 590.
138 Karl Bücher (1915) cited ibid., 592–3.
139 Wenck, 'Soziale Lage,' 223–5.
140 See Engelsing, *Massenpublikum*, 60.
141 Eve Rosenhaft, 'Women, Gender, and the Limits of Political History in the Age of "Mass" Politics,' in *Elections, Mass Politics, and Social Change in Modern Germany: New Perspectives*, ed. Larry Eugene Jones and James Retallack (Cambridge and New York, 1992), 163–9.
142 See, for example, Hannah Barker and Simon Burrows, eds., *Press, Politics and the Public Sphere in Europe and North America, 1760–1820* (Cambridge, 2002).

8 Building a People's Party

Charges of failing to understand the mood of the people were hurled back and forth between Conservatives and antisemites in almost all German states. Yet 'authoritarian' and 'demagogic' solutions to the 'Jewish question' were not defined the same way everywhere. This chapter considers how regional environments affected the willingness and ability of Conservatives and antisemites to work together to win a mass following.

In contrast to the situation just a decade ago, we now have many excellent studies of regional antisemitic movements.[1] To be sure, much work remains to be done on the micro- and macro-planes too. Neither the 'everydayness' of German antisemitism in the countryside nor the role of political violence in shaping Imperial Germany's political culture has fully come into focus.[2] However, these desiderata hint at the usefulness of reconsidering evidence on the meso-level. By taking this approach, this chapter demonstrates that the lines between Conservatism and antisemitism became, for a time, so indistinct as to virtually disappear. Indeed, as this chapter's second section suggests, antisemitic ideas infiltrated German Conservatism more thoroughly and at an earlier date than historians have generally believed. This thesis fits into this volume's larger argument about the difficulty of distinguishing between antisemitic 'populists' and Conservative 'patricians' on the pre-1918 German Right.[3]

Is it appropriate to speak of relations between Conservatives and antisemites at all? Or should we speak instead of Conservatives who were also antisemites and antisemites who were also Conservatives? Can we say whether Conservatives at a particular time and place were 'convinced' antisemites or not? These thorny questions permit no easy answer. But the time has come to abandon the image of German Conservatives as aloof aristocrats unwilling to sully their reputations by adopting radical antisemitism.

The third and fourth sections chart the fortunes of Conservatives and antisemites in the Kingdoms of Bavaria and Württemberg respectively, while the fifth and sixth sections examine these groups in the Grand Duchy of Baden and the Kingdom of Saxony. Each of these sections asks why Conservative leaders felt beleaguered during the formative period of their party movements. Each section also asks why Conservative propaganda was steered in antisemitic directions by the perceived hegemony of a liberal establishment in each state. A seventh section examines the confluence of anti-liberal and anti-Jewish themes in the Conservatives' proclaimed attachment to Christian principles, while an eighth employs a case-study approach to examine representative individuals and their stance on antisemitic agendas. Here, too, we see how often the intermixing of 'Christian,' 'social,' and 'reform' agendas provided the glue that held the Conservative and antisemitic movements closely together.

Conservatives and Antisemites

Historians of German antisemitism have tended to employ analytical categories that only partially reflect the human complexities they try to describe. To a certain extent, this is true of even the most innovative and insightful scholars in the field, including Peter Pulzer and Richard S. Levy (without whose path-breaking studies this chapter could not have been written). Levy's monograph distinguished between 'parliamentary' and 'revolutionary' antisemitic movements.[4] Levy's special contribution was to make historians aware that radicals and moderates could be found in each camp. His book thus refined our understanding of how debates about ends and means evolved in tandem with differing political strategies. Nevertheless, Levy's distinction between such 'democratic' antisemites as Max Liebermann von Sonnenberg and such 'revolutionary' antisemites as Theodor Fritsch comes up short when we apply it to Conservative antisemitism.[5] On the one hand, Conservatives were as resolutely anti-parliamentary and anti-democratic as they were anti-revolutionary. On the other hand, Conservatives of remarkably similar political inclinations were able to work as closely with Liebermann as with Fritsch.

The other principal means of categorizing German antisemites, as advanced by Peter Pulzer (among others), is to differentiate between Christian and racialist strains in antisemitic thought.[6] Because racial antisemitism, in this view, is distinguished from social, moral, ethical, or religious antisemitism, the majority of Conservatives who remained attached to Christian principles are typically said to have had little in common with German racists who radicalized antisemitism after 1871 – except, that is, when they embraced anti-Jewish politics for 'demagogic' purposes. Such 'demagoguery' in turn is equated with Conservative 'insincerity' or even half-heartedness on the 'Jewish question.'

Artificial distinctions between Conservatives and antisemites have been perpetuated in a third way: by overly rigid attempts to use the official programs and public statements of leading Conservatives to chart their changing attitudes towards the Jews. Most historians would agree that we should not see either Conservatism or antisemitism as static. Yet many accounts have overcompensated by constructing a rigid timeline along which Conservatives allegedly moved through various stages of more or less 'demagogic' practices. Thus Conservatives are said to have resisted the siren call of German antisemites until about 1890. Then, during the tumultuous first half of the 1890s, they allegedly 'flirted with' and tried to 'co-opt' radical antisemitism to their own advantage. In the Reichstag election campaign of June 1893 – the orthodox account continues – Conservatives were trumped by radical antisemites and suffered major defeats at the polls. Immediately thereafter, they rejected antisemitic 'excesses' with special vehemence, not least by drawing their own distinctions between 'conservative' members of the antisemitic German Social Party and 'radical' members of the antisemitic German Reform Party. Finally, as the independent antisemitic parties fell into disarray around the turn of the century, Conservatives are said to have incorporated the more popular antisemitic demands at a subterranean level, though they always subordinated such demands to their own agrarian, anti-socialist, and anti-parliamentary goals.

Three elements of this view deserve to be retained. The first is the conclusion that antisemites and Conservatives *together* bear responsibility for bringing antisemitism into the mainstream of German political discourse before 1914. What nonetheless remains to be demonstrated is the relative contribution of each group to what has been called, on the one hand, a 'cultural code' embracing myriad resentments under the rubric of anti-liberalism and, on the other hand, a system of 'post-liberal apartheid.'[7] Second, it has been argued that antisemites of the pre-1918 period were still restrained by a morality, whether Christian or secular, that had its roots in the Enlightenment. In this they differed significantly from Adolf Hitler and his fellow Nazis. However, 'extreme' Christian and 'extreme' antisemitic sentiments were more compatible than this view suggests. Third, the rise and fall of German antisemitism, like the fate of the Jews themselves, was inextricably linked to the fortunes of German liberalism. Past efforts to document this linkage have generally been attempted on the level of national politics. But the fortunes of German liberals (and their opponents) appear in a new light when we focus on local and regional contests for power.

Readers will not be startled by the claim that antisemitism was pervasive in mainstream Conservative thought before 1914. When the antisemitic parties strayed from the 'Jewish question' and championed tangential political issues that threatened Conservative interests, Conservatives publicly disavowed 'illegitimate' and 'excessive' brands of antisemitism, as they did after 1893. However, it is difficult to overemphasize the importance that Conservatives placed on the same acts of distancing long before and long after the 1890s. This decade continues to be cited both by national and regional historians as a 'founding period' when the German political nation was 'reconstituted' and when Conservatives rethought their entire approach to politics.[8] However, an analysis of Conservative antisemitism in the 1870s and 1880s leads to quite a different conclusion. To exaggerate only slightly, Conservatives were conspicuously *unoriginal* in their take on the 'Jewish question' in the 1890s.

These reflections also call into question the appropriateness of claims that Conservatives and antisemites 'paved the way' for or 'funnelled off support' from each other during any particular period. Instead of delineating a series of episodes in which one of these players is categorized as the challenger and the other as the (real or potential) victim, the time has come to identify terrain on which Conservatives and antisemites found real and lasting consensus, rather than looking for where either side drew its 'line in the sand.' Two terms to describe consensus-building – infiltration and interpenetration – are potentially useful. Upon reflection, they may be too open to interpretation to advance the argument much. But emphasizing consensus helps us leave behind the notion that Conservative ideology was free of identifiably antisemitic strains – free, that is, until after a certain date it became receptive to, tinged with, or dominated by such antisemitism. Conservatives, remember, are instinctively suspicious of ideology itself.

Ample evidence shows that antisemitic views had thoroughly penetrated political Conservatism even in the 1860s and early 1870s. Many of the writers who dedicated themselves to formulating a political program for the Conservatives were antisemites.[9] Nevertheless, it was in the last half of the 1870s and the 1880s that the German Conservative Party expanded rapidly into non-Prussian territories. There the party depended much more heavily than historians have previously thought on the efforts of some of Germany's most rabid antisemites. However, Conservatives and antisemites did not merely enter a flirtatious phase or even a marriage of convenience; they came very close to fusing in an unheralded, but nonetheless portentious, political union around 1875. After 1900, too, they cooperated on many fronts. In both periods close attention to regional developments can help to set the record straight. The Saxon and Baden examples, in particular, demonstrate that although Conservatives often disparaged the *style* of Germany's 'extreme' antisemites in public, in private they did nothing to distance themselves from the *content* of antisemitic demands.

This distinction between public and private views on the 'Jewish question' alerts us to the danger of conceiving antisemitism as a carefully thought-out political strategy – as a blueprint for political success worked out 'rationally' and hence not derived from personal emotion or prejudice. Personality mattered. Hellmut von Gerlach, who had a foot in both the antisemitic and Conservative camps, wrote in his memoirs that although poor judgment led many Germans to antisemitism, that journey was rarely embarked upon after careful political calculation. Gerlach described his youthful encounters with antisemites in Saxony, Berlin, and elsewhere under a revealing heading: 'The Fools and the Wise Ones.' 'Among the antisemitic leaders,' he wrote, 'I got to know only a few really decent people. Those whose character was spotless were so ignorant and uneducated that I was appalled when I had the opportunity of observing them at close range. They were demagogues one and all: some against their better judgment, others for lack of judgment.'[10]

Bavaria

In the Kingdom of Bavaria the proselytizing fervour that Gerlach described as demagogic can be seen in the efforts of Imperial Baron Friedrich Karl von Fechenbach-Laudenbach. Fechenbach was a Catholic estate owner from Middle Franconia whose wealth and connections fed an almost insatiable appetite to remain in the eye of political storms.[11]

The details of his plan to rally Protestant and Catholic conservatives behind a Social Conservative Alliance need not concern us directly.[12] His program included resolutions against the 'unchristian' privileges of large capital, 'Manchesterism,' and Jewish 'dominance' in the economy. His 'positive' points included the protection of land ownership, the introduction of a regulated workday, social insurance, progressive income and inheritance taxes, the establishment of Christian cooperatives, and the organization of the three 'productive estates' (workers, artisans, and peasants). More interesting is the reaction Fechenbach elicited from national leaders of the Conservative Party and his role in founding a regional wing of the Conservative Party in Bavaria.

As the second largest state in the empire, Bavaria might have offered the Conservative Party an important foothold in non-Prussian territories. Its population was deeply conservative. This conservatism, however, did not translate into votes for the Conservative Party, for two reasons: The German Conservative Party represented to Bavarian particularists all that was to be feared or loathed from Prussia. The Conservatives were also the defenders of Protestantism and thus unlikely to generate a following in a state that was 71 per cent Catholic. Nonetheless, although the Conservative Party never became a powerful political force in Bavaria, one historian has noted the 'steady advance of Conservatism' in the Protestant areas of Franconia. Another has referred to Middle Franconia as the political proving ground in the state and as the birthplace of Bavarian antisemitism.[13] So an opportunity for Conservative expansion into Bavaria existed, as the Prussian envoy in Munich, Count Georg von Werthern, reported to Otto von Bismarck in March 1881. Bavaria's liberals, Werthern wrote, had 'discredited' themselves of late. Yet there existed 'no real Conservative party' to articulate the discontent of disaffected people or prevent them from joining the Catholic Centre Party.[14] Into this vacuum Fechenbach was more than ready to step.

Fechenbach was not the only one who saw an opportunity in Bavaria. In April 1881 the Bavarian envoy in Berlin, Count Hugo von Lerchenfeld-Koefering, reported to Bismarck that a proposed speaking tour by the antisemitic court preacher Adolf Stöcker had to be forestalled. According to Lerchenfeld, antisemitism had not yet invaded Bavaria. This was wishful thinking. Not only had antisemitic riots broken out in Bavaria and other parts of southwest Germany in 1848, but conflicts over Jewish emancipation in the 1860s had further heightened Christian-Jewish tension in the kingdom. The right of Jews to gather wood from village commons, their allegedly usurious practices, and even the Jews' suspected influence on rising prices – these were typical issues that could transform a local beer riot into an overtly antisemitic demonstration.[15]

Fechenbach's schemes were regarded by some Conservative leaders as revolutionary because he had a clear image of the Conservative Party as a people's party (*Volkspartei*). As he wrote at one point: 'Clearly the masses are coming more into play, and the aims of their movement are going to be decisive for coming events. Our policy, therefore, ... must not fail to steer the currently and yet-to-be active masses as far as possible into our stream ... We must not, through short-sightedness, ... close off access to them.'[16] Fechenbach was able to draw to his side a number of well-known antisemitic propagandists, representatives of the Congress of German Farmers, and regional Conservative activists. As one of these remarked, the common aim was 'to overcome liberalism in state, church, and society.'[17] Many other Conservatives spoke of Fechenbach's untiring efforts to make the Conservative Party 'a people's party in the best sense of the word.'[18]

The majority of Conservative leaders at the national level, however, were too afraid that their young party – the national party had been founded only in 1876 – could be decimated politically by embracing mass politics. Their marginalia on Fechenbach's draft program revealed their doubts, with comments such as: 'This is far too indefinite, and sounds Social Democratic and enticing'; or: 'Unfortunately public opinion is so little prepared for this that the demand will serve to repel rather than attract the masses.'[19] Adolf Stöcker and his antisemitic colleagues in Berlin were more encouraging. But they, too, recognized the uphill battle Fechenbach faced. Beside one of the stronger antisemitic passages in the baron's program, Stöcker wrote that 'for propaganda purposes this point must be omitted; in principle it is correct, but at present impossible. For statesmen and ministers, the point cannot be implemented.' Baron Wilhelm von Hammerstein-Schwartow, the antisemitic chief editor of the Conservatives' leading newspaper, the *Kreuzzeitung*, remarked that the Conservatives in northern Germany would have little sympathy for or understanding of the scope of Fechenbach's proposal. He wrote that the social question was too unfamiliar to them: they recognized only the 'smack of Social Democracy' in any reformist appeals – 'and there is no end to the frightening effect that has here.'

Even greater timidity characterized the Conservative leadership in Bavaria, though Fechenbach could be forgiven for seeing encouraging signs. As the Conservative Party chairman in Nuremberg and, later,

Bavarian party secretary, Rudolf Meyer von Schauensee, wrote to Fechenbach in 1881, dissatisfaction with the nominal Bavarian Conservative leader, August Luthardt, had been brewing for some time.[20] The Nuremberg Conservatives were refusing to nominate Luthardt as their parliamentary candidate because of his lack of popular appeal. As Schauensee wrote: 'Nothing is served by our having a leader who will not or cannot put himself forward and does not even want to have the leadership in name; although I personally admire and esteem Herr Government Councillor Luthardt, I cannot say I agree with the management of south German Conservatives behind closed doors.'[21] When the new Bavarian Conservative Electoral Association was founded in June 1881, it was dominated by supporters of Fechenbach, and its program included antisemitic planks. By the summer of 1882 Schauensee reported confidently that southern Conservatives would soon unite more closely in order to exert pressure on the north German Conservatives for a new social program. Fechenbach subsequently drew up plans for south German 'action committees,' a positive 'action program,' and the establishment of a network of 'party agents' to do the day-to-day work of propaganda.

Little came of this enterprise, however, as pro-Bismarckian sympathies and older notables re-emerged within the Bavarian Conservative Party. In response Fechenbach and Schauensee tacked quickly. Soon they were working hand in glove with leading German antisemites to expand Fechenbach's Association for the Protection of Artisans. By 1884 Schauensee wrote that nothing could be done with either Bavarian or Prussian Conservatives as long as Bismarck encouraged regional and national party leaders to rely on the politics of notables and resist rank-and-file demands for a more popular style. Frustrated and marginalized politically, Schauensee and Fechenbach left the Conservatives to their own devices and joined the Catholic Centre Party.[22] Nevertheless, as events in November 1923 were to demonstrate, Fechenbach's ill-fated revolt was not the last time south German radicals took up arms against a 'high and mighty' leadership in Berlin.

Württemberg

A formal Conservative Party organization existed in the Kingdom of Württemberg only from 1876. Previously, an offshoot of the National Liberal Party, the German Party, had rallied all right-wing elements in the state. When the German Conservative Party was founded nationally, however, Württemberg Conservatives responded. The leading Conservative newspaper, the *Deutsche Reichspost*, began to attack National Liberals and Free Conservatives in the state. This attack drew to the *Reichspost*'s side men who welcomed the chance to declare officially in favour of the Conservative program. But it also alienated many members of the German Party. After disappointments in the Württemberg *Landtag* elections of 1876 and the Reichstag elections of 1878, the Conservatives realized that they could not make their way in Württemberg in direct competition with the German Party. By 1884 they had established separate party associations in only four cities in the state.[23] And so it fell to the *Deutsche Reichspost* to defend its own interpretation of Conservatism as a distinct movement in Württemberg. This it did until the Agrarian League helped to establish a real Conservative presence there in 1895.

In 1879 the *Deutsche Reichspost* was edited by one of Fechenbach's right-hand men, Franz Perrot. In 1875 Perrot had won a national reputation with his 'Era' articles in the *Kreuzzeitung*.[24] In this series he had attacked Bismarck's leading liberal ministers and his Jewish banker, Gerson von Bleichröder. Perrot charged that these men's *'Judenpolitik'* had made Germany a ready victim for economic disaster.[25] With great difficulty, the national chairman of the Conservative Party, Otto von Helldorff-Bedra, had repaired relations with the chancellor in 1876. But Perrot's hand was clearly evident in the anti-liberal orientation of the *Reichspost*, as shown in a typical lead article from 20 April 1880. Perrot argued that the real genesis of the socialist movement in Germany lay in 'that high-finance machinery of exploitation, with its hundreds of millions of workers, that is associated with the stock-exchange swindle, and whose consequences extend to our whole financial, productive, and economic system.' This editorial line continued after 1880 under Perrot's successor. A contributor to the *Reichspost* struck a typical note when he suggested in 1882 that the Reichstag was 'nothing more than an institution for the defence and support of the interests of large mobile capital ... [and] for the enslavement and exploitation of the productive estates.'[26] These polemics linking liberalism and the Jews could not fail to influence those who relied on the *Reichspost* for their information and entertainment.

The expansion of the Conservative Party was also tied directly to the larger view of society and politics that propagandists such as Perrot painted in starkly antisemitic hues. When Conservatives from Baden, Württemberg, and Bavaria met in May 1880, the *Reichspost* highlighted their attempt to give this assembly the character of a 'people's meeting' by citing the attendance of 'all classes,' even the 'most simple worker.' In the five main programmatic speeches of this congress, one was on the 'Christian State,' another was on usury, Perrot spoke on the stock exchange, and two others were about artisans' demands and the party press. Each of these speeches contained obvious references to the Jewish 'threat' facing all Germans.[27]

The *Reichspost* did not limit itself to antisemitism as a means of keeping the Conservatives' quest for popularity alive. A typical call for a Conservative *Volkspartei* was provided in a lead editorial from late 1880: 'If parliamentary parties – which are elected through the universal suffrage by the entire people – want to succeed, they have no choice but to go among the people, to make themselves known to them, and to tell them what they want ... Nothing is accomplished with a reserved, temporizing, supposedly clever attitude. The people do not want to see only wrinkled brows; they want to hear warm words that come from the heart and go to the heart – words with a clear insight into the circumstances and requirements of the day. We therefore call on the Conservative Party: Step lively! Get up to date! Trust in the people, and you will win trust from them!'[28] Although many *Reichspost* editorials eschewed direct reference to the 'Jewish question' in calling for a Conservative people's party, its campaign for party reform usually invoked antisemitic appeals in one form or another.

Model Lands of Liberalism and Reaction?

Baden has long attracted the attention of historians of German liberalism, because of the relative accessibility of its archives and its strong democratic traditions. In recent years historians have begun to examine the fortunes of Conservatives and antisemites in the Grand Duchy, so that a stocktaking is now possible.[29] Research on Saxony has experienced an even more dramatic upswing since 1990. Here, too, historians have thrown light on the activities of Conservatives, antisemites, and radical nationalists in shaping Saxon political culture. This scholarship has modified our image of Baden and Saxon as the model lands of liberalism and reaction in Imperial Germany. National Liberals in Saxony and Conservatives in Baden are now seen to have played more important roles – in local and regional coalition-building, for example – than we once thought.

A brief analysis of each state's occupational, confessional, and political profile suggests why they can be fruitfully compared (see fig. 8.1). In 1882, almost 50 per cent of the Baden population was dependent on agriculture; the corresponding figure for Saxony was just 20 per cent.[30] Whereas less than one-third of Baden's population was dependent on industry and mining, almost 60 per cent of Saxons depended on this sector. The confessional profile of the two states could hardly have been more different either (see fig. 8.2). In 1871 almost two-thirds of Germans were Protestant, slightly more than one-third were Catholic, and 1.25 per cent were Jewish. Saxony's population was far less confessionally mixed than the national average: 97.6 per cent of Saxons were Protestants (overwhelmingly Lutherans). But the Baden case inverted the national ratio of Catholics to Protestants: the latter constituted just one-third of the Baden population. The proportion of Jews in Baden (1.76 per cent) was higher than the national average (1.25 per cent) in 1871. In Saxony it was much lower (0.13 per cent).[31]

Although official Reichstag election results hide all sorts of distinctions on the Right, the different strengths of right-wing parties in the two states is clear. Figure 8.3 illustrates four main points: the consistent strength of the Catholic Centre and the National Liberal parties in Baden, the relatively late rise of Social Democracy, the Right's persistent weakness at the polls, and the minimal electoral impact of Baden's official antisemitic parties. Figure 8.4 presents a contrasting picture for Saxony: Social Democracy expands rapidly after 1871 and keeps growing; the Conservatives increase their strength to the mid-1880s and then decline gradually; the Catholic Centre is wholly insignificant; National Liberalism is slowly squeezed between the Socialist and Rightist blocs; and Saxon antisemites score noteworthy but unsustainable successes in the early 1890s. To simplify somewhat, Conservatism was near-ascendant in Saxony. In Baden it was an also-ran.[32]

Was the Right's divergent fortunes in Germany's federal states related to the shifting political complexions of state-level administrations over time? Conservatives in Baden were thrown on the defensive by the shocks to the political system inaugurated during the 'liberal era' from 1860 to 1866. From this era date many of the resentments that still percolated within Conservative ranks in the 1870s and 1880s. Even in the 1890s the antisemitic editor of the Conservative *Badische Landpost*, Adam Röder, complained that National Liberalism in his state was a 'hothouse plant' for which the Baden government provided all the manure it needed.[33] After 1905 the Baden government's ambivalent stance towards socialism once again gave Conservatives hope that the

284 Tension and Détente

Figure 8.1. Occupational profiles of Baden, Saxony, and the Reich, 1882

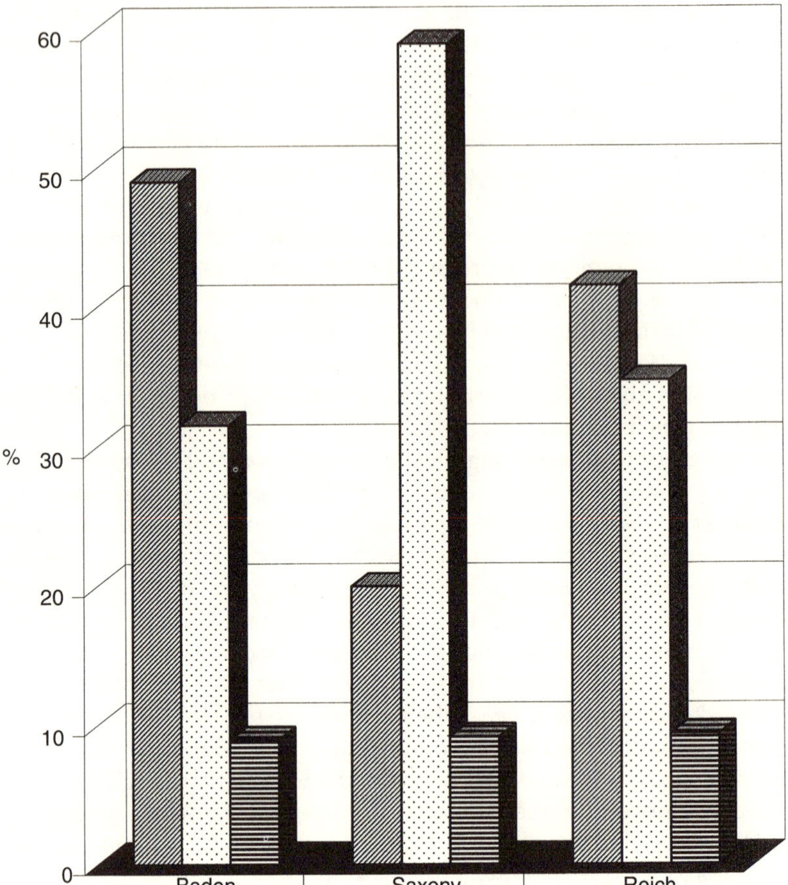

	Baden	Saxony	Reich
Agriculture	49.1	20.0	41.6
Industry	31.6	59.0	34.8
Commerce	9.0	9.2	9.4

Per cent of population dependent on ...

liberals' domination of Baden politics might be broken. Disappointment was not long in coming. Nevertheless, these swings in the general political mood gave Baden Conservatism its characteristic tendency to oscillate between resentment and resignation, on the one hand, and arrogance and attack, on the other.

Figure 8.2. Religious profiles of Baden, Saxony, and the Reich, 1871

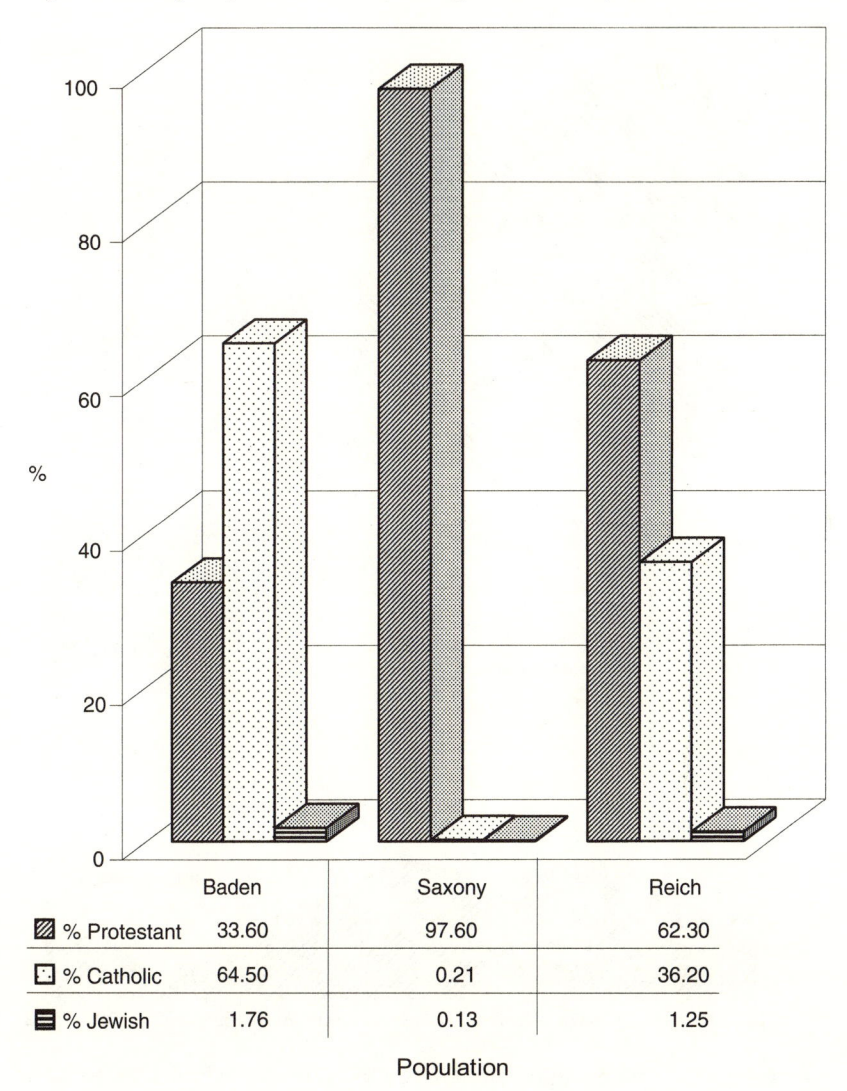

	Baden	Saxony	Reich
% Protestant	33.60	97.60	62.30
% Catholic	64.50	0.21	36.20
% Jewish	1.76	0.13	1.25

Population

Considerable flux also characterized the general orientation of state governance in Saxony. For ten years after 1866 Saxon Conservatives complained that their government capitulated too easily to liberal demands. Many considered this 'liberal era' to be disastrous to their cause. One such Conservative was Baron Heinrich von Friesen-Rötha, a

286   Tension and Détente

Figure 8.3. Reichstag elections in Baden, 1871–1912

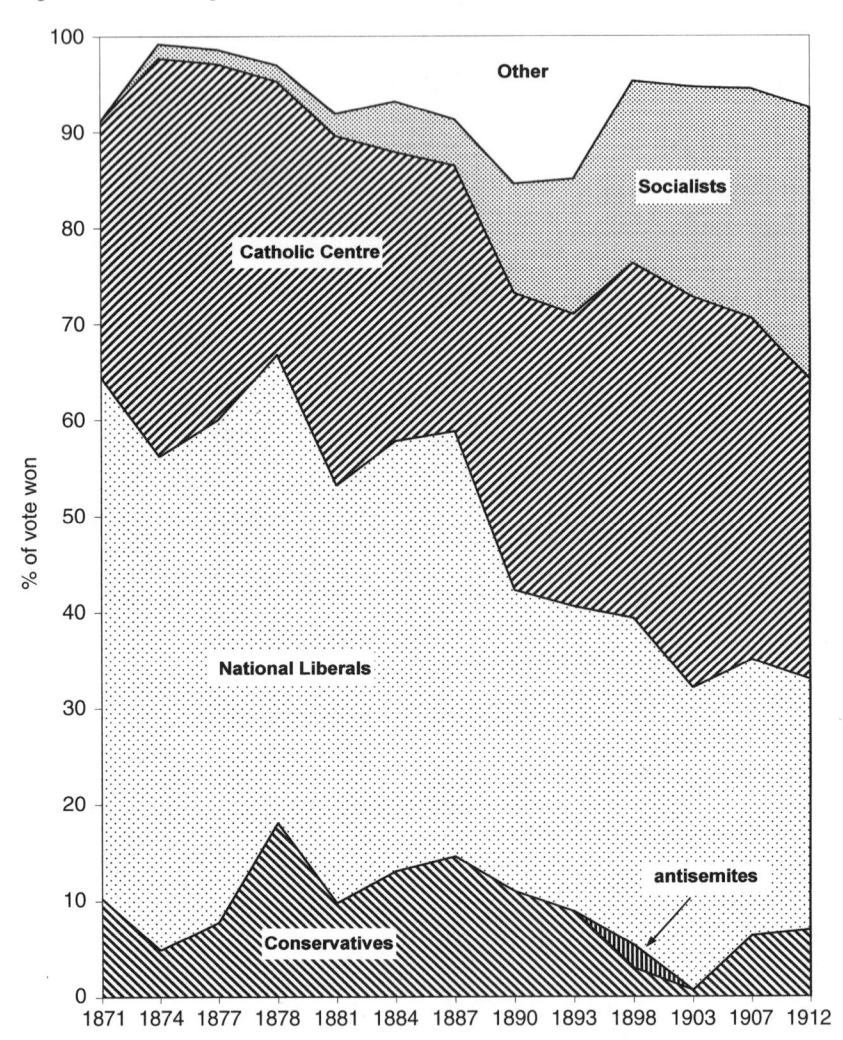

member of the Reichstag from 1887 to 1893 with sufficient rank to host week-long visits from Saxon royal princes on his prosperous estate (Rötha) south of Leipzig.[34] Friesen confided to his diary in 1876 that Conservatives in Saxony lacked the courage to stand up to the more confident liberals. 'How could things be different,' he asked himself, 'considering the official support that [the liberals] receive from the government?'[35] Saxon Conservatives had everything to gain, therefore,

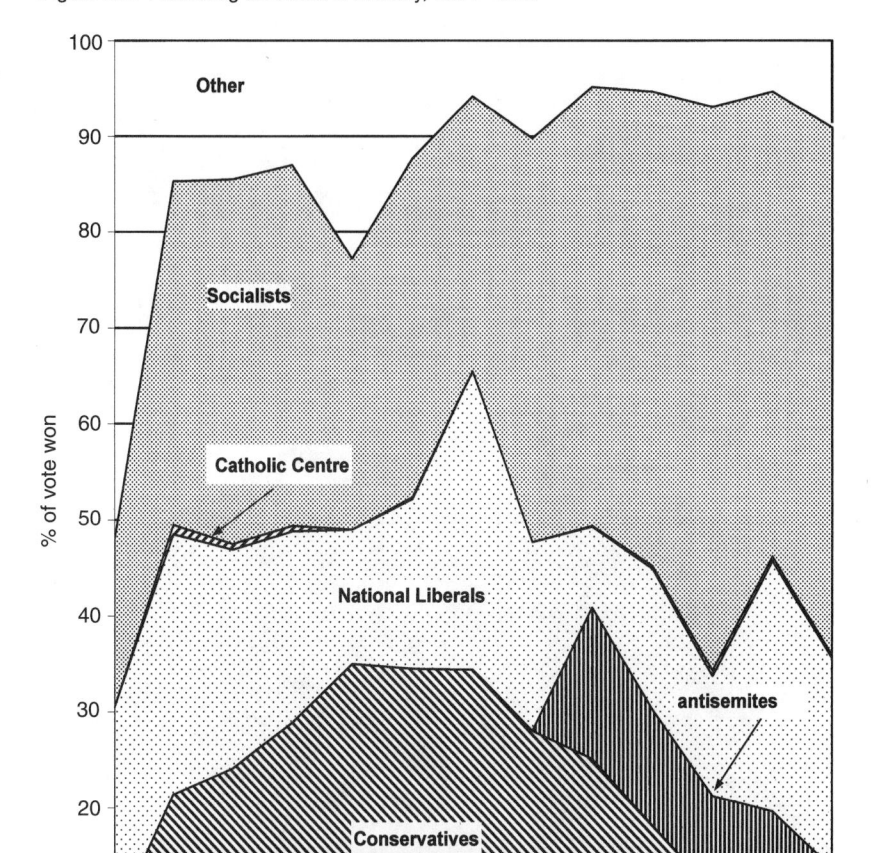

Figure 8.4. Reichstag elections in Saxony, 1871–1912

from the renaissance of Conservatism at the national level that Friesen helped engineer in 1876. Within only a few years, the ties between Saxon Conservatives and the Saxon government were as close as they were extensive. Leading Saxon statesmen and lower officials alike considered it perfectly natural that they should belong to the Conservative Party, appear at its rallies, and support it from their personal finances.

8.1. Baron Heinrich von Friesen-Rötha (1831–1910). 'Today [the Conservative Party] stands as the oldest, most vigorous, most powerful, and most influential of all antisemitic parties' (1892). Undated portrait from *Der Leipziger. Illustrierte Wochenschrift*, no. 12 (8 Dec. 1906): 10–12, in SächsStA Leipzig, RG Rötha, Nr. 1579. Image courtesy of the Sächsisches Staatsarchiv Leipzig.

8.2. Schloss Rötha, interior. From *Der Leipziger. Illustrierte Wochenschrift*, no. 12 (8 Dec. 1906): 10–12, in SächsStA Leipzig, RG Rötha, Nr. 1579. Image courtesy of the Sächsisches Staatsarchiv Leipzig.

Over the long term, the Baden state government is (rightly) seen to have defended Jewish rights more consistently than did any other state ministry.[36] And Saxony is rightly numbered among those states demonstrating the least official tolerance of the Jews. This contrast, however, prompts other questions about how government policy 'from the top down' bumped up against political challenges posed by antisemites 'from the bottom up.' More often than not, Conservatives were caught squarely in the middle – or not so squarely, for their attachment to monarchical principles was as ambivalent as their quest for popularity among the people. What remains to be determined is the extent to which Conservatives managed to balance their own authoritarian and monarchical traditions with the struggle against what many of them deemed to be the most serious threat facing Germany: the Jews. For example, Conservative lobbyists were complicit in legislation that banned kosher slaughtering in Saxony between 1892 and 1910. Conservatives supported arguments put forward locally by Dresden guild leaders, regionally by other *Mittelstand* advocates, and nationally by animal-rights activists. But their arguments also ran with the grain of ritual slaughter mythology propagated by antisemites.[37]

As political environments conducive to antisemitic agitation, Saxony and Baden *seemed* to represent best-case and worst-case scenarios. Kaiser Wilhelm II, whose rabid antisemitism is now well documented, was certainly guilty of wishful thinking in imagining that his problems would disappear if the Saxon model could somehow be replicated at the Reich level. Liberals were equally unjustified in their sanguine belief that Baden's Grand Bloc provided the model for political coalition-building on a national scale. Both examples of self-deception are illustrative, however: they gave political leaders in Baden and Saxony contrasting images of what a future Germany might look like if the struggle over Jewish rights were to be transplanted to the national political arena. Such associations were reinforced by political cartoonists like Max Bewer, who lived near Dresden and whose obscenely antisemitic *Politische Bilderbogen* often depicted a future Germany overrun by Jews (for a relatively tame example, see ill. 9-4 in the next chapter).[38]

After we have drawn contrasts between these two states, four broad similarities must be considered. First, Baden in the 1860s and Saxony in the 1880s were headed by state ministers whose enthusiasm for the imperial idea was conspicuous. In both cases it required considerable effort for regional Conservative leaders to 'opt in' to German nationalism. In both cases Conservatives believed that their state leaders had failed to preserve the requisite sovereignty of the individual federal states within the Reich. And in both cases this dissatisfaction was signalled in Conservatives' decision to preserve the fig leaf of states' rights as they joined a national party. Thus they referred to their party organizations as the State Committee of the German Conservative Party in Baden and as the State Association of Conservatives in the Kingdom of Saxony. Nevertheless, the Bismarckian party *sans phrase*, the Imperial and Free Conservative Party, was considered redundant in both Baden and Saxony, suggesting that Conservatives in these corners of the empire were more willing to accept the legitimacy of the Reich than were Conservatives in Prussia. This acceptance subsequently made it easier for Conservatives in each state to build links with radical nationalists.

Second, neither Saxon nor Baden Conservatives could rely on a strong landed aristocracy to provide the backbone of their party, as Prussian

Conservatives clearly could. One member of the Baden Conservative party was forthright enough to suggest that his party stood perennially on the verge of bankruptcy because its non-noble functionaries always tried to avoid having to ask their social 'betters' to hand over the funds needed for rudimentary party activities. Nor could Conservatives in Baden and Saxony rely wholly on the Agrarian League to do the hard work of political agitation for them, as many Prussians could after 1893. The relationship between Conservative and agrarian leaders in both Baden and Saxony was often strained to the breaking point. On many occasions, Conservative leaders opted for policies that enhanced their own standing regionally while flying in the face of agrarian demands raised nationally. One of the Agrarian League's directors, for example, complained that Baden Conservatives sought to retain all decision-making power in their own hands while deflecting Agrarian League agitation towards electoral districts where the Conservatives stood no chance of winning on their own.[39]

In both states noble Conservatives outranked bourgeois Conservatives in party offices. Yet commoners in both states undertook the bulk of the practical organizational, agitational, and propaganda work that ensured the party's survival. A social profile of the State Association of Conservatives in the Kingdom of Saxony (c. 1877) illustrates that in this highly industrialized and urbanized state, Conservatives could not afford to rely solely on farmers, let alone on *noble* farmers, to support their party (see fig. 8.5).[40]

What do we make of the relatively circumscribed presence of nobles and agrarians in these two regional parties? It would be wrong to suppose that bourgeois Conservatives were simply more receptive to antisemitism than noble Conservatives. If anything, one ought to emphasize that antisemitic Conservatives were drawn from *both* non-noble and noble ranks. During the 1880s, Friesen and other prominent Conservatives aired their antisemitic views freely in the official journal of the German Society of Nobles, the *Deutsches Adelsblatt*.[41] The larger point is that the relative social heterogeneity characterizing these two Conservative organizations appears to have contributed to Conservative leaders' willingness to regard antisemitism as a key weapon in their political arsenal: they hoped it would bring diverse social groups into close enough proximity that a foundation could be built for future political success.

Third, and again in contrast to their comrades in Prussia, Conservatives in both Saxony and Baden were relatively disadvantaged by the

Figure 8.5. Saxon Conservative State Association, social profile, c. 1877

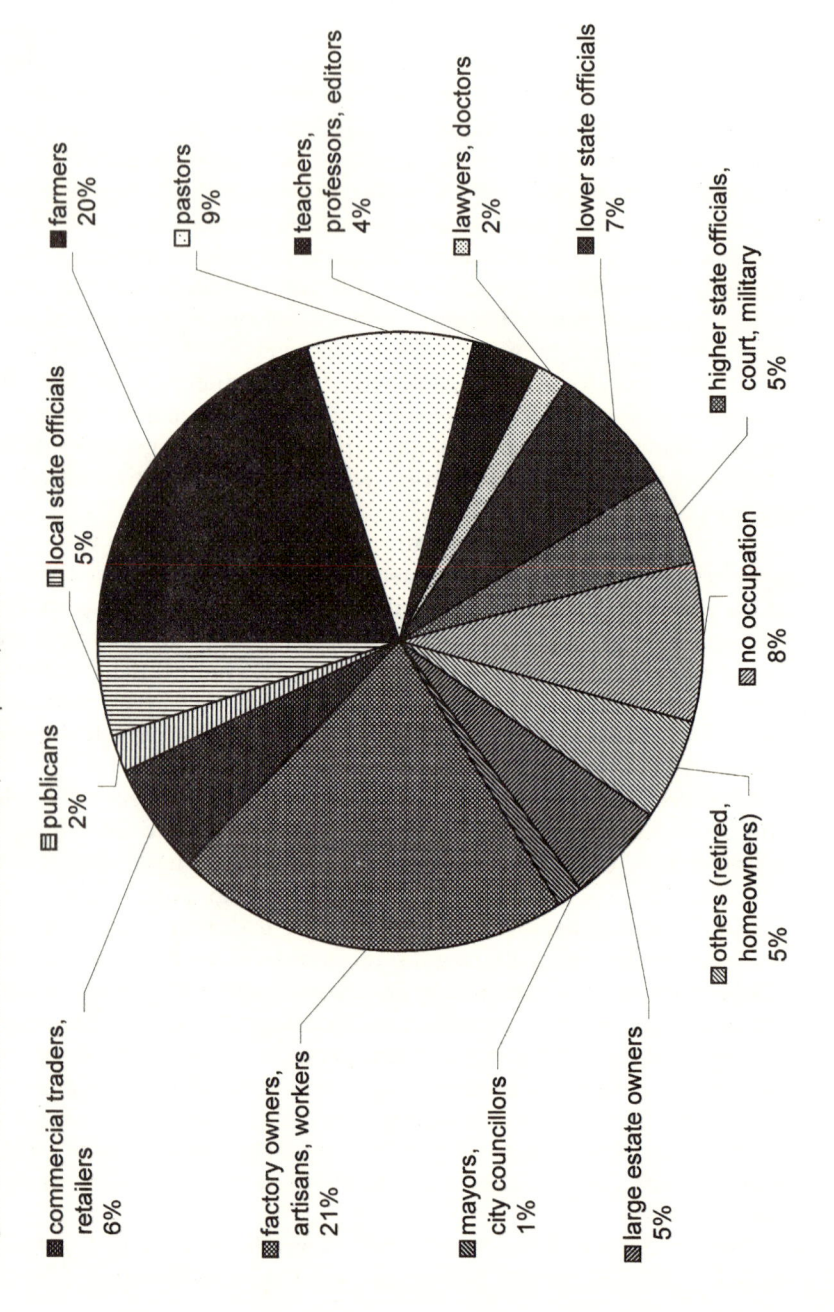

- commercial traders, retailers 6%
- factory owners, artisans, workers 21%
- mayors, city councillors 1%
- large estate owners 5%
- others (retired, homeowners) 5%
- no occupation 8%
- higher state officials, court, military 5%
- lower state officials 7%
- lawyers, doctors 2%
- teachers, professors, editors 4%
- pastors 9%
- farmers 20%
- local state officials 5%
- publicans 2%

Landtag suffrages in their own states, at least for much of the period under consideration here. As a consequence, they were permanently challenged to build election alliances and parliamentary coalitions. In Baden the indirect *Landtag* suffrage up to 1905 gave distinct advantages to the liberal state officials who proved so important in fashioning pluralities at election time. Yet because of Baden's Catholic majority, Conservatives there always faced the threat of being ground between the two rivals that benefited most from the indirect suffrage: the National Liberals and the Catholic Centre Party. In Saxony, on the other hand, the direct *Landtag* suffrage instituted in 1868 initially advantaged Conservative candidates. The tax threshold of 1 thaler (3 marks) effectively barred about one-half (later about one-third) of those permitted to vote in Reichstag elections from casting ballots in *Landtag* elections. Not by coincidence, around the same time that Saxon antisemites began to play an independent role in *Landtag* elections, they also began to agitate in favour of abandoning this threshold.

Fourth, despite their very different strengths regionally, both state-level Conservative organizations – one sooner, one later – were forced to abandon ideological and tactical consistency. In Baden a resurgence of liberalism combined with the rise of Social Democracy after 1900 to convince more and more Conservatives that their party had to ally with the Centre Party or face extinction. Thus antisemitism resonated most loudly in the arguments of those Baden Conservatives who favoured an alliance with the Centre. In this respect Baden Conservatives were merely following the example of Wilhelm von Hammerstein, who in the 1880s used the *Kreuzzeitung* to advocate an alliance of Catholics and Protestants, built on the common ground of antisemitism.[42] Unlike Hammerstein, however, whose governmental rivals eventually succeeded in marginalizing him within the national party, the pro-Centre Conservatives in Baden actually gained control of their state organization in the 1890s. Meanwhile, Saxon Conservative leaders managed to combine antisemitism with a ceaseless struggle against ultramontane influences at the Wettin court in Dresden. Occasionally, Saxon Conservatives drove anti-ultramontanism to a fever pitch. For them, the celebrated flight of the Saxon crown princess into the arms of her children's French tutor under alleged Jesuit intrigue after 1900 ran with the grain of their more familiar charge that the Jews exploited personal calamity, political instability, and other evils of modernity for their own ends.

The Defence of Christian Conservative Principles

Religion brought Conservatives and antisemites together in other ways. A defence of religious principles in confessionally mixed Baden always played a larger role in providing a rallying point for a nascent Conservative movement than it did in Saxony. Especially in the 1860s, Protestantism imbued every facet of Conservative politics in Baden. The leading figure in the party at this time was High-Consistory Councillor Karl August Mühlhäußer, a member of the General Synod in the 1860s, co-founder of the Southwest German Conference for the Inner Mission, and co-founder of the Baden Conservative Party. Mühlhäußer and his closest ally, Baron Ernst August Göler von Ravensburg, who chaired the party from 1881 to 1885, believed that the main enemy was the spirit of anti-church rationalism in the Baden bureaucracy.[43]

It seemed entirely natural to such leaders that their composite picture of the enemy should include freemasons, rationalist theologians, liberals of all sorts, and Jews.[44] A contributor to the leading Conservative newspaper in Baden, *Die Warte*, argued that a person could be devoted to religious principle without engaging in politics, but that the reverse held true only for a liberal politician. Without true religiosity, this writer continued, Conservatism became 'powerless and insipid' – it was reduced either to 'laughable Junkerdom' or to bureaucratic 'despotism.'[45] The list of Protestant newspapers, journals, and serialized pamphlets sponsored by Baden Conservative leaders suggests that their followers took such advice to heart. Conservative arguments linked a general defence of Christian principles to specific charges that the Jews dominated German literature and the press, theatre and music, youth and education, the army, political parties, parliament, family morals, and city life (the list could be extended).[46]

Even this stance proved insufficient to allow the haughty Conservatives to make political headway in the liberal *Ländl* of Baden. Throughout the Imperial period they were as likely to be called 'Jesuit dogs' as they were 'orthodox-pietist full-blooded Junkers.' One pastor wrote to the regional party leadership in 1878 to ask: 'Do you perhaps know of a man from bourgeois society who would be willing to speak [at an election rally], so that the main actors will not be simply "Junkers and priests"?'[47] Another sympathizer advised Conservative leaders not to draw their candidates exclusively from 'castles and churches.'

As other antisemites did with varying degrees of consistency and radicalism elsewhere, Baden Conservatives identified the Jew with the broadest possible threat to the Christian state.[48] Such linkage was clear in the Reichstag election campaign organized in 1878 by one of the most pro-Centre leaders on the Baden Right: County Court Councillor Baron Otto Stockhorner von Starein. Campaigning for the Conservatives in the untested Catholic regions bordering Lake Constance, Stockhorner in his electoral manifesto combined attacks on usurers and Social Democrats and later referred to the 'religion of our Father, Christianity.' Although the word 'Jew' never appeared, Stockhorner's manifesto drew attention to 'the most dangerous enemy of our people': 'the increasing brutalization and licentiousness that have fed mainly on the widespread lack of principle and detachment from God.'[49] This linkage between unchristian morality and economic exploitation persisted in Stockhorner's own thinking. Through the 1890s he tried to build a right-wing coalition of Protestants and Catholics based on antisemitic agitation on behalf of farmers and members of the lower middle classes. In 1898 he supported an antisemitic campaign in the Baden *Landtag* against Jews who were allegedly using state funds to support the 'immoral and unethical' teachings of the Talmud. And in 1903 Stockhorner was still intent on contrasting the 'materialist' and 'Christian' *Weltanschauungen*.[50]

Were these views communicated to potential voters when Stockhorner hit the campaign trail? The evidence on this point seems unambiguous. A notebook he used to deliver his standard stump speech during the 1898 Reichstag campaign contained detailed notes and reminders ('speak *slowly*'). Stockhorner listed in priority the points he wanted to stress each time he spoke: Christianity, monarchy, marriage, family, Fatherland, peace, army, and the struggle against Social Democracy. Under the heading of Christianity, marked in the margin as particularly important and underlined in both red and blue ink, Stockhorner's notes expanded on the initial prompt: 'The more a people is imbued with the Christian spirit, the higher its morality, its power, its energy, its welfare, its intelligence.' He added later in his notes: 'Christianity, in the church, but also in the life of the people and in legislation. *Healthy Christianity*.'[51] And as though he were holding his best ammunition in reserve, Stockhorner carried with him a copy of the Conservatives' 1892 party program with its novel antisemitic plank. He had highlighted the relevant passage in red ink: 'We oppose the intrusive and destructive Jewish influence on our national life. We demand Christian authorities for a Christian people and Christian teachers for Christian students.'[52]

'Authoritarian Types with Democratic Gloves'

That the Conservative movements in Bavaria, Württemberg, Baden, and Saxony after 1875 produced more than their share of antisemitic leaders, functionaries, and propagandists is inexplicable without knowing that the Conservatives' national leadership shared the same profile. Why is this linkage important? Because the existing scholarly literature generally discusses the rise of quasi-independent antisemitic individuals and groups in Germany's non-Prussian regions in the 1880s as though it presented traditional Conservatism with a massive challenge of legitimation – a challenge the party could not meet.[53] Part of this interpretation is correct: the challenge was real. However, to neglect the rise to prominence of radical antisemites *within* Conservative ranks skews the picture.

From the time he edited the *Kreuzzeitung* at mid-century, Bismarck's one-time adviser Hermann Wagener injected antisemitism into all his journalistic, organizational, and electoral activities. Antisemitic articles and cartoons appeared regularly in the *Kreuzzeitung* but also in the *Berliner Revue* and the annual *Kalender* of the Prussian People's Association.[54] By the mid-1870s the early activities of the German Conservative Party and its associated lobby group, the Association of Tax and Economic Reformers, relied heavily on well-known antisemites of the day. Many in the party sympathized strongly with Perrot and his 'Era' articles from 1875. The party's first de facto secretary was Carl Wilmanns, author of *The 'Golden' International and the Necessity of a Social Reform Party*, which appeared in 1877. Wilmanns's scurrilous book appeared from the publishing house of Martin Anton Niendorf, the general secretary of the Tax and Economic Reformers and a well-known propagandist for the agrarian cause. Niendorf published his own, Wilmanns's, and others' antisemitic tracts.[55] He also stood close to two other prominent agrarian publicists: Otto von Diest-Daber and Wagener's personal secretary in the 1870s, Rudolf Meyer.[56] Niendorf's publishing house in Berlin provided a foundation for the Conservative agrarian press, including the *Deutsche Landeszeitung*, which regularly published antisemitic articles.[57]

Whereas the hyper-nationalist, anti-liberal, and antisemitic aspects of the Agrarian League's agitation and propaganda after 1893 are well known, historians have undervalued the antisemitic cultural codes found in these earlier programs. Such codes were also communicated via the Conservatives' leading national newspapers in the early 1880s: the

Kreuzzeitung, the *Deutsches Tageblatt*, and Heinrich Engel's staunchly Protestant *Reichsbote*. In these publications, attacks on Bismarck's Jewish banker and on prominent Jewish National Liberals such as Eduard Lasker frequently served as the focus of sweeping denunciations of 'Manchester liberalism.' Just as common was the call for Christian reforms in economic, religious, and judicial matters. For Conservatives who preferred to avoid Perrot's explicit attacks on Bismarck's '*Judenpolitik*,' the demand for Christian authorities in state and society needed no further elaboration.

The ideological and organizational links between these journalistic enterprises and the nascent Conservative movements in Saxony and Baden are as numerous as they are revealing. One such link can be followed in Perrot's own career. After gaining notoriety in 1875, two years later he was the economic editor of the Conservatives' antisemitic newspaper in Dresden, the *Neue Reichszeitung*. There he worked with two antisemites who would later gain national renown as members of Stöcker's Christian Social Party: Dietrich von Oertzen[58] and Baron Eduard von Ungern-Sternberg.[59] A year later Perrot moved to Frankfurt am Main, where he edited the newspaper that served the Conservative cause in Baden and Württemberg, the *Deutsche Reichspost*.[60] Baron von Ungern-Sternberg moved in the opposite direction. After helping to establish the *Badische Landpost* in the mid-1870s, he was recruited by Saxon Conservatives to edit the *Neue Reichszeitung*, which, like its successor the *Sächsischer Volksfreund*, was open and direct in its antisemitism.

Publicists and functionaries were not the only convinced antisemites within Conservative ranks in this founding period. In Saxony the rejuvenation of the regional party apparatus after 1876 was taken in hand by two relatively unknown figures: Baron von Friesen-Rötha, introduced previously, and Dr Arnold Woldemar (von) Frege-Abtnaundorf, who served as Friesen's political 'adjutant.' These two men engineered the expansion of Conservative party organization in western Saxony. They did so because, as one of Friesen's correspondents put it, it was difficult to find locally 'even one [man] who combines the 3 qualities necessary to take in hand the founding of a local Conservative club: personal competence, social standing, and enthusiasm for the cause.'[61] These men were also determined to combat the local influence of National Liberals in Leipzig and the influence of Jewish traders who travelled to its triennial fairs. Friesen and Frege represent a distinctive type of Saxon Conservative leader: anti-democratic in general and anti-socialist in particular, cognizant of the power of *Mittelstand* demands but not opposed to agrarian interests – and strongly antisemitic.[62] Their careers thus open a window on Conservative antisemitism of word and deed (they are pictured with other Conservative Reichstag deputies in ill. 9.1).

Arnold Frege's political career in the Reichstag alone spanned two and a half decades (1878–1903); he served as Reichstag vice-president from 1898 to 1901. Frege's father had married a famous Berlin singer in 1836 and was ennobled on his golden wedding anniversary. When he died in 1890, the younger Frege inherited his noble patent.[63] Three years later he was named to the upper chamber of the Saxon *Landtag* by the Saxon king. Frege could boast of practical experience in agriculture, numerous writings on cattle-breeding and agricultural tariffs, extensive travel in England, Russia, and Italy, and service as a justice of the peace and chamberlain. He also supported Saxony's Inner Mission for many years. Yet as one of the largest landowners in Saxony – his estate Abtnaundorf, northeast of Leipzig, comprised 305 hectares – Frege rose to prominence as a representative of Saxon agrarian interests on various national councils. He served on the directorate of the Association of Tax and Economic Reformers after 1876, on the German Agricultural Council, and on many other regional agricultural bodies. During the 1880s he was also a Saxon delegate on the German Conservative Party's Committee of Eleven, and in 1892 he was a member of the committee charged with revising the Conservative Party program of 1876. During the 1880s Frege sympathized both with the Christian Social wing of the party under Adolf Stöcker's leadership and with Baron von Fechenbach's efforts in Bavaria.[64]

There is no evidence that Frege was privately troubled by the radicalism of these colleagues' antisemitic proposals. On the contrary, in 1880 he was candid in outlining to Fechenbach why, despite his own enthusiasm for program reform, it was impossible for leading Reichstag deputies in Berlin openly to advocate antisemitic policies. On the one hand, Frege explained that Conservatives could not risk jeopardizing the young party's standing in national politics by undertaking popular agitation that would prove uncomfortable for Prussian Conservatives or Chancellor Bismarck: 'We must refrain from appearing before the masses with promises and slogans, whose sad impossibility of fulfilment is all too clear, at least to those of us in the Reichstag.' On the other hand, Frege already chafed under the *Kartell* yoke that Bismarck had fashioned for the so-called national parties. He declared: 'We unfortunately have in our midst, because of the "might before right" policies of the last twenty years, such a large number of pseudo-Conservative creatures, so many fearful souls who want never to incur the displeasure of the government or the so-called liberal bourgeoisie, that – between us – I think we cannot have doubts about how weak our cause still is, about how many Conservatives ... [would defect to a *Mittelpartei*] if even a few of the decisive demands in Your Excellency's program – of which I personally approve fully – were to be publicized.'[65]

Both Frege and Friesen-Rötha can be included in that 'interlocking directorate of the Right' cited in this volume's introduction. But whereas Frege typified antisemitic Conservatives whose practical experience prevented them from taking action on strongly held but unpopular beliefs, Friesen was more willing openly to pin his flag to the antisemitic mast. In 1892 Friesen grabbed national headlines by suggesting that a revised Conservative Party program should include a statement against all 'unchristian' influences in German life: in schools, parliament, the press, the judiciary, and state bureaucracies.[66] In a keynote speech delivered to a congress of Saxon Conservatives at the height of antisemitic agitation in June 1892, he openly identified those passages in the Conservative Party's 1876 program that had used coded language to defend Christian principles. Those passages, he admitted, were intended to address the 'Jewish question' directly. 'I take it as commonly known,' declared Friesen, 'that the Conservative Party has always taken a stand on the Jewish question.' 'The so-called "political emancipation of the Jews" by legislative means,' he continued, 'has been energetically opposed by the Conservatives in all German states.' Friesen then trumpeted Saxon Conservatives' success in holding back the 'Jewish tide.' He did so in a way carefully calculated to render rival antisemitic parties redundant. But the forthrightness of his antisemitism is striking:

> In the defence of Christianity, monarchy, and *Deutschtum* – as they were clearly identified in the program of 1876 – the Conservative Party has demonstrated its antisemitism since its founding. Today it stands as the oldest, most vigorous, most powerful, and most influential of all antisemitic parties.
>
> It is thanks to the Saxon Conservatives that the Jews have been able to take up citizenship [*einbürgern*] in Saxony less than in any other state. Our judiciary has remained untainted, Jews are rarely found among our teachers, and our parliamentary chambers have remained as insulated from the Jews as has the state bureaucracy. The founding of solid credit institutions have safeguarded our landed proprietors from exploitation by the Jews,

while the establishment of municipal savings banks has created favourable circumstances for depositors and credit-seekers alike, thus contributing to the welfare of the lower classes. The vast majority of our public financial institutions enjoy a reputation for solidity and fair dealing. These are all circumstances that the Conservative Party in Saxony can look upon with satisfaction. Thus when a new antisemitic party, which cannot point to the least practical success, attacks Conservative antisemitism in order to replace it with a new party organization, we are obliged to refute such slander as decisively as possible.

By late 1892 Friesen had already been outflanked by Hermann Ahlwardt and other 'rowdy' antisemites. Perhaps for this reason, historians have failed to appreciate that the Conservatives' second most powerful regional party was shaped and directed for almost two decades by a convinced antisemite. From the mid-1870s until his resignation as Saxon party chairman under a cloud of scandal in 1894, Friesen's personal diaries and correspondence abound with references to the 'Jewish press,' to the 'Semitic leaders' of German liberal parties, and other antisemitic remarks. The same terms are ubiquitous in the letters Saxon Conservative colleagues sent to Friesen applauding his June 1892 speech and in the seven-page résumé on the 'Jewish question' that the prominent Saxon agrarian publicist Georg Oertel supplied to Friesen when he was drafting his remarks.[67]

As we have seen, in his public statements Friesen was typical of many Conservatives in distancing himself from 'unscrupulous' elements within the antisemitic movement.[68] In his candid moments, however, he conceded that antisemitism animated his entire belief system. As he wrote privately to the editors of *Der Kulturkämpfer* in 1888:[69] 'I am a Conservative, and as such [!] I regard the battle against the Jews and their destructive influence on our national development as the most important task of my party. But for that reason I must object when a line of attack is adopted that merely puts weapons into the hands of the Jews and casts a shadow on the higher moral goals of antisemitism.'[70] In retirement more than a decade later, Friesen still clung to familiar Conservative priorities when he wrote that the Catholic 'threat' could not be allowed to distract Saxons from a much more immediate danger to *Deutschtum*: Jewish immigration from eastern Europe. 'The Jews,' he wrote in a political broadside, 'appear to have mistaken our smaller fatherland of Saxony for the promised land of Canaan, and the Elbe for the Red Sea.'[71]

8.3. Two antisemites: Heinrich von Friesen-Rötha and Hermann Ahlwardt. The 'radical' antisemite Ahlwardt will not be domesticated by the 'conservative' antisemite Friesen-Rötha. The caption seems to dismiss the significance of antisemitism's rising tide in 1892–3; it reads: 'Well, that's the way he is!' ('Er ist nun mal so!'). Unidentified cartoon in SächsStA Leipzig, RG Rötha, Nr. 1576, Bl. 91. Image courtesy of the Sächsisches Staatsarchiv Leipzig.

This fear of Jewish immigration from the east had animated Friesen two decades earlier when he drafted an unpublished Conservative manifesto that professed unwavering allegiance to 'German faith, German love, German loyalty, German essence, German song and German word, German morality.'[72] These elements of *Deutschtum*, Friesen noted in 1879, 'must never be taken away by the liberals' ability to devise false, foreign, and demagogic [*volksbeglückenden*] theories!' 'Our forefathers settled on free German soil,' he concluded. 'We want to *be German*, we want to *remain German*!' Completing his memoirs shortly before his death in 1910, Friesen had no energy left for attacks on liberalism. But he returned to the themes of racial purity and nobility of spirit as key elements of his *Weltanschauung*, citing with approval the writings of Houston Stewart Chamberlain.[73] His second son carried on the tradition after 1918.[74]

As we turn now to consider the breakthrough of antisemitism in Baden after 1890, this development met with more than just the tacit approval of Conservatives.⁷⁵ These Conservatives included prominent parliamentarians and newspaper editors, travelling speakers, and ordinary members of local Conservative clubs. One government report cited a Conservative Party member who lost his job as a postal clerk because he offended customers at his window by dispensing antisemitic remarks along with postage stamps. The Conservative mayor of Hugsweier is credited with opening the field for antisemites to organize in the Lahr region, while Conservative schoolteachers were particularly likely to support the increased agitation of Baden antisemites in the early 1890s: a few were actually dismissed from their positions as a consequence of such support. Just as Conservatives were typically the first to believe rumours that Jews paid Social Democratic agitators to disrupt public rallies organized by antisemites, they complained loudly when Jews organized boycotts against cattle markets that fell under antisemitic influence. The interests of Conservatives, antisemites, and agrarian leaders in Baden also converged in the 1890s over the issue of rural credit. Attempts to establish a Baden rural credit institute had both Conservative and antisemitic precursors.⁷⁶

In 1892 Baden Conservatives expressed strong enthusiasm for the *Kreuzzeitung* group around Stöcker and Hammerstein and for the antisemitic plank in the Conservative Party's new program. Both political 'investments' promised the future dividend of cooperation between Conservatives and antisemites at election time. Conservative and antisemitic editors and functionaries may have swapped positions among themselves more often out of careerism than political conviction; yet Baden Conservative journalists maintained ties with the regional wing of the antisemitic German Social movement throughout the 1890s.

To be sure, German Socials began to make inroads into districts previously dominated by Conservatives. Often those activities were accompanied first by violence and then by state action to prevent its recurrence. On such occasions, Conservatives were prone to editorialize in their Sunday news-sheets about the need for 'non-partisanship' and 'Christian love' as principles higher than antisemitism.⁷⁷ But soon thereafter, antisemitic appeals to Baden farmers, artisans, and small businessmen would ring out again in the Conservative press, in club meetings, and on the hustings. Thus, when the Prussian envoy stationed in Karlsruhe reported in early 1893 about Christian love and other traditional Conservative concerns expressed in the Baden Conservative press, he noted that they were conspicuous only by their absence.

'In the Conservative press,' he wrote, 'a fanatical Jew-baiting is underway.' Two months after the founding of the Agrarian League, the envoy reported that the Conservatives' *Badische Landpost* still 'provides its readers with little else but antisemitic and ultra-agrarian polemics.'[78] Baden voters in a number of constituencies were not informed before election day in June 1893 whether the antisemitic candidate seeking their support would join the German Social Party or the German Conservative Party. On more than one occasion, official Conservative flyers adopted antisemitic program points word for word. And despite opposing candidacies in some constituencies, Conservatives and German Socials supported each others' candidates in many run-off ballots.[79] In light of this evidence, a clear distinction between 'conservative' and 'radical' antisemites in Baden becomes untenable.

The 'Dysfunctional' Capitalist System

Exploring the regional power bases and ideological preoccupations of individual Conservatives is only one way to address the questions raised at the outset of this chapter. We can also identify specific economic issues on which Conservatives and antisemites saw eye to eye. One such concern was the scarcity of credit.[80] This issue provided an ideological link not only between anti-capitalism and antisemitism but also between Conservatives and antisemites. Across the bridge of antisemitism, it was possible for the two groups to cooperate and intermingle as they pressed the campaign against industrialization, secularization, democratization, and the 'usurious' Jew.

The provision of credit was of vital significance to many groups within the Conservatives' target constituency, in rural and in urban areas. Such groups included heavily indebted holders of landed estates, small-scale grain farmers and livestock handlers in the German southwest, artisans in Saxony and Baden, and small businessmen and shopkeepers eager to maintain their distance from a proletarian existence. It was in order to rally some of these groups to the Conservative flag that Paul Mehnert senior founded the Saxon Agricultural Credit Association in 1866. Mehnert exemplifies the faceless party organizer who worked behind the scenes to exploit the acute scarcity of credit to provide a foundation for conservative party activities.[81] By the mid-1870s, just when both the (national) Conservative and agrarian movements were getting off the ground, questions about financial propriety had become explosive. The financial scandals of the 'founding era' (1871–3) were making daily headlines and monopolizing parliamentary debate. This environment ensured a hearing for Conservative 'theorists' like Franz Perrot, who lived on 'published governmental statistics and an infrequent scholarly tome.'[82]

As the growth of the rural cooperative movement demonstrated, the issue of credit could easily be folded into larger debates about commodity exchanges, the value of human labour, free trade, stock-market crashes, railway scandals, the protection of 'national work,' and, most broadly of all, the 'moral economy' of capitalism itself. Credit issues steered popular resentments towards the group that could most easily be accused of conspiring to render Germany's economic system dysfunctional by exploiting the little man in society: the Jews. In this way Conservative arguments about the deficiency of liberal capitalism, combined with their gloomy prognosis for religious morals, targeted Germans whose existential struggle centred on the here-and-now. Germany's capitalist economy no longer allowed maximal interest rates to be set by the government; nor was it easy to establish criminal intent to exploit another person's financial vulnerability. But usury could be reinterpreted to include the exploitation of 'need, inexperience, and frivolity.'[83]

Such reinterpretation was all the more attractive to Conservatives and antisemites because it made political attacks on Jewish 'usurers' broadly applicable and morally incontestable. In the process, the notion of the Jew as a speculator in land (*Landwucherer*) became less important as an objective issue of actual hardship or unfair practices than as one whose threatening guise took on physical attributes. Polemics levelled against Jewish 'land butchers' (*Güterschlächter*) conjured up images of rapacious Jews 'who bought up peasant holdings, parcelled them, and resold them at profit to the land-hungry.' These 'heartless' Jewish 'vampires' were immeasurably more alarming than Shylocks of the past, precisely because the combination of sham scholarship, moral authority, political calculation, and occasional physical violence against the Jews promised rich rewards.[84] David Peal has written that radical antisemites such as Otto Böckel in Electoral Hessen wanted 'more from politics than racism, nostalgia for the *Volk*, and a city boy's *Deutschtümelei*.' This yearning, according to Peal, set Böckel apart from racial antisemites such as Theodor Fritsch. Yet the Baden and Saxon examples demonstrate that the issue of rural credit provided Conservatives with a demonology (liberal = Jew) that was functionally equivalent to the one provided by Böckel in Hessen (Junker = Jew).

8.4. Capitalism in crisis! This cartoon carries the title 'The latest rumour' and the caption 'Bankruptcy is coming!' In alarmist fashion, it conflates the economic setbacks and political scandals during the 'founding era' (*Gründerzeit*) of 1871–3. The 'panic' depicted is the result of 'swindles' by banks, joint-stock companies, building societies, railway entrepreneurs, and stock exchange dealers. 'Das jüngste Gerücht,' *Berliner Wespen*, April 1872. Image courtesy of the Bildarchiv Preußischer Kulturbesitz, Berlin.

Conservatives did not necessarily have to behave like the 'extreme' Böckel to seek a power base in the villages of Baden and Saxony. Instead they targeted liberals squarely. This was clearly the intent of a contributor to the Saxon Conservatives' *Neue Reichszeitung* when he combined the discourses of economic and political exploitation during the Reichstag election campaign of 1877: 'In the guise of Jewish businessmen, the National Liberals have sent their agents into the most isolated corners of our land; everywhere these people are working with their characteristic doggedness and energy on behalf of the unitary state.'[85] The British envoy in Dresden reported in 1884 that the Conservatives' equally antisemitic *Dresdner Nachrichten* commonly referred to Saxon left liberals by 'ridiculing them as pedants, professors, and Manchesterians, & reviling them as the representatives of the International Gold League, of Jewry, and of usury.'[86]

Held together with the glue of conspiracy theories, alleged exploitation, and social unfairness, anti-liberalism and antisemitism were used over and over again in Conservative publications from the early 1870s onward to target the (real and potential) victims of liberal economics. Yet to sample such writing is to illustrate the increasingly direct tone of this genre as it singled out Jews as the source of all industrial and agricultural distress. Early in the 1870s Perrot's studies advocating railway reform contained the usual dark allegations of unseen manipulation without mentioning the Jews by name: 'The game in railroad stocks is not only a hazardous one, but one played with marked cards. Some know the cards and play only when they can win, while the rest, who don't know the cards, generally lose.'[87] Near the end of the decade, an anonymous contributor to a Saxon Conservative news-sheet suggested that Christians and Jews had both been overtaken by the spirit of 'dealing' commonly found in high financial circles: 'Things have been so Judaized here that this tendency to jobbery [*Schachern*] is no longer a specific characteristic of the Hebraic race.'[88] But by 1880 the Conservative *Badische Landpost* left no doubt about who was dealing the marked cards: 'The Jews have our *finances* in their hands, the Jews have our *newspapers* in their hands, the Jews have our *trade* in their hands, the Jews have our *farmers* – in their pockets. In a word, the Jews have won superiority in our whole political and social life. That is the situation. How are we once again to escape it? That is the question, that is the Jewish question.'[89]

Helmut Walser Smith has provided a salutary reminder that we should not take at face value antisemitic polemics about exploitative relations between Jewish traders and Gentile farmers in the German countryside.[90] Nevertheless, juxtaposing the public and private views of Conservatives in southeastern and southwestern Germany reveals a striking similarity of tone and an unexpected radicalism in their assessment of Jewish influence in the rural economy. The public side of the equation is exemplified in a starkly antisemitic brochure directed at German farmers, published in 1893 by the Conservative editor of a popular series of quasi-political tracts devoted to contemporary Christian issues.[91] In this brochure, Hermann Dietz drew upon antisemitic arguments he had first published during the 1870s as chief editor of the Conservatives' leading newspaper in Westphalia. Besides attacking Mammonism, materialism, and Social Democracy, Dietz claimed that 99 per cent of usurers were Jewish. He called on readers to establish 'Jew-free' markets wherever possible.

The Baden Conservative leader Göler von Ravensburg was equally convinced that the Jews were to blame for the Conservatives' failure to make headway against their liberal rivals in Baden: 'And how are things with the farmers? The experience of the last *Landtag* elections shows that they lack all understanding and independence. They simply do not possess the judiciousness and the character that would permit [us] to build up a proper following among them. Petty quarrels with their neighbours etc. are the only things that drive them on. If things were otherwise they would not have become the victims of the Jews. They believe whoever addresses them last. However, they vote and they act exactly as the Jews demand and wherever private enmity and suspicion impel them. We cannot gain the least influence over them because they have no understanding for principled ideas. That is why they are increasingly falling prey to keepers of post horses, butchers, and usurers ... Everything is rotten in the state of Baden.'[92]

In 1893 Otto von Stockhorner was less certain about the views of his would-be followers in the Baden countryside. He wrote to the leader of the local farmers' association in Hockenheim to discuss the divergent fortunes of the nascent Agrarian League, on the one hand, and its liberal and Jewish opponents, on the other. Stockhorner's tone suggested that he was searching for clues from the grass-roots level about how well a Conservative brand of antisemitism would play among the farmers in Baden under the new circumstances of the 1890s: 'For a long time I have heard nothing from the farmers' associations, and it would interest me greatly to receive a report about the mood and outlook among their members ... [Farmers] can only be helped if the agrarian movement expands, but that expansion has been limited until now by great impediments, above all by the press and by the liberals' money and in particular by the Jews. The frightful power of the Jews is becoming more dangerous every day, and one's position on the Jewish question is going to be very important in the next elections. I would therefore be grateful for information about the current views and opinions on this question among our friends.'

The report Stockhorner received suggested that Conservative organizers in the Baden countryside, as in Göler's era, still felt powerless in the face of Jewish traders: 'In Hockenheim we can't take up the Jewish question at all,' came the reply; 'so much tobacco is grown here that one cannot risk alienating the Jews; otherwise one would not be able to sell it at all, since they have the whole business in their hands.'[93] Of course, claims that Jews exerted hegemonic control over local economies were often self-serving. They provided Conservative functionaries with a good excuse for inaction or lack of success. They also salved the conscience or lifted the spirits of Conservative leaders who, like Mühlhäußer, believed their service to 'the good cause' was condemned to failure by Jewish domination of the press.[94] Yet such declarations were penned in private correspondence and served no propaganda purpose. They thus reflected Conservatives' inner conviction that reform of Germany's economic, social, and moral life could be achieved only by isolating, disenfranchising, or otherwise restricting the civil rights of the Jews.

Christian / Social / Reform

If antisemitism was a central ingredient in the arguments of party members who sought to 'update' the Conservative Party and make it successful in non-Prussian territories, in those arguments three terms resonated loudly: 'Christian,' 'social,' and 'reform.' Political strategies associated with each of these terms permitted Conservatives to embrace elements of antisemitism consistent with their image of a rejuvenated party. 'Christian Conservatism' held the widest appeal: it subsumed a defence of the Christian state, Christian authorities, and a Christian press.[95] But 'Christian-social' provided a means to combine attacks on the liberal capitalist 'disorder' with arguments identifying the Jews as those most centrally responsible for economic instability. At the same time, it allowed Conservatives to proclaim their abhorrence of Marxist socialism and their determination to help the 'little man' in society in his struggle against the unseen powers of big business and high finance. Hence Adolf Stöcker's vehicle for transforming 'Christian' and 'social' goals into practice was called the Christian Social Party. Until his break with the Conservative Party in 1896, this party served as a beacon for antisemites within the Conservative Party who sought to modernize Prussian Conservatism and create a mass basis for the movement.

Here the third element of the triad, 'reform,' became important, especially as the challenge of Social Democracy loomed larger in the political calculations of Conservatives. Because the struggle against political revolution already served as a common denominator for Conservatives, advocates of Christian and Christian-social Conservatism inaugurated a debate in the 1890s that revolved around the question 'Revolution or Reform?' As it happened, traditional Conservatives used this issue as a means to marginalize Stöcker and other reformist Conservatives within the party. Those Conservatives then retreated to the Evangelical Social Congresses, the rump Christian Social Party, and other organizations where they believed they could pursue their Christian Conservative goals.

What too often gets ignored in this story is that the term 'reform' was associated long before the 1890s with the activities of some of Germany's most dedicated and extreme antisemites. From the time that Alexander Pinkert founded Germany's first Reform Association in Dresden in 1879 until the establishment of the German Reform Party fifteen years later, the overlapping discourses of political reform and the practical work of organizing a new antisemitic party dovetailed in ways that allowed Conservatives to work in tandem with antisemitic leaders to achieve their common goals.[96] Few Conservatives would have objected to the goals announced on the masthead of Dresden's most antisemitic newspaper, the *Deutsche Reform*: 'Organ of the German Reform Movement. Protector of Working People against International Manchesterism and Stock-Exchange Liberalism. Daily Newspaper for Politics, *Honourable* Business Practices, and Conversation.' As early as the 1860s, the German Reform Association had served Saxon particularists and other pro-Austrian (*großdeutsch*) Conservatives who fashioned themselves as sentinels protecting 'Germany' from Prussia and the liberals. Subsequently, Conservatives rarely tried to disassociate themselves from other reformers standing 'on watch' for the German people against the Jewish threat.[97]

Standard works on German antisemitism also tell us that the German Reform Party and the German Social Party were hamstrung and eventually marginalized in national politics by personal rivalries among their leaders, by financial insolvency, and by programmatic inconsistency. That Christian, Christian-social, and Christian-social reformist Conservatives also proved susceptible to these difficulties illustrates why only the combined study of Conservatives and antisemites in their local political environments can explain the pervasiveness of antisemitic prejudice on the German Right. Thus we come to the strange case of Gustav Emil Leberecht Hartwig. An obscure Dresden master builder, Hartwig in the early 1880s fashioned an alliance of Conservatives and antisemitic 'Reformers' in the lower house of Dresden's municipal parliament.[98] The means he used to gain initial prominence, his ability to galvanize Dresden's disaffected lower middle classes, and his frequent run-ins with Dresden Conservative leaders are all illustrative of the complexity of Conservative-antisemitic relations, even though many details of Hartwig's chequered career remain cloaked in obscurity.

As a consequence of rising tax burdens associated with both Germany's new tariff policy and Saxony's income tax introduced in 1877–8, Hartwig burst on the scene during municipal and *Landtag* election campaigns in Dresden in 1881–2. His political bandwagon was a local tax revolt. Despite the highly charged language he used, Hartwig's 'revolt' actually called for all the 'reforms' that Conservative antisemites had been advocating since the mid-1870s. These included opposition to 'bankrupt' liberal economics, Jewish 'domination' of the press, and, not least, misdemeanours in high places. Dresden's powerful Homeowners Association, together with the antisemitic Reform Associations and Christian Social Associations, provided the organizational backing Hartwig needed to penetrate the staid atmosphere of municipal council meetings. Armed with an insider's knowledge of the construction trade and copious statistics, he accused Dresden's Council and its Conservative mayor, Dr Paul Stübel, with multiple counts of financial mismanagement. The imprudent or improper allocation of city contracts, the inaccurate or unfair assessment of property taxes, the unnecessary or untimely expropriation of lands needed for expansion at inflated prices, the disruptive or deleterious stewardship of annual budgets through debate – these issues served Hartwig well in his effort to put an end to 'business as usual,' in both senses of the term.

These charges resonated in the halls of parliament itself, but their echo was louder still in the streets of Dresden. There, strict legality and accepted parliamentary practice mattered little to citizens eagerly awaiting sensational charges of graft and bribery. Hartwig's accusations did not always prove groundless. Nevertheless, he was once sentenced to two weeks in jail (he eventually paid a 1,000-mark fine instead). On another occasion, court proceedings were launched jointly against Hartwig and the radical antisemitic publicist in Dresden, Oswald Zimmermann.[99] Conservative leaders in Dresden were hardly blameless in fanning the flames of controversy throughout the decade; but they floundered politically because they were unwilling to distance themselves from the substance of Hartwig's attacks on the Jews. After political decorum returned to municipal politics in the 1890s, no one could deny that Hartwig and his 'social reformist' backers had secured a power base for themselves that was unequalled in other German cities. Having previously parlayed local notoriety into victories in both *Landtag* and Reichstag elections, for another fifteen years after 1891 Hartwig profited personally from a new company whose contract for services to the city was awarded under circumstances as dubious as those he had originally attacked.

Hartwig transformed Dresden's political culture permanently. The city's Homeowners Association grew so powerful that it served as the model for regional and national organizations whose political influence was still manifest in the Weimar Republic.[100] Long before that, though, Hartwig's activities had already resulted in the last Jewish member of Dresden's city council, Emil Lehmann, losing his seat in 1883.[101] The lack of any significant outcry at the time – except from Jews themselves and from a few left liberals – demonstrated to the Conservatives that there was little political risk in unfurling a campaign to deny Jews political representation in the Saxon capital. Subsequently, an antisemitic coalition of Conservatives and Reformers dominated Dresden politics until the end of the imperial era. Their voice was always heard when the Saxon king, his ministers, or *Landtag* deputies debated Jewish policy.

Were Hartwig and the Conservative-Reform coalition he created in Dresden successful because the city's political culture was amenable to their style of politics? Or did they play a role in preparing the ground for other initiatives that achieved greater national prominence after the 1880s? Such cause-and-effect questions can be posed on other fronts too. Did antisemitic publishing enterprises set up shop in Leipzig, Dresden, and Chemnitz because publishers, editors, and journalists recognized that Saxony's political environment assured them a local readership? Or did the establishment of such enterprises over time make that environment measurably more receptive to antisemitic propaganda? The latter conclusion is more plausible, given how little attention these antisemitic publications actually paid to local affairs. Many of them, including Ernst Schmeitzner's *Internationale Monatsschrift* and Theodor Fritsch's *Hammer*, consciously addressed their antisemitic message to a national audience.[102] Nor did the antisemitic congresses held in Dresden in 1882 and Chemnitz in 1883 take much account of local political affairs.[103] On the other hand, when the *Dresdner Nachrichten* declared in 1890 that steady grain prices were threatened 'by "rings" of radical Jews,' the British envoy in Dresden noted: 'As far as I can judge, this political economy is generally accepted as sound.'[104]

Similarly, were Saxons by the 1890s so animated by resentment of the Jews that the pronouncements of radical nationalists were assured a hearing? Or did the constant stream of propaganda and celebrations organized by nationalist associations actually change Saxony's political culture, placing Saxons in the vanguard of those who promised 'dedicated' and 'principled' action against Germany's enemies (as the local chapter of the Pan-German League claimed). And what are we to make of Saxon Conservatives' willingness to allow the antisemite Theodor Fritsch to spearhead *Mittelstandspolitik* after 1895, leading first to the founding of the Saxon Mittelstand Union and then the Imperial German Mittelstand Association? Although Fritsch is frequently cited as an extreme racial antisemite standing on the margins of the German Right, over many years he worked seamlessly with Saxon Conservatives to assemble Imperial Germany's most powerful regional *Mittelstand* movement.[105]

Against this background, Saxon Conservatives' close integration with local chapters of the Navy League, the Pan-German League, and other radical nationalist organizations comes as no surprise.[106] The authoritarian character of Saxony's political culture and the chauvinism expressed by the Saxon Right were constant objects of comment by foreign diplomats stationed in the kingdom. Indeed, such observers often noted that the rhetorical excess we have discovered in Conservatives' private statements on the 'Jewish question' infiltrated their public rhetoric too. The German imperial adventurer Carl Peters was invited to Dresden in 1890 to address a meeting organized jointly by Saxon Conservatives and the local chapter of the German Colonial Society. On this occasion, the British envoy in Dresden reported that Paul Mehnert junior, chairman of the Dresden Conservative Association, enthusiastically trumped Peters's chauvinism. To use a different metaphor, the British observer might also have reported that Mehnert trumpeted Peters's radicalism in a higher key: 'Where the traveller [Peters] was facetious and satirical, the politician [Mehnert] was acrimonious and malignant. Our [Great Britain's] delinquencies were stated with emphasis, and 2000 intelligent Saxons learned that "England" had ordered Dr Peters be "arrested, and, if possible, placed in chains." If hatred of a country with political and social institutions like ours is, to a German conservative, a second nature, so is servility to the higher powers, and accordingly Dr. Mehnert alluded to the King in language almost fulsome enough for the Tudor age.'[107]

Conclusions

This chapter has tried to suggest that historians should scrutinize the actions of Conservatives and antisemites together and in specific regional settings before they try to sum up how the 'old' and the 'new' Right responded to the challenge of mass politics. Only by penetrating to the local and regional levels can they make sense of the web of relationships that enmeshed German Conservatives and antisemites in common aspirations and joint action against the Jews. Baden and Saxon Conservatives moved in and out of anti-socialist, antisemitic, nationalist, and imperialist communities of spirit, often in unpredictable fashion. In doing so, they engaged in essentially the same acts of probing and retreating, condemning and confessing, that undermined the political success of the antisemitic parties, without, however, suffering their dismal fate.

All this suggests that the relations between insiders and outsiders on the German Right are important, for two reasons. First, Conservatives occupied a central position on the Right and could not easily be dislodged even by challengers such as Fechenbach in Bavaria and Hartwig in Saxony. Nevertheless – second – Conservatives touched realms of the authoritarian imagination that lay beyond the limits of their own activities as members of a political party. Well before Bismarck fell from power, Conservatives knew that they confronted the immense task of reconciling traditional attachments to authority with the search for political scapegoats upon whom they could load all responsibility for Germany's ills. Except for those antisemites who resided on the lunatic fringes of the movement (and there were some of these in Saxony too),[108] most enemies of the Jews grappled with the same challenge. Hence, as historians, we should stop arguing that Conservatives 'discovered,' 'co-opted,' 'instrumentalized,' or 'tamed' radical antisemitism. Instead we should recognize the central role that antisemitism played in Conservative ideology *and* practice at a crucial phase of the party's development. This insight in turn casts new light on a later period of history, when other conservatives also believed they were preserving Christian principles, promoting social reform, providing an alternative to a hated liberal regime, and defending *Deutschtum*. In that later era, the 1930s, they helped deliver Germany to a murderous regime whose Jewish policy moved quickly from social isolation to genocide.

NOTES

1 Three important new additions are Stefan Scheil, *Die Entwicklung des politischen Antisemitismus in Deutschland zwischen 1881 und 1912* (Berlin, 1999); Hansjörg Pötzsch, *Antisemitismus in der Region. Antisemitische Erscheinungsformen in Sachsen, Hessen, Hessen-Nassau und Braunschweig 1870–1914* (Wiesbaden, 2000); and Frank Bajohr, *'Unser Hotel ist judenfrei.' Bäder-Antisemitismus im 19. und 20. Jahrhundert* (Frankfurt a.M., 2003). For Saxony we now have Solvejg Höppner, ed., *Antisemitismus in Sachsen im 19. und 20. Jahrhundert* (Dresden, 2004); and Matthias Piefel, *Antisemitismus und völkische Bewegung im Königreich Sachsen 1879–1914* (Göttingen, 2004). Older works include Thomas Klein, *Der preußisch-deutsche Konservatismus und die Entstehung des politischen Antisemitismus in Hessen-Kassel (1866–1893)* (Marburg, 1995); Karl Friedrich Watermann, 'Politischer Konservatismus und Antisemitismus in Minden-Ravensberg 1879–1914,' *Mitteilungen des Mindener Geschichtsvereins* 52 (1980): 11–64; Daniela Kasischke-Wurm, *Antisemitismus im Spiegel der Hamburger Presse während des Kaiserreichs (1884–1914)* (Hamburg, 1997); Inge Schlotzhauer, *Ideologie und Organisation des politischen Antisemitismus in Frankfurt am Main 1880–1914* (Frankfurt a.M., 1989); Albert Lichtblau, *Antisemitismus und soziale Spannung in Berlin und Wien 1867–1914* (Berlin, 1994); James F. Harris, *The People Speak! Antisemitism and Emancipation in Nineteenth-Century Bavaria* (Ann Arbor, 1994).
2 See Till van Rahden, 'Ideologie und Gewalt. Neuerscheinungen über den Antisemitismus in der deutschen Geschichte des 19. und frühen 20. Jahrhunderts' *Neue Politische Literatur* 41 (1996): 11–29; Helmut Walser Smith, 'Alltag und politischer Antisemitismus in Baden, 1890–1900,' *ZGO* 141 (1993): 280–303. For examples of how small-town notables and antisemites together fomented violence against Jews, see Smith, *The Butcher's Tale: Murder and Anti-Semitism in a German Town* (New York, 2002), esp. 76, 170, 181. See also the recent review essay by Ulrich Sieg, 'Auf dem Weg zur

"dichten Beschreibung." Neuere Literatur zur Geschichte des Antisemitismus im Kaiserreich,' *Jahrbuch für Antisemitismusforschung* 12 (2003): 329–342.
3 The allusion here is to David Blackbourn, *Populists and Patricians* (London, 1987); the issue is treated from a different perspective in Stephan Malinowski, 'Von blauen zum reinen Blut: Antisemitische Adelskritik und adliger Antisemitismus 1871–1944,' *Jahrbuch für Antisemitismusforschung* 12 (2003): 147–68.
4 Richard S. Levy, *The Downfall of the Antisemitic Political Parties in Imperial Germany* (New Haven, 1975).
5 See Andreas Herzog, 'Das schwärzeste Kapitel der Buchstadt vor 1933. Theodor Fritsch der "Altmeister der Bewegung" wirkte in Leipzig,' *Leipziger Blätter*, no. 30 (1997): 56–9; Reginald H. Phelps, 'Theodor Fritsch und der Antisemitismus,' *Deutsche Rundschau* 87 (1961): 442–9; Moshe Zimmermann, 'Two Generations in the History of German Antisemitism: The Letters of Theodor Fritsch to Wilhelm Marr,' *LBI YB* 23 (1978): 89–99; Massimo Ferrari Zumbini, *Die Wurzeln des Bösen. Gründerjahre des Antisemitismus* (Frankfurt a.M., 2003), 321–422; Piefel, *Antisemitismus*, esp. chap. 4. On conservatives, antisemites, and the *völkisch* movement, see Stefan Breuer, 'Gescheiterte Milieubildung. Die Völkischen im deutschen Kaiserreich,' *Zeitschrift für Geschichtswissenschaft* 52, no. 11 (2004): 995–1016, esp. 1012.
6 Peter G.J. Pulzer, *The Rise of Political Antisemitism in Germany and Austria* (orig. 1964), 2nd ed. (London, 1988); Pulzer, 'Third Thoughts on German and Austrian Antisemitism,' *Journal of Modern Jewish Studies* 4, no. 2 (2005): 137–78. See *inter alia* Günter Brakelmann and Martin Rosowski, eds., *Antisemitismus. Von religiöser Judenfeindschaft zur Rassenideologie* (Göttingen, 1989), esp. 5–6. For critical comments on the viability of such distinctions, see Stefan Lehr, *Antisemitismus – religiöse Motive im sozialen Vorurteil* (Munich, 1974), 4 and chap. 7.
7 Werner E. Mosse, cited in Pulzer, *Rise*, xiv.
8 For one example, see Geoff Eley, 'Antisemitism, Agrarian Mobilization, and the Conservative Party: Radicalism and Containment in the Founding of the Agrarian League, 1890–93,' in *Between Reform, Reaction and Resistance: Studies in the History of German Conservatism from 1789 to 1945*, ed. Larry Eugene Jones and James Retallack (Providence, RI, and Oxford, 1993), 194.
9 Including Hermann Wagener, *Die Juden und der Deutsche Staat* (Berlin, 1857); Wagener, *Die kleine aber mächtige Partei* (Berlin, 1885); Philipp von Nathusius-Ludom, *Conservative Position* (Berlin, 1876); Constantin Frantz,

Der Untergang der alten Parteien und die Parteien der Zukunft (Berlin, 1878); Paul de Lagarde, *Programm für die konservative Partei Preußens* (Göttingen, 1884); and Georg Oertel, *Der Konservatismus als Weltanschauung* (Leipzig, 1893).

10 Hellmut von Gerlach, *Von rechts nach links*, ed. Emil Ludwig (Zurich, 1937), 114, where the page head reads: 'Die Narren und die Weisen.'

11 'Fechenbach,' in *Neue Deutsche Biographie* (Berlin, 1961), 5:36–7; Hans-Joachim Schoeps, 'CDU vor 75 Jahren. Die sozialpolitischen Bestrebungen des Reichsfreiherrn Friedrich Carl von Fechenbach (1836–1907),' *Zeitschrift für Religions- und Geistesgeschichte* 9 (1957): 266–77; and Karl Reichsfreiherr von Fechenbach, *Gouvernmental und conservativ oder die Partei Bismarck sans phrase* (Osnabrück, 1885).

12 BA Koblenz, NL Fechenbach, Nr. 28; 'Denkschrift in Sachen der social-conservativen Bestrebungen' [n.d.]; BA Potsdam, NL Hermann Wagener, Nr. 30.

13 See Dietrich Thränhardt, *Wahlen und politische Strukturen in Bayern 1848–1953* (Düsseldorf, 1973), 63–8, 90–1; Hans Fenske, *Konservatismus und Rechtsradikalismus in Bayern nach 1918* (Bad Homberg, 1969), 31–4; Karl Möckl, *Die Prinzregentenzeit. Gesellschaft und Politik während der Ära des Prinzregenten Luitpold in Bayern* (Munich, 1972), 213, 532. Middle Franconia's population was 76 per cent Protestant in 1880.

14 For this and the following, see Werthern to Bismarck, 5 Mar. 1881, Hugo von Lerchenfeld-Koefering to ?, 5 Apr. 1881, and [Reich chancellory] to Kaiser Wilhelm I, 6 Apr. 1881, in PA AA Bonn, I A Bayern, Nr. 50, Bd. 3; Rudolf Meyer von Schauensee to Fechenbach, 12 Jan. 1881, in BA Koblenz, NL Fechenbach, Nr. 52.

15 See James F. Harris, 'Bavarians and Jews in Conflict in 1866: Neighbors and Enemies,' *LBI YB* 32 (1987): 103–15, and Harris, *The People Speak!*

16 Fechenbach to Dr Karl Mühlhäußer, 1 Aug. 1880, in BA Koblenz, Sg F, Bd. 22.

17 Eduard von Ungern-Sternberg to Fechenbach, 2 May 1880, in BA Koblenz, NL Fechenbach, Nr. 38; Ungern-Sternberg was co-editor of the party's official *Conservative Correspondenz* and Hammerstein's deputy on the *Kreuzzeitung* staff.

18 *Reichsbote*, 26 Nov. 1880; see also the *Schlesisches Morgenblatt*, 25 Feb. 1881, 4–9 Nov. 1881; and the *Deutsche Landes-Zeitung*, 7 Dec. 1880.

19 August Luthardt to Fechenbach, 24 Oct. 1880, in BA Koblenz, NL Fechenbach, Nr. 38; for the following, see Franz Perrot to Fechenbach, 18 July 1880, Stöcker to Fechenbach, 20 Aug. 1880, and Stöcker to Perrot, n.d. (copy), ibid.; and Hammerstein to Fechenbach, n.d., in BA Koblenz, Sg F, Nr. 328.

20 See August-Emil Luthardt, *Mein Werden und Wirken im öffentlichen Leben* (Munich, 1901), esp. 259–338.
21 See Schauensee to Fechenbach, 12 Jan. 1881 and 28 Oct. 1881, in BA Koblenz, NL Fechenbach, Nr. 52; for the following, see Schauensee to Fechenbach, 9 June 1882, in ibid; and other materials in BA Koblenz, Sg F, '1888.'
22 But see the antisemitic editorials in the *Süddeutsche Land-Post*, 4 May, 12–22 Oct., and 14 Nov. 1889; see also the Conservative election manifesto in the *Süddeutsche Land-Post*, 23 Jan. 1890.
23 See 'Die Konservative Partei,' *Staats-Anzeiger für Württemberg*, 8–9 Oct. 1857, 2030; *An die Anhänger des deutsch-konservativen Programms in Süd- und Mittel-Deutschland* (broadsheet, Frankfurt a.M., Aug. 1877); *Deutsche Reichspost*, 11 June 1882; 'Die Parteien in Württemberg,' *Preußischer Jahrbücher* 54 (1884): 85–91.
24 Franz Perrot, *Ein parlamentarisches Votum über das Aktienwesen* (Heidelberg, n.d.); Perrot, *Die Börse und die Börsensteuer* (Heidelberg, n.d.); James F. Harris, 'Franz Perrot: A Study in the Development of German Lower Middle Class Social and Political Thought in the 1870s,' *Studies in Modern European History and Culture* 2 (1976): 73–106.
25 Franz Perrot, *Bismarck und die Juden. 'Papierpest' und 'Aera-Artikel von 1875,'* ed. L. Feldmüller-Perrot (Berlin, 1931), 268–83; Philipp von Nathusius-Ludom, *Conservative Partei und Ministerium* (Berlin, 1872).
26 'Der Parlamentarismus,' *Deutsche Reichspost*, 7, 16, and 20 June 1882.
27 Reports in the *Deutsche Reichspost*, 21–22 May and 31 May–4 June 1880.
28 *Deutsche Reichspost*, 3 Oct. 1880.
29 Hans-Jürgen Kremer, 'Die Konservative Partei im Großherzogtum Baden 1876–1914' (unpublished MS). I am grateful to Herr Kremer for providing access to this manuscript. See also Stefan Ph. Wolf, *Konservativismus im liberalen Baden* (Karlsruhe, 1990); Wolf, *Für Deutschtum, Thron und Altar. Die Deutsch-Soziale Reformpartei in Baden (1890–1907)* (Karlsruhe, 1995); Renate Ehrismann, *Der regierende Liberalismus in der Defensive* (Frankfurt a.M., 1993); and Stefan Scheil, 'Aktivitäten antisemitischer Parteien im Grossherzogtum Baden zwischen 1890 und 1914,' *ZGO*, 141 (1993): 304–36.
30 These and other figures from Gerhard A. Ritter with Merith Niehuss, *Wahlgeschichtliches Arbeitsbuch* (Munich, 1980); Gerd Hohorst, Jürgen Kocka, and Gerhard A. Ritter, eds., *Sozialgeschichtliches Arbeitsbuch II*, 2nd ed. (Munich, 1978).
31 By 1910 the proportion of Jews in Saxony had risen to 0.37 per cent of the population; by this time it had fallen for Baden and the Reich to 1.21 per cent and 0.95 per cent respectively.
32 Of Baden's fourteen Reichstag seats, Conservatives never represented

more than three (1884–93); usually they held just one. Of Saxony's twenty-three Reichstag seats, Conservatives held more than half (thirteen) in 1890. The contrast was more dramatic in *Landtag* elections.
33 *Badische Landeszeitung*, no. 225 (24 Sept. 1893), cited in Wolf, *Konservativismus*, 381. See also Adam Röder, *Reaktion und Antisemitismus*, 2nd ed. (Berlin, 1921).
34 Heinrich von Friesen, *Röthaer Kinder-Erinnerungen* (n.p., n.d.), 14.
35 SächsStA Leipzig, RG Rötha, Nr. 1575, pp. 140–1, diary entry of 30 Oct. 1876.
36 See Michael Anthony Riff, 'The Government of Baden against Anti-semitism: Political Expediency or Principle?' *LBI YB* 32 (1987): 119–34.
37 See Adolf Diamant, *Chronik der Juden in Chemnitz* (Frankfurt a.M., 1970), 42; Lehr, *Antisemitismus*, chap. 4; and Dorothee Brantz, 'Stunning Bodies: Animal Slaughter, Judaism, and the Meaning of Humanity in Imperial Germany,' *Central European History* 35, no. 2 (2002): 167–94.
38 *Juden in Deutschland* (Dresden, 1892); *Juden-A-B-C* (Dresden, 1893); *Die Juden im Reichstag* (Dresden, 1895) (Politischer Bilderbogen nos. 2, 8, 16). Cf. Barbara Suchy, 'Antisemitismus in den Jahren vor dem Ersten Weltkrieg,' in *Köln und das rheinische Judentum* (Cologne, 1984), 252–85; Matthew Paul Stibbe, 'Antisemitic Publicists and Agitators in Imperial Germany, 1871–1900' (MA diss., University of Sussex, 1993), 36–8; Lehr, *Antisemitismus*, 60ff.; John C.G. Röhl, 'Kaiser Wilhelm II and German Anti-Semitism,' in Röhl, *The Kaiser and His Court* (Cambridge, 1994), 190–212.
39 Gustav Roesicke to Wangenheim, 31 July 1908, in BA Potsdam, NL Konrad von Wangenheim, Nr. 3, Bl. 53. See also Franz Thierfelder, 'Die Entwicklung und Tätigkeit des Bundes der Landwirte Sachsens' (PhD diss., University of Leipzig, n.d. [1925]).
40 From a list of 2,132 members in SächsStA Leipzig, RG Rötha, Nr. 620, n.d., cited in Wolfgang Schröder, 'Die Armee muß organisiert sein, ehe der Krieg beginnt. Die Entstehung des Conservativen Vereins für den Leipziger Kreis,' *Leipziger Kalender* 1996, 148.
41 Dieter Fricke and Udo Rößling, 'Deutsche Adelsgenossenschaft (DAg) 1874–1945,' in *Lexikon zur Parteiengeschichte 1789–1945*, ed. Dieter Fricke et al., 4 vols. (Leipzig, 1983), 1:530–43, esp. 531. As early as 1875, the society's annual convention debated two key issues in tandem: the 'public danger represented by the dealings of Jews and stock-exchange men' and the question 'What state institutions are most particularly contributing to the general decline of morals among our people?' Immediately after 1918, the

society's official program came out even more openly against the 'Jewish spirit and its culture.'

42 *Neue Preußische Zeitung*, 31 July 1888; see also Helmut Fiedler, *Geschichte der 'Dresdner Nachrichten' von 1856–1936* (Olbernhau, 1939), 96–123.

43 On Mühlhäußer, the 'herald' of the Christian press, see Johannes Reinmuth, *Karl August Mühlhäußer* (Heilbronn, n.d.); Ernst August Göler von Ravensburg, 'Die liberale Ära in Baden,' *Allgemeine Konservative Monatsschrift* 40 (1883): 117–34; Fred Sepaintner, *Die Reichstagswahlen im Großherzogtum Baden* (Frankfurt a.M., 1983), 72–80; Otto von Stockhorner's unpublished memoir, 'Der Konservatismus in Baden bis 1916' (MS); and other materials in GLA Karlsruhe, Hinterlegung Freiherrn von Stockhorn [sic] (hereafter cited as NL Stockhorner), Fasc. 146 and passim.

44 See Wolf, *Konservativismus*, 51–2.

45 *Die Warte*, 27 Aug. 1869, cited ibid., 77.

46 The *Zeitfragen des christlichen Volkslebens* was launched in 1876 by Mühlhäußer and Heinrich Geffcken; in the early 1890s it was co-edited by Heinrich Dietz and Baron Eduard von Ungern-Sternberg. Martin von Nathusius, *Die Unsittlichkeit von Ludwig XIV. bis zur Gegenwart. Ein Beitrag zur Geschichte des sittlichen Urteils*, Zeitfragen Bd. 24, Heft 3 (Stuttgart, 1899), was typical in linking the Jews with everything from French drama and Viennese immorality to press abuses and trafficking in young women (*Mädchenhandel*). Similar themes appeared in other pamphlet series, including the *Zeit- und Streit-Fragen, Sammlung von Vorträgen für das deutsche Volk*, and the *Sächsischer Volkskalender*, 1ff. (1878ff.)

47 Pastor Graebener to Otto von Stockhorner, 18 June 1878, cited in Sepaintner, *Reichstagswahlen*, 76.

48 Cf. Shulamit Volkov, 'Antisemitism as a Cultural Code: Reflections on the History and Historiography of Antisemitism in Imperial Germany,' *LBI YB* 23 (1978): 25–46.

49 'An die Wähler des IV. bad. Reichstagswahl-Bezirks' [1878] and Baden Conservative manifesto of 11 Sept. 1881, in GLA Karlsruhe, NL Stockhorner, Fasc. 133. Compare Pastor H. Nauck to Heinrich von Friesen-Rötha, 22 Nov. 1888, SächsStA Leipzig, RG Rötha, Nr. 275.

50 Kremer, 'Konservative Partei'; Riff, 'Government'; Sepaintner, *Reichstagswahlen*, 77.

51 GLA Karlsruhe, NL Stockhorner, Fasc. 136.

52 See Heinrich von Friesen-Rötha, *Ueber die Notwendigkeit des Zusammenwirkens der kirchlichen und der staatlichen Factoren auf dem ethisch-socialen Gebiete* (Rötha, n.d. [1886]) and the following unpublished manuscripts

by Friesen in SächsStA Leipzig, RG Rötha, Nr. 1577: 'Notwendigkeit der Organisation der konservativen Partei auf sittlichen Grundlage'; 'Die Mißbrauch unser Tagespresse und die von Kirchlichen Seite zu ergreifenden Mittel zur Abstellung derselben'; and 'Ethisch-social!'
53 Geoff Eley's thoughtful review (1977) of new work in German antisemitism perpetuated this view in two ways. First, he suggested that agrarian influences impinged on the DKP and the Agrarian League mainly from the outside. Second, he claimed that antisemitism was 'displaced' onto establishment movements late in the day, after the Conservatives had finished 'dithering' on the issue. Eley is nonetheless correct to emphasize the wide diffusion of antisemitism within the German Right. See *Social History* 2, no. 5 (May 1977): 693–4.
54 *Kalender für den Preußischen Volks-Verein* (Berlin, 1875–81).
55 For example, *Die Fremdlinge in unsrem Heim! Ein Mahnwort an das Deutsche Volk* (Berlin, 1876).
56 Otto von Diest-Daber, *Der sittliche Boden im Staatsleben* (Berlin, 1876); Rudolf Meyer, *Politische Gründer und die Corruption in Deutschland* (Leipzig, 1877); Felix Boh, *Der Konservatismus und die Judenfrage* (Dresden, 1892). See also Donald L. Niewyk, 'Solving the "Jewish Problem": Continuity and Change in German Antisemitism, 1871–1945,' *LBI YB* 35 (1990): 335–70.
57 *Deutsche Landeszeitung*, 29 June 1875, cited in Lehr, *Antisemitismus*, 145; rpt. (by the Verlag M.A. Niendorf) as *Die Sittenlehre des Talmud und der zerstörende Einfluß des Judenthums im Deutschen Reich*, 3rd ed. (Berlin, 1876).
58 Dietrich von Oertzen, *Erinnerungen aus meinem Leben* (Berlin, n.d. [1914]).
59 Eduard von Ungern-Sternberg, *Zur Judenfrage* (Stuttgart, 1892).
60 Harris, 'Franz Perrot,' 90. See also the serialized articles in *Die Juden im deutschen Staats- und Volksleben*, 2nd ed. (Frankfurt a.M., 1878), and *Das Judentum im Staate*, Separat-Abdruck aus dem 'Reichsboten' (Berlin, 1884).
61 Cited in Schröder, 'Armee,' 152.
62 Including the Dresden lawyer Dr Paul Mehnert junior, the privy court councillor and *Mittelständler* Karl Ackermann, and the agrarian publicist Georg Oertel.
63 For enriching my knowledge of Frege and his forebears, I am grateful to Wolfgang Schröder and his communication of 28 Feb. 2005.
64 See Hans Engelmann, *Kirche am Abgrund. Adolf Stöcker und seine antijüdische Bewegung* (Berlin, 1984).
65 Frege to Fechenbach, 24 Oct. 1880, in BA Koblenz, NL Fechenbach, Nr. 38; see also Frege's letters to Friesen in SächsStA Leipzig, RG Rötha, Nrn. 273, 275, 1576.

Building a People's Party 321

66 For the following, see Friesen's 'Gesichtspunkte für ein revidiertes konservatives Program' (MS; from a speech of 9 Dec. 1891), BA Koblenz, Sg F, Bd. XIX. Friesen's speech of June 1892 was reprinted as *Conservativ! Ein Mahnruf in letzter Stunde* (Leipzig, 1892); see esp. 23 for the citation below.
67 See materials in SächsStA Leipzig, RG Rötha, Nr. 1577.
68 See Frege to Friesen, 19 Oct. 1887, ibid., Nr. 273.
69 Friesen to Redaktion, *Der Kulturkampfer* [draft], 24 Sept. 1888, ibid., Nr. 275. For background on this important journal and the man behind it, see Daniela Weiland, *Otto Glagau und 'Der Kulturkämpfer'. Zur Entstehung des modernen Antisemitismus im frühen Kaiserreich* (Berlin, 2004).
70 See 'Conservative Bundesgenossen,' *Conservatives Vereinsblatt*, no. 1 (15 Jan. 1888): 199; 'Semitismus und Antisemitismus,' ibid., no. 20 (30 Oct. 1888): 156–8, 'Die Judenfrage,' *Das Vaterland*, no. 3 (19 Jan. 1889): 32, where one reads: 'We are soldiers of a single army and take the field against one enemy! Only the shoulder straps are different!'
71 Heinrich Freiherr von Friesen-Rötha, *Antwort an den evangelischen Bund in Sachsen auf dessen Zuschrift* (Rötha, n.d. [1900]), 4–6.
72 'Die sittliche Aufgaben der Conservativen Partei [sic]' (MS), SächsStA Leipzig, RG Rötha, Nr. 1577; original emphasis.
73 Heinrich Freiherr von Friesen-Rötha, *Schwert und Pflug*, pt. 1 (Berlin, 1907), 24.
74 Dr. Heinrich Freiherr von Friesen, *Bebel und Bibel* (Dresden, n.d. [1919]), 39–42. Friesen's father had warned against Jewish emancipation in the early 1840s; his *Landtag* speech is printed in Friesen-Rötha, *Conservativ!* 57–8.
75 For the following, see Scheil, 'Aktivitäten'; Smith, 'Alltag'; Kremer, 'Konservative Partei'; and Wolf, *Konservativismus*. The latter should be used with caution, as should Georg Längin, *Zur Charakteristik der kirchlich-konservativen Partei in Baden* (Karlsruhe, 1892); F.G. von Langen, *Das jüdische Geheimgesetz und die deutschen Landesvertretungen* (Leipzig, 1895); and Julius Jacoby, *Die antisemitische Bewegung in Baden* (Karlsruhe, 1897).
76 See esp. Wolf, *Konservativismus*, 354–82.
77 *Brettener Sontagsblatt*, n.d. [Jan. 1892], cited ibid., 363.
78 Carl von Eisendecher's reports of 5 Jan. and 2 March 1893, in *Das Großherzogtum Baden in der politischen Berichterstattung der preußischen Gesandten 1871–1918*, ed. Hans-Jürgen Kremer, 2 pts. (Stuttgart, 1990), pt. 1, 533–6.
79 See the election materials in GLA Karlsruhe, NL Stockhorner, Fasc. 135,

including the transparent attempt to fuse the Conservative and antisemitic messages: *Deutsche Stimme aus dem Volke und für das Volk. Organ der vereinigten deutsch-nationalen und christlich-konservativen Reichspartei* (Freiburg), 2. Probe-Nr., 31 May 1893.
80 David Peal, 'Antisemitism by Other Means? The Rural Cooperative Movement in Late Nineteenth-Century Germany,' *LBI YB* 32 (1987): 135–53.
81 See Carl Paul Mehnert [senior], 'Der landwirthschaftliche Creditverein im Königreich Sachsen,' *Jahrbücher für Volks- und Landwirthschaft* 9 (1868): 51–72; Mehnert, *Wesen und Bedeutung der Hypothek und deren Mobilisirung* (Dippoldiswalde, n.d. [1879]), which draws upon Wilmanns's work, *Die Creditnoth der Grundbesitzer* (Berlin, 1868); and Mehnert, *Wider das Actienwesen* (Dresden, 1877), which draws upon and praises the work of Perrot. By 1905 the Saxon Agricultural Credit Association had 15,393 members.
82 See Harris, 'Franz Perrot.'
83 *Reichsgesetzblatt* cited in Peal, 'Antisemitism,' 138; see also Helmut Walser Smith, 'The Discourse of Usury: Relations between Christians and Jews in the German Countryside, 1880–1914,' *Central European History* 32 (1999): 255–76.
84 Otto Böckel, *Die Güterschlächterei in Hessen* (Leipzig, 1886), cited in Peal, 'Antisemitism,' 140; for the following, ibid, 141–3. See also Germanicus [pseud. for Emil Richter], *Juden und Junker* (Leipzig, n.d.).
85 *Neue Reichszeitung*, no. 6 (10 Jan. 1877), 1.
86 George Strachey, Dresden, to FO, no. 24 (draft), 19 Mar. 1884, in PRO Kew, FO 215, No. 37.
87 Franz Perrot, *Die deutschen Eisenbahnen* (Rostock, 1870), and Perrot, 'Deutsche Eisenbahnpolitik' (1872), cited in Harris, 'Franz Perrot,' 81.
88 *Die socialen Fragen. Beiblatt zum Conservativen Flugblatt für Sachsen* (Crimmitschau), no. 10 (31 Oct. 1878): 79–80; anon., 'Der Mammonsdienst,' ibid., 84–6.
89 'Zur Judenfrage,' *Badische Landpost* (Wochenausgabe), no. 24 (24 Feb. 1880).
90 Smith, 'Discourse'; see also Smith, 'Alltag'; Smith, 'Religion and Conflict: Protestants, Catholics, and Antisemitism in the State of Baden in the Era of Wilhelm II,' *Central European History* 27 (1994): 283–314; Smith, 'The Learned and the Popular Discourse of Antisemitism in the Catholic Milieu of the Kaiserreich,' *Central European History* 27 (1994): 315–28.
91 Heinrich Dietz, *Wer hilft dem Bauernstande?* (Stuttgart, 1893); Emil Richter, *Das Creditsystem der modernen Mißwirthschaft* (Heilbronn, 1884).
92 Göler to Otto v. Stockhorner, 18 Feb. 1884, in GLA Karlsruhe, NL Stockhorner, Fasc. Pfälzer Bauernverein.

93 Herr Bühler to Otto von Stockhorner, 3 March 1893, ibid., 35–9. The preceding letter from Otto von Stockhorner to Bühler, 24 Feb. 1893, is cited in Kremer, 'Konservative Partei,' 35–6.
94 See Karl Mühlhäußer, *Christentum und Presse* (Frankfurt a.M., 1876); Mühlhäußer, *Unsere Presse*, 3rd ed. (Frankfurt a.M., 1874); Theodor Fritsch, *Der jüdische Zeitungs-Polyp*, 2nd ed. (Leipzig, 1922).
95 Kremer, 'Konservative Partei,' 50, describes young aspirants in the Baden Conservative State Association in 1900 as 'now Christian Social, now German Social, now Social Reformer etc. etc.'
96 See Egon Waldegg, *Die Judenfrage gegenüber dem deutschen Handel und Gewerbe*, 2nd ed. (Dresden, 1879); Max Liebermann von Sonnenberg, *Neue Zeiten – Neue Parteien* (Leipzig, 1885).
97 The terms *Wacht, Reform, Manifest,* and *Volk* recur frequently in Conservative propaganda. In the *Sächsischer Volksfreund*, no. 82 (12 Oct. 1881): 514–15, Frege declared that the Saxon Conservative Party legitimately called itself a *Reformpartei*.
98 The following is based on Otto Richter, *Geschichte der Stadt Dresden in den Jahren 1871 bis 1902*, 2nd ed. (Dresden, 1904), chap. 7; *Die Stadtverordneten zu Dresden 1837–1887* (Dresden, 1887); and other materials in the StadtA Dresden.
99 *Prozeß des Kaufmann Carl Weigandt ... und des Geh. Hofrath Rechtsanwalt Ackermann ... gegen Redakteur Oswald Zimmermann und Baumeister Gustav Emil Leberecht Hartwig ... in Dresden* (Dresden, 1888).
100 See K. Häberlin, *Das sogenannte Hausbesitzerprivileg in den Städten Sachsens* (Leipzig, 1913); also the Homeowners Association's *Dresdner Bürgerzeitung* (1901ff.).
101 See Emil Lehmann, *Gesammelte Schriften* (Berlin, 1899).
102 Malcolm B. Brown, *Friedrich Nietzsche und sein Verleger Ernst Schmeitzner* (Frankfurt a.M., 1987).
103 *Manifest an die Regierungen und Völker der durch das Judenthum gefährdeten christlichen Staaten* (Chemnitz, 1882); see also Schmeitzner's *Internationale Monatsschrift* (Chemnitz, 1882–3) and correspondence in BA Koblenz, NL Fechenbach, Nr. 105.
104 George Strachey, Dresden, to FO, no. 8, 7 Feb. 1890, in PRO Kew, FO 68, no. 175.
105 See the documentation of Fritsch's activities in SächsStA Leipzig, Polizeipräsidiums-Vereinsakten Nr. 2859.
106 For example, StadtA Dresden, Bestand 231.01, Vereine und Vereinigungen, Alldeutscher Verband, Ortsgruppe Dresden und Oberelbgau.

107 George Strachey, Dresden, to FO, no. 51, 14 Nov. 1890, in PRO Kew, FO 68, no. 175.
108 Including Ottomar Beta, Max Bewer, and Heinrich Pudor. See Uwe Puschner, Walter Schmitz, and Justus H. Ulbricht, eds., *Handbuch zur 'Völkischen Bewegung' 1871–1918* (Munich, 1996); also Piefel, *Antisemitismus*, esp. 86–90.

9 Conservatives *contra* Chancellor

The development of the Conservative Party has a great and long-lasting significance for the fate of the empire and for the monarchy. The form of all party relationships is influenced by it. – Whether the middle parties gravitate to the left or strengthen a starkly monarchist Right ... will perhaps be decided by the development of the Conservative situation at this moment ... For my part I am only an instrument, and desire to be nothing more, for the rallying of the reasonable conservative elements – to separate these from mindless demagoguery ... An unambiguous statement of position by the Kaiser ... will show the government a firm course and bring the Conservative Party back to order again.

Otto von Helldorff-Bedra to Count Philipp zu Eulenburg-Hertefeld, 23 May 1892[1]

One of two equations that determined the Right's intermediate position in German political society was the relationship between the Conservative Party and the Kaiser's government. Hans-Jürgen Puhle long ago pointed to the estrangement between the agrarian-Conservative community and the government that followed the founding of the Agrarian League in 1893. Yet he did not define the actual nature of this estrangement more precisely than to say that it was 'quasi-oppositional' and that the agrarians and Conservatives 'hovered' between the extremes of governmentalism and opposition.[2] A 1983 Festschrift devoted to German conservatism gave Puhle's thesis a twist. Now the Conservatives 'oscillated between the extremes of a status-bound old-conservative club of notables and a "populist" mass movement of the Right.'[3] Yet more than twenty years further on, writers of general histories of Germany seem unwilling to accept the idea that a serious rift opened between Conservatives and the imperial German state.[4] We still find broad statements about 'those agrarian elites which commanded the Prusso-German political system' or references to the 'hegemony of Conservatives in executive position and the persistent deference to their parliamentary representatives.' A recent textbook follows this pattern: 'Conservatives were not under threat from the establishment because they were the establishment. Aristocratic landowners continued to dominate.'[5] Which interpretation, then, makes more sense: estrangement, oscillation, or hegemony?

The second equation that determined the Conservative Party's middle position was the relationship between the party's leaders and forces below them. Leaving aside for the moment radical nationalists, few of whom displayed much faith in party politics, one can identify three groups of rank-and-file popularizers who sought to broaden the popular base of the German Right. The first was the so-called *Kreuzzeitung* group. The second was the Agrarian League. The third was the collection of dissidents within the party who attempted to rally support for the government's finance reform bill in 1909 and soon thereafter sought to mobilize right-wing groups in Germany's largest cities.

Because the government was continually trying to exploit disunity within Conservative ranks, this chapter analyses the battles waged between popular mobilizers and their critics within the Conservative Party. But it also moves beyond the confines of party to consider how these battles rippled through German political culture more generally. Such ripples disturbed the complacency of Germans who assumed that the Conservative Party would always be able to steer between the charge of governmentalism and the spectre of outright opposition. With this analysis, it becomes possible to embed party politics in larger political and institutional contexts and thus to account for other instabilities in Wilhelmine Germany's political system.[6]

In contrast to the previous chapter, our focus here falls on members of the Kaiser's executive and entourage. Did Germany's chancellors and Wilhelm's unofficial advisers ever seriously contemplate a full break from the Conservative Party? Or did they immediately submit when the Conservatives threatened to withdraw their support from the government? Did *they* regard the Conservative Party as a stabilizing factor in imperial politics, successfully 'hovering' between the monarchy and the masses, between governmentalism and opposition? Or did they conclude that the party 'oscillated' between two extreme courses?

The list of German chancellors who wanted to work with 'enlightened,' 'healthy,' or 'reasonable' elements of the Right extends unbroken from Otto von Bismarck, who sought a middle-party grouping in the 1880s, to Theobald von Bethmann Hollweg, who practised the 'politics of the diagonal' after 1909. To link these two political epochs, this chapter focuses on three occasions when the government's strategy to deal with Conservative opposition was especially revealing: at the time of the Conservative Party's Tivoli congress in December 1892, during the dispute over the Mittelland Canal in 1899, and in the finance reform crisis of 1909.

In arguing, first, that the Conservatives under Kaiser Wilhelm II acted as a kind of 'disloyal opposition' and, second, that this paradoxical orientation profoundly disturbed German statesmen and right-wing leaders alike, we are well advised to reproduce the language of contemporaries as faithfully as possible. Adjectives like 'democratic' and 'demagogic' were used on all sides to vilify opponents' tactics, while government figures often had to reach for extended metaphors to express their outrage at the Conservative Party. Sometimes this language helped contemporaries recognize the larger implications of a possible break between the Right and the state; but at other times it provided welcome cover for ambivalence and indecision. Thus close attention to language offers new insights into the complexity and contingency of party-state relations during the two decades that spanned 1900.

Otto von Helldorff and the Politics of Notables

The German Conservative Party, founded in July 1876, was led by a man whose character, political style, and accomplishments epitomized the politics of notables (*Honoratiorenpolitik*). This individual has never been the subject of a full-scale biography. He does not deserve one. However, even a sketch of his career illustrates his central role in determining real and potential turning points in the political modernization of the German Right.

Otto Heinrich von Helldorff-Bedra was born into an old noble family on 16 April 1833 in Schloss Bedra, in the county of Querfurt in the Prussian province of Saxony.[7] After completing legal and economic studies at four universities, he then served at the county court and with the district administration in Merseburg. After taking part in Prussia's military campaign in 1866, when he was wounded seriously, Helldorff followed in the footsteps of his father. He became a county councillor, or *Landrat*, serving in Wetzlar from 1867 to 1874. He retired from the Prussian administration in the latter year and devoted himself to the management of his estate, Bedra, and three other estates (Leihe, Schalkendorf, and Petzkendorf).

Helldorff's parliamentary activity was restricted to the Reichstag. Even to that august body he twice failed to win election. Hence he represented three different constituencies over the course of his career as a parliamentary deputy. From May 1879 until April 1892 Helldorff chaired the Conservative Party's Reichstag caucus, with the significant interruption of 1881–4. He also led the formal party organization, the Electoral Association of German Conservatives, after its inception in 1876. In May 1890 he was appointed for life to the upper house of the Prussian *Landtag*.

Helldorff first met Otto von Bismarck in 1867, but a personal relationship did not develop between the two men until Helldorff entered the Reichstag and began to gather a following of 'New Conservatives' in the early 1870s. Like Helldorff, these New Conservatives rejected the sterile opposition that had characterized Ludwig von Gerlach's pro-Austrian position in 1866. They also opposed Hans von Kleist-Retzow's position on the Prussian reform of local government of 1872 and Philipp von Nathusius-Ludom's position on religious and social policy later in the 1870s.[8] It was symptomatic that Helldorff played a part in removing Nathusius-Ludom as chief editor of the Conservatives' *Kreuzzeitung* in May 1876. This change was considered essential to marginalize the 'Old Conservatives' and to bring Conservatives back into the government camp (Nathusius-Ludom had agreed to the publication of Franz Perrot's 'Era' articles of 1875).[9] But Helldorff's personal victory over Nathusius-Ludom was symptomatic in another way, for it was neither complete nor permanent. Even in 1876 Kleist-Retzow warned Helldorff that the Conservative Party could not support Bismarck on all questions of the day. Instead of swimming with the tide of the chancellor's changing policies, Kleist-Retzow wrote, the party had to be a 'thorn in the side' of the government.[10] Nor could Helldorff prevent the appointment of Baron Wilhelm von Hammerstein-Schwartow as chief editor of the *Kreuzzeitung* in November 1881.[11]

The founding of the Conservative Party in 1876 can be ascribed mainly to Helldorff's efforts. It was actually his relationship to Bismarck that was decisive.[12] Helldorff understood that Bismarck's impending break with the National Liberals and the chancellor's wish for renewed cooperation with the Conservatives would put emphasis on 'material questions.' Such questions were beginning to take precedence over questions of principle – questions, that is, to which Old Conservatives and Young Turks within the party still wished to give priority. Throughout the 1880s Helldorff regarded the protective tariffs passed in 1879 to be a bedrock of the Conservative alliance with heavy industrial circles and their representatives in the National Liberal and Free Conservative parties. He was thus the staunchest supporter of Bismarck's parliamentary *Kartell* comprising these three parties.

Helldorff was convinced that only a Bismarckian party *sans phrase* could hope to win back a pivotal role in the Reichstag. Hence he discussed the draft Conservative program 'point by point' with Bismarck in 1875–6.[13] There is something of a chicken-and-egg character to Helldorff's assessment of his political options at this juncture. He knew that Bismarck was interested in supporting only a party that commanded enough Reichstag seats to have a critical effect on the passage of legislation. Yet as long as state officials aided only candidates who were 'friendly to the government' at election time, a closer relationship with Bismarck was the precondition to improving Conservative fortunes at the polls.

Many details of Helldorff's early leadership of the party remain obscure. He met with Bismarck frequently on the latter's estates in Varzin and Friedrichsruh to discuss parliamentary strategy. And he attended innumerable parliamentary dinners, often as the only Conservative representative. Neither Bismarck nor Helldorff left behind more than a few veiled remarks about how their relationship developed. It is nevertheless clear that the politics of notables left them considerable room to manoeuvre politically.[14] Bismarck once wrote that the lack of industriousness among members of the Conservative Reichstag caucus greatly eased Helldorff's task as leader. He added, though, that even a Conservative caucus leader had to be sensitive to the charge of being excessively pro-government or 'ministerial.'[15]

What remains of Helldorff's correspondence with Bismarck documents the many advantages the Conservative leader derived from this relationship. His activity during the 1881 Reichstag election campaign is illustrative.[16] Helldorff discussed Conservative propaganda *en détail* with Bismarck and his aides, sometimes changing only the odd word in the chancellor's drafts when preparing Conservative flyers. His fawning stance towards the chancellor was particularly marked when he emphasized the need to identify the Conservative program completely with Bismarck's policies. As he wrote at one point to Bismarck's son-in-law, Count Kuno zu Rantzau: 'With the other leaflets it is above all a matter of presenting the decisive policies and speeches of the chancellor. – The rest of the text is inconsequential ... In any case the authority and popularity of your father-in-law is of the greatest significance – and therefore everything depends precisely on bringing his own words to the masses.'[17] Helldorff did not estimate the intellectual capacity of those masses highly. He believed that Conservative election themes and pamphlets had to be concise and simple if they were to be comprehended by ordinary voters: 'one full sheet of reading material frightens them off.'[18]

When Helldorff drew up a more comprehensive report for Bismarck later in the 1881 campaign, he hoped to illustrate that the Conservative leadership was not inactive, as Bismarck apparently might have thought.[19] Helldorff's pre-eminent position in the party was reflected in all facets of the campaign, from candidate selection to the collection of financial resources, from the publishing of a weekly news-sheet (*Der Patriot*) to editing of last-minute manifestos. Even allowing for some self-substantiation, Helldorff named only one other parliamentarian and the party's secretary as among the Conservative leaders assisting in the campaign. But even that parliamentarian's job supervising the party press was about to be passed on to Helldorff. As a result, the 30,000 marks the party received from the Reich chancellery for *Der Patriot* and other Conservative propaganda – and virtually all questions of policy too – would go (as Helldorff put it) 'through my hands.'

Helldorff never expected that he could conduct Conservative affairs as a one-man operation. He claimed to suffer no illusions about the party's popularity in the provinces or the strength of its press compared to 'the cleverness of the Jewish press barons.' He also complained that he was fighting an uphill battle against the party's rank-and-file members, who, he claimed, were 'unbelievably lazy, indolent, and stingy.' In fact Helldorff often conceded that the party's principal electoral activities remained firmly under the control of local party supporters. The work of these Conservative clubs, he wrote, could never be replaced by any amount of direction from Berlin headquarters.

In 1882 Helldorff tried to establish a firmer organizational plan for the party, and through the 1880s he attempted to expand the party press.[20] On both counts his actual achievement stood in obvious contrast to his (alleged) interest in breaking with the habits of *Honoratiorenpolitik*. By the end of the 1880s his leadership was seen by many party colleagues as oriented exclusively towards backstairs influence-peddling in the Reichstag, to the utter neglect of party activity at the grass-roots level. This perception is ironic in one sense, because Hammerstein's Conservative 'Ultras' in the Prussian House of Deputies had to pay far less attention to the urgencies of political mobilization than did Helldorff in the Reichstag. It was Helldorff, not Hammerstein, who had to try to adapt Conservative practice to the novel proposition of universal male suffrage.

The idiosyncratic mix of desperation and half-heartedness with which Helldorff undertook the task of pulling the Conservative Party into the era of 'mass' politics was evident in a Reichstag speech he delivered during debate on Bismarck's anti-socialist laws in 1878: 'Gentlemen: ... if anything is likely to corrupt the mood in the country and to undermine authority, it is the all-too-frequent use of the universal suffrage. You, gentlemen, you have just emerged fresh from an election campaign. I ask you on all sides of the House: have you actually enjoyed these electoral goings-on [*Wahltreiben*]? I must say, gentlemen, this game, where everyone is more or less obliged to reckon with the prejudices of the masses and to speculate with their passions – this is a highly dangerous business, and we have the most urgent cause to determine whether a means can be found to combat it.'[21]

Through the course of the 1880s, a counter-movement within the Conservative Party grew more vocal in its opposition to Helldorff's style of leadership. Comprising both the *Kreuzzeitung* group around Hammerstein and the Christian Social Party led by Court Preacher Adolf Stöcker, this internal opposition movement sought to overcome the liabilities of Helldorff's elitist approach. Its campaign was three-pronged.

First, it sought a means for those party members outside Helldorff's inner circle to exert more influence on policy formation. In general, this effort yielded meagre results before 1892. Nevertheless, the attempt to foster greater internal party democracy must be understood as part of a broader campaign to make the Conservative Party a 'people's party' (*Volkspartei*). Dissidents demanded in early 1889 that a new steering committee be established to coordinate the party's activity. Of this new body's proposed nine members, Helldorff wanted five – a majority – to be selected from the Reichstag caucus he chaired. But Hammerstein and others pushed through a plan to constitute a Committee of Eleven instead, with four members chosen from the Reichstag, three each from the upper and lower houses of the Prussian *Landtag*, and one from the Kingdom of Saxony. The less-governmental representatives in the Prussian *Landtag* thereby denied Helldorff a dominating influence in policy formation.

This change also illustrated the increased vitality and independence of activists at the party's grass roots and their dissatisfaction with the stagnation of Conservative activity. As one of Helldorff's critics wrote retrospectively of the period before 1892: 'A Conservative Party, in the sense of a firm organization that extended to all corners of the land and encompassed associations and secretaries, simply did not exist. Instead there was a Conservative administrative apparatus and loose committees of Conservative notables, comprised almost exclusively of aristocrats. The current governmental wind determined the course and the strength of the party. In essence the party was not conservative at all; rather, it was governmental.'[22]

Second, the *Kreuzzeitung* group – increasingly called the *Kreuzzeitungspartei* – attempted to attract new social groups to the Conservative Party. As noted in the previous chapter, Hammerstein's antisemitic lead articles in the *Kreuzzeitung* and the propaganda of the Christian Social Party set the tone for countless smaller Conservative news-sheets in the provinces. These organs and the party activists they served tried to de-emphasize the agrarian interests advocated by Helldorff and other landed estate owners. They also tried to redirect the Conservative message towards Protestant workers and the lower middle classes (*Mittelstand*). As a result, starkly anti-liberal, anti-capitalist, and anti-semitic positions were more strongly represented in the *Kreuzzeitung* press than in the official party news-sheet, the *Conservative Correspondenz*, or in the other two Conservative organs under Helldorff's influence: the *Deutsches Tageblatt* and the *Konservatives Wochenblatt*. According to Heinrich Engel – one of Helldorff's strongest critics within the party and chief editor of the Conservatives' 'pastoral news-sheet,' *Der Reichsbote* – new directions in policy and new techniques in agitation had to be implemented hand in hand; both were essential if the party was to be true to its Christian-conservative traditions and yet win 'new blood.'[23]

Third, Helldorff's opponents within the party were determined to see the Protestant church become a more decisive factor in political affairs. In their view, the traditional Christian basis of German Conservatism had been undermined by Helldorff's willing adherence to Bismarck's *Realpolitik*. For them the concept of a reinvigorated 'people's church' (*Volkskirchentum*) was the corollary to a Conservative 'people's party.' Paradoxically, this view induced the *Kreuzzeitung* group to advocate an alliance with the Catholic Centre Party. It hoped thereby to overcome the limitations imposed by Helldorff's adherence to Bismarck's parliamentary *Kartell* (and particularly its anti-Catholic liberal elements). This advocacy of Christian Conservatism injected a significant degree of instability into party alignments after 1881, and it worried Bismarck deeply.

The *Kreuzzeitung* group failed to realign Conservative religious policy in any fundamental way. In this sense, Helldorff's pragmatic strategy remained ascendant. In early 1892, however – to look ahead for a moment – this conflict over religion re-emerged. When the government's School Bill, supported by the Centre Party and by the *Kreuzzeitung* group, failed to find sympathy among the National Liberals, Helldorff counselled Wilhelm II to retract the bill. The Kaiser concurred and the bill was withdrawn. However, it became apparent that Helldorff had fallen between two stools. The National Liberals showed no gratitude for his intervention, whereas his many critics in the Conservative Party now escalated their own criticism of him. They concluded that Helldorff would *never* abandon the government under any circumstances.

By this point, in 1892, the differences in outlook between Helldorff and his opponents could hardly have been more clear. Whereas the party leader continued to subordinate Conservative principles to Bismarck's right-wing coalition of parties, the *Kreuzzeitung* group was steering closer to untested political waters. And whereas the politics of notables still favoured Helldorff's group of insiders, his critics had become convinced that they could realize their goal of creating a vibrant, broadly based Conservative people's party only by expelling Helldorff from the party leadership altogether. After the dismissal of Bismarck in March 1890, Helldorff's chief political strength became his greatest liability.

In explaining how these developments unfolded and led to his fall from grace, one must distinguish carefully between Helldorff's standing in government circles and his standing within the Conservative Party. On the one hand, tactical errors on his part had led to an estrangement between him and Bismarck. Helldorff's most famous error was his alleged failure to understand Bismarck's true intentions regarding renewal of the anti-socialist laws in the winter of 1889–90.[24] But even voters' repudiation of Bismarck's *Kartell* in the Reichstag elections of February 1890 and the chancellor's dismissal from office the next month did not immediately undermine Helldorff's position. Quite the contrary: the Kaiser and his top advisers were initially delighted by the unseemly haste with which Helldorff transferred his allegiance from Bismarck to his successor, Chancellor Leo von Caprivi.

On the other hand, the caesura of 1890 is important as a milestone in the steady growth of anti-Helldorff feeling within the party. Many years after his fall from power, Helldorff in 1905 wrote to the moderate conservative historian and publicist Hans Delbrück. He confided to Delbrück that his greatest mistake in political life was that he failed to destroy Hammerstein when he had the chance to do so in the period 1881–4.[25] Because Helldorff was temporarily absent from the Reichstag at that time and because he had also suffered a bad fall from a horse, he had had to relinquish temporary leadership of the Conservative Electoral Association to Hammerstein. In those years, Hammerstein used that position to expand his power base outside the Prussian House of Deputies to the party at large. Thus he had begun long before 1890 to scheme against Helldorff.

By 1891 the fall of Bismarck had already had a tangible effect on the power struggle within the Conservative Party.[26] In that year Helldorff supported Caprivi's reorganization of local government in Prussia. This reform threatened to reduce the patriarchal authority of Junker estate owners east of the Elbe River. Kleist-Retzow complained that Helldorff was acting like a one-man government committee, pushing through the reform against the wishes of the majority of Conservatives, and other party insiders agreed. Another contributing factor was Helldorff's willingness to support Caprivi's trade treaty with Austria-Hungary in December 1891. This outraged many (though by no means all) agrarians in the Conservative camp. Against this backdrop, Helldorff's unwavering loyalty to the wishes of the Kaiser during the School Bill crisis in early 1892 sealed his fate. Oddly enough, Helldorff was the last one to recognize how precarious his position had become. When Hammerstein declared publicly that Helldorff had finally lost touch with the mood of the party, Helldorff threw down the gauntlet to his rival. On 4 April 1892 he called for a 'clean break' between the warring factions within the party.

Helldorff's *annus horribilis*

The decisive battle for control of the Conservative Party did not last long. Helldorff quickly discovered that distaste for his haughty style of leadership now united his opponents. Those opponents included supporters of the School Bill, critics of the *Kartell*, local party activists,

9.1. Otto von Helldorff-Bedra and members of the Conservative Reichstag caucus, 1889. Standing, 2nd from left: Helldorff; standing, 4th from left: Dr Arnold Frege-Abtnaundorf; sitting, far right: Baron Heinrich von Friesen-Rötha. Photographed in the Reichstag foyer by Julius Braatz. Bundesarchiv Koblenz, Bild 116/121. Image courtesy of the Bundesarchiv Koblenz.

advocates of program reform, radical agrarians, and almost all antisemites within the party. Vitriolic resolutions against Helldorff flooded the Conservative press during April 1892. Members of the Conservative caucus in the Prussian House of Lords demanded that he withdraw from their ranks. On 28 April the Conservative caucus in the Prussian House of Deputies called on Helldorff to resign his position in the party's Committee of Three. A month later Baron Otto von Manteuffel-Crossen was selected as his successor on the Committee of Eleven.

It would be wrong to conclude that Helldorff's brand of governmental Conservatism was now dead. A counter-current of resentment arose in these months, fuelled by outrage over the brutality with which Helldorff had been dispatched by Hammerstein, Stöcker, and other *frondeurs*. Many influential Conservatives feared the implications of handing over control of the party to determined opponents of the Kaiser or to others who might ally themselves with explicitly anti-

Conservative antisemites such as Otto Böckel, Hermann Ahlwardt, and Theodor Fritsch. However, the sudden crest of antisemitic opinion in Germany during the summer of 1892 convinced many vacillating party members that the *Kreuzzeitung*'s radical tone and antisemitic message were now in tune with the times. In their view, that message merited a more sympathetic hearing.

Meanwhile, more local Conservative clubs were demanding that the party revise its official program in the direction of an openly antisemitic policy. Soon it became clear that, if Manteuffel really intended to break with Helldorff's legacy, he would have to demonstrate his goodwill by convening a general party congress – something Helldorff had never considered prudent. Throughout the second half of 1892, Helldorff did his utmost to convince Manteuffel not to take this dangerous step. He argued on more than one occasion that demagogues and 'rowdy' antisemites (*Radauantisemiten*) could not replace the practical party work of experienced parliamentarians (by which, of course, he meant men just like himself). Instead, Helldorff argued, the 'lack of discipline' among party activists would lead the party into 'chaos'; a large party congress could never offer the 'expert opinions' that derived from years of experience in parliamentary life.[27]

On 8 December 1892 the Conservatives finally held their long-awaited general party congress in the Berlin Tivoli brewery.[28] Contrary to the view of many historians, Tivoli was important as a milestone in the history of German Conservatism not *principally* because of the antisemitic program plank that was debated and passed there, but rather because it represented a broader rebellion against Helldorff's aloof style of politics.

Two features of the congress illustrated the historical significance of this new departure. First, the Tivoli congress was well attended and well publicized – a novelty in Conservative Party history. As Stöcker noted later: 'It was not a party congress in dress coat and white gloves, but in street clothes. It was the Conservative Party in the era of the universal, equal suffrage.'[29] This comment puts into its proper context one of the most famous statements made from the floor of the congress. Introducing himself as a 'man of the people,' Eduard Ulrich, a haberdasher from Chemnitz in Saxony, declared that the Conservative Party had to become 'a little more "demagogic."'[30] But the demagoguery Ulrich envisioned as the salvation of the Conservative Party had more to do with overcoming the politics of notables than with any hatred of the Jews: 'Gentlemen, it must be said today to our honourable leaders:

the Conservative Party wishes to be a people's party [*Volkspartei*]; it therefore does not want to see itself all the more insulted with talk of "demagoguery." It is common practice today among the leading circles of the Conservative Party that everything ... that moves the people is very easily dismissed with the stock phrase "demagogic." (Quite right!) I must ask our honourable deputies to become a little more "demagogic" – but not in the bad sense, rather in the good sense. (Bravo!) It is necessary that the leaders of our party become more accustomed to striking the tone of the people [*Volkston*].'

Second, during the Tivoli congress antisemitic agitators barely overcame Helldorff's efforts to censure, not endorse, a 'rabble-rousing' brand of antisemitism. In its program draft the party leaders close to Manteuffel had inserted a clause that stated: 'We condemn the excesses of antisemitism.' The party was deeply divided over this statement. Only the threat of disruptions (and possibly even violence) from the floor persuaded Manteuffel to allow debate of the clause. In the end it was shouted down as much as voted down. Yet even a spokesman for the *Kreuzzeitung* group declared that Conservatives had the moral responsibility to lead the antisemitic movement, as he put it, so that the excesses of antisemitism would cease and so that the 'fanatical spirits' (*Schwarmgeister*) among the antisemites would 'not gain the upper hand.'[31] Thus one of Tivoli's most striking features was the Conservative leadership's lack of commitment to 'rowdy' antisemitism and its desperate attempt to contain antisemitic demagoguery. As Manteuffel declared in his opening remarks at Tivoli and again on later occasions, the Jewish question simply could not be avoided unless the Conservatives wanted to leave the most burning issue of the day to the radicals.

This interpretation throws a different light on the fact that Helldorff, who did not attend the congress, failed to achieve any resonance with a resolution he and twenty other Reichstag deputies sent to Tivoli.[32] With this resolution Helldorff sought to designate the new program as merely a temporary statement of opinion on current issues of the day. His aim was to preserve the program of 1876, which he had been instrumental in formulating. As Helldorff wrote: 'Two programs – one for the summer and one for the winter – we simply cannot have.' But his appeal was rejected. Instead, the new program that was endorsed in December 1892 served the Conservative Party until 1918.

As it turned out, the Tivoli congress marked the high tide, not just the first wave, of *Kreuzzeitung* group victories within the Conservative Party. When independent antisemites won a number of Conservative

9.2. 'A German seven who do not love the Jews.' A contemporary postcard presents a rogues gallery of German antisemites; clockwise from top right: Theodor Fritsch, Paul Förster, Otto Böckel, Adolf König, Bernhard Förster, Max Liebermann von Sonnenberg, and, in the centre, Otto Glagau. Bundesarchiv Koblenz, Nachlaß 105 Karl von Fechenbach, Nr. 200. Image courtesy of Bundesarchiv Koblenz.

constituencies in the Reichstag elections of June 1893, many Conservatives came to the conclusion that Helldorff's warnings about rabble-rousing demagoguery were correct.[33] Yet Conservative activists continued to criticize the 'furtive opportunism' and 'that foolish idea of the *Kartell*' that had been the cornerstones of Helldorff's success before 1890. Hence Helldorff was never able to win back the position of influence he had enjoyed in the 1870s and 1880s. By early 1894 he realized that his chances for a political rebirth were virtually nil. As he wrote to Hans Delbrück around this time: 'For my part it is only a question of whether a personal intervention would be of any use ... The decisive thing is: would a word from me have any effect on the Conservative Party? and after deep reflection I have to answer, no! ... We are at the high point of excitement, of terrorism ..., [and] I have been so discredited by an unconscionable and untruthful press ... that I predict I would have a counter-productive effect.'[34]

In his later years Helldorff retired quietly to Schloss Bedra. He still sought to defend his actions with letters to friends and the occasional journal article.[35] Yet most of Helldorff's former allies willingly abandoned him to his fate. His narrow and unbending conception of Conservative politics was no longer in tune with an age in which 'the masses' were trump. Until his death on 10 March 1908, Helldorff remained bitter that his leadership had been usurped so unceremoniously in 1892. But just as deeply he regretted that the Conservative Party had chosen to 'fish for popularity' in ways he always steadfastly opposed.

The Kaiser's Entourage

In the past twenty years we have become familiar – some would say too familiar – with the Kaiser's entourage of advisers, ministers, courtiers, and hunting companions.[36] Studies have focused on Wilhelm II's friend Count Philipp zu Eulenburg-Hertefeld and his Liebenberg Circle. Most of these men cared little for party politics. However, Eulenburg corresponded with a number of state officials and other observers who offered counsel to Wilhelm on the problem of the Tivoli Conservatives. Besides Helldorff, these included Caprivi's state secretary for foreign affairs, Baron Adolf Marschall von Bieberstein (who had played a prominent role in the Baden Conservative Party before 1890); the later foreign secretary, Alfred von Kiderlen-Wächter; the councillor in the Foreign Office who was most critical of Wilhelm's attempt at personal rule, Friedrich von Holstein; the future chancellor, Bernhard von Bülow; and the Berlin correspondent of the National Liberals' *Kölnische Zeitung*, Dr Franz Fischer. These observers' allergic reaction to the growth of dissent and 'demagoguery' in the Conservative Party drew a direct parallel between internal party affairs and the larger problem of maintaining existing party alignments, domestic peace, and allegiance to the monarch.

The strongest expressions of indignation and bewilderment voiced by Eulenburg's correspondents came in the immediate wake of the Tivoli congress. But attempts had been undertaken long before December 1892 to support Helldorff and his cause within the Conservative Party. Eulenburg, for instance, was relieved when Helldorff resumed his leadership of the Conservatives' Reichstag caucus in December 1890 after victory in a by-election. He wrote to Holstein: 'Men like Helldorff are priceless now, and hopefully he will succeed with an assault on the ... thick-headedness of the Conservatives.'[37] By May 1891, though, Holstein wrote to Eulenburg with more than a hint of desperation: 'Helldorff is being pursued with the most extreme bitterness by the followers of Bismarck ... because of his relation to the Kaiser. The Kaiser, *if* he wants to have support, *must* advance his friends and push back his opponents.'[38]

After Helldorff had been relieved of his title as party chairman in April 1892, government hopes that moderate Conservatives might rally to the royalist side were transferred to the new minister president of Prussia, Botho Eulenburg. Bülow hoped that Philipp Eulenburg's cousin would be able to turn around the Conservatives, without whom, he wrote, 'Prussia cannot in the long run be governed, ... or at least not well.' As he observed: 'The Conservatives against the government – and, indeed, against the Crown – will ruin one another. Government and Conservatives ... must remain together and tolerate each other, like man and woman in marriage.'[39]

Official responses to Tivoli were predictably overwrought. Broadly speaking, Eulenburg and his main correspondents in this crisis identified five principal dangers lying along the political path the Conservative Party seemed to have chosen during the Tivoli congress. They condemned (1) the elimination of governmental moderates and older parliamentarians from positions of influence in the party leadership; (2) the benefit this brought to Bismarck and other *frondeurs*, together with the reciprocal loss of authority suffered by the Kaiser; (3) the future instability of the *Kartell* alliance among the three most dependable state-supporting parties and the effect this disruption would have on such 'national' legislation as the Army Bill of 1893; (4) the transformation of the Conservative Party into a group of radical antisemites; and (5) the advance of 'demagoguery' and the revolutionary potential of any radical appeal to mass sentiments.[40] These five dangers can be examined in turn.

First, the 'courageous' party men who spoke out against antisemitism at the congress, and who were also welcome at the Kaiser's court, received universal praise from Holstein and the Eulenburgs. Holstein complained that some of Eulenburg's East Prussian relatives 'were ridiculed and laid into as "twaddlers"' by rabble-rousers at Tivoli. The consensus, as expressed by Helldorff himself, was that the Conservative Party leadership had capitulated either to 'the mob' or to undisciplined local party associations on 8 December. Holstein agreed: 'The Conservative parliamentarians have the feeling that they have surrendered the leadership to "the clubs." Many to whom I spoke are hanging their heads.'

Second, Wilhelm's advisers also saw Tivoli benefiting Bismarck because in December 1892 rumours of a new Bismarckian National Party were filling the pages of the political press.[41] Alfred von Kiderlen-Wächter referred to the intrigues of the National Party when he observed to Philipp Eulenburg: 'And people call themselves conservative ... who wish to found a party of "dissatisfied ones" and talk of an "absolutist" regime. Muttonheads –.'

Third, only three days after the Tivoli congress, Helldorff warned Philipp Eulenburg about the wisdom of introducing an Army Bill to the Reichstag 'at the high point of the movement that has established Bismarck's oppositional position.' Nor was Kiderlen alone in believing that 'the most dangerous – the only dangerous – opposition is that which will be made by Varzin [Bismarck's estate], Altona [home of Chief of the Prussian General Staff Alfred von Waldersee], and Hammerstein in the *Kreuzzeitung*.'

Fourth, these observers were far more interested in combating the 'revolutionary' form of the antisemitic movement than they were in protecting the rights of the Jews. In fact, there is a clear parallel between the situation in 1892 and the reaction to antisemitism in the early 1880s, when Bismarck complained of the socialist – not the antisemitic – aspect of Stöcker's agitation in Berlin. To be sure, letters exchanged between Helldorff, Eulenburg, and Wilhelm II demonstrate that they sought to deal with the 'awkward question' of antisemitism with 'as little noise as possible.' But it was precisely these latent antisemitic convictions within the Wilhelmine establishment that led many moderates within the Conservative Party to go along with the *Kreuzzeitung* group. Otto Tippel, chief editor of the independent but (at that time) strongly conservative *Tägliche Rundschau*, wrote to Caprivi on 14 December 1892 to protest against the chancellor's Reichstag speech condemning the Tivoli Conservatives two days earlier.[42] Tippel claimed that in its effort to direct antisemitism into a monarchical path, the Conservative Party was acting both honourably and loyally. He added that if the party had become conscious earlier of its duty to take up the Jewish question, 'the antisemitic movement in its present dimensions would have been an impossibility.' Tippel felt that the Conservatives' recent passivity had only benefited the antisemitic – 'and also the democratic' – movements. He concluded: 'I believe that the charge of demagoguery, deeply offensive to wide circles of Conservatives, has been levelled unjustly.'

Eulenburg's correspondents disagreed vehemently with this assessment. Holstein was not untypical when he wrote despairingly to Eulenburg: 'The Reich chancellor had asked His Majesty to express to the Conservatives his disapproval of the demagogic tone of the party congress. Instead of this, His Majesty called over Manteuffel when they next met and said laughingly to him: "You and your friends should all be hanged!" Naturally, Manteuffel regarded that as no censure. His Majesty has not yet recognized the gravity of the situation.' Helldorff tried to convey an equally strong message to Eulenburg and, through him, to Wilhelm. 'We are faced with a frightful brutalization of public opinion,' he wrote; 'all true foundations of social order, the Crown, [and] the empire are in the greatest danger ... In the end, this movement is the certain seed of Social Democracy.' Franz Fischer of the *Kölnische Zeitung* concurred. He claimed that the Conservatives' unwillingness to censure antisemitic excesses at Tivoli signified 'the acceptance of demagoguery in Conservatism, the mixing of fire and water, out of which nothing good can come, either for the party or for the state.'

Fifth, Philipp Eulenburg often regarded it as his special task to pass along to the Kaiser opinions and warnings from others in diluted form. Yet he gave no sign of believing that these observers were indulging in hyperbole. True, he described the Conservatives in childish terms: 'They are sticking their tongues out at all of us – even Your Majesty!' Otherwise, though, Eulenburg was deadly serious. He was particularly worried by antisemitic agitation against large landowners and by the fact

9.3. Court Preacher Adolf Stöcker (1835–1909). Image (c. 1880) from Dietrich von Oertzen, *Adolf Stoecker. Lebensbild und Zeitgeschichte*, 2 vols. (Berlin: Vaterländische Verlags- und Kunstanstalt, 1910), 1: facing 144. From the author's collection.

that Conservatives seemed to be blind to the danger. 'The Social Democrats,' he wrote, 'are making way for the antisemites, because they are clever enough to recognize in them the pioneers of their own interests.' The authoritarian ideal, Eulenburg felt, was being undermined in rural areas by the antisemites in a 'singing match' with the Social Democrats. If Wilhelm failed to make a decisive move, Eulenburg concluded, 'the monarchical principle would be shaken to its foundations.' The Kaiser would become a *'roi des gueux.'*

It is not necessary here to recapitulate the events of 1893–6 that led governmental Conservatives and members of the Kaiser's circle to transfer their antagonism against the antisemites onto the Christian Social faction within the Conservative Party. Nonetheless, a line of continuity can be drawn between government reactions to Tivoli in December 1892, the Kaiser's anti-socialist campaign for 'Religion, Morality, and Order' in the autumn of 1894, and the Conservative leadership's decision to drive Stöcker from the party in February 1896. Wilhelm was forgetting his own early enthusiasm for Christian Socialism when he declared in 1896 that 'Stöcker has ended just as I predicted years ago.' Yet from the moment that radical Conservatism appeared as a major factor in German politics, Wilhelm's policy was a consistent one – at least by his standards.

In May 1892, immediately after the *Kreuzzeitung* group had overthrown Helldorff, Philipp Eulenburg reported a conversation he had had with the Kaiser.[43] Wilhelm and Eulenburg agreed that it was a disgrace 'that men who claim to belong to a party loyal to the king do not meet the wishes of their monarch.' The Kaiser, Eulenburg reported, 'only seeks to strengthen the party on an up-to-date basis, through the invigoration of the moderate elements.' He then quoted Wilhelm's typically indignant response to Conservatives who claimed that they had been left in the dark about whether he preferred the 'middle parties.' Wilhelm had declared: 'This is the sense in which I have *always* spoken to ... the Conservatives, and made the greatest effort in doing so. Each individual Conservative *knows* that, and it is *malevolence* if one claims otherwise. In any case I look gloomily into the future of the party. The subjugation of the moderate elements under the yoke of the extreme wing will destroy the whole party. It has *itself* to blame. It is a mystery to me how reasonable, orderly people can stand under the influence of a Hammerstein press. They are rushing to their ruin with their eyes open.'

The Agrarian League

Older accounts suggest that the Agrarian League was founded in February 1893 primarily to mobilize the agrarian sector – that is, to awaken peasants and farmers from their political torpidity and thereby defeat Chancellor Caprivi's plan to reduce tariffs on foreign grains entering Germany.[44] Newer interpretations offer a contrasting picture. Here, large estate owners of eastern Germany were attempting to deflect spontaneous agrarian revolts – revolts that challenged *their* ascendancy in the countryside as much as they threatened to defeat Caprivi's tariff legislation. In this account, agrarians were not in a position to conjure up rural unrest by a conscious act of will. Instead they were engaged in a desperate rearguard action to gain control over discontents they barely understood. The question remains, however, whether this 'moment of fission' produced a demonstrably new political orientation on the Right.

Let us begin by asking whether the Conservative Party and the Agrarian League drew the same conclusions from the outcome of battles over Caprivi's trade treaties. Here we find that these two organizations diverged fundamentally in their assessments of relations between the Right as a whole and the Kaiser's government. The notion of a 'loyal conservative opposition' to the Crown had been problematic in German history since 1848, perhaps even since 1807. In the crisis of 1890–4, however, it suffered a blow from which it never recovered. This was apparent to most perceptive observers in the mid-1890s. More vexing was the question of what would replace it.

To exploit disagreements between Agrarian League agitators and governmental Conservative parliamentarians, Chancellor Caprivi had a number of weapons at his disposal. One was to cultivate connections to such Conservative leaders as Count Udo zu Stolberg-Wernigerode, who as provincial governor of East Prussia reported on and encouraged Conservative dissent from the Agrarian League in his province. The government, Stolberg declared once, had never previously 'struck sail before such an opposition, which is based not upon real foundations but rather upon the egoism of the leaders and the stupidity of the followers.' He also described a 'scarcely believable agitation' by the Agrarian League designed to ensure that pro-treaty sentiment would be silenced.[45]

In the Russian trade treaty crisis of 1893–4, Caprivi did not have to rely on Stolberg alone. Against the most outspoken agrarians, the chancellor considered or actually launched proceedings on the charge of *lèse-majesté*.[46] To strike at Prussian officials who agitated on behalf of the Agrarian League, he also pressed Botho Eulenburg to issue a decree in late December 1893, 'recalling' Bismarck's own decree of 1882 that forbade Prussian officials from acting contrary to the wishes of the Crown.[47]

By exploiting the symbol of the monarchy to his own advantage, Caprivi was clearly acting in line with the beliefs of the Kaiser and his advisers: Conservatives had to be reminded of their obligation to support the king and his ministers. At a parliamentary dinner, Wilhelm declared that he had no wish to go to war with Russia simply because of 'a hundred stupid Junkers.' This declaration gave one East Prussian Conservative deputy, who was also personally close to Wilhelm, an excuse to convene a local assembly of his voters. That assembly released him from his Agrarian League pledge, and he subsequently broke caucus discipline to vote for Caprivi's treaty. When Wilhelm learned this, he immediately sent the deputy a congratulatory telegram: 'Bravo! Well done like a nobleman!'[48] By contrast, when Caprivi finally won passage of the Russian trade treaty in March 1894, the official Agrarian League news-sheet claimed that the German farmer was 'now inclined ... to see the Kaiser as his political enemy.'[49]

At this point in 1894 some Conservatives agreed with the radical agrarians that their first priority was to take revenge for the reduction of tariffs and topple Caprivi. This they achieved, though certainly not by themselves, in October 1894. In the months and years ahead, however, moderate Conservatives disavowed agrarian radicalism with increasing frequency. This dissent was led in part by the *Reichsbote*'s Heinrich Engel, still the doyen of Conservative editors.[50] Engel voiced the sentiments of Conservatives who feared a break with the government when he wrote that dissatisfaction among farmers and artisans had to be channelled back within proper limits. He claimed that 'opposition in principle' and the 'tactic of arousing and exploiting dissatisfaction and mistrust among the masses' were dangerous new features of agrarian radicalism that did the work of democrats, antisemites, and socialists.[51] By late 1894 many other Conservatives thought agrarian ambitions threatened the party itself.

This concern persisted. On the eve of a joint Conservative Party–Agrarian League congress in late 1896, the *Kreuzzeitung* highlighted the two groups' divergent political aims:[52] 'The direction of the league is a purely agrarian one ... Only the Conservatives follow other goals in their program.' In reply, a contributor to the Agrarian League's largest newspaper, the *Deutsche Tageszeitung*, gave vent to the league's frustration with timid Conservative notables in parliament. He wrote that 'when the individual wants to do something in the Reichstag, the caucus enters, fearful that it could lose control over this individual, that he could embarrass it or disturb it too much from its inactivity.' The threat was unambiguous: if necessary, the Agrarian League would employ radical extra-parliamentary agitation to outflank governmental Conservatives.

These observations illustrate that tension between Conservatives and radical agrarians was generated in part by Conservative notables' continuing access to the government and the Kaiser's court and in part by the relative isolation of the Agrarian League's leaders. The moderates in the DKP felt that their first allegiance was to the Conservative Party, not its agrarian interest group. Unwilling to concede the principle of the imperative mandate – as with the East Prussian nobleman's defection on the Russian vote – members of this group wished to set limits to agrarian extremism. In their view, the party, *not* its auxiliary organization, was responsible for attracting the broadest possible range of electoral support. Only a political party, they felt, could win tactical advantages in parliament and thereby provide the fullest defence of the established order. This distinction helps to explain the persistent tension between Conservatives and radical agrarians through the Mittelland Canal crises of 1899–1905.

Plus royaliste que le roi

The Mittelland Canal Bill of 1899 was introduced into the Prussian House of Deputies, where the Conservative caucus was much stronger than in the Reichstag. The bill proposed the building of a ship canal from the Ruhr industrial area of western Germany to the Elbe River in the east.[53] The government argued that the canal would contribute to industrial expansion and national integration, whereas agrarians claimed that it would open the floodgates to foreign grain imports and enrich Ruhr industrialists.

During the plenary debates that preceded the *Landtag*'s final rejection of the first Canal Bill on 8 August 1899, the Conservatives and the agrarians sustained a united front. Yet the party's official *Conservative Correspondenz* was conspicuously eager to show that the majority of Conservatives had not fallen under the sway of the Agrarian League in voting against the bill. Heinrich Engel in the *Reichsbote* advised Conservatives to make a 'royal sacrifice' and submit to the will of their king. Other pro-canal sentiments were expressed by Conservative newspapers in the Rhineland, Baden, Berlin, and Silesia.[54] An Agrarian League news-sheet, by contrast, warned the Conservative Party that to be popular it must not 'degrade' itself as a 'tool of the government.'[55]

The Conservatives and the Agrarian League forced the government to withdraw a second Canal Bill in May 1901. By the winter of 1904–5, however, a much less comprehensive canal project, together with a disastrous showing in the Reichstag elections of June 1903, provided about one-third of the Conservative caucus with a reason to break with the league on this issue and vote for the canal. In June 1904 a writer in the *Conservative Correspondenz* had defended moderate, pro-canal Conservatives by claiming that the party was better attuned to the voice of the people than was the Agrarian League.[56] Individual Conservatives offered other rationales for their governmental stance. Hermann Lange, editor of the *Neue Westfälische Volkszeitung*, wrote to a radical opponent of the canal that the prospect of a 'liberal era' (namely, if the Conservatives were totally excluded from the Canal Bill majority) left the party's deputies with little option but to vote with the government.[57] The leader of the Conservatives' organization in Westphalia, Pastor Möller-Gütersloh, wrote: 'We cannot agitate against the canal with democratic means, as the league under [Diederich] Hahn and colleagues is doing.'[58]

Conservatives' willingness to compromise with the government infuriated Agrarian League leaders and activists. Baron Conrad von Wangenheim, a member of the league's three-man directorate, rose in the Prussian *Landtag* to denounce the government's 'system of whipping [the Canal Bill] through' parliament.[59] A prominent functionary of the league in Hessen, Franz von Bodelschwingh-Schwarzenhasel, felt the time had come for the agrarians to expose both the backstairs peddling of government favour and the Conservatives' receptivity to it. Otherwise, he claimed, the league's opponents would be able to say: 'See here, the agrarian demands are extreme; the agrarians cannot even manage to win enough ground with their arguments among the parties of the Right.'

Baron Wilhelm von der Reck, a former member of the Conservatives' Committee of Fifty and a confirmed agrarian supporter, also knew how relations were shaped between party and state. He wrote to Hermann Lange that defections to the government's side were 'a symptom that [Chancellor] Bülow has negotiated with us.' He continued: 'Have some sort of offers been made to Manteuffel? Otherwise, the genial wind currently blowing remains a mystery to us.' It was the Kaiser, Reck felt, who had manoeuvred himself into a 'frightful' dilemma: Wilhelm would have to either break his royal pledge (that he would have the canal built) or break the constitution by compelling parliamentary deputies to vote for the canal legislation against their free wishes. Reck observed that it was this dilemma that had sent the Conservative Party into disarray.

The league's Baron von Wangenheim identified the same dilemma but, in a private letter to his wife, presented it in more dramatic fashion: 'Success very doubtful, all the well-known people will likely defect in the end ... In my opinion, that will be the end of the Conservative Party; it only wants to fawn upward, but from there it is trodden underfoot and has meanwhile lost its footing among the people, and will be superseded by the wild antisemites and comrades. *Quos deus perdere vult, dementat pius!* [sic].'[60]

August 1899 may well have been the occasion on which the government most seriously considered abandoning the Conservative Party as a prop of the political status quo. That the more draconian steps against the Agrarian League and Conservatives were undercut from the beginning or abandoned altogether does not detract from the significance of the fact that such ideas were entertained seriously. Indeed, the inability of the Kaiser and his government to reconcile paradoxical views of the Right's place in Germany's authoritarian system becomes clearer when such 'non-events' are considered.

In the early summer of 1899, Chancellor Chlodwig zu Hohenlohe-Schillingsfürst wrote to Philipp Eulenburg: 'If the Canal Bill is defeated, we must have a [*Landtag*] dissolution, and the Prussian state will be moved onto rails further left. That does not frighten me; but it is always a step in the dark, and if it can be avoided, all the better.'[61] By 20 August Hohenlohe believed a dissolution was necessary to preserve the 'authority of the Crown and the government.'[62] The Conservative Party now regarded the issue as 'a question of power,' Hohenlohe told his ministers: 'The whole attitude of the Conservative Party, which has allowed itself to be led by the Agrarian League and by personally embittered leaders, is directed less against the canal than against His Majesty personally.' It was therefore necessary to coordinate a *Landtag* dissolution and the dismissal of government officials who sat in the Conservative caucus and were opposing the Kaiser's wishes.[63] Otherwise, Hohenlohe concluded, 'there exists the danger that the Agrarian League, including the Conservative Party, would force many officials

350 Tension and Détente

Der Handlanger.

9.4. *Deutschtum* endangered. This retrospective on a quarter-century of German achievement probably sprang from the imagination of the rabidly antisemitic publicist Max Bewer. It commemorates the wars Bismarck and Kaiser Wilhelm I waged together (four, including the one against the Prussian liberals), the major battles they won (three), and the assassination attempts they survived (two each). But in 1897, with Bismarck out of office though not forgotten, the German lion slumbers and the threats facing Germany are hydra-like: one set of heads depicts France, ethnic minorities, the court camarilla, German 'discord,' Social Democracy, and anarchy; another set represents the Jewish danger (the 'stock exchange,' 'Cohen'). The authoritarian imagination easily assimilated such associations. *Der Handlanger. Politischer Bilderbogen Nr. 23* (Dresden: Verlag der Druckerei Glöss, n.d.). Image courtesy of the Bildarchiv Preußischer Kulturbesitz, Berlin.

more and more into its following and gradually, in common with the antisemites, reach for means against the government as pernicious as those used by Social Democracy.'

One minister observed in the ensuing discussion that the agrarians 'seek domination and wish to topple the whole ministry.' Prussian Minister of Finance Johannes von Miquel suggested, on the other hand, that new elections were unwise. The reasoning Miquel used is revealing. He claimed that in an election campaign the government would have to offer the slogan 'Here the Crown, there the Agrarian League.' But if the elections should fall to the latter – 'which,' Miquel noted, 'is not entirely impossible' – the situation would become even more critical for the Kaiser.

At the opening of the Crown Council meeting with the Kaiser on 23 August 1899, Chancellor Hohenlohe dismissed Miquel's arguments and did his utmost to make Wilhelm move against the Conservatives. He declared that Conservative intransigence now had the character of a 'systematic opposition, ... indeed, a conspiracy.' He added that because a large number of Conservative deputies appeared dissatisfied with their leaders, a dissolution or the offer of compensations might prompt their rebellion. But despite the advice from the majority of his ministers, the Kaiser in the end feared to launch an election campaign against the Conservatives. Instead he merely adjourned the *Landtag* and had the offending Prussian officials dismissed from their posts. To make the party 'feel his rage,' Wilhelm thought that shutting out their leaders from his court would suffice.

Brief observations from three principals in this crisis illustrate the difficulties inherent in the government's attempt to separate the Conservatives from their agrarian allies. Philipp Eulenburg wrote to Bülow that the government's turn against the Agrarian League was both 'false' and 'dangerous.' To make his point, he cited a conversation he had had with an unnamed agrarian leader, who had told him that the Agrarian League had enrolled many new members 'from radical circles' immediately after the *Landtag* dissolution. This agrarian claimed that these new members clearly saw the league as 'a lever [*Hebel*] against the monarchy.' Eulenburg looked to the Conservative Party to reverse this trend: 'The only element that is capable of keeping in check the decidedly democratic tendency of the league is the Conservative estate owners.' Referring to the 'democratic and demagogic stream' inundating Germany, he concluded that a direct government campaign 'against the league in the form of a fight against the Conservatives makes a hydra out of it.'[64]

The second participant unwilling to proceed decisively was Kaiser Wilhelm himself. After two of his leading court figures resigned their posts in sympathy with the dismissed Conservative officials, Wilhelm complained to Bülow: 'The great men of my court are leaving me.'[65] Soon thereafter he agreed to reinstate a number of county councillors to their posts.

The third observer, Chancellor Hohenlohe, most clearly displayed the extreme ambivalence in government circles. Despite his earlier arguments, Hohenlohe could actually conceive of neither a full alliance nor a full break with the Conservatives. As he wrote to his son: 'To have a dissolution without detaching the officials from the Agrarian League would not have much use. Above all, the administration must be purged. Still, I regret we have not had a dissolution. I am sure the Conservatives would have suffered a healthy defeat. *But of course how would H[is] M[ajesty] work with a liberal ministry?*'[66]

When the Prussian state ministry, now under Bülow's command, began to consider reintroducing a Canal Bill in December 1900, a showdown with the Conservatives was feared as much as ever. By May the following year the government had been forced a second time to withdraw its legislation and adjourn the *Landtag*. The Kaiser, Eulenburg, and others again expressed their frustration with the Conservative Party in stark terms.[67] Eulenburg indulged in metaphors once again. The Conservatives were gnawing like dogs on a stick of dynamite and playing with fire like children: 'Nothing shows the progress of the democratic idea more than the history of this "loyal party."' However, Eulenburg also observed that Wilhelm 'overestimates as much as underestimates' the effects of his banishments from court. Eulenburg's counter-weapon against the Agrarian League was simply to intrigue more earnestly than ever. Because the future Conservative Party leader, Ernst von Heydebrand und der Lase, was 'a poisonous, ambitious viper,' Eulenburg suggested that 'he would likely accept a post if one were offered to him.' Wilhelm's scorn for the Conservative Party, however, remained unabated. He referred to it as the party 'that has outlived itself and no longer understands the modern age – that has ceased to be, for all time, capable of governing [*regierungsfähig*].'[68]

If the Kaiser was lucky enough to be able to maintain the posture of 'no surrender,' his ministers and provincial administrators did not have the same luxury. Through 1901 and 1902 the Prussian state ministry felt that the negotiations to win support for a new tariff bill were too delicate to risk 'upsetting' the Conservatives.[69] Nonetheless, by late 1904 Bülow's chancellery chief, the former Conservative *Landtag* deputy Friedrich Wilhelm von Loebell, was again trying 'under the table and secretly to sway individual [Conservative] members' to vote for the bill. And once again Stolberg was trying to prompt defections in East Prussia.[70] Thirty-nine Conservatives succumbed to government pressure in early February 1905, and the Canal Bill finally passed.[71]

The Conservative *Kreuzzeitung* had already explained away this defection. It claimed that Chancellor Bülow had succeeded where Hohenlohe had failed only because the government avoided many former mistakes and did not make the canal a 'political' issue.[72] In fact, however, the government *did* regard this as a major victory over the radical agrarians. This view is clear from an internal chancellery memorandum, possibly written by Loebell himself, that circulated just three weeks prior to the final canal vote.[73] This unsigned memo focused on the importance of dividing as many Conservatives as possible from the Agrarian League and winning their support for the canal. The author felt encouraged that 'the whole *Conservative* press ... has taken a stand against [agrarian] agitation.' He was also cognizant of the dangers that still lay ahead. In particular, the Conservative Party feared that public knowledge of its ties to the Kaiser would undermine its quest for popular appeal. The memo's author nonetheless concluded that the government stood to win a highly significant political victory over the demagogues in the Agrarian League if the Canal Bill passed: 'It would undoubtedly have a critical effect if it were to become known at the last minute that officials or bearers of court titles were influenced in their votes or threatened with proceedings if they should decide against the canal ... However, if a majority can be won for the Rhine-Hanover Canal, that is at the same time *a desirable strengthening of those Conservative circles who object to the demagogic intrigues of the Agrarian League*. The safe passage of the Canal Bill will therefore be at the same time an auspicious success *for the whole of domestic politics in Prussia*.'[74]

Toppling an Imperial Chancellor

In the period 1900-9, Chancellor Bülow's adeptness at sidestepping political confrontation led Conservatives to believe that the compromises he demanded of both the Left and the Right were actually being delivered up by the latter. These doubts eventually impelled the Conservative Party leadership to follow the Agrarian League on the finance reform issue of 1909. As the final crisis in the history of the Bülow Bloc (1907–9), this reform was opposed by agrarian estate owners who refused to sanction the introduction of a comprehensive inheritance tax.[75]

The strains of the Bülow Bloc brought out older tensions between moderate Conservatives and radical agrarians. In this environment of enmity, Heinrich Engel's warnings about an exclusively agrarian Conservative Party became relevant again. When Bülow defended his planned finance reform in a speech in late November 1907, he told the Conservatives that they must be 'moderate and broad-minded' like their counterparts in England. Engel agreed. But writing in the *Reichsbote*, he took offence at the chancellor's reference to the 'agrarian' essence of the Conservative Party. The word 'agrarian,' Engel claimed, had the negative connotation of 'narrow-minded, self-seeking partisanship opposed to other interests.' He added that with agrarian one-sidedness, Conservatives would be 'in danger of losing the confidence and trust of all serious, national, and truly conservative circles.'[76]

As the finance reform crisis became acute in early 1909, dissent from the Agrarian League's policy of uncompromising opposition to Bülow's legislation grew within Conservative ranks. The later Pan-German leader Baron Georg von Stössel, also chairman of the Conservative Association in Potsdam, sponsored a strongly worded declaration against the Conservatives' Reichstag leaders. Their refusal to break with the extreme agrarians had produced 'strong resentment' and 'great alienation' among urban Conservatives – to the point, Stössel claimed, that those leaders might in the future be neither 'loyally followed' nor considered 'nationally reliable.'[77] The essence of Stössel's argument appeared repeatedly in anti-agrarian resolutions issued by Conservative associations in the spring of 1909. These resolutions stressed five basic points: first, that landowners were duty-bound to make the 'national sacrifice' of 500 million marks in new taxes; second, that Conservative leaders had to pre-empt a popular or royal backlash against the party if Bülow were ousted on an issue of such national importance; third, that the party would appear in an untenable position if the chancellor should fall as a result of collusion between Conservatives and the Catholic Centre Party; fourth, that Conservative opposition to new taxes would cost them votes in the cities and among the lower middle classes at the next election; and fifth, that a kind of 'noble Conservatism' had to stand above demagogic agitation, callous interest politics, and parliamentary intrigue.

This struggle against 'one-sided agrarianism' waged by local Conservative associations in 1909 provided an impetus for further attempts to reform the Conservative Party in the five years before the war, as the next chapter illustrates. Yet the wider implications of this dissent were clear even in 1909. The Conservative Union, a Berlin-based organization of predominantly middle-class Conservatives founded in July 1909, declared that the Bülow Bloc had been destroyed by 'party egoism.' These dissenters presented in their call to arms a comprehensive (if rather contradictory) appeal to all Conservatives who rejected radical interest politics and the sterile opposition: 'More contact with the people! Independence from the Agrarian League! Equity between city and countryside! Away from the Centre Party! Back to the Bloc concept against Social Democracy! *Then the Conservative Party will become a People's Party!*'[78]

Differences of opinion about parliamentary strategy also divided leaders of the Agrarian League and the Conservative Party. In 1908 a writer in the *Kreuzzeitung* called on members of the agrarian-led Economic Union in the Reichstag to join the Conservative caucus; this writer referred to 'the ambitious efforts of sectarians who would rather be leaders in their small circle than mere co-workers in the large Conservative Party.'[79] Around the same time, another member of the Agararian League's directorate, Gustav Roesicke, wrote to Wangenheim that the league needed to remain 'above the parties' and not appear as an auxiliary 'electoral association' of the Conservatives.[80]

When Bülow's attacks on the agrarians in early 1909 prompted the league's leader in West Prussia, Elard von Oldenburg-Januschau, to counter with even more extreme polemics against the chancellor, Conservatives faced an increasingly difficult choice between the opposing fronts. Count Georg zu Dohna-Finckenstein, one of the Conservatives who had been banned from court after the Mittelland Canal vote, attempted to explain this dilemma to Loebell in the Reich chancellery. Oldenburg's style of agrarian radicalism, Dohna asserted, was a necessary tactical ingredient of the Conservative Party's strategy within the Bülow Bloc: '[Oldenburg's] impulsive manner is ... his *strength*, and one must bear with him if he sometimes lays it on too thick ... Within the bloc we Conservatives must press our views energetically. *For that purpose*, there are provincial rallies and other extra-parliamentary meetings. Then, in the committees and in the parliamentary caucuses, the "attainable" is separated from what is "sought after."'[81]

Dohna's letter must have created the impression that Conservatives were merely using Agrarian League radicalism to win concessions from the government and that they did not endorse the agrarians' maximal program. Early reactions to Bülow's conflict with the league also signalled that Conservative Party leaders disapproved of the radical agrarians' attempt to preclude a reconciliation between Bülow and the party. A contributor to the *Kreuzzeitung* noted in March 1909 that the liberals' tactic of blaming all difficulties on agrarian special interests was made easier when the Agrarian League issued declarations of no compromise with the government and set in gear 'systematic agitation in the sharpest tones.' 'That has been neither clever nor necessary,' noted this writer. 'The Conservative Party does not need such backing; it also does not allow itself to be influenced by it. Therefore one can only wish that no more agitational material against the Conservatives ... will fall into the hands of ... [the liberals] through such political declarations.'[82]

Uncertainty about how moderate Conservatives would vote on the finance reform bill troubled Agrarian League leaders well into the spring of 1909. In November 1908 Roesicke warned Wangenheim that Bülow – an 'opportunistic politician' par excellence – would exploit an anti-agrarian backlash among governmental Conservatives if Oldenburg were given free rein to attack the chancellor.[83] 'This initiative would signify a great test of strength for those members of the Right who are of a susceptible disposition and character. The direct attack that Oldenburg wants requires a much greater energy and resoluteness from the Right – that is, the Conservative caucus – which in my view is not to be had ... To precipitate this conflict would alienate a large number of Conservative caucus members.'

In April 1909 Roesicke and Wangenheim complained again to each other that 'things [were] critically shaky on the Right' because of the Conservatives' 'lack of insight, resoluteness, and reliability.'[84] The characteristic feature of the Conservatives' reaction to the finance reform crisis, they felt, was 'the defection of all the weak ones.' Clearly, for these agrarian leaders, compromise with the government or with the other parties that supported its proposed inheritance tax could only be a sign of weakness. In their view, German agriculture had to remain strong in order to provide the rallying point for a 'proper' bloc of state-supporting forces in the empire. Wangenheim expressed this view after Bülow's defeat when he wrote to Roesicke: 'When Bülow says to the Conservatives that they must assimilate liberal viewpoints, he overlooks, I believe, the activity of the Agrarian League, which indeed ensures that the Conservative Party is brought from its former torpidity to a more popular and thereby naturally more liberal [!] course.'[85] Thus Wangenheim's proposal for Conservative 'renewal' linked the same three issues addressed by the Conservative Union: the relationship between a 'new' Right and the state, the moderate Right versus the radical Right, and the mobilization of new political support. Bülow, too, had to deal with these three problems.

The chancellor's efforts to prompt defections from the Conservative Party in 1908–9 were in a way nothing more than a series of measures to banish from his own mind – and from the Kaiser's – the consequences if he should fail. On reports warning him in the autumn of 1908 that the Conservative Party would never accept an inheritance tax, Bülow wrote impulsively in the margin, 'Then the whole reform will fail,' and carried on with his campaign to win renegade Conservatives for his plans.[86] In this campaign Bülow recruited fringe Conservative figures to write brochures in favour of the government's tax reform. He also received indications of support from conservatives of many different political hues. The various viewpoints expressed here did not amount to a tangible or cohesive anti-agrarian argument per se. Yet the chancellor hoped that some of these opportunities could be exploited. Notable successes included the German Mittelstand Congress of 13 April 1909, which called for an end to agrarian opposition to finance reform; a resolution of 6 April 1909 from the executive committee of the Conservative associations in the Kingdom of Saxony, recommending acceptance of the inheritance tax if necessary; and the *Reichsbote*'s consistent advocacy of a flexible and generous Conservative policy. Low-level government officials, who were due to participate in the Mittelstand Congress, were encouraged to believe that their salaries would be raised only after parliament had passed the inheritance tax. Roesicke tried to express his outrage at this action by using the strongest language he could muster: he labelled this strategy 'democratic.'[87]

Many Conservatives were delighted that the government had lent an ear to their views, as the files of the Reich chancellery illustrate. Among this archival material can be found Conservatives' own tax schemes, suggestions to help Bülow gauge the mood of the party, and professions of incomprehension at the party leadership's short-sightedness and intransigence.[88] Taken together, this correspondence must have assumed a great significance in Bülow's political calculations, especially as he grew more desperate to find a way around the impasse presented by the agrarians.

The chancellor's reaction to such evidence of disunity on the Right was by no means passive. For example, in early June 1909 a top-level chancellery figure, Arnold Wahnschaffe, wrote to an influential judicial official in Kiel, Dr Andrae, who planned to resign from the Conservative Party over the finance reform issue.[89] Wahnschaffe still hoped that the Conservatives would have a change of heart; therefore he was intent on informing Andrae that his dissent was not unique. If the Conservatives destroyed the Bülow Bloc, he wrote, it would set itself 'in the sharpest opposition to the feeling of the nation's best elements.' Wahnschaffe was even more concerned to make the best possible use of Andrae's willingness to speak out. He counselled him not to resign from the party; instead he asked: 'Could you not somehow state your opinion in the *Kreuzzeitung* or, if this refuses to accept, in the *Reichsbote*? It is still not impossible that your voice will elicit an echo.'

Bülow and Loebell pursued a similar strategy with the leader of the Saxon Conservative Party, Paul Mehnert junior, the 'uncrowned king of Saxony.' Mehnert admitted that his pro-finance reform position was explicitly calculated not to jeopardize Conservative popularity in Saxony.[90] He was (rightly) fearful of the results expected from upcoming *Landtag* elections in Saxony, to be held for the first time under an expanded plural suffrage. He believed that his first duty was as a regional party chairman, not as a follower of the agrarian program. Mehnert also made no secret of his dislike for the agrarian leaders who had travelled to Saxony and 'left no stone unturned' in their efforts to head off a defection to the government's side. He reported to Bülow at one point that 'in the German Conservative caucus, ... formerly sharp enemies of the inheritance tax are now prepared, with certain reservations, to vote for this tax.'[91]

In the crucial vote of 24 June 1909, the backbone of Conservative opposition was *not* broken. Only six Conservative deputies voted against the party majority, that is, for the government's tax. But other consequences of the finance reform conflict are more significant. One was that Bülow staked his entire career on what turned out to be an exercise in self-deception. We have seen that his self-deception was supported by conflicting signals emanating from the Conservative and agrarian camps.[92] Yet the chancellor's uncharacteristic inability to manoeuvre out of the crisis revealed a fatalistic attitude that the Conservatives were beyond reach, on two counts – beyond reach because they could not be won to the government's side, and beyond reach because they could not save themselves from political suicide. This second aspect emerged most clearly in Bülow's last major Reichstag speech of 16 June

1909, as well as in the notorious interview he gave to the editor of a Hamburg newspaper the day before his resignation from office.

Bülow was not alone in identifying either a new phase in right-wing radicalism or continued conflict between the Right and the state. His loyal chancellery chief, Loebell, felt the same exasperation in 1909 that he had experienced during the canal crisis. He claimed that the Conservatives' 'extremely unclever and irresponsible tactics' had transformed the inheritance tax into a political question.[93] In the draft for an angry letter to a Conservative colleague after the fate of Bülow's reform had been sealed, Loebell wrote of a 'test of strength' (*Kraftprobe*) between Conservatives and the government (this phrase was later deleted).[94] The Kaiser, too, despite his ambiguous and unconvincing support for Bülow since the *Daily Telegraph* affair in November 1908, was utterly alienated by the Conservatives' opposition. Wilhelm read a newspaper account on 6 July 1909 that reported Conservative deputies returning 'in great consternation' from home constituencies they had visited during a brief Reichstag recess.[95] The account claimed that many Conservatives 'now throw up their hands and proclaim that they did not want this end, that they were left in the dark by the leaders, that they did not recognize the possibility of the present consequences.' In the margin the Kaiser wrote: 'Then they are incapable and unworthy as deputies.' In the margin of another article Wilhelm referred to the 'so-called loyal Conservatives.'[96]

The Conservative leader Ernst von Heydebrand implicitly agreed that his party was now profoundly estranged from the government. In a Reichstag speech on 10 July 1909, subsequently printed and distributed as party propaganda, he suggested that no one could claim that the Conservatives had sacrificed their convictions in order to retain favour with the government. The party leadership had overcome 'doubt, lack of courage, dissatisfaction [and] defection' and preserved its independence. Conservative parliamentarians, Heydebrand concluded, had no reason to believe they had lost touch with the mood of the people. '[Our] good conscience will maintain us when we go before the country and the voters to justify what we aimed for and what we have done.'[97] Little was Heydebrand to know that he would be continuing this campaign of self-justification five years later.

Still, it was Bülow who provided the boldest strokes in painting a picture of Conservatism 'digging its own grave.' His most revealing comments here were included in his marginalia to memoranda from Loebell in April 1909.[98] Significantly, Bülow headed his musings about the Right's motivation for a possible destruction of the bloc with two different questions: 'What will the Conservatives achieve?' and 'What will the agrarians achieve?' To the latter question, he replied that the agrarians would be labelled 'base egoists.' But Bülow painted the Conservative Party's prospects more darkly: 'Confusion, bitterness, [and] depression among wide circles of Conservatives, especially in middle Germany, in the cities, among officials, lower middle classes, etc.; ... real (not imaginary) compensations to the liberal-democratic idea in Prussia, in order to defend the party against the odium of a "reactionary" rule by Junkers and priests. The Conservative Party will experience a setback similar to the one in the 70s.' In his Reichstag speech of 16 June 1909, Bülow reiterated this motif; 'a victory in the present,' he declared, 'is often the way to defeat in the future.' And then in 1911, in correspondence with one of the Conservatives who had broken party ranks two years earlier, he offered the same view once again.[99] On Heydebrand's shoulders would rest the responsibility for a 'sharpening of conflicts between Conservatives and liberals, the awakening of dangerous resistance against the Conservative Party, above all a restrengthening of radicalism.'

Conclusions

As in earlier crises, all the principal figures in the finance reform crisis of 1909 believed that the Conservative Party had opted for a political course that repudiated its ties with the Kaiser's government. Instead the party had chosen to appeal to radical oppositional sentiments among 'the people.' From this *perceived* turning point in the history of the German Right, three conclusions can be drawn.

First, one can hardly overestimate the degree to which the Conservative-government relationship was shaped by personal ambition, factional disputes, breakdowns in communication, and divergent understandings of how the normal give and take of politics in an authoritarian polity should work. The mutually reinforcing effect of these factors was as great on the government side as among Conservatives. Finance Minister Miquel was only the most prominent among a number of Prussian state ministers who resisted efforts to accommodate some measure of liberal reform in Imperial Germany. In fact, it was in the realm of 'personal' politics, where Miquel and Bülow seemed to excel, that relations between Conservatives and the state became most opaque and unpredictable.

Chancellor Hohenlohe in 1899 had to consider how he could possibly conduct an election campaign against the Conservatives, but he also had to include in his calculations Wilhelm's inability to work personally with liberal ministers. Philipp Eulenburg thought he might buy off the 'ambitious viper' Heydebrand. Yet Wangenheim and Roesicke, discussing a leadership change for the Conservative Party in 1905, considered Heydebrand to be 'the only one who would lead the cause energetically and along agrarian lines.' All other possible candidates, they felt, 'would be devoutly governmental.'[100] The Saxon Conservative leader Mehnert was condemned by hard-line agrarians in 1909 for his dissenting position, yet his face appeared on the frontispiece of the celebratory *Konservativer Kalender* in 1916. And Chancellor Bethmann Hollweg entered office with the express intent to 'help the Conservatives overcome the errors they made' in 1909. But as early as 1910 he had concluded that his task was impossible as long as Heydebrand led the party; Heydebrand, Bethmann felt, was leading the Reich 'down the democratic path.'[101] After years of polemics hurled across confused battle lines by Conservatives, agrarians, and ministers of the state, exactly what Bethmann meant to condemn with the word 'democratic' was anyone's guess.

The second point is that the questions of governmentalism and reform had large implications both for the Right and for the course of imperial German politics as a whole. On the one hand, without the prospect of cooperation with the moderate Conservatives, the government might have abandoned hope of reliable support on the Right. This factor in turn might have led it to consider compromise with the Left as more attractive than continued reliance on a declining socio-economic group inclined to extremism. Thus if 'demagoguery' had indeed overwhelmed traditional conservatism, the government might have been forced to seek a Leftist majority and might have moved towards parliamentary government. However unlikely that development was, the paradox of this case is that moderate Conservatives actually perpetuated the old system and prevented the final break with unyielding political elites. On the other hand, if the moderate Conservatives had not continually pressed for compromises from their popular auxiliaries and if they had not provided alternative parliamentary support on government bills, the government might have been forced to accept the reactionary policies advocated by the *Kreuzzeitung* group and the Agrarian League.

The most interesting aspect of both these cases is that they prompt us to speculate about how 'system maintenance' works in an authoritarian polity. Neither radical Conservatives nor the government wanted revolution. Yet both sides proved willing to escalate conflicts that always threatened to benefit the Social Democrats directly. Contemporaries refused to identify when 'insignificant' differences of opinion became (or might become) significant. This ambivalent stance has undoubtedly contributed to a lingering vagueness among historians about whether the imperial German state was willing to oppose Junker interests or not.[102] Nevertheless, remaining doubts must not blind us to the occasions when an emerging radical Right was perfectly willing to carry out its threat to mobilize artisans, antisemites, and peasants against the government. Nor can we ignore evidence that the government was willing to proceed with reforms that threatened to undermine the Junkers' power and exclusivity. Parallels between the collapse of the imperial and Weimar systems make this question of system maintenance all the more compelling. When unity on the German Right overshadowed factionalism and dissent, that unity was based on anti-democratic assumptions that fed the authoritarian imagination. But right-wing radicalism often drew on latent anti-establishment sentiments as well. Thus, as events in 1932–3 proved, 1909 was not the last occasion when a radical Right seemed to offer the means to dismiss a troubled and unreliable government.

The major confrontations between Conservatives and the Wilhelmine state discussed in this chapter suggest how complex and difficult these issues of system maintenance and state legitimation had become by the final pre-war years. As we try to understand the ambivalence that characterized contemporaries' assessments of this relationship, we are tempted to describe Kaiser Wilhelm's love-hate relationship with the Conservative Party as a kind of historical soap opera. This analogy underscores the personal idiosyncrasies that helped to determine whether the relationship would in fact 'work.' Yet it prevents us from considering how contemporaries viewed their options should this relationship fail. When a family partnership dissolves, divorce holds the promise of a new life. For members of the Right and for the government, however, total estrangement was seen as an option that could lead only to mutual extinction. Survival, not just happiness, was at stake. Again and again, Conservatives and government figures spoke of the 'dangerous consequences' or the 'fatal situation' that could follow a full-scale conflict between party and state. Neither meaningful parliamentary reform nor a *coup d'état* from above was very likely, given the ebb and flow of sympathy between the Conservative Party and the imperial chancellery. As long as neither partner could proceed with progressive or reactionary initiatives independently of the other, each course of action represented a leap in the dark too fearful for any 'true' conservative to take.

This observation leads to the third point. The Conservative-government relationship, like that between popular mobilizers and Conservative leaders, was a process, not an institution. Therefore, rather than speaking of the Right as though it were a feudal-military-agrarian bloc that governed Germany before 1914, one might speak of a set of blocks that was built up and torn down repeatedly but never assembled in exactly the same way twice.

In the end, the best way to demonstrate that Conservatives enjoyed no 'hegemony' in Imperial Germany may be to draw on the Junkers' martial heritage. That heritage suggests a metaphor that sees the Conservative Party and the government constantly in a state of warfare – latent warfare for the most part, and always limited by the need to maintain the hard kernel of an authoritarian consensus, but warfare nonetheless. These pages have documented many aspects of such warfare: forays into the enemy camp, offers to defect, palace revolts, the overthrow of old generals, occasional truces, deadlock, and a final siege mentality. After 1871, universal manhood suffrage worked in an analogous way to universal conscription: An expanding theatre of war forced all combatants toward an unprecedented mobilization of resources. Raw recruits were enlisted and crude tactics were employed to gain the upper hand. Whenever either side faced a third, more determined enemy on the left flank, hostilities ceased and bilateral talks began anew. But this diplomacy broke down again and again.

In 1914 a crumbling front was shored up for a time. Five years later, both armies had withdrawn from the field.

NOTES

1 John C.G. Röhl, ed., *Philipp Eulenburgs Politische Korrespondenz*, 3 vols. (Boppard am Rhein, 1976–83), 2:877.
2 Hans-Jürgen Puhle, *Agrarische Interessenpolitik und preußischer Konservatismus im wilhelminischen Reich 1893–1914* (orig. 1966; 2nd ed., Bonn–Bad Godesberg, 1975), 204, 212.
3 Dirk Stegmann, Bernd-Jürgen Wendt, and Peter-Christian Witt, eds., *Deutscher Konservatismus im 19. und 20. Jahrhundert* (Bonn, 1983), vii.
4 See also Peter-Christian Witt, 'Konservatismus als Überparteilichkeit: Die

Beamten der Reichskanzlei zwischen Kaiserreich und Weimarer Republik 1900–1933,' ibid., 231–80; Gary Bonham, *Ideology and Interests in the German State* (New York, 1991).

5 Volker R. Berghahn, *Germany and the Approach of War in 1914* (London, Basingstoke, 1973), 12. Berghahn's revised ed. of 1993 refers to 'the traditional political power and influence of the landowners ... [who] were able to exploit their strategic positions within the Prusso-German monarchy to wrest concessions from the government' (25). See also David Schoenbaum, *Zabern 1913: Consensus Politics in Imperial Germany* (London, 1982), 34; and Frank Tipton, *A History of Modern Germany since 1815* (London and New York, 2003), 237. In stating that 'Conservative power rested on the power of Prussia,' Tipton (238) cites Thomas Nipperdey's influential argument that Prussia was 'the hegemonic power of the empire' with a 'conservative internal structure that supported and secured the conservative power complex [of] monarchy, nobility, military, and bureaucracy.'

6 'The political parties have [been] ... neglected, occupying rather a blank space between the wire-pullers of government and the functionaries of the various pressure groups and *Verbände* [associations] ... It was the parties, however, that acted as the essential mediators of change' (David Blackbourn, *Class, Religion and Local Politics in Wilhelmine Germany* [New Haven and London, 1980], 11).

7 See Hermann Diez, 'Helldorff-Bedra,' in *Biographisches Jahrbuch und Deutscher Nekrolog*, ed. Anton Bettelheim (Berlin, 1910), 13:140–1; Friedrich Freiherr Hiller von Gaertringen, 'v. Helldorff,' in *Neue Deutsche Biographie* (Berlin, 1969), 8:474–5; Paul A. Merbach, 'Otto Heinrich von Helldorf-Bedra,' in *Deutscher Aufstieg*, ed. Hans von Arnim and Georg von Below (Berlin, 1925), 243–6.

8 See also Robert M. Berdahl, 'Conservative Politics and Aristocratic Landowners in Bismarckian Germany,' *Journal of Modern History* 44, no. 1 (1972): 1–20.

9 On Perrot and the 'Era' articles, see chapter 8.

10 Letter of 31 July 1876, cited in Hermann von Petersdorff, *Kleist-Retzow. Ein Lebensbild* (Berlin, 1907), 463–4.

11 See Hans Leuß, *Wilhelm Freiherr von Hammerstein 1881–1895* (Berlin, 1905).

12 *Flugblatt des Wahlvereins der deutschen Conservativen*, n.d. [July 1876].

13 'Aufruf zur Bildung einer deutschen conservativen Partei,' ibid., 1–2.

14 For example, see BA Potsdam, Rkz. Nr. 1784, Bd. 1, 1878–81, on efforts to restrict the freedom of speech of Reichstag deputies, esp. Bl. 61–4, Helldorff to Bismarck, 5 Mar. 1879, regarding changes to the legislation. Scribbled at the top was 'Discussed orally with Herr v. Helldorff.'

15 See Heinrich von Poschinger, *Fürst Bismarck und die Parlamentarier*, 3 vols. (Breslau, 1894–6), 2:154ff.
16 See the report on campaign activities and expenditures in the *Mitteilungen des Wahl-Vereins der Deutschen Conservativen*, Dec. 1881, 'II.'
17 Helldorff to Rantzau, 29 Sept. 1881, in BA Koblenz, NL Otto von Bismarck (microfilm), Bestand A, Nr. 4.
18 Helldorff to Rantzau, 23 Aug. 1881, ibid.
19 Helldorff to Herbert von Bismarck, n.d. [Sept. 1881], ibid.
20 See the Wahlverein's *Mitteilungen*, 1882–5, passim; the *Conservative Correspondenz* (1887ff.); the *Deutsches Tageblatt* (1881–91); and Helldorff's *Konservatives Wochenblatt* (1891).
21 *RT Sten. Ber.*, 4. Legislaturperiode, I. Session 1878, Bd. 1, 37–8 (16 Sept. 1878). See also materials in BA Potsdam, 01.01. Reichstag, Nr. 2865, Bd. 1, 1878, Bl. 114ff.
22 Hellmut von Gerlach, *Von rechts nach links* (Zurich, 1937), 131.
23 *Reichsbote*, 16 Nov. 1888.
24 See John C.G. Röhl, 'The Disintegration of the Kartell and the Politics of Bismarck's Fall from Power, 1887–90,' *Historical Journal* 9 (1966): 60–89; Helldorff's retrospective account is in 'Der Fall des Sozialistengesetzes,' *Deutsche Revue* 25, nos. 1 and 4 (1900): 273–84, 41–3.
25 Helldorff to Delbrück, 22 May 1905, in Staatsbibliothek Berlin I, NL Hans Delbrück, Briefe, 'Helldorff-Bedra,' Bl. 7–8.
26 Hammerstein's struggle with Helldorff can be studied in the diary entries of Theodor Schiemann, the writer of the weekly reviews of foreign policy for the *Kreuzzeitung*; see GStAPK Berlin-Dahlem, NL Theodor Schiemann, Nr. 155.
27 E.g., *Konservatives Wochenblatt*, 18 June, 7 Nov., and 5 Dec. 1892.
28 For the following, see Wahlverein der Deutschen Konservativen, ed., *Stenographsicher Bericht über den Allgemeinen konservativen Parteitag. Abgehalten am 8. Dezember 1892 zu Berlin* (Berlin, 1893).
29 From a Stöcker speech in Bielefeld on 28 Feb. 1893; see Walter Frank, *Hofprediger Adolf Stoecker und die christlichsoziale Bewegung*, 2nd ed. (Hamburg, 1935), 233.
30 Wahlverein der Deutschen Konservativen, *Stenographischer Bericht*, 12.
31 Speech by the leader of Wesphalian Conservatives, Dr August Klasing, ibid., 17.
32 Resolution of 6 Dec. 1892, ibid., 21.
33 See the report of 10 Dec. 1892 by the Saxon envoy in Berlin, Count Wilhelm von Hohenthal und Bergen, to the Saxon Foreign Office, SächsHStA Dresden, Außenministerium (Gesandtschaft Berlin), Nr. 3302.

34 Helldorff to Delbrück, 31 Mar. 1894, in Staatsbibliothek Berlin I, NL Delbrück, Briefe, 'Helldorff-Bedra,' Bl. 1–3.
35 See, for example, Otto von Helldorff-Bedra, 'Die heutigen Konservativen in England und Deutschland,' *Deutsche Revue* 22, nos. 3–4 (1900): 285–307, 57–82.
36 Including Isabel V. Hull, *The Entourage of Kaiser Wilhelm II, 1888–1918* (Cambridge, 1982); and Katharine Ann Lerman, *The Chancellor as Courtier: Bernhard von Bülow and the Governance of Germany, 1900–1909* (Cambridge and New York, 1990). John C.G. Röhl, *Wilhelm II: The Kaiser's Personal Monarchy, 1888–1900* (Cambridge, 2004), 465–72, 'The Kaiser and the Conservatives,' confirms the conclusions reached in this section.
37 Philipp Eulenburg to Holstein, 25 December 1890, in Röhl, *Philipp Eulenburg*, 1:617. In 1901 Eulenburg elaborated on the metaphor: 'The thickheadedness of our Junkers has something bullish about it. For breeding and in battle – that is, in war – tremendous. In the stalls of culture, ... unsteerable, unruly. They do not recognize the dangers, and therefore will act accordingly in the canal question' (Philipp Eulenburg to Bernhard von Bülow, 1 March 1901, in BA Koblenz, NL Philipp Eulenburg, Nr. 57, 23ff.).
38 Letter of 23 May 1891, in Röhl, *Philipp Eulenburg*, 1:683.
39 Letter of 18 May 1892, ibid., 2:867–8.
40 The discussion below is based on the following: P. Eulenburg to his mother, 15 Dec. 1892, BA Koblenz, NL Eulenburg, Nr. 22, 792; and Röhl, *Philipp Eulenburg*, 2:988–98, including Helldorff to P. Eulenburg, 11 Dec. 1892; Holstein to P. Eulenburg, 12, 13, and 16 Dec. 1892; Alfred von Kiderlen-Wächter to P. Eulenburg, 12 and 18 Dec. 1892; Franz Fischer to P. Eulenburg, 12 Dec. 1892; P. Eulenburg to Kaiser Wilhelm, 11, 17 Dec. 1892 and 9 Jan. 1893 (the latter in Röhl, *Philipp Eulenburg*, 2:1181).
41 BA Koblenz, NL Bismarck, Bestand A, Nr. 69, Bl. 795ff.
42 BA Koblenz, Rkz. Nr. 680, Bl. 443ff.
43 P. Eulenburg to Alfred von Kiderlen-Wächter, 25 May 1892, in BA Koblenz, NL Eulenburg, Nr. 19, 356ff.
44 Puhle, *Agrarische Interessenpolitik*, 28–36.
45 See Stolberg to Caprivi, 20 and 29 Dec. 1893, in BA Koblenz, Rkz. Nr. 418, Bl. 93ff, 133ff.; Stolberg to P. Eulenburg, 4 Nov. 1893, in BA Koblenz, NL Eulenburg, Nr. 25, 432–4.
46 The title of this chapter was suggested by Baron Karl von Thüngen-Roßbach, *Thüngen contra Caprivi. Verteidigungsschrift*, 6th ed. (Würzburg, 1894).
47 See Caprivi's correspondence with P. Eulenburg in BA Koblenz, Rkz. Nr. 418.

48 See the *Reichsbote* and the *Kreuzzeitung*, both 4 Mar. 1894.
49 Cited in the *Norddeutsche Allgemeine Zeitung*, 18 Apr. 1894.
50 Engel edited the *Reichsbote* from 1873 until his death in 1911.
51 *Reichsbote*, 20 Mar. 1894.
52 By this point Hammerstein had resigned as editor of the *Kreuzzeitung* amid scandal. For the following, see *Germania*, 25 Oct. 1896; *Reichsbote*, 15 Oct. 1896; *Kölnische Volkszeitung*, 27 Nov. and 24 Dec. 1896.
53 Hannelore Horn, *Der Kampf um den Bau des Mittellandkanals* (Cologne, 1964).
54 See Adam Röder in the Conservatives' *Badische Landpost*, 10 Aug. 1899.
55 *Kreuzzeitung*, 18 Aug., 7 Oct., and 6 Dec. 1899; *Deutsche Tageszeitung*, 12 Aug. 1899; *Korrespondenz des Bundes der Landwirte*, 6 May 1899, and *Conservative Correspondenz*, 19 Sept. 1899, cited in Puhle, *Agrarische Interessenpolitik*, 222–3.
56 Cited in the *Berliner Börsen-Courier*, 3 June 1904.
57 Letter to Wilhelm von der Reck, 16 Dec. 1904, in BA Koblenz, Kl. Erw. 455.
58 For this and correspondence cited in the following paragraph, see ibid.
59 Cited in Waltraud Bialke, 'Die Kanalvorlage des Jahres 1899 und die konservative Partei Preußens' (PhD diss., University of Berlin, 1944), 56–7.
60 Letter of 21 Jan. 1904, cited in *Conrad Freiherr von Wangenheim Klein-Spiegel*, ed. H. Freiherr von Wangenheim (Berlin, 1934), 77–8. The last word should be *prius*: 'Whom God would ruin, he first deprives of reason.'
61 Letter of 2 July 1899, in BA Koblenz, NL Eulenburg, Nr. 54, 150b.
62 State ministry protocols in BA Koblenz, Rkz. Nr. 2003, Bl. 40ff., 53ff., and 60–84.
63 See also Hohenlohe's notes in BA Koblenz, NL Chlodwig zu Hohenlohe-Schillingsfürst, Nr. 1612, passim.
64 Letter of 29 Sept. 1899, in BA Koblenz, NL Eulenburg, Nr. 54, 204ff.
65 Correspondence in ZStA II Merseburg, Hausarchiv, Rep. 53 E 111, Nr. 4, Bl. 5–15; for the following, see Bernhard von Bülow, *Denkwurdigkeiten*, 2 vols. (Berlin, 1930), 1:298.
66 Letter to Alexander zu Hohenlohe-Schillingsfürst, 25 Aug. 1899 (emphasis added), in BA Koblenz, NL Hohenlohe, Nr. 1612, Bl. 249ff.
67 For the following, see P. Eulenburg to Bülow, 1 Mar. and 4 June 1901, in BA Koblenz, NL Eulenburg, Nr. 57, 23ff., 85ff.
68 Quoted in P. Eulenburg to Bülow, 4 June 1901, cited in the previous note.
69 Meeting protocols in BA Koblenz, Rkz. Nr. 2005, Bl. 56ff., 65ff.
70 See Loebell's memo to Bülow, 14 Nov. 1904, and Stolberg to [Loebell], 4 Feb. 1905, Rkz., Nr. 2006, Bl. 71, 130ff.

368　Tension and Détente

71　By the final vote (244: 146) the Conservative ayes were not decisive; but this outcome only underscores the government's belief that no legislation should be enacted without the backing of the 'moderate' Conservatives.
72　*Kreuzzeitung*, 21 Dec. 1904.
73　Memorandum, 'Betreff die Aussichten der Kanalvorlage im Abgeordnetenhause,' 19 Jan. 1905, in BA Koblenz, Rkz. Nr. 2006, Bl. 98ff.
74　Ibid.; emphasis added.
75　See Peter-Christian Witt, *Die Finanzpolitik des Deutschen Reiches von 1903 bis 1913* (Lübeck, Hamburg, 1970); Lerman, *Chancellor*, chaps. 5–6; Bonham, *Ideology*, chap. 6.
76　*Reichsbote*, 3 Dec. 1907.
77　*Kreuzzeitung*, 25 Mar. 1909.
78　Konservative Vereinigung manifesto, *Konservative Männer in Stadt und Land!* (13 Nov. 1909); original emphasis.
79　Cited in *Das nationale Deutschland*, no. 26 (3 May 1908): 798–802.
80　Roesicke to Wangenheim, 4 June 1908, in BA Potsdam, NL Conrad von Wangenheim, Nr. 3, Bl. 2.
81　Dohna-Finckenstein to Loebell, 3 Feb. 1909, in BA Koblenz, Rkz. Nr. 1391/5, Bl. 164–5; original emphasis.
82　*Kreuzzeitung*, 28 Mar. 1909.
83　Roesicke to Wangenheim, [14] Nov. 1908, in BA Potsdam, NL Wangenheim, Nr. 3, Bl. 87–8.
84　See the correspondence among Heydebrand, Roesicke, and Wangenheim, 8–10 Apr. 1909, in BA Potsdam, NL Wangenheim, Nr. 4, Bl. 20–30.
85　See Roesicke to Wangenheim, 23 and 28 July 1909; Wangenheim to Roesicke, 26 July 1909; and other correspondence in in BA Potsdam, NL Wangenheim, Nr. 4, Bl. 60–76.
86　Bülow's marginalia to Loebell's notes of 8 Sept. 1908, in BA Koblenz, Rkz. Nr. 208, Bl. 21.
87　Roesicke to Heydebrand, 10 Apr. 1909, in BA Potsdam, NL Wangenheim, Nr. 4, Bl. 29–30.
88　See the copious material in BA Koblenz, Rkz. Nrn. 209–212, and in GStAPK Berlin-Dahlem, Rep. 90, Nr. 1345.
89　Wahnschaffe to Andrae, 1 June 1909, in BA Koblenz, Rkz. Nr. 213; see also Wahnschaffe to Wangenheim, 1 June 1909, ibid., Bl. 11. Wangenheim was Wahnschaffe's uncle.
90　See the correspondence in BA Koblenz, Rkz. Nr. 211, Bl. 89–119.
91　Besides Mehnert's correspondence, ibid., see also the *Kölnische Volkszeitung*, 7 Apr. 1909, cited in Witt, *Finanzpolitik*, 278.

92 See Roesicke to Wangenheim, 23 July and 28 July 1909, and Wangenheim to Roesicke, 26 July 1909, in BA Potsdam, NL Wangenheim, Nr. 4, Bl. 70–6.
93 Loebell to Rudolf von Valentini, 19 June 1909, in BA Koblenz, Rkz. Nr. 213, Bl. 217.
94 Loebell to Dohna-Finckenstein, 29 June 1909, ibid., Bl. 266–7.
95 Clipping in BA Koblenz, NL Bernhard von Bülow, Nr. 35.
96 Wilhelm's marginalia to the *Münchener Neueste Nachrichten*, 30 June 1909, ibid.
97 The printed speech is found in BA Koblenz, ZSg. Nr. 70/1 (7).
98 Marginalia (8 April) to Loebell's notes of 6 Apr. 1909, cited in Witt, *Finanzpolitik*, 275–6.
99 See Bülow to Axel von Kaphengst and Bülow to Loebell, both 31 Mar. 1911, in BA Koblenz, NL Friedrich Wilhelm von Loebell, Nr. 7, Bl. 23ff. I am grateful to Wolfgang von Loebell for access to this collection.
100 Wangenheim to Roesicke, 8 Jul. 1905, in BA Potsdam, NL Wangenheim, Nr. 1, Bl. 74.
101 Bethmann Hollweg to Bülow, 14 July 1911, cited in Willibald Gutsche, *Aufstieg und Fall eines kaiserlichen Reichskanzlers* (Berlin, 1973), 91.
102 See the thoughtful discussion in Witt, 'Konservatismus,' 266–7.

10 The Road to Philippi

Shortly before the outbreak of the First World War, fundamental changes were underway in the structure, style, and orientation of politics on the German Right. Most historians who have studied these changes have concentrated their attention on the leading nationalist and economic pressure groups.[1] Along the way they have neglected the three right-wing parties in Imperial Germany: the German Conservative Party, the Imperial and Free Conservative Party, and the National Liberal Party.[2] Hence these parties have not been integrated into the larger community of the Right, whose members were eager to safeguard their own interests, define the cultural symbols of German nationalism, and rally opposition to the government of Chancellor Theobald von Bethmann Hollweg. The central importance of the German Conservative Party, the furthest right of these three, has been most conspicuously ignored. Geoff Eley and others have pointed out the insufficiency of Hans-Jürgen Puhle's early study of the Agrarian League in defining the Conservative Party's position within the Wilhelmine Right.[3] The previous chapter also addressed this issue. Yet only a few participants in the historical debate have directly addressed one central question: whether or not Conservatives maintained their influence with Bethmann's government after 1909 and, if they did not, how they imagined the consequences that estrangement might hold for the future of German authoritarianism.[4]

To fill this gap, this chapter asks whether leading politicians and statesmen believed that the Conservative Party legitimately represented principles of far-sighted statecraft after 1909 and, if so, whether those principles were deemed to support an authoritarian consensus on the Right. Certainly, Bethmann had supporters on the Right who had been alienated by the Conservative Party or who found other right-wing groups more to their taste. But when we ask why Bethmann could not abandon the party altogether, is the answer simply that he had no alternative source of support for his government? Can we conclude that there was no other party constellation capable of supporting his policies? Or could he simply not *conceive* of an alternative arrangement?

Germany's fifth chancellor, like the first, had many tangible political reasons for not breaking with the Conservatives. When Bethmann discussed these reasons with colleagues, his tone was often one of frustration and resignation – again, not unlike Bismarck's. But at other times, Bethmann's attitude was confident, even arrogant. To understand these changes in attitude, we must understand why he believed he could improve, loosen, or otherwise redefine his ties to the Conservative Party. There was indeed an intangible authority – a right to claim a pivotal position – he ceded to the Conservatives, consciously or not. This intangible factor was the not-so-hard kernel of Bethmann's own authoritarian imagination. For many reasons he could not turn to the Kaiser, the administration, the military, economic interest groups, nationalist pressure groups, other organizations on the Right, or even the forces of the Left as alternative sources of authority. Does this mean Bethmann was incapable of seeing the 'antediluvian' Conservative Party (as one critic described it) for what it was? Is he therefore to be condemned for misjudging it? Or were his options in fact as limited as they appeared? If Bethmann was paying lip service to one political group, was it to the Left or the Right? Can we even speak of 'the Right' in the singular in the half-decade before 1914?

The problem of defining who belonged to the 'old' or the 'new' Right, and why, is bound up with questions about Bethmann's 'politics of the diagonal.' This was the policy whereby the chancellor tried to rely on shifting parliamentary majorities and the collaboration of all non-socialist parties to advance his political agenda. In 1917 Bethmann looked back on the mixed success of this policy and commented: 'The present party alignment and our constitutional structure force [me] to rely basically on a policy of diagonals. But even the diagonal is a straight line, and I believe I have followed it.'[5] Perhaps Bethmann meant to imply here that his policy was less problematic than supposed. Yet it is difficult to say whether his strategies to deal with the emergence of an oppositional Right were mutually reinforcing or contradictory. To some observers, Bethmann's apparent love-hate relationship with the Conservative Party was a carefully considered program to reconcile progressive and reactionary forces in the Reich. Perhaps it could have been as successful as Bismarck's manipulative strategies in the 1870s and 1880s, when ad hoc majorities, sometimes excluding the Conservatives, had yielded an authoritarian and steadfastly 'national' policy. To others, Bethmann's efforts were doomed to failure because he could not decide whether to treat the Conservative Party as an essential prop of the status quo or to regard it as a threat to reasonable, far-sighted policy. Both points of view are explored in what follows.

This chapter has a second theme. Bethmann and his political philosophy have been described as 'enigmatic,' 'without character,' and caught between 'power and morality.'[6] The term 'reformist conservatism,' however, which appears frequently in a biography of Bethmann, is a useful shorthand description of his political outlook.[7] With this concept of reformist conservatism, we can explore new dimensions of party-state relations in Imperial Germany. By examining how the chancellor and Conservatives worked – without ultimate success – to reconcile conservative stasis and conservative reform, this chapter argues that dichotomous thinking and a tendency to see insurmountable polarities where none existed conspired against any 'normalization' of relations between the Right and the government after 1909. Bethmann honestly believed, as he told the Reichstag in February 1912, that the Reich 'could not be governed through either reactionary or radical means.'[8] Yet neither he nor members of the German Right successfully balanced desires for reform and retrenchment. Neither side successfully reconciled new ideas and old prejudices. Neither side successfully found ways to chart a rational political course between the dictates of reason and sentiment.

This concept of reformist conservatism will also be used to study the historical links between efforts to resurrect the Conservative Party's popularity after the debacle of the finance reform crisis of 1909 and efforts to re-establish the party within the phalanx of 'state-supporting' parties in Germany. The party's estrangement from the government in 1909 brought to the fore demands from rank-and-file members for a redefinition of the party's whole political strategy. At the centre of this redefinition lay many troubling questions about how the party should or could be reformed. Conversely, Bethmann hoped that the Conservatives could be 'enlightened' about the realities of political life in a more democratic age. This desire prevented him from abandoning these old, though no longer trusted, allies of the authoritarian state. Whether trying to engineer a reconciliation between Conservatives and National Liberals or to dampen radical nationalist opposition to

10.1. 'Chancellor's love,' 1882. Bismarck embraces his political offspring. The Progressives (<u>F</u>reisinnige) are banished to the shadows, and Bismarck has half-turned away from the <u>C</u>entre Party leader, Ludwig Windthorst. The <u>N</u>ational <u>L</u>iberals get due attention, but 'brother farmer' and another 'agrarian' are conspicuous favourites. 'Kanzlerliebe' (1882), from Wilhelm Scholz et al., *Bismarck-Album des Kladderadatsch 1848–1989*, 31st ed. (Berlin: A. Hofmann & Comp., 1915), 143. From the author's collection.

his foreign policy, Bethmann found that the success or failure of his own reform agenda was inextricably linked to the fate of reformism within the Conservative Party.

In selecting which events could illuminate these relationships, I have given priority to Bethmann's own account, written in July 1914, indicating where he felt the Conservatives' decisive turns towards opposition had been taken: 'Whoever, as in 1909, Morocco, and 1913, not only fails to spare the cabinet, but directly attacks it in an hour of need, and whoever, alleging that the regime does not sufficiently defend public authority, undermines it as the Conservatives ceaselessly do, has lost his right to a special position.'[9] Thus the legacy of Chancellor Bülow's finance reform legislation of 1909 is examined first, followed by a brief survey of the Conservatives' own attempts to popularize their party. Bethmann's efforts to undermine the authority of the Conservative Party's leadership introduces the party-state conflict over Morocco in 1911. A brief analysis of the government's tax and military legislation in 1912–13 sets up concluding remarks that explore the apparent political deadlock on the eve of war. This conclusion once again stresses the interpenetration of personal and structural reasons for the drift of the German Right towards radical nationalist opposition.

Bülow's Legacy

We will see each other at Philippi.
Chancellor Bernhard von Bülow to the Conservatives, upon resigning from office in July 1909[10]

How did contemporaries view the political legacy that Chancellor Bülow handed to his successor in July 1909? When the Conservatives provided the crucial votes to defeat the government's proposed Finance Reform Bill,[11] most observers knew that finance reform was too important to disappear from political debate. In following years the Conservatives claimed that the taxes they passed against Bülow's wishes were fair and provided the necessary added revenue. The liberals claimed, with more justification, that the Conservatives had refused any significant self-sacrifice for the national good: they had defeated an inheritance tax on estates and they had placed the increased fiscal burden of indirect taxation on the shoulders of less prosperous consumers. Thus the finance reform of 1909 came to symbolize the refusal of Germany's agrarian Right to recognize and accept the consequences of economic decline.

At the height of this battle, Bülow painted a stark picture of Conservatism digging its own grave.[12] In his last major Reichstag speech of 16 June 1909, just before the bill's fate was sealed, he told the Conservatives bluntly that that they would wait a long time before another chancellor represented 'true conservative interests' and defended the legitimate long-term needs of agriculture.[13] Overturning the government's proposed finance reform, Bülow continued, would be a grave political error. The Conservatives, however, refused to heed his warning. Therefore on 13 July 1909, the day before his resignation, Bülow declared in an interview[14] that future socialist gains at the polls would prove that the Conservatives had played a 'frivolous gambit' with the interests of the monarchy and the nation. He later wrote that, like Cassandra, he hoped his prophecies would not come true. But he predicted in this interview that the Conservatives' action could be 'the starting point of a trend that creates embittered party conflicts, brings forth unnatural party groupings, and is detrimental to the welfare of the nation.' To the Conservatives he declared: 'We will see each other at Philippi.'

In the summer of 1909, then, Bülow was utterly alienated from the Conservative Party: he sincerely believed that the Conservative Party was rushing to its ruin.[15] In drafting his resignation speech in July, he included more far-reaching criticism than finally appeared in his Reichstag address. In adopting very different attitudes towards the party in his private thoughts and in his public statements, Bülow prefigured the ambivalent, even contradictory positions characteristic of Bethmann Hollweg. Asking his former chancellery chief, Friedrich Wilhelm von Loebell, whom he regarded as his 'political conscience,' for comments on his draft speech, Bülow wrote at this time: 'I might also say: the Conservative Party is using a great national question to initiate a trial of strength [*Machtprobe*] against the government and the chancellor ... It thereby damages the authority of the government ... [and] the foundations upon which the Conservative Party rests.'[16]

In his Reichstag speech of 16 June and over the following years, Bülow continued to assert that he was 'politically conservative.'[17] In his first sustained retrospective look at the events of 1909,[18] he distinguished between 'state conservatism' and 'party conservatism.' The government's espousal of the latter, 'partisan' form of conservatism, he felt, would prove fatal. Nonetheless, he wrote that 'we must never fail to appreciate what the conservative element has achieved for the political life of Prussia and Germany.' It would be a 'sad loss' if the party ceased to occupy a position in parliamentary and political life that was worthy of its past. In fact, the only indication of Bülow's stormy break with the Conservatives was his insistence on referring to 'sound' conservatism or to conservatism's 'best ideals.' With these qualifying words, he groped to identify why a moderate, reformist Right was necessary in modern Germany.

If the Conservative leadership faced a Herculean task in making good the public damage wrought by Bülow's Parthian shot, Bethmann Hollweg's effort to re-establish good relations with the Right could better be described as Sisyphean. Germans in 1909 felt that Bülow had left Bethmann an 'unfortunate legacy.'[19] What was Bethmann's grand strategy to liquidate this legacy?

The new chancellor was not unknown to Conservative leaders, but neither his personality nor his politics much impressed them. In March 1905, when Bethmann first joined the Prussian administration, the Conservative leader Ernst von Heydebrand und der Lase had told Bülow: 'As minister of the interior we need a man with a strong hand and backbone ... Instead you give us a philosopher.'[20] But Heydebrand was neither fair nor accurate with this description, because in 1909 Bethmann indicated quickly that he would take practical steps to mollify public antagonism towards the Conservative Party. In the first Prussian state ministry meeting over which he presided as chancellor,[21] he told his colleagues that his aim was 'to help the Conservatives make good the errors they had committed.' As he later put it, his goal was to help Conservatives 'regain touch with the mood of the people.' With this goal in mind, Bethmann attempted in early 1910 to achieve a compromise between the Conservatives and the National Liberals over a bill to reform the Prussian three-class suffrage, rightly considered one of the most reactionary elements of Imperial Germany's political culture.

The chancellor had reason to expect success with this legislative initiative. As Bülow had predicted, both the Conservatives and the government were under pressure to avoid being tarred with the reactionary brush. A great coup could be scored if, contrary to expectations, the Conservatives proved generous in sharing a small part of their power in Prussia. Bethmann's modest reform bill, however, pleased no one. When the government finally withdrew its legislation, Baroness Hildegard von Spitzemberg, a shrewd observer of Wilhelmine politics and personalities, wrote in her diary in March 1910 that 'the Conservatives are advocating barren, obtuse reaction,' although she added that 'the liberals are turning more and more into radicals.'[22] Bethmann's

10.2. 'The feeling of dependency,' 1910. Clearly under duress, Chancellor Theobald von Bethmann Hollweg stands at the podium holding the ill-fated reform bill of February 1910, intended to revise the Prussian three-class suffrage. Junkers hold Bethmann tightly in check, and Prussian Conservative leader Ernst von Heydebrand – small of stature but here *not* uncrowned – wields an oversized pitchfork to ensure there will be no retreat. With transparent irony, the caption echoes Martin Luther's famous words from 1521: 'Here I stand, God help me, I can do no other!' 'Das Gefühl der Abhängigkeit,' *Kladderadatsch* 63, no. 8, 1. Beiblatt (20 Feb. 1910): 139. Image courtesy of the Universitätsbibliothek, Universität Heidelberg.

choice between the two policy positions, however, was no choice at all, at least when he considered the political realities of the situation, not his personal inclinations. For as the baroness noted, in early 1910 he had become all the more 'firm and "conservative"' as he saw 'how little reliance can be placed on the liberals, with whom he would really gladly govern.'

Because the chancellor's first attempt to 'modernize' the Conservative Party had failed, the government suffered a double defeat. Bethmann recognized in May 1910 that the suffrage reform debate had widened 'the chasm between Conservatives and National Liberals' and driven the latter further to the left.[23] As he put it, the Conservatives, 'with their personal, social, religious, and political hubris and intolerance, ... have succeeded in focusing everyone's disgust and dissatisfaction on the three-class suffrage, which is generally seen as an expression of Junker predominance.' Nonetheless, as Bethmann told his Prussian state ministry colleagues when they were considering another suffrage reform bill in December 1913, any future reform had to be agreeable to the Conservatives. Thus he reaffirmed the impossibility of proceeding decisively against the self-proclaimed protectors of Prussian interests.[24]

Reformist Conservatism

At Philippi, indeed! ... It is now a matter for all positive, constructive forces to *close ranks* ... In this effort may we finally be granted a government that forcefully and decisively takes the lead in the struggle against all destructive elements.

Wilhelm Albers, general secretary of the Conservative Party in Westphalia, 1912[25]

The Conservatives had their own strategy for overcoming the debacle of June 1909. Two parallel efforts can be identified. First, they sought to assert their independence from the government and the other right-wing parties. They emphasized that their party was a people's party (*Volkspartei*) capable of standing alone. They worked to regain the allegiance of groups they had alienated in 1909. And they attempted to expand their constituency to new social groups and geographical regions. Thus they aimed simultaneously to explain their actions in 1909 and to breathe new life into the party apparatus. Second, some Conservatives, especially at the provincial level, sought to re-establish contact with whoever in government or National Liberal circles was willing to consider an alliance on terms that did not require an abandonment of fundamental Conservative policies. These two strategies were contradictory in some ways but complementary in others. The second strategy more directly affected the party's relationship with Bethmann. However, as noted previously, the chancellor could not afford to ignore any signs from within the Conservative Party that a new orientation might be considered.

For Heydebrand, for the Conservative Reichstag caucus chairman, Oskar von Normann, and for Normann's eventual successor, Count Kuno von Westarp, the first priority after the summer of 1909 was to dampen dissent among the party rank and file. Between the defeat of the government's finance reform in June and the staging of a general party congress in November, the German political press was filled with reports of defections from the party. The National Liberals printed a twenty-eight-page brochure chronicling this disaffection with the party leadership in virtually all regions of Germany.[26] Pastors, government officials, retired army officers, members of the lower middle classes (*Mittelstand*), and Conservatives in urban areas figured prominently in this rebellion. Bülow's prophecy about the internal agonies the party would experience seemed to be coming true with a vengeance.[27]

When Conservatives met for their long-postponed general party congress in November 1909, the party's leaders regarded the congress, not incorrectly, as a useful outlet for party members to vent their frustrations. Those leaders thus called on local and regional Conservative associations to establish new and 'independent' organizations throughout the empire. A deeper and more critical self-evaluation, however, was impossible. The need to present an image of party unity and steadfastness overwhelmed all other considerations. Hence, despite these efforts to suppress the issue, the debate about Conservatism's 'renewal' and 'modernization' persisted. In response, Heydebrand abandoned his disinclination to speak at provincial rallies and did his utmost to emphasize the party's confidence, unity, and progressive character.[28] As he declared at a congress of Pomeranian Conservatives in late 1910: 'We are destined to be a party of the future, ... a true people's party, ... a liberally oriented party.'[29]

The Conservative Party's storm-and-stress period prompted a number of other new campaigns to increase its following. One of these was the so-called drive to the west. In December 1909 the Conservative *Kreuzzeitung* published a letter from Cologne in which the correspondent noted that most western Germans believed in liberal demonologies of reactionary, boorish east-Elbian Junkers. To counter this notion, Conservative test candidacies were to be launched in the west. The west's rising demographic importance, the potential reservoir of Protestant conservatives there, and the dissatisfaction with the leftward trend of the National Liberal Party under its leader, Ernst Bassermann, also argued for a new commitment from the Conservatives, demonstrating that the Conservative Party was 'a people's party in the best sense of the word.'[30]

By prompting discussion about conservatism's role in an industrializing society and the Conservative Party's function as a party of all interests and classes, the 'drive to the west' prompted another controversy, about urban conservatism. In 1910 Heydebrand announced that party secretariats would be set up in Westphalia and the Rhine Province, two of the most urbanized provinces in Prussia. Then in May 1911 the Conservatives staged their first large party congress in a western German metropolis, attracting two thousand supporters in Cologne. In the next two years urban associations were founded or expanded in many localities, including the Hansa cities. These initiatives were greeted enthusiastically by less-traditional editors of Conservative newspapers. A contributor to the influential *Reichsbote*,[31] for example, wrote that 'in the age of universal suffrage, a party must *go out among the people*: it must show the masses where their true friends lie.' What was needed was 'a Conservative people's party,' this writer added, true to old Christian-Conservative principles but incorporating 'the challenge of Conservative progress!' However, the Conservatives' opponents heaped scorn on the party's achievements in this westward drive. After the Reichstag elections of 1912, the Conservatives' failure was obvious: their share of the vote in cities of over 100,000 inhabitants was only 2.2 per cent.

The crisis of 1909 also compelled the party to seek support from another 'new' demographic: women. Press reports as early as 1909 alleged that Conservative women were organizing themselves. In 1912 the *Kreuzzeitung* printed a letter from an unnamed Conservative countess who claimed that previous Reichstag elections would have turned out very differently if Conservative women had been more active in politics.[32] Educated women from the upper classes were discovering too late that they had a duty to protect 'everything that is holy to mankind.' (As this countess observed, many of the 110 Social Democratic deputies elected to the 1912 Reichstag had had 'bad mothers.') A positive but careful tone was adopted by the Conservative press when a Conservative Women's Union was finally established in April 1913. The

Reichsbote saw the union as another defence against 'disbelief' and 'cosmopolitan anti-nationalism,' while the *Kreuzzeitung* observed (with no hint of double entendre) that although 'politics is without doubt a hateful business,' the new age demanded 'new comrades in arms.' Yet doubts quickly arose in Conservative circles about the organization's reliability as a bulwark against women's emancipation. By the beginning of the war, the majority of Conservatives probably felt that the organization of Conservative women in 1913 had merely opened another Pandora's box full of modern, progressive, democratic spirits.

The same conclusion emerges from the shorter pre-war history of the Young Conservative movement. In early July 1914 an Imperial Young Conservative Association was founded by a collection of academic youths in Bonn. This founding presented Heydebrand and Westarp with a *fait accompli* that was made all the more painful by the left-wing press's emphasis on the association's idealism. The liberal press linked the group's manifesto to earlier calls from within the Conservative Party for a broader commitment to urban, academic, and non-agrarian elements.[33] Worried by this new departure, Westarp spoke of putting a 'good face on a bad affair.'[34]

The party congress of November 1909 and the provincial rallies at which Heydebrand spoke the following year were Conservative, not merely right-wing, assemblies. There was no serious talk of forming unified associations with either women or youth groups within the National Liberal and Free Conservative parties. Even urban conservatism and the 'drive to the west' were hailed in the Conservative press as means to make the Conservative Party independent. But running parallel to these efforts was another campaign to revive the party's influence. This campaign was pursued by those who wanted to moderate Conservative policies, to engineer a Conservative–National Liberal rapprochement, and to resurrect a parliamentary majority against the Left.

A great deal is known about certain features of this effort, and little is known about others. The early work of Dirk Stegmann confirmed the important ties between Conservative agrarians and large industrialists in 1909 and after.[35] We also know of extensive cooperation among the Agrarian League, the Central Association of German Industrialists, and specific *Mittelstand* groups. Essentially, these efforts were carried out in boardrooms, in the halls of parliament, in government offices, and in correspondence among the leaders of the party caucuses and executive committees. However, they were all complicated by the need to find a workable anti-Left consensus at the middle and lower party levels. The rallying together of agricultural, industrial, and *mittelständisch* interest groups failed to overcome the gulf between the National Liberal and Conservative parties, reflected in the continuing polemics between Bassermann and Heydebrand. This was true even after the 1912 elections, which are too easily assumed to have compelled these parties to bury the hatchet (as the contemporary press frequently, but incorrectly, announced).

In many regions of Germany, it was the antagonism between the National Liberals and the Conservatives, not their cooperation, that led to marked increases in organizational and agitational activity. Far from subsiding after the 'red' elections of 1912, this activity accelerated.[36] On 14 January 1912, at the height of the Reichstag election campaign, Bassermann wrote to the left-wing National Liberal leader in Saxony, Gustav Stresemann, to complain that the National Liberals had failed to win the provinces of Pomerania and East Prussia from the Conservatives.[37] In 1913 the debate over whether the National Liberals' efforts in the eastern provinces of Prussia would pay off still raged in the party's executive committee meetings. Local National Liberal chairmen expressed confidence that Conservative ascendancy could be broken, and they concentrated more than ever on problems associated with the disruptive relationship between the two parties.[38] Although the Conservatives claimed the socialists were their main enemies, the National Liberals saw themselves in a two-front war against 'radicals' on both the Left and the Right.

As both parties attempted to invade the traditional political territory of the other, spectacular clashes resulted. Old Conservative domains in the east suddenly came within the view of National Liberal eyes still smarting from the finance reform defeat. The German Peasants League, formed in 1909 to attract farmers who did not condone the Agrarian League's chauvinistic interest politics, spearheaded this 'drive to the east.' Conversely, the Conservatives' 'drive to the west' signalled their unwillingness to concede constituencies west of the Elbe River to the National Liberals. Even the Free Conservative Party, despite its claim to be the ideal 'middle party,'[39] had to shape its policies within the constraints imposed by this conflict. Still, it managed to expand into some regions where it had previously been willing to support candidates from the other two parties.[40] Thus the period after 1909 saw many conservative 'refoundings' on the local level, as the two conservative parties strove to build up their separate provincial organizations.

These continuing tensions among the right-wing parties provide a salutary reminder that the goals espoused by leading economic and nationalist interest groups were restated, compromised, and often condemned to failure because it was politically necessary to work through the established parties, even though those party organizations were themselves undergoing disruptive and unpredictable changes.[41]

Va banque

Heydebrand is leading the Conservatives down demagogic paths. If in our non-parliamentary system the government no longer finds support ... even from the Conservatives and the moderates, then in the end there will be no one left to carry on.

Chancellor Theobald von Bethmann Hollweg, November 1911[42]

In the course of 1910–11 it gradually became apparent that Heydebrand's personal authority within the Conservative Party, together with Bassermann's refusal to seek an alliance on the Right, was undermining all efforts to end the impasse between Conservatives and National Liberals. In December 1910 and then again almost a year later, Bethmann wrote to the Prussian envoy in Baden, Carl von Eisendecher, that Heydebrand was leading the Conservatives down 'disastrous' and 'demagogic' paths.[43] By February 1912 he had concluded that 'as long as Bassermann and Heydebrand remain as leaders, I see a very black future.'[44] By May that year Baroness von Spitzemberg reported that Bethmann was 'disconsolate' over 'the lack of political maturity and reliability among the leaders of the bourgeois parties.'[45]

During these years Bethmann sought to overcome the personal antagonism between Bassermann and Heydebrand, and between them and himself, through personal diplomacy. He repeatedly attempted to engineer personal meetings between these party leaders; but invariably he failed, and not only because of Heydebrand's obstinacy. In August 1910, for example, Bethmann tried to act as a middleman, allegedly having received conciliatory gestures from both men. However, the attempt misfired, this time 'because of the stupidist blindness of the National Liberals.'[46] Bethmann then turned his attention to recruiting pro-government figures within the Conservative Party to report on internal party relations and to undermine the authority of official party leaders. In doing so, he merely continued strategies employed by each of his predecessors in the Reich chancellery – Bismarck, Caprivi, Hohenlohe, and Bülow.[47]

A confidential letter Bethmann wrote in mid-1911 to a leading Conservative who also happened to be president of the Reichstag, Count Hans von Schwerin-Löwitz, illustrates the tense and ambiguous relationship between the Conservatives and the government.[48] Because Schwerin was highly respected within the party and had just received national press attention by disavowing Heydebrand's campaign tactics, this letter is especially noteworthy. Bethmann appealed to Schwerin's more traditional anti-parliamentary and anti-popular instincts by linking criticism of Heydebrand to a broader attack on recent developments in party politics. He claimed that he could understand how the Conservatives might feel provoked and made more stubborn by the 'flagrant' fraternization of left liberals and Social Democrats, the unreliable policies of Bassermann, and the radicalism of the liberal Hansa League. However, it would be 'to deny the traditions of the Conservative Party' and to 'parliamentarize' it if the Conservatives were to compete with the other parties for partisan profit: 'Political principles are thereby thrown overboard.'[49]

Then Bethmann pointed out the dangers of a Conservative policy explicitly calculated to appear 'popular.' The Conservatives, he claimed, seemed to fear that if their party did not fish for votes like other parties, it would not remain competitive at the polls. This might be the case, the chancellor wrote, 'if we were steering towards the parliamentary system of government.' But such a system was 'constitutionally impossible' for both Prussia and the empire. 'Therefore, all this newly inaugurated policy achieves is that the Conservatives, by giving up the traditions that provide their strongest support in the countryside, are degraded to the level of the other parties who live from party egoism, and that the long-standing reciprocal relationship between it and the government is destroyed. The end result will be the weakening of the conservative principle and thereby the acceleration of democratization. I am watching this unhealthy process with growing concern.' Lastly, Bethmann praised Schwerin for speaking out against 'party egoism' in his recent speech, because he wanted to encourage such independent thinking in the party. Although he did not express himself so explicitly in the final version, the deleted phrases in Bethmann's draft clearly suggest this strategy. He wrote that 'improvement can emerge only from the midst of the Conservative Party itself.'

Schwerin's correspondence with Bethmann reinforces other evidence that leading Conservatives outside Heydebrand's small circle were deeply worried by antagonisms among Conservatives, National Liberals, and the government. As so often previously, such worries were voiced mainly by Conservative leaders in the provinces. The reasons these men were willing to speak out against Heydebrand's policies are not difficult to discern. For it was they who faced the difficult task of reconciling local and national interests by adapting official Conservative doctrine to circumstances and attitudes in their smaller homelands. In middle and western Germany these regional leaders tried to de-emphasize the Prussian roots of Conservatism, highlighting instead the party's alleged progressive, enlightened, and up-to-date character. Yet they also had to respect Heydebrand's immense personal authority within the party and work within the limitations of the National Liberal-Conservative conflicts that his attitude perpetuated. Moreover, the Conservative Party's national leaders and their war cry of 'no surrender' after 1909 made it difficult, if not impossible, for these regional leaders to form ad hoc *Landtag* alliances.[50] This was especially true in regions where members of both parties recognized that only right-wing unity could hold back the socialist tide.

That provincial observers were aware of the party's difficulty in reconciling regional and national priorities is illustrated by observations in the unpublished memoir of a leading Conservative *Landtag* deputy from Silesia, Alfred von Goßler.[51] Like many others, Goßler's retrospective commentary on caucus life under Heydebrand's leadership was filled with contradiction and inconsistency. For example, he combined an enthusiasm for traditional Conservative ideals with a regret that the party 'defended its position in such an obstinate manner' by pursuing 'partisan and interest politics.' At one point Goßler reported his outrage at Heydebrand's boast that 'the Prussian ministers dance to my tune.' Yet later he praised Heydebrand's 'eminent talents.' In a similar tone, a Baden party leader, Baron Udo von La Roche-Starkenfels, wrote to Arnold Wahnschaffe, chief of the Imperial chancellery, in October 1910, asking for government funds to support his 'energetic' and 'loyal' Conservative organization struggling in Baden, that 'little land of liberalism.'[52] La Roche described Conservatism in Baden as 'not feudal-conservative in the narrow Prussian sense, but rather more Christian-conservative, with inclusion of the Christian-national workers and also with the wish to see the right-wing elements of the National Liberals à la Heyl[53] join us.'

The urgency with which Conservatives in the Kingdom of Saxony confronted this dilemma was particularly acute because of the socialist threat there. As the leader of the Saxon Conservative Party, Paul Mehnert junior, wrote to Loebell in the late summer of 1911, it was a 'duty to the Fatherland' for the right-wing elements to 'stress what unites them and push into the background what divides them.'[54] Mehnert hoped that the 'expected' ouster of left-wing National Liberals such as Stresemann would remove an 'extremely unfortunate influence' on Bassermann. As he wrote: 'If one allows the National Liberals to march further and further to the left, without making the attempt to hold to our side the better and – at least in national affairs – relatively sympathetic elements,' then one could not later complain that the empire was drifting into 'liberal-democratic channels.'

Tellingly, Mehnert had not turned to the official party leadership to express these worries: 'I fear that at the moment they are not to be won for such considerations.' Although he described himself as a 'strict party man' – and he was – he wrote to Loebell that his allegiance to Conservative principles compelled him 'to keep in mind the general political situation.' When Loebell sent a copy of Mehnert's letter to Bethmann, he acknowledged that Mehnert's opinion was shared by all 'reasonable men on the Right and on the right wing of the National Liberals.' Loebell also emphasized that Mehnert was correct 'when he thinks sceptically about the Conservative Party leadership – that is, Heydebrand,' and he added: 'The errors have not yet ceased, and there is no understanding for farsighted politics.'

At this point preoccupied with the Morocco crisis, Bethmann replied that if the government were 'not to come wholly and irrevocably under the domination of the Centre Party, a bridge between the National Liberals and the Conservatives must be established.' This, he wrote to Loebell, was exactly what had been attempted a year earlier. But at that point the plan had been torpedoed by the National Liberals: 'They demanded as conditions for a reconciliation with the Conservatives Prussian suffrage [reform] and [an] inheritance tax!' Displaying his characteristic ambivalence, Bethmann wrote that 'in the intervening time the chances [for this reconciliation] have become worse and become better.' Most of what followed, however, was pessimistic. Bethmann's pessimism was predicated on Bassermann's 'unreliability' and 'radicalism,' but also on Heydebrand's 'intractable dictatorial strain' and his clear signals that he wanted nothing to do with the National Liberals. As if struggling to identify his own allegiance, Bethmann finally conceded that he blamed conflicts between National Liberals and Conservatives more on Bassermann and Stresemann than on Heydebrand. The National Liberals' criticism of the government's position in the Morocco question was evidence of the party's 'lack of political understanding,' its 'parliamentary swagger,' and its 'unscrupulousness' in exploiting national crises for partisan purposes. It was 'no wonder,' Bethmann observed, 'that Conservative men feel their gorge rise' in the face of such conduct.[55] On the positive side, he saw a possibility for improvement because members of both parties were 'beginning more and more to recognize the errors of leadership.'

The 'Uncrowned King of Prussia'

Were Bethmann and Loebell realistic in hoping that Heydebrand's opposition to reform or his authority within the Conservative Party could be shaken? The evidence suggests they were not. In fact, both men seriously underestimated Heydebrand's personal and political influence. A common thread running through contemporary descriptions of Heydebrand is the single-minded commitment with which he worked to preserve the power of the Conservative Party and of his native Prussia. Franz Sontag, the Pan-German enthusiast who once served on the staffs of the Conservatives' *Kreuzzeitung* and the Free Conservatives' *Post*, remarked in his unpublished memoirs that, for Heydebrand, the logic of the Reich ended at the Prussian border: 'On these frontier posts stood Herr v. Heydebrand, ... always ready to fight for Prussia, even against his king.'[56] Eugen Schiffer, a leading right-wing National Liberal who periodically met secretly with Heydebrand, was also impressed by the directness of his manner and the sureness with which he pursued his goals.[57] Theodor Wolff, chief editor of the left-liberal *Berliner Tageblatt*, referred to the Conservative leader as a 'huge talent.'[58] And Goßler described him as the 'most important' and 'most interesting' personality in parliament – 'not only within the Conservative Party but in the whole political world of the day.' Heydebrand possessed an 'exceptional power-consciousness' that, in combination with 'a steel-like, unbending will,' made him 'a born leader.'[59]

The state secretary of the Reich treasury, Reinhold von Sydow, recalled in his own memoirs that one question was repeatedly asked in the Prussian state ministry when a crucial issue of domestic policy was discussed: 'What does von Heydebrand say about this?'[60] When Heydebrand and Bethmann clashed in early 1911, Bethmann's secretary and confidant, Kurt Riezler, spoke of Heydebrand's ambition to topple the chancellor in almost titanic terms: he referred to the conflict as 'German chancellor versus Prussia.'[61] With similar language, Sontag described Heydebrand as a 'knight without fear or reproach.'[62]

10.3. The 'uncrowned king of Prussia.' Ernst von Heydebrand und der Lase (1851–1924) was also known as 'the little one' (*der Kleine*). Image from Kuno Graf von Westarp, *Konservative Politik im letzten Jahrzehnt des Kaiserreichs*, 2 vols. (Berlin: Deutsche Verlagsgesellschaft, 1935), 1: facing 112. From the author's collection.

Eugen Schiffer provided what remains the most compelling portrait of Heydebrand: 'He is actually called, not without reason, the uncrowned king of Prussia. In parliament and in the government he is known as "the little one," also not without justification. For he is remarkably small of stature, and therefore never stands behind, but rather beside, the speakers' podium. Naturally on the right-hand side, in order to remain close to his *gardes du corps* and as far as possible from the Left. There he stands, shaking his little head back and forth, while, in a not very strong voice, he formulates his phrases, which are often more like a throne speech than a parliamentary one. Time and again he addresses the government benches and upbraids the men sitting there, sometimes with condescension, sometimes in a challenging or even threatening way; or he hurls lightning bolts upon the Left, which are accompanied by the thunder of applause from his myrmidons.'[63]

Heydebrand, then, was a superstar among Wilhelmine politicians. But was Bethmann justified in describing his attitude within the party as 'dictatorial'? Could governmental Conservatives have moderated or disavowed Heydebrand's policies? If this second question were answered in the affirmative, Bethmann's strategy of undermining Heydebrand's position would appear less baffling. However, contemporary reports suggest that Bethmann was simply deluding himself. Franz Sontag noted that Heydebrand headed an 'absolutist regime' in the party executive. Other memoirs confirm this view. Although the Conservative Party had its 'magnates wing' and its governmentalists, who often caused Heydebrand consternation, he always carried the day. The bankruptcy of his personal war on democracy became open to world view in 1918. But to party insiders, the consequences of Heydebrand's intransigence were evident even before 1914, which partly explains why so many radical nationalists turned away from the party shortly before and during the war.

The Nationalist Opposition

To reform Prussia is impossible; it will remain the Junker state [*Junkerstaat*] it is at present or go to pieces altogether ... Everything works for a great crisis in Germany.

August Bebel, leader of the Social Democratic Party, 1910 [64]

The story of Bethmann's unsuccessful policy in the second Moroccan crisis of 1911 is well known.[65] On 9 November – now a fateful date in

German history – the chancellor defended his French settlement in the Reichstag.[66] It was on this occasion that Heydebrand, scheduled to speak after Bethmann, chose to prove that the Conservative Party was indeed a 'nationally minded' party. He called the Morocco settlement a 'worthless' agreement and charged that 'these yieldings ... will not secure us peace, ... only our good German sword can do that.' The import of Heydebrand's speech was not lost on anyone. For the first time, his pugilistic attitude – towards Britain and towards Bethmann himself – rivalled what radicals in the Pan-German League had been saying for years. The Prussian crown prince highlighted the occasion by applauding conspicuously from the royal box when Bethmann's policy was called 'a *defeat*, whether we say so or not.'

Heydebrand's dramatic attack on the government suggested that the Conservatives were willing to join the nationalist opposition to Bethmann. But Heydebrand was also attempting to redefine the Conservative Party's popular image and to reinvigorate a moribund anti-socialist campaign for the Reichstag elections scheduled for January 1912. The SPD charged in its propaganda that the Conservative Party was a chauvinistic agrarian interest group responsible for the new taxes of 1909 that had created such economic hardship for German consumers in 1911. Therefore Heydebrand was determined to show that his party was dynamic, committed, independent, and 'national' – that is, worthy of the allegiance of all the little men of Germany who shared his shame over the defeat of Bethmann's Moroccan policy.

The confrontation between Heydebrand and Bethmann in November 1911 opened more questions about the direction of both foreign and domestic policy than most Conservatives wished to address at this juncture. Liberals immediately anticipated new departures and a new alignment of pro-government parties.[67] Some even dared to hope for a 'grand bloc' of left-wing parties from the National Liberals to the socialists.[68] But just as interesting is the response from members of what might be called the moderate conservative establishment.[69] Rudolf von Valentini, chief of the Kaiser's civil cabinet, wrote to the shipping magnate Albert Ballin in mid-November 1911 that Bethmann's political standing had been 'considerably improved' with the help of two people: 'Heydebrand and the crown prince!'[70] Baroness von Spitzemberg concluded that the Kaiser must be firmly behind Bethmann if the latter was able to reply to Heydebrand's attack with equally harsh words. Bethmann's speech, she noted, had 'thrown the house into blank astonishment and brought about the "retreat to a standstill."'[71] For many

Conservatives, that standstill – or stand-off – was preferable to acute conflict in the Reichstag. A contributor to the *Konservative Monatsschrift* in December 1911 spoke for these Conservatives in suggesting that the current political situation was 'infected with the spirit of negativism.' This writer called for the party to preserve its 'political independence' not through opposition but through 'moderate governmentalism.'[72]

The upcoming elections, however, precluded a normalization of relations. When the crown prince, after his 'childish, student-like' display, remarked that 'Heydebrand's speech was certainly splendid!' the Bavarian envoy in Berlin had said to him: 'Y[our] H[ighness], that was an election speech!' Another moderate conservative was pleased that Bethmann had shown his teeth in replying sharply to Heydebrand on 10 November. Count Karl von Wedel, the senior official in Alsace-Lorraine, had once been considered likely to become Bülow's successor. Wedel regretted that the Conservatives under Heydebrand had used the 'most hateful, demagogic means to further their party goals.' They had done so under Bismarck too, Wedel noted; but now the Conservatives were 'seeking to excite the chauvinistic instincts of the people in order to secure their votes.'[73]

One of the most enlightening perspectives on the Moroccan crisis was provided by a moderate Conservative who had already proven himself able to bridge the gap between party and state. Before he accepted the position as Bülow's chancellery chief in 1904, and in the midst of a distinguished civil service career that culminated in his appointment as Bethmann's minister of the interior, Friedrich Wilhelm von Loebell had served on the Conservative Party's Committee of Five, to which Heydebrand also belonged. Yet like the two chancellors he served, Loebell was incapable of reconciling a critical stance towards the Conservative Party with a deeper commitment to authoritarian rule. In his unpublished memoirs, he wrote that 'even though I was naturally aware of the constraints and weaknesses of any party institution, I still always believed that one could work productively within the bounds of the German Conservative Party, if one always kept its great goals in sight.'[74] To be sure, this creative enterprise required more clever tactics as the party's program became 'sharper' and 'more rigid,' Loebell commented. Experience in later years further tempered his original optimism about how easily one could pursue these larger goals, and replaced it with a 'certain scepticism.' Nevertheless, he concluded, 'in my innermost heart I always remained loyal to the fundamental beliefs of my party.'

In November 1911, just one day after Heydebrand's outburst in the Reichstag, Loebell wrote to Bethmann. He, too, was critical of Heydebrand, but he appealed to the chancellor not to abandon moderate Conservatives. With reference to Heydebrand's speech, Loebell asked: 'Is it loyal, conservative policy to speak of washing away sins, to excite popular passions ... and to bellow for the applause of the rabble?' Loebell acknowledged that Heydebrand had delivered 'a fine speech, a spirited and clever speech,' but it had been 'the speech of an *advocatus diaboli*.' Heydebrand's words had been neither respectful nor fair, Loebell continued, and they had done more harm than good to the Fatherland by 'tearing down the authority that, according to tradition and the party program, one should protect.' Heydebrand erred if he believed that such a speech represented the mood of the party. Therefore, Loebell advised Bethmann to take no action against the Conservatives: 'we must first survive [the elections of] 12 January without new complications.' Loebell saw the possibility that the Reichstag elections might represent 'the beginning of an improvement in our situation.' Yet it was clear that he conceived of this new beginning as a repudiation of Heydebrand's tactics: 'It will indeed be a terrible Philippi for my poor party, which is led so falsely.' Posterity would be hard on Heydebrand, Loebell concluded: 'One will later say of him that he was a courageous man but a calamitous party leader.'[75]

A similarly revealing retrospective on the crisis of November 1911 was provided by the National Liberal Eugen Schiffer, who felt that Bethmann's indecisive character had caused a great opportunity to be missed. At a parliamentary dinner, Bethmann once asked Schiffer why the National Liberals seemed to regard him as a 'political ox.' 'Do I not do what I can?' inquired the chancellor: 'In plenary session I am attacked by Heydebrand. I answer him and earn generous applause. I do not believe I exaggerate when I say that I almost always emerge the victor from speaking duels with him. But after three days everyone has forgotten my triumph, and I am dealt with, attacked, and mobbed precisely as if I had not beaten him.' Schiffer's (alleged) reply to Bethmann was startling in its insight and forthrightness. The chancellor did not exploit his victories over the Conservatives, Schiffer explained, because he believed that he had to excuse himself for striking out at them too harshly. He told Bethmann: 'You lay Heydebrand out in the sand; but then you help him up, shake the dust off his coat, and ask him if he has been hurt.' Perhaps Bethmann felt himself 'inwardly too closely bound to this party and its members.' Or maybe it was his nature to avoid 'brutal decisiveness.' Perhaps he found it tactically important that things not come to a climax, to a full break. But what was at stake was not a matter of personal or party enmity but of great objective issues. One could not evade such issues, Schiffer warned Bethmann: 'Evasion can prepare the battle,' he wrote, but ultimately the battle had to be 'taken up and fought out.'[76]

Did Schiffer's admonition have any effect on Bethmann's attitude towards the Conservatives? In his correspondence with Loebell, Riezler, Bülow, Valentini, and the Kaiser during November 1911, Bethmann explained why he had replied so sharply to Heydebrand's attack and how he viewed the Conservatives' new strategy for popularity.[77] To Loebell he wrote that 'you know me and understand that I do not like to speak in this tone, and all the less towards a Conservative.' But the Conservatives, Bethmann added, 'could have kept the national wind in their sails without making such irresponsible noises and distancing themselves so openly from the government.' Thus, instead of leading them back into the government fold, the Conservatives' effort to achieve popular appeal had set them further at odds with the chancellor. 'I follow no policy of revenge,' Bethmann wrote to Loebell, 'but I fear that the imperial government – whether it is led by me or by another chancellor – will find it more and more difficult to preserve a fundamentally conservative orientation in its policies if there is no change in the leadership of the Conservative Party.'

His Majesty's Disloyal Opposition?

Now the Conservative Party has sunk to complete insignificance, and the Centre and the Social Democrats are trump. Philippi is here.
    Ernst Bassermann, leader of the National Liberal Party, April 1912 [78]

After November 1911 the chancellor drifted towards more explicit criticism of the Conservatives, and they more directly opposed his policies. Bethmann still claimed that he could steer a diagonal course, enlighten the Conservative Party, and avoid his own Philippi. Just as vehemently, the Conservatives claimed that their uncompromising policy towards liberalism had been the correct one, in 1909 and afterward. The government's military and fiscal legislation in 1912/13 illustrated that Bethmann and his ministers were objectively aware that there existed an alternate parliamentary majority – one excluding the Conservatives. Yet the government continued to regard a decisive anti-Conservative policy as incompatible with authoritarian principles.

Addressing a Prussian state ministry meeting of March 1912, Bethmann still thought he could help the Conservatives overcome their errors of political judgment.[79] He told his colleagues that the same Reichstag majority should pass the upcoming Army Bill and the new taxes necessary to cover its expense. The Conservatives had declared that they would support the army increases but would never vote for an inheritance tax. In refusing to compromise, Bethmann felt, they were merely reopening the political wounds they had first inflicted – on themselves and the nation – in 1909. On the other hand, if they were prepared to sacrifice for the needs of the military, the Conservatives would thereby remove forever the hatred and demagoguery that had been directed against the party in the winter of 1911/12.[80]

Despite these determined words, Bethmann proposed entering into negotiations with the parties with no firm program. He conceded that this tactic left his government open to the charge of 'indecisiveness' and that negotiations were made more difficult by the National Liberals' 'wavering attitude.' But the issue was too serious to approach any other way. The Conservatives could not be challenged directly. As Bethmann concluded: 'If the Army Bill were to be defeated because no agreement as to funding could be achieved, should one then dissolve the Reichstag? From which parties would one want to draw support?' In any case, a new Reichstag 'would be no better than the present one.'

By May 1912 'a kind of truce' had been reached in 'the wretched war over the inheritance tax.'[81] The army increases had been approved. But the left liberals and the National Liberals were outraged that the government had paid more heed to Conservative wishes than to those of the Left. In the Reichstag Bassermann pointedly asked the chancellor why the National Liberals were always called upon to abandon *their* principles.[82] And in private Bassermann complained to former chancellor Bülow that his prophecy had been fulfilled: 'Philippi has arrived. In the Wilhelmstraße [the government quarter], complete helplessness ... Everything has fallen through!'[83] Because of this frustration and anger at the government's apparent rebuff, the National Liberals and the Centre Party pushed through a resolution calling for the government to reintroduce a comprehensive inheritance tax within a year, leaving the Conservatives standing on the sidelines.

By late 1912 the Reich treasury again had to draft a tax bill acceptable to the Conservatives.[84] In notes Bethmann prepared after reading this draft, the chancellor indicated his expectation that the Centre Party and the Conservatives, now loosely allied in the Black-Blue Bloc, would oppose the tax.[85] But if the government were to force the tax through parliament with the help of the Left, the bloc's defeat would be 'so devastating that the conservative principle would suffer a blow from which it could hardly recover.' This defeat, in turn, would 'put off the possibility of renewed cooperation among the bourgeois [i.e., non-socialist] parties far into the future.' Bethmann observed that 'the government could not retreat from such a conflict, even against the conservative elements in the country, if it were a matter of national necessity and if the liberal elements found themselves in a mood that would make it appear possible that we could govern with them for some length of time.' However, the chancellor concluded that 'both prerequisites are not at hand.'[86]

Bethmann was frustrated and angered by the Conservative Party's continued opposition when a compromise tax bill was finally passed in June 1913. He countered Westarp's and Heydebrand's denunciation of the government's 'feeble performance' with an attack of his own in the semi-official *Norddeutsche Allgemeine Zeitung*.[87] Privately, Bethmann evidently derived some satisfaction from the Conservatives' isolation. He complained that they demanded that 'the government march through thick and thin for them,' but that they did not 'want to support it in return.' Bethmann was even happy to see 'this democratic Reichstag' accept 'such a gigantic military bill.' Yet he was fully aware that further difficulties loomed on the horizon.

The consequences of his failure to win over the Conservatives were going to be large, for three reasons. First, the liberals' 'revenge' for 1909 would not make them less eager to break down the bastions of conservatism and expand the powers of the Reichstag. Second, Bethmann had aroused the indignation of the Kaiser by appearing to concede too much to the Left on an issue that touched on Wilhelm's unchallenged authority in military matters.[88] Third and most important for our discussion, the Conservatives' defeat did not induce them to be more reasonable in the future.

The Conservatives were not yet willing to campaign openly for Bethmann's dismissal, as the nationalist opposition was already doing. As in 1909, Conservatives had no wish to convey the impression that a parliamentary crisis had caused the resignation of a German chancellor. Nonetheless, as they began to spin their 'secret intrigues' against

Bethmann – intrigues that were not dissimilar to those of leading Pan-Germans – Westarp, Heydebrand, and the leaders of the Agrarian League saw little chance of a reconciliation with the chancellor.[89] Bethmann's hope that the two sides could commit themselves to an 'objective program' for the future was regarded by Westarp as too dangerous a 'blank cheque' to give the government. Heydebrand agreed.[90] In July 1913 he observed that Bethmann had 'the correct impression that we ... cannot govern [!] with him, that is, with the policy he represents.' The chancellor was 'finally beginning to see that even he, properly speaking, cannot do so.' The preceding four years had provided ample evidence of that, Heydebrand believed: Bethmann's 'scoffing remarks,' 'connivance,' and 'declarations of loyalty' could neither change the Conservatives' attitude nor induce 'votes or promises of support, to which he cannot lay claim.' As Heydebrand wrote to Westarp, it was Bethmann himself who would be kept in check[91] by 'the pentacle in Prussia' (by which Heydebrand meant the five bastions of Conservative power: the Prussian House of Deputies, the Prussian House of Lords, the Prussian civil service, the Prussian ministry of state, and the Prussian royal court). Thus Germany's last major battle over domestic legislation before the war, originally planned to bring together the government and the right-wing parties, had ended in another stand-off. Further crises in party-government relations in the winter of 1913/14 – over the Zabern Affair, tariffs, and rumours of another Prussian suffrage reform bill – added no new ingredients to the volatile mixture of optimism and pessimism on both sides.[92]

Conclusions

What can we conclude about the relative importance of structural and personal factors shaping the relationship between Conservatives and the imperial German government? We have seen that Bethmann's hopes, insights, and expectations were a mass of contradictions. The chancellor at the same time hoped for a change of Conservative leadership, recognized that it had to come from within the party, and (in his more fatalistic moments) expected that Heydebrand would prevail. Yet these perceptions, however idiosyncratic, were all reactions to the larger, more general problem of reconciling a semi-parliamentary political system with maintenance of the authoritarian state. This dilemma, too, was recognized by all the principal figures involved.[93] Westarp condemned Bethmann primarily for his willingness to consider parliamentary cooperation with the Social Democrats. Heydebrand claimed the mistrust between him and the chancellor was rooted in the latter's 'inner sympathy for liberalism and democracy [and] insufficient consideration of Prussia and Prussian circumstances.' Bethmann, of course, had often considered the larger question of conservatism's role in Prussia and the Reich. As he wrote to Gustav Schmoller in 1910: 'Our Prussian landed aristocracy is certainly not free of faults. However, it provides us, in the army, state administration, and local government, with forces that we can as little do without in the present as in the past.'[94] Believing that the Conservative Party could be shown the way towards a reformist conservative policy, Bethmann observed that one could never think of marginalizing the Conservatives; instead, one had to 'modernize' them.

Unable to turn to the forces of the Left after 1909 because he considered them politically radical or intellectually mediocre, Bethmann proved unable to overcome political deadlock on the domestic front. Because so many conservatives in the German establishment shared his view of liberalism, the prospect of a reformist conservative course remained an ideal that was inspiring but, in the long run, disastrous. It prevented a break from unyielding men such as Heydebrand, and it blinded Bethmann and others to the possibilities for fundamental reform. Instead it was the Conservatives who saw more clearly than Bethmann the options that lay open for a liberal, reformist policy in Germany, a policy that might have arisen directly from a head-on clash between the Conservative Party and the authoritarian state. Heydebrand conjured up this calamitous future in speaking with a left-liberal parliamentarian in 1910: 'The future does indeed belong to you; the mass will assert itself and deprive the aristocrats of their influence. A strong statesman may stem this tide, but only for a while. We will not, however, abandon our position of our own free will. Nevertheless, if you force us to, then you will have what you want.'[95]

The agrarians were not blind to such possibilities either. In May 1912 Gustav Roesicke replied to a proposal from an Agrarian League member that the league should leave the government 'high and dry' if it failed to defend agriculture. 'From the Conservative side,' replied Roesicke, 'we cannot render the government too afraid that we will abandon it, because 1. it no longer draws support from us, and does not even want to, and 2. it will find, as soon as it is liberal, a cooperative, jubilant reception on the Left.' That such hard-nosed politicians as Heydebrand and Roesicke should have seen these options, and that the philosophical Bethmann did not, may be regarded as either wholly obvious or highly ironic. In any case, because of the person who occupied the highest political office in the land, it was the *perception* of deadlock that prevailed.

Despite the importance of these structural dimensions of the problem – the problem of modernizing Germany *and* the German Right – neither contemporary assessments nor more scholarly ones since have managed to divert our attention from the personalities involved. Heydebrand may have criticized Bethmann's sympathy for liberalism and democracy, but he concluded that it was the 'weakness of his character that precluded an energetic, firm, purposeful, and determined policy, either domestically or in foreign affairs.' Westarp was unsure whether Bethmann's apparent willingness to compromise with democracy was the result of a 'personal liberalizing policy' or due simply to 'indecisiveness' and 'lack of fighting spirit.' Westarp remembered conversations in which he and Heydebrand 'could not decide which of the two faults appeared to us to be the more fateful.'[96] Because Bethmann's personal relationship with the Conservative Party reflected unresolved paradoxes of governmentality in Imperial Germany, it is perfectly legitimate to concentrate on human shortcomings, not merely the pressures of circumstance, to explain the disasters that befell Germany in the summer of 1914. Thus, too, the political limits of the authoritarian imagination are inseparable from the personal shortcomings that contributed to blinkered thinking among statesmen and other Germans during the entire imperial era.

In the July crisis of 1914 Bethmann appeared to be as ready to oppose the plans of the Conservative Party as Bülow had been in 1909. He insisted that a 'reasonable' policy for the authoritarian German state did *not* entail fighting a war to preserve the Conservatives' ascendance domestically: 'If the Conservatives demand special consideration from the government, they themselves must show it first.'[97] Kurt Riezler, in close contact with Bethmann during the crisis, described the chancellor's attitude more starkly: 'The chancellor expects from a war, whatever its outcome, a revolution of all existing order.' Bethmann felt that 'everything has grown so old,' Riezler reported. Germany's spiritual and intellectual decline weighed heavily on the chancellor. But in this crisis Bethmann dwelt on the practical problems he faced in an age when the authoritarian state confronted the challenge of democracy more directly than ever before. In Bethmann's eyes, some of the blame for bringing Germany to this point lay with the liberals – the 'intelligentsia' and the 'professors.' But in the end he turned against much of what Heydebrand, not the liberals, stood for. As Riezler reported: 'Heydebrand has said that a war would strengthen the patriarchal spirit and order.' Bethmann, however, was 'outraged at such nonsense.'[98]

Was it insight about the effects of modern industrialized warfare that caused Bethmann to react to Heydebrand's 'nonsense' in this manner? Was it a feeling of helplessness? Or was it a sign that he finally had begun to see the necessity of breaking with the old order in Prussia? We will never know. As Riezler seemed to realize during those final days before Imperial Germany's own Philippi, the chancellor did not understand the implications of his struggle to identify and reconcile conflicting aspects of German authoritarianism. '[Bethmann] is not at all one-dimensional. His shrewdness is probably as great as his ineptitude. The two are mixed and variable.'

NOTES

1 Geoff Eley, *Reshaping the German Right: Radical Nationalism and Political Change after Bismarck* (New Haven, 1980); Eley, *From Unification to Nazism: Reinterpreting the German Past* (Boston, 1986); Dirk Stegmann, *Die Erben Bismarcks. Parteien und Verbände in der Spätphase des Wilhelminischen Deutschlands* (Cologne, 1970); Stegmann, 'Zwischen Repression und Manipulation: Konservative Machteliten und Arbeiter- und Angestelltenbewegung 1910–1918. Ein Beitrag zur Vorgeschichte der DAP/NSDAP,' *Archiv für Sozialgeschichte* 12 (1972): 351–432; Stegmann, 'Vom Neokonservatismus zum Proto-Faschismus: Konservative Partei, Vereine und Verbände 1893–1920,' in *Deutscher Konservatismus im 19. und 20. Jahrhundert*, ed. Stegmann, Bernd-Jürgen Wendt, and Peter-Christian Witt (Bonn, 1983), 199–230; Stegmann, 'Literaturbericht. Konservatismus und nationale Verbände im Kaiserreich,' *Geschichte und Gesellschaft* 10 (1984): 409–20. See also Roger Chickering, *We Men Who Feel Most German: A Cultural Study of the Pan-German League, 1886–1914* (Boston, 1984); Abraham J. Peck, *Radicals and Reactionaries: The Crisis of Conservatism in Wilhelmine Germany* (Washington, DC, 1978); and Marilyn Shevin Coetzee, *The German Army League: Popular Nationalism in Wilhelmine Germany* (New York and Oxford, 1990).
2 I do not regard it as self-evident that the National Liberal Party was right-wing – or, indeed, that the Catholic Centre Party should not also be included under that rubric.

400 Tension and Détente

3 Hans-Jürgen Puhle, *Agrarische Interessenpolitik und preußischer Konservatismus im wilhelminischen Reich 1893–1914* (orig. 1966; 2nd ed., Bonn-Bad Godesberg, 1975).
4 In David Blackbourn and Geoff Eley, *The Peculiarities of German History* (Oxford, 1984), Eley notes (119) our continuing uncertainty about Bethmann's political philosophy.
5 Bethmann to Clemens von Delbrück, 8 Sept. 1917, cited in Konrad H. Jarausch, *The Enigmatic Chancellor: Bethmann Hollweg and the Hubris of Imperial Germany* (New Haven, 1973), 349.
6 Klaus Hildebrand, *Bethmann Hollweg – der Kanzler ohne Eigenschaften?* (Düsseldorf, 1970); Eberhard von Vietsch, *Bethmann Hollweg. Staatsmann zwischen Macht und Ethos* (Boppard am Rhein, 1969); Willibald Gutsche, *Aufstieg und Fall eines kaiserlichen Reichskanzlers* (Berlin, 1973).
7 See Jarausch, *Enigmatic Chancellor.*
8 *RT Sten. Ber.*, Bd. 283, 64–5, 16 Feb. 1912.
9 Bethmann's marginalia on the *Vossische Zeitung*, 18 July 1914, in BA Koblenz, Rkz. Nr. 1392, Bl. 37.
10 Bernhard von Bülow, *Denkwürdigkeiten*, 4 vols. (Berlin, 1930), 2:520–1.
11 For details and further references, see chapter 9.
12 Marginalia (8 Apr.) to notes of 6 Apr. 1909, cited in Peter-Christian Witt, *Die Finanzpolitik des Deutschen Reiches von 1903 bis 1913* (Lübeck, Hamburg, 1970), 275.
13 *RT Sten. Ber.*, Bd. 237, 8585–9.
14 For the following, see Bülow, *Denkwürdigkeiten*, 2:520–2; Kuno von Westarp, 'Die Konservative Partei und das Ende des Bülowblocks,' *Süddeutsche Monatshefte* 28, no. 6 (Sonderheft: *Fürst Bülow*): 416ff.
15 See Bülow to Loebell, 23 Jan. 1910, in BA Koblenz, NL Friedrich Wilhelm von Loebell, Nr. 6, Bl. 91. I am grateful to Wolfgang von Loebell for access to this collection.
16 Undated notes [July 1909] and Bülow to Loebell, 9 Aug. 1909, ibid, Bl. 48, 58.
17 Bülow to Rudolf von Valentini, 31 Aug. 1909, in ZStA II Merseburg, NL Rudolf von Valentini, Nr. 3, Bl. 6–7; Bülow to Axel von Kaphengst, 31 Mar. 1911, in BA Koblenz, NL Friedrich Wilhelm von Loebell, Nr. 7, Bl. 23; Bülow, *Denkwürdigkeiten*, 2:522.
18 Bernhard von Bülow, *Imperial Germany* (New York, 1914), 163ff.
19 *Das Tagebuch der Baronin Spitzemberg*, ed. Rudolf Vierhaus (Göttingen, 1960), 520; see also Crown Prince Wilhelm to Bülow [n.d.] in Bülow, *Denkwürdigkeiten*, 2:520, and Wilhelm II to Bethmann, 31 Dec. 1911, cited in Hans-Günter Zmarzlik, *Bethmann Hollweg als Reichskanzler 1909–1914* (Düsseldorf, 1957), 43.

20 Bülow, *Denkwürdigkeiten*, 2:181; see also Walther Rathenau, *Tagebuch 1907–1922*, ed. Hartmut Pogge von Strandmann (Düsseldorf, 1967), 141.
21 Prussian state ministry meeting protocol in ZStA II Merseburg, Rep. 90a B III 2 b Nr. 6, Bd. 158, 14 July 1909, Bl. 200–1 (hereafter cited as Pr. St. Min., Bd., date, Bl.).
22 *Tagebuch ... Spitzemberg*, ed. Vierhaus, 519.
23 For this and the following, see Jarausch, *Enigmatic Chancellor*, 78–9, 445.
24 Pr. St. Min., Bd. 162, 31 Dec. 1913, Bl. 192ff.
25 Wilhelm Albers, *Die Besiegten von Philippi! Ein Wort zu den Reichstagswahlen von 1912* (Bielefeld, 1912), 1, 18–19.
26 *Konservative unter sich* (Berlin, 1909). Provincial reverberations are found in *Die Reichsfinanzreform 1909 im Lichte der Öffentlichkeit*, ed. Wilhelm Schmidt, 2nd ed. (Karlsruhe, 1909), and *Zur Steuer der Wahrheit*, 'von einem ostpreußischen Konservativen' (Königsberg, 1909).
27 *Konservative Männer in Stadt und Land!* (13 Nov. 1909), manifesto of the Konservative Vereinigung.
28 Kuno von Westarp, *Konservative Politik im letzten Jahrzehnt des Kaiserreiches*, 2 vols. (Berlin, 1935), 1:397–8.
29 *Parteitag des Konservativen Provinzialvereins für Pommern* (n.p., n.d. [1910]), 31, 87, 94.
30 *Kreuzzeitung*, 10 Feb. 1910.
31 *Reichsbote*, 13 Aug. 1912; original emphasis.
32 See *Kreuzzeitung*, 4, 8, and 11 Mar. 1912; *Deutsche Tageszeitung*, 15 Nov. 1912.
33 *Freisinnige Zeitung*, 12 July 1914; *Berliner Tageblatt*, 22 July 1914.
34 Westarp to Heydebrand, 8 and 15 Jul. 1914, typewritten MS transcription from the archive of the late Dr Friedrich Freiherr Hiller von Gaertringen, Gärtringen.
35 See Stegmann, *Erben Bismarcks*, passim.
36 At a delegates' meeting of the East Prussian Conservative Association in October 1913, every point on the agenda dealt with some aspect of organization. See ZStA II Merseburg, NL Wolfgang Kapp, CVIII Nr. 3, Bl. 255.
37 BA Koblenz, NL Eugen Schiffer, Nr. 9, H. 1, Bl. 23.
38 See 'Sitzungen des geschäftsführenden Ausschusses' [1913], meeting of 12 Nov. 1913, in BA Koblenz, R 45 I, Nationalliberale Partei, Nr. 4, Bl. 65ff.; the NLP's 'Organisations-Statistik 1907–1912' (ibid., Bl. 19); and the 'Jahresberichte landschaftlicher Organisationen und Wahlkreise' (ibid., Bl. 21ff. and 31ff.), to compare reports for 1911 and 1912. Also A. Wynecken to the NLP's executive committee, 18 Oct. 1913, in BA Potsdam, NL Ernst Bassermann, Nr. 9, Bl. 87.

39 The *Frankfurter Zeitung*, 19 Oct. 1912, referred to the 'little club with room for all.'
40 See *inter alia* Ernst Deetjen, *Freikonservativ! Die nationale Mittelpartei* (Breslau, 1913); *Die Partei der Zukunft*, 'von einem Deutschen' (Leipzig, 1914); *Die Bayerische Reichspartei 1911–1913* (Munich, 1914); and the Free Conservatives' circular (n.d. [early 1912]), to regional party leaders, in BA Koblenz, NL Alfred Hugenberg, Nr. 31, Bl. 22ff.
41 David Blackbourn, *Class, Religion and Local Politics in Germany* (New Haven and London, 1980), 11.
42 Bethmann Hollweg to the Prussian envoy in Baden, Carl von Eisendecher, letter of 26 Nov. 1911, in PA AA Bonn, NL Carl von Eisendecher, Nr. 1/2, Bl. 24–5.
43 For this and the following, see Bethmann Hollweg to Eisendecher, letters of 27 Dec. 1910, 16 Nov. 1911, and 22 Feb. 1912, ibid., Nr. 1/2, Bl. 20–1, 24, 29–30.
44 The double meaning here derived from the 'black' Centre Party, which was loosely aligned with the Conservatives after 1909 in the Black-Blue Bloc.
45 Diary entry for 27 May 1912, in *Tagebuch ... Spitzemberg*, ed. Vierhaus, 545.
46 Bethmann to Loebell, 16 Aug. 1911, in BA Koblenz, Rkz. Nr. 1391/5, Bl. 192.
47 This was certainly not a novel practice; see also chapter 2.
48 Bethmann to Schwerin-Löwitz, 29 June 1911 [draft], in BA Koblenz, Rkz. Nr. 1391, Bl. 110.
49 See also Bethmann to Eisendecher, 27 Dec. 1910, in PA AA Bonn, NL Eisendecher, Nr. 1/2, Bl. 20–1; Bethmann to Bülow, 14 July 1911, in BA Koblenz, NL Bernhard von Bülow, Nr. 64, Bl. 26–36.
50 For example, Wilhelm Schmidt, *'Großblock' oder 'bürgerlicher Block'? Ein politischer Wegweiser für alle rechtsstehenden Wähler in Baden* (Heidelberg, n.d. [1911]).
51 BA-MA, Freiburg i. Br., NL Alfred von Goßler, Nr. 1, Bl. 40ff., 'Erinnerungen.' I am grateful to Frau Toni von Goßler for allowing me access to this collection.
52 La Roche to Wahnschaffe, 7 Oct. 1910, in BA Koblenz, Rkz. Nr. 1391, Bl. 86. The Baden case is illuminated in an unpublished manuscript by Hans-Jürgen Kremer, 'Die Konservative Partei im Großherzogtum Baden 1876–1914.'
53 He is referring to the National Liberal agrarian Baron Cornelius von Heyl zu Herrnsheim.
54 Correspondence between Mehnert, Loebell, and Bethmann in Aug. 1911 is in BA Koblenz, Rkz. Nr. 1391/5, Bl. 192–8.

55 In late 1910 Bethmann had written that the Conservative defeat he foresaw in the next elections would lead to a more stable situation only if that defeat signified the victory of 'moderate' (i.e., not left-wing) liberalism.
56 BA Koblenz, NL J. Alter [pseud. for Franz Sontag], Nr. 6, 'Kampfjahre der Vorkriegszeit' (MS), 27–8, for this and the following remarks.
57 BA Koblenz, NL Eugen Schiffer, Nr. 1, 'Memorien' (MS), Heft 1, Bl. 34–47; unfortunately, these entries cannot be dated precisely.
58 Theodor Wolff, *Tagebücher 1914–1919*, ed. Bernd Sösemann (Boppard, 1984), pt. 1, 160, 350.
59 BA-MA, Freiburg i. Br., NL Goßler, Nr. 1, Bl. 43.
60 Cited in David Schoenbaum, *Zabern 1913: Consensus Politics in Imperial Germany* (London and Boston, 1982), 34.
61 Kurt Riezler, *Tagebücher, Aufsätze, Dokumente*, ed. Karl Dietrich Erdmann (Göttingen, 1972), 168, 172.
62 BA Koblenz, NL Alter, Nr. 6, 'Kampfjahre der Vorkriegszeit,' 27–8.
63 BA Koblenz, NL Schiffer, Nr. 1, 'Memorien,' Heft 1, Bl. 46.
64 Cited in Volker R. Berghahn, *Germany and the Approach of War in 1914* (London, 1973), title page.
65 See *inter alia* Fritz Fischer, *War of Illusions: German Policies from 1911 to 1914* (London, 1975), 71–94; and Chickering's briefer account in *We Men*, 262–7.
66 RT Sten. Ber., Bd. 268, 7721ff. (9 Nov. 1911) and 7756ff. (10 Nov. 1911).
67 See Bethmann to [Rudolf von Valentini], 17 Nov. 1911, in ZStA II Merseburg, 2.2.1, Nr. 667, Bd. 2, Bl. 86–7; and Arthur von Huhn (of the NLP's *Kölnische Zeitung*) to Bülow, 20 Nov. 1911, in BA Koblenz, NL Bülow, Nr. 108, Bl. 55.
68 See Beverly Heckart, *From Bassermann to Bebel: The Grand Bloc's Quest for Reform in the Kaiserreich, 1900–1914* (New Haven and London, 1974).
69 BA Koblenz, Rkz. Nr. 1391/5, Bl. 204; PA AA Bonn, I.A.A.b Deutschland Nr. 125, Nr. 3, Bd. 25, and I.A.A.m Sachsen (Königreich), Nr. 48, Bd. 20; Jürgen Bertram, *Die Wahlen zum Deutschen Reichtag vom Jahre 1912* (Düsseldorf, 1964).
70 Valentini to Ballin, 15 Nov. 1911, in ZStA II Merseburg, 2.2.1., Nr. 667, Bd. 2, Bl. 80–1; see also Ballin to Valentini, 19 Nov. 1911, ibid., Bl. 82–5, and Ballin to Wilhelm II, 12 Dec. 1911, ibid., Bl. 88–9.
71 *Tagebuch ... Spitzemberg*, ed. Vierhaus, 537–8, and on the crown prince.
72 'Die Regierung und die konservative Partei. Ein Exkurs in die deutsche Verfassung,' *Konservative Monatsschrift* 69, no. 3 (Dec. 1911): 233.
73 Wedel to Eisendecher, 12 Nov. 1911, in PA AA Bonn, NL Eisendecher, Nr. 2/3, Bl. 95–6.
74 BA Koblenz, NL Loebell, Nrn. 26–7, 'Erinnerungen.'

75 Loebell to Bethmann Hollweg, 12 Nov. 1911, in BA Koblenz, Rkz. Nr. 1391/5, Bl. 201.
76 BA Koblenz, NL Schiffer, Nr. 1, 'Memorien,' Heft 2, Bl. 85–6.
77 Bethmann to Loebell, 20 Nov. 1911 (reply to letter from Loebell of 12 Nov. 1911), in BA Koblenz, Rkz. Nr. 1391/5, Bl. 201ff.; cf. Bethmann to Eisendecher, 16 Nov. and 26 Dec. 1911, in PA AA Bonn, NL Eisendecher, Nr. 1/2, Bl. 24ff.; Bethmann to Bülow, 21 Nov. 1911, in BA Koblenz, NL Bülow, Nr. 64, Bl. 26ff.; Bethmann to [Valentini], 17 Nov. 1911, and Bethmann's telegram to Wilhelm II, 11 Nov. 1911, both in ZStA II Merseburg, 2.2.1, Nr. 667, Bd. 2, Bl. 86–7, 74–5.
78 Letter of 3 April 1912, in BA Koblenz, NL Bülow, Nr. 107, Bl. 153.
79 Pr. St. Min., Bd. 161, 4 Mar. 1912, Bl. 25ff., and for the following. See also Kuno von Westarp, *Die Wehr- und Deckungsvorlagen des Jahres 1913 und die konservative Partei* (Berlin, 1913); Witt, *Finanzpolitik*, 337–76; Shevin Coetzee, *German Army League*, 30–43.
80 See the SPD's *Worte und Taten der Konservativen* (Berlin, 1911), 21, 38–9.
81 Wahnschaffe to Valentini, 19 May 1912, cited in Zmarzlik, *Bethmann Hollweg*, 59.
82 *RT Sten. Ber.*, Bd. 284, 1301 (22 Apr. 1912).
83 Cited in Bülow, *Denkwürdigkeiten*, 3:89.
84 For this and the following, see [Reichsschatzamt], 'Denkschrift über die Einführung einer allgemeinen Besitzsteuer im Reiche,' n.d. [Oct. 1912], and Bethmann's 'Aufzeichnungen,' n.d., both in ZStA II Merseburg, 2.2.1, Nr. 27426, Bl. 8ff.
85 Witt, *Finanzpolitik*, 357ff.
86 Pr. St. Min., Bd. 162, 24 Feb. 1913, Bl. 36ff.
87 For this and the following, except where noted, see Jarausch, *Enigmatic Chancellor*, 98–99, 104–7, and Witt, *Finanzpolitik*, 372–3.
88 By the end of the year, the combination of the Kaiser's displeasure and the Conservatives' intrigues had already prompted Bethmann to consider resignation. He wrote to Eisendecher on 1 Oct. 1913: 'Precisely the factors that should ease my burden professionally, H[is] M[ajesty] and the Conservatives, make things more difficult for me, according to their whims and powers. I should have drawn the consequences of this fiction at the beginning of July, since in any case it is unavoidable in the long run' (PA AA Bonn, NL Eisendecher, Nr. 1/2, Bl. 44ff.).
89 See Westarp to Heydebrand, 3 July 1913, in Westarp, *Konservative Politik*, 1:388; Wangenheim to Roesicke, 20 June 1913, in ZStA I Potsdam, NL Conrad von Wangenheim, Nr. 7, Bl. 50.

90 Heydebrand to Westarp, 5 July 1913, in ZStA I Potsdam, NL Kuno von Westarp, Nr. 1, Bl. 162.
91 Literally, 'made small': 'das Pentagram in Preußen macht ihn klein!'
92 See further, Westarp to Heydebrand, 18 and 25 Dec. 1913, and Heydebrand's replies, 20 and 27 Dec. 1913, in ZStA I Potsdam, NL Westarp, Nr. 1, Bl. 190ff.
93 For the following, see Westarp, *Konservative Politik*, 1:338ff. and 378ff.; and Ernst von Heydebrand und der Lasa, 'Beiträge zu einer Geschichte der konservativen Partei in den letzten 30 Jahren (1888 bis 1919),' *Konservative Monatsschrift* 77 (1920): 605–6.
94 Bethmann to Gustav Schmoller, 9 Apr. 1910, cited in Zmarzlik, *Bethmann Hollweg*, 44; compare Philipp Eulenburg to Bülow, 1 Mar. 1901, in BA Koblenz, NL P. Eulenburg, Nr. 57, Bl. 23 ff. (cited chap. 9, note 37).
95 For this and the following passage, see Hermann Pachnicke, *Führende Männer im alten und im neuen Reich* (Berlin, n.d. [1930]), 63; Roesicke to Joachim von Levetzow-Sielbeck, 2 May 1912, in ZStA I Potsdam, NL Wangenheim, Nr. 7, Bl. 37ff.
96 See the works by Heydebrand and Westarp cited in note 93 above. For the period up to 1920, see also James Retallack, 'Zwei Vertreter des preußischen Konservatismus im Spiegel ihres Briefwechsels: Die Heydebrand-Westarp Korrespondenz,' in *'Ich bin der letzte Preuße.' Der politische Lebensweg des konservativen Politikers Kuno Graf von Westarp*, ed. Larry Eugene Jones and Wolfram Pyta (Cologne, etc., 2006), 33–60.
97 From Bethmann's marginalia (July 1914) on a newspaper clipping in BA Koblenz, Rkz. Nr. 1392, Bl. 37.
98 Diary entry of 7 July 1914, in BA Koblenz, Kl. Erw. 584–1, Bl. 2ff., for this and the concluding observation.

Acknowledgments

As noted in the introduction, this book has had a dual focus: historical and historiographical. Each chapter has aimed to convey the drama of historical processes that transformed the German Right over sixty or more years; each has also considered how modern scholars have studied such transformations and the historical patterns they have discerned.

Readers will have to judge for themselves, but neither this book's method nor its central findings can easily be ascribed to any one scholarly camp in the field of modern German history. The revisionists of the 1960s spawned the revisionists of the 1980s. Now, twenty years further on, no clear division exists between orthodox and revisionist views. It seems appropriate, therefore, to point out that these chapters were conceived in the context of a generational anomaly that situated the author, as it were, between the fronts. Relatively few historians of Imperial Germany emerged from graduate school in the early 1980s. Hence the only available option was to draw eclectically on the work of colleagues from more than one generation. Doing so has been gratifying and, I hope, beneficial to the conclusions offered here.

Among scholars who have already reached retirement or soon will, this book reflects the inspiration of Gerhard A. Ritter (Berlin), James J. Sheehan (Stanford), Hartmut Pogge von Strandmann (Oxford), and Hans-Ulrich Wehler (Bielefeld). A somewhat younger group has been even more influential in shaping the questions that inform these chapters. This group includes Margaret Lavinia Anderson (Berkeley), David Blackbourn (Cambridge, Mass.), Roger Chickering (Washington, DC), Geoff Eley (Ann Arbor), Richard J. Evans (Cambridge), and Peter Steinbach (Karlsruhe). Lastly, a younger group of scholars has influenced these chapters so deeply that it is difficult to say where inspiration ends and imitation begins. These scholars include Celia Applegate (Rochester), Brett Fairbairn (Saskatoon), Thomas Kühne (Worcester, Mass.), Simone Lässig (Washington, DC), and Helmut Walser Smith (Nashville).

This chronicling of scholarly debts is not presented simply to express my gratitude to fellow travellers or to say how much I admire scholars who think like me. It is intended to convey a sense of the institutional and intellectual environments within which this work was originally undertaken. Although these chapters contribute most directly to a social history of politics, each of them emerged from a running debate with many contending voices. As such, they combine intense engagement with others' interpretations and critical distancing from them. For that reason, this book seeks its ideal reader among those who are similarly engaged and critical.

Besides the colleagues already mentioned, each of whom was by turns appropriately supportive and demanding, it is a pleasure to express my gratitude to other friends and colleagues. Since 1987 I have been privileged to work with many talented graduate students at the University of Toronto, including my own PhD supervisees. In roughly chronological order of their completion dates, these supervisees include Thomas Bredohl, Marven Krug, Richard Steigmann-Gall, Marline Otte, Erwin Fink, Lisa Todd, and Deborah Neill. I have also received important assistance from other graduate students: John Bingham, Robin Brownlie, Krystyna Cap, Michael Cavey, Todd Craver, Ralph Czychun, Hilary Earl, Darla Fraser, Valerie Hébert, Benjamin Hett, Erin Hochman, Eric Lund, Ken Mills, Bill Newbigging, Andrea Geddes Poole, John Ondrovcik, Nadine Roth, Greg Smith, Johann Vollmer (Göttingen), Geoff Wichert, and Rebecca Wittmann. That some of these individuals have now become faculty colleagues in Toronto gives me special pleasure, as has the opportunity to host two Humboldt Foundation Feodor Lynen fellows in Toronto, who often provided selfless assistance and advice: Thomas Adam and Stefan Grüner.

My thinking on German history has received an important impetus each time I have had the opportunity to study and research abroad. I therefore owe a great debt to my hosts in Stanford (1983–5), James J. Sheehan; in Berlin (1993–4 and 1997), Peter Steinbach; and in Göttingen (2002–3), Bernd Weisbrod. For opportunities to read, write, and research abroad I am grateful to the Rhodes Trust, the Social Sciences and Humanities Research Council of Canada, the German Academic Exchange Service (DAAD), the TransCoop Program, the DAAD / University of Toronto Joint Initiative in German and European Studies, the Connaught Program at the University of Toronto, and especially the Alexander von Humboldt Foundation.

Other individuals who have supported or provided critical commentary on my work include Lynn Abrams, Robert Beachy, Gary Bonham(†), John Breuilly, Eckart Conze, Christian Jansen, Larry Eugene Jones, Alf Lüdtke, Thomas Mergel, Jan Palmowski, Karl Heinrich Pohl, Stuart T. Robson, and Siegfried Weichlein. The time I have spent in Britain and Germany would have been diminished in innumerable ways without the friendship and hospitality of Johannes Hahn and Gurli Jacobsen, Hans Horn, Jef McAllister, Ann Olivarius, and Ute and Friedrich Schilfert.

My wife, Helen E. Graham, and my children, Hanna and Stuart, have paid many times over for my distraction – so many, indeed, that it is impossible either to calculate or to dispatch this debt here. Since they know another project is nearing completion, perhaps they will begin thinking about how to collect. Instead I have dedicated this book – with equal affection and gratitude – to my father, who still reads everything I write, and to my mother, who does not.

Chapter 1, 'Habitus and Hubris,' draws on three sources. The first is a review essay entitled '"Ideology without Vision"? Recent Literature on Nineteenth-Century German Conservatism,' in the *Bulletin of the German Historical Institute, London* 13, no. 2 (May 1991): 3–22. The second source is my half of an essay, originally co-authored with Larry Eugene Jones, introducing a multi-authored study of German conservatism: 'German Conservatism Reconsidered: Old Problems and New Directions,' in *Between Reform, Reaction, and Resistance: Studies in the History of German Conservatism from 1789 to 1945*, ed. Larry Eugene Jones and James Retallack (Providence, RI, and Oxford, 1993), 1–30. I am grateful to Larry for permission to publish part of our joint essay here and relieve him of any responsibility for errors of fact or interpretation that remain. The third source is a half-dozen book reviews written for scholarly journals in the 1980s and 1990s.

Chapter 2, 'Fishing for Popularity,' was first rehearsed at a conference held at the University of Pennsylvania in February 1990. For that meeting I gave my paper the tongue-in-cheek title of 'Paradigms and "P-Words": Populism, Participation, and Propaganda in the *Kaiserreich*.' I returned to this essay and added more material while at the Free University Berlin in 1997. A shorter version appeared as

'Demagogentum, Populismus, Volkstümlichkeit. Überlegungen zur "Popularitätshascherei" auf dem politischen Massenmarkt des Kaiserreichs,' in the *Zeitschrift für Geschichtswissenschaft* 48, no. 4 (2000): 309–25, and then, more briefly still, as 'Deutsche Demagogie vor und nach dem Umbruch 1918/19,' in *Deutsche Umbrüche im 20. Jahrhundert*, ed. Dietrich Papenfuß and Wolfgang Schieder (Cologne, Weimar, Vienna, 2000), 163–72. This text appears here in English for the first time. Despite adding new material and fuller citations, I have tried to preserve the iconoclastic, inquiring tone of the original oral presentation.

Chapter 3, 'Meanings of Stasis,' originally appeared as 'Ideas into Politics: Meanings of "Stasis" in Wilhelmine Germany,' in *Wilhelminism and Its Legacies: German Modernities, Imperialism, and the Meanings of Reform, 1890–1930*, ed. Geoff Eley and James Retallack (Oxford and New York, 2003), 235–52. This chapter reflects my long engagement with the work of Geoff Eley. Over the years Geoff's critical reading and generous advice have made me rethink (though not always change) many points of the larger argument found in this book.

Chapter 4, 'Culture/Power/Territoriality,' is a new composite. Part of the text was published in German as 'Politische Kultur, Wahlkultur, Regionalgeschichte: Methodologische Überlegungen am Beispiel Sachsens und des Reiches,' in *Modernisierung und Region im wilhelminischen Deutschland. Wahlen, Wahlrecht und Politische Kultur*, ed. Simone Lässig, Karl Heinrich Pohl, and James Retallack (Bielefeld, 1995, 2nd rev. ed., 1998), 15–38. Other versions appeared as 'Politische Kultur in der Region,' in *Politische Kultur in Ostmittel- und Südosteuropa*, ed. Werner Bramke and Thomas Adam (Leipzig, 1999), 15–46, and as 'Kultur, Politik und regionenbezogene Identifikationsprozesse: Neuere Forschungen zum Thema "Sachsen in Deutschland,"' in *Comparativ* 10, no. 1 (2000): 112–31. Later parts of this chapter derive from introductions to three volumes of essays: 'Saxon Signposts: Cultural Battles, Identity Politics, and German Authoritarianism in Transition,' in *Saxon Signposts*, ed. James Retallack (special issue of *German History* 17, no. 4 [1999]), 455–69; 'Locating Saxony in the Landscape of German Regional History,' in *Saxony in German History: Culture, Society, and Politics, 1830–1933*, ed. James Retallack (Ann Arbor, 2000), 1–30; and 'Einleitung. Sachsen und Deutschland, Sachsen in Deutschland,' in *Sachsen in Deutschland. Politik, Kultur und Gesellschaft 1830–1918*, ed. James Retallack (Bielefeld and Gütersloh, 2000), 11–32.

Chapter 5, 'Governmentality in Transition,' originally appeared as 'Suffrage Reform, Corporatist Society, and the Authoritarian State: Saxon

Transitions in the 1860s,' in *Saxony in German History*, ed. Retallack (2000), 215–34.

Chapter 6, 'Citadels against Democracy,' was co-authored with Thomas Adam. I am grateful to Thomas for allowing me to publish it in English for the first time and in revised form; it goes without saying that I alone take responsibility for its present deficiencies. It originally appeared as James Retallack and Thomas Adam, '*Philanthropy* und politische Macht in deutschen Kommunen,' in *Zwischen Markt und Staat. Stifter und Stiftungen im transatlantischen Vergleich*, ed. Thomas Adam and James Retallack, which appeared as a special double issue of *Comparativ* 11, nos. 5–6 (2001): 106–38.

Chapter 7, 'Publicity and Partisanship,' took stock of ideas that were intended to receive more comprehensive treatment in a study that will probably never be completed but was provisionally entitled 'Political Journalism and Propaganda in Germany, 1770–1920: The Right-wing Struggle against Rationalism, Revolution, and the Jews.' The chapter first appeared as 'From Pariah to Professional? The Journalist in German Society and Politics, from the Late Enlightenment to the Rise of Hitler,' in *German Studies Review* 16 (1993): 175–223. In this chapter I deliberately omitted a discussion of right-wing allegations that Germany's press was controlled by the Jews, hoping to return to this subject at a later date.

Chapter 8, 'Building a People's Party,' is a new consolidation of material drawn from two principal sources. One part derives from my Oxford DPhil dissertation (1983) but adds new material I gathered in German archives later in the 1980s. This section was published as 'Anti-Semitism, Conservative Propaganda, and Regional Politics in Late Nineteenth-Century Germany,' *German Studies Review* 11, no. 3 (Oct. 1988): 377–403. In the 1990s I was able to pursue more intensive research in German regional archives. Some of this research was included in the essay entitled 'Conservatives and Antisemites in Baden and Saxony,' in *Saxon Signposts*, ed. Retallack, 507–26, and in longer form as 'Herrenmenschen und Demagogentum. Konservative und Antisemiten in Sachsen und Baden,' in *Sachsen in Deutschland*, ed. Retallack, 115–41.

Chapter 9, 'Conservatives *contra* Chancellor,' is based in part on material that was cut from my Oxford dissertation at the final stage of revision. The argument nevertheless benefits greatly from the questioning of my two DPhil examiners, John Röhl and Peter Pulzer. Part of this material was published as 'Conservatives *contra* Chancellor: Official Responses to the Spectre of Conservative Demagogy from Bismarck to

Bülow,' *Canadian Journal of History* 20 (August 1985): 203–36. The section focusing on Helldorff and the politics of notables presents new archival material and draws on an essay previously published only in German: 'Ein glückloser Parteiführer in Bismarcks Diensten – Otto von Helldorff-Bedra (1833–1908),' in *Konservative Politiker in Deutschland*, ed. Hans-Christof Kraus (Berlin, 1995), 185–203.

Chapter 10, 'The Road to Philippi,' was drafted while I was at Stanford University in the mid-1980s. It was intended to appear in a Festschrift for Otto Pflanze. Because of a disastrous series of delays with that Festschrift and then its final abandonment, the chapter was withdrawn, thoroughly revised, and published as 'The Road to Philippi: The Conservative Party and Bethmann Hollweg's "Politics of the Diagonal," 1909–1914,' in *Between Reform, Reaction, and Resistance*, ed. Jones and Retallack, 261–98.

For permission to republish whole essays, consolidated fragments of previously published work, and illustrations drawn from archives or other publications, I am grateful to the authors, editors, publishers, librarians, and archivists who have made this possible. I welcome any communication from holders of copyright whom I have not been able to reach directly. For his assistance in bringing this book to press and helping to launch the new series, German and European Studies, in which it appears, I am indebted to Len Husband, editor at the University of Toronto Press, and to my colleagues on the editorial board of that series. For compiling the index, Krystyna Cap deserves my sincere thanks.

On a final note, I am deeply grateful to the students, mentors, colleagues, friends, and general listeners who have heard oral presentations of these arguments over the years. Members of those audiences, like the individuals listed above, have helped me in my effort to remain an eager student of modern German history, rather than become a crusty advocate of entrenched viewpoints. In lieu of citing the many forums in which these chapters were first rehearsed orally, I offer participants in those discussions a collective thanks. I am particularly indebted to friends and colleagues who provided feedback on the final draft of the entire manuscript and offered innumerable suggestions to improve it: Roger Chickering, Thomas Kühne, Helmut Walser Smith, and two anonymous referees for the University of Toronto Press. All these people have contributed immensely to whatever originality these chapters once had and may retain.

Index

Page numbers in italics refer to illustrations.

absolutism, 16, 49, 54, 55
'achievement' (*Leistung*), 193, 195–6, 201, 210–11
Ackermann, Karl, *155*, 320n62
advertisements, 227, 234, 241, 251–2
agrarianism, agrarians, 7, 20, 36, 42, 45, 48, 50–1, 60–1, 81–2, 87, 111, 117, 134n42, 170, 174, 180, 184, 275, 279, 283–4, 291, 295–6, 298, 300, 302–4, 306–7, 320n53, 325–6, 332, 335, 345–8, 351, 353–8, 360–1, 363, *373*, 374–5, 381–2, 390, 396–7, 402n53. *See also* Agrarian League; Junkers; rural society and economy; estates, landed
Agrarian League, 42, 43, 58, 81–4, 87, 90, 97, 103n15, 104n22, 281, 291, 296, 303, 307, 320n15, 325–6, 345–9, 351–6, 361, 370, 381–2, 396, 397. *See also* agrarianism, agrarians; Junkers
Ahlwardt, Hermann, 97, 300, *301*, 336
Ahrweiler, 113

Albert (Saxon Crown prince), *155*
Allgemeine Zeitung, 229
Alltagsgeschichte, 142, 144, 148, 150, 154, 158, 162
Alsace-Lorraine, 391
'Alter, Junius.' *See* Sontag, Franz
Anderson, Margaret Lavinia, 12, 124
Anderson, Pauline R., 82
Andrae, Dr, 358
Anhalt-Dessau, Duchy of, 157
anti-capitalism, 48, 87, 332. *See also* capitalism
anti-democracy, 11–12, 23, 42, 195, 197, 212, 250, 253, 274, 297, 362. *See also* democracy, democratization
anti-feminism, 11, 258–60. *See also* women
anti-liberalism, 11, 23, 48, 87, 274–5, 281, 296, 306, 332. *See also* liberalism, liberals
anti-modernism, 42, 88. *See also* modernity
anti-parliamentarism, 11, 20, 23, 274–5, 384. *See also* parliament, parliamentarism
anti-revolutionary, 48–9, 56, 244, 247. *See also* revolution, revolutionary

antisemitism, antisemites, 3, 7, 11, 20, 22–3, 24n4, 30n46, 42, 58, 62, 83, 90, 94, 160, 203, 212, 273–83, *288*, 289–300, *301*, 302–13, 320n53, 322n79, 332, 335–7, *338*, 341–2, 344, 346, 349–51, 362

anti-socialism, 20, 100, 134n42, 193, 212, 275, 313, 344, 390. *See also* Social Democratic Party, Social Democrats; socialism, socialists

anti-socialist laws, 127, 197–8, 331, 333

Applegate, Celia, 138, 146

aristocracy, aristocrats, 3, 6, 14, 20, 35–9, 42–3, 45–50, 54, 56, 63, 82–3, 116, 137, 212, 274, 290–1, 322, 326, 364n5, 397. *See also* Prussia: aristocracy

Arndt, Ernst Mortiz, 232

army, 6, 15, 44, *155*, 294–5, 321n70, 379, 394, 397. *See also* military

Army Bill, 341, 394

art galleries, 206–8, 215

artisans, 3, 82, 111, 180, 210, 278, 281–2, 302–3, 346, 362

Association for Social Policy, 208

Association for the Distribution of Conservative Journals, 252

Association for the Distribution of Good, Popular Literature, 252

Association for the People's Welfare, 252

Association for the Protection of Artisans, 280

Association of German Editors, 257

Association of German Newspaper Publishers, 252, 256

Association of Tax and Economic Reformers, 296, 298

associations, associational life, 12, 45, 51, 57–9, 87, 92, 94, 96–9, 144, 173, 178, 211–12, 228, 234, 255–6, 258, 290, 307, 332, 341, 354–5, 357, 364n6, 379–81

Augustinus Association for the Cultivation of the Catholic Press, 255

Austria, 42, 170, 309, 328, 334

authoritarianism, authority, 7, 8, 9–18, 20, 23–4, 35, 45, 49, 55–6, 59, 65, 67, 70, 76, 80, 82, 95, 117, 120–4, 127–8, 137, 140, 151–4, 156, 158, 160, 172, 184–5, 193, 197, 199, 206, 212, 217, 225, 244, 251, 261, 263n6, 273, 289, 295–7, 304, 312–13, 331, 334, 340, 344, 349, *350*, 360, 362–3, 370–2, 374–5, 383, 385, 391–2, 394–9. *See also* political culture

Bachem, Julius, 244

Bachem, Karl, 244

Baden, Grand Duchy of, 200, 274, 277, 281–6, 289–91, 293–4, 296–7, 301–4, 306–8, 313, 317n31, 339, 348, 383, 385, 402n52; *Landtag*, 293, 295, 307

Badische Landpost, 283, 297, 303, 306

Badische Post, 250

Ballin, Albert, 390

banks, 111, 300, *305*

Barth, Theodor, 122, 251

Bassermann, Ernst, 380, 382–4, 386, 394

Bavaria, Kingdom of, 51, *86*, 200, 207, 274, 277–81, 296, 298, 313, 391; *Landtag*, 54

Bavarian Conservative Electoral Association, 280

Bavarian Peasants League, 50

Beachy, Robert, 153

Bebel, August, 185, 186
Bendix, Reinhard, 61
Berdahl, Robert M., 36, 45–9, 51, 61, 68
Berghahn, Volker R., 44
Berg-Schlosser, Dirk, 149
Berlin, Isaiah, 92, 146
Berlin, 3, 8, 21, 45, *53*, 55, 59, 63, 65, 72, *98*, 139, 173, 181, 247, 250, *253*, 256, 277–80, 296, 298, 330, 336, 340–1, 348, 355, 391
Berliner Revue, 296
Berliner Tageblatt, 260, 387
Berlin Parliament (1848), 59, 63
Berlin Press Association, 242, 255, 258
Berlin Workers Press, 255
Berly, Karl Peter, 248–9
Beta, Ottomar, 324n108
Bethmann Hollweg, Moritz August von, 41
Bethmann Hollweg, Theobald von, 57, 94, 117, *119*, 120, 327, 361, 370–2, 374–6, *377*, 378–9, 383–4, 386–7, 389–99, 403n55, 404n88
Beust, Friedrich Ferdinand von, 170, 172, 174, 181
Bewer, Max, 290, 324n108, *350*
Biedermann, Karl, 174, 189n, 229, 255
'Bielefeld school,' 43–4, 79
Bildung, 154, 157, 230. See also education
Bismarck, Otto von, 8, 10, 23, 41, 57, 75n106, 78, 84, 90, *93*, 94, 101, 105n47, 109, 111, 115, *118*, *119*, 121, 124, *125*, 126–9, 139, 168, 172, 175, 178, 180, 184, 197–8, 226, 237, 249, 278, 280–1, 290, 296–8, 313, 327–34, 340–1, 346, *350*, 371–2, *373*, 383, 391

Black-Blue Bloc, 126, 395, 402n44
Blackbourn, David, 78, 84–5, 87, 90–1, 94, 96, 124, 168
Blanckenburg, Moritz von, 57
Blaschke, Karlheinz, 144–5, 185–6
Bleichröder, Gerson von, 281
Bodelschwingh-Schwarzenhasel, Franz von, 348
Böckel, Otto, 304, 306, 336, *338*
Bödeker, Hans Erich, 230
Bonaparte, Napoleon, 245
Bonn, 381
Book Dealers Association, 234
Bourdieu, Pierre, 46
Bowman, Shearer Davis, 61, 62
Brandenburg, 45
Brandmann, Paul, 212
Bremen, 209
Briggs, Asa, 180
Brunner, Otto, 46
Buddenbrooks (Thomas Mann), 23–4
Bücher, Karl, 257, 260
Bülow, Bernhard von, 339–40, 348, 351–60, 374–6, 379, 383, 391, 393–4, 398
Bülow Bloc, 126, 354–5, 358
Bülow-Cummerow, Ernst von, 56
bureaucracy, bureaucrats, 6, 15, 17, 38, 44, 51–2, 112, 115, 123, 143, 150, 152, 173, 175, 178–80, 183, 212, 215, 226, 287, 294, 299, 351, 364n5, 379. *See also* Prussia: bureaucracy
burghers, 7, 51, 59, 95, 140, 175, 177, 192, 196, 200, 204–6, 209–212, 216. *See also* citizenship; citizens; middle classes
Burke, Edmund, 35, 67–8

Camus, Albert, 195
capitalism, 22, 38, 54, 62, 80, 82, 111,

117, 186, 262, 278, 281, 303–4, *305*, 308, 311. *See also* economy, economic development
Caprivi, Leo von, 334, 339, 342, 345–6, 383
Carlsbad decrees, 54, 247
Carsten, Francis L., 45
Cartel of German Writers Associations, 256
Cartel of Productive Estates, 66
Catholicism, Catholics, 94, 124, 134n42, 151, 240, 252, 278, 283, 285, 293, 295, 300, 333. *See also* church; clergy; German Centre Party; religion
censorship, 54, 245
Central Association of German Industrialists, 381
Central Information Bureau for the Catholic Press, 252
Centre Party. *See* German Centre Party
Chamberlain, Houston Stewart, 301
Chemnitz, 196, 198, 203–6, 208–15, 218n4, 220n28, 221n47, 311–12, 336
Chickering, Roger, 25n11, 66, 97, 99
Childers, Thomas, 99
Christianity, the 'Christian state,' 3, 6, 37, 56, 247, 252, 254, 274–6, 278, 282, 294–5, 297, 299, 302, 306–10, 314, 323n95, 332–3, 385. *See also* church; Protestantism, Protestants; religion
Christian Journal Association, 252
Christian Social Party, 67, 297–8, 309–10, 323n95, 331–2, 344. *See also* *Kreuzzeitung* group; Stöcker, Adolf
church, 56, 117, 124, 147, 279, 294, 332
cities. *See* urbanism, urbanization

citizenship, citizens, 17, 54, 91, 109, 139–40, 156–7, 159, 161, 169, 170, 173, 183, 185, 188n13, 193, 198–200, 205–7, 210–11, 213, 215–16, 220n28, 299, 310
civil liberties, 59, 127, 174, 228
civil society, 140, 152–3, 157, 169, 172
class, 8, 19, 38, 43–7, 50, 52, 60, 83, 87, 89, 109, 113, 138, 151–2, 156, 161, 169, 172, 177, 179–80, 184–5, 195, 200, 203, 205, 209, 282, 284. *See also* aristocracy; middle classes; suffrage; working classes, workers
Claß, Heinrich, 11, 12, 63, *64*, 65–6
clergy, 3, 44, 47, *86*, *125*, 178, 205, 229, 240, 294, 360, 379
Cologne, 379–80; Trade Academy, 56
Committee of Eleven, 331, 335
Committee of Fifty, 348
Committee of Five, 391
Committee of Three, 335
Communists, 89
Concordia, 255
Congress of German Farmers, 279
Conradi, Hermann, 229
Conservative Correspondenz, 250, 332, 347, 348
Conservative Women's Union, 380
constituencies, 45, 116, 120, 178–9, 185, 203, 303, 328, 339, 359, 382; rural, 44, 60, 116, 170, 179, 303; urban, 116, 178, 179, 180, 303
constitutionalism, constitution, 8, 10–11, 17–19, 39, 41, 44, 49, 55–6, 88–9, 115–16, 121, 127, 143, 156, 170, 175–7, 179, 183, 190n35, 349, 370–1
Constitutionelle Zeitung, 174
corporatism, 61, 84, 99, 111, 123, 169, 183

Cotta, Johann, 229–32
court: judicial, 7, 45, 188n13, 311, 327; royal, 6, 38, 44, 46, 54, 59, 100, 145, 249–50, 278, 293, 331, 339, 341, 347, *350*, 351–3, 355, 396
Craig, Gordon A., 24
Crowe, Joseph Archer, 176
culture, 17, 22–3, 67, 78, 108–10, 114–15, 120, 122, 137–40, 148–54, 156–8, 166n43, 206, 215–16, 231, 256, 257, 261, 366n37; popular, 153, 157
Czok, Karl, 144–6

Dahrendorf, Ralf, 43, 82
Daily Telegraph affair (1908), 121, 359
Darmstadt: Technical University, 256
Debit and Credit (Gustav Freytag), 100
Delbrück, Hans, 236, 244, 256–7, 334, 339
demagoguery, demagogues, 11, 13, 65, 76–85, 87–92, 94–7, 100, 101n1, 102n2, 103n15, 160, 193, 229–30, 238, 242, 248, 262, 273, 275, 277, 301, 303, 325, 327, 336–7, 339–42, 351, 353–4, 361, 383, 391, 394
democracy, democratization, 3, 6, 8, 10–15, 17–18, 20, 22, 28n35, 43–4, 49, 51–2, 57, 59, 67, 79, 81–2, 84, 89, 100–1, 104n22, 113, 123–4, 127, 134n42, 137, 139, 148, 160, 168–9, 172–3, 175, 177–8, 180–1, 183–4, 191n44, 192–3, 195–7, 199, 200, 211–12, 214, 216, 261, 274, 282, 303, 327, 331, 342, 346, 348, 351–2, 357, 361, 372, 380–1, 384, 386, 389, 395, 397, 398
Democracy and Kaiserdom (Friedrich Naumann), 82
Deutsche Allgemeine Zeitung, 229

Deutsche Landeszeitung, 296
Deutsche Reform, 309
Deutsche Reichspost, 281–2, 297
Deutsches Adelsblatt, 291
Deutsches Tageblatt, 297, 332
Deutsche Tageszeitung, 347
Deutschtum, 8, 299–301, 313, *350*
Diamond, Larry, 172
Diest-Daber, Otto von, 296
Dietz, Hermann, 307
Disraeli, Benjamin, 180–1
Dittmer, Lothar, 51–2, 54, 58
Dohna-Finckenstein, Georg zu, 355
Dresden, 150, 153, *155*, 160, 161, 172, 174, 179, 181, *182*, 196, 198, 203–6, 208, 212, 214, 218n4, 290, 293, 297, 306, 309–12
Dresden Historical Association, 146
Dresden Uprising (1849), 172
Dresdner Nachrichten, 306, 312
Drexler, Anton, 63

East Germany. *See* German Democratic Republic
East Prussia, 46, 60, 341, 345–7, 353, 382
East Prussian Conservative Association, 401n36
Economic Union, 355
economy, economic development, 8, 12, 15, 43, 45–6, 50, 54, 56, 60–1, 80–1, 94, 99, 109–12, 117, 123–4, 126, 130, 139, 142, 148, 152–3, 161–2, 169–70, 173–4, 177, 186, 197, 201–2, 208, 211, 217, 226, 230, 237, 239, 242, 256, 278, 281, 295, 297, 303–4, *305*, 306–8, 310, 312, 327, 370–1, 374, 383, 390
Economist, 57
editors, 7, 20, 51–2, 145, 233–6, 238,

243, *246*, 249, 257–8, 300, 302, 311, 346, 380
education, 44, 47, 81, 83, 112, 115, 157, 169–70, 193, 195, 202–4, 207, 233, 241, 245, 258, 260, 294
1848, revolution of, 36, 44, 46, 49, 52, 54–9, 62, 92, 228, 247
Eisendecher, Carl von, 383
Eksteins, Modris, 115
Elbe River, 20, 61, 347, 382
election campaigns, 21, 57, *86*, 89, 101, 116, 127, 150, 174, 193, 197, 275, 295, 306, 310, 329–30, 351, 384
elections, 11–13, 17, *21–2*, *53*, 89, *98*, 101, 116, 144, 173, 177, 179, 181, 193–4, *195*, 197–202, 210–13, 293, 330, 340, 351, 382, 391, 403n55; *Landtag*, 57, 116, 189n15, *194*, 214, 281, 307–8, 310–11, 318n32, 358; municipal, 199, 200, 202, 209, 310; Reichstag, 11–12, 26n18, *53*, 134n42, 189n15, 197, 218n4, 275, 281, 283, 286–7, 293, 295, 306, 329, 333, 339, 348, 380, 390, 392
Electoral Association of German Conservatives, 328, 334
electoral culture, 96, 116, 127, 184, 206
electoral systems, 120, 124, 126, 196–205, 208–14; *See also* democracy, democratization; elections; parliament, parliamentarism; suffrage
Eley, Geoff, 66, 78, 80, 84–5, 87–9, 91, 94, 96–7, 124, 133n41, 134n53, 148, 150, 320n53, 370, 400n4
elites, 6, 10, 16, 18, 38, 43–5, 48, 54, 56, 61–2, 79, 81, 83, 90–1, 95, 98, 115, 123, 153, 184, 197, 201, 208, 212, 231, 236, 326, 361. *See also* aristocracy, aristocrats
emancipation, 11, 13, 22, 91, 110, 129, 143, 145, 157; Jewish, 278, 299, 308, 321n74; of women, 381
Engel, Heinrich, 297, 332, 346–7, 354
Engels, Friedrich, 37
Enlightenment, 41, 225, 227, 233, 237, 261, 276
Epstein, Klaus, 41, 48–9
estates, landed. *See* landowners, landed estates
estates, social, 41, 47, 55, 111, 169–70, 179, 184, 204, 254, 278
Eulenburg, Botho zu, 340–1, 346
Eulenburg-Hertefeld, Philipp zu, 339, 340–2, 344, 349, 351–2, 361, 366n37
Evangelical Social Congress, 309
Evangelische Kirchenzeitung, 56, 247
Evans, Richard J., 50

Fairbairn, Brett, 12
Farr, Ian, 50
fascism, 44, 60, 62–3, 82–4, 88–90
Fatherland Party. *See* German Fatherland Party
Fechenbach-Laudenbach, Friedrich Karl von, 277–81, 298, 313
Federal Council (*Bundesrat*), 115–16
federalism, federal states, 19, 115, 126, 128, 139, 143, 157, 177, 181, 290. *See also* regionalism, regional politics
Feldman, Gerald D., 61
Female Danger in the Literary Field, The (Theodor Wahl), 258
feudalism, 17, 38, 43, 45
finance reform, 327, 354, 358, 374–6, 382
First World War, 11, 14, 62, 65–6, 84, 95, 109, 114, 126, 215–16, 228, 252, 257–8, 260, 370

Index 419

Fischer, Franz, 340, 342
Fischer, Fritz, 44
Förster, Bernhard, *338*
Förster, Paul, *388*
Fontane, Theodor, 11, 38, 83, 236, 249
Foucault, Michel, 137, 154, 156, 158
France, 168, *350*
Franco-German War (1870–1), *155*
Franconia, 277–8
Frankfurt am Main, 297
Frankfurt Parliament (1848–9), 59, 185
Frederick the Great, 38, 48
Frege-Abtnaundorf, Arnold Woldemar (von), 297–9, *355*
Freiligrath, Ferdinand, 235
Frevert, Ute, 94
Freytag, Gustav, 101, 235–7, 239–40, 242–3
Friedrich, Norbert, 62
Friedrich Wilhelm IV, 56, 229, 247
Friesen, Richard von, 170, *171*, 172–3, 176, 178–81, 184, *288*
Friesen-Rötha, Heinrich von, *158*, 285–7, *288*, 291, 297, 299–300, *301*, *335*
Fritsch, Theodor, 274, 304, 312, 336, *338*
Fritzsche, Peter, 80
'Frymann, Daniel.' *See* Claß, Heinrich
Füßl, Wilhelm, 36, 54–8, 68

Garber, Jörn, 48
Geffcken, Heinrich, 319n46
General Civil Code (1794), 47
General German Writers Club, 255
General Writers Association, 256
Gentz, Friedrich von, 48
Gerlach, Hellmut von, 277
Gerlach, Leopold von, 247
Gerlach, Ludwig von, 56, 58, 67–8, 247, 328
German Agricultural Council, 298
German Army League, 94
German Assembly of Writers, 235
German Centre Party, 8, 82, 85, 87, 127, 278, 280, 283, 293, 333, 354, 355, *373*, 386, 394–5, 399n2, 402n44. *See also* Catholicism, Catholics
German civil war (1866), 170
German Colonial Society, 312
German Confederation, 228
German Democratic Republic, 50, 67, 113, 143, 145
German Empire, The (Hans-Ulrich Wehler), 44
German Fatherland Party, 62–3, 65–6, 74n97
German Journalists Congress, 255
German Mittelstand Congress, 357
German Peasants League, 382
German Reform Party, 275, 309
German Social Party, 275, 302–3, 309
German Society of Nobles, 291
German Workers Party, 96
German Writers Association, 255
German Writers Club, 256
Gerschenkron, Alexander, 43, 81–2
Geßler, Ernst von, 184
Gneist, Rudolf von, 181
Goethe, Johann Wolfgang von, 114
Glagau, Otto, *338*
Göler von Ravensburg, Ernst August, 294, 307
Göttingen, 48
'Golden' International and the Necessity of a Social Reform Party, The (Carl Wilmanns), 296

Gordon, Colin, 184
Goßler, Alfred von, 385, 387
Grabowsky, Adolf, 257
Gramsci, Antonio, 173
Great Britain, 37, 43–4, 111, 168, 181, 298, 313, 390
'Great Depression' (1873–96), 61, 110
Grebing, Helga, 199
Grenzboten, 100, 235, 242–3
Griepentrog, Gisela, 50
Grimm, Jacob, 229
Gutzkow, Karl, 231, 235, 238

Habermas, Jürgen, 151
Hacking, Ian, 183
Hagen, William W., 45, 49–51
Hagenlücke, Heinz, 62–3, 65–6, 74n97
Hahn, Diederich, 87, 348
Haller, Karl Ludwig von, 49, 54
Hamburg, University of, 44
Hamerow, Theodore S., 44
Hammer, 312
Hammerstein-Schwartow, Wilhelm von, 244, 279, 293, 302, 328, 331–2, 334–5, 341, 365n26, 367n52
Hannah Arendt Institute for the Study of Totalitarianism, 146
Hanover, 45
Hansa League, 112, 384
Harden, Maximilian, 242, 244
Hardenberg, Karl August von, 120
Harmony Society, 210
Harnisch, Hartmut, 50
Hartwig, Gustav Emil Leberecht, 310–11, 313
Haußmann, Conrad, 122
Hegel, Georg Wilhelm Friedrich, 235
Heidelberg, University of, 256, 258, 260

Heine, Heinrich, 81
Heinrich, Christel, 50
Heinze, Rudolf, 122
Helldorff-Bedra, Otto Heinrich von, 91, 281, 327–44, *335*, 365n26
Hengstenberg, Ernst Wilhelm, 56, 244, 247
Hermes, Justus, 257
Herrschaft, 14, 37, 46, 47
Heß, Klaus, 60, 61
Hessen, 304, 348
Heßling, Diederich, 3, 7, 12, 23
Hewitson, Mark, 120, 121
Heydebrand und der Lase, Ernst von, 121, 166n39, 359, 360–1, 376, *377*, 379–87, *388*, 389–92, 394–9
Heyl zu Herrnsheim, Cornelius von, 402n53
Hindersmann, Ulrike, 45
Hinrichs, Ernst, 142–3
historiography, 7–10, 12–13, 17, 19–20, 22–4, 26n15, 36–7, 40–51, 60–3, 66–8, 77–9, 80–5, 87–8, 90–2, 94, 97, 99, 116, 121–2, 124, 129, 137–51, 162, 225–6, 228, 239–40, 274–7, 282, 296, 300, 304, 306–7, 313, 345, 362, 370, 381
Hitler, Adolf, 13, 63, 65, 78, 80, 89, 92, 95–9, 276
Hockenheim, 307–8
Hoetzsche, Otto, 257
Hoffmann, Leopold Alois, 244–5, 247
Hohenlohe-Schillingsfürst, Chlodwig zu, 349, 351–2, 361, 383
Holstein, Friedrich von, 339–42
Homeowners Association, 310–11
Hopwood, Robert, 95
housing, social, 207, 215, 222n48
Huber, Ernst Rudolf, 41
Huber, Victor Aimé, 55

Hübschmann, Johannes, 208–9, 211
Hugsweier, 302

ideology, 6, 7, 9, 12–13, 18–20, 35–7, 39–40, 42, 45–6, 48–52, 54–5, 58–60, 62, 67–8, 79, 82–5, 87–9, 94, 99, 124, 145, 225, 229, 273–4, 276, 295, 297, 302–3, 313, 329, 346, 358
If I Were the Kaiser (Heinrich Claß), 12, *64*
illiberalism, 78–9, 82–3, 90–1. *See also* anti-liberalism; liberalism, liberals
Imperial and Free Conservative Party, 19, 290, 370
Imperial German Mittelstand Association, 312
Imperial German Press Club, 257–8
imperialism, imperialists, 37, 44, 90–1, 134n42, 160, 290
Imperial League against Social Democracy, 252
Imperial Young Conservative Association, 381
industrialism, industrialization, industrialists, 38, 44, 48, 54, 109, 111–12, 117, 139, 157–8, 186, 197, 205, 213, 291, 303, 306, 347, 381–2
Institute for Saxon History, 146
Institute for the Study of Newspapers, 257
interest groups, 12, 22, 44, 94, 124, 257, 289–90, 296, 370, 382–3, 390. *See also* associations, associational life
Internationale Monatsschrift, 312
Italy, 298

Jahrbuch für Regionalgeschichte, 145
Japan, 181
Jeggle, Utz, 50, 51

Jelavich, Peter, 114
Jesuits, 294
Jewish Rifles (Hermann Ahlwardt), 97
'Jewish question,' 276–7, 282, 299–300, 337, 342
Jews, 3, 6, 29, 30n46, 54, 97, *125*, 157, 273, 275–6, 278–79, 281, 283, 285, 289, 293–5, 297, 299–300, 302, 304, 306, 308, 311–13, 317n31, 318n41, 330, 336, *338*, 341, *350*. *See also* antisemitism, antisemites
journalism, journalists, 36, 51–2, 101, *125*, 225–62, 263n6, 297, 302, 311, 334
Journalism Academy (Richard Wrede), 256, 260
Journalisten, Die (Gustav Freytag), 225, 227, 233, 236, 240, 242, 254, 261
'Judenpolitik,' 281, 297
'Junker Parliament' (1848), 42, 46, 56
Junkers, 20, 37–8, 43–7, 49–50, 56, 60–1, 67, 75n106, 80–3, 91, 111, 197, 294, 334, 346, 360, 362, 363, 366n37, 377, 380. *See also* aristocracy, aristocrats; Prussia: aristocracy

Kaase, Max, 149
Kant, Immanuel, 113
Kapp, Wolfgang, 63, 65–6
Kapp Putsch, 66
Karlsruhe, 302
Kartell, 127, 298, 329, 333–4, 339–40
Kaschuba, Wolfgang, 50
Keim, August, 88
Kessler, Harry, 129
Kiderlen-Wächter, Alfred von, 90, 339, 341
Kiebingen, 51

Kiel, 358
Kierkegaard, Søren, 106n65
Kladderadatsch, 55, *118*, *119*, *373*, *377*
Kleist-Retzow, Hans von, 328, 334
Knigge, Adolph von, 238
Koch, Adolf, 256, 258, 260
Kölnische Zeitung, 340, 342
Kötzschke, Rudolf, 144
Kolinsky, Eva, 149
Kondylis, Panajotis, 36, 37
Konservative Monatsschrift, 391
Konservativer Kalender, 361
Konservatives Wochenblatt, 332
Kretzschmar, Hellmut, 144
Kreuzzeitung. See *Neue Preußische (Kreuz-) Zeitung*
Kreuzzeitung group, 302, 326, 331–3, 337, 342, 344, 361
Krug, Wilhelm Traugott, 152
Kühne, Thomas, 111, 128
Kulturkampf, 92–4, 127, 184
Kulturkämpfer, 300

Lässig, Simone, 157
La Roche-Starkenfels, Udo von, 385
Lagarde, Paul de, 42
Lahr, 302
Lamprecht, Karl, 144, 162, 257
landowners, landed estates, 36, 38–9, 41, 43, 45–8, 56, 60–1, *125*, 179, 326, 332, 342, 354, 364n5. See also agrarianism, agrarians; Junkers
Landtag (state parliament), 54, 57, 115–16, 122–3, 143, 168–86, 189n15, *194*, 197–8, 201–4, 206, 212–14, 218n3, 221n32, 293, 295, 298, 310–11, 318n32, 328, 331–2, 347–9, 351–3, 358, 385. See also under names of states
Langbehn, Julius, 42

Lange, Hermann, 348
Langewiesche, Dieter, 23, 84
Lasker, Eduard, 297
Lassalle, Ferdinand, 239
Laube, Heinrich, 236, 238
lawyers, 101, *125*, 205, 258
League of German Editors, 257
Lee, W.R., 50
Lehmann, Emil, 311
Leibl, Wilhelm, *259*
Leipzig, 145, 150, 152–3, *158*, 159–62, 174–6, 193, 196, 198–204, 206, 208, 210–16, 218n3, 222n48, 233–5, 242, 257, 286, 297, 311
Leipzig Literary Association, 234
Leo, Heinrich, 55, 57
Lerchenfeld-Koefering, Hugo von, 278
Lessing, Gotthold, 238
Levy, Richard S., 20, 30n46, 274
liberalism, liberals, 11, 18, 23, 36, 37, 39, 43, 49, 51–2, 54, 58–9, 79–80, 85, 87, 88, 90, 92, 109, 116, *118*, 121–2, 124, 127–8, 137, 140, 148, 150–1, 152, 156, 158, 169, 174–5, 178, 181, 184, 186, 192, 195, 206, 212, 217, 226, 229, 231–2, 239, 242–4, 256–7, 274, 276, 281–6, 290, 293, 299, 300–1, 306–7, 309, 313, 333, *350*, 356, 360, 381, 386, 393, 395, 397–9, 403n55
Liebenberg Circle, 339
Liebermann von Sonnenberg, Max, 274, *338*
Linz, Juan, 17, 18
localism, local politics, 7, 18–19, 38, 47, 58, 60–1, 65, 73n80, 80, 87, 116, 128, 137, 139, 140–1, 149–51, 154, *155*, 156, 158, 162, 178, 186, 198, 201–15, 251, 255–6, 297, 300, 302,

308, 310–13, 328, 330–1, 334, 341, 346, 355, 379, 382; historiography, 97, 138, 142, 148, 161, 162, 167n46
Loebell, Friedrich Wilhelm von, 353, 355, 358–9, 375, 386–7, 391–3
London, 237
Lorenz, Moritz Heinrich, 175
Loyal Subject, The (Heinrich Mann), 3, 6, 7, 24n1, 236
Ludwig-Wolf, Leo, 212, 213
Lübeck, 23
Luthardt, August, 280

Magdeburg, 50
Malinowski, Stephan, 63
'Manchesterism,' 278, 297, 306, 309
Mann, Heinrich, 3, 7, 22–4, 236
Mann, Thomas, 14, 22–4, 83
Mannheim, Karl, 8, 20, 35, 40, 41
Manteuffel-Crossen, Otto von, 335, 336, 337, 342, 348
Marr, Wilhelm, 20
Marschall von Bieberstein, Adolf, 339
Marwitz, Ludwig von der, 41, 46, 48
Marx, Karl, 67, 235
mass media, 80, 228
'masses, the,' 6, 8, 9, 13, 15, 20, 43, 66, 77–9, 84, 85, 91, 92, 95, 97, 98, 100, 102n6, 231, 245, 248, 251, 253, 260, 279, 298, 326, 330–1, 339, 346, 380
Masters and Lords (Shearer Davis Bowman), 61
Mehnert, Carl Paul, Sr, 303
Mehnert, Karl Paul, Jr, 166n39, 312, 313, 320n62, 358, 361, 385–6
Merquior, José G., 95
Merseburg, 327
Metternich, Klemens von, 54, 228, 231, 236

Meyer, Herrmann Julius, 206
Meyer, Johann, 206
Meyersche Foundation, 216, 217
middle classes (*Bürgertum*), 3, 6, 42–5, 80, 94–6, 98–100, 102n6, 117, 137, 148, 150, 151, 157, 185, *194*, 195–6, 204, 206–8, 210–13, 226, 231, 233, 239, 291, 299; lower (*Mittelstand*), 6, 7, 42, 66, 87, 90, 111, 127, 203, 207, 212, 221n42, 229, 290, 295, 297, 303, 310, 312, 332, 354–5, 360, 379, 381, 382
militarism, 20, 24n4, 61
military, 38, 127, 147, 395; service, 188n13, 198. *See also* army; navy
Mill, John Stuart, 19, 202
Minogue, Kenneth, 92
Miquel, Johannes von, 351, 360
Mirbach-Sorquitten, Julius von, 9, 20
Mittelland Canal, 327, 347–9, 352, 353, 355
Mittelstand. *See* middle classes: lower
modernity, 10, 22, 23, 26n13, 37, 78–9, 82–3, 92, 101, 108, 115, 122, 123, 124, 140, 147–9, 156, 169, 172–3, 181, 184–5, 192, 197–8, 208, 211–12, 226, 251, 293, 352, 381
modernization, 13, 22, 43, 45, 84, 112–14, 139–40, 148, 150, 156, 158, 177, 261, 174, 398–9; economic, 177, 186; social, 45, 140, 151, 153, 183, 238, 242; theory, 22, 148, 149
Moeller, Robert G., 50
Möller-Gütersloh, Pastor, 348
Moeller van den Bruck, Arthur, 42
Möser, Justus, 41
Mommsen, Hans, 199
Mommsen, Theodor, 235
Mommsen, Wolfgang J., 114

Monarchical Principle, The (Friedrich Julius Stahl), 49
monarchism, monarchy, 6, 11, 12, 14, 17, 39, 49, 61, 289, 299, 364n5, 375
Mooser, Josef, 50
Moritz, Karl Philipp, 230
Moroccan crisis (1911), 386, 389–91
Mosse, George L., 7, 41, 42, 81, 83
Mühlhäußer, Karl August, 294, 308, 319n46
Müller, Adam, 48, 49
Münchner Neueste Nachrichten, 259
Mumm, Reinhard, 62
Munich, 96, 200, 278
museums, 152, 159, 206–8, 215, 216

Napoleonic Wars, 153
Nathusius-Ludom, Philipp von, 328
nationalism, 7, 13, 15, 19, 63, 65, 67, 79, 83–5, 94–7, 102n6, 147–8, 150, 156, 158, 184, 206, 253, 280, 290–1, 311, 370, 383, 385, 395; radical, 7, 12–13, 15, 19, 65, 78, 80, 85, 87–8, 90, 97, 290, 337, 372, 374, 389. *See also völkisch* movement
nationalist camp (*Lager*), 65, 117, 134n42
nationalist opposition, 54, 89, 94, 97, 372, 374, 389–90, 395
National Liberal Party, 67, 87, 122–3, 125, 127–8, 174–6, 212, 214–15, 218n3, 280–3, 293, 297, 306, 328, 329, 333, 340, 370, 372, 376, 378–87, 390, 392, 394, 399n2, 402n53. *See also* liberalism, liberals
National Socialism, Nazism, 13, 42, 50, 60, 63, 78, 80–1, 84, 89, 94, 99, 108, 111, 113, 117, 157, 276
Naumann, Friedrich, 67–8, 82, 121
navy, 63

Navy League, 85, 88, 97, 312
Neue Preußische (Kreuz-) Zeitung, 55, 59, 67, 236, 250, 257, 279, 281, 293, 296–7, 302, 326, 328, 330, 332–3, 336–7, 341–2, 344, 346, 353, 355–8, 361, 365n26, 367n52, 379–81, 387
Neue Reichszeitung, 297, 306
Neues Archiv für sächsische Geschichte, 146
Neue Westfälische Volkszeitung, 348
Neumann, Sigmund, 41–2
Niendorf, Martin Anton, 296
Nietzsche, Friedrich, 24, 114
1918, revolution of, 22, 66, 81, 98, 214
Nipperdey, Thomas, 51, 144
nobility. *See* aristocracy, aristocrats
Nolde, Emil, 114
Norddeutsche Allgemeine Zeitung, 395
Nordhausen, Richard, 251
Normann, Oskar von, 379
North German Confederation, 170, 175–6
Nostitz-Wallwitz, Hermann von, 176–7, 181
Nuremberg, 279–80

Oberpostamts-Zeitung, 248–9
O'Boyle, Lenore, 236
Oertel, Georg, 300, 320n62
Oertzen, Dietrich von, 297
Oldenburg-Januschau, Elard von, 355–6
Oncken, Hermann, 257
Ordinary Prussians (William W. Hagen), 49
Ottaway, Marina, 17
Otte, Marline, 153, 160

Palmowski, Jan, 122

Pan-German League, 11–12, *64*, 85, 97, 102n6, 150, 252, 390, 396
Pareto, Vilfredo, 43
Paris, 237
parliament, parliamentarism, 8, 10, 22, 27n26, 36, 39–40, 49, 66, 87, 89, 91, 96, 116–17, 120–4, 127, 143, 152, 156–7, 159–60, 168, 172–7, 180–5, 189n14, 198–9, 201, 203–5, 209, 211–15, 274, 280, 282, 293–4, 299, 302, 304, 310, 326, 328–30, 333, 336, 340–1, 345–50, 355, 357, 359, 361–2, 370–1, 372, 381, 384, 387, 389, 394–7
particularism, 145, 148–9, 175, 309. *See also* regionalism, regional politics
paternalism, 39, 46, 47
Patriot, 330
Payer, Friedrich von, 122
Peal, David, 304
peasantry, 20, 45–7, 49–51, 90, 100, 111, 345, 362
Peculiarities of German History, The (David Blackbourn and Geoff Eley), 84–5
Penny, H. Glenn, 153, 159
People's League to Combat Filth in Word and Image, 252
Perrot, Franz, 281, 282, 296–7, 306, 322n81, 328
Peters, Carl, 312–13
Pfotenhauer, Friedrich Wilhelm, *155*
philanthropy, 192–3, 195–6, 202, 206–11, 215–16, 245
Pinkert, Alexander, 309
Plaul, Hainer, 50
Poland, 67
police, policing, 115, 178, 237
political culture, 10, 13, 17, 22, 39, 42, 78, 80, 117, 123, 140–1, 149–51, 161, 169, 172, 181, 186, 212, 225, 273, 282, 311–12, 326
'political mass market,' 8, 92, 99. *See also* 'masses, the'; politics, popular and mass
political mobilization, 6, 8, 11, 13, 17, 20, 22, 36, 39, 43–4, 58–60, 63, 66, 77–8, 81, 87, 89–90, 97–8, 126, 133n41, 134n42, 148, 193, 326, 331, 357
political modernization, 6, 8, 10, 13, 20, 22–3, 45, 77, 84, 99–100, 124, 139, 148, 168, 186, 227, 309, 327, 378–9, 381, 397
political platform, political program. *See* ideology
political styles, 10, 11, 12, 15, 17, 23, 42, 44–5, 59, 63, 77–9, 83, 85, 87, 89, 90, 98, 116, 124, 131n10, 277, 280, 311, 327, 336, 355, 370, 372, 385
political system, 10, 17, 43, 90, 123, 128, 283, 326, 396
political violence, 20, 39, 63, 89, 160, 273, 291
politics, popular and mass, 8, 13, 20, 22, 44, 54, 57–8, 62, 65, 77–8, 87–8, 90, 92, 94, 97, 101, 158, 173, 313, 325, 330–1, 337, 393
'politics of notables' (*Honoratiorenpolitik*), 8, 12–13, 58, 62–3, 66, 78, 80–1, 85, 87–8, 96, 99–101, 116, 150, 325, 327, 330, 332–3, 336, 347
Politics of the Prussian Nobility, The (Robert M. Berdahl), 45
Politische Bilderbogen, 290, *350*
Pomerania, 382
populism, populists, 15, 43, 63, 77–80, 83–5, 87–92, 95, 97–9, 124, 273, 325

Populists and Patricians (David Blackbourn), 90
Post, 387
Potsdam, 354
press, 12, 22, 48, 52–3, 55, 57, 58–9, 80, 127, 170, 227–38, 243–60, 294, 300, 308, 310, 319n43, 330, 344, 353, 380, 381, 384. *See also* editors; journalism, journalists; propaganda, propagandists
Preußische Jahrbücher, 175, 236
propaganda, propagandists, 21, 49, 51–2, 54, 57, 59, 65, 80, 83, 88, 90, 98, 99, 178, 225, 251, 254, 278, 281, 291, 296, 297, 300, 308, 311–12, 323n97, 329–30, 332, 359
Protestantism, Protestants, 44, 56, 278, 283, 285, 293–5, 297, 332, 380. *See also* church; clergy; religion
Protestant Press Association, 252
Prussia, Kingdom of, 7, 15, 19–20, 27n26, 36, 51, 54, 57–8, 60–2, 74n97, 111, 116, 122, 139, 143, 168, 177, 197, 199, 201, 207, 214, 278, 290–1, 309, 334, 340, 353, 360, 376, 380, 387, 389, 394, 396, 397, 399; aristocracy, 20, 36, 38, 45–9, 52, 54, 83, 351; bureaucracy, 38, 44, 51, 52, 54, 115, 245, 345, 352, 394, 396; House of Deputies (*Landtag*), 194, 331, 334, 347, 396; House of Lords (*Landtag*), 335, 396; *Landtag* (state parliament), 57, 115–16, 172, *194*, 201, 328, 331–2, 347–8, 351–3, 358, 385; suffrage (three-class). *See* suffrage: Prussian (three-class).
Prussian People's Association, 58, 96
publicists. *See* journalism, journalists; propaganda, propagandists
public opinion, publicity, 12, 52, 54, 57–8, 90, 100, 185, 228–9, 232, 245, 248
public sphere (*Öffentlichkeit*), 49, 151–2, 225
publishers, 234–5, 249, 252, 254, 258, 261, 311
Pudor, Heinrich, 324n108
Puhle, Hans-Jürgen, 43–4, 50, 60, 83–5, 87, 89–91, 325, 370
Pulzer, Peter G.J., 42, 274–5

racism, race, 13, 20, 42, 61, 97, 120, 275
radicalism, radicals, 13, 19, 109, 298, 307, 312–13, 335, 346–7, 353, 355–6, 360, 376, 382, 384, 386, 390. *See also* nationalism: radical
Radkau, Joachim, 112–13
Radowitz, Joseph Maria von, 41
Rantzau, Kuno zu, 330
Rassow, Hermann, 88
Rathenau, Walther, 117, 120–2, 129
Rauh, Manfred, 116
Realpolitik, 46, 57, 332
Reck, Wilhelm von der, 348–9
Reform Association, 309–10
regionalism, regional politics, 6, 7, 9, 18–20, 61–2, 65, 67, 74n97, 109, 116, 120, 127–8, 137, 141, 144, 147, 149, 151, 156, 183, 199, 200, 206, 214, 273, 277, 279–80, 282, 291, 295, 300, 302–3, 311–3, 332, 352, 378, 380, 382, 385; historiography, 97, 137–40, 142–8, 150, 153, 157, 161–2, 167n46, 276
Reichsbote, 297, 332, 346–7, 354, 357, 380–1
Reichstag, 11, 12, 22, 26n18, 91, *93*, 115–16, 121, 127, 134n42, 169, 174, 176–7, 185, 189n15, 193, 197, 200,

218n4, 250, 275, 281, 283, 286–7, 293, 295, 298, 306, 311, 317n32, 328–9, 331, 333–4, *335*, 339–42, 347–8, 354–5, 358–60, 364n14, 372, 375, 379–80, 382, 384, 390–2, 394–5
religion, 8, 13, 44, 115, 122, 174, 285, 294, 304, 328, 332
Requate, Jörg, 263n6
Reshaping the German Right (Geoff Eley), 87–8, 97
revolution, revolutionary, 13, 35, 38–9, 44, 46, 55–7, 59, 66, 68, 84, 110, 123, 137, 196–7, 235, 274, 309, 362; French, 39, 41, 48, 54, 229, 231, 244–5, 262; industrial, 39, 109, 112. See also 1848, revolution of; 1918, revolution of
Rhine-Hanover Canal, 353
Rhineland, 139, 348, 380
Riehl, Wilhelm Heinrich, 238, 249
Riezler, Kurt, 387, 393, 398–9
Ritter, Gerhard, 81
Ritter, Gerhard A., 111, 144
Robespierre, Maximilien de, 245
Röder, Adam, 250, 283
Roesicke, Gustav, 355–6, 361, 397
Roesler, Hermann, 181
Role of Force in History, The (Friedrich Engels), 37
Rosenberg, Hans, 8, 43, 46, 67, 81–2, 92
Rosenhaft, Eve, 22, 262
Rossiter, Clinton, 39, 56
Rothe, Karl, 215
Ruhr district, 347
rural society and economy, 7, 38, 45–7, 49–51, 59, 60–2, 111, 116, 249, *259*, 273, 307–8, 344–5, 355, 384
Russia, 181, 298, 345–6

Sächsischer Volksfreund, 297
Sahlins, Marshall, 22
Saxon Agricultural Credit Association, 303, 322n81
Saxon Conservative State Association, 292
Saxon Mittelstand Union, 312
Saxony, Kingdom of, 20, 74n97, 122–3, 137, 140, 143–6, 150, 153, *155*, 156–7, 161, 168–81, *182*, 183, 185, 189n14, 190n36, 193, 196–208, 212–14, 217, 218n4, 219n9, 234, 274, 277, 282–7, 290–4, 296–300, 303–4, 306, 309–13, 317n31, 318n32, 327, 331, 336, 357–8, 382, 385. *Landtag*, 122–3, 168–81, *182*, 183–6, 189n15, 197–8, 202–6, 212–14, 218n3, 293, 298, 310–11, 318n32, 358
Schäfer, Michael, 210
Schauensee, Rudolf Meyer von, 280, 296
Scheck, Raffael, 62–3
Schiemann, Theodor, 365n26
Schiffer, Eugen, 387, 389, 392–3
Schiller, Friedrich, 114, 235
Schiller, René, 45
Schissler, Hanna, 46, 50
Schlesinger, Walter, 144
Schleswig-Holsteinische Zeitung, 235
Schlick, Moritz, 28n32
Schlözer, August Ludwig, 230
Schloss Rötha, *158*, *289*
Schmeitzner, Ernst, 312
Schmoller, Gustav, 397
Schopenhauer, Arthur, 237
Schorske, Carl, 8
Schreck, Hermann, 174
Schulze-Delitzsch, Hermann, *93*
Schwabe, Emil, *125*

Schwabe, Gustav, 206, 208
Schwentker, Wolfgang, 36–7, 57–9, 68
Schwerin-Löwitz, Hans von, 384
Second World War, 50
Sheehan, James J., 25n10, 162, 231
Silesia, 348, 385
Simon Dubnow Institute for Jewish History and Culture, 146
Smith, Helmut Walser, 124, 306
Social Conservative Alliance, 278
Social Democratic Party, Social Democrats, 8, 44, 81, 85, 122–4, 126, 128, 134n42, 146, 175–6, 181, 185, 192–3, 196, 198–9, 201, 203–5, 208, 211, 213–15, 218n4, 221n32, 252, 279, 283, 293, 295, 302, 307, 309, 342, 344, *350*, 351, 355, 362, 380, 384, 390, 397–8
socialism, socialists, 37, 39, 79, 89, 116–17, 151, 197, 206, 211, 213, 221n42, 308, 341, 346, 375, 382, 385. *See also* anti-socialism
Society and Democracy in Germany (Ralf Dahrendorf), 43, 82
Sonderweg, 9, 40, 43, 83, 149
Sontag, Franz, 98–9, 387, 389
Spahn, Martin, 257
Spenersche Zeitung, 235, 247
Spielhagen, Friedrich, 256
Spitzemberg, Hildegard von, 376, 383, 390
Stahl, Friedrich Julius, 36, 39, 49, 54–7, 72n71
State Association of Conservatives in the Kingdom of Saxony, 290–2
State Committee of the German Conservative Party in Baden, 290
StatsAnzeigen, 230
Stechlin, The (Thedor Fontane), 38

Steel Helmets (Stahlhelm), 94, 99
Stegmann, Dirk, 62–3, 65–6, 381
Stein, Karl vom und zum, 48
Stein, Lorenz von, 181
Steinbach, Peter, 142, 144
Stern, Fritz, 41–2, 81–3
Stockhorner von Starein, Otto, 295, 307–8
Stöcker, Adolf, 97, 278–9, 298, 302, 309, 331, 335–6, 341, *343*, 344
Stössel, Georg von, 354
Stolberg-Wernigerode, Udo zu, 345, 353
Stosch-Sarrasani, Hans, 159
Stratz, Rudolf, 250
Stresemann, Gustav, 128, 382, 386
Studnitz, Cecelia von, 239–40
Stübel, Paul, 310
Süddeutsche Conservative Correspondenz, 250
suffrage, 6, 9, 20, 68, 82, 101, 126–7, 143, 147, 168–70, 172–7, 179–81, 183–4, 186, 192, 195–6, 198, 199, 200–7, 209–10, 212–14, 216–17, 218n3, 282, 293, 331, 363, 376, 378, 380, 386, 396; Prussian (three-class), 122, 126, 177–8, *194*, 197, 201–8, 210, 213, 218n4, 376–7, *378*, 386, 396; reform, 127–8, 168–70, 172–3, 175, 180–1, 183–5, 192–3, 196, 198, 203–8, 212, 214, 218n3, 378, 386, 396. *See also* electoral systems
Swabia, 51
Sydow, Reinhold von, 387

Tägliche Rundschau, 342
Taylor, A.J.P., 36, 44
taxation, 43, 45, 60, 111, 156, 169, 180–1, 193, 196, 198, 201–2, 203–4,

207–8, 214, 278, 310, 345, 354, 356–7, 359, 374, 386, 390, 394–6
teachers, 205, 240, 295, 302
Third Reich, 80, 84. *See also* National Socialism, Nazism
Thompson, Alastair P., 122
Thompson, E.P., 46, 138
Thoughts on the Cause of the Present Discontents (Edmund Burke), 67–8
Thüringische Zeitung, 100
Thuringia, 199
Tippel, Otto, 342
Tirpitz, Alfred von, 62–3, 66
Tivoli party congress, 327, 336–7, 340–1
Treitschke, Heinrich von, 150, 175, 235
Tucholsky, Kurt, 60, 67
Twain, Mark, 139

Ungern-Sternberg, Eduard von, 297, 319n46, 336
Union of German Journalists and Writers Associations, 256–7
universities, 207, 256–7
Untertan, Der (Heinrich Mann). *See Loyal Subject, The*
urbanism, urbanization, 115, 139, 142, 151–2, 156–8, 197, 200, 203–4, 206–7, 209, 212, 214–15, 217, 222n48, 234, 281, 291, 311, 326, 354, 360, 379–80

Valentini, Rudolf von, 390, 393
Valjavec, Fritz, 41, 48–9
Vienna, University of, 256
Vierhaus, Rudolf, 229
völkisch movement, 7, 13, 19, 24n4, 42, 58, 62, 96, 127. *See also* nationalism: radical; racism, race

Vogel, Julius, 215
Vormärz, 36, 46, 52, 54, 62, 67, 231, 233, 237, 244, 247
Vossische Zeitung, 230, 247

Wagener, Hermann, 57, 244, 296
Wahnschaffe, Arnold, 358, 385
Wangenheim, Conrad von, 348–9, 355–6
Warte, 294
Weber, Alfred, 257
Weber, Max, 11, 14–16, 90, 94, 238–9, 260, 262
Wedekind, Frank, 114
Wedel, Karl von, 391
Wehler, Hans-Ulrich, 25n11, 43–4, 158
Weimar Republic, 42, 44, 51, 63, 66, 80, 88–9, 92, 95–6, 127, 240, 260, 311, 362
Weltpolitik, 90, 128. *See also* imperialism, imperialists
Werthern, Georg von, 278
Westarp, Kuno von, 89, 379, 381, 395–6, 398
Westphalia, 50, 307, 348, 380
West Prussia, 60, 355
Wetzlar, 328
Wiener Zeitschrift, 244–5
Wilhelm I, 350
Wilhelm II, 12, 113, 116, 129–30, 239, 290, 326–7, 333–5, 339–42, 344, 346, 349–53, 359, 361–2, 390, 393, 395, 404n88
Wilmanns, Carl, 296
Wolff, Theodor, 387
women, 9, 22, 51, 63, 67, 214, 227, 257, 258, 259, 260, 380–1
working classes, workers, 6, 44, 50, 82, 117, 137, 203–4, 206–7, 209, 211–12, 215–16, 229

Wrede, Richard, 256, 260
writers, 227–9, 231, 233, 236–7, 239, 242, 249, 254, 256, 258, 260, 277. See also journalism, journalists; propaganda, propagandists
Württemberg, Kingdom of, 87, 184, 274, 280, 296. *Landtag*, 281

Young Conservatives, 381

Young Germany, 231

Zabern Affair (1913–14), 396
Zeitfragen des christlichen Volkslebens, 319n46
Zimmermann, Oswald, 311
Zurich, University of, 256
Zwahr, Hartmut, 144

GERMAN AND EUROPEAN STUDIES

General Editor: James Retallack

1 Emanuel Adler, Federica Bicchi, Beverly Crawford, and Raffaella A. Del Sarto, *The Convergence of Civilizations: Constructing a Mediterranean Region*
2 James Retallack, *The German Right, 1860–1920: Political Limits of the Authoritarian Imagination*
3 Silvija Jestrovic, *Theatre of Estrangement: Theory, Practice, Ideology*
4 Susan Gross Solomon, *Doing Medicine Together: Germany and Russia between the Wars*
5 Laurence McFalls, *Max Weber's 'Objectivity' Revisited*